THE OPERATION REINHARD DEATH CAMPS

THE OPERATION REINHARD DEATH CAMPS

Belzec, Sobibor, Treblinka

Revised and Expanded Edition

YITZHAK ARAD

INDIANA UNIVERSITY PRESS

THE INTERNATIONAL INSTITUTE
FOR HOLOCAUST RESEARCH

This book is a publication of

Indiana University Press
Office of Scholarly Publishing
Herman B Wells Library 350
1320 East 10th Street
Bloomington, Indiana 47405 USA

iupress.indiana.edu

Yad Vashem—The World Holocaust Remembrance Center
P.O.B. 3477
Jerusalem 9103401, Israel
publications.marketing@yadvashem.org.il

Library of Congress Cataloging-in-Publication Data

Names: Arad, Yitzhak, author.
Title: The Operation Reinhard death camps : Belzec, Sobibor, Treblinka /
    Yitzhak Arad.
Description: Revised and expanded edition. | Bloomington, Indiana : Indiana
    University Press ; Jerusalem : Yad Vashem, [2018] | Includes
    bibliographical references and index.
Identifiers: LCCN 2018001492 (print) | LCCN 2018017770 (ebook) | ISBN
    9780253025791 (e-book) | ISBN 9780253025302 (hardback : alk. paper) | ISBN
    9780253025418 (pbk. : alk. paper)
Subjects: LCSH: Operation Reinhard, Poland, 1942-1943. | Concentration
    camps--Poland. | Holocaust, Jewish (1939-1945) | Belzec (Concentration
    camp) | Sobibor (Concentration camp) | Treblinka (Concentration camp)
Classification: LCC D805.P7 (ebook) | LCC D805.P7 A728 2018 (print) | DDC
    940.53/18538--dc23
LC record available at https://lccn.loc.gov/2018001492

1 2 3 4 5 23 22 21 20 19 18

CONTENTS

PREFACE

THIS BOOK IS A STUDY of Operation Reinhard—the name the SS chose for the plan to exterminate the Jews who lived in the General Government of occupied Poland—and of three death camps in particular, Belzec, Sobibor, and Treblinka, established with the goal of implementing this plan. Concentration camps and death camps were an integral component of Nazi Germany's governing system and a tool for achieving its political aims. These camps were the responsibility of the SS, headed by Heinrich Himmler. The concentration camps served as places of detention and torture, centers of forced labor, and instruments for the physical elimination of those whom Nazi Germany considered hostile elements, including the Jews. Conversely, the death camps served but one purpose: the physical and total extermination of the Jewish people, regardless of their age or gender; human beings whose only "crime" was to have been born Jewish, or who were born to at least one Jewish grandparent. The crimes, cruelties, and murders committed by Nazi Germany against the Jews reached their peak in these death camps. Five death camps were erected and operated, all in Nazi-occupied Poland: Auschwitz-Birkenau, Chelmno, Belzec, Sobibor, and Treblinka.

This book describes the process and execution of the deportations from the ghettoes and relates the complete story of three camps in the General Government—Belzec, Sobibor, and Treblinka—from the preparations for their construction at the end of 1941 until their final razing in the fall of 1943. It depicts in full the physical layout of the camps, the transports to the camps, the process of extermination, and the methods and deeds of the SS men who commanded and operated the camps, as well as of the Ukrainian guards, who comprised the majority of the armed forces tasked with guarding the camps.

This book also tells the tale of the hundreds of thousands of people who were brought for extermination—although their stay in the camps usually lasted no more than a few hours—from the time they disembarked onto the railway platform until their corpses were removed from the gas chambers and buried in mass graves. In each of the camps, a few hundred Jews were removed from the transports and held in the camps to do the physical work involved in the extermination process, as well as some service jobs. Most of these Jews survived for only a short time, from a few days to several months, and were ultimately murdered, as were their brethren who were sent directly from the transports for extermination in the gas chambers. The book describes the daily life and work of these Jews, their underground organization, the revolts, and escapes from the camps. The number of victims in each camp, grouped by location of residence on the eve of deportation, and the timetables for the transports and murder are also included.

The death camps were the final station for the Jews of the General Government. But before reaching this destination, and their ultimate extermination, they were subjected to persecutions, deportations, torture, and murder. This book describes in general terms the German policy toward the Jews of Poland before the implementation of Operation Reinhard, how the decision regarding the operation was taken and its place within the general framework of the "Final Solution of the Jewish Question," and the decisions regarding the physical extermination of all of European Jewry. In addition to the Jews of Poland, tens of thousands of Jews from Holland, France, Greece, Yugoslavia, Germany, Czechoslovakia, Austria, and the Soviet Union were murdered in these three camps.

This book is the fruition of extensive research on the camps of Belzec, Sobibor, and Treblinka. The primary sources were testimonies of the few survivors of these camps, German documents, sources of the Polish underground, testimonies by Poles and Germans, and German trial protocols. Nazi criminals who served in these camps stood trial in West Germany. The trial of the SS men who had served in Belzec was held in Munich in January 1965. The primary defendant was Josef Oberhauser; seven other SS men were also tried with him. The trial of the SS men who had served in Sobibor was held in Hagen from September 1965 until December 1966. The primary defendant was Kurt Bolender; eleven other SS men were tried with him. The first Treblinka trial, at which ten of the SS men who served in the camp were brought to trial, among them Kurt Franz, the deputy commander, was held in Dusseldorf between October 1964 and August 1965. The second Treblinka trial, at which Franz Stangl, the commander of the camp, was tried, was also held in Dusseldorf, from September 1969 to December 1970.

The first hardcover English edition of this book appeared in 1987. Since then, new studies have been published on Operation Reinhard and on how the operation was decided on. These studies—including the research of

German historians Dieter Pohl, Götz Aly, and Ulrich Herbert; Polish historian Bogdan Musiał; American historian Christopher R. Browning; and Israeli historians David Silberklang and Sara Bender, along with many other historians—are reflected in this book.

The research involved in the study of any topic concerning the Holocaust and, above all, the extermination camps is emotionally difficult for any historian, and especially for one who personally experienced those times. My parents, Chaya and Yisroel Moshe Rudnitski, who spent time in the Warsaw ghetto, died in all probability in Treblinka; it is only luck and resourcefulness that staved off the same fate from my sister, Rachel, and myself.

ACKNOWLEDGMENTS

Judith Appleton and Ita Shapiro Haber contributed to the translation from Hebrew to English of additions and updates for the new edition.

THE OPERATION REINHARD DEATH CAMPS

INTRODUCTION

THE POLICY OF NAZI GERMANY toward the Jews in the years 1933–1945—which has been termed in the historiography of the period the "Final Solution of the Jewish Question in Europe"—was overtly aimed at exterminating the Jewish people. This policy was rooted in the racist Nazi ideology, according to which the Aryan race is the superior "master race" and the German nation, which embodies this race, fulfills the role of "master nation"; in this ideology, everything beautiful and useful in the world is the product of this race. On the opposite end of the racial continuum are the Jews, the root of all evil. All that is destructive and ugly in the world was introduced by them and from within them, and they embody all that is totally negative in humanity. The Jew is a subhuman, a germ that attempts to infect the pure German blood. An unending struggle transpires between these two races, the outcome of which will determine the fate of the world and humanity. This is an uncompromising struggle for life or death. Only the destruction of the Jewish people can ensure the victory of Nazi Germany in this battle for the future.

When Adolf Hitler rose to power, there were more than five hundred thousand Jews living in Germany; with the annexation of Austria in 1938, they were joined by an additional two hundred thousand Jews. Various stages can be discerned as the Nazis labored to realize their racial ideology toward the Jews, but the general process constantly moved in the direction of growing extremism. From the time the Nazis came to power on January 30, 1933, until the outbreak of World War II, their conscious policy was to force the Jews to leave Germany and to confiscate their property, awarding it to the Aryans. In the course of implementing this policy, the Germans ostracized the Jews from German society, cut them off from the economy, rescinded their rights as citizens, and discriminated against them in all areas of life. A series of anti-Jewish laws, culminating in the Nuremberg Laws, which were promulgated on September 15, 1935, provided the legal basis for these anti-Jewish acts. This policy reached its peak on the night of November 9, 1938, *Kristallnacht*. On this night, the Nazis waged a pogrom on the Jews of Germany. Hundreds of synagogues, businesses, and Jewish institutions were set on fire, and windows were smashed by the thousands (hence the name, the "Night of Broken Glass"). About one hundred Jews were killed, and thirty thousand were arrested and interned in concentration camps. In the aftermath, thousands of German and Austrian Jews left their homes in search of a refuge somewhere in the world. But the nations of the world did not open their gates to the Jews.

Finding refuge countries for these Jews became an international problem. Jewish opinion in the United States pressured the administration to absorb more refugees than Germany; to quell this pressure, President Franklin D. Roosevelt convened an international conference in an attempt to divide the burden of absorbing the emigrants among other countries. The conference met in Evian, France, between July 6 and July 15, 1938, with the participation of representatives from thirty-two other countries as well as of various organizations. The conference resulted in failure. Not one country acquiesced to increase their immigrant quota. Britain went as far as to require assurances that the topic of the immigration of the Third Reich's Jews to Mandatory Palestine would not even be broached before confirming its participation in the conference.

Germany closely followed the conference, and with its failure, Hitler concluded that the world's countries were not interested in the fate of Germany's Jews and that no government would get involved if he decided to take more extreme steps in solving the Jewish problem. Despite the fact that the Evian Conference resulted in no practical measures, over 300,000 German Jews and close to 130,000 Austrian Jews were able to emigrate by the time World War II began. Germany's attack on Poland and the start of the war put an end to further emigration. With the conquest of Poland, an additional 2 million Jews fell under German control; they could not be disposed of through emigration. Moreover, although the war's circumstances barred the expatriation option, it opened the way for other possibilities and solutions to the Jewish problem.

Hitler, in a speech to the Reichstag on January 30, 1939, referred to one of these possibilities that World War II would later offer Germany when he announced: "Today I will once more be a prophet: If the international Jewish financiers in and outside Europe should succeed in plunging the nations once more into a world war, then the result will not be the Bolshevization of the earth, and thus the victory of Jewry, but the annihilation of the Jewish race in Europe!"[1]

It should be noted that this speech was not a clear instruction to exterminate the Jews. It was a form of prophecy, expressing a trend. Hitler would only provide the instruction regarding extermination three years later. No detailed instructions or plans regarding Polish Jewry or European Jewry that entailed the consolidation of a general policy followed this speech. However, Nazi Germany's governing elements, mainly the SS, which was tasked with dealing with the Jews, viewed the speech as "the spirit of the leader," in a sense—the legitimacy to harass the Jews, abuse them, and even exterminate them. And indeed, World War II provided Hitler, Heinrich Himmler, Reinhard Heydrich, the SS factions, and the Nazi government with the opportunity to fulfill this "prophecy," which resulted in the murder of six million Jewish victims.

PART I

THE EXTERMINATION MACHINE

Operation Reinhard Death Camps
Occupied Poland 1942-1943 – Pre-WWII Borders

Bee Graphic Design, Jerusalem

Administrative Borders during German Occupation   – – – – – –

Main Cities   • Lublin

Death Camps   ■ Chełmno

Operation Reinhard Death Camps   ■ Sobibór

Territories annexed to the Third Reich   ▨

THE JEWS OF THE GENERAL GOVERNMENT, SEPTEMBER 1939–JUNE 1941: DEPORTATIONS AND GHETTOIZATION

ON SEPTEMBER 1, 1939, THE German army invaded Poland at dawn; two days later, Great Britain and France declared war on Germany. On September 17, 1939, under the Ribbentrop-Molotov Pact signed on August 23, the Red Army crossed the border with Poland and within a few days controlled its eastern regions. Warsaw, the capital, surrendered on September 28, 1939, and the German army took over control of central and western Poland.

Thus, in accordance with the Ribbentrop-Molotov Pact, Poland was divided between Nazi Germany and the Soviet Union. Eastern Poland (today's western Belarus, western Ukraine, and southeastern Lithuania), including the big cities of Vilna, Bialystok, and Lvov (Lemberg), with their large Jewish communities, was annexed to the Soviet Union. Central and western Poland, including Warsaw, Lodz, Lublin, and Cracow, major cities with a large Jewish population, became occupied German territories. On October 26, 1939, these occupied zones were transferred from military rule to a civilian government. The districts of Poznan, Lodz, and Shleswig in western Poland were annexed administratively to Germany to become part of the Third Reich, while central Poland became an administrative unit called the General Government. The latter comprised four districts: Warsaw, Cracow, Lublin, and Radom.

On the eve of World War II, there were approximately 3.3 million Jews living in Poland, about 10 percent of Poland's entire population. An estimated 2.1 million Jews lived in western and central Poland, under German control, while approximately 1.2 million lived in the Soviet-controlled areas. About 200,000 Jews fled from German-controlled areas to the areas under Soviet control. Between 1.8 and 1.9 million Jews remained under German control: between 1.3 and 1.4 million in the General Government and the rest in western Poland annexed to Germany.

The German policy toward the Jews in Poland from September 1939 to June 1941 was one of deportations and ghettoization. It was only during September 1939 that this policy was formulated by the very top of the Nazi hierarchy in conversations among Adolf Hitler, Heinrich Himmler, and Reinhard Heydrich, who was head of the RSHA (*Reichssicherheitshauptamt*, the Reich Main Security Office). The major trend for the long term was to expel the Jews from Nazi Germany; enclosing the Jews in ghettos was supposed to be an interim measure until deportation would be possible. On September 21, 1939, Heydrich called a meeting with the heads of the RSHA and the *Einsatzgruppen* commanders, together with Adolf Eichmann, in charge of Jewish affairs in his office. At the time, the Red Army had already taken control of eastern Poland, and the trend of deportation, which had no realistic basis, was to deport the Jews to the border with the Soviet Union. Heydrich announced at that meeting that "Hitler approved the deportation of Jews into the non-German area, their expulsion over the demarcation line."[1]

Heydrich expressed this policy in writing in his *Schnellbrief*—an express letter—to the *Einsatzgruppen* commanders operating in Poland. The letter was sent on September 21, 1939, on the date of the aforementioned meeting, as the battles in Poland were still raging. He stated that the Jewish policy would be executed in two stages: the first stage was for immediate execution, while the second stage, defined as the *Endziel*—the final goal that they would implement—would require more time.

For immediate implementation at the first stage, the Jews were to be concentrated in the big cities, near major railroad junctions, while Jews residing in western Poland, areas annexed to Germany, were to be deported from their homes to the General Government. This order was intended to serve the *Endziel*, whose essential nature was not set out in detail but involved deportation of the Jews to some place in the future. Heidrich's urgent letter also included the order to establish a *Judenrat*—a Jewish council—in each Jewish community to be in charge of carrying out the instructions to be given to it. The directives also ordered that during implementation of the instructions, the *Einsatzgruppen* should make sure that the occupied areas would not sustain economic damage.[2] We must note that Heydrich's order to concentrate Jews in large cities near railway junctions, intended to be carried out immediately, could have been understood as a directive to set up ghettos in these places of concentration. It was not binding on local authorities of the military government, nor did it obligate Hans Frank and the civil government—which had controlled the Jews since October. This order was not actually carried out.

Between October and December 1939, several orders were publicized in the General Government referring to the Jews. On October 26, a directive was issued on introducing forced labor for Jews, both men and women, for those between fourteen and sixty years of age. According to an ordinance referring to this directive, from January 1, 1940, Jews were forbidden "to move their residence or place of lodging outside of the locality where they have been living until now, or to wander beyond the borders of the locality by leaving their permanent lodging or residence."[3]

A directive published on November 23, 1939, stated, among other orders: "All of the Jews and Jewesses staying in the General Government over the age of 10 must, beginning from December 1, 1939, wear a white band with a Jewish Star on their right arm of their clothing and outerwear, of a width of at least 10cm," and it was stated that "anyone failing to fulfill this order will be punished by imprisonment."[4] These orders did not mention concentrating Jews and imprisoning them in ghettos.

Already during the first few months of the occupation, thousands of Jews were murdered, including the intelligentsia or those accused (without proof) of Communism; synagogues torched, often with people praying inside; and Jews abused—all through local initiatives, especially by the SiPo (*Sicherheitspolize*, Security Policei) and the SD (*Sicherheitsdienst*, Security Service), without directives from above, and sometimes also by soldiers. Thus, in the towns of Mielec and Sanok, synagogues were burned with scores of Jews inside; in Przemyśl already in September 1939, immediately after the Germans marched in, about 500 of the Jewish intelligentsia were shot. And so it was in many other places. In late 1939, a unit of the Waffen SS shot 440 Jews on the road between Chelm and Hrubieszów. On January 12, 1940, 420 Jewish and Polish inmates of a mental hospital in Chelm were shot, and the next day, 600 Jews were shot in the town.[5]

What was the motive for the immediate deportation of the Jews and some of the Poles from the areas of Poland annexed to the Reich to the General Government pursuant to Heydrich's directives of September 21, 1939? The top Nazi leadership—Hitler, Himmler, and senior SS officials—crystallized their decision to concentrate the *Volksdeutsche* (ethnic Germans) dispersed throughout eastern Europe in the expanded Reich into the areas that became an integral part of Germany. The immediate deportation of the Jews from areas of western Poland annexed to Germany was intended to make room for the intake of the *Volksdeutsche* who would come from eastern Polish areas annexed to the Soviet Union and later from the Baltic states, as well. German historian Götz Aly has written on this subject: "In his Reichstag speech of 6 October 1939, Hitler proclaimed the new principles of 'a farsighted ordering of European life.' He viewed as the 'most important task' the creation of 'a new order of ethnographic constellations, meaning a resettlement of nationalities so that at the conclusion of this development better lines of division arise than exist today.'" The speech continues: "In this context the attempt ought to be made to achieve 'an ordering and settlement of the Jewish problem.'"[6]

The following day, on October 7, 1939, Hitler appointed Himmler by secret order as the Reich Commissioner for the Consolidation of German Nationhood (RKFDV, *Reichskommissar für die Festigung deutschen Volkstums*), in addition to his position as head of the SS (*Reichsführer* SS) and chief of German police. As part of this appointment, Himmler was charged with three major missions:

1. To restore to the homeland all *Volksdeutsche* living outside of Germany considered suitable for returning permanently to the Reich.
2. Erase the damaging influence of foreign elements endangering the Reich and Germany society.
3. Establish new settlement areas for Germans by resettling others, especially by awarding lands to ethnic Germans.[7]

In this new role, Himmler became the sole authority for transferring populations, meaning moving people from areas occupied by Germany in eastern Europe to settle *Volksdeutsche* in their place. Himmler's general staff as RKFDV prepared a plan called "Home to the Reich" (*Heim-ins-Reich*) to deal with the approximately five hundred thousand *Volksdeutsche* from eastern Poland's areas annexed to the Soviet Union, from the Baltic states, Romania, south Tyrol, and other areas of Europe. The first stage involved about one hundred thousand Germans from Volhynia in eastern Poland and from Ukraine, plus approximately forty thousand Germans from the Baltic states. Consent to this project was achieved during Ribbentrop's second visit to Moscow on September 28, 1939. The agreement also comprised transferring the Lublin district, located between the Wisla and Bug Rivers, to German control in exchange for transferring Lithuania to the Soviet zone of influence. The following day, Hitler said to his advisor Alfred Rosenberg, his expert on Eastern European affairs, that all of the Jews, including Jews living in the Third Reich, would be moved to the area between the Wisla and the Bug.[8]

The program, headed by Reinhard Heydrich and named the Nisko Plan (Nisko was a city south of Lublin, close to the new border with the Soviet Union), began to be implemented from mid-October 1939. In addition to being the head of the RSHA, he was also appointed to the Central Bureau for Resettlement, the *Umwandererzentralstelle* (UWZ). In this capacity, he was busy transferring *Volksdeutsche* "home to the Reich" and preparing places where they could live, which involved deporting Jews and Poles.[9] The Nisko Plan was designed to transfer to the area dubbed the *Reservat* not only the Jews deported from the areas of Poland annexed to Germany but also Jews from Germany, Austria, and Bohemia and Moravia.

The Germans began deporting Jews from the General Government to the Soviet zone. Thousands of Jews living near the border, along the Bug and San Rivers, were deported over the border. The Soviets refused to allow them to remain and transported them back to the area under German control. One of the men deported in early December 1939, in a group of two thousand Jewish men from the Chelm area, testified:

> We advanced to Gawusze, Sokal's sister-city. This was the border between the General Government and the Soviet Union. It was just before the Bug.... When darkness fell, they told us what we were going to do. They said to us that we were about to advance towards the border where there was a bridge...and they ordered us to walk: on the first part of the bridge, we would walk slowly, in the middle section we were to step up the pace, and in the far section, they told us to raise our hands and yell out "Long live Stalin!".... They explained to us that this would influence the [Soviet] border guards not to shoot us. When we reached the Soviet side...they sent us back there [to the General Government].... At 10 p.m. the Germans reappeared and pressed us to cross the border.[10]

Hundreds of people in this group were shot by the Germans on the way, before they reached the Soviet border.[11] These deportations led to tension between the Germans and the Soviets. Director General of the German Foreign Office Ernst von Weizsäcker's internal memorandum of December 5, 1939, stated: "Generaloberst Keitel [head of the Wehrmacht General Staff] telephoned me today on this subject: Recently there was repeated friction on the border between Russia and the General Government, in which the Wehrmacht was involved. Especially involving the deportation of Jews to Russian soil. The procedure was, for example, that in a quiet place in the forests, 1,000 Jews were deported beyond the Russian border. At a distance of 15km from there, they returned, escorted by a Russian commander, who attempted to force the German officer to accept the group back again."[12] The Soviet Foreign Ministry raised the issue of the deportations with the German ambassador in Moscow. To prevent friction with the Soviet Union, the German Foreign Office intervened, and the deportations ceased.[13] The Soviet government was always was suspicious of foreigners and viewed the refugees similarly. An NKVD document referring to the large number of refugees arriving at the annexed areas stated: "Together with the refugees, the Germans are inserting their agents into our territory as well. Under these conditions of mass [border] crossings, some of the refugees undergo no screening. . . . Most of these trespassers from the direction of Germany are residents of the German-occupied areas who do not want to remain under their rule . . . as well as Jews, whom they are forcibly deporting."[14]

The Nisko Plan was under consideration for a very short time, from October 1939 to March 1940. Although several transports arrived at the area, the plan foundered in light of Hans Frank's opposition as governor of the General Government (supported by Hermann Göring). This opposition stemmed from the small area designed to take in hundreds of thousands of Jews, logistical and economic reasons, and from the lack of possibility of deporting them to the Soviet Union. The plan to create a *Reservat* of hundreds of thousands of Jews in the Lublin district was a utopian plan thought up by SS officials without forethought. It lacked basic planning, since it could not take place without transferring a large population of Poles, and it lacked the transportation means or any examination of the question of whether the Soviet Union would be willing to take in dozens if not hundreds of thousands of Jews. The Nisko Plan was a foreordained failure.

GHETTOIZATION

Concentrating Jews and establishing ghettos was intended to serve as a temporary means moving toward the *Endziel*. Heydrich wrote about this in his *Schnellbrief* of September 21, 1939. On November 4, 1939, SS *Standartenführer* Dr. Rudolf Baatz ordered the Warsaw *Judenrat* to concentrate all of the Jews in the city in a few city blocks within three days. Baatz issued the order in the name of the military commander, General Karl-Ulrich von Neumann-Neurode. The next day, a delegation from the *Judenrat* appealed to the general, but he knew nothing at all about it, and the order to form the ghetto was postponed for a few months.[15] When the Nisko Plan collapsed with its opportunity to deport Jews to the Soviet Union, and genocide had not yet become part of the Nazi regime's agenda, incarcerating the Jews in ghettos became almost the only alternative. Indeed, local German authorities began, on their own initiative, without any clear official order from above, to concentrate the Jews from the villages and towns and establish ghettos in the bigger cities. Section 7 of the order by the director of the Department for Jewish Affairs in the General Government regarding policy guidelines and plans for the Jews dated April 6, 1940, stated: "All measures must be directed at the target that later the whole of [the]

Jewry will be concentrated in a specific district and in one area of Jewish settlement, as a self-supporting society under the control of the Reich." These directives also noted that there was still a plan extant to transfer approximately four hundred thousand Jews from the Polish areas annexed to Germany to the General Government.[16] However, these directives did not yet contain any order to establish ghettos throughout the entire General Government. Establishing the ghettos was under the authority of regional and local authorities, taking into consideration of conditions such as the accessibility of a suitable area, the need to remove the Poles residing there, economic problems, a road system and resolving any disruption to the public transportation system that might arise from establishing a ghetto on its thoroughfares, and other similar details. During this period, it was the local German administration that was empowered with the authority to establish ghettos.

The risk that the Jews of Warsaw would be deported to the Lublin *Reservat* once again led to rejection of the establishment of a ghetto in the city. A similar situation took place also in the district capitals of Cracow, Lublin, and Radom, from where Jews were deported to smaller cities and towns in their districts, due to certain considerations.[17] Further postponement in implementing the ghettoization program for the General Government was due to the background hope that the Jews would be deported beyond the German-occupied zone as part of what was called the Madagascar Plan.

The Madagascar Plan

Madagascar, an island in the Indian Ocean east of the African continent, was then under French rule. In May–June 1940, when the Nisko Plan became obsolete, the Madagascar Plan came to the fore. The Germans expected a victory over France momentarily and expected to conquer Great Britain or, at the very least, reach some sort of settlement with it. Against the backdrop of these expectations, a plan arose to deport all of the Jews of Europe to the island of Madagascar. The idea was suggested even before the war. In 1937, the French government allowed the Polish government to send a research delegation to the island headed by Major Lepecki and with two Jewish members to examine the possibility of settling Polish Jews there. The idea to settle Jews there had also been raised by the British government and the Joint Distribution Committee had looked into it.[18]

Following the German victories and occupation in Western Europe, additional hundreds of thousands of Jews came under German control, and the "Jewish problem" facing the Nazi top brass became even more acute. The idea of deporting the Jews to Madagascar from the German zones of occupation in Europe had arisen in the German Foreign Office as well as in the SS. Hitler confirmed the Madagascar Plan in principle, while agencies in the aforementioned two agencies were engaged in working out the details. It must be noted that the intention of the plan was not that the Jews would live out their lives in Madagascar but that they would gradually reduce their numbers and die out due to famine, illnesses, and the climate. Hans Frank was enthusiastic about the plan since it would have prevented the transport of Jews from western Poland and Germany into "his" territory and would enable him to rid himself of the Jews already in the area of the General Government. Since the implementation of the program was planned for August, Frank even froze the plan for establishing additional ghettos.[19]

Work on the plan was canceled in the early fall of 1940, since, following Germany's failure in the Battle of Britain, the sea transportation routes remained under the control of the British navy. Following the shelving of the Madagascar Plan and other problems that arose, including the danger of contagious disease, Hans Frank decided to incarcerate the Jews of Warsaw in a ghetto, and on November 16, 1940, the gates of the ghetto were sealed. Despite the Jews of Warsaw being imprisoned in the ghetto, the ghettoization of the Jews in other cities of the General Government remained under the authority of the German local administration in the various districts.

By the time the Madagascar Plan was permanently shelved, the decision was already made to attack the Soviet Union; this campaign opened up possibilities for new solutions. One of these was the deportation of the Jews of Poland, Germany, and other European countries to the soon-to-be-conquered areas of the Soviet Union. German researcher Dieter Pohl has written on this subject:

> In conjunction with preparations for the campaign against the Soviet Union, early in 1941 new plans arose in Berlin for the "Solution of the Jewish Question." For the first time, however, they now concerned more than the Jews in Germany or Poland. Under consideration were plans to expel all Jews from territories under German rule to the occupied Soviet Union, either to the Pripyat marshes in Belorussia or to the Arctic Sea. Accordingly, on 17 March 1941 Hitler remarked to Hans Frank that all Jews were to be expelled from the General Government eastward. Thereafter the General Government administration halted until further notice all plans for Jewish policies. In particular, plans to construct more ghettos were put on hold.[20]

The order of Friedrich-Wilhelm Krüger, the HSSPF (*Höhere SS-und Polizeiführer*, the higher SS and police leader of the SS and the police) of the General Government, regarding the obligation to concentrate the Jews in a limited number of ghettos was published in *General Government*

Verordungsblatt, the official mouthpiece of the General Government only on November 14, 1942, when the process of extermination of the Jews of the General Government was nearing its end. This order named the thirty-two cities in which Jews had to be confined to ghettos; most were cities whose Jewish residents worked in plants important to the war economy. Jews were prohibited from living in other cities. In addition to these ghettos, there were closed labor camps in which Jews who worked for the army and plants vital to the German war effort were incarcerated.[21]

CHAPTER TWO

THE ROAD TO OPERATION REINHARD

OPERATION REINHARD WAS THE NAME given to the entire framework of actions undertaken in the destruction of the Jews in Poland's General Government. The name was chosen for the operation after the death of Reinhard Heydrich, following the injury he sustained in the assassination attempt by the Czech underground on May 27, 1942. The decision to exterminate the Jews of the General Government was taken months earlier, and its execution began months prior to the decision on the operation's title.

In the discussion on the extermination policy of European Jewry and the decision-making process on the subject, historians are generally in agreement that the decision to annihilate all of Soviet Jewry was taken separately, before the decision on exterminating the rest of European Jewry. Historians disagree on the question of whether, when deciding on the extermination of the rest of European Jewry, it was a single decision by Adolf Hitler and the Nazi leadership in Berlin or whether there were several decisions taken while considering the war's progress in 1941–1942 and problems that arose in the occupied areas during those years. Was it a series of decisions that ultimately led to the total destruction of the Jews, with Operation Reinhard a part of it? Undoubtedly, at the base of the decision—whether it was a single or a series of decisions—lay the Nazi ideology with its racist anti-Semitism originating from Hitler and the Nazi leadership. Yet the discussion was on the timing of the decision—single or multiple decisions—and on the interests of local German authorities, their "rational" explanations, and their influence on the decision-making process on the total annihilation. The mass murder of the Jews in the Soviet occupied areas, perpetrated while the Nazis were discussing the fate of the Jews in the rest of occupied Europe, implied to the Nazi hierarchy in Berlin—and to Heinrich Himmler and the SS—as well as to the senior officials in the General Government, that extermination was a possible final solution to the Jewish question in all of Europe.

The mass extermination of the Jews of occupied Europe by Nazi Germany began with the Nazi invasion of the Soviet Union on June 22, 1941, the so-called Operation Barbarossa. Soviet Jews were taken into consideration in the German plans to attack the Soviet Union and in several of the orders issued in preparation for Operation Barbarossa. The Jews were defined as a most hostile element, requiring "cruel and aggressive means." This, in the terms of terror employed by Nazi Germany, implied physical destruction.[1] Four SiPo and SD *Einsatzgruppen* units were established under Heydrich's command in preparation for the invasion. The *Einsatzgruppen* advanced with the front units of the German army, and one of their "special tasks" was to murder Jews. On June 17, 1941, Heydrich held a meeting with *Einsatzgruppen* commanders in Berlin, where he informed them verbally of their missions in the Soviet Union. There is no extant summary of this meeting or of what they discussed, nor is there a written order from Heydrich to the *Einsatzgruppen*. However, in a document from July 2, 1941, that Heydrich conveyed to the three HSSPF who were annexed to the headquarters of the three armies at the front and in the Soviet-occupied areas, he informed them of the orders given orally to the *Einsatzgruppen* commanders. The document about the executions, communicated as a telegram, also stated: "All of the following are to be executed: Officials of the Comintern (together with professional communist politicians in general); top and medium level officials and radical lower level officials of the Party; ... People's Commissars; Jews in Party and State employment, and other radical elements (saboteurs, propagandists, partisans, murderers, inciters, etc.).[2]

It is evident from this document that the *Einsatzgruppen* were not given any orders regarding the total murder of the Jews in the Soviet Union prior to Germany's invasion. Despite this, the *Einsatzgruppen*, from the time they became operational in the region—the end of June 1941 and during July—indiscriminately apprehended and murdered Jewish men of work or military age, without clarifying whether they belonged to the Communist Party or whether they had any role whatsoever in the Soviet regime. The decision to exterminate all of Soviet Jewry regardless of age or gender was taken during an excursion Himmler took in the occupied areas of the Soviet Union between the second half of July and the beginning of August 1941, during the conversations he held with *Einsatzgruppen* commanders and the HSSPF. At that time, the decision was taken only with regards to Soviet Jewry, and they were the first to be destined to total physical annihilation.[3]

The *Einsatzgruppen*, in their execution of the extermination *Aktionen* (actions), adopted the same modus operandi throughout their sphere of action, making the necessary adjustments based on conditions in each locality. In certain towns they murdered thousands of Jews in an *Aktion* that lasted between one to three days; in other places, they murdered the Jews in several *Aktionen* at different time intervals. In rural areas and townships the extermination *Aktionen* were executed by small, mobile *Einsatzgruppen* units, which would arrive at a specific place for a day or two, and, assisted by local police officials, would murder all the Jews in a single *Aktion*. The exterminations took place in the open. Both the Wehrmacht soldiers stationed in the area and the local residents knew about them and were sometimes, out of curiosity, eyewitnesses to them.

There were not many *Einsatzgruppen* men, and they required additional forces to execute the extermination *Aktionen*. These additional forces included the German Orpo and Ordnungspolizei battalions and tens of thousands of local collaborators. The General Government SiPo commander also dispatched three units subordinated to him to Lvov, Brest-Litovsk, and Bialystok to assist the *Einsatzgruppen* in their mission. Thousands of Jews were murdered by these units.[4]

The locations selected for these killings were either natural ravines, antitank ditches, or pits specially dug for the purpose. The Jews were concentrated at assembly points and taken in groups to the killing sites. As a rule, the men were taken first, then the women, and finally the children. The victims were lined up either inside the ditch or at its edge; then they were shot. After one group had been killed, the next was brought over. In cities with a large Jewish population, the killing sometimes went on for days or even weeks. Karl Jäger, the commander of *Einsatzkommando 3*, which carried out the murder operation of Jews in Lithuania, wrote in his report:

> The carrying-out of such *Aktionen* is first of all an organizational problem. The decision to clear each sub-district systematically of Jews called for a thorough preparation for each *Aktion* and the study of local conditions. The Jews had to be concentrated in one or more localities and, in accordance with their numbers, a site had to be selected and pits dug. The marching distance from the concentration points to the pits averaged 4 to 5 kms. The Jews were brought to the place of execution in groups of 500, with a distance of at least 2 kms distance between groups.[5]

The *Einsatzgruppen* left behind hundreds of thousands of victims in mass murder valleys in Ponar near Vilna, Fort IX at Kovno, Rumboli near Riga, Babi Yar at Kiev, Drobitzki Valley near Kharkov, in the Crimea, and at numerous other sites in the occupied areas of the Soviet Union.

However, this method of mass murder—shooting the victims in the vicinity of their homes—raised problems for the Nazi authorities. The shooting of thousands of people was a slow process, and large numbers of SS men were required for each killing operation. The executions were carried out simultaneously in hundreds, even thousands of different locations, rendering it almost impossible to keep them secret from the local population and prospective victims. Instances of last-minute flight and even resistance were recorded by the Germans. It was also evident that what could be done in the occupied territories of the Soviet Union and near the front lines could not be accomplished so openly in most other European countries, where negative reactions were to be expected from sections of the local population. Furthermore, the prolonged exposure of members of the *Einsatzgruppen* to the murder of women, children, and the elderly produced a cumulative psychological effect on some of them and even caused mental breakdowns.

Himmler was aware of these difficulties. An eyewitness describes what happened during his visit to Minsk in late summer 1941, while watching the killing of a group of one hundred Jews: "As the firing started, Himmler became more and more nervous. During every volley, he looked down to the ground. . . . The other witness was *Obergruppenführer* von dem Bach-Zelewski. . . . Von dem Bach addressed Himmler: 'Reichsführer, those were only a hundred. . . . Look at the eyes of the men in this Kommando, how deeply shaken they are! These men are finished [*fertig*] for the rest of their lives. What kind of followers are we training here? Either neurotics or savages!'"[6] As a result of these drawbacks, Himmler and the SS authorities, who were in charge of the Nazi extermination machine, began looking for additional methods and improved technical means that would enable them to carry out the killings more efficiently, more quickly, and with less effort. Rudolf Höss, the commander of Auschwitz, wrote in his evidence:

In the summer of 1941, I cannot remember the exact date, I was suddenly summoned to the SS *Reichsführer* Himmler, who received me without his adjutant being present. Himmler said: 'The *Führer* has ordered that the Jewish question be solved once and for all and that we, the SS, are to implement that order. The existing extermination centers in the East are not in a position to carry out the large *Aktionen* which are anticipated.'"

Shortly afterwards, Eichmann came to Auschwitz and disclosed to me the plans for the operations as they affected the various countries concerned. . . . We discussed the ways and means of effecting the extermination. This could only be done by gassing, since it would have been absolutely impossible to dispose by shooting of the large numbers of people that were expected, and it would have placed too heavy a burden on the SS men who had to carry it out, especially because of the women and children among the victims.[7]

"Operation Euthanasia": Mass Killings by Gas

The first time gas had been used in Nazi Germany for murdering people was for the "euthanasia program." Over seventy thousand mentally or otherwise "hopelessly" ill Germans—not Jews—were killed between September 1939 and late summer 1941. For this operation, Hitler had established a secret organization known as T4 (a reference to the organization's headquarters at 4 Tiergartenstrasse in Berlin) subordinated to Hitler's chief of chancellery, *Reichsleiter* Philipp Bouhler.[8]

At the beginning of World War II, Hitler signed the following order: "*Reichsleiter* Bouhler and Dr. [Karl] Brandt [Hitler's personal physician] are charged with the responsibility for expanding the authority of individual physicians, with a view to enable them, after the most critical examination in the realm of human knowledge, to administer to incurably sick persons a mercy death."[9]

The first to be killed under the euthanasia program were "deformed newborns" reported by health officials complying with the decree of August 18, 1939. A panel of three doctors was set up to review the infants selected for consideration. Over time, the age limit moved from infants and children under the age of three to older children and, even in some cases, teenagers. By the end of the war, some five thousand children had been murdered by the program.[10]

The man who was directly in charge of the euthanasia operation was Viktor Brack, a senior official in the chancellery of the *Führer* and subordinate to Bouhler. The T4 organization established several institutions throughout Germany. The mentally ill destined for elimination were placed in hermetically sealed rooms into which carbon monoxide was introduced; they died within a short time. Some victims were killed by injections of poison. All the bodies were cremated.

A request from Himmler to Bouhler in the summer of 1940 expanded the euthanasia program to apply to sick concentration camp detainees from the camps inside Germany under SS supervision. Some of the detainees were Jews. They were removed from their camps to the euthanasia centers and were murdered there. The code name for this operation was 14F13. As a result of internal pressure within Nazi Germany, Hitler ordered the termination of the euthanasia program at the end of August 1941. However, sporadic killings of small groups of "incurable victims" continued in some euthanasia institutions after this date.[11]

On September 3, 1941, the gas Zyklon B was first used for extermination in Auschwitz on an experimental basis. Zyklon B was an alcohol acid preparation that had been used until then at Auschwitz for exterminating vermin. The group chosen for this first experiment consisted of Soviet prisoners of war. Further experiments followed shortly thereafter. Rudolph Höss, the commander of Auschwitz, wrote in his testimony:

> The gassing was carried out in the detention cells of Block 11. Protected by a gas mask, I watched the killing myself. In the crowded cells, death came instantaneously the moment the Zyklon B was thrown in. A short, almost smothered cry, and it was all over . . .
>
> I must even admit that this gassing set my mind at rest, for the mass extermination of the Jews was to start soon, and at that time neither Eichmann nor I was certain as to how these mass killings were to be carried out. It would be by gas, but we did not know which gas and how it was to be used. Now we had the gas, and we had established a procedure.[12]

Concurrent to these experiments in Auschwitz, the *Einsatzgruppen* looked for additional and simpler methods for mass killings. The new facility developed and supplied to the *Einsatzgruppen* was gas vans. The idea of the gas van originated with SS *Brigadeführer* Artur Nebe, commander of *Einsatzgruppe B*, which operated in territories close to the central front and which had carried out in Belorussia large-scale shooting actions of Jews, Communists, and other "asocial elements." Nebe, as former leader of the Reich's Criminal Police Department (*Kripo Kriminalpolizei*), was familiar with the euthanasia program and killing by gas.

In September 1941, *Einsatzgruppe B* was faced with the task of liquidating the patients of the lunatic asylums in the cities of Minsk and Mogilev. Nebe decided to find a simpler way for his men to kill the mentally diseased, other than by shooting them. He contacted Kripo headquarters and asked for their help in carrying out the killing of the insane with either explosives or poison gas. Dr. Albert Widmann of the Criminal Police was sent to Nebe in Minsk, but before he left, Dr. Widmann discussed with the director of the Criminal Police Technological Institute, Dr. Heess, ways of using the carbon monoxide gas from automobile exhaust for killing operations in the East, based on the experience gained from the euthanasia program. Dr. Widmann took to Minsk four hundred kilograms of explosive material and the metal pipes required for the gassing installations.

Nebe and Dr. Widmann carried out an experimental killing using explosives. Twenty-five mentally ill people were locked into two bunkers in a forest outside Minsk. The first explosion killed only some of them, and it took substantial time and trouble until the second explosion killed the rest. Explosives, therefore, were unsatisfactory.

A few days later an experiment with poison gas was carried out by Nebe and Dr. Widmann in Mogilev. In the local lunatic asylum, a room with twenty to thirty of the insane was closed hermetically, and two pipes were driven into the wall. A car was parked outside, and one of the metal pipes that Dr. Widmann had brought connected the exhaust of the car to the pipe in the wall. The car engine was turned on, and the carbon monoxide began seeping into the room. After eight minutes, the people in the room were still alive. A second car was connected to the other pipe in the wall. The two cars were operated simultaneously, and a few minutes later all those in the room were dead.

After these experimental executions, Nebe came up with the idea of constructing a car with a hermetically sealed cabin for killing purposes. The carbon monoxide from the car's exhaust would be channeled into the sealed cabin, in which the victims stood. Nebe discussed the technical aspects of the idea with Dr. Heess and together they brought the proposal before Heydrich, who adopted it.[13]

The Technical Department of the Reich Security Main Office, headed by SS *Obersturmbannführer* Walter Rauff, developed a special vehicle for killing purposes. This vehicle resembled an ambulance or refrigerator truck and contained a hermetically sealed rear cabin. The victims were placed in the cabin and carbon monoxide was introduced by means of a pipe. The gassing process took between fifteen and thirty minutes. During this time the van was driven from the loading site to prepared graves.

Two types of gas vans had been built: a larger one, 5.8 meters in length, and a smaller one, measuring 4.5 meters. Both were about 2.5 meters wide and 1.7 meters high. The bigger one could accommodate between 130 and 150 people, when densely packed inside, and the smaller one from 80 to 100.[14]

The first gas vans were supplied to the *Einsatzgruppen* and to the Chelmno death camps in November–December 1941. The killing in Chelmno began on December 8, 1941. By the middle of 1942, about thirty gas vans had been produced by a private car manufacturer, the Gabschat Farengewerke GMBH, Will-Walter Strasse 32–38, Berlin.[15]

A few weeks before the first gas vans were supplied to the *Einsatzgruppen*, in late October 1941, Dr. Alfred Wetzel of the Ministry for the Eastern Occupied Territories wrote to the *Reichskommissar* for Ostland, Hinrich Lohse, of a proposal suggested by Viktor Brack to set up permanent gassing facilities in Ostland for mass extermination based on the experience and help of the euthanasia program. With the cessation of the euthanasia program in Germany, its personnel were available and looking for new tasks.[16]

The permanent gassing facilities were intended to lighten the task of Nazi authorities in the occupied territories of the Soviet Union in carrying out their killing operations. But the proposal of Dr. Wetzel and of Brack was not implemented in Ostland. The unemployed "euthanasia" personnel were assigned to another and bigger task—the erection of camps with gassing facilities, where the annihilation of the Jews in the Nazi-occupied territories of Poland would be carried out. The successful experiments in Auschwitz and the development of the gas vans had provided the solution to the technical problems involved.

WANNSEE CONFERENCE

At the same time that the extermination activities were being carried out by the *Einsatzgruppen* in the Soviet Union and the technical experiments with gassing were being conducted, the governing authorities of the Third Reich were beginning to prepare for the implementation of the "final solution" of European Jewry.

On July 31, 1941, Heydrich was assigned by Reich Marshal Hermann Göring the task of preparing a plan for the "final solution of the Jewish question" within the realm of German rule and influence in Europe. He was to make "all necessary preparations with regard to organizational, practical and financial aspects for an overall solution [*Gesamtlösung*] of the Jewish question in the German sphere of influence in Europe."[17] The various components of the German governing apparatus—the SS; the Nazi party; the ministries, with their bureaucratic machinery; and the army—were to play specific roles in carrying out the "final solution."

Heydrich was to draw up a comprehensive plan for all of European Jewry—and not only for the Jews residing within areas governed by Nazi Germany and the Axis alliance, but also for Jews in neutral countries as well as Great Britain, which was at war with Germany. The conference at which Heydrich was to present his plan was scheduled to convene on December 9, 1941, but was postponed to January 20, 1942, on several grounds. These included the Japanese attack on the United States on December 7, 1941, and the German declaration of war on America on December 11, which precipitated a far-reaching strategic change, rendering the war a global one; and the Soviet counterattack on the Moscow front, which worsened Germany's situation in its war against the Soviet Union.

Nevertheless, the six-week postponement of the conference was also related to Hitler's speech from December 12, 1941, before the leaders of the Nazi Party and its regional leaders. The content of this speech necessitated a reform in the plan that Heydrich was to present at the Wannsee Conference. German historian Christian Gerlach quotes from notes taken by Joseph Goebbels and others at the meeting:

> Regarding the Jewish problem, the *Führer* is determined to make a clean sweep. He has forewarned the Jews that they will be exterminated if they bring about another world war. These were not mere words. We are now facing a world war. Exterminating the Jews is the natural outcome. We cannot afford to be sentimental in this matter. It is not our business to be sympathetic toward the Jews. We need to focus our sympathy on our own German nation. If the German people are required to sacrifice 160,000 victims on the altar of an additional battle in the east—then those responsible will have to pay with their own lives.[18]

Hitler's warning to the Jews lest they bring about another world war would lead to their destruction echoed his speech from January 30, 1939. Many of the historians who have researched this subject agree that December 12, 1941, was the day on which Hitler approved of or decided on the destruction of European Jewry. This was not an order but rather a declaration before a large forum, which included Himmler, Alfred Rosenberg, Hans Frank, and others from the Nazi leadership. Those present clearly understood that, as far as they were concerned, this was indeed Hitler's decision to destroy the Jews in Europe. Hitler did not require explicit directives to annihilate the Jews. His words were sufficient for the upper echelons of the Nazi leadership to understand that this was the *Führer's* intention, the "spirit of the commander."

Hans Frank, the Nazi governor general of the General Government, at a meeting of his top officials held in Cracow on December 16, 1941, spoke openly of the purposes of the forthcoming conference:

> I want to say to you quite frankly that we shall have to finish with the Jews one way or another. The *Führer* once spoke these words: If united Jewry should again succeed in causing another world war, the peoples who have been hounded into this war will not be the only ones to shed their blood; the Jew of Europe will also find his end . . .
>
> I will therefore, on principle, approach Jewish affairs in the expectation that the Jews will disappear. They must go. I have begun negotiations to send them to the east. In January a big conference regarding this question will be held in Berlin and I will send *Staatssekretär* Dr. Bühler as a representative. This conference will be held in the Reich Security Main Office under the auspices of *SS-Obergruppenführer* Heydrich. A major migration is about to start. . . . But what is to happen to the Jews? Do you think they will actually be resettled in Ostland villages? We were told in Berlin: Why all this trouble? We can't use them either in Ostland or in the *Reichskommissariat*, liquidate them yourselves.[19]

Gerlach details several factors to explain Hitler's decision to totally exterminate European Jews at that time. Hitler fanatically believed that the Jews were behind the Allied powers' opposition to his "just" territorial demands and that they were to blame for the war, which after the entrance of the United States had become a world war. The possibility of a second European front as well as Germany's defeat in the Moscow front in December 1941 confronted Hitler and the Nazi leadership with a new concerning reality. Hitler now viewed the Jews under his rule all over Europe as terrorists, spies, and "partisans" endangering the German home front who therefore must be eliminated. This was Hitler's intent when saying the Jews were "to be exterminated as partisans," during his December 18, 1941, meeting with Himmler.[20]

After a postponement caused by the entrance of the United States into the war, the conference was held on January 20, 1942, at Wannsee, a suburb of Berlin. The participants of the Wannsee Conference included the director generals (*Staatssekretär*) of the relevant ministries, senior representatives of the German ruling authorities in the occupied countries, and SS senior department heads.

At the conference convened by Heydrich, he informed the relevant authorities in Nazi Germany of the "final solution" as decided on by Hitler and that the SS and he personally would be in charge of it. In addition, the conference was to discuss the different political and organizational aspects of the implementation of the "final solution" and the problem of the *mischlinge* (a person of mixed blood; specifically, a person with at least one Jewish grandparent).

Dr. Josef Bühler, *Staatssekretär* of the General Government (the areas of central Poland occupied by Germany) demanded at the conference that the "final solution" be applied first to the Jews of the General Government. The conference protocol states:

Staatssekretär Dr. Bühler announced that the General Government would welcome it if the final solution of this problem would begin in the General Government, as, on the one hand, the question of transport there plays no major role and consideration of labor supply would not hinder the course of the *Aktionen*. Jews must be removed as quickly as possible from the General Government, because it was there in particular that the Jew, as a carrier of epidemics, constituted a great danger, and, at the same time, caused constant disorder in the economic structure of the country by his continuous black-market dealings. Furthermore, of the approximately two and a half million Jews under consideration, the majority were in any case unfit for work. *Staatssekretär* Dr. Bühler further stated that the solution of the Jewish question in the General Government was primarily the responsibility of the Chief of

Security Police and the SD and that his work would have the support of the authorities of the General Government. He had only one request: that the Jewish question in this area be solved as quickly as possible.[21]

Bühler's request that the Jews of the General Government in Poland be destroyed first was in fact accepted.

The conference protocol also states that:

> Emigration has now been replaced by evacuation of the Jews to the East, as a further possible solution, with the appropriate prior authorization by the Führer....
>
> In the course of this final solution of the European Jewish question approximately 11 million Jews may be taken into consideration, distributed over the individual countries as follows: ...
>
> General Government   2,284,000 ...
>
> Under appropriate direction the Jews are to be utilized for work in the East in an expedient manner in the course of the final solution. In large [labor] columns, with the sexes separated, Jews capable of work will be moved into these areas as they build roads, during which a large proportion will no doubt drop out through natural reduction. The remnant that eventually remains will require suitable treatment; because it will without doubt represent the most [physically] resistant part, it consists of a natural selection that could, on its release, become the germ cell of a new Jewish revival.[22]

The conference's protocol does not mention the word "extermination," but it is clear that during the deliberations, the participants were made to understand the implication of the words "evacuation of the Jews to the East" denoted extermination and that this had already received "appropriate consent by the *Führer*." The conference participants surely knew about Hitler's speech from December 12, 1941, where he used the word "extermination"; repeating it at the conference or in its protocol was superfluous. It was Heydrich's goal at the conference to elucidate that from this point forward there would be no more partial solutions or initiatives by the various agencies regarding the anti-Jewish policy, but rather, that there was now a comprehensive solution to all of European Jewry, and that SS *Reichsführer* (Himmler) and the RSHA, which he directed, would be dealing with the issue en bloc. German historian Ulrich Herbert wrote, in relation to the importance of the Wannsee Conference: "The approach presented by Heydrich at the conference needs to be viewed as a proposal to unite the various developments in anti-Jewish policy, in other words, to create a foundation that would encompass Europe in its entirety."[23]

The Decision to Exterminate the Jews of the General Government: Operation Reinhard

The preparations for the extermination of the Jews of the General Government had actually started months before the Wannsee Conference. At the end of July 1941, about a month after the attack on the Soviet Union, Himmler, in his role as the reichcommissar for the Strengthening of German Ethnic Stock, decided to settle *Volksdeutsche* in the Lublin area, and tasked Odilo Globocnik, the SSPF (*SS- und Polizeiführer*, SS and police commander) of the Lublin district, with the mission.[24]

Globocnik was an Austrian, a member of the Austrian Nazi party, and in 1933 received a prison sentence for his part in the murder of a Jew in Vienna. He had earned Himmler's high esteem for his contribution to the annexation (*Anschluss*) of Austria to Germany, and when Austria became part of the Reich, he was appointed *Gauleiter* of Vienna. In January 1939, he was accused of illegal speculation in foreign currency and was stripped of his post and all his party honors. After Globocnik's demotion to the ranks of the Waffen SS, Himmler pardoned his friend and in November 1939 appointed him as SS and police leader of the Lublin district. The SS and police leader was the highest SS authority in the district. Globocnik felt a personal gratitude to Himmler for his rehabilitation and became his loyal trustee.

He was not an "ordinary" district SS and police leader. Through Globocnik's initiative, the Lublin district became the center of SS industrial plans, and as early as December 1940, the DAW (Deutsche Ausrüstungswerke, German supply and armaments factories) company had established a branch there. Over five thousand Jewish prisoners, including Jewish POWs from the Polish army, were employed in its factories. In the summer of 1941, the SS clothing workshops were established in Lublin, which also employed Jewish slave laborers. Majdanek concentration camp in Lublin was designed to absorb twenty-five thousand to fifty thousand prisoners who would work in the financially productive SS factories slated for expansion and enlargement.

On July 17, 1941, Globocnik was appointed by Himmler as his commissioner in organizing the SS and police stations in the newly occupied eastern territories as settlements for the families of SS men who would be serving there. Globocnik initiated plans for the extensive resettlement of Germans, comprising special settlements of SS in the Lublin district. The SS settlements were intended to serve as a link with the areas of the future German colonization in the newly occupied territories of the Soviet Union.[25]

During the summer of 1941 it appeared that a victory over the Soviet Union was imminent, within a matter of weeks or several months; and once the war in the east was over, Germany could deport to the Polesie bogs or the Arctic Circle in the far north the three hundred thousand Jews residing in the Lublin district and replace them with German settlers. This plan was ready at the end of September 1941; however, by the fall, the war was clearly still ongoing, and, so as not to delay the plan to resettle Germans in the region despite not being able to deport the Jews—Himmler and Globocnik decided to murder them. A meeting was held on October 13, 1941, with Himmler, Globocnik, and Krueger, the General Government HSSPF. The consensus is that the decision was taken at that meeting to expand the extermination plan and apply it to all the Jews of the General Government.[26]

There is no doubt that Himmler received Hitler's consent to a decision of such an extent, and there is no doubt that Hans Frank knew about the plan and expressed his consent even before the meeting.[27]

SS officials in the General Government knew from reports coming out of occupied areas in the Soviet Union that it was possible to physically exterminate multitudes of people. The decision to exterminate the Jews of the General Government was but a continuation of the activity in the Soviet Union. This decision also fit the Nazi racial perception and anti-Semitism. However, the method of shooting victims employed in areas of the Soviet Union was unsuitable for the extermination of two and a half million Jews living in the General Government. Beyond the various difficulties involved with this method, the General Government lacked the necessary manpower. The use of gas in the euthanasia program together with the experience garnered during this campaign, as well as the use of gas to exterminate the mentally ill in Mogilev and to murder Soviet POWs at Auschwitz, provided the solution—extermination in gas chambers and cremating the corpses in special camps.

The euthanasia program was terminated in August 1941. In the second half of October its personnel, who were unemployed for but a few weeks, were placed at the disposal of Globocnik and Operation Reinhard—bringing with them their experience in extermination by gas. Belzec, the first extermination camp, was established in November 1941, followed by Sobibor and Treblinka.

THE WAVE OF POGROMS AND MURDERS
IN THE DISTRICT OF GALICIA

Even before the decision was made to embark on Operation Reinhard and the extermination of all the Jews of the General Government, thousands of Jews were murdered in pogroms in Galicia. Eastern Galicia, which was part of the Soviet Ukraine, was conquered by the German army during the first ten days of Operation Barbarossa. An estimated six hundred thousand Jews were living there at the time of its occupation. In July, during the days of the military rule and before it was annexed to the General Government on August 1, 1941, becoming yet another of its districts—"District Galicia"—a wave of pogroms swept through eastern Galicia. In many places these riots took place as soon as the Soviets took their leave, and sometimes even before they were replaced by the German army.

The local Ukrainians welcomed the German army wholeheartedly, and thousands of them joined the police force serving the Germans. The pogroms were an expression of the anti-Semitism that had grown following the Soviet rule. Violence toward the Jews increased after hundreds of corpses were found in the prisons the Soviets had deserted as they fled eastward; these prisoners had been murdered by the NKVD as they escaped to the east. The majority of those murdered were Ukrainians (though there were also a number of Poles and Jews), and the Ukrainian rabble took their rage out on the Jews. The pogrom's victims included men, women, and children.

Based on various estimates, at the time of the German occupation there were 160,000 Jews living in Lvov, including thousands of refugees from other areas of west and central of occupied Poland. A pogrom that began on June 30, the day the German army entered the city, continued until July 3, during which close to 4,000 Jews were murdered. Pogroms against Jews took places in dozens of cities, towns, and villages throughout eastern Galicia: In Złoczów, for example, between 3,000 and 4,000 Jews were murdered; in Tarnopol, 5,000.[28]

An additional pogrom began in Lvov on the fifteenth anniversary of the murder of Symon Petliura and was named *Aktion Petliura*. This pogrom began on July 25 and continued until July 28, resulting in the killing of almost 1,500 Jews.[29]

During the first few days of July 1941, following *Einsatzgruppe C*, and in order to assist it, a special unit of 150 SiPo and SD men came to Lvov from the General Government. They carried out a series of *Aktionen* against Jews in various places in the district of Galicia, beginning in July. Several of these men formed the permanent SiPo and SD extensions in the central cities of the Galicia district.[30]

In September 1941, a *Julag*, or *Judenlager*—a slave labor camp for Jews— was established on Janówska Street, located in northwest Lvov. The camp was under the SS, but several of its workshops also served the army. In late October, with six hundred forced Jewish laborers already working there, the camp was turned into a closed camp: the Jews who worked there were prohibited from returning at night to their residences and their families, severing them from the outside world. With the closure, a concentration camp regime was gradually introduced, and the number of Jews sent to the camp also increased. The camp became the nightmare of the Lvov Jews.[31]

With the annexation of eastern Galicia to the General Government, Karl Lasch was appointed district governor of Galicia, while Friedrich Katzmann was named SSPF. Hans Frank demanded that additional areas of the former Soviet zones be annexed to the General Government, especially the Pripet Marshes area, to which he intended to deport the Jews of the General Government. Frank's request was denied.[32]

The policy implemented toward the Jews of the district of Galicia was similar to the policy applied in other areas of the General Government, but its actual implementation was much more drastic, similar to the Jewish policy in the Soviet occupied areas. All of the anti-Jewish laws enacted in the General Government—establishment of the *Judenräte*, obligatory white armband with Jewish star, forced labor, and the like—were also implemented in Galicia. In addition to these laws and the looting of Jewish property in the district, the Germans also executed groups of Jewish intelligentsia who were active in Soviet government institutions or suspected of being Communist sympathizers, exactly as they did in areas they occupied in former Soviet territory. The Germans set up ghettos in several cities in the first few months of the occupation, but in the majority of the towns the Germans established ghettos only during 1942.

The extermination *Aktionen* began in the district of Galicia in early October 1941, with the first mass murders of Jews throughout the General Government prior to Operation Reinhard. In September 1941, discussions were held in Katzmann's office in Lvov on the extermination of the Jews. The decision was made to begin the roundups in the Stanislawow area (now Ivano-Frankovsk) in the southern Galicia district.[33]

The biggest roundup of Jews during that period of time took place in Stanislawow, settled by more than twenty-five thousand Jews—which was, after Lvov, the second-largest Jewish community in eastern Galicia. During the second half of 1939, thousands of refugees from German-occupied Poland streamed into Stanislawow.

During the first few weeks of the German occupation, in July 1941, when the Hungarian army was in control of Stanislawow, several thousand Jews who had been deported from Carpatho-Rus, which was at that time part of Hungary, were transported to the city in early August. There were already thirty-five thousand to thirty-eight thousand Jews in the city, including Jews who had fled there from the surrounding townships and villages out of fear of the local Ukrainians.[34]

During the first half of August 1941, about five hundred Jews of the intelligentsia were shot to death. On the eve of the "Big *Aktion*" a reinforcement made up of men from the German Police Battalion 133 and of Ukrainian policemen arrived in the city. On Sunday, October 12, 1941, nearly twenty thousand Jews were plucked out of their homes and brought to the Jewish cemetery. There they were ordered to strip and hand over their valuables, while group by group they were shot standing near open pits prepared in advance. That same day, ten thousand to twelve thousand Jews were shot near the pits; thousands who still remained at nightfall were taken back to their homes. During the *Aktion*, rabble in the city went searching for Jews in hiding and looted the homes of those taken to the cemetery. The Stanislawow ghetto was established in the first half of December 1941 in the city's poorest quarters where the very poorest of the Jews lived. The ghetto was officially sealed by the end of December, incarcerating between twenty-three thousand and twenty-six thousand Jews.[35]

Before the war, about 15,000 Jews lived in Kolomyya; in October 1941, 2,850 of its Jews were murdered, based on a list prepared by the Ukrainians. On December 23, another 1,200 Jews were murdered; these were refugees from Germany and Hungary. On January 24, 1942, another 400 of the Jewish intelligentsia were shot. These murders took place near the village of Sheparovtse, a distance of eight kilometers from the city.[36] Additional roundups and murders took place from October through December 1941 in the Stanislawow area.[37]

On December 8, 1941, the Germans announced the establishment of a ghetto in Lvov, ordering the Jews to move into the ghetto by December 15, 1941. On the way to the ghetto they had to pass underneath an iron railroad bridge, alongside which stood German and Ukrainian police guards. They abused the Jews and looted their possessions. They then took all those who looked elderly and ill out of the line, marched them in groups to the forest outside of the city, and murdered them. Approximately five thousand Jews were murdered during this roundup, called the "Bridge of Death *Aktion*." Until December 15, 1941, tens of thousands of Jews had not yet managed to move into the area set for the ghetto, and the Germans accepted this situation: whoever had not moved was permitted to remain in their home, creating an open ghetto, which was only sealed in September 1942.

Roundups in which hundreds of Jews were killed, and in some places thousands murdered, took place in most of the Jewish communities in Galicia. Except for the *Aktionen* in the Stanislawow area, at this stage the *Aktionen* did not yet take on the character of mass murder. The victims were Jews whose names were on lists drawn up by local Ukrainians. Among those murdered were members of the intelligentsia, Jews in the free professions, those active and holding office in the Soviet regime, and Jews whom the Ukrainians wanted to be rid of for their own personal reasons. By the end of 1941, about sixty thousand Jews of Galicia had been murdered—10 percent of all of the Jews of Galicia—even before Operation Reinhard.[38]

THE ESTABLISHMENT OF THE CHELMNO DEATH CAMP AND THE DECISION TO EXTERMINATE THE JEWS OF THE WARTHEGAU

The Warthegau was one of the areas of western Poland annexed to the Third Reich and not part of the General Government. The protocol of the Wannsee Conference stated that there were 420,000 Jews in these areas. Like the decision taken in October 1941 to annihilate the Jews of the General Government—which arose at first from the plan for the resettlement of Germans in the Lublin area—the decision to kill all the Jews in the Warthegau, prior to Hitler's decision on genocide in December 1941 and prior to the Wannsee Conference, was not directly associated with the Jews.

During the second half of 1941, the British Air Force bombed many cities in Germany, including Hamburg, Cologne, and others. Houses were hit, leaving many Germans homeless. The Gauleiters and mayors appealed to Göring and through him to Hitler, asking them to deport the Jews still remaining in Germany, evacuating them from their apartments, which could then be given to Germans. The initial plan called for about sixty thousand Jews from the bombed cities to be deported to the General Government, but Frank's objections prevented this. On October 2, 1941, Hitler held a meeting in the presence of Himmler and Heydrich, at which he authorized the deportations, with the destinations as Minsk, Riga, and Tallinn.

However, at the time, the Wehrmacht was engaged in fierce battles on the Moscow and Leningrad fronts and needed the trains. Consequently, the first deportees, approximately twenty thousand, were sent to the Lodz ghetto, the nearest location, instead of to the planned destinations. To make room for the new arrivals, the German authorities in Warthegau decided to kill the Jews who were already living in the Lodz ghetto, and so they established the Chelmno death camp. Mass murder at Chelmno began on December 8, 1941, using gas vans. Chelmno was the first extermination camp; the Jews killed there were transported from the Lodz ghetto and other ghettos in the Warthegau.[39]

SUMMARY

The decision to exterminate the Jews of Europe was not taken as one single decision by Hitler regarding the total annihilation of European Jewry but rather as a series of decisions relating to the Jews in different countries. These decisions were along the lines of his speech in the Reichstag on January 30, 1939, which stated that if another world war broke out, it would culminate in the destruction of the Jewish race in Europe. It was Himmler and Heydrich who initiated most of these decisions, after receiving Hitler's consent to their implementation.

The first decision regarding mass extermination was taken concerning the Jews of the Soviet Union, between the end of July and the beginning of August 1941. The decision applied to the Jewish population within the June 22, 1941, borders of the Soviet Union—more than 5.0 million Jews. It was close to 46 percent of the 11.0 million Jews mentioned in the Wannsee Conference protocol. The second decision regarding the mass annihilation was taken in October 1941 and related to the extermination of close to 2.3 million Jews in the General Government and another close to 400,000 Warthegau Jews, comprising almost 25 percent of the Jews mentioned in the Wannssee Conference protocol. To these numbers one must add the thousands of Jews who had already been murdered in occupied Yugoslavia and the thousands of Jews of the Third Reich who were deported to the Baltic states and murdered there.[40] Hitler's speech on December 12, 1941, had to be seen and understood as the third decision for total extermination of European Jewry that was expressed at the Wannsee Conference. This decision was taken after it had already been decided to exterminate nearly 75 percent of the 11.0 million Jews accounted for in the protocol of the Wannsee Conference.[41] This third decision was the de facto consent to the previous decisions regarding the extermination, which primarily related to the Jews of Eastern Europe. The decision's novelty was that it included in the extermination process the Jews of Western Europe, the Jews in the countries that were Germany's allies, the Jews in neutral countries, and the Jews in Great Britain. When Hitler decided to exterminate all of European Jewry, Operation Reinhard had already been put into effect: Organizing the manpower was already underway, and construction of the first extermination camp, Belzec, had already begun.

CHAPTER THREE

OPERATION REINHARD: ORGANIZATION AND MANPOWER

FOLLOWING THE DECISION OF OPERATION Reinhard, on October 13, 1941, Heinrich Himmler appointed Odilo Globocnik as its commander. Himmler did not provide Globocnik with any written orders regarding Operation Reinhard and the extermination of the Jews. These orders were given verbally, as were the orders given to the *Einsatzgruppen* relating to their killing operations in the occupied territories of the Soviet Union. Himmler, for secrecy reasons, opposed written orders and documents on the extermination of the Jews. In a speech before an audience of high-ranking SS and police officers in Poznan on October 4, 1943, he stated:" I am referring here to the evacuation of the Jews, the extermination of the Jewish people. . . . This is an unwritten and never-to-be-written page of glory in our history."[1] As chief of Operation Reinhard, Globocnik was a direct subordinate of Himmler and not to the HSSPF of the General Government. However, as the SSPF of the Lublin district, Globocnik did continue to be subordinate to Friedrich-Wilhelm Krüger. In early 1941, the operation headquarters (*Einsatzstab Reinhardt*) was established in Lublin. SS *Hauptsturmführer* Hermann Höfle was appointed as chief of staff and was directly in charge of the operation's organizational setup as well as all its activities. The main tasks imposed on Globocnik and his staff within the framework of Operation Reinhard were:

- the overall planning of the deportations and extermination activities of the entire operation;
- organizing the manpower;
- building the death camps;
- coordinating the deportations of the Jews from the different districts to the death camps;
- seizing the assets and valuables of the victims and handing them over to the appropriate Reich authorities; and
- killing the Jews in the camps.

Operation Reinhard set the guidelines and directives for the deportations, and its staff was in charge of coordinating the timetable of the transports in accordance with the absorption capacity of the camps. The specific organization and guarding of the transports of Jews from all over the General Government—and later from other European countries—to the death camps were not under the command of Globocnik's Operation Reinhard staff. These tasks were handled by the Reich Security Main Office and its branches and by higher SS and police leaders in each locality (SSPF and HSSPF). Nevertheless, teams of officers and noncommissioned officers, from units subordinated to Operation Reinhard, were sent to different localities to extend help and even to carry out the deportations to the death camps. The staff of each of the camps included German SS men and Ukrainian guards.

THE GERMAN PERSONNEL

The first task required by the headquarters of Operation Reinhard was to organize the manpower required for the construction and operation of the killing centers. The people assigned to Operation Reinhard came from the following sources:

1. SS and policemen who served under Globocnik's command in the Lublin district until Operation Reinhard—153
2. Members of the SS and police staff or units transferred from other districts of the General Government—205
3. Chancellery of the *Führer*—Euthanasia program—92
   a total of 450 men[2]

The most important professionals who were put at the disposal of Operation Reinhard came from the euthanasia program. They brought with them knowledge and experience in setting up and operating gassing institutions for mass murder. They filled the key posts involved with the extermination methods, the planning and construction of three death camps—Belzec, Sobibor, and Treblinka—and the command over these camps. It was they who were involved in the euthanasia program in the actual extermination operations: leading the victims to the gas chambers, filling the chambers with gas, removing the corpses, and cremating them. Irmfried Eberl was the only doctor among the euthanasia personnel to be transferred to Operation Reinhard. During the operation, all the Jews were sentenced to death and therefore did not require an examination of their mental or physical condition or health. Viktor Brack gave evidence in his trial after the war about the transfer of the euthanasia personnel to

Operation Reinhard: "In 1941, I received an order to discontinue the euthanasia program. In order to retain the personnel that had been relieved of these duties and in order to be able to start a new euthanasia program after the war, Bouhler asked me—I think after conferring with Himmler—to send this personnel to Lublin and place it at the disposal of SS *Brigadeführer* Globocnik."[3]

The first group of euthanasia personnel, numbering a few dozen men, arrived in Lublin between the end of October and the end of December 1941. Among them was SS *Kriminalkommissar* of Police Christian Wirth, the highest-ranking officer from the euthanasia program assigned to Operation Reinhard, and SS *Oberscharführer* Josef Oberhauser. Additional people from the euthanasia program arrived in Lublin during the first months of 1942. Viktor Brack visited Lublin at the beginning of May 1942 and discussed with Globocnik the contribution of the euthanasia organization to the task of exterminating Jews. Globocnik asked for more euthanasia personnel to be placed under his command. His request was accepted. Brack wrote to Himmler after this meeting:

> In accordance with my orders from *Reichsleiter* Bouhler, I have long ago put at *Brigadeführer* Globocnik's disposal part of my manpower to aid him in carrying out his special mission. Upon his renewed request, I have now transferred to him additional personnel. Globocnik took this opportunity to explain to me his idea that the action against the Jews should be carried out with all deliberate speed, in order to avoid getting stuck [in the middle of] one of those days when some sort of difficulty may force us to stop. You, yourself, *Reichsführer*, once voiced to me your opinion that even while considering the camouflage requirements, we are obliged to act as quickly as possible. Both conceptions are thus directed in principle toward the same result, and according to my experience, they are more than justified.[4]

Some euthanasia personnel arrived in Lublin in May–June 1942, after having served on the eastern front in the Kursk area in a medical unit. While serving in the front area, they each carried a red paper in their pay books, signed by the German army headquarters, stating that they were not to be employed at the forward front line. This was to prevent any danger that some of them might be captured by the Soviet army and taken as prisoners. The secrecy of the euthanasia program had to be preserved. When a need for them arose in the rear areas, like the need for people for Operation Reinhard, they were withdrawn from the front area.[5]

The euthanasia personnel transferred to Operation Reinhard became SS members and, like the others, wore gray uniforms and held SS ranks. They were under Globocnik's operational orders but on personal matters continued to be connected to their headquarters in Berlin and took their vacations at the euthanasia recreation center in Austria. A special courier from euthanasia headquarters came to Lublin every week and brought them additional payments and mail. Almost all of the euthanasia personnel who served in Operation Reinhard were appointed to serve in the death camps and not on staff assignments in Lublin.

The majority of euthanasia personnel assigned to Operation Reinhard were born between 1908 and 1911 and were in their thirties when they served in the operation's death camps. They had lived through the great difficulties of Germany's financial crises at the end of the 1920s and the early 1930s—a reality that led most of them to support the Nazi Party and its economic policies, political positions, radicalism, and anti-Semitism. Several of them even became party members. They had not undergone an especially nationalistic indoctrination and had no criminal record. Their upbringing and education did not prevent them from filling—without any pangs of conscience—their roles in the euthanasia program's institutions and in the death camps of Operation Reinhard thereafter.[6] Up until their service in the euthanasia program they were run-of-the-mill Germans.

SS members, including the euthanasia personnel assigned to Operation Reinhard, reported to the headquarters in Lublin and were instructed on their duties by SS *Hauptsturmführer* Höfle. They were all forced to sign the following declaration of secrecy:

I have been thoroughly informed and instructed by SS *Hauptsturmführer* Höfle, as Commander of the main division of *Einsatz Reinhard* of the SS and Police Leader in the District of Lublin (Leiter der Hauptabltelung "Einsatz Reinhard" beim SS-und Polizeiführer im Distrikt Lublin):

1. That I may not under any circumstances pass on any form of information, verbally or in writing, on the progress, procedure or incidents in the evacuation of Jews to any person outside the circle of the *Einsatz Reinhard* staff;
2. That the process of the evacuation of Jews is a subject that comes under "Secret Reich Document," in accordance with censorship regulation *Vershl V.* [Reserved]; ...
4 [*sic*]. That there is an absolute prohibition on photography in the camps of *Einsatz Reinhard*; ...

I am familiar with the above regulations and laws and am aware of the responsibilities imposed upon me by the task with which I have been entrusted. I promise to observe them to the best of my knowledge and conscience. I am aware that the obligation to maintain secrecy continues even after I have left the Service.[7]

Among the high-ranking staff of Operation Reinhard were many Austrians—Globocnik and Höfle, who commanded the operation, and three of the six SS officers commanding the camps: Dr. Irmfried Eberl, Franz Reichleitner, and Franz Stangl.

The organizational framework of Operation Reinhard was developed according to the tasks imposed on Globocnik. The experience gained during the first three months of the extermination activities—March to May 1942—influenced the organizational structure. The Operation Reinhard organization included the three camps of Belzec, Sobibor, and Treblinka and the training camp in Trawniki. The SS clothing workshops, which in the past had been subordinated to SS central authorities, were transferred to the command of Operation Reinhard in March 1942. These workshops were located in the old Lublin airport. The clothes and goods of the victims would be brought to this camp and treated there. Operation Reinhard headquarters was located in Lublin at Pieradzkiego 11, in the former Stefan Batory college. Because Globocnik was SS and police leader of the Lublin district, his headquarters were located separately from Operation Reinhard headquarters.[8]

THE UKRAINIAN AUXILIARIES

The SS unit assigned to each of the camps was too small to meet all its requirements: security, guard duties in and around the camp, and ensuring the smooth extermination of the thousands of victims brought in each transport. An additional security force was necessary for these tasks. Such a unit, composed mostly of Ukrainian nationalist collaborators, was formed.

Friendly ties between Ukrainian nationalists and Nazi Germany had existed for years. Nationalist Ukrainian emigrants who had found refuge in Germany after World War I and Ukrainian legal and illegal organizations active in the Polish West Ukraine hoped to obtain Nazi Germany's help in establishing their own independent state in Polish and Soviet Ukraine. Nazi Germany used these organizations for subversive activity when they attacked Poland at the beginning of World War II.

Nazi Germany's preparations to attack the Soviet Union in the summer of 1941 raised hopes among the Ukrainian nationalists. Two Ukrainian military battalions, the "Nightingale" (*Nachtigall*) and "Roland," were organized by the German *Abwehr* (army intelligence) to render assistance once the invasion began. Underground ties were maintained with Ukrainian clandestine organizations and groups in Soviet Ukraine.

On June 23, 1941, with the German invasion of the Soviet Union, the nationalist Ukrainians in west Galicia staged an anti-Soviet revolt. In the city of Lvov a rally of Ukrainian nationalist leaders proclaimed an independent Ukrainian state and government on June 30, 1941, the day the city was captured by the Germans. The invading German troops were welcomed to the Ukraine by large segments of the local population, who staged extensive anti-Jewish pogroms. But Nazi Germany did not intend to grant the Ukrainians any form of self-rule or independence. The fertile Ukraine was slated as an area for German colonization.

In the beginning of July, the Ukrainian government was dissolved and its leaders were arrested. In spite of this, collaboration of Ukrainians with Germany continued. Tens of thousands of Ukrainians enlisted in the local police and volunteered for the German security forces. The majority of these Ukrainians were former Red Army soldiers who had fallen into German captivity. Nazi Germany encouraged Ukrainian prisoners of war, as well as Lithuanians, Latvians, Estonians, and others, to join their ranks, and thousands responded to the call. Some of them did it to escape the horrible conditions in which Soviet prisoners of war were kept; others did so for nationalistic reasons, hoping to receive some kind of Ukrainian independence within the framework of Nazi Europe as a reward for their services. Many joined the ranks of the Nazis for reasons of anti-Semitism, which was quite common among the Ukrainians and other East European nations, or for economic profit. Other Ukrainians who joined the German security forces were local people, most of them inhabitants of Polish West Ukraine. The Ukrainians served in special units of the German army, the SS, and the police. A special unit was organized for Operation Reinhard.

In addition to the Ukrainians, this unit also included *Volksdeutsche* who lived in the Ukraine. These *Volksdeutsche* were descendants of Germans who had come to Russia in the second half of the eighteenth century. They numbered about four hundred thousand on the eve of World War II. Their knowledge of the German and Ukrainian languages, and their German identity and identification, rendered them the most suitable element to serve in such units, where they made up the low command staff. Most of these *Volksdeutsche* were also former Red Army soldiers who had been removed from the prisoner of war camps.

Those Soviet war prisoners or local Ukrainians from West Ukraine who volunteered for Operation Reinhard were sent to the SS training camp at Trawniki. In October 1941, SS *Sturmbannführer* Karl Streibel was appointed commander of this camp. He toured the Soviet prisoner of war camps in the Lublin district and in the Kiev area and traveled to the Galicia district to find Ukrainian and *Volksdeutsche* volunteers for Trawniki.[9] Feodor Fedorenko, a Ukrainian who had been captured by the Germans, testified in an American court about how he had enlisted in the

German service, trained in Trawniki, and was sent to Treblinka as a guard. According to the court's protocol:

> Evidence as to Defendant's conduct, 1941–1949.
>
> The defendant was mobilized on June 23, 1941, almost immediately after the invasion of the Soviet Union by Nazi Germany. He was a truck driver, and the truck he drove was also mobilized. He had no previous military training, and in the next two or three weeks his group was encircled twice by the German army. He escaped the first time, but was captured three days later by the Germans.
>
> The Germans transported several truckloads of prisoners to Zhitomir, a former Soviet training camp, and the defendant described the conditions as very bad and with little water or food. The camp housed about 50,000–100,000 prisoners, with no barracks available for them. After two to three weeks he was transferred to Równe. Next he was transferred to Chelm, Poland, to a camp surrounded by barbed-wire rolls. . . . The defendant estimated the population at Chelm at about 80,000 prisoners. He described the conditions at Chelm as so bad that if you became ill you rarely recovered. He also indicated that food was at an absolute minimum and that approximately 40,000 prisoners of war died over the winter of 1941/42.
>
> One day at Chelm, the Germans assembled the Soviet prisoners and walked down the line selecting 200 to 300 who were sent to Trawniki. . . . At Trawniki most of the guards were *Volksdeutsche*. The defendant is not a *Volksdeutsche* but Ukrainian. . . . In the spring of 1942 the Germans gave black uniforms to all of the prisoners. *Volksdeutsche* also wore black uniforms, but theirs were well tailored and of better material. After the barracks had been constructed at Trawniki, the Germans instructed them in the firing of rifles, field training, and in [long] marches. . . . In the spring of 1942 the defendant was sent to Lublin where at first the prisoners guarded their own camp and then were sent to the Jewish ghetto. At Lublin the Soviet prisoners guarded houses and furniture—whatever was left. They were issued rifles which were not fired. The Soviet prisoners were switched from being workers to guards at Lublin. From Lublin, the defendant was sent to Warsaw along with about 80 to 100 others. . . . The defendant was transported to Treblinka and served as a prisoner guard sometime approximately in September 1942.[10]

Upon their arrival at Trawniki, the volunteers were required to sign the following declaration as part of their enlistment process: "I declare under oath that all information I provide is true. I furthermore declare that I am of Aryan descent (meaning, I have no Jewish ancestors), and that I was never a member of the Communist Party or the Komsomol Youth Communist League."[11]

These volunteer units were called by a variety of names by the local population: "Ukrainians," "Trawniki men," or "Askaris." The Germans called them *Hilfswillige* (auxiliaries), or "Hiwis" for short, and the volunteers themselves *Wachmanner* (guardsmen). In Trawniki, the "guardsmen" received abbreviated military training and exercises, including tactics for the deportation of Jews. One of these guardsmen, Engelhand, testified about such tactical training in the village of Trawniki: "The first action against Jews that I participated in took place after my arrival in Trawniki. . . . We were told that this was a tactical exercise. We surrounded the whole village, and were told by the translator that Jews were living there. He told us to go there [in groups of] two men and tell them to get dressed, take with them whatever they can. . . . Soon the car will come and take all of them to Lublin."[12]

The Trawniki training camp operated for two and a half years. About 3,000 guardsmen passed through the military and police training. In the summer of 1942, as Operation Reinhard was operating at full capacity in all three death camps, there were close to 2,500 Trawniki men. Approximately 1,000 were organized into two battalions with four companies each, and about 1,500 additional men were divided into companies that operated throughout the General Government on security missions and deportation *Aktionen* to the death camps. Each company was composed of between 90 and 130 men. The entire force of 2,500 men were under the command of 30 to 50 men of different rank from the SS and German police. A company-size unit was allotted to each Operation Reinhard death camp—Belzec, Sobibor, and Treblinka. Most of the squad commanders (*Zugwachmänner*) were *Volksdeutsche* who spoke German and Ukrainian. Some of the squad commanders were Ukrainians. Privates were given the rank *Wachmann* (guard). One of the companies was a training company for squad (*Zug*) commanders, which included Ukrainians. The Trawniki men were equipped mainly with firearms taken as loot from the Soviets; the remainder were German guns.

One or two companies were stationed permanently in the city of Lublin for security and other duties there, including deporting Jews to the death camps. During July–September 1942, one Trawniki company was active in deporting three hundred thousand Jews from the Warsaw ghetto to Treblinka. Eight months later, in April 1943, a battalion of Trawniki men participated in suppressing the Warsaw ghetto uprising and deporting the last of its Jews, some to the death camps, some to the Majdanek concentration camp, and others to the Poniatowa and Trawniki labor camps. Trawniki men also participated in the murder of Jews during *Aktion Erntefest* (Operation Harvest Festival, see chapter 46).

The companies stationed in the death camps were under the camp commanders' operational subordination. However, for administrative purposes they were connected to their home base, the Trawniki training

SS *Brigadeführer* Odilo Globocnik (second from right), SS and police commander of the Lublin district, appointed to carry out Operation Reinhard. Yad Vashem Archives (YVA), 1869/551

camp, which provided their wages, uniforms, arms, and various necessities. Those who were not suitable for service in the death camps, for health or discipline reasons (drunkards, for example), were sent back to Trawniki and were replaced by others.[13] Guards were paid half a Reichsmark a day. Families of *Wachmann* who were in poor financial condition were supported by the local authorities in their place of residence.[14] The Trawniki men were the main force at Globocnik's disposal to execute Operation Reinhard and the main security force at the Belzec, Sobibor, and Treblinka death camps.

CHAPTER FOUR

BELZEC: CONSTRUCTION AND ESTABLISHING THE METHOD OF ANNIHILATION

THE LEADERS OF OPERATION REINHARD, who at the end of October 1941 initiated the preparations for the extermination of the Jews in the General Government, did not foresee how many death camps would have to be constructed and operated for this purpose. Up to that time, no death camp operated in Nazi Germany or in the occupied countries, and there was therefore no model on which the Operation Reinhard planners could base their plans. However, some guidelines did exist for selecting the sites on which to build the death camps. The camps would have to be near the main concentration of Jews in the General Government and near the railways, to facilitate the transports and deportations. The location of the camps had to be desolate places, as far as possible from inhabited areas, to maintain secrecy and to keep the knowledge of what was transpiring within them from the local population. And third, the camps had to be in the vicinity of the occupied territories of the Soviet Union so as to encourage the belief that the Jews who had disappeared had eventually reached labor camps in the vast areas of the East.

But no previous experience could be used to determine the optimal extermination technique to be employed or to estimate the annihilation capacity of a gas chamber or a death camp. Such information could be gained only through experimentation. Then, based on early results, decisions regarding the size and structure of each camp and the number of camps required for Operation Reinhard could be made. Belzec was to be the camp where these experiments would be initiated, and additional camps would be planned and constructed according to the results obtained there.

Belzec was a small town in the southeast of the Lublin district, located on the Lublin–Zamosc–Rava Russkaya–Lvov railway line. At the beginning of 1940, the Germans had established in Belzec a labor camp for Jews. Thousands of Jews from the Lublin district were sent there as slave-workers to build fortifications on the Soviet-German line of demarcation, which was close to Belzec. This labor camp was liquidated in the autumn of 1940.[1]

In August 1941, five weeks after the German attack on the Soviet Union, formerly Polish East Galicia, with a population of over half a million Jews, was annexed to the General Government. Consequently, Belzec became the center of a large Jewish population in the General Government—that of the Lublin, Cracow, and Lvov districts. Belzec's location, as well as the fact that it was on an efficient railway line, would facilitate the transportation of Jews to a camp there.

The exact location selected for the death camp was about half a kilometer from the Belzec railway station, along a railway spur. The area included antitank trenches that had been part of the border fortifications built there in 1940. This was a further advantage, as the trenches could be used as burial pits for the victims.

The construction of the death camp began on November 1, 1941, by the SS Central Building Administration (SS *Zentralbauverwaltung*) in the Lublin district. SS *Oberscharführer* Josef Oberhauser, a former euthanasia man, was placed in charge of building the camp. In the second half of December 1941, SS *Hauptsturmführer* Christian Wirth was appointed commander of Belzec and Oberhauser became his adjutant.[2]

SS *Scharführer* Erich Fuchs, who was engaged in the euthanasia institution at Bernburg, testified about Wirth and his arrival to Belzec:

> *Polizeihauptmann* [police captain] Christian Wirth conducted the *Aktionen* in Bernburg. Subordinate to him were the burners, disinfectors, and drivers. He also supervised the transportation of the mentally ill and of the corpses. One day in the winter of 1941 Wirth arranged a transport [of euthanasia personnel] to Poland. I was picked together with about eight or ten other men and transferred to Belzec. . . . I don't remember the names of the others. Upon our arrival in Belzec, we met Friedel Schwarz and the other SS men, whose names I cannot remember. They supervised the construction of barracks that would serve as a gas chamber. Wirth told us that in Belzec "all the Jews will be struck down." For this purpose barracks were built as gas chambers. I installed shower heads in the gas chambers. The nozzles were not connected to any water pipes; they would serve as camouflage for the gas chamber. For the Jews who were gassed it would seem as if they were being taken to baths and for disinfection.[3]

Before coming to Belzec, Wirth became acquainted with the gas vans in operation in Chelmno and in the eastern occupied territories of the Soviet Union and learned their advantages and disadvantages. This experience in euthanasia—where permanent gas chambers had existed, and with the gas vans—inspired his solution. He decided to combine in Belzec the permanent gas chamber with the internal combustion car engine as the gas supplier. Wirth objected to the bottles of carbon monoxide gas that had been used in euthanasia institutions. The bottles, which were produced in private factories and which would be supplied to Belzec in large quantities, could arouse suspicion. In addition, the factories were located at great distances from Belzec and the steady supply of the bottles might cause a logistical problem. Wirth preferred to set up a self-contained extermination system, based on an ordinary car engine and easily available gasoline and not dependent on supply by outside factors.[4]

Stanislaw Kozak, a Pole who participated in the building of Belzec, described the first stages of construction:

> In October 1941, three SS men came to Belzec and requested from the municipality twenty men for work. The municipality allotted twenty workers, residents of Belzec, and I was among them. . . . We began the work on November 1, 1941. We built barracks close to the side track of the railway. One barrack, which was close to the railway section, was 50 meters long and 12.5 meters wide. . . . The second barrack, 25 meters long and 12.5 meters wide, was for the Jews destined for the "baths." Not far from this barrack we built a third barrack, 12 meters long and 8 meters wide. This barrack was divided into three chambers by a wooden wall, so that each chamber was 4 meters wide and 8 meters long. It was 2 meters high. The inside walls of this barrack were of double boards with a vacant space between them filled by us with sand. The walls inside the barracks were covered with pap. In addition, the ground and walls up to 1.10 meters were covered by sheet-metal. . . . From the second to the third barrack led a closed corridor, 2 meters wide, 2 meters high, and 10 meters long. This corridor led to a corridor in the third barrack where the doors to its three chambers were located. Each chamber of this barrack had on its northern side a door 1.80 meters high and 1.10 meters wide. These doors, like those in the corridor, were covered with rubber. All the doors in this barrack could be opened from the outside only. These doors were built with strong boards 7.5 cm in diameter and were secured from the outside with a wooden bar held by two iron hooks against pressure from inside the barrack.
>
> In each of the three chambers of this barrack a water pipe was installed 10 cm above the floor. In addition, on the western wall in each chamber in the corner, was a water pipe 1 meter above the ground, with an open joint, turned toward the center of the room. These pipes with the joint were connected through the wall to a pipe that ran under the floor. In each of the three chambers of this barrack was installed an oven weighing 250 kg. It was expected that the pipe joint would later be connected with the oven. The oven was 1.10 meters high, 55 cm wide and 55 cm long. . . . During the time that we Poles built the barracks, the "Blacks" [Ukrainians] erected the fences of the extermination camp, which were made of dense barbed wire. After we Poles

had completed building the three above-mentioned barracks, the Germans dismissed us, on December 22, 1941.[5]

When the Polish workers had finished their work and left, a group of Jews from ghettos in the vicinity of Belzec, mainly from Lubycze-Krolewska and Male-Mosty, were brought to the camp. Some of these Jews were skilled workers—carpenters, smiths, and builders. They continued the construction of the camp.[6]

The installations and buildings required to begin the mass killings were ready by the end of February 1942. The first transports of Jews were used for experimental killings, to check the efficiency and capacity of the gas chambers and the technique of the extermination process. There were two or three such experimental transports of four to six freight cars with 100 to 250 Jews in each of them. These experimental killings lasted a few days and the last group to be murdered were the Jewish prisoners who had been engaged in building the camp.

Mieczyslaw Kudyba, a Pole who lived in Belzec, testified about these experimental killings:

> The Germans took out a group of Jews from Lubycze-Krolewska and brought them by car to the Belzec camp. One Jew from that group told me that he had been in the camp some time cutting pine trees. One day all the Jews were driven into a barrack. This Jew was able to hide and later to escape. While in hiding, he heard long screams from the barrack in which the Jews had been locked and then silence. This was the first experimental killing in Belzec. I heard that this Jew who escaped was later caught by the Germans and killed.[7]

When these experimental killings were carried out, the system that would supply the gas was not yet ready. Therefore, the gas used for these killings was bottled carbon monoxide. Shortly afterward, however, a self-contained monoxide gas system was developed, and an armored car engine of 250 horsepower was installed in a shed outside the gas chamber. From it, a pipe channeled the gas inside.

Adolf Eichmann, who visited Belzec at that time and saw the gas chambers, wrote:

> At the turn of the year 1941/42, the chief of the Security Police and SD Heydrich told me . . . "I come from the *Reichsführer*; the *Führer* has now ordered the physical extermination of the Jews." He informed me further that the *Reichsführer* had instructed Globocnik, the SS and Police Leader of Lublin, to use the Soviet antitank ditches for the mass annihilation of the Jews. I myself should travel there and submit to him a report about the implementation of the operation. . . . I traveled in the direction of Lublin; I don't know what the place

is called. A *Hauptsturmführer* accompanied me. I met there a *Hauptmann* of the Order Police [Wirth]. I expressed astonishment that the small house, completely secluded, was built, and he told me: "Here the Jews are being gassed now."[8]

Wirth carried out experiments to determine the most efficient method of handling the transports of Jews from the time of their arrival at the camp until their murder and burial. He developed some basic concepts for the process of extermination and for camp structure. The basic structure of the camp and the various actions the victims were made to do as soon as they left the train were intended to ensure that they would not grasp the fact that they had been brought for extermination. The aim was to give the victims the impression that they had arrived at a labor camp or a transit camp from where they would be sent to a labor camp. The deportees were to believe this until they were closed into the gas chambers camouflaged as baths.

The second principle of the extermination process was that everything should be carried out with the utmost speed. The victims should be rushed, made to run, so that they had no time to look round, to reflect, or to understand what was going on. This also supported the basic principle of deceiving the victims. They should be shocked, and their reactions paralyzed in order to prevent escape or resistance. The speed of the extermination process served yet an additional purpose: it increased the killing capacity of the camp. More transports could be brought and annihilated in one day.

According to Wirth's annihilation scheme, the Jews themselves should carry out all physical work involved in the extermination process of a transport. A group of a few dozen or even a few hundred young, strong Jews were selected from among the victims after they disembarked the train. It was their duty to remove the corpses from the gas chambers and bury them. They also collected and arranged the clothes, suitcases, and other goods left behind by the murdered Jews. These Jews were kept working for a day or so; then they were murdered and were replaced by others who would be taken from the arriving transports.

Another group of Jews, among them tailors, shoemakers, carpenters, and other skilled workers, had to be kept in each camp to carry out services for the German and Ukrainian staff. This group, which numbered a few dozen Jewish prisoners, were called *Hofjuden* (court Jew). They had to be kept entirely separate from the Jews selected from the arriving transports and engaged in the extermination process. They were kept for longer periods, but even from among them people were sent frequently to the gas chambers and were replaced by others.

The entire camp occupied a relatively small, almost square area; the north, west, and east sides each measured 275 meters, and the south side

265 meters. It was surrounded by a high fence of wire netting, topped by barbed wire and camouflaged with branches. Young trees were also planted around it to prevent observation from outside. Three watchtowers were placed in the corners of the camp, two on the east side, the third on the southwest corner. An additional watchtower was in the center of the camp close to the gas chamber. A railway spur, about 500 meters in length, ran from the station in Belzec and led through the gate on the north side of the camp. The southern and eastern sides were bordered by a pine forest.

As construction continued, Belzec was divided into two sub-camps. Camp I, in the northern and western part, was the reception and administration area; Camp II, on the eastern part, was the extermination area. The reception area included the railway ramp, which could accommodate twenty railway cars; the assembly square for the arriving deportees; and two barracks, one for undressing and the second to store the clothes and goods the victims had brought with them. The administration area included two dwelling barracks for the Jewish prisoners; their laundry, kitchen, and store barracks; and the *Appellplatz* (roll-call square). Close to the entrance gate, which was on the north side of the camp, was the guardhouse, permanently attended by SS men and Ukrainians. On the left of the entrance gate was the Ukrainians' area, separated from the other parts of the camp by barbed wire. It included three barracks: living quarters, a kitchen, and a barrack for their clinic, dentist, and barber.

Camp II, the extermination area, included the gas chambers and the burial ditches, which were in the east and northeast sections of the camp. The gas chambers were surrounded by trees, and a camouflage net was stretched over the roof to prevent aerial observation. At a later stage two barracks were erected in this area: living quarters and the kitchen of the Jewish prisoners who worked in this part of the camp. Camp II was fenced off from the other parts of the camp with a specially guarded entrance gate. A narrow passageway, two meters wide and a few dozen meters long, called *der Schlauch* (the tube), was enclosed on both sides by barbed wire and partly by a wooden fence. It connected the undressing barrack in Camp I to the gas chambers in Camp II.

Construction in Belzec continued for months, even as the entire extermination procedure was being carried out.

The living quarters of the SS men were close to the Belzec railway station, about five hundred meters outside the camp. They consisted of three houses; one contained the headquarters and kitchen. The houses were fenced off, and a Ukrainian guard was posted at the entrance gate. Close to the SS living quarters were some houses where Polish civilians lived.[9]

While construction was going on and experiments were being carried out, the organizational structure was also taking shape. Christian Wirth was the commander of the camp and the dominant figure there. One of his subordinate SS men in Belzec described him: "Wirth was the absolute ruler in the Belzec camp. Every one of the camp personnel received orders from him. He was seen everywhere and supervised the execution of his orders. But even during general briefings he personally allotted us specific duties and gave us detailed orders, what we were to do or what we were to say. During his absence the orders were given by Schwartz."[10]

SS *Oberscharführer* Gottfried Schwartz was deputy commander of the camp. SS *Oberscharführer* Josef Niemann (later promoted to the rank of *Untersturmführer*) was in charge of Camp II, the extermination area. SS *Oberscharführer* Josef Oberhauser, Wirth's adjutant, was the third in the camp's chain of command and was in charge of construction. He organized the Ukrainian unit in Trawniki for its duties in Belzec. SS *Scharf-führer* Lorenz Hackenholt was in charge of operating the gas chambers, with two Ukrainians subordinate to him. SS *Unterscharführer* Heinrich Unverhau was in charge of the storerooms where the clothes and personal belongings of the victims were kept and sorted to be sent on to Lublin. The storeroom was located outside the camp in the locomotives garage, close to Belzec station.

All the SS men were given assignments in the camp administration and were in charge of specific activities. Some of them had several duties. From time to time, there were changes in these assignments. Close to the expected arrival of a transport with Jews, the SS men were assigned specific duties in handling the liquidation of the deportees—from disembarkment to gassing of the victims and shooting those unable to be brought to the gas chambers.

The Ukrainian unit under the command of *Oberscharführer* Feiks included sixty to eighty men organized in two platoons. SS *Scharführer* Fritz Jierman and, later, SS *Scharführer* Werner Dubois were in charge of their training and discipline. The platoon and squad commanders were mainly *Volksdeutsche* and, like the other members of this unit, former soldiers in the Soviet army. They had the police ranks of *Hauptzugwachmänn* and *Zugwachmänn*.

The Ukrainians manned the guard positions in the camp, at the entrance, at the four watchtowers, and with some patrols. Some of them helped in operating the gas chambers. Before the arrival of a transport with Jews, the Ukrainians took up guard positions around the railway ramp, the undressing barrack, and along the "tube" leading to the gas chambers. During the experimental killings and even the first transports,

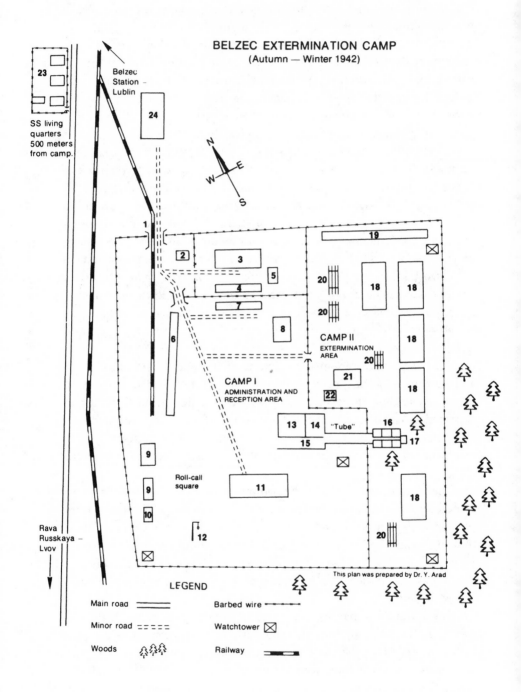

BELZEC EXTERMINATION CAMP
(Autumn — Winter 1942)

23

SS living
quarters
500 meters
from camp.

Belzec
Station –
Lublin

24

N
E
W
S

CAMP I
ADMINISTRATION AND
RECEPTION AREA

CAMP II
EXTERMINATION
AREA

Roll-call
square

1
2
3
5
4
7
8
6
9
9
10
12
11
13 14 "Tube" 16
15   17
19
18 18
18
18
21
22
18
20
20
20
20

Rava
Russkaya –
Lvov

This plan was prepared by Dr. Y. Arad

LEGEND

Main road ——————

Minor road = = = = =

Woods 🌲🌲🌲

Barbed wire ·—·—·—·

Watchtower ⊠

Railway ▬▬▬

Belzec Extermination Camp

Camp I—Reception and Administration Area

1. Entrance gate
2. Guards' house
3. Ukrainian living quarters
4. Barber, clinic, dentist for the SS and Ukrainians
5. Ukrainian kitchen
6. Railway ramp
7. Garage
8. Tailor's and shoemaker's workshops for the SS and Ukrainians
9. Living quarters for Jewish prisoners
10. Kitchen and laundry for Jewish prisoners
11. Storeroom for belongings taken from the victims
12. Gallows
13. Undressing barrack
14. Room in which women's hair was cut
15. A courtyard enclosed by a wooden fence leading to the "tube"

Camp II—Extermination Area

16. Gas chambers
17. Gas engine
18. Burial pits
19. Antitank trench used as a burial pit
20. Shelves for cremating the bodies
21. Living quarters for Jewish prisoners
22. Kitchen for Jewish prisoners

Outside the camp

23. The SS living quarters and offices
24. Warehouse for the belongings taken from the victims—former locomotive shed

The Belzec labor camp, 1940. YVA, 16FO5

SS *Hauptsturmführer* Christian Wirth, first commandant of the Belzec death camp, later the supervisor
of the death camps of Operation Reinhard. YVA, FA
245/34

SS *Obersturmführer* Franz Stangel, the first commandant of the Sobibor death camp; from September 1942, commandant of the Treblinka death camp. YVA, 4577/115

SS *Hauptsturmführer* Hermann Höfle, one of the chief architects of Operation Reinhard. YVA, 4577/610a

the Ukrainians were in charge of removing the bodies from the gas chambers and burying them.

The organizational structure of the camp's staff took its final shape after weeks and months of experimental operation of the camp. As Belzec was the first death camp of Operation Reinhard, its manpower and organizational needs were improved as more and more experience was attained. Toward the middle of March 1942, Belzec death camp was ready to absorb the first transports.

CHAPTER FIVE

CONSTRUCTION OF SOBIBOR

SOBIBOR WAS THE NAME OF a small village in a wooded area on the Chelm-Wlodawa railway line, eight kilometers south of Wlodawa. The Bug River, the border between the General Government and the *Reichskommissariat* of Ukraine, was five kilometers east of Sobibor. The whole area was swampy, wooded, and thinly populated. The exact location for the death camp was selected by the SS Central Building Administration in the Lublin district. The camp was built alongside the railway, west of Sobibor station, and was surrounded by a sparse pine forest. Close to the railway station buildings was a spur that was included in the camp site and was used for disembarkation of the transports. In the area selected for the camp two wooden buildings existed—a former forester's house and a two-story post office. The entire camp area encompassed a rectangle six hundred by four hundred meters. At a later stage it was enlarged.

The construction of the Sobibor camp began in March 1942, at the same time that extermination actions were beginning in Belzec. SS *Obersturmführer* Richard Thomalla, from the SS Central Building Administration in Lublin, was put in charge of the construction of Sobibor. The workers employed at building the camp were local people from neighboring villages and towns. A group of eighty Jews from the ghettos in the vicinity of the camp was brought to Sobibor for construction work. A squad of ten Ukrainians from Trawniki arrived to guard these Jews. After completing their work, the Jews were shot.[1]

By the beginning of April 1942, construction of the camp had fallen behind schedule. To speed things up, Odilo Globocnik appointed SS *Obersturmführer* Franz Stangl commander of Sobibor. Stangl was ordered by Globocnik to travel to Wirth in Belzec for guidance and to obtain experience in preparation for the operation of Sobibor. Stangl described his visit to Belzec:

> I went there by car. As one arrived, one first reached Belzec railway station.... Oh God, the smell! It was everywhere. Wirth wasn't in his office. I remember they took me to him . . . he was standing on a hill next to the pits . . .

the full . . . they were full. I cannot tell you; not hundreds, thousands, thousands of corpses . . . that's where Wirth told—he said that was what Sobibor was for. . . .

Wirth told me that I should definitely become the commander of Sobibor. I answered that I was not qualified for such a mission. . . . I received from Globocnik the task to erect the camp. That it was not to be an ammunition camp but a camp for killing Jews I learned finally from Wirth. During the discussion with Wirth he told me if I would not do it, another would come. He would then put me back at the disposal of the *Brigadeführer* [Globocnik]. Actually, I was not relieved [of my post]. I stayed in Sobibor. Transports arrived and were liquidated.[2]

After Stangl's arrival in Sobibor, the building of the camp was accelerated, and a second group of Jews from ghettos in the Lublin district was brought there for construction work.

The first gas chambers erected in Sobibor were in a solid brick building with a concrete foundation. They were located in the northwest part of the camp, more isolated and distant from the other parts of the camp than in Belzec. There were three gas chambers in the building, each four by four meters. The capacity of each chamber was about two hundred people. Each gas chamber was entered through its own separate door leading from a veranda that ran along the building. On the opposite side of the building, there was a second set of doors for removing the corpses. Outside was a shed in which the engine that supplied the carbon monoxide gas was installed. Pipes conducted the gas from the engine exhaust to the gas chambers.[3]

In the middle of April 1942, when the building of Sobibor was close to completion, experimental killings were carried out there. About 250 Jews were brought from the Krychow labor camp, which was close to Sobibor, for this purpose.[4] Wirth arrived in Sobibor to attend these experiments. With him came a chemist from the euthanasia program whose pseudonym was "Dr. [Karl] Blaurock." SS *Scharführer* Erich Fuchs, who served in Belzec, described the preparations and the first experimental killing in Sobibor:

As ordered by Wirth, I drove an LKW [a car] to Lvov, fetched a gas motor and transported it to Sobibor. When I arrived at Sobibor, close to the railway station I saw a tract of land with a concrete construction and some other solid buildings. The *Sonderkommando* there were commanded by Thomalla. Other members of the SS who attended were F. B. Stangl, F. Schwartz, Kurt Bolender, and others. We unloaded the motor. It was a heavy Russian benzine engine (presumably a tank or tractor motor) at least 200 horsepower (V-motor, 8 cylinders, water cooled). We installed the engine on a concrete foundation and set up the connection between the exhaust and the tube.

I then tested the motor. It did not work. I was able to repair the ignition and the valves, and the motor finally started running. The chemist, whom I knew from Belzec, entered the gas chamber with measuring instruments to test the concentration of the gas.

Following this, a gassing experiment was carried out. If my memory serves me right, about thirty to forty women were gassed in one gas chamber. The Jewish women were forced to undress in an open place close to the gas chamber, and were driven into the gas chamber by the above-mentioned SS members and by Ukrainian auxiliaries. When the women were shut up in the gas chamber I and B [Bolender] set the motor in motion. The motor functioned first in neutral. Both of us stood by the motor and switched from "Neutral" (*Freiauspuff*) to "Cell" (*Zelle*), so that the gas was conveyed to the chamber. At the suggestion of the chemist, I fixed the motor on a definite speed so that it was unnecessary henceforth to press on the gas. About ten minutes later the thirty to forty women were dead. The chemist and the SS leader gave the sign to stop the motor. I packed my tools and saw how the corpses were removed. The transportation was done with a lorry trail that led from the gas chambers to a remote plot.[5]

After this experiment, which verified the smooth working of the gas chambers, and with the completion of some other construction work, Sobibor death camp was ready for its task. The structure of Sobibor was similar to that of Belzec and was based on the experience that had been gained there. The camp was divided into three parts: the administration area, the reception area, and the extermination area. The reception area and administration were close to the railway station. The extermination area was in the remote part of the camp.

The administration area, which was in the southeast of the camp, was divided into two sub-camps: the "Forward Camp" (*Vorlager*) and Camp I. The Forward Camp included the entrance gate, the railway ramp, and the living quarters and services of the SS men and Ukrainians. Unlike Belzec, in Sobibor all the SS men lived inside the camp. The Jewish prisoners who worked in Sobibor were kept in Camp I. This area included their living quarters and workshops, where some of them worked as shoemakers, tailors, blacksmiths, and so on.

The reception area was called Camp II. The Jews who arrived with the transports were, after disembarking, driven inside this area. It included the undressing barracks of the victims and the barracks where their clothes and belongings were stored. The former forester's house, located in this area, was used for camp offices and living quarters for some of the SS men. A high wooden fence, which prevented observation, separated the main part of the forester's house from the area where the victims passed. At the northeast corner of this fence began the "tube." This "tube," which connected Camp II with the extermination area, was a narrow passageway, about 3 to 4 meters wide and 150 meters long. Through here the victims were driven into the gas chambers located at the end of the "tube." Close to the entrance of the "tube" was a stable, a pigpen, and a poultry coop. Halfway through the "tube" was the "barber shop," a barrack where the hair of the Jewish women was cut before they entered the gas chambers.

The extermination area, called Camp III, was on the northwest side of the camp. It included the gas chambers, burial pits, a barrack for the Jewish prisoners employed there, and a guard barrack. The burial pits were fifty to sixty meters long, ten to fifteen meters wide, and five to seven meters deep. For easier absorption of the corpses into the pits, the sandy sidewalls were made oblique. A narrow railway with a trolley led from the railway station up to the burial pits, bypassing the gas chambers. People who had died in the trains or those who were unable to walk from the platform to the gas chambers were taken by the trolley.

The whole camp was fenced off by barbed wire intertwined with tree branches to prevent observation from the outside. Along the fence and in the corners of the camp were watchtowers. All the sub-camps, and particularly Camp III, were fenced off from each other by dense barbed wire.[6]

While the basic installations necessary for initiating the killing operations were being completed, the organization of manpower was also taking shape. Stangl's deputy, second in command in Sobibor, was the camp *Oberscharführer*, Hermann Michel, who was replaced a few months later by *Oberscharführer* Gustav Wagner. Camp I, where the Jewish prisoners were kept, and Camp III, the extermination area, had their own commanders, subordinate to Stangl. The commander of Camp I was *Oberscharführer* Bruno Weiss, who was replaced by *Oberscharführer* Karl Frenzel. It was his duty also to supervise the Jewish prisoners when they worked in Camp II. Kurt Bolender served as commander of Camp III from April until autumn 1942. He was replaced by *Oberscharführer* Erich Bauer. Alfred Ittner was in charge of the camp administration; he was later transferred to Camp III.

The Ukrainian guard unit in Sobibor was organized in three platoons. They came from the Trawniki training camp with commanders who for the most part had served in the German police and held police ranks; Erich Lachman, a former policeman who trained the Ukrainians in Trawniki, became their commander in Sobibor. Being an "outsider" among the euthanasia members, he was replaced as commander of the Ukrainians by Kurt Bolender in autumn 1942.[7]

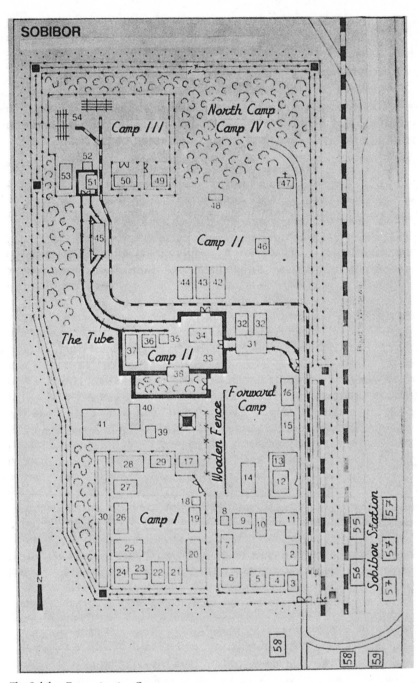

The Sobibor Extermination Camp

Watchtower
Minefield
Railroad
Narrow-gauge railroad
Barbed wire fence
Camouflaged barbed wire fence
Forester's tower

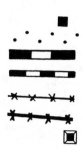

Forward Camp
   1. Unloading platform
   2. Dentist and jail for Ukrainian guards
   3. Guard house
   4. SS clothing store
   5. SS quarters
   6. SS quarters
   7. Laundry
   8. Well
   9. Showers and barbershop for SS
   10. Garage
   11. SS kitchen and canteen
   12. Living quarters of the camp commanders
   13. Armory
   14. Barracks for Ukrainian guards
   15. Barracks for Ukrainian guards
   16. Barracks for Ukrainian guards
   17. Bakery

Camp I
   18. Dispensary
   19. Tailor shop for D
   20. Shoemaker and saddler shop for SS
   21. Smithery
   22. Carpentry
   23. Latrine
   24. Painters' shop
   25. Barracks for male prisoners
   26. Barracks for male prisoners
   27. Prisoners' kitchen
   28. Barracks for female prisoners
   29. Shoemaker shop for Ukrainian guards
   30. Water ditch

Camp II

31. Undressing barracks where deportees deposited their clothing and luggage
32. Barracks where luggage was sorted and stored
33. Undressing yard
34. Storage warehouse for food brought by the deportees
35. Electrical generator
36. Storage of silverware
37. Stable and barns
38. Administration building and storeroom for valuables
39. SS ironing room
40. Shoe warehouse
41. Garden
42. Barracks for storing property
43. Barracks for storing property
44. Barracks for storing property
45. Barracks where women's hair was cut
46. Incinerator
47. Former chapel
48. Latrine

Camp III

49. Barracks for Camp III prisoners
50. Barracks for Camp III prisoners' kitchen and "dentist" workshop
51. Gas chambers
52. Engine room for gas chambers
53. Fenced yard
54. Mass graves and outdoor crematoria

Sobibor station and village

55. Railway station building
56. Living quarters of Polish railway workers
57. Houses of local agricultural workers
58. Farms of Polish peasants
59. Living quarter of railway workers

In Sobibor, as in Belzec, each member of the German staff in the camp was in charge of a specific function and duty. When a transport of Jews arrived, most of the SS men carried out particular duties in the process of annihilation. SS *Oberscharführer* Erich Bauer, who served in Sobibor, testified at the Sobibor trial in 1964: "Normally, inside the camp, each member of the permanent staff had a specific function (for example, commander of the Ukrainian auxiliaries, leader of a working group, excavation of pits, erection of barbed-wire fences, etc.). However, when a transport with Jews arrived, there was so much 'work' that the regular activity was interrupted, and everyone on the permanent staff had to participate somehow in the routine extermination process. Primarily, each member of the permanent staff took part occasionally in the unloading of the transports."[8]

Toward the end of April 1942, Sobibor death camp was ready for operation. Dov Freiberg, who was brought to Sobibor with the first transports in May 1942, described his first impression of the camp: "The appearance of the camp was like an ordinary farm, except for the barbed-wire fences that surrounded it and some barracks. Actually, it was a farm, with all its buildings, in the midst of a beautiful green forest. . . . It seems that the camp was erected in a hurry and had few basic installations. I mean Camp I and Camp II [reception and administration areas]; about Camp III [extermination area], we did not yet know of its existence. But the area was big."[9]

CHAPTER SIX

CONSTRUCTION OF TREBLINKA

THE CONSTRUCTION OF TREBLINKA DEATH camp began after Belzec and Sobibor were already operational. The expertise gained in the building and in the killing operations in the other two camps were applied in the planning and construction of Treblinka. It became the most "perfected" death camp of Operation Reinhard.

The Treblinka death camp was located in the northeast section of the General Government, not far from Malkinia, a town and station on the main railway, Warsaw-Bialystok, and close to the railway Malkinia-Siedlce. It was built in a thinly populated area near the village of Wolka Okranglik, some four kilometers from Treblinka village and train station. The site chosen for the camp was wooded and naturally concealed from both the Malkinia-Kosov road to its north and the Malkinia-Siedlce railway, which ran to its west. Near the camp's southwest boundary, a rail spur connected Treblinka station with a gravel quarry in the region that had been worked before the war. In the spring of 1941, the Germans decided to exploit the quarry for raw materials for the fortifications then being constructed on the Soviet-German line of demarcation, and in the summer of that year they established Treblinka I penal camp, to which they brought a thousand to twelve hundred Polish and Jewish detainees for forced labor. This camp, like the entire region, was under the authority of the Warsaw area SS and police leader (SSPF).

In late April or early May 1942, an SS team arrived in the Treblinka area, toured the region, and determined the site where a death camp would be erected.[1] The plan of the camp was almost identical to Sobibor, but with some improvements. The construction of the death camp began in late May or early June 1942. The contractors were the German construction firms Schönbronn of Leipzig and Schmidt-Münstermann. In charge of the construction of Treblinka was SS *Obersturmführer* Richard Thomalla, who had completed his building mission in Sobibor and had been replaced there by Franz Stangl in April 1942. Technical assistance in the erection of the gas chambers was also made available.

SS *Unterscharführer* Erwin Herman Lambert, a former foreman of a building team in the euthanasia program, testified: "I and Hengs [a euthanasia man] went to Treblinka by car. SS *Hauptsturmführer* Richard Thomalla was the camp commander. The Treblinka camp was still in the process of construction. I was attached to a building team there. Thomalla was there for a limited time only and conducted the construction work of the extermination camp. During that time no extermination actions were carried out. Thomalla was in Treblinka for about four to eight weeks. Then Dr. Eberl arrived as camp commander. Under his direction the extermination *Aktionen* of the Jews began."[2]

The SS and police leader of the Warsaw district was responsible for the erection of the camp. Polish and Jewish prisoners from Treblinka penal camp, as well as Jews from neighboring towns, were provided for labor. Along with the building construction—including the gas chambers, barracks, and stores—work commenced on a railroad spur running from the nearby rail line into the camp; shortly thereafter, a station platform was constructed.

None of the Jewish workers who were employed at the building of the camp survived. Jan Sulkowski, a Polish prisoner from Treblinka penal camp who was engaged in building the death camp, stated: "The Germans killed the Jews either by beating them or by shooting them. I witnessed cases where the SS-men . . . during the felling of forests, forced Jews to stand beneath the trees which were about to fall down. In both cases 4 Jews were thus killed. Besides, it often happened that the SS-men raided the huts of the Jewish workers and killed them in cold blood. . . . I was told by the SS-men that we were building a bath-house and it was after a considerable time that I realized that we were constructing gas-chambers."[3]

The death camp formed a rectangle, six hundred by four hundred meters, surrounded by two sets of fences and barbed-wire obstacles. The inner fence was three to four meters high and intertwined with tree branches that hid the camp from outside view. A second fence, some forty to fifty meters from the first, included chains of antitank obstacles ("Spanish horses") wrapped in barbed wire. The ground between the fences was left barren—devoid of any vegetation or possible hiding place—to facilitate observation by the guards. Fences also surrounded areas within the camp. In each corner of the camp, an eight-meter-high watchtower was constructed. An additional tower was built along the southern perimeter, between the two corner towers and near the gas chambers. It was later transferred to the center of the extermination area.

The camp was divided into three zones of nearly equal size: the living area (*Wohnlager*), the reception area (*Auffanglager*), and the extermination area (*Totenlager*). The living and reception areas were called the Lower Camp, while the extermination area was known as the Upper Camp.

The living area was in the northwest section of the camp. It comprised the living quarters for the German SS personnel and the Ukrainians, and other administration buildings—an office, an infirmary, stores, and workshops. Unlike at Sobibor, the living quarters of the SS men were concentrated in one area. Part of this area, a square one hundred by one hundred meters, was set off by a barbed-wire fence. It contained three barracks forming a U, where the Jewish prisoners lived, workshops where they worked, and a roll-call square. At the far side of the square were about thirty toilets covered by a straw roof.

The reception area was in the southwest section of the camp, and it was there that the transports of Jews first arrived. It included the train platform and the three-hundred-meter railway spur. At the end of the railway spur was a wooden gate, wrapped with barbed wire intertwined with tree branches.

In front of the platform was a large structure where the victims' belongings were stored. Aside from the platform and the rail spur, no facilities or signs were to be seen that could identify the site as a train station. Near the platform, north of the storehouse, was "Railway Station Square," an open area, and past it a fenced-in area called "Transport Square" (*Transportplarz*) or "Undressing Square," which was entered through a gate. This gate was where the men were separated from the women and children. Transport Square was flanked by two large hut barracks. In the left-hand barrack, the women and children undressed and deposited their money and valuables. The right-hand barrack served the men for the same purpose. South of Transport Square was "Sorting Square" (*Sortierplatz*), where the victims' clothing and belongings were sorted and piled up for shipment out of the camp. At one end of Sorting Square, in the southeast corner of the camp, were large ditches for burying those victims who had died in the trains on their way to the camp.

The entrance gate to the camp was in the northwest section, near the railway. It was built of two wooden pillars, each decorated with a flower styled from metal and crowned by a small roof resting on the pillars. At night floodlights lit the entrance. Ukrainian guards and SS men were posted at the gate and at the guardhouse, which was close to it, twenty-four hours a day. The entrance gate served mainly the SS and Ukrainians; transports with Jews entered the camp by train.

The extermination area, or Upper Camp, as it was called by the Germans, was in the southeastern section; there the mass murders were carried out. This area was completely isolated from the rest of the camp by a wire fence camouflaged with branches, which prevented observation from the outside. The entrances were hidden by a special screen. The upper camp was approximately 200 by 250 meters.

The gas chambers were located inside the extermination area. There were three gas chambers, each 4 by 4 meters and 2.6 meters high, similar to the first gas chamber constructed in Sobibor. A room attached to the building contained a diesel engine, which introduced the poisonous carbon monoxide gas through pipes into the chambers, and a generator, which supplied electricity to the entire camp.

The entrance doors to the gas chambers opened onto a wooden corridor at the front of the building. Each of these doors was 1.8 meters high and 90 centimeters wide. The doors could be closed hermetically and locked from the outside. Inside the gas chambers, opposite each entrance door, was another door made of thick, strong wood beams, 2.5 meters wide and 1.8 meters high. These doors, too, were hermetically sealed. Inside the chambers the walls were covered with white tiles up to a certain height, and shower heads and piping crisscrossed the ceiling—all designed to maintain the illusion of a shower room. The piping actually served to carry the poison gas into the chambers. When the doors were closed, there was no lighting in the chambers.

East of the gas chambers, and close to them, were huge ditches for burying the dead. The ditches were fifty meters long, twenty-five meters wide, and ten meters deep. They were dug by an excavator brought from the quarry at Treblinka penal camp, and by the prisoners. To facilitate the transport of bodies from the gas chambers to the ditches, a narrow-gauge railway was laid, with trolleys pushed by prisoners. South of the gas chambers, a barrack was erected for prisoners employed inside the extermination area. This barrack and a small surrounding yard were fenced with barbed wire; the entrance gate faced the gas chambers. The barrack served as living quarters and included a kitchen and toilet. A watchtower and a guardroom were built in the center of the extermination area.

Transport Square in the Lower Camp was connected to the extermination area by the "tube," or, as the Germans in Treblinka called it derisively, "the road to heaven" (*Himmelstrasse*). The "tube" was nearly 100 meters long and 4.5 to 5 meters wide. It began near the women's undressing barrack, continued east and then south to the extermination area. It was fenced on both sides with barbed wire 2 meters high and intertwined with tree branches so that it was impossible to see in or out. The "tube" crossed a thin grove of trees, which continued eastward up to the camp fence. At the entrance to the "tube," near the women's undressing hut, a sign said: "To the Showers" (*Zur Badeanstalt*).[4]

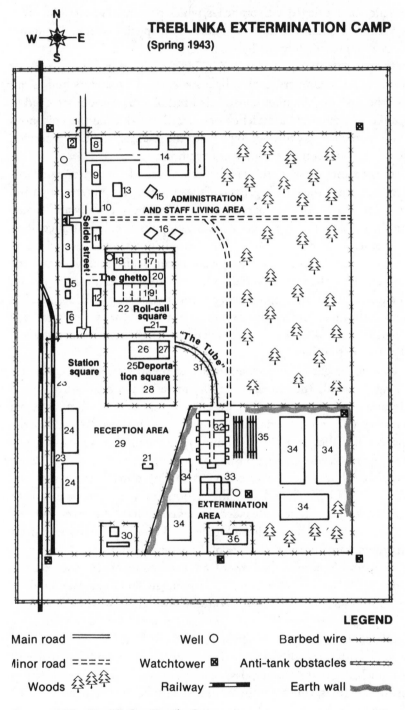

The Treblinka Death Camp

Administration and Staff Living Area

1. Entrance to the camp and Seidel Street
2. Guard's room near the entrance
3. SS living quarters
4. Arms storeroom
5. Gasoline pump and storerooms
6. Garage
7. Entrance gate to Station Square
8. Camp Command and Stangl's living quarters
9. Services for SS—barber, sick bay, dentist
10. Living quarters of domestic staff (Polish and Ukrainian girls)
11. Bakery
12. Foodstore and supply storeroom
13. The barrack in which "gold Jews" worked
14. Ukrainian living quarters—"Max Bialas barracks"
15. Zoo
16. Stables, chicken coop, pig pen
17. Living quarters for capos, women, tailor shop, shoe-repairs, carpentry, shop, and sick-room
18. Prisoners' kitchen
19. Living quarters for men prisoners, prisoners' laundry and tool room
20. Locksmithy and smithy
21. Latrine
22. Roll-call square

Reception Area

23. Station platform (ramp) and square
24. Storeroom for belongings taken from victims—disguised as a station
25. Deportation square
26. Barrack in which the women undressed and relinquished their valuables
27. Room in which women's hair was cut
28. Barrack in which men undressed, also used as a storeroom
29. Reception square
30. "Lazarett"—execution site
31. "The Tube"—the approach to the gas chambers

Extermination Area

32. New gas chambers (10 chambers)
33. Old gas chambers (3 chambers)
34. Burial pits
35. "The Roasts" for burning bodies
36. Prisoners' living quarters, kitchen, and latrines

Part of the building material and the equipment needed for constructing the camp were taken from the Warsaw ghetto workshops. Dr. Irmfried Eberl, who was in charge of constructing Treblinka, wrote to Dr. Heinz Auerswald on June 19 and 26 and on July 7, 1942, and demanded the immediate supply of various items required for the completion of the narrow-gauge railway and electrical installations.[5]

Unterscharführer Erich Fuchs, who took part in the construction of Treblinka, testified: "Subsequently I went to Treblinka. In this extermination camp I installed a generator which supplied electric light for the barracks. The work in Treblinka took me about three to four busy months. During my stay there transports of Jews who were gassed were coming in daily."[6]

The camp's main facilities for implementing the extermination of the Jews were completed in the middle of July 1942. The killings began on July 23, 1942, although construction work continued for months after.

CHAPTER SEVEN

PREPARING FOR THE DEPORTATIONS

ORGANIZING THE DEPORTATION OF THE 2,284,000 Jews who, according to German data, lived in the General Government in hundreds of ghettos dispersed all over the country demanded thorough planning. The geographical dispersion of the Jewish ghettos, the location and killing capacities of the death camps, the available means of transport, and their projected optimal use would all have to be considered.

In charge of planning and activating the deportations of Operation Reinhard was *Hauptsturmführer* Hermann Höfle. The deportation orders were coordinated and channeled through SS authorities from Höfle's office in Lublin, through the district SS and police leaders, down to the localities where the expulsions were to take place. In the first months of Operation Reinhard, the Jews in the General Government were under the jurisdiction of the German civilian administration. Therefore, the deportations required coordination of the SS authorities with the civilian officials. The SS chiefs of Operation Reinhard tried at first to keep the purpose of the deportations and the fate of the Jews secret—even from the German civilian authorities. The earliest known German document regarding any cooperation between SS authorities and civilian officials in the deportation of Jews in the framework of Operation Reinhard is a note written by Dr. Richard Turk, the head of the Department of Population Affairs and Welfare (*Bevölkerungswesen und Fürsorge*) in Lublin district. The document states:

> Notice, Lublin, 17 III 1942, Ref (event) II, R/We
> On March 4, 1942, I received a telegram from the government in Cracow, signed by Mr. [Friedrich] Siebert, the chief of the SS department, in which the concluding sentence reads as follows: I ask you to be helpful to the SS and Police Leader of Lublin in his actions.
> On March 7 I received a telephone call from the government [in Cracow], from Major Regger, in which I was strictly requested, in connection with the resettlement of the Jews from Mielec to the Lublin district, to reach an agreement with the SS and Police Leader, and it stressed the highest importance of this agreement. . . . I arranged a conference with *Hauptsturmführer* Höfle

for Monday, March 16, 1942, and it took place at 17.30. In the course of this conference, Höfle explained the following:

1. It would be appropriate if the transport of Jews that arrive in the Lublin district were split in the departure stations into those who are able to work and those who are not. If this division is impossible in the departure stations, eventually it should be considered to divide the transport in Lublin, according to the aforementioned point of view.
2. All the Jews incapable of work would arrive in Belzec, the final border station in the Zamosc region.
3. *Hauptsturmführer* Höfle is preparing the erection of a big camp, where the Jews capable of work will be held and divided according to their professions and from where they will be requested [for work].
4. Piaski will be cleared of Polish Jews and will become a concentration point for Jews arriving from the Reich.
5. In the meantime Trawniki will not be populated by Jews.
6. The *Hauptsturmführer* asks whether on the train section Deblin-Trawniki 60,000 Jews can be disembarked. After having been informed about the transports of Jews dispatched by us, Höfle announced that out of the 500 Jews who arrived from Suziec, those unable to work can be sorted out and sent to Belzec. . . .

In conclusion, he announced that every day he can receive four to five transports with 1,000 Jews each for the destination of Belzec station. These Jews would cross the border [of the occupied territories of the Soviet Union] and never return to the General Government.[1]

The initial plans of the Operation Reinhard staff were intended to thoroughly clear the whole General Government of Jews. Those fit for work, mainly craftsmen and skilled workers, were to be concentrated in labor camps in the Lublin district subordinate to the SS. All others were to be sent to the death camps. Concomitant with these deportations, Jews from Germany and the Protectorate of Bohemia and Moravia would repopulate the empty ghettos in the Lublin district—until their turn came to be sent to the death camps. A report of Dr. Richard Türk dated April 7, 1942, states:

Routine talks about the limited accommodation possibilities along the railway of Deblin-Rejowiec-Belzec were and are being conducted with [authorized] competent representatives of the SS and Police Leader. Alternative possibilities were checked.

On the basis of my proposals the matter was cleared up. The number of Jews brought from the west will be equal to the number of local Jews deported.

The present situation of the settlement movement is that about 6,000 [Jews] arrived from the Reich; and from the district [of Lublin]

7,500 were deported, and from the city of Lublin another 18,000.[2]

The deportation plan to the death camps was based on the administrative division of the General Government into five districts, each of which was divided into subdistricts. Each camp was intended to receive Jews from specific districts and subdistricts. The basis for planning the transports was the geographical proximity of a district or subdistrict to the camp's location, the principle of dividing the extermination activity equally and efficiently among the three camps, and the optimal exploitation of the railroad network. At times Jews from a particular subdistrict were sent to a more distant extermination camp because train transportation there was faster and more convenient than to a nearer camp. The general deportation plan called for the Jews of the Lublin district to be deported to Belzec; after Sobibor was completed, however, they were deported there also. Jews from the Lvov district (eastern Galicia) and Cracow district (western Galicia) were sent to Belzec. Jews from Warsaw and Radom districts were to be sent to Treblinka and partly to Sobibor. This was the basic master plan that could and would be adapted to changing circumstances and conditions. On June 3, 1942, Hans Frank issued a directive to transfer all Jewish affairs from civilian authorities in the General Government to the SS and Security Police to simplify the deportations and their procedures and to avoid misunderstandings.[3] From that point on, sole authority over the Jews and their fate in the General Government was in the hands of the SS.

The total deportation of the Jews from the ghettos of the General Government, as planned by the SS authorities, produced economic dislocations and a shortage of manpower. On June 22, 1942, Max Frauendorfer, the director of the labor department of the General Government, spoke about these difficulties at a meeting of German high officials in Cracow. He said that out of the manpower sources of the General Government, about 100,000 skilled workers were employed in the arms industry, eight hundred thousand workers were sent for work to Germany, and one hundred thousand workers were employed by the military authorities. Therefore, he "is now entirely dependent on Jewish labor. This point of view is shared also by the arms inspector of the General Government, General Lieutenant Max Schindler. Because of the shortage of Polish skilled workers, the Jews are irreplaceable. Indeed, they should not be excluded from the actions carried out by the SS, but in wartime, their labor should be exploited."[4]

In mid-July 1942, on the eve of the "great expulsion" of the Jews from Warsaw, the largest ghetto in Europe, Heinrich Himmler visited the Operation Reinhard death camps in the Lublin area. He closed his tour with a visit to operation headquarters in Lublin. Discussions with Odilo Globocnik led Himmler to conclude that with the completion of the three death camps, the Operation Reinhard staff was equipped with the means and facilities for the extermination of the Jews of the General Government. While still in Lublin, on July 19, Himmler issued an order to complete the deportation of all the Jews from the General Government to the death camps by December 31, 1942. By the time he issued the order, hundreds of thousands of Jews in the General Government had already been deported and murdered in the death camps. This order was intended to provide the "legal" basis for the deportations and killings already carried out, as well as for future operations. But to solve the manpower problem raised by this order, some camps where working Jews were to be kept had to be erected in the main towns of the General Government. Himmler's order was sent to SS *Obergruppenführer* Friedrich-Wilhelm Krüger, and it stated:

> I herewith order that the resettlement of the entire Jewish population of the General Government be carried out and completed by December 31, 1942.
>
> From December 31, 1942, no persons of Jewish origin may remain within the General Government, unless they are in the collection camps in Warsaw, Cracow, Czestochowa, Radom, and Lublin. All other work on which Jewish labor is employed must be finished by that date, or, in the event that this is not possible, it must be transferred to one of the collection camps.
>
> These measures are required with a view to the necessary ethnic division of races and peoples for the New Order in Europe, and also in the interests of the security and cleanliness of the German Reich and its sphere of interest. Every breach of this regulation spells a danger to quiet and order in the entire German sphere of interest, a point of application for the resistance movement and a source of moral and physical pestilence.
>
> For all these reasons a total cleansing is necessary and therefore to be carried out. Cases in which the date set cannot be observed will be reported to me in time, so that I can see to corrective action at an early date. All requests by other offices for changes or permits for exceptions to be made must be presented to me personally.[5]

Globocnik and his men on the Operation Reinhard staff received Himmler's order to eliminate the Jews of the General Government with great satisfaction. A few days after the July 22, 1942, visit, Globocnik wrote to the head of Himmler's personal staff, SS *Obergruppenführer* Karl Wolff: "The SS *Reichsführer* was just here and gave us so many new tasks that from now on all our hidden ambitions will be directed toward carrying them out. I am so thankful to him for this that he can rest assured that the thing he is interested in will be executed in the shortest time."[6]

Himmler's order, however, met with objection from German army authorities, who had been using Jewish forced labor in their industrial enterprises and workshops. General Kurt von Gienanth, commander of the

Military District of the General Government, sent a memorandum to the general staff on September 18, 1942:

> The evacuation of the Jews without advance notice to most sections of the Wehrmacht has caused great difficulties in the replacement of labor and delay in correct production for military purposes. Work for the SS, with priority "Winter," cannot be completed in time. . . .
>
> According to the figures supplied by the [General] Government's Central Labor Office, manpower in industry totals a little over a million, of which 300,000 are Jews. The latter include roughly 100,000 skilled workers.
>
> In the enterprises working for the Wehrmacht, the proportion of Jews among the skilled workers varies from 25 to 100 percent; it is 100 percent in the textile factories producing winter clothing. . . .
>
> The immediate removal of the Jews would cause a considerable reduction in Germany's war potential, and supplies to the front and to the troops in the General Government would be held up, at least for the time being. . . .
>
> Unless work of military importance is to suffer, Jews cannot be released until replacements have been trained, and then only step by step. . . .
>
> It is requested that the orders be carried out in this manner. The general policy will be to eliminate the Jews from work as quickly as possible without harming work of military importance. . . .
>
> It is requested that the evacuation of Jews employed in industrial enterprises be postponed until this has been done.[7]

General von Gienanth's memorandum was handed over by the German general staff to Himmler. Himmler's reply of October 9, 1942, stated:

Secret

With reference to the memorandum from the Commander of the Military District [*Wehrkreisbefehlshaber*] in the General Government to the OKW [High Command of the Wehrmacht] concerning the replacement of Jewish labor by Poles, I have the following comments:

1. I have given orders that all so-called armament workers who are actually employed solely in tailoring, furrier, and shoemaking workshops be collected in concentration camps on the spot, i.e., in Warsaw and Lublin, under the direction of SS *Obergruppenführer* [Friedrich] Krüger and SS *Obergruppenführer* [Oswald] Pohl. The Wehrmacht will send its orders to us, and we guarantee the continuous delivery of the items of clothing required. I have issued instructions, however, that ruthless steps be taken against all those who consider they should oppose this move in the alleged interest of armament needs, but who in reality only seek to support the Jews and their own businesses.

2. Jews in real war industries, i.e., armament workshops, vehicle workshops, etc., are to be withdrawn step by step. . . .

3. Our endeavor will then be to replace this Jewish labor force with Poles and to consolidate most of these Jewish concentration-camp enterprises into a small number of large Jewish concentration-camp enterprises—in the eastern part of the General Government, if possible. But there, too, in accordance with the wish of the *Führer*, the Jews are some day to disappear.

[signed] H. Himmler[8]

The request by the German army caused changes and delays in carrying out the total elimination of the ghettos and the extermination of their inhabitants, but it did not change their final fate—to be wiped out entirely. This was Hitler's wish, and Himmler and his men carried it out enthusiastically.

The German army and civilian authorities did not object in principle to the liquidation of the Jews in the General Government. Their objections were temporary and relevant to only a small segment of the victims and were based on immediate manpower needs. When it came to the actual deportations, the SS authorities received all the help they needed from the civilian and military authorities; this included the vital transportation necessary for the task.

THE DEPORTATION TRAINS

The deportation of the Jews to the death camps was based on railway transportation. The railways in the General Government were run by the *Generaldirektion der Ostbahn* (Directorate General of the Eastern Railroad), called "Gedob" for short. This organization, headed by Dr. Adolf Gerteis, operated the expropriated Polish railways. It was subordinate, operationally, to the German railways (the *Reichsbahn*), which were under the Ministry of Transport. Transports to the German eastern front (that is, the Soviet Union) and military supplies crossed through the area of the General Government and came under the jurisdiction of Gedob. Gedob's headquarters were in Cracow, but there were five distinct operational branches: in Cracow, Lublin, Radom, Warsaw, and Lvov. Personnel included about 9,000 Germans, 145,000 Poles, and a few thousand Ukrainians.[9]

Gedob was responsible for the allocation of trains for deportations within the framework of Operation Reinhard. It had to coordinate the traffic schedule with the SS authorities in charge of the deportations to determine at which railway stations the trains were to be waiting, the number of freight cars needed, the timetable, and the destinations of the trains. Gedob was in charge of planning the traffic schedule in accordance with military and other important priorities and of carrying out the transportation of the deported Jews from the embarkation stations, which were close to where they lived, to the death camps.

The trains with Jewish deportees were classified "special trains" (*Sonderzuge*). Usually they were closed freight cars; only on rare occasions did Jews travel in open cars. But, as a rule, each train included one or two passenger cars for the guards attached to the transport.

Within Gedob, Department V (Operations), headed by Erwin Massute, and, subordinate to him, Section 33 were in charge of the "special trains." Railway-inspector Stier was the man directly responsible for them.[10] The requests for the trains came from the SS and police leaders in charge of the deportation of the Jews from their districts. It was their duty to bring the Jewish deportees to the railway station, to supervise the embarkation, and to provide the police escort for the trains heading for the death camps.

The legal basis for the allocation of "special trains" for "resettlement" purposes was Hitler's secret order of October 7, 1939, which had appointed Himmler Reich Commissioner for the Consolidation of German Nationhood (RKFDV, *Reichskommissar für die Festigung deutschen Volkstum*). As previously indicated, this order imposed on Himmler three main tasks:

1. the repatriation of persons of German race and nationality resident abroad and considered suitable for permanent return to the Reich;
2. the elimination of the injurious influence of those sections of the population which were of foreign origin and constituted a danger to the Reich and the German community; and
3. the formation of new German settlement areas by means of transfer of population.[11]

To carry out these tasks, Himmler was authorized by this decree to issue directives to all the governing authorities in the Third Reich and to take any administrative measures he considered necessary. Among other things, this order obliged the Ministry of Transport of Germany to meet Himmler's demands for trains for the purpose of resettlement and deportation. Dr. Max Leibbrand, head of the Operations Department in this ministry, sent a telegram to Gedob authorizing it to meet transport requests for resettlement. Himmler empowered the higher SS and police leaders to submit their requests for trains directly to the railway authorities.[12]

During the first four months of Operation Reinhard, from the middle of March to the end of July 1942, when only Belzec and Sobibor were active, there were some transport problems and difficulties in getting the trains needed for the deportations. Although the number of trains requested during that period was small—because of the relatively limited killing capacity of the gas chambers in Belzec and Sobibor at that time—requests could not be met by the transportation authorities. At a conference of the highest German officials in the General Government, held by Hans Frank in Cracow on June 18, 1942, the problem of the lack of trains and the request to speed up the deportation of the Jews were raised. This conference was attended by the heads of the five districts, by Higher SS and Police Leader Krüger, and by the SS and police leaders of the districts. Krüger responded to complaints by the civilian authorities that the deportation of the Jews was going too slowly by stating that the police were prepared for a wider scale of deportations but the shortage of trains was causing delays. He promised that in the weeks and months to come the situation would improve.[13] At that time the German army was engaged in a major offensive on the eastern front directed at the Volga and Caucasus, and the German railways were heavily burdened with military traffic. As a result there were difficulties in allocating trains for the deportation of the Jews.

After Himmler's order of July 19, 1942, to complete the "resettlement" (that is, extermination) of the Jewish population within the framework of Operation Reinhard by the end of that year, and especially with the beginning of the mass expulsion from the Warsaw ghetto to Treblinka, transportation problems became acute. Himmler, who had checked out the transport problems during his visit to Operation Reinhard headquarters in July 1942, ordered his chief of personal staff, SS *Obergruppenführer* Karl Wolff, to contact the secretary of state of the Ministry of Transport, Dr. Theodor Ganzenmüller, on the matter. In his testimony at Ganzenmüller's trial, Wolff told of a phone conversation he had had with the accused on July 16, 1942:

> In July 1942, while I was at the *Führer's* headquarters, Himmler ordered me to contact Secretary of State Dr. Ganzenmüller and inform him that serious transportation difficulties had arisen in the course of the concentration of Jews from several ghettos to one central place near Lublin. Complaints had been received from those responsible for the operation, the SS and Police Chief in Poland SS *Obergruppenführer* Krüger and Lublin Police Chief SS *Brigadeführer* Globocnik. The SS *Reichsführer* has ordered me to request most urgently that Secretary of State Dr. Ganzenmüller personally ask those responsible for railroads in the General Government to eliminate these transportation difficulties as quickly as possible.[14]

Dr. Ganzenmüller responded to Himmler's request, and in a letter to Karl Wolff on July 27, 1942, he wrote:

> Since July 22, a train load of 5,000 Jews has departed daily from Warsaw via Malkinia to Treblinka, and in addition a train load of 5,000 Jews has left Przemysl twice a week for Belzec. . . .
> Gedob is in constant contact with the Security Police in Cracow. It has been agreed that the transports from Warsaw through Lublin to Sobibor be suspended for as long as the reconstruction works on that section make those

transports impossible (approximately until October 1942). These trains have
been agreed upon with the commander of the Security Police in the General
Government, and SS *Brigadeführer* Globocnik has been advised.
Heil Hitler!

Yours faithfully,

[Ganzenmüller][15]

In reply, Wolff wrote to Ganzenmüller on August 13, 1942: "Hearty
thanks, in the name of the *Reichsführer* SS, for your letter of July 28, 1942.
With great joy I learned from your announcement that, for the past fourteen days, a train has gone daily to Treblinka with 5,000 'members of the
chosen people' (*Angehörige des auserwählten Volkes*)."[16]

To work out the transportation requirements for the deportation of an
additional six hundred thousand Jews from the General Government and
the expulsion of two hundred thousand Jews from Rumania to Belzec, a
conference was held at the Ministry of Transport in Berlin on September
26 and 28, 1942. At this conference, attended by Eichmann or Rolf Günther
from the IV B 4 Gestapo, Stier of Gedob, and headed by Klem of the Ministry of Transport, the following was decided:

Evacuation of the Polish Jews

Urgent transports as proposed by the Chief of the Security Police and
the SD:

2 trains daily from the Warsaw district to Treblinka
1 train daily from the Radom district to Treblinka
1 train daily from the Cracow district to Belzec
1 train daily from the Lvov district to Belzec

These transports will be carried out with the 200 freight cars already
made available for this purpose by order of the Directorate of the German
railways in Cracow, as far as this is possible.

Upon completion of the repair of the Lublin-Chelm line, about November 1942, the other urgent transports will also be carried out. These are:

1 train daily from the Radom district to Sobibor
1 train daily from the north Lublin district to Belzec
1 train daily from the central Lublin district to Sobibor

insofar as this is practicable and the required number of freight cars are
available. With the reduction of the transport of potatoes, it is expected that
it will be possible for the special train service to be able to place at the disposal of the Directorate of the German railway in Cracow the necessary freight
cars. Thus the train transportation required will be available in accordance
with the above proposals and the plan completed this year.[17]

These decisions afforded the transportation requests of the SS authorities high priority. As the distances from the ghettos to the death camps, according to the deportation plans of Operation Reinhard, were not great—on the average, between 100 and 120 kilometers—the two hundred freight cars allocated within the General Government could transfer as many as twenty-five thousand Jews daily. With the solution of the transport problems, Himmler's order to complete Operation Reinhard by the end of 1942 could be realized.

However, the expulsion plan for the 280,000 Jews from Rumania to Belzec, which was the closest death camp to this country, met with several obstacles. The representatives of the Rumanian railways, who were asked to attend a special conference regarding their participation in transporting the Jews, never arrived. Nevertheless, the deportation was still planned, and it was decided to dispatch fifty freight cars, carrying 2,000 Jews, along with one passenger car for the escort, every two days. The departure point in Rumania had to be Adjud on the Ploesti-Cernauti line through the border station of Sniatyn in the General Government and from there through Lvov to Belzec.[18]

Notwithstanding all these plans, the deportation of the Rumanian Jews to Belzec did not materialize. A combination of squabbles within the Rumanian administration, a protest submitted by the United States to the Rumanian government in September 1942 regarding the planned deportation, and various efforts by Jewish leaders within Rumania prevented the implementation of the German plan.[19]

CHAPTER EIGHT

EXPULSION FROM THE GHETTOS

THE EXTERMINATION PROCESS BEGAN WITH the deportations from the ghettos. A master plan was formulated to determine to which death camps Jews from each district would be sent; this was determined in accordance with the killing capacity of each camp and the available transportation (mainly trains). The deportations executed within the framework of Operation Reinhard were coordinated by *Sturmbannführer* Hermann Höfle.

The SS authorities in charge of the deportations developed a method that became routine procedure in all the ghettos. The basic principles were surprise, speed of execution, terror, and ensuring that the victims were unaware of their destination and fate. The Jewish councils and general Jewish population were informed of their imminent expulsion and what they were permitted to take only a few hours or, at most, one day before the deportations actually started. At the same time, the ghetto was surrounded by security reinforcements to prevent escape and resistance. With the onset of the deportation itself, small security units, composed of SS men, Ukrainians, local Polish police, and sometimes members of the Jewish police in the ghettos, dispersed throughout the ghetto and ordered the Jews to leave their homes and congregate at the assembly points. From there they were taken on foot, under police escort, to the embarkation stations. The sick and elderly, those who were unable to walk, and those who refused to leave their homes were very often shot on the spot.

In the trial records of Karl Streibel, the commander of Trawniki training camp, whose units took part in the deportations from the ghettos in the Lublin district, we find the following description of the deportations:

The Conduct of the Evacuation Aktionen

All the deportations were carried out according to the same scheme. The Jewish living quarter that was to be evacuated was cordoned hermetically by the local [police] units in the early morning hours. The blocking forces were under order to shoot any person attempting to escape the blockade. Then, the so-called "cleaning units," which were formed under the command of members of the local gendarmerie or security police, entered the living quarter. The Jews were ordered to go to a designated assembly square.

Afterward, the houses and apartments were searched for Jews who had gone into hiding or had remained behind, and they were driven into the streets violently. The old, sick, and feeble who could not go to the assembly square and the Jews who tried to escape were shot. . . .

At the assembly square, the Jews, who usually carried hand baggage, had to sit down to enable the guard units better observation of the crowd. Jews who stood up or somehow aroused the attention of the guards were beaten or shot. At the beginning, some of the Jews who were employed by German enterprises or institutions as skilled workers, and as such were indispensable, were individually or with their families separated [from the others] and exempted from deportation. In *Aktionen* in which the whole locality had to be "cleansed of Jews," all Jews were deported.

When all the Jews slated for transport were assembled, they had to line up in marching columns and, under heavy guard, were taken to the railway station. Sometimes they had to cover distances of many kilometers. The Jews, on their way to the railway stations, were urged on by shouting and beatings. Jews who could not keep up with the marching columns and lagged behind were beaten, and if that did not help, they were shot. Those who tried to escape were shot immediately.

At the railway station the Jews were made to sit down. When the freight cars were ready, embarkation began. Usually, the number of Jews assembled exceeded the normal capacity of the cars. The Jews were then pushed in by force. Up to 150 people were crammed into one freight car. On these occasions, there were shootings into the cars to create more places. The freight cars were then closed, and the Jews were taken to the extermination camps, and there they were killed.

When for some reason the deportation to an extermination camp was impossible, the Jews were shot on the spot. Sometimes they themselves had to dig the mass graves and later fill them up. Usually, for this purpose a working group was selected and later, after finishing the work, they were also shot.

The Units Participating in the Evacuation Aktionen

Jewish affairs were in the jurisdiction of the local commander of the security police branch. The members of this branch always took part in the evacuation *Aktionen* in their locality. In almost every locality where a Jewish living quarter [ghetto] existed, there was also a gendarmerie post. The members of this post were in charge of security and order, which included regularly guarding the Jewish quarter. To the gendarmerie were subordinated the local Polish or Ukrainian police. The members of the gendarmerie post took part in the evacuation *Aktionen*.

However, the local security police branch and gendarmerie post could not carry out large evacuation *Aktionen* with only the people who were under their command. In such cases they were reinforced by SS or police units from their locality or vicinity. To support the local forces in the execution of some of the *Aktionen* in the district, the SS and Police Leader of the Lublin district had reinforced the local forces with [Ukrainian] guardsmen from Trawniki.

The size of the Ukrainian unit assigned to such *Aktionen* varied. It was fixed according to the extent of the planned evacuation *Aktion* and the strength of the other forces in disposition. Smaller units numbered about thirty people; larger ones reached company strength (90–120 guardsmen).... These units were used to encircle the Jewish living quarter, to search and evacuate the houses, to guard the Jews at the assembly place and on their way to the railway station. They provided the shooting unit during the mass shootings. The members of this unit behaved particularly brutally and ruthlessly with the Jews and carried out the shootings willingly. They drank a lot of alcohol and tried to extract money and valuables from the victims. ... The *Aktion* usually lasted two days or even more.[1]

In each locality this basic scheme was adapted to local conditions: the size of the Jewish community doomed to deportation, the strength of the German forces allotted to the *Aktion,* the transportation means, and time limits.

LUBLIN DISTRICT

On the eve of the deportations there were close to three hundred thousand Jews in the Lublin district, many of whom had not yet been incarcerated in ghettoes. The Lublin ghetto, established at the end of March 1941, held almost thirty-six thousand Jews. Approximately ten thousand Jews were expelled to other cities prior to the ghetto's establishment.[2] The first large-scale deportation within the framework of Operation Reinhard was from the Lublin ghetto to the Belzec death camp. Odilo Globocnik wanted first of all to get rid of the Jews from the Lublin district, who were directly under his jurisdiction and in his immediate vicinity. The closeness to Belzec caused no transportation problems, and the priority of deporting the Jews from Lublin district served some additional purposes. Globocnik had a colonization plan, confirmed by Heinrich Himmler, to create in the future in the city of Lublin a German quarter as a first step in repopulating the entire city by Germans. The removal of the Jews from the city left vacant places and served this purpose. The deportation of the Jews from the ghettos in the Lublin district also enabled Nazi authorities to bring Jews from Germany, Slovakia, and the Protectorate of Bohemia and Moravia to Lublin and keep them there temporarily, until they would be sent to the death camps.

The deportation from Lublin began on March 16, 1942, late in the evening. The heads of the Jewish council (*Judenrat*) were called to the SS office and were handed the deportation order. On March 17, 1942, a meeting of the Jewish council was called, and the deportation order was read out to those present.

The following are the minutes of that meeting:

Protocol No. 14/138

The plenary meeting of the Jewish Council of Lublin of 17/3/42.
Attendance: 22 members
Chairman: Head of the Council, Eng. H. Becker
Protocol written by: The member of the Council and Secretary, Advocate,
[David] Hochgemein.

Deportation Order

In the city of Lublin there will remain only those Jews who have a stamp of the Security Police on their work permits. They will remain with their wives and children. Those who are to be deported may take with them one handbag weighing 15 kg, all their money and valuables. . . . They should be prepared to walk about 3 kms on foot; from then on, there will be transportation. The epidemic hospital, with its patients and staff, will remain. About 1,400 people will be deported every day. The deportation will start from the hill, from Unitzky Street. Those Jews who remain after the departure in the empty flats will be shot.[3]

At the trial held in Wiesbaden, Germany, of a group of SS men who had operated in Lublin, a description was given of the deportation of the Jews of Lublin:

The fenced-off ghetto was surrounded from the outside by forces of the Order Police and Ukrainian auxiliaries [Trawniki men]. Inside the ghetto, along Lubartowska Street, the expulsion commandos operated in accordance with their orders: small units of Trawniki men, under the command of Germans, woke up the sleeping inhabitants with shouting and ordered them to leave their apartments without delay and to congregate in the street; otherwise they would be shot. . . .

The *Aktion* was carried out with cruelty. In their surprise, the people became panic-stricken. The drunken Ukrainians used their weapons indiscriminately and many were killed on the spot. No selection was held at this deportation. The people, with no distinction of age or sex, were lined up in marching columns and led under escort to the synagogue. There they had to remain until dawn, when they were taken on foot to the *Umschlagplatz* [transfer station] near the slaughterhouse, where they embarked for Belzec.[4]

The deportations continued in this way for several months. A survivor of the Lublin ghetto described them:

The expulsions were carried out at night. Every night there were "selections." The people, with their personal documents in their hands, had to pass along tables placed in the streets at which German policemen and men of the

Jewish Order Service sat. Every night brought a new surprise. The families of the craftsmen who worked at Lipowa Street 7 were confident that nothing would happen to them. They went to the checkpoints and were deported; those who did not have work permits went into hiding and survived. The Germans needed a certain quota of people for deportation, and they did not care who went for destruction....

The SS men spread rumors that the deportation was to Russia where there was a need for working men. The bewildered people believed them....[5]

Close to fourteen hundred Jews were deported daily from Lublin to Belzec. During each of the shooting *Aktionen*, Jews who did not leave their apartments were shot dead. Jews were also shot as they made their way to the assembly points and the trains. After being removed from their homes, and an entire area has been cleared of its residents, Trawniki men would search the apartments to make sure no Jews remained there in hiding, including any invalids or the ill who could not walk to the assembly points. Hundreds of those found during these searches were shot on the spot. Toward evening, a group of Jewish men would collect the corpses of the murdered off the streets and out of the apartments and bury them in the Jewish cemetery.

The Germans did not bother transporting to Belzec any of the Jewish orphans and the patients in the ghetto hospitals; they were shot on site. Nearly two hundred children were shot dead on March 24 and were buried in pits that had been dug outside the city. On that day, the Germans also shot one hundred Jews hospitalized in the hospital for contagious diseases, its medical staff, and ninety residents of the old age home. At dawn on March 27, the SS informed the staff of the Jewish hospital on Lubartówska Street to prepare the patients for "resettlement in the East." Trawniki men surrounded the hospital, ordering the staff to remove the patients, including children, to the trucks awaiting them outside. The patients were driven outside the city, to the outskirts of Lubartów, and were shot dead into pits that had been prepared beforehand. At the end of March, close to half of the *Judenrat* members were murdered. By April 14, approximately thirty thousand Jews had been deported from Lublin to Belzec, and several thousand others had been shot on the spot. At the end of the deportation all work permits (*Scheine*) held by Jews were canceled and were replaced with new ones—*J-Ausweis*—which were given to only a few of the remaining Jews.

After the deportation, close to seven thousand Jews were left in Lublin, several thousand of them without a *Scheine*. They were all ordered to move to the new ghetto in Majdan Tatarsk by April 19. At dawn the next day, the ghetto in Majdan Tatarsk was surrounded and its residents ordered to line up for roll call. The Germans conducted a selection, and the Jews were divided into two groups: The new *Scheine* holders, numbering between thirty-three hundred and four thousand Jews, remained in the ghetto; the approximately three thousand others were expelled on foot outside of the city, where they were shot.[6]

DEPORTATIONS FROM SMALL GHETTOS

The Jews from hundreds of small ghettos were expelled from their homes and forced to walk to the railway stations. Horse-drawn carts were sometimes mobilized from the neighboring villages by the local police for the transportation of small children and the elderly. Jews from ghettos close to the death camps were expelled on foot or by means of horse-drawn carts directly into the camps. Where the capacity of the train was larger than the number of Jews from one ghetto, Jews from several ghettos were concentrated and expelled together. A survivor of one such expulsion described the event:

I lived in the township of Turobin in the Lublin district. On May 10, 1942, Jews from neighboring townships were brought into Turobin. On May 12, SS men and Ukrainians surrounded the town. Early in the morning, they announced that we were going to be deported and that by 9 o'clock all Jews should be in the town square. I came there with my aunt. My uncle and their children went into hiding. I was so fed up with the life we had been leading that I decided to go, but it didn't occur to me that we were going to be sent to a death camp. At the square were carts for the children and for the bundles. All the rest were compelled to go on foot. Many people, the elderly and sick and those found in the houses, were shot on the spot. Close to me was a paralyzed man in a wheelchair. An SS man approached him, put his gun to the man's head and pressed the trigger. No shot came. The man's face convulsed, his eyes filled with tears, but the SS man continued his "game" and finally shot him. I stood close by, frozen, unable to cry.

After some hours came the order to move. We left the town, mainly families with their old, their babies, and their bundles. On the way we were joined by Jews from Wisokie. We marched silently, guarded by Germans and Ukrainians on horses and bicycles. The weak fell and remained behind. From time to time we heard shots; those who had remained behind were shot. We marched for two days and two nights—about 30 km. We passed through Polish villages. People stood and watched us. Some of them laughed, others closed themselves into their houses, but there were also some who gave us water.

When we passed through Zolkiew and Gorzkow, the local Jews joined our marching column, and our number increased to 4,000. We continued walking. The sky became cruel to us. After the burning sun, which weakened us and caused deaths, came a storm with torrential rain, thunder, and lightning. We were soaking wet and the marching column became part of the mud. It was hard to walk.

We arrived at the railway station in Krasnystaw, where we stayed for a few hours. Then the Ukrainians pushed us into the train, about 150 to each freight car. We were told that we were going to the Ukraine to work. On the other hand, there were people who were told that we were being sent to Majdanek camp. But when we looked out through the small window, we realized that we were not going in the direction of Lublin. That meant that our destination was not Majdanek. We were delighted. After a few hours of traveling, we arrived at Sobibor.[7]

Globocnik—the SSPF of the Lublin district, commander of Operation Reinhard throughout the General Government, and the person directly in charge of the deportation from Lublin, both the city and district—transferred the deportation model from his district, together with any conclusions drawn from the process, to the SSPF in the General Government's other districts. This model, with appropriate changes to suit different localities, was copied for conducting the deportations from the other districts.[8]

SHOOTING *AKTIONEN*

In the final stages of this process, the Jews from most of the ghettos in the General Government were sent to death camps. There were, however, some townships in which the Jews were not sent to the death camps, but were shot in their own vicinity. There were a few reasons for these *Aktionen*: the lack of transportation, the inability of the death camps to receive these deportees on a definite date, and, in some cases, the desire of local Nazi authorities to collect for themselves the goods and valuables of the victims.

One of these shooting *Aktionen* took place in Lomazy, in the northeast section of the Lublin district, and was described in the Streibel-Trawniki trial:

About 1,600–1,700 Jews lived in Lomazy in August 1942. They were kept in a separate quarter. This township was subordinate to the security police post of Biala Podlaska. In September 1942 the reserve police battalion 101 was stationed in the northern part of the district of Lublin. The *Aktion* against the Jews in Lomazy lasted from the middle of August 1942 until the end of the month. The 2nd company of the reserve police battalion 101, including the witness Franke, surrounded the Jewish living quarter in the early morning hours. Then the members of the battalion, under the command of the officers of the security police branch of Biala Podlaska, evacuated the people from the houses and apartments. The Jews were assembled on the sport grounds. Following instructions, the children and elderly, the sick and weak, who were not able to walk, were shot on the spot.

At the sports stadium, the Jews were divided by sex; they had to sit on the ground for a long time.

During this period of waiting, a police unit received an order to organize a working group of fifty Jews and take them to a forest at a distance of 1 km. There they had to dig a large pit. In the morning hours Jews were taken to the execution place by groups, as they had been divided, according to sex; they had to lie down, close to the pit. Any contact between men and women was prevented and forbidden. The pits where the executions were carried out were only 40–50 meters away from the place the Jews were being kept, but could not be seen by them. The whole execution area—the waiting place, the way to the pits, and the pits themselves—was surrounded by members of the police units.

The Jews had to undress right before the shootings and hand over their valuables. Then, in groups of ten to twenty people, they had to run the 40–50 meters to the pits between two rows of guards. In doing this they were rushed on by shouting and the rifle butts of the guards. The Jews had to lie in the pits face down, and then they were shot. The next group of victims had to lie down in a row behind those who had already been killed or on top of them, and then they, too, were shot. The executions continued in that way until the pit 1.80 meters deep was filled to the edge with corpses.

The Jewish working group, which had dug the pit, had to cover it with earth at the end of the *Aktion*. Finally, these people had to dig a small pit in which they themselves were killed and buried.

In the shooting *Aktion* in Lomazy a unit of about 40 guardsmen from Trawniki participated. They arrived in Lomazy after the members of the reserve police battalion 101 had driven the Jews to the sport grounds. The guardsmen were sent to the *Aktion* as an execution unit because members of the police battalion which had carried out the shooting *Aktion* in Josefow were unwilling to repeat it.

The guardsmen stood by the pits and carried out the shootings with their rifles. They drank so much liquor that during the shooting inconceivable scenes took place. Because of their drunkenness their shots missed the target, many times, and the shots did not cause the victims' immediate death. In the afternoon the guardsmen were so drunk that they could not continue the executions. The members of the police battalion continued with the executions while the guardsmen slept out their drunkenness close to the execution area. Later in the afternoon the guardsmen returned and continued with the shootings until the end of the *Aktion*. Afterward they supervised the Jewish working group which had covered the pit, and finally they also shot those people.[9]

THE DEPORTATION FROM WARSAW

The first deportation transports to Treblinka were from the Warsaw ghetto, which was the largest ghetto in Nazi-occupied Europe. The Jews from the entire region west and southwest of Warsaw were concentrated there. At the beginning of 1941, the population of the ghetto had reached four hundred fifty thousand. However, owing to the terrible conditions—hunger and disease—the death rate assumed dire proportions, and by the time the deportations had begun, the ghetto population numbered approximately three hundred fifty thousand Jews.

Between the spring of 1942 and the beginning of summer, during the deportation transports from the areas of Lublin, Lvov, and Cracow to the Belzec and Sobibor camps, the Jews in the Warsaw ghetto heard rumors about the deportations but not about the destination or the fate of the deportees. The rumors spread and increased and were reported in the ghetto's Underground newspapers, stirring fear and unrest among the residents that they, too, were to be deported. Adam Czerniakow, the *Judenrat* chairman, decided to approach the German authorities with whom he had been in contact for close to three years as part of his responsibilities, to inquire whether the rumors had any basis. On July 20, 1942, he contacted the SiPo. By that time the deportation was already set to take place, and the German authorities in charge of the ghetto were aware of it. Upon returning to the ghetto that day Czerniakow wrote in his diary:

> In the morning at 7:30 at the Gestapo, I asked Mende how much truth there was in the rumors. He replied that he had heard nothing. I turned to Brandt; he also knew nothing. When asked whether it *could* happen, he replied that he knew of no such scheme. Uncertain, I left his office. I proceeded to his chief, *Kommissar* Böhm. He told me that this was not his department but Hoeheman [Höhmann] might say something about the rumors. I mentioned that according to rumor, the deportation is to start tonight at 7:30. He replied that he would be bound to know something if it were about to happen. Not seeing any other way out, I went to the deputy chief of Section III, Scherer. He expressed his surprise hearing the rumor and informed me that he too, knew nothing about it. Finally, I asked whether I could tell the population that their fears were groundless. He replied that I could and that all the talk was *Quatsch* and *Unsinn* [*utter nonsense*].[10]

The deportation from the Warsaw ghetto began on July 22 and continued through September 12, 1942. *Sturmbannführer* Höfle, of Operation Reinhard headquarters in Lublin, was in charge of the deportation. On the morning of July 22, 1941, Höfle, accompanied by SS and government officials, arrived at the *Judenrat* offices of the ghetto and announced to Czerniakow that the Jews, regardless of sex or age and with but a few exceptions, were to be evacuated to the East. That same day the *Judenrat* was ordered to supply six thousand Jews for transportation and to announce the evacuation to Warsaw Jewry. The announcement explained that the only exceptions to the deportation rule would be workers in German factories who had valid work permits, *Judenrat* employees, the Jewish Order Service, hospital patients and employees, and the families of the exempt. The deportees would be permitted to carry with them fifteen kilograms of baggage, food for three days, money, gold, and other valuables. The *Judenrat* was told that, from that day on, it had to ensure that six thousand Jews reported to the embarkation place (*Umschlagplatz*) every day by 4:00 p.m. to board the trains.

That day Czerniakow noted in his diary: "*Sturmbannführer* Höfle (*Beauftragter* [plenipotentiary] in charge deportation) asked me into his office and informed me that for the time being my wife was free, but if the deportation were impeded in any way, she would be the first one to be shot as a hostage."[11]

Posters were placed around the ghetto, detailing the names of the deportees and those who had been released. In the afternoon hours of July 22, crowds gathered in front of the posters announcing the deportation. On the first day the designated contingent of deportees was delivered to the *Umschlogplatz*. It consisted partly of inmates of the psychiatric hospital and partly of inmates of the central detention station who had been arrested mostly for failure to obey administrative orders. The following day, July 23, Czerniakow was required to supply seven thousand Jews to be deported, including children. That day, Czerniakow committed suicide. He was not willing to hand over Jews, preferring to take his own life. His deputy, engineer Marek Lichtenbaum, was appointed as head of the *Judenrat*.

The appearance of the ghetto streets changed according to the intensity of the *Aktion*. The technique of hunting the victims varied. During the initial stage, it consisted of blocking house exits; later, whole streets were closed by German security forces. The street blockade consisted of surrounding the exits of the given section by squads of police, and a stringent examination of the documents of all who were caught. Those who did not hold a valid *Ausweis* (worker identification) were loaded into cars and taken to the *Umschlagplatz*. The Jewish hospital at Stawki Street, whose patients and staff had been evacuated previously, and which was in the immediate neighborhood of the *Umschlagplatz*, became an assembly point for deportees prior to loading them into the trains. There was a side railroad track at the *Umschlagplatz* from which freight trains loaded with Jews departed. The deportees were pushed into the crowded train cars, almost 100 people to a carriage. A transport of 6,000 to 7,400 deportees left daily. Loading took place in the afternoon hours, from 4:00 to 5:00 p.m. All those assembled were driven out of the hospital building to the accompaniment of brutal beatings with guns and sticks. During the first ten days, which can be defined as the first phase in the deportations that continued until the end of July, approximately 65,000 Jews were removed from the ghetto.

To speed up the process and to encourage the ghetto Jews to report to the *Umschlagplatz* of their own volition, the German authorities announced through the Jewish Order Service that every person reporting on their own free will between July 29 and July 31 (and thereafter from August 2 to 4) would receive a travel ration of three kilograms of bread and one kilogram of jam. In view of the prevailing famine conditions in the ghetto, this offer brought many to the assembly point. But the results still did not satisfy the deportation authorities. They changed their tactics.

The second phase of the deportation began on July 31 and continued through mid-August. This phase was more violent than the previous one. Houses and streets were cordoned off, German-owned enterprises were liquidated, and the workers were sent to the *Umschlagplatz*. The entire *Aktion* was accompanied by shooting. Besides the SS, Ukrainian Trawniki men and police units, as well as Lithuanians and Latvians, took part in the kidnappings and the deportations. The Jewish police assisted in assembling those to be deported; however, as the deportation turned more violent, and Jews were kidnapped from their homes and off the streets, their involvement decreased. During the first week of August, two hundred children were taken to the deportation trains from Janusz Korczak's orphanage. Dr. Korczak was given the option to remain in the ghetto and not accompany the children; he rejected the proposal, and, together with the institution's entire educators' staff, they went to their deaths with the children. The third phase of the deportation began in mid-August and continued through September 6. The deportation now took on the nature of a wide-ranging transport. Thousands of people had already either found hiding places in the ghetto or had fled it. To meet the deportation quota, the Germans and their collaborators would break into factories and workshops whose workers were *Schein* holders and were not intended for deportation, and these workers, together with their families, would be taken to the trains to be deported to Treblinka.

During the deportation's final phase, on September 6, thirty-five thousand permits were distributed to the various factories and workshops and the *Judenrat*. The Germans intended on leaving in the ghetto 10 percent of its residents on the eve of the deportation. Once the deportation was completed, in mid-September, the ghetto was reduced in size and divided into three separate, cut off areas. In addition to the thirty-five thousand "legal" Jews who remained in the ghetto, there were an additional twenty-five thousand "illegals" who survived the deportations while in hiding.

The surviving Jews, mainly youngsters, knew that this was but a brief deferment until their time would come.[12]

THE RADOM DISTRICT

In 1941, there were about four hundred thousand Jews living in the entire Radom district. Most were incarcerated in ghettos or concentrated near railroad junctions prior to being deported to Treblinka during Operation Reinhard. Before the deportations began, district SSPF, SS *Standartenführer* Herbert Böttcher, issued an order to shoot on sight any Jew found outside a ghetto or labor camp once the deportations began.[13]

The Radom district was characterized by numerous munitions plants that had belonged to Poland's arms industry. The Germans continued operations for their own needs, employing Polish workers. When they needed more laborers in Germany itself, between May and August 1942, the Germans transferred three hundred forty thousand Polish workers from the Radom district to Germany to alleviate the need. To further help the dire situation in the workforce and munitions plants, in the summer of 1942, the Wehrmacht, police, and SS concluded that simultaneously with liquidation of the ghettos they would bring Jews to work in the munitions factories. A special commission discussing the transfer of Jews to the arms industry decided to construct housing for the Jewish slave laborers adjacent to the plants. Each complex would thus be a *Betriebslager*—a factory-camp.[14]

The Radom ghetto, established in early April 1941, was divided into two ghettos erected in two neighborhoods on two opposite sides of the city: the large ghetto, in which about twenty-five thousand Jews were concentrated, and the small ghetto with about eight thousand Jews. In the early summer of 1942, rumors reached the ghetto about evacuating Jews from the Lublin district and deportations "for labor, in the East." Jews were deported from the city of Radom in two roundups. The *Aktion* in the small ghetto began on August 5, 1942. About eight hundred Jews with work certificates were transferred to the large ghetto; about one thousand Jews were murdered on the spot; and about six thousand transported to Treblinka.

When the news of the liquidation of the small ghetto reached the large ghetto, thousands of Jews attempted to be accepted to work in the vital plants, while others attempted to find hiding places inside the ghetto. On the morning of August 16, the roundup began in the large ghetto in which about ten thousand Jews were transported to Treblinka, and another ten thousand transported the next day. During the evacuation of the large ghetto, about fifteen hundred Jews were shot to death on site, including the children in the orphanage, residents of the old age home, and all patients in the hospital. We may assume that after the deportations and murders in the ghetto, about forty-five hundred Jews remained in the large ghetto— needed for labor to assist the Reich's war effort.[15]

On August 19, 1942, upon completion of the deportations from Radom, the Germans began to deport the Jews from Ghetto Kielce, which contained about twenty-four thousand Jews. The deportations were originally planned to take place from August 20 to August 24. The *Aktion* was especially violent. Thousands of Jews ran through the streets while the Germans and their collaborators cruelly urged them to gather at the evacuation points, ordered dogs to savage them, beat them with clubs and rifle butts, and shot into the crowds. On August 20, nearly a thousand Jews were murdered, while on Friday, August 21, more than six thousand residents were transported to Treblinka. Over the next two days, August 22–23, approximately six thousand more Jews were transported to Treblinka. Among those murdered during the *Aktion* were seventy children living in the orphanage, patients and staff of the hospital, and their family members hidden in the hospital that day, for a total of about nine hundred dead. On the final day of the deportation, August 24, another seven to eight thousand Jews were transported to Treblinka. Thirty pregnant women caught in the *Aktion* were shot. Our data show that during the five days of liquidating the Kielce ghetto, between August 20 and 24, 1942, three transports brought about twenty thousand Jews to Treblinka. Furthermore, during the *Aktion,* about twenty-five hundred Jews were murdered and buried there—about 10 percent of the ghetto residents. Another seventeen hundred Jews who survived the selection in Kielce were kept alive for slave labor in the ghetto. Hundreds survived in hideouts or fled outside of the ghetto.[16]

The liquidation of the Jews of Czestochowa, the third-largest city in the Radom district, began about one month after concluding the deportations from Kielce, and lasted about two weeks. When the ghetto was established in April 1941, it incarcerated about 35,000 Jews; by the time the deportation began in September 1942, the population had increased to 36,500. The Czestochowa ghetto was liquidated in several *Aktionen* over a two-week period, between September 22 and October 7, 1942. A total of about 30,000 Jews were deported to Treblinka, leaving 6,000 Jews in the ghetto, Jews who had undergone selection and were found fit for labor.[17]

With completion of the deportations from the three largest cities of the Radom district—Radom, Kielce, and Czestochowa—the Germans began deporting the Jews from the small towns and villages in the district's remaining administrative areas. These evacuations had an entirely different character, primarily because the small towns had no train stations. Jews who were not murdered on the spot were forced to walk distances of twenty to forty kilometers to locations where trains awaited them. These forced marches were often death marches in practice.

Within approximately three months, from early August to mid-November 1942, nearly three hundred sixty thousand Jews, out of the approximately four hundred thousand residents in 1941, were deported from the Radom district to Treblinka, where they were murdered. Thousands were shot to death on the spot during the roundups. After each wave of deportations, some tens of thousands of Jews remained in the entire Radom district, imprisoned in small ghettos or work camps adjacent to plants important for the German war effort, where they worked. Thousands more Jews were brought to the arms factories in the district from the Płaszów camp and other places during 1943–1944. Over these two years, a total of about fifty thousand Jewish prisoners were employed at the arms factories in the Radom district, not all at the same time, and about thirty thousand of this total perished. As the Red Army advanced toward the Radom district in August 1944, the Germans liquidated the labor camps. A few of the workers were transported to Auschwitz-Birkenau, and some were sent to camps in Germany.[18]

THE CRACOW DISTRICT

There were approximately 250,000 Jews residing in the Cracow district when the war began, about 60,000 in the city of Cracow itself. During the first few months of the war, about 20,000 Jews who were deported from Lodz arrived in Cracow, but since many fled from the city to eastern Poland, which was under Soviet Union occupation, and thousands of others were shot by police and SS officials as well as by the initiative of locals, by June 1940, the Cracow district contained 215,000 Jews. Following deportations to other districts of the General Government, in May 1941 there were 200,000 Jews in the district.

Governor General Hans Frank governed the General Government from the city of Cracow. As early as September 1940, over thirty-five thousand Jews were forced to leave Cracow and settle in neighboring small towns, leaving about eleven thousand Jews in the city. This evacuation, extremely extensive for its period, was designed to keep the governor general's city as *Judenrein* as possible, while simultaneously intending to concentrate the Jews in as few locations as possible. This policy forced Jewish residents of small towns and villages to move into ghettos established in the main administrative cities. The majority of ghettos in the Cracow district were established just prior to or during Operation Reinhard.

The Cracow ghetto had been established on March 20, 1940. In addition to the Jews who remained in the city, Jews were transferred there from the adjacent towns, resulting in a total of about 18,000 residents of the ghetto. Deportation from Cracow and the district cities to Belzec began on June 1, 1942, and continued until mid-September 1942. The first deportation *Aktion* in Cracow lasted from June 1 to June 8, during which about 6,000 Jews were transported to Belzec and hundreds were shot to death in the ghetto. The second *Aktion* took place on October 27–28, 1942; about seven thousand Jews were transported, mostly to Belzec and a minority to Auschwitz-Birkenau; about six hundred people were shot to death in the ghetto. The final liquidation of the Cracow ghetto took place on March 13–14, 1943. Since the Belzec death camp was liquidated in late 1942, about two thousand of the ghetto residents were sent to the Płaszów slave labor camp located southeast of Cracow, while about twenty-three hundred were transported to Auschwitz-Birkenau to be murdered. About seven hundred people were shot to death during the liquidation *Aktion* within the ghetto.[19]

Between June and September 1942, Jews residing in other ghettos in the Cracow district were also deported. During these months, about 140,000 people were transported to their death, with thousands of others shot during the *Aktionen* while still in the ghettos. In other ghettos, Jewish laborers were spared to slave for the war effort.

The remaining ghettos in the district after September 1942 were split into "productive" and "nonproductive" sections. Jews residing in the "nonproductive" section received no food rations, and whoever did not die of hunger was shot in the course of local *Aktionen* during 1943. During that year, all remaining ghettos were converted into slave labor camps under SS and police command. In 1944, any remaining Jews were concentrated in the Płaszów camp, which had been converted into a concentration camp by January of that year. The last prisoners in Płaszów were transported to Auschwitz on January 14, 1945, and from there sent on Death Marches toward Germany and Austria.

The Galicia District

The annihilation of the Jews of the district of Galicia as part of Operation Reinhard was characterized by the large number of Jews murdered near their homes. An estimated more than one-third of the Jewish population of the district were shot to death near their homes simultaneously with the deportations to Belzec and after it ceased operating in late 1942. The first wave of deportations from Galicia to Belzec began on March 20, 1942, and continued until mid-April 1942. Estimates of the number of Jews residing in the district of Galicia in mid-March 1942 place the figures between 507,000–522,000 Jews. The majority of those deported to Belzec in this wave of deportations were classified by the Germans as "unfit for labor."

The first deportees were the Jews of the city of Lvov. Between March 19 and April 1, 1942, about fifteen thousand Jews were deported from Lvov to Belzec. The *Judenrat* and Jewish police who cooperated in the roundup had no knowledge of the death camp at the time, as it had just become operational. News began to arrive in the city only later. Nevertheless, even without concrete knowledge, the *Judenrat* and the Jewish police helped send the Jews to an unknown location, which later turned out to be a death camp.

In Stanislawow, after thousands of young people were transported to labor camps, executions, and many deaths from diseases and starvation, in March 1942 there were still twenty thousand to twenty-three thousand Jews. On Passover Eve, March 31, 1942, the German and Ukrainian police surrounded the ghetto and ordered all the Jews to concentrate at one of the ghetto's main squares. Many hid and many others attempted to flee. Police shot at those who fled, set several houses on fire, and lobbed grenades into possible hiding places to flush out anyone concealed there. At the square, all work permits were examined; permit holders and their families were released. About five thousand people, including beggars, indigent residents of the poorhouse, residents of the old age homes, the remnants of the Hungarian Jewish deportees (see chapter 2), and children living in the orphanage, were most of the victims transported to Belzec in this roundup. Several hundreds were shot on the spot. After the *Aktion*, Jews from the villages in the vicinity were brought to Stanislawow and, within a short time, were shot to death.[20]

The Kolomyya ghetto was made up of three separate neighborhoods. The process of enclosing the Jews in the ghetto took several months and was completed on March 25, 1942. The ghetto population was approximately 18,000 people. During March 3–5, 1942, Germans and Ukrainians went through each section of the ghetto already settled with Jews; removed about 5,000 people, most of whom had been classified unfit for work; and sent them on transports to Belzec. Many hid, but while searching for Jews who fled or hid, the Germans shot to death about 250 people and burned dozens of others to death by setting fire to the houses.[21]

In Tarnopol, the *Judenrat* was ordered to draw up a list of all the elderly, disabled, welfare cases, and orphans—that is, those whom the Germans called the "nonproductive" in order to "transfer them to other locations to make life easier in the ghetto," according to the German directive. The Jewish police concentrated six hundred to seven hundred of these Jews in the old synagogue; German and Ukrainian police took them to an adjacent forest and shot them to death in the woods.

In mid-April 1942, murder operations in Belzec were suspended until mid-June. This ended the first wave of deportations in which 35,000 Jews were transported from the district of Galicia. Thousands more were murdered in that period during the roundups as they tried to hide or flee. This "first wave" encompassed a relatively small number of Jewish communities, but in terms of population, they were the largest, leaving about 472,000–487,000 Jews in Galicia.[22]

The Second Wave of Murder and Deportations: "The Big Aktion"

Once construction of the new gas chambers at Belzec was completed, with an increased capacity, the "Big Aktion" began at the end of July 1942, deporting most of the Jews of the Galicia district to be gassed in the camp. The Big Aktion lasted about four and a half months until early December 1942, when murder operations ceased at Belzec.

The first step taken by the SiPo, who were given all of the authority to handle "Jewish affairs" already in June 1942, was to nullify the authorization granted by the German Labor Office to determine which Jews were vital to the war effort and the power to grant the work permits (Scheine) that would save their bearers from deportation to death. SS officials accused the German civil administration, the Labor Office, and the German private corporations employing Jewish labor with corrupt practices in employing Jews.[23] Thus, Jews fit for work were also deported and murdered in the Big Aktion that began in the summer of 1942.

On June 26, 1942, SS units burst into the Lvov ghetto, having arrived specially for the roundup. With the assistance of local Ukrainian police, they removed six thousand to eight thousand Jews from the ghetto and took them to the sandy area on the outskirts of the Janowska camp, where they tormented and then shot the Jews. The German administration had canceled all work permits before the Aktion, forcing the employers to submit lists to the German Labor Office (Arbeitsamt-Judeneinsatz) of Jews in their employ considered vital. The Judenrat was also ordered to submit a list of employees. All of the above received a "Registration Certificate" with a personal number, on which spouse and children were also recorded. To the bearers was added an external sign: in the center of the Star of David on their armband, the letter A was added in red thread, as well as their personal number appearing on the Registration Certificate. The June 26 Aktion deported those who lacked Registration Certificates, primarily older and elderly adults, women and children without a working head of family, and orphans.[24]

The largest Aktion in this wave of deportations was from Lvov in August 1942. The SiPo first examined all of the Registration Certificates issued by the German civilian administration. Certificates belonging to the Jews they considered "vital" received a special stamp; all others were considered "not vital." Concurrent with this inspection, German and Ukrainian police units were brought into the city to reinforce the forces already deployed. The deportation began on August 10, 1942, under the command of Katzmann himself. An estimate of the number of Jews deported to Belzec, murdered in Lvov itself, or those who committed suicide puts the figure between fifty thousand and sixty thousand. After the deportation, fifty thousand to sixty thousand Jews remained in Lvov.[25]

At the end of the August *Aktion*, the German authorities announced that they were sealing the Lvov ghetto: They set the final date for transferring all of the Jews living in Lvov into the ghetto for September 7, 1942.

On November 18, 1942, the Germans conducted a census classifying all ghetto workers according to how vital they were to the war economy. Those working in plants manufacturing for the army received the letter W (Wehrmacht) or R (*Rüstungsindustrie*, that is, munitions factories). About twelve thousand people received these labels. In the transport at the end of November, five thousand to seven thousand Jews who lacked such a label were deported; some were transported to Janowska and some to Belzec. The murder of "non-vital" Jews continued without cessation from September to December 1942. In early January 1943, about ten thousand Jews who lacked the aforementioned labels with a W or an R were removed from the ghetto to "the sands" (Piaski) and shot to death. When mass murder by gassing ceased in Belzec in late 1942, the sands became the main murder site for the Jews of Lvov. On January 30, 1943, most of the *Judenrat* members were executed, making the ghetto officially a *Judenlager*, or "*Julag*"—a slave labor camp for Jews. An *Oberjude* ("head of the Jews") was appointed as liaison between the Jews and the German authorities.[26] By the end of January 1943, an estimate of the number of Jews remaining in the *Julag* was about twenty-five thousand, more or less half the number of Jews remaining alive after the August 1942 *Aktion*.

While the deportations were taking place in Lvov, similar *Aktionen* were being conducted in other regions of the district of Galicia throughout the second half of 1942 and until early 1943.

By July 1942, there were still fourteen thousand to seventeen thousand Jews remaining in the Stanislawow ghetto. During that month, the head of the *Judenrat*, several of its members, and hundreds of additional Jews were murdered in the Pawelce forest adjacent to the city. By the end of July or early August, about a thousand more Jews were shot near a ditch dug inside the city, under the pretext that a Jew had hit a Ukrainian policeman. In an additional *Aktion* carried out on September 12, 1942, about five thousand

Jews were deported to Belzec and hundreds more were murdered in the ghetto, leaving about four thousand Jews alive in the Stanislawow ghetto by December. On January 24–26, 1943, about a thousand Jews were removed from the ghetto and shot to death, while another fifteen hundred to two thousand were transferred to the Janowska camp in Lvov. On February 22 or 23, 1943, the last remaining Jews in the ghetto were murdered and the ghetto was liquidated. Several thousand Jews were still in the camps adjacent to the factories where they worked.[27]

In the Tarnopol ghetto, there were about eleven thousand to twelve thousand Jews in July 1942, including Jews transported there a short time previously from the small towns and villages in the area. On August 28, 1942, the ghetto was surrounded; all residents were evacuated from their homes and brought to an assembly point. Those bearing work certificates were released along with their families. Some of the healthy young men were sent to labor camps. The remaining three thousand were brought to the railroad station and herded into freight cars. Jews from nearby villages were also added to the transport. On August 31, 1942, the train departed for Belzec. Deportations continued throughout September, October, and November, sending thousands of Jews to Belzec. Between the end of 1942 and early 1943, with about six thousand to seven thousand Jews still remaining in the ghetto, a section of the ghetto was separated for the establishment of a labor camp that became a branch of the *Julag* on Janowska Street in Lvov, imprisoning twenty-five hundred to three thousand people there, all of whom were workers.[28]

The history of the Jews of the town of Buczacz in the east of the district of Galicia is characteristic of the fate of the smaller concentrations of Jews in Poland. On the eve of World War II, there were about 4,500 to 5,000 Jews in the town. In late July 1941, during the first weeks of the German occupation, about 350 of the intelligentsia were murdered and hundreds of young people were sent to labor camps. Refugees from other communities increased the Jewish population of the town to 5,000. There were no industrial plants or German civilian or military institutions considered vital to the German war efforts, and so the Germans considered the vast majority of the Jews of Buczacz expendable. Two roundups, the first on October 17, 1942 and the second on November 27, deported more than 4,000 Jews to Belzec. Many attempted to hide or flee to the forests around the town, but guards posted around the town caught most of those fleeing, and many Jews were discovered in hiding. Groups of locals participated in the hunt for the escaped and concealed Jews and handed many of them over to the Germans. In late 1942, several thousand Jews were brought to the ghetto from towns in the area. On February 1–2, 1943, with the cessation of operations at Belzec, more than 2,000 Jews were taken out of the ghetto to the Fedor Hill and shot to death there. After the *Aktion*, all of the craftsmen were removed from the ghetto and concentrated in a labor camp in one of the town's suburbs.[29]

An unusual incident occurred during the deportation from the city of Przemyśl on the San River. More than twenty thousand Jews were concentrated in its ghetto, which was established on July 14, 1942, and included thousands from the towns and villages in the area. The deportation *Aktion* to Belzec lasted from July 27 to August 3, 1942. Laborers in industries manufacturing for the German army were among those rounded up on July 27. The chairman of the *Judenrat*, Ignatz Duldig, contacted Major Max Liedtke, military governor of the city, and his adjutant, Lieutenant Dr. Alfred Battel, asking them to intervene. Liedtke and Battel in turn approached SiPo officials; the SiPo refusal prompted the two to use the army to prevent the train from leaving to Belzec by blocking the bridge over the San. After negotiations, which involved upper echelons in Cracow, some of the Wehrmacht workers were taken off the transport. Battel sent military trucks to the part of the ghetto where the Jews slated for deportation were concentrated and removed about one hundred workers and their families from the group. A short time afterward, Duldig and another member of the *Judenrat* were ordered to appear before the SiPo, where they were tortured and executed for the "crime" of daring to appeal to the army. SS officials began a secret inquiry against Liedtke and Battel, Nazi party members since May 1933. The affair became known to Himmler; the latter described it in a letter to Martin Bormann, the head of Hitler's office, and noted that Liedtke and Battel would be tried after the war. Several months later, Liedtke was sent to the front, where he perished, apparently as a POW of the Soviets. Battel was demobilized in 1944 due to heart disease and died in 1952. Yad Vashem officially recognized the two as Righteous Among the Nations.[30]

As far as we know, this was the only case in which the army intervened to use force to prevent SiPo personnel from deporting the Jews it employed. This singular incident is evidence that had the Wehrmacht wished to do so, it could have prevented the annihilation of tens of thousands of Jews employed in its service or at least postpone their destruction.

The number of those actually murdered in each and every place was far greater than the number of deportees and victims of the mass roundups that took place from mid-1942 to early 1943 on specific dates in specific locations, since the murder of Jews, individually or in groups, continued without cessation between and after the mass roundups. During these murder operations for which we have no figures, thousands of Jews—who are not included in the statistics of death for each location—were murdered. Similarly, the figures do not include the vast numbers of Jews who died during this time from starvation or diseases in the ghettos and camps. We can estimate that about three hundred fifty thousand Jews were murdered during this time. The statistics of natural deaths should also be added to the number of the victims of the mass murder, starvation, and diseases. Thus, the estimated number of Jews in the district of Galicia in early 1943 is between one hundred forty thousand and one hundred fifty thousand in the ghettos, *Julags*, dozens of different types of labor camps, and a small number of "illegals."[31]

After murder operations ceased in Belzec, the murder *Aktionen* by shooting continued. The vast majority of remaining Jews were murdered by mid-1943. Friedrich Katzmann, SSPF of the Galicia district, reported to his superiors: "The district of Galicia has been made . . . *judenfrei* [free of Jews], save for the Jews in the camps, under the supervision of the Commander of the SS and the Police. Individual Jews who are captured are subject to 'special handling' [*werden sonderbehandelt*] by the Ordnung Police and the gendarmes. As of June 27, 1943, a total of 434,329 Jews were evacuated [*ausgesiedelt*] . . . [followed by a list of 21 camps in which 21,156 Jews still remain]."[32]

CONCLUSION

The deportations and roundups were similar in most of the ghettos in the General Government. Overall, the process began with terminating the authority of the labor offices, which were part of the German civil government, to engage in Jewish affairs; transferring the authority of determining who were vital to the war efforts into the hands of SiPo officials; and a drastic minimization of the number of work certificates issued to Jews.

The next step was usually to deport to death camps the Jews lacking work certificates, and, finally, the Germans would liquidate the ghetto, leaving a certain number of Jews behind in labor camps, usually adjacent to their place of work. Assembling the Jews before leading them to their deaths was usually accompanied by setting their homes on fire and throwing grenades to lure those hiding out of their concealment. The Jews murdered in the city were, on the whole, those who attempted to hide, resulting in the Germans setting their homes on fire or blowing them up; and those incapable of marching to the assembly points: the elderly, disabled, ill, and patients in the ghetto hospitals. The process also included liquidation of the local *Judenrat*. The Germans would kill all members of the *Judenrat* and appoint in their stead people who the Germans found to be easier to deal with or more committed to them. Gradually, the number of "vital" Jews who remained in the labor camps was decreased. And, as the Germans retreated from the regions of the General Government, the last Jews were led on death marches to concentration camps or labor camps in Germany or, as occurred in the district of Galicia, shot on site.

CHAPTER NINE

THE TRAINS OF DEATH

THE EXTERMINATION OF THE JEWS was planned to be executed in the gas chambers, but, in practice, death and destruction began while the Jews were still in the freight cars rolling toward the death camps. Designed to carry a maximum of sixty to seventy people, including their belongings, the cars were packed with double that number. Deprived of air and water, with no sanitary facilities, forced to spend endless hours traveling or waiting in stations in the packed freight cars, many died en route. Personal belongings were stolen by the train guards—a few dozen SS men, Ukrainians, Lithuanians, and occasionally Polish Blue Police (police that served the Germans and were nicknamed "blue" by the local population because of their blue uniforms).

Ada Lichtman described the journey to Sobibor:

> We were packed into a closed cattle train. Inside the freight cars it was so dense that it was impossible to move. There was not enough air, many people fainted, others became hysterical. . . . In an isolated place, the train stopped. Soldiers entered the car and robbed us and even cut off fingers with rings. They claimed that we didn't need them any more. These soldiers, who wore German uniforms, spoke Ukrainian. We were disorientated by the long voyage, we thought that we were in Ukraine. Days and nights passed. The air inside the car was poisoned by the smell of bodies and excrement. Nobody thought about food, only about water and air. Finally we arrived at Sobibor.[1]

The most terrible scenes took place on the trains to Treblinka at the end of July and in August 1942. Jakub (Abraham) Krzepicki described one such experience that the deportees from Warsaw went through:

> Over 100 people were packed into our car. . . . It is impossible to describe the tragic situation in our airless, closed freight car. It was one big toilet. Everyone tried to push his way to a small air aperture. Everyone was lying on the floor. I also lay down. I found a crack in one of the floorboards into which I pushed my nose in order to get a little air. The stink in the car was unbearable. People were defecating in all four corners of the car. . . . After some time, the train stopped suddenly. A Shaulist [Lithuanian volunteer in the Nazi service]

entered the car . . . at first I didn't understand why. It quickly became apparent that he had simply come to rob us. We had to approach him one by one and show him all our possessions. The Shaulist took everything that had not been well concealed previously: money, watches, valuables. . . . The situation inside the car was becoming worse. Water. We begged the railroad workers. We would pay them well. Some paid 500 and 1000 zlotys for a small cup of water. The Polish railroad workers and the Shaulists took the money. I paid 500 zlotys (more than half the money I had) for a cup of water—about half a liter. As I began to drink, a woman, whose child had fainted, attacked me. I drank; I couldn't take the cup from my lips. The woman bit deep into my hand—with all her strength she wanted to force me to leave her a little water. I paid no attention to the pain. I would have undergone any pain on earth for a little more water. But I did leave a few drops at the bottom of the cup, and I watched the child drink. The situation in the car was deteriorating. It was only seven in the morning, but the sun was already heating the car. The men removed their shirts and lay half naked. Some of the women, too, took off their dresses and lay in their undergarments. People lay on the floor, gasping and shuddering as if feverish, their heads lolling, laboring to get some air into their lungs. Some were in complete despair and no longer moved. . . . We reached Treblinka. . . . Many were inert on the freight-car floor, some probably dead. We had been traveling for about twenty hours. If the trip had taken another half day, the number of dead would have been much higher. We would all have died of heat and asphyxiation. I later learned that there were transports to Treblinka from which only corpses were removed.[2]

Abraham Goldfarb testified about a Treblinka transport in which most of the passengers died en route:

At the end of August 1942, the Germans carried out the expulsion from Mazaritz. . . . When the Jews were brought to the railway station, the Germans forced 150–200 of them into a freight car designed for sixty or seventy. The cars were closed from the outside with boards. Water and food were not provided. People were suffocating; there was no air to breathe. Before we moved off, the Germans sprinkled chlorine in the cars. It burned the eyes. The weaker among us fainted. People climbed on top of each other and banged on the walls with whatever they could find. The children were so thirsty they licked their mothers' sweat. . . . There were 150 people in our freight car. During the two-day trip to Treblinka, 135 suffocated.[3]

A Polish engineer, Jerzy Krolikowski, who was working on the construction of a railroad bridge near Treblinka, wrote in his memoirs: "On July 23, 1942 (dates like that are not easily forgotten), while we were working on the railroad bridge between Malkinia and Siedlce, a rather strange train passed, with closed freight cars whose air apertures were covered with barbed wire. Between the bunched wires, one could make out pale and hunger-stricken faces. . . . One day in late July or early August 1942, I heard groaning voices from a train crossing the bridge; they wanted water . . . the people packed into those freight cars had been there for hours. They were simply dying of thirst."[4]

In the latter half of August, several dozen Jews were summoned from the Siedlce ghetto to the train station to unload a stalled freight car. When they opened the car, they were confronted by a horrible sight. The car was littered with the corpses of about a hundred Jews. It turned out that they were from the Radom ghetto and had been on their way to Treblinka. They had suffocated from lack of oxygen, the heat, and the lime sprinkled on the freight-car floor.[5]

A German soldier, Hubert Pfoch, saw a transport of Jews for Treblinka at the Siedlce train station while on his way to the front by military transport. He wrote in his diary:

> The next morning, August 22, 1942, our train was moved to a track near the platform. A rumor spread that the train in front of us was carrying a transport of Jews. The Jews began calling out to us that they had been without food or water for days. As they were forced into the freight cars, we witnessed a disgusting scene. The bodies of those shot the night before were thrown into a truck. It had to make four trips to remove them. . . . Calls of "Water! I'll give my gold ring for water," issued from the cars. Some offered 5,000 zlotys for a cup of water. When a few managed to get out of the cars through the air apertures, they were shot before they reached the ground. . . . By the time our train left the station, at least fifty dead women, men, and children, some of them entirely naked, were lying along the track. . . . Our train followed the transport, and we kept seeing bodies on both sides of the track—children and others. When we reached Treblinka station, the transport train was again alongside. Some of us vomited from the stench of decomposing bodies. The pleas for water were more intense, and the guards' aimless firing continued.[6]

Thousands of Jews died en route to the death camps during that summer from thirst, suffocation, and lack of minimum sanitary facilities in the crowded freight cars. The trip from Warsaw and other ghettos to Belzec, Sobibor, and Treblinka, which should have lasted a few hours, sometimes lasted a day or two. The combination of conditions in the freight cars and the extended journey led to mass deaths.

The SS personnel in charge of Jewish transport purposely overloaded the freight cars. For example, Gedob placed a single daily train at the disposal of the Warsaw deportation. It consisted of fifty-eight or fifty-nine freight cars for the transport of five thousand Jews in stifling conditions. However, one train daily, with this number of freight cars, was not nearly adequate to meet the demands of the deportation authorities. Therefore, in practice, six thousand to seven thousand Jews were forced to board the train. The SS personnel in Warsaw in charge of the expulsion were so enthusiastic about their job of transporting the Jews to their death in a minimum of time that they disregarded entirely the optimum absorptive capacity of the trains.

The Gedob transport directive of early August 1942 set the travel time for deportee trains from Warsaw to Treblinka at four hours. The train was to leave Warsaw at 12:25 and arrive at Treblinka at 16:30. An additional two and one-half hours were calculated as turnaround time at Treblinka. The train was planned to arrive empty back at Warsaw at 23:19. Warsaw to Treblinka and back was to take about eleven hours.[7] In reality, the plan met with difficulties, and the Treblinka round trip took much longer.

The deportation trains left Warsaw only in the evening, whereas in Treblinka the staff was unprepared to receive transports in the darkness. The trains, therefore, entered the camp only in the morning hours. Warsaw-Treblinka-Warsaw took almost twice the time planned and caused a decrease in the available trains for the deportations.

There was an additional and unexpected problem that caused an increase in the number of transports to Treblinka. According to the plan, Jews deported for extermination from the Warsaw district were to be sent to both Treblinka and Sobibor. However, on July 28, 1942, the general director of the German Transportation Office, Dr. Theodor Ganzenmüller, informed Heinrich Himmler's headquarters that the Warsaw-Lublin-Sobibor rail line would be out of commission until early October 1942, due to repair work, and that the Warsaw-Sobibor transports could not, therefore, be carried out. With the Sobibor camp out of operation, all deportee trains from Warsaw and a number of other ghettos were directed to Treblinka.[8]

Treblinka alone was incapable of absorbing all the transports from the ghettos in the Warsaw and Radom districts. There were also many organizational and technical difficulties in this camp in the first months of its operation, which decreased killing capacity there (see chapter 13). Although Belzec was in operation at that time, receiving transports of Jews from the Lublin, Lvov, and Cracow districts, it was doubtful whether it could absorb additional deportees. As a result, the overloaded trains to Treblinka were delayed at the way stations.

Due to lack of coordination between the size of the transports, their frequency, and Treblinka's absorptive capacity, the deportees would be held in the trains for days en route, and in the interim many died. Even at the last station, Treblinka village, they would be delayed for hours. Franciszek Zabecki, a Pole in Treblinka village, noted:

> There were days when two or three trains stood at Treblinka station with their unfortunate cargo, waiting their turn to be sent to the death camp. The

transports sometimes waited all night, because transfer to the camp was not carried out in darkness. The cruelty of the security guards, Germans, Latvians, and Ukrainians, is difficult to describe. Sadism and torture seemed to know no bounds. I saw how guards, who were always drunk, would open the freight-car doors at night and demand money and valuables. Then they would close the doors and fire into the cars. . . . During the day, the corpses remaining at the station were collected, loaded onto a car and sent to the death camp. This task was attended to by a group of Jews from the camp, under SS and Ukrainian supervision.[9]

The train delays en route to the death camps were not planned in advance by those in charge of the transports and extermination. Rather, they were the result of inefficient planning, and they in turn caused additional overloading of a railway system already overburdened by the logistical requirements of the eastern front. However, the extreme crowding in the freight cars, which, indeed, was a deliberate act on the part of the deportation authorities, and the inhuman behavior of the train guards turned the journey into a shocking nightmare. Treblinka's initial "running-in" difficulties contributed to additional delays. These factors, taken together, accounted for the high mortality rate of the Jews on the trains to the death camps.

CHAPTER TEN

BELZEC: MARCH 17 TO JUNE 1942

THE FULL-SCALE EXTERMINATION OF JEWS in Belzec began on March 17, 1942, with the onset of the deportation of the Jews of Lublin. This date marks the actual start of Operation Reinhard.

In an entry in his diary regarding the beginning of Operation Reinhard, ten days after the killings started in Belzec, on March 27, 1942, Joseph Goebbels wrote:

> Beginning with Lublin, the Jews in the General Government are now being evacuated eastward. The procedure is a pretty barbaric one and not to be described here more definitely. Not much will remain of the Jews. On the whole it can be said about 60 percent of them will have to be liquidated whereas only about 40 percent can be used for forced labor.
>
> The former *Gauleiter* of Vienna [Odilo Globocnik], who is to carry this measure through, is doing it with considerable circumspection and according to a method that does not attract too much attention. Fortunately, a whole series of possibilities presents itself for us in wartime that would be denied us in peacetime. We shall have to profit by this. The ghettos that will be emptied in the cities of the General Government will now be refilled with Jews thrown out of the Reich. This process is to be repeated from time to time.[1]

The reception and treatment of the transport from its arrival at Belzec station until the completion of the killing process was developed by Christian Wirth. Secrecy and deception of the victims were the cornerstones of this extermination technique.

Upon arrival at Belzec station, the train stopped. There, the train, which usually numbered between forty to sixty freight cars, was split into two or three sections; each was driven separately into the camp, because the absorption capacity of the ramp inside the camp was no more than twenty cars. When the empty cars returned, after they had been unloaded, another section of the train was driven in. The guards who had escorted the train and the German and Polish railroad workers who had driven the train from the embarkation stations were not permitted to enter the camp.

There would be no unnecessary eyewitnesses to what was going on inside. The train was driven into the camp by a select and trusted crew of German railroad workers.

A Polish locomotive driver, Stefan Kirsz, who was in the Belzec station, testified to what he saw from the vicinity of the camp:

> As a co-driver of a locomotive, I led the Jewish transports from the station of Rava-Russkaya to Belzec many times. . . . These transports were divided in Belzec into three parts. Each part, which consisted of twenty freight cars, was taken to the railway spur inside the camp pushed by the locomotive, and stopped near the former border wall of 1939/40 [outside the camp]. Immediately after the freight cars stopped inside the camp, they were emptied of the Jews. Within 3–5 minutes the twenty cars were empty of Jews and their luggage. I saw that in addition to the living, corpses were taken out. . . . The Germans did not allow us to watch the camp, but I was able to see it when I approached the camp and deceptively pretended that I must put the coal closer to the entrance gate.[2]

The view of the camp and the "treatment" that greeted a transport of Jews was as follows:

- The camp looked "peaceful"; no graves, pits, or gas chambers could be seen by the victims. They believed that they had arrived in a "transit camp," and an SS man strengthened this belief by announcing that they should undress and make their way to the baths for cleaning and disinfection. They were told that afterward they would receive clean clothes and be sent to labor camps. The barbed-wire fences and the armed guards that were around also kept the victims submissive and calm.
- The separation between the sexes, the undressing, and even the haircuts given to the women convinced them even more that they were going to the baths. At this stage they were hurried along and beaten so as to prevent any thought of escape or resistance. For reasons of security, and also to prevent escape and resistance, the men were taken to the gas chambers first, before they grasped what was happening. Afterward, the women and children were taken.[3]
- The gas chamber resembled ordinary baths. When they were closed and the victims were packed inside, they still did not know what was happening. Even if they finally realized that they were being gassed, it was too late. The building and doors were strong enough to resist any pressure from inside. Within minutes those inside the gas chambers lost consciousness, and a few minutes later, their lives.

When a transport of Jews disembarked, usually a group of young, strong men was removed from the crowd. They numbered a few dozen, or sometimes even a few hundred men. Most were taken to Camp II and put to work. It was their duty to pull the bodies out of the gas chambers, carry them to the open ditches, and bury them. Some of them collected the clothes and goods left behind by the victims and transferred them to the sorting place. Others had to remove from the train the people who had died on the way and those who were unable to walk and take them to the pits in Camp II. These Jews were organized in work groups under their own capos. They were kept for a few days or even weeks, tortured, and weakened through work. Each day some were murdered and replaced by others taken from the transports.

SS *Unterscharführer* Karl Alfred Schluch, a former euthanasia employee who served in Belzec from February or March 1942, when the killing operations began, for some sixteen months, described the handling of a transport:

> In the morning or noon time we were informed by Wirth, Schwartz, or by Oberhauser that a transport with Jews should arrive soon.... The disembarkation from the freight cars was carried out by a group of Jewish prisoners under the command of their capos. Two or three Germans from the camp staff supervised this action. It was my obligation to carry out such supervisions. After the disembarkation, the Jews were taken to the assembly square. During the disembarkation, the Jews were told that they had come here for transfer and they should go to baths and disinfection. This announcement was made by Wirth and translated by a Jewish capo. Afterward the Jews were taken to the undressing barracks.[4]

Kurt Franz, who served under Wirth in Belzec, testified: "I heard with my own ears how Wirth, in a quite convincing voice, explained to the Jews that they would be deported further and before that, for hygienic reasons, they must bathe themselves and their clothes would have to be disinfected. Inside the undressing barrack was a counter for the deposit of valuables. It was made clear to the Jews that after the bath their valuables would be returned to them. I can still hear, until today, how the Jews applauded Wirth after his speech. This behavior of the Jews convinces me that the Jews believed Wirth."[5]

After undressing, first the men and later the women with the children were taken through the "tube" to the gas chambers. SS *Unterscharführer* Schluch testified:

> My post in the "tube" was close to the undressing barrack. Wirth briefed me that while I was there I should influence the Jews to behave calmly. After leaving the undressing barracks, I had to show the Jews the way to the gas chambers. I believe that when I showed the Jews the way they were convinced that they were really going to the baths. After the Jews entered the gas chambers, the doors were closed by Hackenholt himself or by the Ukrainians subordinate to him. Then Hackenholt switched on the engine which supplied the gas. After five or seven minutes—and this is only an estimate—someone

looked through the small window into the gas chamber to verify whether all inside were dead. Only then were the outside doors opened and the gas chambers ventilated. . . . After the ventilation of the gas chambers, a Jewish working group under the command of their capos entered and removed the bodies from the chambers. Occasionally, I had to supervise at this place; therefore, I can describe the whole process, which I saw and witnessed personally.

The Jews inside the gas chambers were densely packed. This is the reason that the corpses were not lying on the floor but were mixed up in disorder in all directions, some of them kneeling, according to the amount of space they had. The corpses were besmirched with mud and urine or with spit. I could see that the lips and tips of the noses were a bluish color. Some of them had their eyes closed, others' eyes rolled. The bodies were dragged out of the gas chambers and inspected by a dentist, who removed finger-rings and gold teeth. . . . After this procedure, the corpses were thrown into a big pit.[6]

The number of gas chambers in operation during the first months of the extermination activity in Belzec is hard to establish. As a result of technical problems or breakdowns, probably only one or two out of the three gas chambers were in operation at any given time.[7] There were also some difficulties concerning the burial of the victims. After a pit was full of corpses, it was covered with a thin layer of earth. From the heat, putrefaction, and in some cases water that penetrated into the pits, the corpses swelled, and the thin layer of earth split. What happened then is described by Franz Stangl, who visited Belzec in April 1942: "Wirth was not in his office, they said he was up at the camp. . . . I asked what was the matter. The man I was talking to said that one of the pits had overflowed. They had put too many corpses in it and putrefaction had progressed too fast so that the liquid underneath had pushed the bodies on top up and over, and the corpses had rolled down the hill. I saw some of them—oh God, it was awful.[8]

Those people who had no strength to go through the ordinary extermination procedure, from the train to the gas chambers, were taken directly to the pits, and there they were shot. SS *Unterscharführer* Robert Jührs, who arrived in Belzec in the summer of 1942 and took part in such shootings, described how they were carried out:

I had to carry out the shooting of Jews once. . . . In that transport the cars were overloaded; some of the Jews were unable to walk. Maybe, in that confusion, some of the Jews had been pushed down and had been crushed underfoot. Therefore, there were Jews that, by no means, could cover the way to the undressing barrack. [Gottlieb] Hering gave me an order to shoot these Jews. He told me verbally: "Jührs, take these Jews to Camp II immediately and shoot them there." . . . These Jews were taken to the gate [of Camp II] by a Jewish working group, and from there they were taken to the pits by other working Jews. As I remember, there were seven Jews, men and women, who were taken inside the pit. . . . It is hard to describe the condition these people were in, after their long journey in the unimaginably packed freight cars. I regarded the killing of these people in this way as a mercy and redemption. . . . I shot these Jews with a machine gun, as they stood on the edge of the pit. I aimed directly at their heads so that everyone died instantly. I am absolutely sure that nobody felt any torment.[9]

The first large Jewish community that was deported for extermination in Belzec was Lublin. During less than four weeks, from March 17 to April 14, close to 30,000 Jews, out of 37,000 who lived in the Lublin ghetto, were sent to Belzec. During this same period, an additional 13,500 Jews were deported from the Lublin district to Belzec, among them 3,000 from Zamosc, 3,400 from Piaski, 2,200 from Izbica and other places. (See Appendix A.)

The first transport with Jews from the Lvov district came from Zolkiew, a town fifty kilometers southeast of Belzec. This transport, with about seven hundred Jews, arrived in Belzec on March 25 or 26, 1942. Within a period of three weeks after the first transport from Zolkiew, almost thirty thousand Jews arrived in Belzec from the Lvov district. Among them were fifteen thousand Jews deported from Lvov during the so-called March *Aktion*, five thousand from Stanislawow, five thousand from Kolomyya, and others from Drogobych and Rava-Russkaya. During the wave of deportations from the Lvov district, most of the Jews sent to Belzec were, according to the Germans' classification, "nonworking" Jews.

After about four weeks of intensive activity, during which approximately seventy-five thousand Jews had been killed, the transports stopped. Toward the end of April or beginning of May 1942, Wirth, along with the SS men stationed there, left the camp. Josef Oberhauser related:

After those first gassing operations, Wirth, Schwartz and all the German personnel disappeared from Belzec. As his final official act, Wirth had, before his departure, gassed or shot the fifty working Jews, including their capos. When Wirth and his people departed, I was in Lublin. I had a big transport of material to bring. When I came again to Belzec, nobody was there. In the camp there were about twenty Ukrainian guards. They were under the command of SS *Scharführer* Feiks. Curiously enough, SS and Police Leader Globocnik had no knowledge of the departure of Wirth and his men. He sent me to Belzec to find out in which direction Wirth had gone. I found out that he had left for Berlin via Lvov and Cracow, without reporting to Globocnik.[10]

At that time it was not clear whether Wirth was subordinate to Globocnik or to the euthanasia program in Berlin.

The reasons for Wirth's departure from Belzec and the intermission in the killing operation there are unknown. It is possible that Wirth saw his task as completed after he had erected Belzec, had experimented, and had developed the extermination process there. At that time the Sobibor death camp had also become operational, with Wirth's help, and he could see his task as fulfilled. No doubt Wirth had aspirations for a higher post than commander of Belzec, especially as he had held important assignments in the past in the euthanasia program.

At the beginning of May 1942, SS *Oberführer* Viktor Brack, one of the euthanasia leaders in Berlin, visited Globocnik in Lublin. Globocnik demanded the return of Wirth and his men to Belzec and additional euthanasia people for Operation Reinhard. Following this request Wirth returned to Belzec in the middle of May 1942.

In the last week of May, two small transports with 1,350 Jews arrived from two small ghettos near Zamosc (Laszczow, 350; Komarow, 1,000). At the beginning of June 1942, new transports, this time from the Cracow district, began arriving in Belzec. Three transports with 5,000 Jews from the city of Cracow arrived between June 1 and 6. From June 11 to 19, an additional 11,600 Jews arrived in Belzec from Cracow district.[11] (See Appendix A.)

With the beginning of the deportations from Cracow district and the deportations from the Lvov and Lublin districts, it was clear to Wirth that the three wooden gas chambers in Belzec would no longer be sufficient to hold the increased number of Jews arriving in the transports. New, larger gas chambers would have to be built. To facilitate construction, the deportations to Belzec were stopped temporarily in the middle of June 1942 with the approval of Operation Reinhard headquarters in Lublin. The first stage of the Belzec operation was terminated. During this stage, from the middle of March until the middle of June 1942, about ninety-three thousand Jews had been murdered in Belzec.

The old wooden building with its three gas chambers was dismantled, and on the same site a bigger, a more solid building was erected. The new building was twenty-four meters long and ten meters wide. It had six gas chambers, each of them four by eight meters. (According to other sources, the size of the new gas chambers was four by five meters each.) Toward the middle of July, the new gas chambers were operational.[12]

Rudolf Reder, one of the two survivors of Belzec, described the gas chambers:

> The building was low, long, and wide. It was of grey concrete, had a flat roof covered with pap, and above it a net covered with green branches. Three steps without railings, 1 meter wide, led into the building. In front of the building was a big flower pot with colorful flowers and a clearly written sign reading: *"Bade und Inhalationsräume"* [Bath and Inhalation Rooms]. The steps led to

a dark, long, and empty corridor, 1.5 meters wide. On the right and left of the corridor were doors to the gas chambers. These were wooden doors, 1 meter wide. . . . The corridor and the chambers were lower than ordinary rooms, no higher than 2 meters. On the opposite wall of each chamber was a removable door, 2 meters wide, from which the gassed bodies were thrown out. Outside the building was a shed, 2 x 2 meters, where the engine for the gas was installed. The chambers were 1.5 meters above ground level.[13]

Karl Schluch described the inside of the gas chambers:

I can relate that I saw the gas chambers in the euthanasia institutions, and I was shown the gas chambers in Belzec. . . . These were each about 4 x 8 meters. They had a friendly, bright appearance. Whether the color was yellow or grey, I don't remember. Maybe the walls were painted with oil colors. In any case, the floor and part of the walls were made so that cleaning would be easy. The newly arriving Jews must not guess the purpose the room served, and they should believe that it was a bath. Vaguely I remember that there were shower-heads on the ceiling.[14]

These new gas chambers could absorb over two thousand people at a time, the capacity of a transport of about twenty freight cars. Belzec was now ready to renew activity on an even larger scale.

CHAPTER ELEVEN

SOBIBOR: MAY TO JULY 1942

AFTER THE EXPERIMENTAL KILLINGS WERE carried out in Sobibor in April 1942, routine mass extermination began there in the first days of May 1942. Franz Stangl, the commander of Sobibor, who had visited Belzec, had studied the extermination technique there, and had introduced it in his camp, received additional advice and instructions when Christian Wirth visited Sobibor during the experimental killings there.[1] The killing process in Sobibor was in effect an improved version of what had been implemented in Belzec.

The deportation trains stopped at the station of Sobibor. No more than eighteen to twenty freight cars were taken into the camp. When the train was composed of more cars, it was split into two or three parts. The escort and railway workers remained outside the camp, and only a specially trusted team of German railway workers drove the train inside. In the camp, the train stopped along the ramp, and the cars were opened by the Ukrainians. The people were ordered to disembark and were driven into Camp II, which was the reception area.

Dov Freiberg, a survivor of Sobibor, described his arrival at the camp:

> Germans and Ukrainians opened our freight cars and expelled us. It was May 15, 1942. We were taken through a gate into a square surrounded by barbed wire.... We were separated there, men on the one side, women and children on the other. After a short period, the women and children were taken away by SS men. Where they were taken to, we did not know, but we could hear screams and laughter of the SS men when they undressed. Afterward we heard a mixture of noises, a running engine, the playing of an orchestra.... We were kept overnight. It was terrible. The Ukrainians hit us and did not allow us to go to the toilet. We had to relieve ourselves sitting on the spot. They told us that nothing bad would happen to us and that the women had already been sent to work.... In the morning some SS men appeared and selected skilled workers.... Then they pointed out some young and strong men. I was among them.... We were about thirty men. We had to put the clothes and parcels in order.[2]

SS *Oberscharführer* Kurt Bolender, who served in Sobibor, testified about the killing process:

> Before the Jews undressed, *Oberscharführer* [Hermann] Michel [deputy commander of the camp] made a speech to them. On these occasions, he used to wear a white coat to give the impression [that he was] a physician. Michel announced to the Jews that they would be sent to work. But before this they would have to take baths and undergo disinfection so as to prevent the spread of diseases.... After undressing, the Jews were taken through the so-called Schlauch. They were led to the gas chambers not by the Germans but by Ukrainians.... After the Jews entered the gas chambers, the Ukrainians closed the doors.... The motor which supplied the gas was switched on by a Ukrainian called Emil and by a German driver called Erich Bauer from Berlin. After the gassing, the doors were opened, and the corpses were removed by a group of Jewish workers.[3]

A survivor from Sobibor, Ada Lichtman, described how Michel addressed the people as they arrived: "We heard word for word how *Oberscharführer* Michel, standing on a small table, convinced the people to calm down. He promised them that after the baths all their belongings would be returned to them and that it was time for Jews to become a productive element. At present all of them would be going to the Ukraine to live and work. This address aroused confidence and enthusiasm among the people. They applauded spontaneously and sometimes even danced and sang."[4]

Elderly people, the sick, and invalids who were unable to walk were told that they would be taken to a *Lazarett* (infirmary) where they would receive medical treatment. Actually they were put on carts, pushed by men or pulled by horse, and at a later stage on a narrow-gauge railway carriage, and were taken into Camp III, directly to the open pits, and there they were shot.[5]

The alleged "transfer" of the disabled to the *Lazarett* also served as part of the deception—the deportees had been taken to a labor camp, and those unable to work were undergoing medical treatment.

After the first few weeks, during which the undressing took place on the open square of Camp II, a barrack for this purpose was erected (see chapter 5 for the plan of Sobibor, Camp II). Inside this barrack were signs indicating the direction to the "cashier" and the "baths." At the "cashier" the Jews were ordered to submit their money and valuables. In the forest house was a room that overlooked the path where the naked people had to pass on their way to the "tube" and gas chambers, and the victims handed over their money and valuables through the window of this room. They were warned that those who attempted to hide anything would be shot.

The cashier was SS *Oberscharführer* Alfred Ittner, who was the accountant of the camp. Later he was replaced by SS *Scharführer* Hans Schutt and SS *Scharführer* Herbert Floss. When time permitted, the Jews received numbers as receipts for the money and valuables they had submitted, to make them believe that they would truly receive everything back after the baths.[6]

SS *Oberscharführer* Erich Bauer, one of the men in charge of Camp II, testified:

> Usually the undressing went smoothly. Subsequently, the Jews were taken through the "tube" to Camp III—the real extermination camp. The transfer through the "tube" proceeded as follows: one SS man was in the lead and five or six Ukrainian auxiliaries were at the back hastening the [Jews] along. The women were taken through a barrack where their hair was cut off. In Camp III the Jews were received by SS men. . . . As I already mentioned, the motor was then switched on by Go[t]ringer and one of the [Ukrainian] auxiliaries whose name I don't remember. Then the gassed Jews were taken out.[7]

When transports arrived in the evening or night, they disembarked and were kept under guard in Camp II until the morning. Then they were taken to undress and to the gas chambers.[8] Usually no extermination activity was carried out in the dark.

Many times the whole process, from disembarkation until entering the gas chambers, was accompanied by beatings and atrocities carried out by some of the Germans and the Ukrainians. For example, there was a dog called Barry that was trained by the SS men to bite the Jews, especially when they were naked on the way to the gas chambers. The beatings, the bitings from Barry, and the shooting and shouting of the guards caused the Jews to run through the "tube" and push themselves into the "baths," hoping to find some escape from the hell around them.

Sometimes the SS men mocked the victims and gave them "special treatment." For example, on June 10, 1942, a transport arrived with Jews from the ghetto of Biala Podlaska. The people believed that they had been sent to a labor camp. When they disembarked from the train, a *Judenrat* member who had arrived with this transport handed over a letter to one of the SS men who was on the ramp. The letter included a request from the municipality of Biala Podlaska for decent treatment of the arriving Jews. For the "insolence" and "impudence" of bringing such a letter, two hundred of the Jews were taken for "special treatment"; all the others were taken directly to the gas chambers. The two hundred Jews were forced to take luggage from Camp II and load it on a train, while the Germans and Ukrainians created a cordon around them. While carrying the luggage, the Jews had to run between the guards, and as they ran by they were whipped and clubbed. The dog Barry was also set to bite them. After the "special treatment," these Jews were also gassed.[9]

A limited number of skilled workers, among them carpenters, tailors, and shoemakers, and a few dozen strong young men and women were selected from some of the transports. It was their duty to carry out the physical work. Every day some of them were shot or sent to the gas chambers, and their ranks were filled by arrivals from new transports. Their work was to unload the corpses of those who had died in the trains and take them to the pits and to transfer the old, sick, and invalids to Camp III, where they were shot. Some of the Jews selected for work were taken to Camp III, where their duty was to remove the gassed bodies and bury them. Others were engaged in collecting and sorting out the goods left behind by the victims and preparing them for transferal from the camp. The selection of some of the arriving Jews for work was frequently used to make them believe that they had been brought to a labor camp.

Herszl Cukerman, who arrived at Sobibor on May 13, 1942, described the process of forming groups of men to be sent to the gas chambers: "Every few minutes some SS men approached and inquired who among us was a shoemaker, tailor, etc. People believed it was worthwhile to appear as a skilled worker and therefore responded. Then they marched in groups consisting of 300–400 men who believed they were being sent to a labor camp. Actually they were taken directly to Camp III, to the gas chambers."[10]

From some of the transports, however, young men and women were indeed selected and sent to labor camps in Ossowa, Sawin, and Krychow, which were not far from Sobibor. These groups numbered a few hundred people, and most of them were returned to Sobibor several months later, when these camps were liquidated.[11]

The unawareness of what happened to the Jews who were taken to Camp III weighed heavily on the daily life of those selected to work. Days and even weeks passed until the Jewish prisoners who worked in Camp I and Camp II found out that those who had been taken there were gassed. In Sobibor, unlike Belzec, the extermination area with the gas chambers was more isolated from the other parts of the camp, and nothing could be seen. Dov Freiberg, who came to Sobibor in May 1942 and was selected for work, said that "for two weeks he and those with him hoped that the people had not been murdered, but had been sent to the Ukraine. This in spite of the fact that they worked only a few hundred meters away from the gas chambers."[12]

The two hundred to three hundred Jewish prisoners who were kept in Camp III, who removed the bodies from the gas chambers and buried them, had no contact with those in the other parts of the camp. The food for them was cooked in Camp I and taken by Jewish prisoners to the gate of Camp III. No physical contact was permitted between the Jewish prisoners from the different parts of the camp. But the Jewish prisoners in Camp I wanted desperately to find out what was going on in Camp III. Herszl Cukerman, who was a cook and prepared the food for prisoners in Camp III, testified:

> I came up with an idea. Every day, I used to send twenty or twenty-five buckets with food for the workers in Camp III. The Germans were not interested in what I cooked, so once I prepared a thick crumb pie and inside I put the following letter: "Friends, write what is going on in your camp." When I received the bucket back, I found in one of them a piece of paper with the answer: "Here the last human march takes place, from this place nobody returns. Here the people turn cold." . . . I informed some other people about the substance of this letter.[13]

The truth of what was going on in Camp III became known to the Jewish prisoners in Sobibor at the beginning of June 1942.

The extermination machine of Sobibor operated for months without interruptions and in an orderly way. The structure of the camp was adapted to the extermination technique and enabled a more efficient treatment of the arriving transports than in Belzec. Moreover, the frequency of the transports to Sobibor was lower than in Belzec and, in most cases, fewer people were in each train. Usually only one train with deportees arrived daily, and there were even days without any transports. The size of the transports rarely exceeded twenty freight cars carrying from two thousand to twenty-five hundred people.

Stangl was the leading figure in Sobibor and supervised the work. His personality and years of experience as a police officer and with the euthanasia program provided him with the most suitable training for the assignment of commander of a death camp. The order and smooth operation of the camp should be attributed to him. His name or his attendance is seldom mentioned in the testimonies of the survivors—contrary to other SS men like Michel, Gustav Wagner, Bauer, Karl Frenzel, and others, who are referred to many times—but he was the dominant figure behind the scenes. The following event sheds some light on Stangl's personality.

In the spring of 1942, a Jewish woman from Chelm came to Sobibor on her own to search for her husband, who had been taken with a transport of Jews to the camp. She was brought to Stangl and asked him to allow her to visit her husband. This innocent woman did not know what was going on in Sobibor and that her husband had already been gassed. Stangl called in the SS man Alfred Ittner and ordered him to take the woman to Camp III.

The Sobibor train station; the tracks had a branch line that led to the extermination camp. YVA, 1561/2

When the woman turned her back to Stangl, he signaled to Ittner the pulling of a trigger. Stangl made it clear to Ittner that the woman should be shot in Camp III. Ittner took the woman and handed her over to a Ukrainian guard, who shot her. Returning from Camp III, Ittner met Stangl, who was waiting for him and who asked him whether Ittner himself had shot the woman. When Ittner replied that it had been done by a Ukrainian, Stangl said: "You coward." Stangl wanted all the SS men in the camp to be individually involved in the killing, making them all partners to the murder.[14]

The first stage of killing operations in Sobibor lasted from May until the end of July 1942. In this period Jews were sent there from ghettos in the Lublin district and from Czechoslovakia and Austria. The Jews who came from foreign countries were deported either to ghettos in the Lublin district and from there to Sobibor or directly to the camp. In May (6–12) 1942, close to 21,000 Jews arrived in Sobibor from ghettos in Pulawy county. Between May 12 and 15, 1942, about 9,500 Jews arrived from Krasnystaw county. Between May 3 and 15, 7,200 Jews arrived in Sobibor from Zamosc county. In the second half of May 1942, over 6,000 Jews arrived from Chelm county. In the first half of June 1942, over 10,000 Jews arrived from Hrubieszow county and 3,000 Jews from Biala Podlaska and 800 from Krasniczyn, both in Krasnystaw county. Altogether about 57,500 Jews arrived in Sobibor from identified localities in the Lublin district. But the actual number can be estimated at approximately 15,000 to 20,000 more. In addition, during these months 10,000 Jews arrived from Austria and Germany and 6,000 arrived from the Protectorate of Bohemia and Moravia, as did part of the 24,378 Jews from Slovakia who would be murdered in this camp by the end of 1942.

During the first stage of the killing operations in Sobibor, which lasted three months, at least ninety thousand to one hundred thousand Jews were murdered there (see Appendix A).

At the end of July 1942, the large-scale deportation to Sobibor ceased because of the reconstruction work on the railway between Lublin and Chelm, which meant that no trains from the General Government could reach the camp. A few transports arrived in Sobibor at the beginning of August from the ghettos that were close to the camp and located east of the section of railway that was under construction. But, for the most part, during the next two months there was a lull in operations at Sobibor.

CHAPTER TWELVE

TREBLINKA: JULY 23 TO AUGUST 28, 1942

THE TRAINS WITH DEPORTEES DESTINED for the death camp at Treblinka stopped at the Treblinka village station, some four kilometers from the camp. The train, which was usually composed of close to sixty freight cars, was then divided into three sections, and each section was driven separately into the camp. Like in Belzec and Sobibor, from that point the train was driven by two German railway workers. In Treblinka they were Rudolf Emmerich and Wili Klinzman. The arrival of the first deportation transport from the Warsaw ghetto to Treblinka station was described by a Pole, Franciszek Zabecki:

> The first transport of "deportees" left Malkinia on July 23, 1942, in the morning hours. The train announced its approach not merely with a shriek of wheels as it crossed the Bug bridge, but with a volley of rifle and machine-gun fire from the security guards. The train entered the station. It was loaded with Jews from the Warsaw ghetto. . . . Four SS men from the new camp were waiting. They had arrived earlier by car and asked us how far from Treblinka the "special train with deportees" was. They had already received word of the train's departure from Warsaw. . . . A smaller engine was already at the station, waiting to bring a section of the freight cars into the camp. Everything was planned and prepared in advance. The train was made up of sixty closed cars, crowded with people. These included the young and elderly, men and women, children and babies. The car doors were locked from the outside and the air apertures barred with barbed wire. On the car steps on both sides of the car and on the roof, a dozen or so SS soldiers stood or lay with machine guns at the ready. It was hot, and most of the people in the freight cars were in a faint. . . . As the train approached, an evil spirit seemed to take hold of the SS men who were waiting. They drew their pistols, returned them to their holsters, and whipped them out again, as if they wanted to shoot and kill. They came near the freight cars and tried to calm the noise and weeping; then they started yelling and cursing the Jews, all the while calling to the train workers, "Tempo, fast!" Then they returned to the camp to receive the deportees. [1]

As the train neared the death camp, the engine pushing the freight cars would issue a long whistle to warn of the deportees' approach. This was a signal for the Ukrainians to take up their guard positions around the reception area and on the roofs of the buildings overlooking it. A group of SS and Ukrainians also took up positions on the platform. As the train moved onto the spur inside the camp, the gate was closed behind it. One of the deportees described the arrival into the camp:

> The train moved slowly through a strange, sad countryside. A moment later it came to a stop. The door opened noisily. The emptiness and sadness of the sandy countryside disappeared. Within seconds a strange fear seized us all. "Get out, out!" came the familiar shouts. People began to push. . . . We held one another's hand and jumped down into the sand. . . . Everyone went toward the wall of crowded pine trees. Suddenly I had a strange thought. Those trees aren't growing, they're dead. They had made a fence, a tight fence that looked like a forest, made out of trees that were cut down. I looked at the fence and saw something else—barbed wire between the branches. I thought—concentration camp. That moment we went through a wide gate in the fence; in front of us was a square. . . . Several SS men with whips jumped at us. "Fast! Fast!" they yelled, and lashed with the whips. Women to the barrack, men form up in groups of six. . . . The confusion was tremendous, difficult to describe. We ran.[2]

The deportees were removed from the freight cars to the platform and shunted through a gate to a fenced-in square inside the camp. As they passed the gate, they were separated: men were directed to the right, women and children to the left. A large sign proclaimed in Polish and German:

Jews of Warsaw, Attention!

> You are in a transit camp [*Durchgangslager*], from which you will be sent to a labor camp [*Arbeitslager*]. In order to avoid epidemics, you must present your clothing and belongings for immediate disinfection. Gold, money, foreign currency, and jewelry should be deposited with the cashiers in return for a receipt. They will be returned to you later when you present the receipt. Bodily cleanliness requires that everyone bathe before continuing the journey.[3]

The women and children were sent to a barrack on the left side of the square, where they undressed before entering the "showers." Their clothing was wrapped by them into bundles and left aside. Valuables were deposited by them with the cashier at the end of the hut. The way in which the clothing was arranged and the valuables were deposited created the illusion that, after the "shower," each one would retrieve her valuables and receive fresh clothing. The men were held outside until the women and children had been taken to the "showers." Several dozen men were selected for the work of cleaning the freight cars and taking care of the clothes and baggage left behind by the victims.

The women and children were forced to run naked along the "tube"—the narrow, fenced path that led to the gas chambers. Then the men were ordered to undress, deposit their valuables, and they, too, were taken to the gas chambers.

After the murder of the Jews who had arrived that day, those men who had been selected for various jobs were rounded up and murdered—either in the gas chambers or by shooting at the burial ditches.

During the first weeks of extermination activity at Treblinka, the Germans succeeded in their ruse of presenting Treblinka as a transit camp. The Jews who arrived at Treblinka were misled about the true nature of the camp. David Novodvorski, from Warsaw, who was taken to Treblinka and escaped during the first week of August 1942, related, after returning to the ghetto, that when his transport had first arrived in the camp, no one was suspicious. Only after two days did he discover its true purpose.[4]

During this early period, before mid-August, five thousand to seven thousand Jews arrived in Treblinka every day. Then the situation changed, the pace of transports increased, and there were days when ten thousand to twelve thousand deportees arrived, including thousands who had died en route and others in a state of exhaustion. This state of affairs disrupted the "quiet welcome" designed to deceive the deportees into believing they had arrived at a transit station and that before continuing their journey to a labor camp they must be disinfected. Blows and shooting were needed to force those still alive but exhausted to descend from the freight cars and proceed to the square and the undressing barracks. Abraham Goldfarb, who arrived at the camp on August 25, related: "When we reached Treblinka and the Germans opened the freight car doors, the scene was ghastly. The cars were full of corpses. The bodies had been partially consumed by chlorine. The stench from the cars caused those still alive to choke. The Germans ordered everyone to disembark from the cars; those who could were half-dead. SS and Ukrainians waiting nearby beat us and shot at us."[5] The platform and the nearby square were filled with corpses removed from the cars and the bodies of those shot on the spot. Oskar Berger, who was brought to Treblinka on August 22, described the scene: "As we disembarked we witnessed a horrible sight: hundreds of bodies lying all around. Piles of bundles, clothes, valises, everything mixed together. SS soldiers, Germans, and Ukrainians were standing on the roofs of barracks and firing indiscriminately into the crowd. Men, women, and children fell bleeding. The air was filled with screaming and weeping. Those not wounded by the shooting were forced through an open gate, jumping over the dead and wounded, to a square fenced with barbed wire."[6]

Jakub (Abraham) Krzepicki gave a detailed description of what went on in Transport Square:

The square where we sat was guarded on all sides. By a telephone pole were two notice boards. I read the announcements on them printed in large letters: "Jews of Warsaw, Attention . . ." These were instructions for people arriving at a labor camp; they were told to deposit their clothes for disinfection and were promised that money and valuables would be returned. . . . An SS man arrived and selected ten young men out of our group; he didn't want older men. A while later another SS man demanded sixty men; I was among that group. They marched us two by two through the square we had traversed when we left the freight cars, then to the right, to a larger square, where we were confronted by a staggering sight: a huge number of corpses, lying one next to the other. I estimate there were 20,000 corpses there . . . most of whom had suffocated in the freight cars. Their mouths remained open, as if they were gasping for another breath of air. . . . Hundreds of meters away, a scoop-shovel dug large quantities of earth from the ditches. We saw a lot of Jews busy carrying the bodies to these huge ditches. Some of them transported the bodies in handcarts to the ditches at the edge of the square. These Jews did everything at a run. . . . The bodies were laid in the ditches, row upon row. A group of laborers were pouring chlorine on the corpses. . . . I should mention that those buried at this square were not gas-chamber victims, but rather the bodies removed from the transports and those who had been shot at Treblinka. . . . Often we heard pistols shooting and bullets whistling. We didn't hear the screams of those shot; the Germans fired at the nape of the neck, and the victim never even moaned. . . .

The German who brought us to work had the impression that one of the youths in our group was working sloppily. He took his rifle from his shoulder, and before the youth knew what was happening, he was no longer alive. A few minutes later the same thing happened with another Jew, shot by a Ukrainian, who took a packet of money from the man he shot. . . . Within a short time, only ten men remained in our group. . . . At night another transport arrived at the camp. We ran toward the cars. I was shocked. All the cars were filled only with the dead—asphyxiated. They were lying on top of one another in layers, up to the ceiling of the freight car. The sight was so awful, it is difficult to describe. I asked where the transport had come from; it turned out from Miedzyrzec. . . . There was nowhere to place the corpses. Near the railroad tracks were large piles of clothing, and under these were still-unburied bodies. We laid the bodies in layers, near the railway. Occasionally, moans could be heard from under the piles of clothes as people recovered consciousness and asked in a weak voice for water. There was nothing we could do to help; we were dying of thirst ourselves. . . . Those still alive were moved to the side, nearer to the clothes. It was dark, and the Germans didn't notice. Among those living I found a baby, a year or a year and a half old, who had woken up and was crying loudly. I left him by the side. In the morning he was dead. The next day, our first job was to remove the bodies of the people from Kielce from the barrack. . . . Later we had to remove the bodies of people who had drowned in a well. How they had drowned, what had happened to them, I didn't know. I was told they had committed suicide.[7]

Those who had not died en route or been shot on the platform passed through Transport Square, then the "tube" to the gas chambers. Abraham Goldfarb described what happened to those who arrived alive and were taken through this route: "On the way to the gas chambers, on both sides of the fence, stood Germans with dogs. . . . The Germans beat the people with whips and iron bars so they would run and push to get into the 'showers' quickly. The women's screams could be heard far off in other sections of the camp. The Germans urged the running victims on with yells of 'Faster, faster, the water's getting cold, and others have to use the showers, too.'"[8]

To avoid the blows, the victims ran as fast as they could to the gas chambers, the stronger pushing aside the weak. At the entrance to the gas chambers stood two Ukrainians, Ivan Demianiuk and Nikolai, one armed with an iron bar and the other with a sword, and they, too, urged the people on with blows to push their way in—200 to 250 in a chamber of sixteen square meters. When the gas chambers were full, the Ukrainians closed the doors and started the engine. Twenty to twenty-five minutes later, an SS man or one of the Ukrainians would peep into the chambers through a window in the door. When they thought everyone had suffocated, they ordered the Jewish prisoners to open the rear doors and remove the bodies. When the doors were opened, all the corpses were standing; because of the crowding and the way the victims grasped one another, they were like a single block of flesh.[9]

To drown out the victims' screams on their way to the gas chambers—so that they would not be heard throughout the camp—the SS arranged an orchestra. Krzepicki related:

> As I stood near the "shower" at Treblinka, I discovered something new. For some time I had thought I was hearing music. I thought it was a radio receiver installed by the Germans so that—God forbid—they should not be removed from their native culture in this out-of-the-way spot. Now I could ascertain that their concern for musical culture was even greater. Forty meters from the gas chambers, near the path where the Jews were led to the "showers," a small musical ensemble stood under a tree. Three Jews with yellow patches, three musicians from Stock, stood and played there on their instruments. . . .They played enthusiastically. It was difficult to make out their repertoire . . . these were apparently the latest hit songs favored by the Germans and Ukrainians.[10]

Even in this smoothly efficient process there were sometimes break-downs and disruptions in the operation of the gas chambers. In the initial phase, the operators did not know how long the victims should be left in the chamber until they had suffocated. There were instances when the gas chambers were opened too early and the victims were still alive; the doors would have to be closed again. The engines that produced and fed the gas into the chambers also broke down, causing stoppages in the extermina-tion operation. Breakdowns of this nature also occurred when the victims were already inside the gas chambers, and they would then be held there for long hours until the engines had been repaired. The removal of bodies from the gas chambers and their transport in trolleys to the ditches was also a slow process, and it delayed the arrival of new victims to the gas chambers. The hand-pushed trolley used to transfer the corpses to the pits would often derail and overturn, and it finally was decided to dispense with it altogether. Instead, the prisoners dragged the bodies by their feet to the ditches.

During the first five weeks of the killing operation in Treblinka, be-tween July 23 and August 28, about 245,000 Jews were deported there from the Warsaw ghetto and Warsaw district; from Radom district, 51,000; and from Lublin district, 16,500, bringing the total in this period to about 312,500.[11] (See Appendix A.) SS *Unterscharführer* August Hingst, who served at that time in Treblinka, testified that "Dr. Eberl's ambition was to reach the highest possible numbers and exceed all the other camps. So many transports arrived that the disembarkation and gassing of the people could no longer be handled (*nicht mehr bewaltigt werden konnte*)."[12] From the technical and organizational standpoint, the camp was simply unable to absorb such a large number of victims.

The three gas chambers, with their frequent technical breakdowns, were the main bottleneck, and the surplus from each transport had to be shot in the reception area. Many prisoners and more pits were required for burying the thousands of people who were shot, in addition to those thousands who died inside the densely packed freight cars on their way to the camp. The problem of digging more burial pits was partially solved by a scoop-shovel that was brought from the quarry in the nearby Treblinka penal camp. But since new transports arrived several times daily, still more and more corpses were left unburied.

Near the barracks and the adjacent square, the scattered piles of vic-tims' belongings multiplied, as no one processed them. The barrack de-signed to serve as a storehouse for victims' belongings filled up quickly; the barrack originally intended for the men to undress in was also turned into a storeroom and filled with clothes. Every new transport added to the

The entrance sign to Treblinka. YVA, 143CO2

The Treblinka Village train station. YVA, 2CO1

piles of clothing; there was no ordered attempt to remove the belongings from the camp. There was total confusion in the reception area. The camp was in chaos. Even security became lax, and there were several instances of escape.

Railroad tracks leading from Treblinka station to the Treblinka death camp. YVA, 2B04

Dr. Irmfried Eberl, the commander of Treblinka, was incapable of maintaining control over the situation. With transports coming in all the time and both corpses and clothing piling up in the reception area, transports would have to be delayed at way stations. The result was a higher death toll in the freight cars themselves—with all its ramifications once the transport reached the camp.

Information on what was going on in Treblinka finally reached Odilo Globocnik. Operation Reinhard headquarters was also made aware of reports that large sums of victims' money and valuables, which should have been forwarded, were disappearing into the camp staff's pockets, while part of the money was finding its way from Dr. Eberl's Treblinka camp headquarters directly to Eberl's superiors in the euthanasia program, at Hitler's chancellery in Berlin.[13] The entire situation demanded the immediate intervention of Operation Reinhard headquarters.

CHAPTER THIRTEEN

REORGANIZATION IN TREBLINKA

IN THE SECOND HALF OF July 1942, the three death camps were in operation; however, serious administrative problems were involved in keeping them active. It became necessary for Odilo Globocnik to establish an authority within Operation Reinhard headquarters that would be directly in charge of the camps. Himmler's order of July 19, 1942, which stated that by the end of December 1942 all the Jews within the General Government, with a few exceptions, should be liquidated, set a time limit for the entire operation. This made the need for a commanding authority to supervise and guide the activities in the camps even more urgent. The main problem was how to shorten the time it took to liquidate a transport after its arrival at the camp and thereby accelerate the extermination process. This required streamlining the extermination process and increasing the absorptive capacity of the gas chambers. To carry out this improvement and to achieve more control and more efficient supervision over the activities in the camps, Christian Wirth was appointed inspector of the three death camps at the beginning of August 1942. This was after he had completed the reconstruction of the gas chambers in Belzec and had been replaced there by SS *Hauptsturmführer* Gottlieb Hering. Wirth took with him from Belzec *Oberscharführer* Josef Oberhauser, who became his aide-de-camp. Wirth's new headquarters were in Lublin in the "old airport" camp.

The first problem Wirth had to deal with as inspector of the death camps was the chaotic situation in Treblinka. In the last week of August 1942, Globocnik and Wirth visited Treblinka. Oberhauser, who accompanied him to Treblinka, testified:

> In Treblinka everything was in a state of collapse. The camp was overstocked. Outside the camp, a train with deportees was unable to be unloaded as there was simply no more room. Many corpses of Jews were lying inside the camp. These corpses were already bloated. Particularly I can remember seeing many corpses in the vicinity of the fence. These people were shot from the guard towers.

I heard then in Treblinka how Globocnik and Wirth summed up the following: Wirth would remain in Treblinka for the time being. Dr. [Irmfried] Eberl would be dismissed immediately. In his place, [Franz] Stangl would come to Treblinka from Sobibor as commander. Globocnik said in this conversation that if Dr. Eberl were not his fellow countryman, he would arrest him and bring him before an SS and police court.[1]

At that time, Sobibor had been inactive for over a month due to the repairs being done on the railway leading to the camp, so Stangl was available. Furthermore, Globocnik had faith in Stangl's ability, on the basis of his accomplishments in Sobibor. Stangl was replaced in Sobibor by *Obersturmführer* Franz Reichleitner, who had served in the euthanasia program. Dr. Eberl left Treblinka at the end of August 1942, and Stangl arrived at the beginning of September. Stangl described his arrival in Treblinka:

> When I arrived at Treblinka the first time, a large board was located in Reception Square. As I remember, on this board were noted ten clauses. These clauses stressed how the arriving Jews should behave. . . . It is clear that in this written announcement the mission of this camp, in some way, was disguised. Maybe it related to a resettlement camp. . . . But I know that it alluded to the fact that all have to go to the baths and in the meantime the clothes would be disinfected. . . . In the framework of the reorganization, Wirth ordered the signboard removed. In its place, the low ranking SS men would verbally announce (to the deportees) the directions which were until then written on the board. These short announcements were translated by the working Jews.[2]

SS *Oberscharführer* Kurt Franz, who had been appointed Stangl's deputy, arrived a few days later. Kurt Franz, like Stangl, had been with the euthanasia program. Prior to his arrival at Treblinka, he had served at Belzec under Wirth. There Franz had excelled in his display of zeal and cruelty in dealing with the Jewish victims. His transfer to Treblinka and his promotion to deputy camp commander were Wirth's decisions. Kurt Franz described his arrival in Treblinka:

> It was late summer or the beginning of autumn 1942, when I came from Belzec to Treblinka. I went by foot from the railway station of Malkinia to Treblinka; when I arrived it was already dark. Everywhere in the camp there were corpses. I remember that these corpses were already bloated. The corpses were dragged through the camp by working Jews. . . .
> These working Jews were driven by the guardsmen [Ukrainians] and also by Germans. . . . I reported to Wirth in the dining room. As I remember, Wirth, Stangl, and Oberhauser were there.[3]

Wirth remained in Treblinka for approximately three to four weeks to help Stangl restore order to the camp. To regain control over the situation, and first of all to evacuate the thousands of corpses piled in the reception area, Wirth and Stangl asked Operation Reinhard headquarters to stop the transports to Treblinka temporarily. Globocnik agreed, and on August 28, 1942, the deportations from Warsaw and other places ceased.[4]

With the suspension of the transports to Treblinka, work commenced on clearing the multitude of corpses piled up near the station platform and around the reception area. It was carried out by Jews who had remained from the last transports, left alive by camp command decision until the cleanup was completed. Jakub (Abraham) Krzepicki described the prisoners' living and working conditions at the time:

> At seven in the evening there was a roll call; they counted us—we were about 500. They appointed a Jewish commander—a capo, the engineer [Alfred] Galewski. That day, like every day, the roll call lasted two hours. The next morning there was another roll call. Since first counting us they had instituted some order, and the roll calls were held three times a day. Food distribution was also organized. A field kitchen was set up near the well, and there they gave us half a liter of soup three times a day. We received no bread, but there was no lack of food, since we could take it from the bundles left behind by the Jews brought for extermination. The kitchen food also came from these bundles.... After roll call we were taken to work at the big square, where there were mass graves. This time I worked at transferring corpses to the big ditch near the fence. After a few days, the scoop-shovel stopped working. A new system was instituted—burning the corpses in the ditches. All kinds of articles were used to light the fires, including empty valises and the junk which was collected in the course of cleaning the square. The body-burning continued day and night, and the entire camp was filled with smoke and the stench of burned and burning bodies. Still there were endless quantities of bodies. It was necessary to clean the area fully of the remains of the last transports . . . bodies, dozens of bodies, hundreds, thousands of men, women, and children who had been murdered. Corpses of people of different ages, in different positions, with different expressions frozen on their faces the moment they breathed their last. All around, just earth, sky, and corpses! A factory of horror whose sole product was bodies. Evidently only a German could become accustomed to a place like this. I didn't get used to the sight of corpses until the end. . . .
>
> The quantity of bodies in the large square gradually decreased, until one day the entire field was clear. What will happen to us now? New transports aren't arriving. Our hearts tell us that our last hour has arrived. . . . but a miracle happened. . . . they selected eighty of our group and shot them, while the rest, several hundred, were directed to other jobs.[5]

With the cessation of deportations on August 28, the SS men murdered all the prisoners who had worked in the extermination area in removing and burying bodies. Considerations of secrecy caused the camp command to prevent any contact between the Jews employed in the extermination area and those in the Lower Camp; thus, the latter were not used for clearing the corpses from the reception area. As preparations proceeded for renewing the transports, a group of prisoners from the reception area was transferred to work in the extermination area. This group was reinforced with dozens of men from the first transports to arrive after extermination activities were resumed.[6]

Simultaneously, and in order to ensure that the renewed transports and extermination process would be carried out with all possible efficiency, steps were also taken to give traffic priority to deportee trains and to prevent delays at the way stations en route to Treblinka. One cause of these delays had been the regularly scheduled passenger trains passing through the Treblinka village station. Transport order no. 243 of the Gedob issued on August 27, 1942, stated that "in order to facilitate special evacuation trains [*Umsiedlersonderzüge*] activity without malfunctions, Treblinka train station will be closed to normal passenger traffic from September 1 until further notice."[7]

This order to eliminate civilian railroad traffic through Treblinka station also contributed to the maintenance of secrecy regarding the transports' destination and fate. Part of every transport was held at this station for hours, since the death camp's platform could only handle twenty cars at a time. By limiting civilian traffic at the station, unwanted observers of events at the station were also reduced.[8] Wirth was the leading personality in the reorganization of Treblinka and in guiding the German staff in handling the transports. SS *Scharführer* Franz Suchomel testified:

> I remember that in the time when the whole camp was entirely disorganized, Wirth conducted talks with the German staff, mainly at 1 o'clock in the evening. These talks took place in the presence of Stangl.... Wirth gave detailed instructions as to the liquidation of the transports and to the incorporation of the Jewish working commandos in this process. His instructions were detailed. For example, they described how to open the doors of the freight cars, the disembarking of the Jews, the passage through the "tube" to the upper part of the camp. Wirth personally gave an order that when the Jews were taking off their shoes they had to tie them together.... Wirth's instructions were carried out even after he left Treblinka.[9]

The pause taken for the reorganization in Treblinka was short. The continuation of the liquidation of the largest ghetto in Europe—the Warsaw ghetto—could not be postponed long.

Deportations from the Warsaw ghetto to Treblinka were renewed on September 3, and the first transport arrived at the camp the following morning. To prevent a new accumulation of corpses and piles of belongings in the reception area, the new camp commanders decided to alter the transport reception system. Several hundred Jews, some who had remained in the camp from the last deportations of late August and others who had arrived with the first new transports, were assigned jobs in the reception area.

One group of workers waited for the transport at the train platform. It was charged with removing the bodies of those who had died en route and taking them to the ditches. This group also carried to the ditches those deportees who were incapable of walking on their own from the train to the gas chambers. An additional ditch was prepared in the southern corner of the camp, near the train platform, where these Jews were shot by the SS men and Ukrainians. Wirth and Stangl were at the platform when the transport from Warsaw arrived on September 4, and they supervised the work closely. Boris (Kazik) Weinberg, who was deported from Warsaw on September 4 and arrived in Treblinka among the first of the renewed transports, related:

> We arrived at a kind of train station. Jewish laborers opened our freight-car doors, and we saw in front of us a lot of Germans and Ukrainians. . . . They started screaming and hitting, and we had to run. . . . Jewish workers gave us string to tie our shoes. It turned out they needed about 400 men for work. A "selection" was held among the men, and I was among those chosen. We stood in the courtyard and waited. Through the gate they brought in a group of workers who had already been in the camp for a while. They started hitting them: the scene was indescribable. They hit them with iron and wooden clubs, and a dog bit them. Those in the first rows fell, then the others fell on top of them. They were all pushed into a hut, then removed in groups of twenty men and shot. . . . *Hauptsturmführer* Stangl arrived and told us that those who had been shot had intended to kill the Germans and wipe out the camp. "I have orders to do the same to you," he added, "but I don't want to. There is work here for years. Whoever works well will be treated humanely. . . ." Our daily work was sorting clothes and searching in pockets and elsewhere for gold and valuables. They would beat us endlessly, until our faces swelled up. Usually every two days they eliminated the weak and the beaten. During roll call the German in charge would remove those who had been beaten, line them up in a row, and transfer them to the ditch we later called "Lazarett." Initially this was just a hole with no fence and no name. . . . This situation continued for some time.[10]

The Jewish worker's constant companion was the threat of selection during one of the thrice-daily roll calls, the fear that if he appeared weak, or if he simply displeased the German inspecting the roll call, his fate was sealed. Krzepicki wrote:

> The selection was a constant threat, like a drawn sword over our heads. . . . In the morning we would awaken before the signal and arrange our appearance

to look better. Never, even in the best of times, did we shave so often as in Treblinka. Every morning everyone would shave and wash his face in eau de cologne taken from the bundles left by [dead] Jews. Some powdered their faces and even rouged their lips, pinched their cheeks till they were rosy, and all this to gain another few days of life, perhaps a few weeks, who knew.[11]

The number of Jewish workers employed in the reception area varied between five hundred and six hundred. Every day some of them were murdered and replaced by strong young men taken by the Germans from the new transports.

On September 10 (or 11), on the eve of Rosh Hashanah (Jewish New Year), one of the last transports of Jews arrived from the Warsaw ghetto. As was the practice with early transports, a group of men was selected for work in the reception area. Everyone else in the transport, about five thousand to six thousand people, were taken to the gas chambers. At the evening roll call, after the day's work, *Oberscharführer* Max Bialas, who was in charge, held a selection and pulled out of the rows those who were to be shot by the edge of the ditches. Weinberg described what happened:

> When we had formed up at the evening roll call, the German in charge ordered all those who had arrived in the camp that same day to form up separately. The men hesitated as to where to stand—were the Germans going to eliminate the new arrivals, or the veterans? At first no one moved, then a few left the ranks. The Germans began beating the men brutally. At that moment a man jumped out of the ranks, ran toward the German Max Bialas with a drawn knife, and stabbed him in the back. He did the deed—then stood by, hesitating. One of the Ukrainians, Corporal Manchuk, saw what happened and ran over and hit the assailant on the head with a shovel he was holding. . . . With Bialas lying on the ground bleeding from his wound, the Ukrainians began hitting and shooting into the crowd. Dozens were killed and wounded. The deputy camp commander, Kurt Franz, who was nicknamed "Lalka," arrived on the scene. [Lalka, "the doll," was the name given Franz by the prisoners because of his innocent face, like that of a doll.] Franz had the wounded Bialas evacuated, stopped the wild shooting, and ordered the Jews to form up again. He ordered the "camp elder," Galewski, to stand in front of the roll call, beat him with a whip he carried, and announced that if such an event occurred again, he, Galewski, would be executed. Christian Wirth, who was still in Treblinka, was summoned. He ordered ten men to be selected and shot. Kurt Franz chose them, and they were shot in front of the roll call. The others were put into barracks and held there all night. The next day there was no usual 6 a.m. roll call. The Jews locked in their barracks feared the worst. At 7:30 a.m. they were taken to roll call. It was held under a heavy guard of SS and Ukrainians. One hundred and fifty men were selected, taken to the ditches and shot as punishment for the killing of Max Bialas.[12]

SS *Oberscharführer* Kurt Franz, deputy commander of Treblinka from September 1942. YVA, FA 245/34-45

As further punishment the prisoners received neither food nor water for three days; they had to make do with whatever they found in the victims' belongings. Max Bialas, who was badly wounded, was taken immediately to the army hospital in Ostrow. He died of his wounds either en route or at the hospital.[13]

The Jew who killed Bialas was Meir Berliner, an Argentinian citizen who was visiting Warsaw with his wife and daughter when war broke out. They were sent to Treblinka despite their Argentinian citizenship. The wife and daughter were taken straight to the gas chambers, while Berliner was selected for labor.[14] The killing of Max Bialas was carried out by Berliner at his own initiative, without assistance and without revealing his intentions to the others. He planned his action in advance and hid a knife specifically for this purpose, but his timing was dictated by the knowledge that his end was near. His was an individual act of heroism and despair.

Berliner's act aroused shock and fear among the SS personnel in the camp. It was the first instance of resistance at Treblinka after over a month and a half of operation, during which a quarter of a million Jews had been murdered. The Germans realized that in their despair the Jews could be very dangerous. During the first days after the incident, the Germans were very suspicious; they ordered every Jew who passed near them to raise his hands, and they checked for knives or other hidden weapons. To perpetuate the name of the dead SS man, the camp command decided to name the Ukrainian guards' barracks after him. A sign was affixed to the barracks' entrance—"The Max Bialas Barracks."[15]

There was, however, no basic change as a result of the killing. The Treblinka death factory continued operating at full capacity. Transports arrived daily and the mass murder continued, including the killing of Jewish workers employed in the reception area. Between September 3 and September 12, some fifty-two thousand Jews, all from Warsaw, were murdered. The last transport of the "big expulsion" from the Warsaw ghetto arrived on September 21, 1942. It comprised about twenty-two hundred people, including the Jewish police, who had taken part in the deportations from the ghetto, and their families. Nearly two hundred fifty-four thousand Jews taken from the Warsaw ghetto between July 23 and September 21, 1942, were murdered at Treblinka.[16]

CHAPTER FOURTEEN

THE MISSION OF GERSTEIN AND PFANNENSTIEL

THE GASSING SYSTEM THAT HAD been developed and introduced by Christian Wirth in the Operation Reinhard death camps proved only partially satisfactory. The frequent engine breakdowns caused disturbances and delays in the entire extermination process. Odilo Globocnik was aware of these shortcomings and, in coordination with the higher authorities of the SS, decided to look into the possibility of introducing an alternative gassing system. The prevailing opinion among the higher SS authorities in charge of the extermination of Jews was that Zyklon B was more suitable for this task.

Obersturmführer Kurt Gerstein, the chief disinfection officer in the Main Hygienic Office of the Waffen SS, and SS *Obersturmbannführer* Wilhelm Pfannenstiel, professor and director of the Hygienic Institute at the University of Marburg/Lahn, who had also served as hygienic adviser of the Waffen SS, were sent to Lublin in the middle of August 1942. Gerstein's main mission was to check the possibility of introducing the gas Zyklon B into the gas chambers. Zyklon B had already been successfully used in Auschwitz instead of the engines that were still supplying the monoxide gas in the death camps of Operation Reinhard. In addition, Gerstein was to advise regarding the disinfection of the clothes left behind by the Jews.[1]

Gerstein submitted a written report of his mission when he was incarcerated in an American army prison at the end of the war in April–July 1945. The report described his visit to Lublin, Belzec, and Sobibor.

> On June 8, 1942, SS *Sturmbannführer* [Rolf] Günther of the *Reichssicherheitshauptamt*, dressed in civilian clothes, walked into my office. He was unknown to me. He ordered me to obtain for him, for a top secret mission, 100 kilos of prussic acid and to take it to a place known only to the truck driver. A few weeks later, we set out for the potash plant near Kolin (Prague)....
>
> I understood little of the nature of my mission. But I accepted....
>
> On the way to Kolin, we were accompanied by SS *Obersturmbannführer* and MD, Professor Pfannenstiel, Professor of Hygiene at the University of Marburg/Lahn....

We then set off with the truck for Lublin (Poland). SS *Gruppenführer* Globocnik was waiting for us. He told us: "This is one of our most secret matters, indeed the most secret. Anyone who talks about it will be shot. Only yesterday two babblers were shot." He then explained to us: "At present"— this was August 17, 1942—"there are three installations":

1. Belzec, on the Lublin-Lvov road. Maximum per day: 15,000 persons (seen)!
2. Sobibor, I don't know exactly where: not seen: 20,000 persons per day.
3. Treblinka, 120 km northeast of Warsaw: 25,000 persons per day; seen.
4. Majdanek, near Lublin; seen in preparation.

Except for the last one, I made a thorough inspection of all these camps, accompanied by Police Chief Wirth, the head of all these death factories.

Globocnik said: "You will have to disinfect large quantities of clothing ten or twenty times, the whole textile accumulation. It is only being done to conceal that the source of clothing is Jews, Poles, Czechs, etc. Your other duty will be to improve the service in our gas chambers, which function on diesel engine exhaust. We need gas which is more toxic and works faster, such as prussic acid. The *Führer* and Himmler—they were here on August 15, the day before yesterday—instructed me to accompany personally all those who have to see these installations." Then Professor Pfannenstiel: "But what did the *Führer* say?" Globocnik replied: "The *Führer* ordered all action speeded up! Dr. Herbert Lindner, who was with us yesterday, asked me: 'But wouldn't it be wiser to cremate the corpses instead of burying them? Another generation may perhaps judge these things differently!' I replied: 'Gentlemen, if there were ever, after us, a generation so cowardly and so soft that they could not understand our work which is so good, so necessary, then, gentlemen, all of National Socialism will have been in vain. We ought, on the contrary, to bury bronze tablets stating that it was we who had the courage to carry out this gigantic task!' The *Führer* then said: 'Yes, my good Globocnik, you are right!'"

We left for Belzec two days later. . . .

Next morning, a few minutes before seven, I was told: "In ten minutes the first train will arrive!" Indeed, a few minutes later a train arrived from Lvov, with 45 cars holding 6,700 people, of whom 1,450 were already dead on arrival. . . .

Then the march began. To the left and right, barbed wire; behind, two dozen Ukrainians, guns in hand.

They approached. Wirth and I were standing on the ramp in front of the death chambers. Completely nude men, women, young girls, children, babies, cripples, filed by. At the corner stood a heavy SS man, who told the poor people, in a pastoral voice: "No harm will come to you. You just have to breathe very deeply, that strengthens the lungs, inhaling is a means of preventing contagious diseases. It's a good disinfection!" They asked what was going to happen to them. He told them: "The men will have to work, building roads and houses. But the women won't be obliged to do so; they'll do housework, cooking." For some of these poor creatures, this was a last small hope, enough to carry them, unresisting, as far as the death chambers. . . .

. . . *Unterscharführer* Hackenholt was making great efforts to get the engine running. But it doesn't go. Captain Wirth comes up. I can see he is afraid because I am present at a disaster. Yes, I see it all and I wait. My stopwatch showed it all, 50 minutes, 70 minutes, and the diesel did not start. The people wait inside the gas chambers. In vain. They can be heard weeping, "like in the synagogue," says Professor Pfannenstiel, his eyes glued to a window in the wooden door. Furious, Captain Wirth lashes the Ukrainian assisting Hackenholt twelve, thirteen times, in the face. After 2 hours and 49 minutes—the stopwatch recorded it all—the diesel started. Up to that moment, the people shut up in those four crowded chambers were still alive, four times 750 persons in four times 45 cubic meters Another 25 minutes elapsed. Many were already dead, that could be seen through the small window because an electric lamp inside lit up the chamber for a few moments. After 28 minutes, only a few were still alive. Finally, after 32 minutes, all were dead. . . .

. . . Two dozen workers were busy checking the mouths of the dead, which they opened with iron hooks. "Gold to the left, without gold to the right!" . . . Dentists hammered out gold teeth, bridges and crowns. In the midst of them stood Captain Wirth. He was in his element, and showing me a large can full of teeth, he said: "See for yourself the weight of that gold! It's only from yesterday and the day before. You can't imagine what we find every day—dollars, diamonds, gold. You'll see for yourself! . . ."

The next day we drove in Captain Wirth's car to Treblinka, about 120 km. northeast of Warsaw. The equipment in that place of death was almost the same as at Belzec, but even larger. Eight gas chambers and veritable mountains of clothing and underwear, about 35–40 meters high. Then, in our honor, a banquet was held for all those employed at the establishment. *Obersturmbannführer* Professor Doctor Pfannenstiel, Professor of Hygiene at the University of Marburg/Lahn, made a speech: "Your work is a great work and a very useful and very necessary duty." To me, he spoke of the establishment as "a kindness and a humanitarian thing." To all present, he said: "When one sees the bodies of the Jews, one understands the greatness of your work!"[2]

This report was one of the first and most important documents relating to Operation Reinhard. It includes facts and events that Gerstein personally witnessed and some that were told to him by Globocnik or Wirth. The report of what Gerstein saw as an eyewitness is reliable; the "facts" based on what his hosts told him were to some extent exaggerated by them or simple boasting. Globocnik's story about the visit of Hitler and Himmler on August 15, 1942, was untrue. Hitler never visited Operation Reinhard headquarters, and it is unlikely that he met Globocnik at some other place. The visit and conversation were Globocnik's own invention, probably to stress his high status and the importance of his mission. There is, however, a possibility that such a conversation transpired with Himmler during his visit to Lublin in the middle of July 1942. Its veracity aside, this story is important as an insight to Globocnik's view and ideological approach to the extermination of the Jews.

The number of people murdered per day in Belzec, Sobibor, and Treblinka as given by Globocnik was also exaggerated. This could only be an estimate of the theoretical absorption capacity of the gas chambers in the camps if they were to operate twenty-four hours a day without pause or disturbance.

SS *Obersturmbannführer* Dr. W. Pfannenstiel testified about his visit to Belzec before the Land-Court of Darmstadt in the Federal Republic of Germany, on June 6, 1950. This eyewitness evidence of the mass extermination of Jews in Belzec, as given by a high SS officer, a physician and university professor, is extremely important. According to his own evidence, Pfannenstiel's mission was to advise on prophylactic problems in the Lublin district. Regarding the circumstances that made him visit Belzec and what he saw there, he stated:

> As a disinfector, I received an order to go to Lublin in the summer of 1942. There I had to advise about the reconstruction of the city's water supply and sewer system. I went to Berlin to get a car because at that time a journey by train took too much time. I could not get a car. I was told that Dr. Gerstein was going to Lublin, too, and I should contact him. I did so. Dr. Gerstein explained to me that he had to travel through Prague. I agreed. Our car was followed by an empty truck. While traveling, Dr. Gerstein told me that he had to pick up prussic acid from a factory in Kolin near Prague. He did not tell me for what purpose. I did not even ask, as it was obvious that it was for disinfection and that Dr. Gerstein was in charge of disinfections.
>
> In the factory, which was a small one, I found out that the prussic acid was in the form of gas. . . . Then together with Dr. Gerstein we went to Lublin. . . . There I devoted my time to the task assigned to me. At that time I found out that there was a camp in Belzec where Jews were being murdered. I wanted to see this camp. The commander was a certain Wirth. . . . I made a request to visit the camp. Globocnik, who was very proud of his creation, gave permission. Globocnik took Gerstein and me to the camp. The next day, before noon, a transport with Jews arrived, including men, women, and children. They were decently received by the Jews who worked in the camp, and they were told not to be afraid. They had to undress and to give away their belongings. It was announced to them that they would be directed for

work, and in order to prevent epidemics, they had to be deloused. They were told that they must inhale something. Then, after the women's hair was cut off, the whole transport was taken to a building of six chambers. Only four chambers were needed. When the people were closed in the chambers, the gas from an engine was piped in. When the Jews were led into the chambers, an electric light was on inside and everything went quietly. But when the light was extinguished, screams were heard from the chambers. Gradually they became silent. When silence prevailed in the chambers, the outside doors were opened. Then the corpses were taken out, checked for gold teeth, and afterward they were put, layer upon layer, in a pit. This work was again carried out by Jews. No physician was present. The corpses were not exceptional. Some of the faces were blue. This was not surprising, because death was caused by suffocation. As I remember I traveled back to Lublin with Globocnik that same day.

When Globocnik granted me permission to visit the camp he stressed that I should not speak about what I would hear and see with anybody, for that would be punishable by death. When I returned to Berlin, I reported to the SS Reich physician Professor Dr. Ernst Grawitz what I saw and my disgust at what I had observed. He promised me that he would take care to stop these matters. What happened henceforth, I do not know. . . .

Why I actually asked to visit the camp can be explained by curiosity. I wanted especially to find out whether any atrocities were carried out during the extermination of these people. I found the atrocity particularly in the fact that the killing took eighteen minutes. I told this to Globocnik. He thought that with prussic acid it would go faster. As a matter of fact, prussic acid was not used, because Gerstein drew his attention to the dangers of prussic acid in the form of gas. If I was correctly informed, the containers with the prussic acid were buried.[3]

This evidence and the earlier testimony, which is almost identical, given by Dr. Pfannenstiel at the main office of the Land Justice Administration in Marburg/Lahn on November 9, 1959, both verify the basic facts of Gerstein's report.

Gerstein's mission did not bring about any changes in the gassing system in the Operation Reinhard death camps. Carbon monoxide, supplied by truck or tank engine, as introduced by Wirth, remained the means of killing used in these camps. The fact that Gerstein witnessed in Belzec a breakdown of the diesel engine that supplied the gas and during which people were locked inside the gas chambers for almost three hours until the engine started working did not cause any change in the procedure. Wirth refused to give up the gassing system he had developed. His professional pride did not permit him to admit that the use of Zyklon B for mass killings, as developed by Rudolf Höss, the commander

The sign posted in front of the gas chambers in the Belzec death camp

"Attention! Fold all of your clothes. Everything you have brought with you must be left where you undress except for money, valuables, documents, and shoes. Hold your money and valuables until they are collected at the window and keep them with you. Tie your shoes together, and leave them in the places marked. You must come to the baths and vapor room entirely nude."

YVA, 2590/1

of Auschwitz, was preferable to carbon monoxide. He asked and subsequently persuaded Gerstein not to propose to Berlin any other type of gas or gas chamber for Belzec, Sobibor, and Treblinka. Gerstein did not even carry out any killing experiments with the Zyklon B he had brought with him from Kolin. The gas was buried on the pretext that it had been spoiled in transit.[4]

CHAPTER FIFTEEN

JEWISH WORKING PRISONERS

THE LACK OF A PERMANENT and experienced cadre of Jewish prisoners to carry out the physical work involved in the extermination process, and the daily murder of some of those already engaged in this work and their replacement by others taken from the newly arriving transports, caused a constant disruption and slowdown of the liquidation activities in the camps. Realizing the source of the problem, the authorities in each camp decided to turn the temporary Jewish prisoner workforce into a permanent one. According to this plan, each Jewish prisoner would belong to a particular working group and would become a specialist in the work he was assigned. These people would be kept working as long as they were fit and selections and executions would continue for those who became too weak or too ill to keep up to the required pace.

The first camp in which such a change was instituted was Sobibor, in May/June 1942. Moshe Bahir, who arrived in Sobibor at that time with a transport of Jews from Zamosc, wrote: "To my great good fortune I was part of the second transport, some of whose members were selected as permanent workers. Before that, they would take out 200 men from each transport to load the belongings. As soon as the work was finished, they shot them. I, however, was privileged to be counted among the 'permanent workers' of the camp."[1]

Franz Stangl, as commander of Sobibor, grasped at an early stage the importance of a permanent work cadre and subsequently introduced it in his camp. In Belzec, the establishment of a permanent cadre of Jewish prisoners took place sometime toward the end of the first period of its activity (June/July 1942). Rudolf Reder wrote that when he arrived in Belzec on August 11, 1942, he already met there Jewish prisoners who were engaged in different activities and that he was attached to such a "permanent" work group.[2]

In Treblinka this change took place only in September 1942, after Stangl became commander of the camp. There the killing of Max Bialas had prompted the camp command to rethink its approach regarding the Jews working in the reception area. While the thousands of Jews who were transported daily to Treblinka knew nothing of their fate until they were actually inside the gas chambers—and in their ignorance they were not expected to show resistance—the Jews selected for temporary work were a potential danger to the Germans, and the Berliner incident had proved it. These Jews quickly learned of what was happening around them—that their families were no longer alive and that it was their fate to die, too, in a few hours or days. Under such circumstances, when people knew they had nothing to lose, an act of despair like that of Meir Berliner could happen again and again.

Stangl understood this well. In view of his own experience as commander of Sobibor, Stangl decided to stop the existing practice of constant selections and replacement of the reception area workers and to organize a permanent cadre of Jewish prisoners. Accordingly, the daily mass killings of the Jews employed in the reception and extermination areas were stopped. Tanhum Greenberg, a Treblinka prisoner, described Wirth's announcement of the change in their status:

> An SS *Obersturmführer* arrived from Lublin. He wore glasses. They lined us up at the barrack entrance, and he made a speech: You Jews, you should work hard. Whoever works will have everything. He shall get good food and drink. Workers will get medical treatment. There will be a hospital with doctors. The sick will be taken to the hospital and receive special food until they recover and return to work. ... You Jews should remember that Germany is strong. Five cities will be built for Jews; there they will work and live well, and no one will be taken away. Treblinka will be one of these cities where Jews will live. There will be no more selections.[3]

The Jewish prisoners were transferred to the living quarters of the "court Jews," where conditions improved. Kalman Taigman described the merging of these two groups of prisoners in Treblinka:

> After the roll call they put us into two barracks fenced with barbed wire. Everyone got a place to sleep. There we met a group of Jews who were called the "court Jews." They were from the region of Treblinka, mostly skilled craftsmen. ... The "court Jews" were not as restricted in the camp as the rest of the prisoners. They could move about freely ... they had their own kitchen and plenty of food. ... At first they kept their distance from us, didn't want any contact with us, as if they weren't interested in what was happening in the camp. They were even afraid to approach us. It was only after the camp commander announced that there was no longer any special status to the "court Jews," that all the Jews were equal and no further distinctions would be made between them, that the "court Jews" began to approach us.[4]

The guiding principle in the reorganization of the Jewish prisoners' work was that at each station along the route of death—from the freight car, via the train platform, the undressing area, to the gas chambers and burial ditches—work teams would be assigned specific tasks with specific responsibilities at which they would become expert. In charge of each work team was a capo, who was one of the prisoners. The capo was responsible for the prisoners' work, and they had to obey his orders. The capo wore a yellow armband bearing the black letters c-a-p-o; he was armed with a club or whip. Larger work teams were subdivided, and each sub-group was headed by a foreman (*Vorarbeiter*), who wore his title on a black armband. At the top of the hierarchy of Jewish prisoners was the "camp elder" (*Lageraltester*), whose title was emblazoned in white letters on a black armband. The first "camp elder" in Treblinka was Engineer (Marceli?) Galewski from the Lodz region. When he was sick, he was replaced for a short time by Rakowski, but later he was reappointed.

In Sobibor, the "camp elder," who was there called "chief capo" (*Oberkapo*), was Moshe Sturm, nicknamed "the Governor." In the late summer of 1943 he was executed and replaced by a man the Jews nicknamed "the Berliner" because of his German origin. There is no information about the "camp elder" in Belzec.

A separate hierarchy, headed by a different "camp elder," was organized among the Jewish prisoners of the extermination area, who were kept isolated from the other Jews in the camp. In Treblinka the first "camp elder" in the extermination area was named Blau; he was replaced by a prisoner named Singer. Both were from Austria. Stangl, who was himself an Austrian, gave preference to Austrian Jews as camp functionaries.[5] In each barrack a "barrack elder" was appointed to be in charge of everything that happened in the barrack, including cleanliness, the sleeping places of each prisoner, and ascertaining that all the prisoners left the barracks for work. The "camp elder," "barrack elder," and capos had the authority to punish prisoners and were exempted from physical labor.

Prisoner work teams were labeled according to the tasks for which they were responsible. The prisoner teams that came into direct contact with deportees on the train platform and at Transport Square were given a special insignia, a colored armband. As the camp prisoners wore normal civilian clothing, the colored armband was intended to identify the members of the work team from among the transport deportees and prevent prospective victims from saving themselves by joining work teams—a subterfuge which had hitherto been exploited often. In choosing the work teams for the platform and Transport Square, the Germans gave preference to German-speaking Jews who could transmit the orders to the Jewish victims when they arrived.

An SS man from among the German staff of the camp was in charge of each prisoner work group. In some cases one SS man supervised two or three work groups. The capos generally served as intermediaries between the SS man and the prisoners.

THE ORGANIZATION OF LABOR IN THE MAIN CAMP (RECEPTION AREA)

Platform Workers (Bahnhofkommando)

This group of forty to fifty prisoners worked at the train platform. The team's job was to open the freight cars and transfer the orders of the SS man in charge to disembark from the train. After the victims disembarked, the team workers removed the bodies of those who had died en route and transferred them to the burial ditches. Then they cleaned the cars and removed any remaining belongings to eliminate any traces of the transport cargo. Two or three prisoners would clean each freight car, and within ten to fifteen minutes the entire train had been cleaned. In Treblinka the platform workers' team wore blue armbands and thus were known as "the blues."

Transport Square Workers (Transportkommando)

This group of about forty prisoners was engaged in the activities carried out on the square where the victims undressed. They directed the victims, relayed the German orders to undress, and distributed string for tying shoes together so they could be easily reused in the future without having to sort them. The team workers aided in undressing small children and in taking the clothes and baggage left by the victims to the sorting area or stores. They also carried deportees who were too weak to make their own way to the gas chambers to the shooting ditches. (In Treblinka these were located in the reception area, and in Sobibor and Belzec in the extermination area.) In Treblinka this team wore red armbands and became known as "the reds," or, in the prisoners' special slang, the "burial society" (Chevra kadisha).

The "Gold Jews" (Goldjuden)

This group comprised nearly twenty people, most of them former jewelers, watchmakers, and bank clerks. Their task was to receive and sort the money, gold, valuables, foreign currency, and bonds taken from the arriving Jews. Some of the group worked at the undressing area, receiving money and valuables from the victims on their way to extermination. Members of this group had to carry out body searches on the women after they had stripped and before they were taken to the gas chambers. The women had to lie on a special table, where they would be thoroughly searched, including in their genitalia.

One section of this group worked at the square and stores where the belongings left by the victims were sorted and checked. They received the money and valuables and prepared them for shipment from the camp. These "gold Jews" were considered extremely privileged, because they could secretly siphon off money and valuables of considerable worth, even in the camp. On their part, the SS personnel needed them to secure their share of the wealth that passed through the camp.

The Hair Cutters (Friseurs)

This group comprised those prisoners who cut the hair of the women victims before they entered the gas chambers. They numbered about ten to twenty men, mostly professional barbers. The hair cuttings in the camps began in September or October 1942, after the SS Main Office for Economic Affairs and Administration had issued the following order on August 16, 1942: "The Head of the SS Main Office for Economic Affairs and Administration, SS Obergruppenführer [Oswald] Pohl, has ordered that care is to be taken to make use of the human hair collected in all concentration camps. This human hair is threaded on bobbins and converted into industrial felt. After being combed and cut, the women's hair can be manufactured as slippers for submarine crews and felt stockings for the Reichsbahn."[6]

This order related to the women prisoners in the Nazi concentration camps and to Jewish women brought for extermination to the death camps.

In Sobibor the barbershop was in a special barrack in the middle of the "tube," and in Belzec it was in a barrack close to the gas chambers. In Treblinka the barber room was set up at the end of the barrack where the women disrobed, near the entrance gate to the "tube," and near the site where the "gold Jews" worked. Adjacent to the barbershop, a disinfection room was established, where several prisoners were engaged in cleaning the hair.[7] The initiation of the cutting of women's hair at Treblinka was described by Stangl: "One day we received a disinfecting machine without having been told what it was for. I asked about it in Lublin. I was told in reply that from now on we were to cut the women's hair. The hair should be cleaned and packed in bags. ... I recall that at Lublin they explained that the hair was intended for insulating submarines. Wirth himself must have told me that."[8]

The Sorting Team for Clothing and Belongings (Lumpenkommando)

This was the largest labor team, numbering 80 to 120 men, and was subdivided into several smaller groups. The team worked in the square, where the victims' belongings were piled, and in the storage sheds. Its main job was to collect the victims' clothing and belongings, examine them, sort them by categories, tie them in bundles of ten or twenty-five units in each category, prepare them for shipment, and load them on freight cars. The team workers were each given a personal number that they wore on their collars and had to list on each bundle they prepared. The clothing was first examined for documents, photographs, hidden money and valuables, and the yellow patch or any other mark that could identify the clothing and other items as having belonged to Jews. All these were to be removed. Any sloppiness, or Jewish identifying marks left on the clothing or other belongings, could be traced to the perpetrator by his personal number on the bundle. In such an event the worker paid for his mistake with his life.

The Forest Team (Waldkommando) and the Camouflage Team (Tarnungskommando)

A special group known as the forest team, which numbered a few dozen prisoners, was set up to cut wood for heating and cooking in the camp. It was put to work in the forests near the camp. When the cremation of the corpses started, this team was enlarged, for it also had to supply the wood for the bonfires on which the corpses were burned.

In Treblinka a second prisoners' group worked outside the camp. It was called the camouflage team and numbered approximately twenty-five. Its task was to camouflage with branches the camp's outer and inner fences, especially the fences around the extermination area and the "tube." This was intended to prevent outside observation of camp activities, as well as observation from within the camp of what transpired on the way to the gas chambers and in the extermination area. The team workers would cut branches in the forests near the camp and weave them into the barbed-wire fences. Since it was constantly necessary to replace dried-out branches with fresh ones, the camouflage work was continuous. These groups of prisoners left the camp confines under a strong guard of Germans and Ukrainians.

In addition to these groups in the main camp, whose work was connected with the extermination process, part of the prisoners were employed at other activities. Groups of prisoners were engaged in construction of barracks, in stringing barbed-wire fences, and in paving roads inside the camps. In the autumn and winter a special "potato team" was established. Potatoes were the camp's principal food, and as winter approached, large quantities were brought to the camp. To prevent the potatoes from freezing and spoiling, special cellars were prepared where they would be processed daily. The potato workers supplied the potatoes to the kitchens of the SS, the

Ukrainians, and the Jews. Some prisoners worked in the vegetable garden, pigsty, chicken coop, and cowshed, and in the SS personnel's baths. A few prisoners were employed in cleaning and disinfecting the huts and toilets.

There were also prisoners who supplied direct personal services to the SS and Ukrainians. They included doctors, a dentist, and several barbers. A small group of boys was employed to polish and clean the shoes and uniforms of SS personnel. These boys worked in and around the SS barracks. In addition, there were groups of skilled workers, like tailors, shoemakers, smiths, mechanics, carpenters, and others, known as the "court Jews," who continued to extend services to the German and Ukrainian staff, as they had since the first stages of the camps' activity.

THE PRISONERS IN THE EXTERMINATION AREA

The decision to establish a permanent prisoner staff in the camp applied to the extermination area as well. The Jews there faced more difficult living and working conditions than those throughout the rest of the camp. They had to remove the bodies of the dead from the gas chambers and carry them to the burial ditches, located up to one hundred meters away. This work was carried out at a constant run, since the extermination rate, and consequently the work pace of the entire camp, was determined by it. Prisoners who could not stand up to this pace of work were beaten and shot. Moreover, the nature of their work affected the men to an extreme, and before they would collapse physically they would often break emotionally. Thus the attrition rate in the extermination area was high; workers there survived but a few days, and dozens were shot daily, sometimes for no reason at all. Others were brought to replace them from among the prisoners in the other part of the camp or directly from the incoming transports. The decision to create a permanent camp workforce brought about a drop in the rate of executions of workers in the extermination area and some improvement in their living conditions. A core of prisoners who could handle the work for longer periods began to form. Here, too, the prisoners were divided into work teams.

The Gas Chamber Body-Disposal Team

This group of several dozen men had the job of removing the bodies from the gas chambers and taking them through the rear doors to the concrete platform built alongside the chambers. There they laid the bodies for removal by the body transport team. The body-disposal team's work was the hardest physically and emotionally. After gassing, the hundreds of people packed standing up in the gas chambers became a solid block of bodies. Separating and removing them was extremely difficult. At times the workers who entered the chambers immediately after they were opened were themselves poisoned by the residue of gas remaining there.[9]

Gas Chamber and "Tube" Cleaners

This group cleaned the blood and excrement off the floor and walls of the gas chambers, as the chambers had to be clean before introducing a new group of victims. This group also cleaned the "tube" and scattered fresh sand on the ground.

The Body-Transport Team (Leichenkommando)

This was the largest prisoner work team in the extermination area, comprising some one hundred men. Its task was to carry the bodies from the platform next to the gas chambers to the mass burial ditches. After experimenting with various methods of conveying the bodies, the Germans fixed upon stretchers as the fastest way. Two men carried the stretcher, which looked like a ladder with leather carrying straps. The bodies were placed on the stretchers face up to facilitate the work of the *Dentisten*.

The "Dentists (Dentisten)"

The prisoner work team known as the *Dentisten* was located between the gas chambers and the burial ditches. It numbered about twenty to thirty men whose job was to extract, with pliers, the gold, platinum, and false teeth from the corpses. The dentists also examined the bodies, especially those of the women, for valuables hidden in the body orifices. Part of the team worked at cleaning and sorting the extracted teeth and preparing them for shipment.

The Burial Detail

This group of several dozen men worked at the burial ditches. After the victims' bodies were thrown into a pit by the body-transport workers, the corpses were arranged in rows by the burial detail. To save space, the bodies were arranged head to foot; each head lay between the feet of two other corpses, and each pair of feet between two heads. Sand or chlorine was scattered between the layers of bodies. Approximately half the team worked inside the ditches arranging the corpses at the same time that the other half was covering a layer of bodies with sand. When a ditch filled up, it was topped off with earth and a new ditch was opened.

Kitchen and Service Workers

A kitchen and a laundry for the prisoners were established in the extermination area to prevent any contact between the prisoners in the two sections of the camp. A group of craftsmen was also organized in the extermination area for building and maintenance tasks, again in order to avoid contact with the main camp. These innovations caused the Jewish prisoner group in the extermination area to grow to around two hundred; at times it neared three hundred.

The absolute division of the Jewish prisoners between those in the main camp and those in the extermination area existed in Sobibor and Treblinka. There is no certainty whether such a division existed in Belzec. One of the two survivors of Belzec, Rudolf Reder, in his book about this camp, referred to all the Jewish prisoners in this camp as one group. However, in the testimonies given by SS men who served in Belzec, the Jews were divided into two separate groups.[10]

Work team assignments were not permanent, with the exception of certain specialists. The size of the work groups also varied from time to time. Men would be transferred from group to group according to requirements and priorities determined by the Germans. When the number of deportee transports increased, the groups engaged in the work connected directly with the extermination process were expanded. When transport frequency dropped, more prisoners were sent to the sorting team to prepare clothing and belongings for shipment from the camp and to maintenance and construction works. Occasionally, work teams were set up ad hoc for a specific task and then disbanded. Prisoner traffic between the main camp and the extermination area was one way only. Those sent to the extermination area for work never returned to the main camp. Details of what went on in the extermination area were to remain secret from the rest of the camp's prisoners.

The process of reorganizing the Jewish prisoner cadres in the camps and converting them into a permanent staff continued for many weeks. In Treblinka, the last camp where this change took place, it lasted from the second half of September until the end of October. To ensure control and identification of prisoners, each received a number, which he had to wear on the left side of his chest. The number was backed by a triangular piece of leather, and each work team's triangle was of a different color.[11] The numbers were given out in late 1942.

Even after the reorganization, the executions of Jewish prisoners from the work staff continued, but on a far more limited scale than had existed in the past. Nor were such executions within the framework of a fixed policy of renewing the cadres every few days. Now the victims were prisoners whom the SS men found unfit to continue working, or those punished either individually or collectively for real or imagined violations. Those who were executed were replaced by new deportees. This was the procedure that would be maintained for the remainder of the camps' existence.

CHAPTER SIXTEEN

WOMEN PRISONERS

THE PERMANENT PRISONER STAFF IN the camps also included Jewish women. In Sobibor Jewish women prisoners were employed from the early stage of the camp's activity. From a transport that arrived in Sobibor on June 2, 1942, three girls were taken by SS *Oberscharführer* Gustav Wagner and left there to work. Ada Lichtman, one of those girls, described her first day in Sobibor:

> We were ordered to clean thoroughly a villa where the Germans lived. After work we were taken to an area with some barracks, surrounded by a barbed-wire fence where we were given a room with three wooden beds, one over the other. Close to our room lived the skilled workers.... In the evening, two men brought two big boxes with dirty laundry, and a Ukrainian guard told us that it should be ready within two days.... The washing required many different kinds of work. The laundry was full of lice, so first of all it had to be disinfected. We had to raise the water from a deep well with heavy wooden buckets tied to a rope. The laundry had to be boiled at a distant place. The wet laundry was transported in a baby carriage.[1]

The number of women in Sobibor increased gradually. They cleaned the SS living barracks, worked in the kitchen, and ironed the clothes of the SS men. In the autumn about fifteen young women and girls, who were asked whether they knew how to knit, were taken by SS *Oberscharführer* Gustav Wagner from a transport and put in a special room. Wagner brought them wool, taken from baggage left by the murdered Jews, and ordered them to knit knee-high socks and pullover sweaters. These would warm the SS men of the camp in the coming winter. Wagner made the women work and sleep in the same barrack, away from the other prisoners, who were infected with lice. He gave them clothes, soap, and water so that they could keep clean and not infect the woolen socks and pullovers with lice. The capo of this knitting group was Mrs. Shapiro, a Viennese woman.[2]

From the transports from Holland and other European countries to Sobibor, additional girls and young women were selected. From a transport that arrived from Holland on April 9, 1943, twenty-eight women were selected for work. At that time the women were employed not only in services, but also in sorting and packing the clothes and other articles left by the victims. Other women were engaged in the vegetable garden and flower beds that were planted at the gate and along the roads in the camp. The SS men selected some women singers for entertainment. From one of the transports from Vienna, they selected three beautiful singers, who were forced to perform. After a short period, when the SS men had enough of their performances, they were executed.[3]

In the last months of the camp, women were even engaged in construction works. At that time the number of Jewish women in Sobibor had reached 150.[4] According to available evidence and documentation, there were no women among the Jewish prisoners in the extermination area of Sobibor. At the end of the war, eight Jewish women prisoners from Sobibor had survived.

In Treblinka, among the Jews originally employed in building the camp, there were a few women who worked in the SS kitchen as helpers to the Polish female cooks from the surrounding villages.[5] With the organization of a permanent prisoner staff, camp authorities decided to set up a Jewish women's work team for the laundries. The Lower Camp held three such laundries—for the SS men, the Ukrainians, and the Jewish prisoners. About twenty-five to thirty women were selected from the transports that arrived during the second half of September 1942. Of these, most were sent to work in the laundries; a few professional seamstresses were attached to the men working in the sewing shop; and others were placed in the kitchen. Their number gradually grew, until by the end of the winter of 1942–1943, there were about fifty women in the camp.

Occasionally additional women were selected from new transports. Bronka Sukno, who arrived from Warsaw in Treblinka on January 18, 1943, related how she alone was selected:

> After we arrived at Treblinka, they separated the women from the men and ordered us to remove our shoes and clothing. I stood at the [transport] square without disrobing. A moment later I was pushed by SS man Franz Suchomel into a hut where clothing was being sorted. . . . After about two hours there, Suchomel took me to the laundry where the Germans' clothing was washed and ironed. On the way Suchomel told me not to ask any questions, and to remember that I had neither heard nor seen a thing. The next day they took me to work in the tailor's shop.[6]

Most of the women at Treblinka were young, between eighteen and thirty, although there were a few younger girls and a few older women. The women's capo in the Lower Camp was a woman named Perla or, as she was usually called, "Paulinka." She was notorious for her poor treatment of women prisoners and her informing to the Germans.[7]

There were no women among the prisoners in the extermination area until mid-February 1943. A typhus epidemic had swept the camp that winter and claimed many victims, particularly in the extermination area. As a result, camp authorities decided to improve sanitary facilities in that part of the camp by setting up a laundry for the clothing of the prisoner work teams there. Until then the prisoners had been wearing the same filthy clothes, soaked with the blood of the corpses they handled, for weeks and even months on end, seldom receiving a fresh change of clothing from the Lower Camp. A group of young women was selected from a transport of Jews brought from the Grodna area in February 1943, and transferred to the extermination area. Eli Rozenberg described their arrival: "At that time thirteen girls were brought to the camp: six were employed in the laundry, three in the kitchen, one by the camp doctor as an aide, and the others were allotted to the various capos."[8] As few women were also transferred from the Lower Camp to the extermination area, this meant that the total number in the Upper Camp reached fifteen or twenty. The women's capo there was Lila Ephroimson. Sonia Lewkowicz, the sole survivor of the group of women who worked in this part of the camp, gave highly favorable testimony on Ephroimson's behavior as women's capo.[9]

There was also a married couple, the Blau family from Vienna, in the extermination area—a highly unusual circumstance. Treblinka commander Franz Stangl knew the Blau family from his own days in Vienna; when they arrived at Treblinka in a transport, Stangl recognized them by chance and saved them. A while later Blau was appointed "camp elder" in the extermination area, and his wife was transferred there, too. Later, Blau was exempted from this task for health reasons, following which, as Suchomel related: "Stangl then appointed him and his wife as cooks for the Jews. The old lady Blau was a good cook and she often made me meals. I ate the food in our dining hall and she often cooked me special dishes."[10]

From all the women prisoners at Treblinka, only two survived.

Since most of the women were young and pretty, they caught the eyes of the SS men. Suchomel told of one: "Chesia Mendel was the only true blond in the camp. . . . Everyone agreed that she stood out for her intelligence, and she was proud and bold. She was one of the few Jews whom we Germans all addressed not in the familiar *du* but in the third person *sie*."[11]

The women prisoners, who were at the mercy of the SS men, were in some cases sexually abused and later murdered. Two women from Austria, Ruth and Gisela, who were film or theater actresses, were kept in Sobibor in the kitchen of the forester house, where some SS men lived. After being used by the SS men, they were shot. SS *Oberscharführer* Erich Bauer testified:

> I was blamed for being responsible for the death of the Jewish girls Ruth and Gisela, who lived in the so-called forester house. As it is known, these two girls lived in the forester house, and they were visited frequently by the SS men. Orgies were conducted there. They were attended by [Kurt] Bolender, [Hubert] Gomerski, Karl Ludwig, Franz Stangl, Gustav Wagner, and Steubel. I lived in the room above them and due to these celebrations could not fall asleep after coming back from a journey. . . . One evening Karl Ludwig banged on the girls' door. Evidently he wanted to enter. The girls opened the door in my presence. Ludwig ordered the girls to put on their dressing gowns, and both of us took them in the direction of Camp III. I went halfway only and then returned. Ludwig went with them alone. Next day Ludwig told me that by his order a Ukrainian had shot the two girls.[12]

Another case, what may be considered a love affair, transpired in Sobibor between an SS man, Paul Groth, and a Jewish girl. Favorably affected by his love, Groth changed his behavior toward the Jewish prisoners and acted more humanely. This relationship was viewed by the commanders of Sobibor as an abuse of the Aryan race (*Rassenschande*), and one day, while Groth was outside the camp, the Jewish girl was taken to Camp III and killed.[13]

The women in the camps lived in separate barracks from the other prisoners, and at morning and evening roll call they formed up separately from the men. They slept on double-decker bunks and their food was like that served the men—though occasionally they received extras from the SS men or Ukrainians at their place of work. The camp guards treated the women more humanely than they did the men, and there were few instances of women being beaten or otherwise punished.

Women also had easier access to the means for maintaining personal hygiene. In the laundries and kitchen they could use the water to wash daily, while the male prisoners were denied this "luxury."

Men also assisted the women in their work, carrying out the more physically strenuous tasks. In the laundries the men carried the water in buckets from the wells, while the women washed and ironed. A similar setup existed in the kitchen and elsewhere where men and women prisoners worked together.

The last Operation Reinhard camp to introduce Jewish women prisoners to work was Belzec. This was in October 1942. Rudolf Reder wrote:

> A transport with Jewish women from Czechoslovakia arrived in October. . . .
> It was decided that from this transport a few dozen women would remain. . . .

Forty women were assigned to work in the kitchen, in the laundry and in the tailor shop. . . . I don't know what happened to them. No doubt, they shared the fate of all the others. They were intelligent women. They brought their baggage with them. Some of them had butter with them. They gave us what they had. Those who worked in the kitchen helped us with food. They lived in a separate barrack and had their own capo. . . . They were not so badly treated as we were. They finished their work at dusk and waited in line for soup and coffee. As we, they were dressed in their own dresses and had no particular mark. . . . Through the windows of the kitchen and tailor shop they watched the daily arrival of the transports of death.[14]

No women survived Belzec death camp.

The presence of the women in the camps influenced the behavior of the male prisoners and even the SS men there. The small, closed world of the doomed prisoners took on an added dimension. They had some reference point, some vague reminder of a different life they had once led.

CHAPTER SEVENTEEN

IMPROVING EXTERMINATION TECHNIQUES AND INSTALLATIONS

IN THE COURSE OF THE reorganization that followed the first stage of operation, larger gas chambers and other attendant facilities were erected in Treblinka and Sobibor. The new gas chambers that had been built in Belzec in June/July 1942 served as a model in the other two camps.

TREBLINKA

The commanders of Operation Reinhard were of the opinion that the most urgent need was to increase the absorptive capacity of the gas chambers in Treblinka; as a result of their limited capacity, the extermination process suffered from complete chaos as early as the first month of activity. Therefore, one of Franz Stangl's first priorities when appointed commander of the camp was to erect a new building for the gas chambers next to the old one. This was carried out while the extermination activities in the old one continued. Christian Wirth, as inspector of the death camps, dispatched *Scharführer* Lorenz Hackenholt, who was in charge of the gas chambers in Belzec, to assist in the erection of the new gas chambers in Treblinka.

Construction of the new gas chambers began in early September. The new building comprised ten gas chambers, each 4 by 8 meters, although according to some sources the new building included only six gas chambers.[1] In place of the three old chambers, which together covered 48 square meters, the ten new chambers had a combined area of 320 square meters (or 192 square meters if there were only six). The height of the new rooms was 2 meters—about 60 centimeters lower than the old ones. There had been instances in the old chambers in which little children had not been asphyxiated because the gas rose to the ceiling, and this was taken into account in planning the height of the ceilings in the new chambers. Lowering the ceiling also reduced the chambers' total cubic volume, reduced the total gas requirement for killing the victims, and shortened asphyxiation time.

The new structure was rectangular. A corridor ran through the length of the building down the middle, with gas chambers on either side. The entrance doors and body-removal doors for each chamber were similar to the old setup. The doors contained a small glass window, through which the SS men and Ukrainians checked to see what was happening and ascertained whether the victims were already dead. The entrance to the corridor was covered by a dark Jewish ceremonial curtain taken from an unidentified synagogue. On it was inscribed in Hebrew: "This is the Gateway to God. Righteous men will pass through." A gable over the entrance door bore a large Star of David. To reach the door, one climbed five wide steps with potted plants on either side.

The new building, with its decorative steps, plants, and curtain, was located at the end of the "tube." The victims who were forced to run through the "tube" continued straight up the entrance steps and into the corridor flanked by the gas chambers. The engine room was at the end of the building close to the old gas chambers.

To speed up the pace of construction, a group of Jewish builders was brought from Warsaw. They were selected from a transport that had been scheduled to be sent to Treblinka in early September 1942. Forty Jewish prisoners were employed in building the new gas chambers.[2] Jacob Wiernik described the emotional state of the Jewish prisoners engaged in the construction work:

> The work of building the new chambers lasted five weeks. To us it seemed an eternity. The work went on from sunrise to sunset, under the whips and rifle butts. One of the guards, Woronikov, beat and maltreated us mercilessly. Every day a few workers were murdered. While our physical distress was far beyond normal human concepts, it was our morale that suffered even more. Every day new transports arrived; the deportees were ordered to strip, and then they were taken to the three old gas chambers. The way to the chambers passed near the construction site. Several of us discovered their children, wives, or relatives among the victims. If anyone was moved by his anguish to run to his family, they shot him on the spot. Thus we built the death chambers for ourselves and for our brothers.[3]

The new gas chambers could absorb a maximum of twenty-three hundred people (six chambers) or thirty-eight hundred people (ten chambers) simultaneously, whereas the old one could hold only six hundred. With the inauguration of the new gas chambers, in the middle of October 1942, the old ones ceased to function. The old structure was now converted into a tailor's shop, where several prisoners from the extermination area worked. The SS officials in charge of the gas chambers were Gustav Münzberger and Fritz Schmidt.[4]

When asked during his trial how many people could be murdered in one day, Stangl answered: "Regarding the question of what was the optimum amount of people gassed in one day, I can state: according to my estimation a transport of thirty freight cars with 3,000 people was liquidated in three hours. When the work lasted for about fourteen hours, 12,000 to 15,000 people were annihilated. There were many days that the work lasted from the early morning until the evening."[5]

SS *Oberscharführer* Heinrich Matthes, who was in charge of Camp III (with the gas chambers), described the killing operations there:

> During the entire time that I was in Treblinka, I served in the Upper Camp. The Upper Camp was that part of Treblinka with the gas chambers, where the Jews were killed and their corpses laid in large pits and later burned.
>
> About fourteen Germans carried out services in the Upper Camp. There were two Ukrainians permanently in the Upper Camp. One of them was called Nikolai. The other was a short man, I don't remember his name. . . . These two Ukrainians who lived in the Upper Camp served in the gas chambers. They also took care of the engine room when Fritz Schmidt was absent. Usually this Schmidt was in charge of the engine room. In my opinion, as a civilian he was either a mechanic or driver. He came from Pirna. . . .
>
> I carried out the roll calls of the working Jews in the Upper Camp. There were about 200–300 such working Jews. They took away the corpses and later burned them. There were also working Jews who had to break out the gold teeth from the corpses. When I asked whether a special working group examined the corpses for hidden jewelry and valuables, I answered: "About this I don't know." In the Upper [Camp] in the area of the gas chambers were stationed about six to eight Ukrainians. These Ukrainians were armed with rifles. Some of them also had leather whips. . . .
>
> The people who were brought through the passage were forced to enter the separate [single] gas chamber. Later, in summer 1942, the new gas chambers were built. I think that they became operational only in the autumn. All together, six gas chambers were active. According to my estimate, about 300 people could enter each gas chamber. The people went into the gas chambers without resistance. Those who were at the end, the Ukrainian guards had to push inside. I personally saw how the Ukrainians pushed the people with their rifle butts. . . .
>
> The gas chambers were closed for about thirty minutes. Then Schmidt stopped the gassing, and the two Ukrainians who were in the engine room opened the gas chambers from the other side.[6]

Another extermination facility in Treblinka was the *Lazarett*. Near the camp's southern fence were huge pits, where the tens of thousands who had died in the freight cars on their way to Treblinka were buried alongside those who had been shot on or near the camp train platform. At these pits, too, the prisoners who worked in the camp during the first stage of operation were shot and killed after a day or so of work.

The need for these pits had stemmed from the high mortality rate inside the transport trains and the insufficient capacity of the three original gas chambers. After construction of the new gas chambers and the resultant reduction in the time of the train journey to Treblinka, the need for these pits was sharply reduced. Henceforth, they were used for executing those deportees who lacked the strength to walk to the "showers" on their own, as well as the Jewish prisoners from the camp.

Following these changes, the area set aside for execution by shooting was reduced in size. The camp command decided to give the area the appearance of a hospital, which became known in the camp as *Lazarett*. The *Lazarett* covered an area of 150 to 200 square meters and was surrounded by a barbed-wire fence laced with branches. The entrance to the *Lazarett* area was decorated with a red cross, and next to it was a sign, "Lazarett." Inside was a small hut, and behind it a ditch twelve meters long and four meters deep. Next to the ditch was an earth rampart with benches. Those about to die were told to strip and sit on the benches. One of the Germans or Ukrainians shot them. The dead bodies fell or were pushed into the ditch, where a fire was always burning, which consumed the bodies.

Scharführer August Miete, who was in charge of the *Lazarett* and was called the "Angel of Death" by the prisoners, described the *Lazarett* executions in his testimony at the Treblinka trial:

> There were always sick and crippled people in the transports. . . . There were also those who had been shot and wounded en route by SS, policemen, or Latvians who guarded the transports. These ill, crippled, and wounded passengers were brought to the *Lazarett* by a special group of workers. Inside the *Lazarett* they placed or lay these people at the edge of the pit. When all the sick and wounded had been brought, it was my job to shoot them. I fired at the nape of the neck with a 9 mm pistol. Those shot would fall . . . into the pit. . . . The number of people shot in this way from each transport varied. Sometimes two or three, and sometimes twenty or even more. They included men and women, young and old, and also children.[7]

The construction work on various camp facilities continued for months. Originally the train platform where deportees arrived had none of the accoutrements of a normal railroad station. Stangl, as camp commander, decided that, to enhance the illusion and deception that was intended to dupe the arriving victims—and particularly those in transports coming from outside Poland—the platform should be made to look like a genuine train station. The front of the northern barrack, which was adjacent to the platform and served as a storage shed for victims' belongings, was altered completely. Fake doors and windows were installed, along with signs that read "Ticket Counter," "Waiting Room," "Information," "Telegraph

Office," "Station Manager," "Rest Rooms," and so on. An incoming and outgoing train schedule was posted at the station, complete with signs and arrows directing passengers "To the Bialystok Train" or "To the Volkovysk Train." A large dummy clock was affixed to the building. Trees and flower beds were planted nearby. The barrack itself continued to serve as a storage shed.[8]

These changes were carried out at the end of 1942. Deportees arriving in Treblinka disembarked into what seemed to be an ordinary railroad station from which trains continued in various directions.

Sobibor

The last camp at which the new, larger gas chambers were installed was Sobibor. The three single-room gas chambers, with a killing capacity of a mere six hundred people, could not cope with the tasks imposed on this camp. During the two-month lull in extermination activities in the autumn of 1942, the old gas chambers were partially dismantled and the three additional gas chambers were built. The construction of these gas chambers was done under the guidance of SS *Unterscharführer* Erwin Herman Lambert, who had erected the new gas chambers in Treblinka, and SS *Scharführer* Lorenz Hackenholt, who was in charge of the gas chambers in Belzec. They were both sent to Sobibor by Christian Wirth. Lambert testified:

> As I mentioned at the beginning, I was in the extermination camp of the Jews for about two to three weeks. It was sometime in autumn 1942, but I don't remember exactly when. At that time I was assigned by Wirth to enlarge the gassing structure according to the model of Treblinka. I went to Sobibor together with Lorenz Hackenholt, who was at that time in Treblinka. First of all, I went with Hackenholt to a sawmill near Warsaw. There Hackenholt ordered a big consignment of wood for reconstruction in Sobibor. Finally, both of us went to Sobibor. We reported there to the camp commander, [Franz] Reichleitner. He gave us the exact directives for the construction of the gassing installations. The camp was already in operation, and there was a gassing installation. Probably the old installation was not big enough, and reconstruction was necessary. Today I cannot tell exactly who participated in the reconstruction work. However, I do remember that Jewish prisoners and so-called "Askaries" [Ukrainian auxiliaries] took part in the work. During the time that building was in progress, no transports with Jews arrived.[9]

The new six-room gas chamber building had a corridor that ran through its center, and three rooms on either side. The entrance to each gas chamber was from the corridor. The three gas chambers were the same size as the existing one, four by four meters. The killing capacity of the gas chambers was increased to nearly thirteen hundred people simultaneously. With the renewal of the extermination activities in Sobibor, in October 1942, the new gas chambers became operational.

Another technical improvement introduced in Sobibor was a narrow railway trolley that ran from the disembarking platform to the burial pits in Camp III. It was to replace the carts pushed by prisoners or the horse-drawn carts on which the dead, the sick, and those unable to walk from the train were transferred to the pits. According to *Oberscharführer* Hubert Gomerski, who was in charge of Camp III, the length of the narrow railway was about three hundred to four hundred meters. It included five or six trolleys and a small diesel locomotive.[10]

Scharführer Erich Bauer testified:

> Part of the trolleys and rails originated from the sawmill that bordered the Sobibor camp. Additional trolleys and rails arrived by train from Trawniki. The locomotive of this train came later, about two months after the trolley was in operation. At the beginning horses pulled the trolleys. As I explained in previous interrogations, the trolley was laid to transport the sick and handicapped Jews from the arriving trains to Camp III. I know that these people, including the handicapped and sick, children, and particularly infants, were taken to the so-called *Lazarett*, and there they were shot by those serving in Camp III. . . . It was known in the camps that this *Lazarett* was used not for healing but for the extermination of the people.[11]

CHAPTER EIGHTEEN

THE ANNIHILATION OF THE JEWS IN THE GENERAL GOVERNMENT

AFTER THE CHANGE IN COMMAND and the reorganization of the manpower in the camps, the enlargement of the gas chambers and improvements in the killing process, the extermination pace was stepped up considerably. The death camps turned into murder factories that could meet all the demands of those in charge of Operation Reinhard.

The large-scale deportations of the General Government Jews proceeded without disruption. Planned and coordinated from Operation Reinhard headquarters in Lublin, the expulsion of the Jews was carried out by the district SS and police leaders. From their headquarters in Cracow, German railroad authorities in occupied Poland (*Gedob*) planned the train schedule and allocated cars and engines accordingly. As transports to the death camps were outside the framework of normal passenger or freight-train traffic, their movements along the track system and via the way stations en route to the camps were coordinated by "travel timetable orders" (*Fahrplananordnung*) issued by the railroad authorities in Cracow. These detailed each station stop, the number and type of freight cars in the transport, arrival and departure times to and from the camps, the train's destination once empty, and the fact that the train would be cleaned by prisoners before leaving the camp.

The trip-plans used a code to indicate a transport's region of origin. Deportations from the General Government were indicated by the code PKR; those from the Bialystok district were PJ; and from Germany—or other countries that necessitated crossing Germany—DA. Railroad personnel were ordered to report to railroad authorities the number of people in each transport before it reached the camps.[1]

A series of new documents was published over a decade ago, particularly those of the British Secret Service's wiretapping of telephones from the beginning of January 1943. These documents state a lower number of victims than the numbers discussed here. See chapter 48 for reference and analysis of these numbers.[2]

The deportations to Belzec were renewed in the second week of July 1942 and lasted until the middle of December 1942. Rudolf Reder wrote:

> From August up to the end of November 1942, I was in the death camp. It was the period of the mass gassing of the Jews. The few of my friends of suffering who had succeeded in surviving there a longer time told me that in that period there was the largest number of transports of death. They came every day, without interruption, three times daily. Each train numbered fifty cars, with hundreds of people in each one of them. When the transports arrived at night, the victims of Belzec waited in closed cars until 6 o'clock in the morning. Sometimes the transports were larger and more frequent. Jews arrived from everywhere—and only Jews. Never were there any other transports. Belzec served only to kill Jews.[3]

From the district of Cracow, over 140,000 Jews were deported to Belzec between July 7 and November 15, 1942. From the Lvov district, about 240,000 Jews were deported between the end of July and mid-December 1942. About 8,000 Jews were deported to Belzec from the towns of Sandomierz and Zawichost from the district of Radom, and an additional 25,600 from the southern parts of the Lublin district (Bilgoraj and Janow counties).

From the second half of December 1942, no further transports arrived in Belzec, and the mass murder there ceased. The fact that the plan to deport 200,000 Jews from Rumania had been abandoned (see chapter 7) meant that there were no more potential victims for this camp.

The number of Jews deported and murdered in Belzec from identified towns and townships in this stage of the operation was about 414,000. From hundreds of small towns and villages located in these districts, thousands of Jews were deported to Belzec, but no documents or survivors were left and therefore no exact numbers can be determined. Thousands of Jews from Germany, Austria, the Czech Republic and Slovakia, and other countries who had been deported to the ghettos in the Lublin district were also sent to Belzec and murdered there. Hence, we need to include the 93,000 Jews annihilated in Belzec between March and June 1942 to the number mentioned previously. The number of 600,000 Jews, as estimated by the official Polish committee to investigate Nazi crimes in occupied Poland, seems to be the most accurate we have. At the Belzec trial, SS Scharführers Heinrich Gley and Robert Juhrs estimated that 500,000 to 540,000 corpses of murdered Jews had been burned in the months between November 1942 and March 1943. The estimated number of 600,000 was also accepted by the Landgericht München in the Federal Republic of Germany in the Belzec-Oberhauser Trial.[4]

The deportations to Treblinka, which were renewed on September 3, 1942, included transports from the Warsaw district, the Radom district, and the northern part of the Lublin district, all of which were in the vicinity of this camp. The deportations continued without pause until mid-November 1942. During this period 438,600 Jews from the ghettos of the General Government were murdered in Treblinka. Aron Gelberd, who was deported to Treblinka from Czestochowa in October 1942 and was there for nineteen days until his successful escape, wrote that during that time each day three or four transports arrived in the camp, and some of them even came at night.[5]

From mid-November 1942 until January 1943 there were almost no transports from the General Government to Treblinka. During that period transports from Bialystok were sent there. (See chapter 19.) In January 1943, some small ghettos were finally liquidated, and the Jews were deported to Treblinka. From the Warsaw ghetto some transports with between five thousand and six thousand Jews were sent to this camp in the second half of January 1943. The Warsaw ghetto with its sixty thousand Jews was totally liquidated at the end of April 1943. The ghetto uprising began with the start of the liquidation on April 19 and the fighting continued until the second half of May.

During the first days of the uprising, the Germans were met with fierce opposition from the Jewish fighters resulting in German deaths and casualties. They then adopted a systematic strategy of setting fire and then bombing house after house. The thousands of Jews who did not respond to the deportation warrants found their deaths among the debris of the burned and destroyed homes—or were burned to death in their hideouts. Those who survived the burned down and destroyed houses were deported to Madjanek and the work camps at Trawniki and Poniatowa. Several transports reached Treblinka. From one of the transports that arrived in Treblinka late in April 1943, some 220 young men were selected and sent to a labor camp in Budzyn, near Lublin. In the period from January to April 1943, 31,500 Jews were deported to Treblinka from the General Government.

From the beginning of the extermination activities in Treblinka, on July 23, 1942, until the end of April 1943, about 763,000 Jews from the ghettos of the General Government were murdered there (see Appendix A).[6]

Sobibor

The deportations and killing operations were renewed in Sobibor at the beginning of October 1942, after the repair works on the Lublin-Chelm railway were accomplished. This stage of the deportations from the ghettos in the General Government continued at a relatively slow pace, until the beginning of May 1943.

Dov Freiberg, who was in Sobibor at that time, wrote about these transports from Poland:

> The people who arrived from the last ghettos and labor camps of Poland had already passed through the seven circles of hell before they reached Sobibor. They were in despair; they already knew what awaited them; and there was no need to tell them stories. The Germans did not even address them. They shouted at them to take off their clothes quickly, maltreated and struck them until the last moment. The deportees asked whether it would take much time until the gas chambers. There were among them people who had escaped from the *Aktionen*, who had jumped from the trains, who had been in the forests, who had gone into hiding, but did not find refuge and had returned to the ghettos knowing exactly what awaited them.[7]

One transport to Sobibor that left an especially shocking impression on the prisoners there included Jews from Majdanek concentration camp. In this transport there were about five thousand prisoners. They wore the striped prisoners' clothes, and many of these utterly weakened Jews had died en route. When this transport arrived, the gas chambers were inactive because of a mechanical breakdown, so the prisoners were kept during the day and night in an open area between Camp I and Camp II. During the night, two hundred of them died, some of exhaustion and others from the blows and shootings of the SS men. The people were so weak that they could not even cry; only groans were heard. In the morning those who still had some strength were forced to support the weak, and all of them were taken to the gas chambers.[8] A group of Jewish prisoners from the camp staff was ordered to remove the corpses that remained on the square. Dov Freiberg, one of these prisoners, wrote:

> The SS man Frenzel selected twenty prisoners and told us that we should work naked because the corpses were dirty and full of lice. We had to take the dead to the trolley, a distance of about 200 meters. In spite of the fact that we were used to this kind of work, I cannot describe our feelings when we carried the dead on our naked bodies. The Germans urged us with shouts and blows. While I was dragging a man's body, I stopped for a while and, not seeing a German nearby, I laid it on the ground. And then the body, which I thought was of a dead man, rose up, looked at me with great eyes and asked: "Is it still far?" He said these words with great effort and collapsed.... At that moment I felt lashes on my head and back. The SS man Frenzel whipped me. I caught the living dead by his feet and dragged him to the trolley.[9]

In October and in the beginning of November 1942, close to 28,000 people were deported to Sobibor from the Lublin district. From that time until the beginning of May 1943, more transports arrived sporadically from the Lublin district with an additional forty-five hundred Jews. (See Appendix A.)

In the winter of 1942–43 and in the spring and summer of 1943, transports arrived in Sobibor with Jews from the Lvov district. In some of the transports the Jews were naked. They were forced to undress before entering the freight cars, to make it more difficult for them to escape from the train. One of these transports during the winter stopped at Belzec, but this camp was already in its closing stage and could not receive the human cargo; the transport was subsequently dispatched to Sobibor.[10]

In her testimony Ada Lichtman told of a transport that arrived from Lvov in the winter; nude corpses were removed from the closed freight cars. "The prisoner 'Platform Workers' said that the corpses were frozen and stuck to one another, and when they were laid on the trolley, they disintegrated, and parts of them fell off. These people had had a long voyage and their corpses crumbled."[11]

Leon Feldhendler, a prisoner in Sobibor, wrote about a transport that arrived from Lvov in June 1943: "There were fifty freight cars all together—twenty-five of them with living prisoners, and twenty-five with corpses. The living were nude. In the freight cars with the killed, the corpses were mingled, without any wounds, only swollen. The prisoners were forced to unload the freight cars and put the corpses on the trolley to the crematorium. The smell of the corpses made it impossible to enter the freight cars. The Germans whipped us to force us to enter them. From the state of disintegration of the bodies, these people had been dead for about two weeks."[12]

From these testimonies it is difficult to evaluate the number of Jews from the Lvov district who were deported to Sobibor and murdered there after the Belzec camp stopped its extermination activities. There were some such transports, and the number of Jews in them can be estimated at between 15,000 and 25,000.[13] The number of Jews deported to Sobibor from the General Government from October 1942 through June 1943 was between 70,000 and 80,000. The total number of Jews from the General Government deported to Sobibor was between 145,000 and 155,000 (see Appendix A).

MAJDANEK

Majdanek was similar to the Third Reich's other concentration camps, though it was unique due to the additional roles it filled. The camp, established in the suburbs of Lublin, was initially founded as a camp for Soviet POWs; following an agreement between Heinrich Himmler and the Wehrmacht command, a number of POWs were to be given to the SS for its own purposes. Construction began in July 1941; the first prisoners and Soviet POWs began arriving in October. In April 1942, Himmler designated the camp as a "camp for prisoners of war, as well as a concentration camp";[14] until the spring of 1943 the camp's description was the Waffen-SS POW Camp.

Officially, the camp fell under the supervision of the SS Main Economic and Administrative Department (*SS-Wirtschafts-Verwaltungshauptamt*). Odilo Globocnik was in charge of the camp's additional and specific functions, namely Germanization of the East and to be part of Operation Reinhard. Given these roles, and the camp's location in Lublin, the camp was actually under Globocnik's command. The camp served as a selection site for Jews—eligible for work—from among those arriving on transports, which would later be redirected to other extermination camps. This selection took place at the Lublin train station. A number of these able-bodied Jews worked in forced labor within the camp—including working on its establishment and expansion—while others were sent to work camps and SS economic enterprises in the Lublin area. Majdanek served as a base for receiving money, valuables, clothes, and any other items left behind by victims deported from the ghettos and from within the extermination camps. Thousands of Jews—men and women—before being sent on to their various destinations, were employed at Majdanek sorting through and dealing with the possessions of Operation Reinhard's victims. (See chapter 22.)[15]

There is no exact data regarding total number of people—including Jews, Poles, and Soviet POWs—who were held in the camp or spent any amount of time there, as well as to the total number of victims there.

Regarding Jews specifically, one can ascertain they were brought to, and passed through the camp, starting from when it became operational in the fall of 1941 and up until the summer of 1944. During the Warsaw ghetto uprising and liquidation in April–May 1943, fifteen thousand Jews were brought from Warsaw to the camp; close to one-third were taken directly to the gas chambers and the remainder were employed in various jobs. Polish historian Tomasz Kranz writes that, based on recent data and estimations, the total number of Jews who passed through Majdanek was seventy-four thousand, the majority of whom were Polish Jews, although the camp also had Jews from Slovakia and Germany. Kranz estimates that approximately sixty thousand Jews perished at Madjanek, either those who were murdered, or whose death was a result of their living conditions. Close to fifteen thousand Jews were sent to other camps, including Auschwitz, where they suffered a similar fate to the Jews already there.[16] This number of victims in Madjanek must be added to the total number of Operation Reinhard victims (see chapters 46 and 48).

The mass deportations in the General Government were completed by mid-November 1942. Following the intervention of German army authorities in charge of military enterprises and supply, Jewish workers and their families were left in some ghettos. On October 9, 1942, in response to the army's request, Himmler issued an order that Jews who worked for the military as tailors, furriers, and shoemakers should be collected in concentration camps in Warsaw and Lublin, where they would continue their work for the army under the direction of the SS. The order further stated that Jews who were directly employed as workers in war industries should temporarily remain at their workplaces, but that efforts should be made to replace them with Poles and then send the Jews to concentration camps in eastern Poland. Himmler stressed that all these measures were temporary because, "in accordance with the wish of the *Führer*, the Jews are some day to disappear."[17]

Friedrich-Wilhelm Krüger, the higher SS and police leader of the General Government who received Himmler's order, himself issued an order on November 10, 1942, that listed fifty-four ghettos where Jewish workers would temporarily remain.[18] According to the March 23, 1943, report by Richard Korherr, the head of the Statistics Department in Himmler's office, on December 31, 1942, the estimated number of Jews in the Cracow district was 37,000; Radom district, 29,400; Lublin district, 20,000; Warsaw district, 50,000; and Lvov district, 161,514, for a total of 297,914. When Kruger's order was issued, with the exception of the Lvov district, the bulk of the Jews had already been exterminated.[19]

These few remaining Jewish ghettos in the Warsaw, Radom, and Lublin districts were liquidated between January and May 1943. About 36,000 Jews from these ghettos were sent to Treblinka and Sobibor, and the remainder to concentration camps. The last ghettos in the Lvov district were liquidated by June 1943. According to a report by Fritz Katzmann, the police and SS leader of the Lvov district, until Kruger's order of November 10, 1942, 254,989 Jews had been evacuated.[20] All these Jews had found their death in Belzec, where the killing operations stopped after this mission had been completed. The remaining Jews of the Lvov district were killed in local *Aktionen* in the first half of 1943. Some transports were sent via Belzec to Sobibor.[21] On June 27, 1943, 21,156 Jews remained in the Lvov district in closed camps.

Operation Reinhard, which had begun in March 1942, was completed. No ghettos remained in the General Government and, with a few minor exceptions, it was free of Jews. In an address given by Hans Frank in Cracow on August 2, 1943, the Nazi head of the General Government said: "We started here with three and a half million Jews, and what remains of them—a few working companies only."[22]

DEPORTATIONS FROM BIALYSTOK GENERAL DISTRICT (BEZIRK BIALYSTOK) AND REICHSKOMMISSARIAT OSTLAND

General District Bialystok

General District Bialystok comprised the regions of Bialystok, Grodno, and Volkovysk. It constituted an independent administrative district within the German regime in occupied Poland and was under the authority of Erich Koch, the *Gauleiter* of East Prussia and *Reichskommissar* of the Ukraine. Bialystok General District was divided administratively into seven *Kreiskommissariats* or subdistricts.

During the first months of the German occupation, at the end of June 1941, the Jewish population of the Bialystok General District were subjected to a wave of mass murders. From July to September 1941, 30,000 Jews, mostly men, were shot by the *Einsatzgruppen* or ORPO battalions near their homes. In some localities like Stawiski, Radzilow, and Jedwabne the murderers were local Polish inhabitants. On the eve of the mass deportations to Treblinka and Auschwitz, in the autumn of 1942, there were about 140,000 Jews in the district, concentrated in ghettos. The largest of these were Bialystok ghetto, with about 40,000 Jews, and Grodno ghetto, with 25,000 Jews.[1]

In the first half of October 1942, the Reich Security Main Office issued an order to the SiPo and SD commander in the Bialystok General District, Wilhelm Altenloh, to liquidate all the ghettos in the district and deport the Jews. In the beginning of November the authority over the Jews was transferred to the SiPo and SD. But after the intervention of the German army and German civilian authorities that employed Jewish labor in war-economy enterprises, it was decided that the liquidation of the Bialystok ghetto would be postponed.[2]

The deportation of the Jews from the Bialystok district, most of them to Treblinka and some to Auschwitz, commenced after the deportation of

GENERAL GOVERNMENT AND BIALYSTOK GENERAL DISTRICT
Deportations to the Death Camps

Death Camp ▲
Direction of Deportation →
District Borders ～

The General Government and Bialystok General District

most of the General Government Jews had been completed. It began in
the first week of November 1942, and continued until mid-February 1943.
The first to be deported were the Jews from the small ghettos; the last were
from the Grodno ghetto and some from the Bialystok ghetto. At the end
of this period, only thirty thousand Jews from the entire General District
remained in the Bialystok ghetto.

When the deportation began, on November 2, 1942, most of the Jews in
the district, except those from Bialystok, Grodno, and a few other ghettos,

were concentrated in five collection camps (*Sammellager*), located at Bialystok, at Kelbasin near Grodno, at Bogusze near Grajewo, and at Volkovysk and Zambrow near Lomza. All the Jews in these camps were sent to Treblinka, with the exception of the Zambrow Jews, who were deported to Auschwitz. The Jews of Bielsk Podlaski, numbering approximately nineteen thousand, which was in the southern part of the district and thus relatively close to Treblinka, were sent directly to the extermination camp, without passing through a collection camp.

The transports moved according to plan during November and early December 1942. Toward mid-December, the deportation plan from the Bialystok General District, as well as from other parts of Poland, was disrupted due to a lack of rolling stock. German defeats on the Stalingrad front had necessitated a diversion of rolling stock for the military, and German railroad authorities announced a cessation of train allocations for transport of Jews between December 15, 1942, and January 15, 1943. SS *Obergruppenführer* Friedrich-Wilehlm Krüger, higher SS and police leader in the General Government, cabled Heinrich Himmler on December 5, 1942: "SS and Police chiefs are all informing me that due to transport cessation from 15.12.1942 to 15.1.1943 there is at present no possibility of transports for the purpose of evacuating Jews. This step most seriously endangers the plan for the deportation of Jews in its entirety. I entreat you to contact the central authorities of the Reich, the Wehrmacht Supreme Command (OKW), and the Transportation Ministry to obtain the placing of at least three pairs of trains at the disposal of this mission of highest importance."[3]

Krüger's intercession was of little avail, and in practice no deportations were carried out from Bialystok General District to Treblinka during this period. When rolling stock was again provided and deportations from the Bialystok area were renewed, the number of cars was insufficient, and Himmler personally intervened with Dr. Theodor Ganzenmüller, secretary of state of the German Transport Ministry. In his letter of January 23, 1943, Himmler wrote:

> Now I wish to present another important question: a precondition for bringing peace and quiet to the General District of Bialystok and the Russian territories is the deportation of all those aiding the gangs or suspected of belonging to them. This also includes, over and above all else, deportation of the Jews, as well as the Jews from the West, because otherwise we will have to take into account a rise in the number of assaults from these territories as well. Here I need your help and your support. If I wish to finish things up quickly, I must have more trains for transports. I well know what dire straits the railroads are in and what demands are always being made on them. Nevertheless I am forced to appeal to you: help me and supply me the trains. Himmler.[4]

The requested transportation was supplied as a result of the intervention, and the deportations from Bialystok General District continued. Himmler and RSHA officials in Berlin had not given up entirely on the idea of decreasing the area of the Bialystok ghetto and reducing the number of Jews residing there. The *Judenrat* was ordered to draw up a list of Jews who were not employed in plants important for the war effort. Rumors of the impending deportation of ten thousand Jews spread throughout the ghetto, and numerous Jews went into hiding. The roundup in the Bialystok ghetto began on February 5, as described by Sara Bender:

> Before dawn on Friday morning, February 5, 1943, at precisely 3:30 in the morning, about 80 armed Germans entered the ghetto . . . and marched toward the Judenrat building. Within minutes they had surrounded the streets and alleys in the neighborhood designated for evacuation, and opened fire with submachine guns. The Germans made sure to remain in the rear, having instructed the Jewish policemen to knock on the doors of the houses to make sure all of the Jews come out. Any policeman refusing these orders and instead had warned the Jews and prevented their evacuation were viciously beaten for sabotage. The Germans said they would kill 10 Jewish policemen if they failed to provide them with the Jews. Nevertheless, several policemen managed to escape and go into hiding, leaving the hunt for Jews to the Germans. Except for a group of refugees living in the synagogue on Neuwelt Street, it was impossible to locate the Jews from the Judenrat's list . . . since during the first few hours of the roundup unexpected difficulties arose. The Germans caught everyone they could lay their hands on. They caught workers from the mechanized carpentry shop in the ghetto and even those with work permits were unable to escape.[5]

Five transports departed from Bialystok during the week of the *Aktion*. Two trains departed to Auschwitz-Birkenau on February 5 and 6; three others departed from Treblinka between February 8 and 12. A total of close to ten thousand Jews were deported from Bialystok. Nearly nine hundred Jews were shot in the ghetto during the *Aktion*.[6]

As with all the transports to Treblinka, the deportees were usually taken directly to the gas chambers. But at least from one of these transports a few hundred young men were selected and sent for work. Out of 1,600 Jews from the Grodno ghetto who arrived in Treblinka on February 14, 1943, 150 men were sent to Treblinka I labor camp. Some of them even succeeded in escaping from the camp.[7] Rumors about Treblinka and what was going on there reached the ghettos of General District Bialystok and, as a result, the deportation *Aktionen* became much more difficult to carry out. Dov Freiberg, who witnessed the arrival of these transports to Treblinka, wrote:

> There were transports, like those from the eastern areas, which were very strongly guarded by SS men and Ukrainians. In these trains there was no

one car left undamaged. Each freight car looked like a battlefield and inside were more dead and wounded than living people. Some of the people were nude and white from the chlorine powder. . . . These people resisted, they refused to undress, they attacked the Germans with their fists. . . . Many were shot and many went to the gas chambers dressed. We worked late in the night to clean the area from the dead and wounded.[8]

The transports from General District Bialystok to Treblinka, which started on October 15, 1942, continued until February 19, 1943. In these four months, over 105,000 Jews were deported and annihilated in Treblinka, and about 4,000 were sent to Auschwitz. No other Jews were left in the General District Bialystok besides the nearly 30,000 Jews who remained in the Bialystok ghetto.

On February 19, 1943, at a conference held in Bialystok about the continuation of the deportations, the deputy commander of the Security Police announced that, for economic reasons, the Bialystok ghetto, with its remaining Jews, would be left intact until the end of the war. He said that it was expected that the Reich Security Main Office in Berlin would accede to this attitude of the local Security Police.[9]

Despite this reassuring message, in the summer of 1943, Himmler issued an order to *Gauleiter* Erich Koch, the head of the Bialystok General District, and to the local commander of the Security Police to liquidate the Bialystok ghetto and deport its inhabitants to the General Government. The background reasons was the deteriorating situation on the eastern front and the Soviet partisans' increased activity in the district, as well as the trend to transfer to the Lublin district the industrial plants that employed the ghetto's Jews. German civilian authorities in Bialystok, as well as the army authorities, again claimed that the Jews in Bialystok were vital to the war economy. But Himmler did not accept this argument. He ordered the immediate implementation of the deportation, and, as he no longer relied on the local German authorities, he entrusted the mission to the Operation Reinhard staff and the police forces subordinate to them. Globocnik personally came to Bialystok to coordinate the liquidation of the ghetto with the local German authorities.[10]

The deportations were carried out on August 18–19, 1943. From Bialystok 7,600 Jews were sent to Treblinka. Some other transports, with about 4,000 Jews, were deported to Majdanek and Auschwitz-Birkenau. About 13,000 working men and women were sent to labor camps and concentration camps. The final liquidation of the ghetto met with stiff resistance from the Jewish Underground, which fought back, and many Jews found their death inside the ghetto during this uprising. But the Bialystok ghetto, the last ghetto in the entire district, was finally liquidated in the second half of August 1943. The total number of Jews from the General District of Bialystok who were deported and murdered in Treblinka came to about 118,000 and about 8,000 were deported to Auschwitz-Birkenau. (See Appendix A.)[11]

REICHSKOMMISSARIAT OSTLAND

Reichskommissariat Ostland comprised the areas of Lithuania, Latvia, Estonia, and the western parts of Belorussia, including the city of Minsk, capital of Russian Belorussia, which were occupied by the Germans after their invasion of the Soviet Union on June 22, 1941. The head of Ostland was the *Reichskommissar*, Hinrich Lohse. He was subordinate to Alfred Rosenberg, the minister of the "Eastern Occupied Territories."

The majority of the Jews in these territories, mainly men, were killed during the *Aktionen* of the mobile SS *Einsatzgruppen*, which had operated there in the first months after the occupation, in the summer of 1941, and later by the civilian German administrative authorities in Ostland. The large-scale killing operations were carried out in Lithuania, Latvia, and Estonia in the summer and fall of 1941 and in parts of Belorussia that were under German civil administration during 1942. The extermination actions were carried out by taking the Jews out to locations in the vicinity of the places in which they lived and shooting them there. Thousands of local people participated in the extermination actions in the Baltic countries. These locals comprised the main force at the disposal of the German authorities, and of the SiPo and SD in particular, to exterminate the Jews throughout Ostland.

After these *Aktionen*, Jews remained only in the few ghettos that existed in the larger cities. At the beginning of the summer of 1943, there were seventy-two thousand Jews in these ghettos. They were concentrated in six ghettos, in the cities of Vilna, Kovno, Shavli, Riga, Minsk, and Lida. On June 21, 1943, Himmler issued an order to liquidate these ghettos. The able-bodied Jews who were needed for work were to be sent to concentration camps that would be erected in Ostland to service the war economy and to build fortifications. According to Himmler's order, the "nonessential" inhabitants of the Jewish ghettos were to be evacuated to the East. This term—"evacuation to the East"—meant that they would be sent for extermination.[12] Three ghettos—Vilna, Minsk, and Lida—were liquidated, and the other three ghettos were turned into concentration camps. The "nonessential" Jews from these ghettos were sent to Sobibor.

The Lida ghetto, with its remaining approximately three thousand Jews, was liquidated on September 18–19, 1943. Several hundred ghetto Jews successfully escaped to the forests and joined the partisans, while the ghetto's remaining twenty-seven hundred Jews were deported to Sobibor in two transports. The first transport comprised fourteen hundred Jews. Regarding the deportation of the thirteen hundred Jews in the second transport, a German engineer, Otto Weisbecker, who was a *Bauführer* in the Organization Todt, testified at the Sobibor trial:

> As a building engineer I came to Lida and worked there on the railways. . . . In the ghetto, which was subordinated to the *Gebietskommissar* [district commissar], were 1,400 Jews. At the building site that I headed, 1,300 Jews and their families, who were accommodated in a camp, were engaged [in work]. . . . Approximately in the middle of 1943, the Security Police arrived in Lida. . . . All the Jews were then subordinated to the Security Police. One day, these Jews from the ghetto—men, women, and children—were loaded onto freight cars and, under the direction of *Haupttruppführer* Bache from Organization Todt they were transferred to Sobibor. The next day I received an order from the head of my department, the architect Hans W., to transfer our Jews to Lublin for a working mission. The Jews were loaded on the train that day, sixty people to a freight car. I was the commander of the transport, and I had at my disposal a police sergeant and nine or ten Polish policemen. . . . In spite of the security measures, between twenty and twenty-five Jews escaped on the way. . . . One of the guards at Sobibor told me that the transport was to be exterminated in the morning. The next morning, I came into the camp and was brought to the commander, who was in the breakfast barrack. . . . On the wall of this barrack was a big plan of the camp. I could see on it that the 1,400 Jews that Bache had brought the day before could not possibly be accommodated in the existing barracks. In reference to my question to the camp commander, where can he accommodate the Jews I had brought, he told me that of the 1,400 Jews of yesterday's transport, nobody remained.[13]

On the eve of the liquidation of the Minsk ghetto, in the summer of 1943, there were six thousand to eight thousand Jews out of the seventy-five thousand who had lived there at the beginning of the German occupation at the end of June 1941. About five hundred of them, skilled workers, were kept in the SS labor camp on Shiroka Street, where an additional one hundred Jewish prisoners of war from the Soviet army were employed. Before the deportation more Jews were brought from the ghetto to the Shiroka Street labor camp.

On September 18, 1943, a transport with two thousand Jews left Minsk for Sobibor. First Lieutenant Alexander (Sasha) Pechersky, a prisoner of war who was with this transport, wrote:

> On September 18, all the Jews were ordered to assemble in the courtyard. It was four o'clock in the morning, still dark. We stood in a line to get the 300 grams of bread we received for the journey. The courtyard was full of people, but no noise could be heard. Scared children kept close to their mothers.

Commander Wat announced to us: "Soon you will be taken to the station. You are going to Germany; there you will work. Hitler has made it possible to grant life to each Jew who will work honestly. You are going with your families." The women and children were taken to the station in trucks, the men by foot. . . . We were pushed—seventy people in a freight car. . . . On the fifth day of traveling, we arrived in the evening at an isolated station. A white sign bore the name: Sobibor. . . . We were kept in the closed freight cars overnight. On September 23, in the morning, a locomotive pushed the train into the camp. . . . Tired and hungry we left the cars. *Oberscharführer* Gomerski shouted: "Cabinetmakers and carpenters without families, forward." Eighty men, most of them war prisoners, reported. We were rushed into a fenced area inside a barrack. . . . A Jew from the camp who returned from some work approached us. During the conversation I noticed grey smoke rising in the northwest direction and a sharp smell of burning hovering in the air. I asked: "What is burning there?" "They are burning the bodies of your friends who arrived with you," the Jew answered. I was shocked.[14]

The Jews from Minsk, who had witnessed mass extermination in their ghetto, as tens of thousands of them were shot in the vicinity of the city from the beginning of the German occupation, knew nothing about the existence of the death camps. The Minsk ghetto was a remote and isolated ghetto. Moreover, since Minsk was part of the Soviet Union, the Jews of Minsk had almost no connections with the Jews in the ghettos of Poland, and no messengers with information arrived there, as was the case among the ghettos in Poland itself. The very existence of the death camps and of Sobibor was a secret to them. They came to Sobibor and filed into the gas chambers without knowing what fate awaited them.[15]

Additional transports arrived in Sobibor from Minsk. Although Pechersky mentions in his diary transports that arrived in Sobibor on September 27, October 8, and October 11, 1943, he does not mention from where the victims came.[16] It is, however, quite plausible that these transports indeed came from Minsk. We may estimate that about six thousand to eight thousand Jews from the ghetto of Minsk, brought in three or four transports, were murdered in Sobibor.

The liquidation of the Vilna ghetto took place on September 23–24, 1943. In the ghetto at that time were about eleven thousand to twelve thousand inhabitants left from the fifty-seven thousand Jews who had been in Vilna at the beginning of the German occupation. Most of these Jews were shot in Ponar, near Vilna, in the months of July through November, 1941. During the final liquidation, all the Jews were taken outside the ghetto to Rossa Square; there the men were separated from the women and children. The men and women who were able to work were selected and sent to concentration camps—men to Estonia and women to Latvia. About forty-three hundred to five thousand elderly women and children were sent to Sobibor in the last days of September 1943.[17]

There were no survivors from this transport, so no direct testimony exists about their arrival in Sobibor. Leon Feldhendler, who escaped from Sobibor, mentions in his testimony "transports which arrived from Minsk and Vilna."[18] The assumption that the last Vilna Jews were sent to Sobibor is also based on the fact that all the other Jews who were deported from Ostland to the General Government, that is, those from Lida and Minsk, reached Sobibor. They definitely did not reach any other death camp. The lists of transports that arrived in Auschwitz-Birkenau and Majdanek exist, and this transport is not mentioned in either. As Belzec and Treblinka were no longer in operation at that time, this leaves Sobibor as the only camp where the transport from Vilna could have been brought and annihilated without a trace. The number of Jews from Ostland who were annihilated in Sobibor in the second half of September 1943 was about 12,700.[19]

CHAPTER TWENTY

TRANSPORTS FROM OTHER EUROPEAN COUNTRIES

BELZEC, SOBIBOR, AND TREBLINKA WERE established for the implementation of Operation Reinhard, that is, for the purpose of exterminating the Jews of the General Government in Poland. There were, however,
Jews from other European countries who were also sent to these camps for
extermination—Jews from Germany, Austria, Czechoslovakia, Holland,
France, Greece, the Soviet Union (Ostland), and Yugoslavia.

Some of the Jews deported from these countries were sent directly
to the extermination camps. Yet many others first arrived at the ghettoes
outside of the Lublin district, which served as transit ghettos (*Durchgangs-
getto*); after staying there briefly, they were deported to the extermination
camps. These transit ghettos were located in small towns, near railroads,
making the deportation from there to extermination camps easier for the
Germans. They were situated in Izbica, Piaski, Opole Lubelskie, Rejowiec, and other small towns, and the deportees mingled with the locals. The
ghettos were terribly crowded, with appalling living conditions. The transports from other countries began arriving in the ghettos from mid-March
1942, continuing till the beginning of June 1942. Thereafter, the transports
were sent directly to the extermination camps.[1]

The deception perpetrated on these Jews regarding their destination
and the fate awaiting them there was complete. They were convinced they
were traveling to labor camps or would be employed on agricultural farms
in the East. Part of these transports were in passenger cars, and, in some
cases, Jews even had to buy tickets with their own money. During the journey the conductors would occasionally check the tickets and tear off the
stubs. When the train stopped at way stations, the Jewish passengers were
occasionally permitted to walk around the platform and buy drinks at food
stands. Franciszek Zabecki wrote that he witnessed how a Jew riding in
one of these trains got off at a station to go to a food stand and while he
was still standing on the platform the transport started off without him.

He turned to the railroad officials at the station, presented his ticket, and asked the location of the industrial plants to which the others were being taken, so that he might join them.[2]

GERMANY AND AUSTRIA

Tens of thousands of Jews from Germany and Austria were deported to the Lublin district at the end of 1939 or beginning of 1940, and, on a smaller scale, in the years following. After the Wannsee Conference, Adolf Eichmann's office, early in March 1942, ordered that most of the deportation trains from the Third Reich be rerouted from the ghettos of Minsk and Riga in Ostland to ghettos and camps in the Lublin district.[3] This change coincided with the opening of the death camp of Belzec in mid-March 1942, and the building of Sobibor and Treblinka. Tens of thousands of Jews from the Third Reich arrived in the Lublin district from April 1942, and from there they were later sent to the death camps of Operation Reinhard.

On March 27, Goebbels wrote in his diary about these deportations: "The ghettos which will be emptied in the cities of the General Government will now be refilled with Jews thrown out of the Reich. This process is to be repeated from time to time."[4]

Between March 13, 1942, and June 20, 1942, 19,046 Jews were deported from Germany to the Lublin district; 7,700 were sent directly to Sobibor, and another 1,000 were deported directly to Belzec. Six transports from Austria reached the Lublin district in April, May, and June 1942, carrying a total of 6,000 Jews. Several of these transports were taken directly to Sobibor. Even earlier, in 1941, 2,087 Jews were deported to the Lublin district. A total of 8,987 Austrian Jews were sent to the Lublin district.[5]

According to the evidence given at the Sobibor/Bolender trial, at least ten thousand Jews from Germany and Austria found their death in Sobibor in the months of April, May, and June 1942.[6] Some of the transports were sent directly to the death camp. A report dated June 20, 1942, from the commander of the Number 152 police precinct of Vienna, described the deportation of a transport of Austrian Jews directly to Sobibor:

> The transport commando consisted of Lieutenant Fischmann as commander, two sergeants and thirteen policemen of the "First Police Reserve Company East. . . ." The embarkation of the Jews to the freight cars of the allocated "Special Train" at the Aspang station started at 12:00 hours under the command of SS *Hauptsturmführer* Brunner and SS *Hauptscharführer* Girzik from the [local] "Main Office for the Deportation of Jews" and went smoothly.
>
> At that time the transport commando assumed the guard duty. All together, 1,000 Jews were deported. . . .

The DA-38 train left Vienna on June 14, 1942, at 19:08 and crossed Brno, Neisse, Oppeln, Czestochowa, Kielce, Radom, Deblin, Lublin, Chelm to Sobibor and not, as expected, to Izbica. The arrival in Sobibor was on June 17, 1942, at 8:15. At the station of Lublin, where we arrived on June 16, 1942, at 21:00 hours, SS *Obersturmführer* Pohl was waiting, and he ordered that fifty-one able Jews between the ages of fifteen and fifty disembark and be brought to a labor camp. . . . At that time he gave an order that the remaining 949 Jews were to be taken to Sobibor. The list [of the people], three freight cars [with food], and 100,000 zloty were handed over to the SS *Obersturmführer* Pohl in Lublin. At 23:00 we left Lublin for Sobibor. In the Jewish camp of Trawniki, 30 km before Lublin, we handed over the three freight cars with food and luggage to SS *Scharführer* Mayerhofer.

The train arrived at 8:15 on June 17 at the labor camp, which was close to the Sobibor station, where the camp commander, *Oberleutnant* Stangl, received the 949 Jews. The disembarkation began immediately and was completed at 9:15. The departure from Sobibor to Lublin with the "special train" followed immediately after the unloading of the Jews, at 10:00.[7]

Some transports with Jews from Germany also arrived in Belzec. Some sources mention a transport with Jews from Würzburg which was sent for liquidation in Belzec.[8]

In addition to the 10,000 or more Jews from Germany and Austria who were killed in Sobibor, tens of thousands more found their death in Belzec and Treblinka. At the Wannsee Conference on January 20, 1942, Reinhard Heydrich mentioned the number of 175,500 Jews who lived at that time in Germany and Austria. It is hard to estimate how many of these Jews were sent to the Lublin district and found their death in Operation Reinhard death camp.

An unusual instance in which a non-Jewish German woman was murdered at Treblinka together with her two children was described by Jacob Wiernik:

A transport arrived. Everything proceeded normally. While they were undressing, a woman stepped out of the line with her children—boys. She identified herself as a German by birth who had been included in the transport by mistake. All her papers were in order, and the two boys weren't circumcised. The woman was attractive, and her eyes showed fear. She held her children, calmed them, and promised that everything would be cleared up quickly and they would go home to their father. The Germans ordered her and her children to leave the group. She thought she had been saved, and calmed down. But that's not the way it was. They had sentenced her to die with the Jews, since she had seen too much and might spread it around. Whoever enters Treblinka was doomed, and this woman and her children marched together with the others—to die.[9]

The deportation of the Jews from Slovakia to the ghettos in the Lublin district and to Auschwitz-Birkenau, which began on March 25, 1942, was based on an agreement between the Slovakian and German governments. By October 20, 1942, about fifty-eight thousand Slovakian Jews had been deported, forty thousand of them to the Lublin district, the remainder to Auschwitz.[10] The transports were carried out on Slovak trains and under Slovak guard up to the border. At the first station within the confines of the General Government, the train and its human cargo passed into the hands of the Germans, who escorted the train to its destination. In some of the ghettos to which the Slovakian Jews were brought, there were still some local Jews left. In some places they found empty ghettos; the former inhabitants had already been annihilated in the death camps. A survivor of such a journey, who passed through Sobibor and some labor camps but who succeeded in escaping and returning to Slovakia, testified about his experience:

> On May 21, 1942, our transport, consisting of about 1,000 Jews, was deported from Sabinov via Zilina, Cadca, directly to Poland. At the boundary we were told to line up. We were counted by the SS [men] on the station platform, while the women were counted in the carriages. Then we continued our journey for three or four days until we reached Rejowiec-Lubelski [Lublin district], where we left the carriages. During the entire time we suffered from thirst, as we had been given water only on two occasions and no food at all; but we had left provided with plenty of provisions. . . .
>
> On the next day, May 27, two transports of a size similar to ours arrived from Stropkov and Humenne, so that we were then all together 3,000 Slovakian Jews. . . .
>
> On August 9, 1942, German police suddenly ordered a general lineup. The entire Jewish population, including the Jews of the ghetto as well as the labor camp, all together about 2,700 people, had to line up on the main square before the school with their luggage. All those who had not been able to obey the order owing to illness or exhaustion were shot in their quarters. . . .
>
> We were taken over at Rejowiec railway station by the so-called "Black Ukrainians." There we were squeezed into waiting cattle trucks, 120 to 150 persons per truck, without being registered. The doors were then closed from the outside, and the trucks were left standing at the station till 8 p.m. . . .
>
> We arrived at Sobibor shortly past midnight, where SS men with *nagaikas* [horse whips] received us. There at last we got a little water, though no food. We were subsequently lined up in a pine alley, divided by sexes, and twenty-five men were told to fall out to clear luggage and corpses out of the trucks. We never saw these men again. In the morning we saw most of the women move in ranks of four to a yard some distance away. At 8 a.m. the SS lieutenant came to us and told all those who had previously worked at draining swamps to fall

out. About 100 men and 50 women stepped forward, 155 in all, to whom the lieutenant remarked cryptically: "You are born anew." From the remaining group, mechanics, locksmiths, and watchmakers were separated, while the rest had to follow the women to the yard in the distance, and shared their fate....

Our group of 155 was brought to Ossowa, where we spent one night. We were very well received and fed there by the Jews. At Ossowa there were about 500 German and Czech Jews. Jewish Ghetto Police accompanied us to Krychow....

On October 16 we were told that a certain proportion of workers was to be sent to the "Jewish City" of Wlodawa on the Bug, 25 km from Krychow.... Four days after they arrived at Wlodawa, the entire Jewish population there was deported to Sobibor.[11]

From the 40,000 Slovakian Jews who had been deported to the Lublin district, about 24,500 were murdered in Sobibor, 7,500 in Belzec, and 7,000 in Treblinka.[12]

The Transports from Theresienstadt Ghetto (Protectorate of Bohemia and Moravia)

The Jews from the Protectorate of Bohemia and Moravia, before their deportation to the Operation Reinhard death camps or Auschwitz-Birkenau, were sent to the Theresienstadt ghetto.

Fourteen transports, comprising about fourteen thousand Jews, were sent from Theresienstadt to ghettos of the Lublin district between March 11 and June 13, 1942. At least six thousand of these Jews were murdered in Sobibor and about seven thousand in Belzec.[13] Other transports, with about four thousand Jews, reached ghettos of the Lublin district in October 1942. They were most likely deported to Sobibor or to Belzec. Five transports, comprising about eight thousand Czech, German, and Austrian Jews, were sent to Treblinka from the Theresienstadt ghetto between October 5 and October 25, 1942. The first two transports departed on October 5 and 8, and carried one thousand Jews each. The last three, each of two thousand Jews, departed on October 15, 19, and 22. The trip to Treblinka took two days. Richard Glazer, one of the survivors of these transports, described what transpired on the way and upon arrival:

> After a month in Theresienstadt I was notified that I was to leave the next day for another camp, in the East....
>
> We, our Czech transport, traveled on a passenger train; later I was to find out how rare that was; only transports from the "West"—Germany, Austria, Holland, etc.—traveled on passenger trains with their comparative comfort; everybody else went in cattle trucks. The people supervising our transport were police—in green police uniform. They appointed some of

the young men as monitors and gave them armbands. It wasn't particularly rough, or frightening. True enough, the police officer in charge expressed himself rather oddly. "I am to bring a thousand pieces," he said, "and a thousand pieces I am going to bring. So anybody who puts his head out of the window is going to have it blown off; we shoot." We thought he was being unnecessarily crude; no need, we thought, to frighten the women and children that way; but we didn't really give it a second thought. We left Theresienstadt on October 8 and we traveled two days. First we thought we were going in the direction of Dresden, but then the train turned and we went east. During the nights it stood more than it moved. The last morning we saw in the distance the outline of a city; it must have been Warsaw. We got to Treblinka at 3 p.m. We all crowded to look out of the windows. I saw a green fence, barracks, and I heard what sounded like a farm tractor at work. I was delighted. The place looked like a farm. I thought, "This is *prima* [marvelous]; it's going to be work I know something about...."

I saw men with blue armbands on the platform, but without insignia.... There were loud announcements, but it was all fairly restrained: nobody did anything to us. I followed the crowd: "Men to the right, women and children to the left," we had been told. The women and children disappeared into a barrack further to the left and we were told to undress. One of the SS men—later I knew his name, Küttner—told us in a chatty sort of tone that we were going into a disinfection bath and afterward would be assigned work. Clothes, he said, could be left in a heap on the floor, and we'd find them again later. We were to keep documents, identity cards, money, watches and jewelry with us.... And just then another SS man (Miete was his name) came by me and said, "Come on, you, get back into your clothes, quick, special work." That was the first time I was frightened. Everything was very quiet, you know. And when he said that to me, the others turned around and looked at me—and I thought, my God, why me, why does he pick on me? ... and of course, never forget that we had no idea at all what this whole installation was for.[14]

The Theresienstadt deportees were taken directly to the gas chambers, but a few dozen had been selected to reinforce the Jewish prisoner cadres in the camp. Thus a few were saved.

GREECE AND YUGOSLAVIA

On February 22, 1943, the SS *Hauptsturmführer* Theodor Dannecker and representatives of the Bulgarian government signed an agreement that specified that fourteen thousand Jews living in areas recently annexed to Bulgaria would be delivered to the Germans for transport to the East no later than April 15 of that year. These annexed areas included Thrace in Greece and Macedonia in Yugoslavia.

Some 5,500 Jews lived in the parts of Greece annexed by Bulgaria, in the towns of Kavalla, Drama, Xanthi, Serrai (Serres), Dede-Agatch

(Alexandroupolis), Souphlion (Soufli), and Komotini. Over 4,000 of them were arrested on March 4, 1943, and taken to Dupnitsa and Gorna-Dzhumaia internment camps in the new territories of Bulgaria. After ten days in the camps, on March 18–19, they were transferred by train to the port of Lorn on the Danube. Jews from the Yugoslav town of Pirot, which also had been annexed to Bulgaria, were also brought to this river port. At Lorn, the Bulgarian authorities transferred the Jews, who numbered 4,215, to the Germans. On March 20–22, the Jews boarded four boats headed for Vienna. The trip on the Danube to Vienna took five to eight days. According to several accounts, Jews on one of the boats were drowned—either accidently or deliberately. From Vienna, the Jews were sent by train to Treblinka on March 26 and 28, 1943, and they all were exterminated upon arrival.[15]

The parts of Yugoslav Macedonia transferred to Bulgaria after the German conquest contained a Jewish population of about eight thousand, in the communities of Skopje, Bitola, and Stip. From March 11, 1943, they were concentrated in an internment camp established at the tobacco warehouse called the Monopoly in Skopje. About the conditions at that camp, Elena Leon Ishakh from Bitola testified as follows:

> In one room there were over 500 persons. . . . We arrived at Skopje about midnight and were locked up in the Monopoly building. We and the Jews from Stip were kept locked in during whole of the next day, because the plundering-search of the Jews from Skopje was still in progress. The day before we had been locked up in the wagons, and now a whole day in a building without a single latrine. The inmates were compelled to relieve themselves in the corners so that the air soon became stifling. . . . When some of us tried to peep through the windows, a policeman fired in the air.
>
> On March 13, they opened the door for the first time and allowed us to go to the latrines. . . . They let out the 500 that were in our room and gave us a half an hour, whereupon they locked us up again so that more than half the people never managed to relieve themselves or to get water. . . . They let us out only once a day, compartment by compartment, for a short while only, so that many weak people, sick or invalids, never managed to get to the bottom of the stairs. . . . We were hungry. . . . Only on the fifth day did the camp authorities organize the kitchen. . . . For more than 7,000 inmates there were too few cooking stoves. Food distribution started at eleven o'clock, but only at five o'clock did the last ones get their ration.
>
> The food was distributed once daily and it consisted of 250 grams of bread and, usually, a watery dish of beans or rice. . . . They gave us smoked meat from time to time, but it was so foul that we could not eat it in spite of our hunger. . . . Not even the fifth part of the inmates had any receptacles so that several had to use the same dish.
>
> Under the pretext of searching us for hidden money, gold, or foreign currency, they forced us sadistically to undress completely. . . . Sometimes

they would even take away baby diapers. . . . If anything was found on some-body . . ., he was beaten.[16]

The Jews from Skopje camp were deported to Treblinka in three successive transports. The first transport, with 2,338 Jews, left on March 22 and arrived at Treblinka on March 28. In each of the freight cars was a small barrel of water and several buckets into which people could relieve themselves. The luggage that people were permitted to take was forty kilograms per adult and twenty per child. An eyewitness described the departure of this transport:

> The first transport departed on 22 March 1943. The day before merely 1,600 persons were chosen for this transport and were provided with food for fifteen days. They received 1¼ kgs. of bread, ½ kg. *Katchkaval*-cheese, 2 kgs. 2 kgs. Jam, 2 kgs *peksimit*a [a kind of bread or biscuit], and 1 kg. of unboiled smoked meat each; all of us refused the meat in protest.
>
> During the morning of that same day, March 22, 1943, we were suddenly informed that another 800 persons were to be added to the transport; they were hurriedly forced into the wagons since the transport was already about to leave, so that many of them were unable to provide themselves with any food.
>
> When one's turn came to be transported no one asked whether he or she was sick or pregnant or even whether it was a woman who had given birth only the day before.[17]

The second transport, with 2,402 Jews, left on March 25 and arrived at Treblinka on March 31 in the evening. The third transport, with 2,404 Jews, left on March 29 and reached Treblinka on April 5. The trip from Skopje to Treblinka lasted six days.[18]

The first transport from Skopje was guarded by a platoon of Bulgarian soldiers up to the Lapovo train station in Yugoslavia, where responsibility was transferred to the German military police. The two other transports were guarded by the German military police from their departure from Skopje (which was under Bulgarian rule) all the way to Treblinka. A report given by the German officer who was in charge of the third transport described the route and events on the way from Skopje to Treblinka:

> Work Report 12 April 1943
> Subject: Escorting the Jewish Transports
> On the basis of a telephoned command from SS *Hauptsturmführer* Danker, the train left Skopje on March 23, 1943, at 12:00, escorted by platoon No. 1, which comprised thirty men and was commanded by Police Sergeant Buchner. The train arrived at 23:00. On March 29, at 06:00, the loading of 2,404 Jews onto freight cars commenced at the former tobacco sheds. Loading was completed at 12:00, and at 12:30 the train departed. The train passed

through Albanian territory. The final destination, Treblinka (the camp), was reached on April 5, 1943, at 07:00, via Czestochowa, Piotrkow, Warsaw. The train was unloaded that same day between the hours 09:00 and 11:00. *Incidents:* Five Jews died on route. On the night of March 30—an elderly woman of seventy; on the night of March 31—an elderly man, aged eighty-five; on April 3—an elderly woman, aged ninety-four and a six month-old child. On April 4 an elderly woman aged ninety-nine died.

Transport Roster: received 2,404
                         less   5
total delivered at Treblinka 2,399

[signed] Karl, Military Police Lieutenant and Company Commander.[19]

Reports like this were prepared for every transport. All told, 7,144 Jews were sent from Yugoslav Macedonia to Treblinka, and, with the exception of twelve who had died en route, they all died in the gas chambers.

The transport trains from those parts of Greece and Yugoslavia under Bulgarian rule, as well as those from Salonika, traveled via Vienna and Cracow to the extermination camps. The regional administrations of the German railway authority in Vienna and Cracow issued trip-plan orders for these trains, including a demand that the railway workers deliver an exact report of the number of people in each transport. A cable sent by the *Gedob* in Cracow on March 28, 1943, detailed this request:

German Railroads

Service Cable, received March 28, 4:25
From Malkinia . . . original: Generaldirektion der Ostbahn, Cracow.
To Treblinka train station, in regard to DA trains from Bulgaria and Greece. In accordance with special train trip-plan orders, arriving passenger count and careful check of data on transport certificate are mandatory. Irregularities in data should be noted, e.g., received 490 people here and not 510, transport certificate, etc., should be sent immediately to Cracow VK WEMI.

Gedob Cracow.[20]

Between March 15 and May 9, the Jews of Salonika, Greece, were sent to Auschwitz-Birkenau for extermination. A document of the German railroad authority in Vienna, dated March 26, 1943, mentions a forty-eight-car train carrying deportees loaded at Salonika that passed through Cracow and from there to Malkinia.[21] Since in many documents relating to transports to Treblinka Malkinia is noted as the destination station, it would appear that at least one transport from Salonika, carrying twenty-eight hundred Jews, arrived at Treblinka. Stangl also testified that transports from Salonika arrived at Treblinka. Shmuel Wilenberg bore witness to such a transport:

> During those days of March 1943, a train's whistle signaled the arrival of a new transport. This time, a most strange crowd issued forth from the cars. The new arrivals, with tanned faces and jet black, curly hair, spoke among themselves in an unrecognizable language. The baggage they took with them from the cars was tagged "Salonika." Rumors of the arrival of Greek Jews spread like lightning. Among the arrivals were intellectuals, people of high station, a few professors and university lecturers. While they had come all this way in freight cars, the strangest thing to us was that the cars had not been locked and sealed. Everyone was well-dressed and carried lots of baggage. Amazed, we eyed marvelous oriental carpets; we couldn't take our eyes off the enormous reserve of food. We began salivating as we stared at bags loaded with delicacies, fruits, and drinks. Besides food, these Jews took along a reserve of clothing, various and sundry accessories, trinkets....
>
> They all disembarked from the freight cars in perfect order and serenity. Attractive, well-dressed women, children as pretty as dolls, gentlemen tidying up their lapels. ... Miete found three German speaking Greeks and appointed them translators; they moved about with armbands embellished with the Greek colors. Not a single one of the new arrivals had grasped where he was and what his fate was to be. The truth only penetrated when they were being led naked, supposedly to the baths, and suddenly the first blows began to fall.[22]

Wiernik described the Yugoslav and Greek Jews at the gas chambers:

> Transports from Bulgaria began to arrive. ... They were eliminated like the others. The Bulgarian Jews were tall, strong and manly. When we looked at a man like that, we didn't want to believe that only twenty minutes later he would end his life in the gas chamber. These fine-looking Jews would hardly let the hangmen kill them so easily.
>
> A small quantity of gas was introduced into the chambers, and the asphyxiation process went on all night. They suffered for a long time until they breathed their last. They also suffered terribly before entering the chambers. The hangmen were jealous of the victims' fine appearance and maltreated them that much more.[23]

FRANCE

The deportation of Jews from France to the death camps in occupied Poland began on March 27, 1942, and continued sporadically until the summer of 1944, close to the liberation of France. The deportations were carried out in full cooperation with the French Vichy government, which divided the Jews into two categories: (1) native French Jews and those who had been naturalized for a long time; (2) refugees, stateless Jews, or those unprotected by a foreign power. The Vichy government protected the first category, and few of them were deported, but they cooperated and handed over for deportation the Jews belonging to the second category.

Over 75,000 Jews from France were deported to the death camps. The deportations were carried out in freight cars, and most of the transports departed from the Drancy internment camp, near Paris. There were about eighty transports, with about 1,000 people each. The lists of these transports, which include the names, places, and dates of birth of the deportees, were preserved. The destination of most of the transports was Auschwitz-Birkenau, but four transports in March 1943 were sent to the Lublin district. Transports nos. 50 and 51, with a total of 2,001 people, almost all of them males from the Gurs internment camp, left on March 4 and 6, 1943. They reached Majdanek, where part of the people were left for work; the others were sent to Sobibor and murdered there. Transport no. 52, with Jews from Marseille, left Drancy on March 23 for Sobibor. Transport no. 53 departed on March 25, 1943.[24]

Josef Dunitz, who was in transport no. 53, testified:

I remember that we left Drancy on March 25, 1943. We traveled four days and arrived at Sobibor on March 29/30, 1943. We passed through Majdanek and the same day came to Sobibor. Before we left Drancy, the Germans told us that we were going to Poland for work. They said that we should take part in the war effort and not walk around the cities of France. We were just being tricked. The transports that left Drancy were quite big, 1,000 people in each, fifty people in a freight car.... We were a group of friends from Drancy, and, in spite of the fact that we did not know what awaited us there, we wanted to escape. We wanted to jump from the train when the other people in the car were sleeping, otherwise they would try to prevent the escape, as they were afraid of collective punishment. We made a hole in the floor. We started to jump, without knowing that in the last car were Gestapo with machine guns. When the Germans understood that people were escaping, they started to shoot. Some were killed. I do not know how many of those who jumped succeeded in escaping. We reached Sobibor....

After we left the train, some SS men ordered that thirty people be selected for work. We did not know what was better, to be among the thirty people taken for work or among those who were going in the other direction. Where were they going? I saw that one of my friends from Drancy was among the thirty people taken to work. I joined this group. The Germans counted and found that we were thirty-one people. "Let there be thirty-one," he said. In this way I remained in the group.[25]

Josef Dunitz and one other man, Antonius Bardach, both of them from transport no. 53, were the only survivors from the four thousand Jews deported from France to Sobibor.[26]

The mass deportation of the Jews from Holland to Auschwitz-Birkenau and Sobibor began in July 1942. The Jews marked for deportation were concentrated mainly in the Westerbork camp, with some of them in the Vught camp. The deportations were carried out by the German authorities in Holland and with the full collaboration of the Dutch "Green Police." About 105,000 Jews from Holland were deported in ninety-eight passenger trains between July 15, 1942, and September 3, 1944. Sixty-four transports, with about 60,000 Jews, were sent to Auschwitz. Nineteen transports, with at least 34,363 Jews, were sent to Sobibor. There is a possibility that some transports marked for Auschwitz eventually reached Sobibor. The other transports were sent to Theresienstadt and Bergen-Belsen.[27]

The deportation from Westerbork to Sobibor was carried out between March 5 and July 23, 1943. Selma Wijnberg wrote in her testimony:

> In 1942, I was arrested with my family and interned in Westerbork. We were 8,000 prisoners, and the German officers in charge announced that we were going to work in Poland or the Ukraine, and we were to take with us shoes, clothes, and food. Letters were arriving from Wlodawa confirming that life was pleasant in Poland. Later I knew it was a lie, as the prisoners were forced to sign printed post cards. The name Sobibor was never mentioned. I did not want to go to Poland, and I ran away from Westerbork. I hid for a long time among Dutch families, but a *Volksdeutsche* denounced me. I spent two months in an Amsterdam prison. . . . In March 1943, we were on our way to Poland. Many of us hoped to meet our families there, again. Sick Jews were treated during the journey; German nurses distributed medicines to patients. We reached Sobibor on April 9. . . . A German chose twenty-eight women to work in camp no. 2.[28]

Ilana Safran testified:

> At Vught there were many Jewish families and many children. . . . Later we were transferred to Westerbork, the place where the Dutch Jews were concentrated, and we remained there for one week. In April 1943, we left for Poland. The journey to Poland was dreadful; the prisoners from Western countries believed that we were going to labor camps. . . . When we reached Sobibor, a selection took place—young girls were placed on one side, the others, including children, went to the gas chambers. We were given postcards. "Write to your families that you have arrived safely." I wrote a card to some Dutch friends; it reached its destination and I found it after the war.[29]

According to information gathered by the Red Cross, from all the transports from Holland that arrived in Sobibor, only nineteen persons survived.[30]

Dov Freiberg described the arrival of a hospital, complete with doctors and patients: "I remember the arrival of a hospital, I believe it was from Holland. The patients were carried on stretchers, and the whole hospital team accompanied them. A table was put on the square, and a doctor, perhaps the director of the hospital, was sitting there. Doctors and nurses went around, checked the patients, gave injections, served water and pills. The director was busy writing and giving some notes to the nurses. There was an impression that the whole area had turned into a hospital. After a few hours there were no more patients or hospital personnel."[31]

Leon Feldhendler, a prisoner in Sobibor, wrote about the treatment of the transports from Western Europe:

> These transports were treated entirely differently. They arrived in passenger trains. The *Bahnhofkommando* [platform workers] helped them carry their baggage to a special barrack near the station. The deception was carried on to such an extent that they were given tickets in order to reclaim their baggage. On the square was a special table with writing instruments to write letters. They were ordered by the SS men to write that they were in Wlodawa and to ask the recipients to send them letters to Wlodawa. Sometimes answers to these letters were indeed sent. These letters had a double purpose: to make the recipients believe that the deportation did not mean liquidation and to reveal the addresses of the families of the deported.[32]

The Jews who were brought to the Operation Reinhard camps from Western, central, and southern Europe had never heard of Belzec, Sobibor, and Treblinka and knew nothing of their destination or the fate awaiting them there. They believed what they were told—that they were being sent to labor camps in eastern Europe, or that they would be employed on agricultural farms. Some were placed temporarily in transit ghettoes, and some were sent directly to the extermination camps. Even after they had arrived in these camps, until they were actually in the gas chambers, they did not realize what was being done to them. More than 131,000 Jews from European countries other than Poland and the Soviet Union were murdered in Operation Reinhard death camps.[33]

THE EXTERMINATION OF GYPSIES

THE GYPSIES ORIGINATED IN NORTHERN India and are part of the Indo-Germanic Aryan race. The Gypsies left India over one thousand years ago and came to Europe through Asia Minor to the Balkan peninsula. They reached central Europe in the fifteenth century. They did not constitute a homogeneous people but split into tribes, each with its own king, dialect, and beliefs. Eventually, they adopted Christianity. During the generations of wandering over Europe as nomadic tribes, they endured prejudice, expulsions from one country to another, and persecutions. Anti-Gypsy laws and restrictions were imposed on them in many countries, particularly in Germany and Austria.

For Nazi Germany the Gypsies became a racist dilemma. The Gypsies were Aryans, but in the Nazi mind there were contradictions between what they regarded as the superiority of the Aryan race and their image of the Gypsies. Their treatment of the Gypsies was an indication of the lack of sincerity with which the Nazis regarded their racial theories. Nazi racial "specialists" and "scientists" had to find a way to prove that Gypsies were not Aryans and thus lay the ideological basis for their persecution. It was not an easy task, as they had to deny ethnographic and anthropologic facts. But Professor Hans Günther, a leading Nazi racial scientist, found a definition that could solve the Nazis' racial dilemma. He wrote: "The Gypsies have indeed retained some elements from their Nordic home, but they are descended from the lowest classes of the population in that region. In the course of their migration, they absorbed the blood of the surrounding peoples and thus became an Oriental, West-Asiatic racial mixture with an addition of Indian, mid-Asiatic, and European strains. Their nomadic mode of living is a result of this mixture. The Gypsies will generally affect Europe as aliens."[1]

Germany's Ministry of Interior established a department to deal solely with the Gypsies. It identified a group of "pure Gypsies" (*reinrassiger Zigeuner*)—a small minority comprising less than 10 percent of the total Gypsy population. The remainder were clarified as part-Gypsy

(*Zigeunermischling*)—Gypsies who over generations of wanderings merged with humanity's most inferior and criminal elements. Based on these definitions, the "pure Gypsies" were a harmless element, particularly the small minority that settled in dwellings and ended their nomadic lifestyle; the remaining majority comprised a criminal and parasitic element that needed to be eliminated.[2]

Notwithstanding this definition, the Nazis did not feel confident that ideologically they could base the persecution of the Gypsies on racist theories alone. Using the prevailing negative stereotype of the Gypsies among large segments of the population, they preferred to justify the persecutions of the Gypsies by defining them as "asocial elements." The Gypsies were regarded as aliens in Nazi German society; they endangered the purity of Aryan blood and the public health. Many restrictions, which included special identity cards, were imposed on them even before the outbreak of World War II. After the beginning of the war, their situation in Germany worsened. At a conference held in Berlin on January 30, 1940, a decision was taken to expel thirty thousand Gypsies from Germany to the territories of occupied Poland. Due to the general situation in occupied Poland at that time, and because of transportation difficulties, this plan was postponed but not canceled; five thousand Gypsies were sent along with twenty thousand Jews from Germany to the Lodz ghetto—which was in that part of Poland annexed to Germany—in November 1941. Most of them died from typhus within a few months; those who survived were sent to the Chelmno extermination camp, together with the Jews from this ghetto, in March/April 1942. Smaller transports of Gypsies were sent to other Jewish ghettos and suffered the same fate as the Jews. The reports of the SS *Einsatzgruppen* that operated in the occupied territories of the Soviet Union mention the murder of thousands of Gypsies along with the massive extermination of the Jews in these areas.[3]

The deportations and executions of the Gypsies came under Himmler's authority. On December 16, 1942, Himmler issued an order to send all Gypsies to the concentration camps, with a few exceptions. Exempted from deportation were those Gypsy tribes within the Third Reich who had succeeded in maintaining both Aryan purity and a lifestyle and standards of behavior that could, according to Nazi judgment, justify their being spared the fate of expulsion and later extermination. Among those who evaded the deportation from Germany were the Sinte and Lalleri Gypsy tribes. Such an exemption was never given to any segment of the Jewish population, neither in Germany nor in any other part of occupied Europe.[4]

The deported Gypsies were sent to Auschwitz-Birkenau, where a special Gypsy camp was erected. Over twenty thousand Gypsies from

Germany and some other parts of Europe were sent to this camp, and most of them were gassed there.[5]

The data collected about Gypsies sent to Jewish ghettos in the General Government is very limited. Gypsies lived in only a few places (ghettos) from which the inhabitants were expelled to the death camps of Sobibor, Belzec, and Treblinka. But hundreds of Gypsies, some of them from Germany, were expelled to the Warsaw ghetto in April–June 1942. Adam Czerniakow, the head of the Jewish council there, mentioned them in his diary. He wrote that at the end of April 1942, a few dozen Gypsies were brought to the ghetto and put in the prison. After being deloused, they were set free in the ghetto. Other groups of Gypsies arrived in the ghetto, went through the prison, and were set free in June 1942. In the entry for June 16, 1942, Czerniakow mentions 190 Gypsies who were released from prison.[6] The Gypsies in the Warsaw ghetto had to wear armbands with the letter Z for *Zigeuner* ("Gypsy" in German).

Emmanuel Ringelblum wrote in his diary on June 17, 1942, that 240 Gypsy families were brought to the ghetto and located in Pokorna Street. As a possible reason why the Germans sent them to the ghetto, Ringelblum assumed that "they wish to toss into the ghetto everything that is characteristically dirty, shabby, bizarre, of which one ought to be frightened and which anyway has to be destroyed."[7] The final fate of the Gypsies in the Warsaw ghetto was the same fate that befell the Jews—they were sent to Treblinka and murdered there.

Several groups of Gypsies were brought to Treblinka for extermination without passing through a ghetto. The first group, some seventy people from the Warsaw area, arrived and was exterminated in the summer of 1942. Later, in February 1943, several hundred more Gypsies arrived.[8] These Gypsies were brought to the camp in their wagons; they usually entered through the main gate and were taken to the gas chambers via Seidel Street to the extermination area. On a few occasions the Gypsies arrived in one or two special railroad cars.[9] Small groups of Gypsies, a family or a few individuals, who were brought to Treblinka were shot at the Lazarett rather than being taken to the gas chambers.[10] The Gypsies' clothing and meager belongings were not brought to Sorting Square for shipment; rather, they were destroyed or thrown outside the camp and burned there.

Wiernik described the arrival of the largest of the Gypsy groups brought to Treblinka, apparently in the spring of 1943:

> One day, while I was working near the gate, I noticed the Germans and Ukrainians making special preparations. The *Stabsscharführer*, a short, squat man of about fifty, with a face of a murderer, left the camp several times in a car. Meanwhile the gate opened, and about 1,000 Gypsies were brought in (this

was the third transport of Gypsies). About 200 of them were men, and the rest women and children. All their belongings were piled up with them on the wagons—filthy rags, torn bedding, and other beggar's belongings. They arrived with nearly no security escort; they were brought in by two Ukrainians in German uniform who themselves did not know the entire truth. The latter asked to take care of the formalities and get a receipt for delivering the transport. They weren't even allowed into the camp. Their request was honored with a sarcastic smile. As this procedure was being carried out, they learned from the Ukrainians in the camp that they had brought victims to an extermination camp. They paled, didn't believe what they had been told, and made an attempt to enter the camp. Then the *Stabsscharführer* came out and gave them a sealed envelope. They left. All the Gypsies were taken to the gas chambers and then burned.[11]

The Gypsies did not realize what was happening until they were actually inside the closed gas chambers. Only then did they try to break out. Shimon Goldberg, who worked near the gas chambers, wrote:

> While I was there, they killed about 2,000 Gypsies. The Gypsies went wild, screamed awfully and wanted to break down the chambers. They climbed up the walls toward the apertures at the top and even tried to break the barred window. The Germans climbed onto the roof, fired inside, sealed off the apertures and asphyxiated everyone.[12]

The number of Gypsy victims at Treblinka can be estimated at over 2,000. There is almost no evidence about Gypsies brought for extermination in Sobibor and Belzec. A Jewish survivor from Sobibor, Dov Freiberg, mentioned in his testimony that "he remembers a transport with Gypsies that arrived in Sobibor" but he gave no details or approximate numbers.[13]

In all the documents relating to Belzec, there is no mention of Gypsies having been brought there. But a Polish woman, Maria Damiel, who lived in the township of Belzec, testified: "In the year 1942, when I was going on the Rava-Russkaya-Belzec highway, I saw Germans who were bringing two trucks full of Gypsies. The Gypsies implored on their knees to be released."[14] However, from this testimony it is unclear whether these two trucks with the Gypsies were taken to the death camp and exterminated there. In any case, there were no survivors among the Gypsies brought to any of the Operation Reinhard death camps.

Gypsies from the General Government who were not sent to Auschwitz or to the Operation Reinhard camps were shot on the spot by the local police or gendarmes. In the eastern region of the Cracow district, in the counties of Sanok, Jaslo, and Rzeszow, close to one thousand gypsies were shot. About one hundred Gypsies were shot in some places in the county of Radomsk in the Radom district during the second half of

1943. There are testimonies that hundreds of Gypsy families were shot in the counties of Siedlce and Ostrow-Mazowiecka in the Warsaw district.[15] There were many other places where Gypsies were shot, but no information or testimonies were left. Likewise, the total number of Gypsies from the General Government of Poland who were exterminated in the death camps or shot in the localities they lived in, or even of those who survived the Nazi occupation, is unknown. No comprehensive research on the subject has been carried out, and no further data are available.

THE ECONOMIC PLUNDER

THE HIGH AUTHORITIES OF THE SS took steps to ensure that all the belongings, especially those of any value, of the Jews that were exterminated in the death camps would remain under their control and further their goals. The belongings and valuables were slated for distribution among the SS men and their families, to the Department for *Volksdeutsche* (VoMi), an organization in the SS responsible for the affairs of the *Volksdeutsche* whose purpose was to aid the Germans living in the German-occupied European countries, as well as to the Economic Ministry and the Reichsbank.

In an order dated September 26, 1942, from SS *Brigadeführer* August Frank, one of the heads of the Economic and Administrative Main Office (*Wirtschaft Verwaltungs Hauptamt*, WVHA) of the SS, to Operation Reinhard headquarters and to the commandant of Auschwitz, the guidelines for the treatment and distribution of the belongings of the Jews who had been brought to the death camps were set out:

1. All money in bills of the Reichsbank (i.e., German money) will be deposited in Account No. 158/1488 of the WVHA in the Reichsbank.
2. Foreign currency, rare metals, diamonds, precious stones, pearls, gold teeth, and pieces of gold will be transferred to the WVHA for deposit in the Reichsbank.
3. Watches, fountain pens, lead pencils, shaving utensils, pen knives, scissors, pocket flashlights, and purses will be transferred to the workshops of the WVHA for cleaning and repair and from there will be transferred to the troops (i.e., SS) for sale.
4. Men's clothing and underwear, including shoes, will be sorted and checked. Whatever cannot be used by the prisoners in the concentration camps and items of special value will be kept for the troops; the rest will be transferred to VoMi.
5. Women's underwear and clothing will be sold to the VoMi, except for pure silk underwear (men's or women's), which will be sent directly to the Economic Ministry.
6. Feather-bedding, blankets, umbrellas, baby carriages, handbags, leather belts, baskets, pipes, sunglasses, mirrors, briefcases, and material will be transferred to VoMi. Payment will be arranged later.

7. Bedding, like sheets and pillowcases, as well as towels and tablecloths will be sold to VoMi.

8. All types of eyeglasses will be forwarded for the use of the Medical Authority. Glasses with gold frames will be transferred without the lenses along with the precious metals.

9. All types of expensive furs, styled or not, will be transferred to the SS-WVHA. Furs of lesser quality will be transferred to the Waffen SS clothing workshops in Ravensbrück bei Furstenberg in accordance with Order BII of the SS-WVHA.

10. All articles mentioned in paragraphs 4, 5, 6, or little or no value will be transferred by the SS-WVHA for the use of the Economic Ministry. With regard to articles not specified in the aforementioned paragraphs, the Chief of the SS-WVHA should be consulted as to the use to be made of them.

11. The prices for the various articles are set by the SS-WVHA. . . . Therefore the price of a pair of used pants will be 3 marks, a woolen blanket—6 marks. . . . Check that all Jewish stars have been removed from all clothing before transfer. Carefully check whether all hidden and sewn-in valuables have been removed from all articles to be transferred.[1]

This comprehensive written order was a summary of existing verbal instructions and procedures. Its aim was to institute formally the transfer of the goods and to prevent substantial sums of the money, valuables, and better clothing left by the victims from being pilfered by individuals or establishments outside the SS Economic and Administrative Main Office.

To exploit these goods maximally and to carry out Frank's order, a detailed work system had to be developed. Inside the camps the prisoners had to be put to work sorting the articles according to their destination and preparing them for transportation. In addition, a central location and authority, where the goods from the death camps would be transferred, had to be put into operation in the framework of Operation Reinhard. In the camps all the work involved in preparing the goods was carried out by special work teams of Jewish prisoners. They sorted and subdivided the belongings left by the victims. It was their responsibility to search the clothes for money or valuables and to remove the yellow stars, documents, or any other mark that could in any way identify the items as having belonged to Jews. Those who would use these goods should not know for certain their source or former owners; they could only surmise. For neglecting this order and leaving valuables or any Jewish identification, the prisoners who were in charge of this work were taken to the gas chambers or shot. The SS men who were in charge of the prisoner work groups also bore responsibility for strictly carrying out these orders. SS *Unterscharführer* Heinrich Unverhau, who was in charge of such a work group in Belzec, testified: "SS *Sturmbannführer* Hering accused me of being a saboteur because of the fact that during the sorting of the clothes that were sent for utilization in Germany, a yellow Jewish star was found. Some money was also found there. These clothes belonged to Jews who were killed in Belzec."[2]

In Belzec, the victims' belongings were temporarily stored in the locomotive shed, a few hundred meters outside the camp, close to the railway station. The clothes and other articles that were left in the undressing barrack or on the train platform were transferred to the locomotive shed by hand lorries pushed on the railway track by a work group of Jewish prisoners. Another group of prisoners sorted the belongings there and prepared them for transport. The money and valuables were put in valises and taken by prisoners, escorted by SS men, to camp headquarters near the railway station.

In Sobibor, the undressing barrack and the sorting and storing barracks were close to one another, and were adjacent to the railway station. These storing barracks could accommodate all the goods until their dispatch, because there were considerably fewer articles than in Belzec or Treblinka, proportionate to the smaller number of victims in this camp. From the stores, the goods were taken to the station and loaded by the prisoners onto a train. A Polish railway worker at Sobibor station, Jan Piwonski, testified: "I saw how the goods which were of no value to the Germans were burned. The other goods were loaded on freight cars and sent to Germany. Such transports with objects and clothing departed twice a month. Valuables, gold, and money were packed in an iron box and sent to Berlin twice a week. . . . I myself saw these boxes. The guards [Ukrainians] said that inside those boxes were gold, money, and valuables."[3]

In Treblinka the situation was different. In the first months of the camp's operation there were so many transports that the barracks that had been constructed for clothes storage could hold only a small fraction of the belongings. Therefore, the victims' belongings began to be concentrated in the reception area. After they were sorted into categories, a large amount, mostly clothing, was left in the reception area until it was ready for transport by train. Another part of the belongings, mostly small but more valuable articles, were stored in a barrack near the train platform and in a barrack near the transport yard that at first had been intended to serve as an undressing barrack for the men. However, its purpose was altered, and the men were made to undress outside. The sorting of the belongings was done by prisoners working in sorting groups.

Oscar Strawczinski, a Jewish prisoner who was put to work at sorting, related:

> The group to which I belonged, consisting of several hundred people, reaches the yard and begins working. . . . On the blankets and tablecloths that are spread on the ground are piled all kinds of articles, from imported material

and expensive suits to plain rags. . . . From the suitcases we remove notions, cosmetics, soap, matches, medicines. It seems that there is nothing that we do not remove here in quantities—all sorts, from the most expensive tins to the few potatoes that the poor Jews brought with them. The sorted articles are brought nonstop to the edge of the yard, where they are piled up and up. The suitcases with valuables have a special place; into them are put things made of gold, watches, rings, diamonds. Wedding rings make up the greatest quantity of valuable articles. There are also great quantities of foreign exchange, dollar bills and coins, pounds sterling and gold Russian coins. Polish money is gathered into large piles. From time to time some "gold Jews" come to the yard and take suitcases full of valuables and money to their workshops and leave behind the empty suitcases that they brought with them. These are also filled up within a short time. . . .

The entire yard gives the impression of a market. There is a special place for housewares and bottles. Among the housewares there are utensils of the most expensive nickel or aluminum as well as old broken pots. . . .

I work in a group of twenty men. They make us sort packages from the transport from Czechoslovakia. I open a package and find underwear, suits, shoes, notions, and so on. I am still new at this work so I am not sure what to throw onto the pile of silk clothing, of partially silk clothing, wool, cotton. . . . One must always be in motion; to rest or sit down is prohibited—one could pay for that dearly.[4]

After the initial sorting of the belongings in the sorting yard, there was an additional sorting according to the quality and value of the articles. Household goods and old, poor-quality articles, which were not worth sending even as raw material, were burned on the spot in a special pit prepared for this purpose.

The gold teeth that had been extracted from the corpses of the victims after they had been removed from the gas chambers were packed, transferred to the camps' headquarters, and from there sent to their destinations. Abraham Lindwaser, who was made to extract teeth in Treblinka, related that during the period that the transports arrived, every week an average of two suitcases full of gold, each with eighteen kilograms, were sent from Treblinka. The money, gold, and valuables were sent from Treblinka in an armored car or in a special railway car with an SS and Ukrainian guard escort.[5]

SS *Unterscharführer* Gustav Münzberger related: "I know that Matthes [who was in charge of Camp III], at the end of each day when a transport arrived, used to take the gold to the Lower Camp. This relates to gold teeth and valuables of gold that had been found on the corpses. This gold was brought in a small case."[6]

Shmuel Rajzman testified that he, the "camp elder" Galewski, and the capo of the *Lazarett*, Ze'ev Korland, kept a secret watch on the number of transports of Jews that were brought to the gas chambers in Treblinka and then the transports leaving Treblinka with the belongings of the victims. According to Rajzman, the transports with belongings included 248 railway cars of clothing, 100 cars of shoes, 22 cars of material, 260 cars of bedding, about 450 cars with various different articles and household goods, and hundreds more cars with various rags—all in all, about 1,500 cars full of belongings.[7]

Franciszek Zabecki, a Pole who worked in the railway station at Treblinka, wrote that from the account that he kept while watching the railway station at Treblinka, more than 1,000 cars full of the victims' belongings passed through the station. This estimate is very close to exact, as verified by documents that have come into our possession from the Gedob relating to three freight trains with clothing that were sent from Treblinka to Lublin by way of Siedlce. The first was on September 9, at which time 51 cars left; the second was on September 13, on which date 50 cars left; and the third on September 21, with 52 cars. In all, in a matter of twelve days in September 1942, 153 cars full of victims' clothing left Treblinka.[8] If we assume that the clothing was approximately one-third, or a little more, of the victims' luggage, which also included bedding, kitchen utensils, and other possessions, then besides the 153 cars of clothes that were sent from Treblinka, there were between 250 and 300 cars with other articles, which means a total of 400 to 450 cars. This, then, was the amount of the belongings that were accumulated in the camp during its first few months of operation, during which time approximately one-third of the Jews who would eventually be killed there were brought to Treblinka. Therefore, we may estimate the quantity of belongings that the Jews brought with them during the entire period of the camp's operation at a minimum of 1,200 railway cars.

All the trains with clothing were sent to the camp in the old airport of Lublin. In this camp the SS clothing workshops were located; they were subordinate to the central Waffen SS clothing workshops in Ravensbrück, Germany. At the beginning of March 1942, these clothing workshops in Lublin were transferred to the command of Globocnik as a sub-camp of Majdanek. This became the collection, disinfection, repair, and sorting place for the clothing taken from the victims of Operation Reinhard before their belongings were distributed to the various authorities stipulated in the order of SS *Brigadeführer* August Frank.

About five hundred to seven hundred Jewish prisoners, mainly women, worked in this camp. The old hangars were converted into stores for the clothing. In March 1943, the camp was placed under the command of Christian Wirth, as an integral part of Operation Reinhard. Wirth's headquarters were even located in this camp. Ernst Gollak, an SS man who served for three years in the SS clothing workshops, from January 1942 onward, testified:

> From May or June 1942, in this clothing camp of Lublin, furs and coats of Jews who were in the extermination camps of Belzec, Treblinka, and Sobibor were disinfected and sent to Germany. These articles were brought by freight trains, unloaded by the [Ukrainian] auxiliaries and later by the working Jews, disinfected, and loaded again in the freight cars. I was in charge of a group of twenty to thirty Jewish women who were trained as disinfectors.... The clothing was divided according to men's, women's, and children's clothing. Then it was subdivided again; outer and under clothing, shoes, etc. Where these sorted clothes were sent I don't know exactly. I once saw on the freight cars the names of the train stations: Berlin, Glogau, Breslau, and Hirschberg.[9]

There are some very important Nazi documents concerning the economic aspects of Operation Reinhard and the quantity of goods, money, and valuables that Germany aggregated from the extermination actions. A report submitted by SS *Sturmbannführer* Georg Wippern, the administrative head of Operation Reinhard, to Heinrich Himmler's headquarters gave details of Jewish property received for delivery up to February 3, 1943. The summarized total sum in German marks of this four-page report is as follows:

1. Cash and cash balance delivered	RM	53,013,133.51
2. Foreign currency in notes		1,452,904.65
3. Foreign currency in gold coins		843,802.75
4. Precious metals		5,353,943.00
5. Miscellaneous		26,089,800.00
6. Textiles		13,294,400.00
	RM	100,047983.91[10]

SS *Obergruppenführer* Oswald Pohl, head of the SS Economic and Administrative Main Office, issued a report on February 6, 1943, regarding "hitherto utilization of textile materials originating from the evacuation of the Jews." This report includes the textile materials forwarded from Auschwitz and from Operation Reinhard and to whom they were submitted. According to this report, the Reich Economic Ministry received 262,000 complete men's and women's outfits, over 2.7 million kilograms of rags, 270,000 kilograms of bed feathers, and 3,000 kilograms of women's hair—all transported in 570 freight cars. The *Volksdeutsche Mittelstelle* (VoMi) received 211 freight cars full of men's, women's, and children's clothing. The *Reichsiugendführung* (command of the youths of the Reich), the I. G. Farben industry, the Todt Organization, concentration camps, and the General Inspector of Transport Leaders all received an additional 44 freight cars full of clothing. The total was 825 freight cars containing textile materials.[11]

This report relates to the textile materials transferred during 1942. That year the majority of deported Jews were sent to the death camps of Operation Reinhard rather than to Auschwitz; therefore, these camps were the main source of the textiles mentioned in Pohl's report.

Fritz Katzmann, the SS and police leader in the district of Galicia, from where most of the Jews were deported to Belzec, submitted a report to higher SS and police leader of the General Government Friedrich Kruger on the "Solution of the Jewish Question in Galicia." This report, dated June 30, 1943, describes the sequence of the persecution and liquidation of the Jews in East Galicia (Lvov region) and relates also to the property of the victims: "Simultaneously with the evacuation *Aktionen*, Jewish property was collected. Valuables were secured and handed over to the 'Reinhard Special Staff.' Apart from the furniture and large quantities of textiles, etc., the following were confiscated and delivered to the 'Reinhard Special Staff.'"

Then came a long, detailed list of coins, rings, watches, and other valuables, subdivided into gold, silver, and other metals—all this in kilograms. Further on was a list of currencies, mainly foreign, collected in bank notes.[12]

On January 5, 1944, Globocnik submitted to Himmler a report summarizing the money, gold, and valuables taken from the Jews in Operation Reinhard. The summary was given in Reichsmarks; it included money from forty-eight countries; gold coins from thirty-four countries; 2,910 kilograms of gold bars; 18,734 kilograms of silver bars; 16,000 diamond carats; and more. The total value of all the valuables (money, valuables, and belongings) taken from the Jews by Operation Reinhard headquarters was also listed in the report's summary:

Money in zlotys and German marks	RM	73,852,080.74
Precious metals		8,973,651.60
Foreign currency in bills		4,521,224.13
Foreign currency in gold		1,736,554.12
Precious stones and other valuables		43,662,450.00
Fabric		46,000,000.00
Total in German marks		178,745,960.59[13]

(2.5 German marks were equal to $1 at that time.)

All the written reports contain only what was transferred by Operation Reinhard headquarters to the higher authorities of the Reich, but they did not contain the money, gold, valuables, and belongings the SS pilfered for themselves—by those who were occupied with deporting the Jews as well as those serving in the camps or as commanding officers in Lublin, Warsaw, and Berlin. A rough estimate would be in the millions. The treasures that the victims left were a source of enrichment for the SS and German institutions and caused internal struggles among the various organizations.

The extermination of the Jews by the German Nazis stemmed from Nazi racial ideology; the resultant control over the Jews' property, money, and valuables should be seen as an important byproduct of this ideology.

While Dr. Irmfried Eberl was commander of Treblinka, the money and valuables were not sent through Operation Reinhard headquarters or to the higher authorities of the SS, but directly to those in charge of the euthanasia program in Hitler's Chancellery. Since Eberl and some of his advisers had originally come from the ranks of the euthanasia program, they retained their connections there. Franz Suchomel, the SS man in charge of the "gold Jews" in Treblinka, tells of a messenger from Hitler's Chancellery who came to the camp with an order from SA *Oberführer* Werner Blankenburg, one of the heads of the euthanasia program, instructing the SS to hand over to him one million marks. "We filled his suitcase with a million marks, and he returned with it to Berlin," related Suchomel.[14] Franz Stangl confided to Odilo Globocnik his suspicion that his direct superior, Christian Wirth, together with Dr. Eberl, had decided to bypass Operation Reinhard headquarters and transfer the money and valuables from Treblinka directly to Berlin. Stangl promised he would ensure that all property and valuables would be transferred to Globocnik's headquarters. Stangl related that when he reached Treblinka, he chatted with the SS men serving there: "They said they had great fun: shooting was 'sport': there was more money and stuff around than one could dream of, all there for the taking: all one had to do was help oneself."[15]

And, indeed, the SS men and Ukrainians in the camp did help themselves to large amounts of money, gold, valuables, and belongings. Jakub (Abraham) Krzepicki, a prisoner in Treblinka, related:

Some of the Germans enjoyed collecting all sorts of "curios." They made no effort to hide it from us, but among themselves, the Germans were wary of each other. They would come right over to us and take away a nice gold watch which they would immediately take to one of the six Jewish watchmakers to put in working order. Or they would pick out a particularly unusual ring or some other item of women's jewelry, no doubt as a gift to their sweethearts in the Fatherland. All of them, both Germans and Ukrainians, had so much money that they did not even bother to touch it. I think that they all became millionaires in Treblinka.[16]

Stanislaw (Shlomo) Szmajzner, a jeweler, was put to work in Sobibor making jewelry for the SS officials. He made a monogrammed ring for Stangl, the commander of the camp, and other SS men liked the idea and also began bringing him gold rings for monogramming. But despite his expert work, Szmajzner was constantly subjected to threats on his life by various SS personnel who wanted the work kept secret from other SS men and from the prisoners. Once Gustav Wagner was already in the process of leading Szmajzner to the gas chambers because another prisoner had revealed his knowledge of Szmajzner's work. Only by a miracle was he saved that time.[17]

When the SS went on vacation to Germany, they would take suitcases and parcels full of Jews' belongings. So as not to be too conspicuous when leaving the camp with their packages, the SS in Treblinka would send their parcels ahead with the two German railroad workers, Wili Klinzman and Rudolf Emmerich, who would bring the transports from Treblinka train station to the camp and return with the empty cars. After the SS men left the camp for their vacation, they would stop by Treblinka or Malkinia train station and pick up the packages they had forwarded. In return for this service and as a reward for their silence, Klinzman and Emmerich were bribed accordingly.[18]

Part of the money taken from the victims was used by the Operation Reinhard staff for purchasing camp equipment, barracks, vehicles, and other articles, as well as for financing activities connected with the implementation of the deportations and extermination.[19]

The money that was taken from the Jewish victims was also used by the camp commanders to improve the living conditions of the SS men in the camps. This, however, was in violation of orders. SS *Oberscharführer* Alfred Ittner, who was the treasurer of Sobibor, testified that the camp commander, Stangl, ordered him to buy additional food for the camp staff with part of the victims' money. Ittner claimed that special funding had been provided for this purpose and that it was against orders and therefore he was reluctant to comply. Ittner was subsequently replaced as treasurer by another SS man.[20]

The Ukrainian guards and, through them, the local population also grew rich as a result of the murder of the Jews and the property that the victims had brought with them. Even the speculators of Warsaw and other cities benefited. Jerzy Królikowski, a Polish engineer who worked in the vicinity of Treblinka, wrote:

> The events that I have described [the extermination of the Jews in Treblinka] caused a real revolution in the vicinity of Treblinka. The poor areas of Podlassia overflowed with gold, and riffraff from all over the country came there

to get rich quickly and easily. Even among the local population there was, unfortunately, a certain group that wanted to make a fortune from the Jewish tragedy at any cost. It was our luck that as far as I know the workers in our construction company were not tempted to go along with this. I scorned the frequent offers I was made to buy watches, gold coins, and various articles for almost nothing. The Ukrainian fascists who were on the staff of the death camp were the ones who brought the gold coins, valuables, and money from the camp. At first they were not aware of the real value of the articles, and one could buy all kinds of things for next to nothing. Men's watches were sold literally for pennies, and local farmers kept dozens of them in egg baskets to offer them for sale.

The Ukrainian fascists, who were totally corrupted by the wealth they had acquired with no effort, were contemptuous of its worth. For example, they would pay for a drink without even counting the bills. . . . The avarice that was rampant among a certain section of the local population destroyed all moral foundations. In the neighboring villages near the camp the Ukrainian fascists were welcomed by some of the local farmers. Their daughters, as it was widely known, became the girlfriends of the murderers and enjoyed the benefits of their generous hearts. It is no wonder that, even though it was wartime, one could see in the neighboring villages extensive construction on the farms and the village women wearing furs and clothes of expensive material whose source was well known.[21]

Testimonies as to the widespread trade between the Ukrainians in Treblinka and the farmers and speculators in the area and even as far as Warsaw have been given by SS men Stangl and Suchomel, as well as by Jewish prisoners. They have even related that prostitutes from Warsaw, in addition to their professional "services" to the Ukrainians, also speculated for them.

The Ukrainian guards in the camps stole the money and valuables directly from the people in the transports as they were brought to the camps, as well as from the "gold Jews." In Treblinka they would usually barge into the barracks where the "gold Jews" worked and swipe gold and valuables from them under threats to their lives if the Germans were told. Wiernik writes that once when the Germans discovered what was going on they tortured and then murdered half of the "gold Jews."[22]

The true value of the property, money, and valuables taken from the Jews who were murdered in the Operation Reinhard camps can never be accurately estimated. The figures that appear in the Operation Reinhard headquarters' report of January 5, 1944, quoted earlier in the chapter, are only a part of the total value: these figures were what was officially submitted to the Reich authorities. A tremendous amount of Jewish property crept into the private pockets of Germans and Ukrainians who had any connection with the expulsions or who served in the camps, and through them to the local neighboring population. Moreover, large amounts of money and valuables were lost forever with the tens of thousands of Jews who died en route on the trains or who were shot when they arrived in the camps, for they were buried with their clothes.

Along with the hundreds of thousands of victims of the Operation Reinhard camps, an inestimable amount of property, which had been earned and accumulated over a period of several generations by the Jewish inhabitants of Poland and other European countries, was lost with them. The murderers inherited all.

HIMMLER'S VISIT TO SOBIBOR AND TREBLINKA

In late February or early March 1943, Heinrich Himmler visited Operation Reinhard headquarters and the death camps of Sobibor and Treblinka. Himmler had already paid a visit to Operation Reinhard headquarters in the first stage of the extermination action, in the middle of July 1942. The second visit also included the death camps, places he had not inspected on his first tour. The February 1943 visit was in the closing stage of Operation Reinhard, which, according to Himmler's order of July 19, 1942, had to be accomplished by December 31, 1942.

Belzec had actually ceased its killing activity before the end of 1942, but Himmler's deadline was extended for several months for the other two camps after the extermination of the Jews from the Bialystok General District was included in Operation Reinhard. In the middle of February 1943, this operation had also come to its end. On February 16, 1943, Himmler issued an order for the final liquidation of the Warsaw ghetto, the last large ghetto in the General Government. For him this symbolized the end of Operation Reinhard.[1]

Of the 1.7 million Jews murdered during Operation Reinhard in the liquidation of ghettoes and in the death camps of Belzec, Sobibor, and Treblinka, 1.65 million of them had been exterminated until the second half of February 1943, when Himmler came for his second visit. The aim of this visit was mainly to inspect the camps during their final stage of operation and to determine their future and that of their personnel. By that time there was no longer a need for the death camps of Operation Reinhard. Auschwitz-Birkenau had increased its killing capacity by constructing more and larger gas chambers and crematoria, and it could now meet all the needs of the Nazi extermination machine for all of occupied Europe.

In anticipation of Himmler's visit, the camps were cleaned. The prisoners were put to work tidying the camps to impress this "most important" guest, whose arrival was imminent. Himmler was accompanied by a group of ten to fifteen dignitaries in SS or army uniforms. SS *Oberscharführer* Karl Frenzel testified about Himmler's visit to Sobibor: "The visit was announced a few days ahead. The leadership of the camp took steps to make order in the camp.... I was ordered, together with some *Unterführers* [SS men] and Ukrainian guards, to take over the outside security of the camp and guarantee Himmler's personal security. When Himmler visited the gassing installation in Camp III, I guarded the surrounding area. I remember that afterwards all the *Unterführers* were assembled in the canteen, and Himmler delivered an address to them."[2]

On the day that Himmler was to visit Sobibor, no regular transport with Jews for extermination was scheduled to arrive. But the commanding authorities of Operation Reinhard, whether at their own initiative or at Himmler's request, planned to show their guest a gassing in action. Therefore, a special group of young Jews was selected from a transport that had arrived in Sobibor a few days before Himmler's visit. Ada Lichtman testified about what happened to this group:

> During the preparations for Himmler's visit, a transport arrived with over 1,000 people. A group of young people was taken out and kept overnight. They were given food and drinks. We did not know what was going to happen; we thought that they would be attached to us, for work. But it happened differently. These youngsters were not sent to work.... Himmler arrived. The commanders of the camp welcomed the important guests and toured the area with them. The youngsters were taken to Camp III for extermination. Himmler and his group attended the gassing and cremation of the youngsters. After this killing operation, all of them went to the canteen, where tables with food and flowers had been prepared for these murderers.[3]

According to other testimonies, there were no ordinary transports on the days of Himmler's visit. A special group of several hundred young Jewish girls was brought to Sobibor from one of the labor camps in the Lublin district, and their gassing was carried out as a show for Himmler.[4]

SS *Oberscharführer* Hubert Gomerski mentioned this gassing in his testimony: "I remember the visit of *Reichsführer* Heinrich Himmler in Sobibor. All the SS men, members of the police, and the Ukrainian volunteers were lined up in a parade. I personally reported my platoon to Himmler for inspection. I know that on the day when Himmler was in Sobibor a certain number of Jews was gassed.... I can tell for sure that Himmler visited Camp III. I saw Himmler with the whole group going in the direction of Camp III."[5]

Himmler's visit to Treblinka is described by Tanhum Greenberg:

> One day we received orders that someone extremely important was about to arrive for a visit. We were not told who the man was, but we had to clean

the camp thoroughly. They ran us and beat us to make us clean quickly. There was a great commotion. Then they locked us in a hut, and we could only see through a window. Seven cars arrived, with Himmler in one of them. His entourage comprised about twenty people. The "Doll" [Kurt Franz] and the *Obersturmführer* [Stangl] showed them the camp. They passed by the huts quickly on their way to the *Lazarett*. Then they went to the extermination area, where they stayed half an hour. Later they got into their cars and drove off.[6]

Himmler learned from his visit to Treblinka that, in spite of his orders, the corpses of the Jews who had been exterminated in this camp had not been cremated, but buried. Immediately after this visit, the big cremating operation began in the camp. This was the main task imposed on Treblinka during the last months of the camp's existence.

Himmler found the camps of Sobibor and Treblinka virtually idle of new transports. It was apparently his decision that, until the camps were dosed, transports from Holland would be directed to Sobibor, and some transports from the annexed Bulgarian area of Yugoslav Macedonia and Greek Thrace would be sent to Treblinka. However, this did not change the decision Himmler had reached during his visit—Operation Reinhard was basically accomplished, and its camps were to be closed after the completion of their final tasks: in Sobibor, the annihilation of the transports with Jews from Holland, and in Treblinka, the burning of the hundreds of thousands of corpses buried there.

Himmler, impressed with the efficiency and dedication of the Operation Reinhard staff, concluded his visit with a decision to promote the commanding officers of the operation and a group of noncommissioned officers who had excelled in the extermination action. In a letter written to SS *Gruppenführer* Maximilian von Herff, the head of the SS Personnel Main Office, dated April 13, 1943, Odilo Globocnik stated: "The SS *Reichsführer*, on the occasion of his visit to Operation Reinhard installations in March, as I have already verbally informed you, has approved the promotion of the best men and commanders who are engaged in this action. Attached is the promotion list, which I have already sent you."[7]

The promotion list included twenty-eight members of the SS and German Police, among them Wirth and the commanders of Belzec, Sobibor, and Treblinka. There were, however, some bureaucratic obstacles to their promotion, and Globocnik wrote a second letter to the SS Personnel Main Office on May 22, 1943: "To explain the whole matter, I would like to add the following. The above-mentioned Wirth, Hering, Reichleitner, and Stangl are the commanders who were at the forefront of the action in Operation Reinhard."[8]

Christian Wirth was promoted to the rank of SS *Sturmbannführer* and his adjutant, SS *Oberscharführer* Josef Oberhauser, to the officer rank of *Untersturmführer*. The three camp commanders, Gottlieb Hering (Belzec), Franz Reichleitner (Sobibor), and Franz Stangl (Treblinka), were promoted to the rank of *Hauptsturmführer*. In his recommendation to promote Stangl, Globocnik noted that of all his subordinate extermination camp commanders, "Stangl is the best camp commander and had the most prominent part in the whole action. While still in the Austrian police, he served as an undercover SS man." The three deputy commanders of the camps, Gottfried Schwartz (Belzec), Josef Niemann (Sobibor), and Kurt Franz (Treblinka), who held the rank of SS *Oberscharführer*, were promoted to SS *Untersturmführer*.

The decrease in the pace of extermination activities in the death camps of Operation Reinhard had begun at the end of 1942, with the cessation of the killing activities in Belzec and the reduction of these activities in the other two camps during the winter of 1942–43. Himmler's visit to Operation Reinhard installations, in February or early March 1943, marked the beginning of the closing stage of the entire operation. The annihilation of the Jews in the General Government had almost been achieved.

After Himmler's visit, the date for closing and liquidating the camps of Belzec, Sobibor, and Treblinka became dependent on the completion of the cremation of the victims' corpses and the erasure of all traces of the crimes that had been carried out in these camps. The timetable for carrying out this decision lay mainly in the hands of the camp commanders and in their ability and desire to accomplish the erasure of the crimes as quickly as possible.

The decision to close and dismantle the camps of Belzec and Treblinka remained unchanged, but the fate of Sobibor underwent alteration. On July 5, 1943, Himmler issued an order not to dismantle Sobibor but to transform it into a concentration camp. This order was addressed to SS *Obergruppenführer* Oswald Pohl, who was in charge of the concentration camps, and to Globocnik and to the higher SS and police leaders in the General Government and in the German-occupied territories of the Soviet Union. The first paragraph stated: "The transit camp Sobibor in the District of Lublin has to be transformed into a concentration camp. In the concentration camp a depot for booty ammunition has to be established."[9] Further, the order stressed that the higher SS and police leaders had to deliver to this camp all kinds of ammunition taken from the enemy, and it specified how it should be treated there.

The order that Sobibor was to become a concentration camp meant it would now be subordinate to Pohl instead of Globocnik. Both Pohl and

Globocnik were not satisfied with this change in subordination. On July 15, 1943, Pohl wrote to Himmler: "*Reichsführer*, following your order that the transit camp Sobibor in the District of Lublin should be transformed into a concentration camp, I had a talk on this subject with SS *Gruppenführer* Globocnik. Both of us propose to give up the idea of the transformation into a concentration camp. Your desired aim, namely to install in Sobibor a depot for confiscated ammunition, can be achieved without change. Everything else in the above-mentioned order can remain. Please let me have your endorsement, which is important for *Gruppenführer* Globocnik and myself."[10]

On July 24, 1943, Pohl was informed that Himmler agreed to his proposal: namely, that Sobibor would be transformed into a confiscated ammunition camp but would remain subordinate to Globocnik.[11]

Construction work on barracks and bunkers, where the confiscated ammunition would be stored and treated, was then begun in Sobibor. The camp was enlarged, and the whole northeast section close to the railway station was rebuilt. This new part of the camp was called Camp IV or North Camp. The construction work was carried out by prisoners, whose ranks were reinforced by more Jews removed from new transports.

THE ERASURE OF THE CRIMES

THE HUNDREDS OF THOUSANDS OF Jews who had been murdered in the death camps of Operation Reinhard in the spring and summer of 1942 were originally buried in the huge pits that had been prepared for this purpose. The cremation of the corpses in the camps of Sobibor and Belzec began in the autumn of 1942 and in Treblinka in March 1943.

The idea of burning the bodies of Nazi Germany's victims in eastern Europe to erase any traces of the crimes had come up earlier. In the spring of 1942, Heinrich Himmler decided that the corpses of Jews and the Red Army prisoners who had been shot in Soviet-occupied territories and buried there in mass graves should be removed and all trace of the killing should be erased. The same would be applied to those who were to be killed in the death camps operating at that time. Reinhard Heydrich, chief of the Reich Security Main Office and the commander of the *Einsatzgruppen* of the SS that had carried out the mass killings in the Soviet-occupied territories, was entrusted with this task.

In March 1942, Heydrich met in Warsaw with SS *Standartenführer* Paul Blobel, the former commander of *Einsatzkommando* 4a, who had carried out the killings in Kiev and other places in the Ukraine. Heydrich discussed with Blobel the matter of his appointment to lead the operation of erasing all traces of the mass murders and the ways it would be implemented. Blobel's appointment to this task was postponed for about three months because of Heydrich's death, but in June 1942, SS *Gruppenführer* Heinrich Müller, the head of the Gestapo, formally appointed Blobel the task of covering up the traces of the mass executions carried out by the *Einsatzgruppen* in the East. This task was top secret, and Blobel was ordered that no written correspondence should appear on the subject. The operation was given the code name "*Sonderaktion* 1005." Blobel's duty was to find the proper technical means and system for destroying the victims' bodies, to coordinate and supervise the entire operation, and to issue the verbal orders for its implementation.[1]

After his appointment, Blobel, along with a small staff of three or four men, began experimenting with systems for burning bodies. The place chosen for these experiments was Chelmno, the first death camp that had been established and had been operating since the end of 1941. At that time, tens of thousands of Jews from the Lodz area had already been killed there; they were buried in pits in a wooded area. The pits were opened, and the first experiments were carried out. Incendiary bombs were tried, but these caused large fires in the surrounding woods. Then they started to cremate the bodies on wood in open fireplaces. The bones that remained were destroyed by a special bone-crushing machine. The ashes of the bodies and small fragments of bones were buried in the pits from which the bodies had been removed. At the conclusion of these successful experiments, Blobel had found a simple and efficient way to erase the crimes perpetrated by the SS elements.[2]

Following these experiments, the burning of the corpses of the victims murdered in Chelmno and in Auschwitz was begun, this as early as the last months of 1942. The results of Blobel's experiments were sent to Odilo Globocnik so that he could introduce cremation of the corpses in the Operation Reinhard camps. But Globocnik was not eager to carry out the erasure mission; he even had "ideological" objections to it. He felt that the German people should be proud of having exterminated the Jews and should not hide this fact from future generations. According to Kurt Gerstein's affidavit, Globocnik said, in August 1942, that instead of cremating the corpses and erasing the traces of the mass graves, they must be left and "one should bury bronze plaques [with the bodies], on which is inscribed that it was we, we who had the courage to complete this gigantic task" (see chapter 14).[3] For this reason Globocnik did not immediately enforce cremation of the corpses in the Operation Reinhard camps. Eventually, however, in spite of Globocnik's attitude, the burning of the corpses was undertaken in the camps subordinate to him.

Sobibor was first. The reasons for the operation there were local. As a result of the hot weather in the summer of 1942, the buried corpses swelled, and the fully packed mass graves rose up above the surrounding surface. The entire area became infested with vermin, and a terrible stench pervaded the camp and its surrounding areas. The camp commanders feared that the drinking water, which came from dug wells, could be contaminated and poisoned. Therefore the decision was made to start burning the bodies in Sobibor. A big excavator was brought to the camp; a special group of Jewish prisoners was also assigned to this work. The decomposed corpses were taken out of the pits by the excavator and arranged on a big roaster built from old railway tracks laid over an empty pit.

Unterscharführer Becher Warner, who served as a driver in Sobibor from August through November 1942, testified at the Sobibor trial: "The corpses were taken out from the gas chambers and cremated on a specially prepared roaster. The ashes and the remains of the bodies were buried in a specially designated place, and later a forest was planted there. . . . As I have already said, I used to bring foodstuffs to the camp and also wood for cremating the killed."[4]

The commander of Trawniki camp, SS *Sturmbannführer* Karl Streibel, testified about the cremating sites he saw during his visit to Sobibor at the end of 1942: "Wirth led me through the Sobibor camp. I saw the gas chambers and the other facilities. I saw the ditches near the gas chambers. I could not see any corpses in the ditches, because they were covered with a layer of earth. But I saw the roaster made of railway lines where the corpses were burned. During my visit, there was no extermination operation. There were also no corpses burned, but I could see the cremating sites. The roaster made from the railway lines was supported by a stone base."[5]

There were no survivors from among the Jewish prisoners who worked in the extermination area of Sobibor and were engaged in cremating the corpses. Therefore, no evidence, oral or written, was left by them about this operation. There are, however, some testimonies of Jewish prisoners who were in the other part of the camp. Leon Feldhendler wrote about the start of the cremation of the corpses in the camp: "In the first period, there was no crematorium. After gassing, the people were laid into the graves. Then, out of the soil, blood and a bad odor of gas began to surface; terrible smells spread over the whole camp, penetrating everything. The water in Sobibor became rancid. This forced the Germans to build a crematorium. It was a large pit with a roaster above it. The bodies were thrown on the roaster. The fire was ignited from beneath, and petrol was poured on the corpses. The bones were crushed into ashes with hammers."[6]

The corpses of those who were gassed after cremation was instituted were not buried; they were taken directly to the roaster and cremated. The burning of the corpses of the newcomers and of those murdered earlier went on simultaneously. The smell of burned flesh prevailed throughout the camp and its vicinity.[7]

The opening of the mass graves in Belzec and the cremating of the corpses removed from them began with the interruption of the arrival of transports and of the killing activities there in mid-December 1942. At that time there were about six hundred thousand corpses of murdered Jews in the pits of the camp. SS *Scharführer* Heinrich Gley, who served at that time in Belzec, testified:

> From the beginning of August 1942 until the camp was closed in September 1943 I was in Belzec. . . . As I remember, the gassing stopped at the end of 1942, when snow was already falling. Then the unearthing and cremation of the corpses began. It lasted from November 1942 until March 1943. The cremation was conducted day and night, without interruption. At first, the burning took place at one site, and later, at two. One cremating site had the capacity to burn 2,000 corpses in twenty-four hours. About four weeks after the beginning of the cremation operation, the second burning site was erected. On the average, during five months, at the first burning site about 300,000 corpses were cremated, and in four months at the second burning site, about 240,000 corpses. Naturally, these are average estimations.[8]

An official Polish committee investigating German crimes in the Lublin area wrote in its concluding report:

> From December 1942 the arrival of transports with Jews to the Belzec camps came to a standstill. The Germans then started to erase systematically the trails of their crimes. They started to remove from the graves, with special cranes, the corpses of the murdered, pour over them some highly flammable material, and cremate them in large heaps.
>
> Later the procedure of burning the corpses was improved, and a roaster of railway tracks was built. The corpses were laid in layers, alternated with a layer of wood. The ashes from the burned corpses were put through a screening machine so that the valuables that might have remained with the corpses could be separated and removed. Subsequently, the ashes were buried. . . . The burning of the corpses was finished in March 1943.[9]

Maria Damiel, a Polish woman who lived in the township of Belzec, testified: "We could see a machine that took out the corpses from the graves and threw them into the fire. There were a few such fires going simultaneously. At that time a dreadful smell dominated the whole area, a smell of burned human bones and bodies. From the moment they began burning the corpses, from all directions of the camp came the smell of the corpses. When the Germans completed the burning of the corpses, they dismantled the camp.[10]

As in Sobibor, also in Belzec there were no Jewish survivors from the prisoners who were engaged in the cremation of the corpses. But unlike Sobibor, in Belzec there were also no survivors from any other part of the camp who could give evidence about the cremating. Rudolf Reder escaped from Belzec at the end of November 1942, shortly before the cremation began, so he could not give firsthand testimony about the cremation of the corpses there.

The cremation of all the murdered in Belzec was accomplished by the end of April 1943.

The last camp where cremation of the corpses was instituted was Treblinka. During Himmler's visit to the camp at the end of February/beginning of March 1943, he was surprised to find that in Treblinka the corpses of over seven hundred thousand Jews who had been killed there had not yet been cremated. The very fact that the cremation began immediately after his visit makes it more than possible that Himmler, who was very sensitive about the erasure of the crimes committed by Nazi Germany, personally ordered the cremating of the corpses there. A cremation site was erected for this purpose in the extermination area of the camp.

Some of the Jewish prisoners who were employed in the cremation operations in the camp escaped during the uprising in Treblinka and survived the war. Therefore, there is more information and evidence on the cremation process and installations in Treblinka than in the other death camps. The cremating structure consisted of a roaster made from five or six railroad rails laid on top of three rows of concrete pillars each 70 cm high. The facility was 30 meters wide. The bodies were removed from the pits by an excavator. Franz Stangl, the camp commander, related:

> It must have been at the beginning of 1943. That's when excavators were brought in. Using these excavators, the corpses were removed from the huge ditches which had been used until then [for burial]. The old corpses were burned on the roasters, along with the new bodies [of new arrivals to the camp]. During the transition to the new system, Wirth came to Treblinka. As I recall, Wirth spoke of a *Standartenführer* who had experience in burning corpses. Wirth told me that according to the *Standartenführer*'s experience, corpses could be burned on a roaster, and it would work marvelously. I know that in the beginning [in Treblinka] they used rails from the trolley to build the cremation grill. But it turned out that these were too weak and bent in the heat. They were replaced with real railroad rails.[11]

The *Standartenführer* mentioned by Wirth in his conversation with Stangl was Paul Blobel, commander of Commando 1005. To introduce the cremation of corpses in Treblinka, experts were sent there from the other Operation Reinhard camps. SS *Oberscharführer* Heinrich Matthes, the commander of the "extermination area" in Treblinka, testified: "At that time SS *Oberscharführer* or *Hauptscharführer* [Herbert] Floss, who, as I assume, was previously in another extermination camp, arrived. He was in charge of the arrangements for cremating the corpses. The cremation took place in such a way that railway lines and concrete blocks were placed together. The corpses were piled on these rails. Brushwood was put under the rails. The wood was doused with petrol. In that way not only the newly accumulated corpses were cremated, but also those taken out from the graves."[12]

A special working group composed of Jewish prisoners in the extermination area was organized for the cremation operation. Additional prisoners were transferred for this operation to the extermination area from the Lower Camp, where the work had decreased significantly due to a reduction in the pace and number of transports.

After the cremation installation had been constructed, the process of removing the bodies from the pits began. The work was initiated by a single excavator; later, a second excavator was brought in. The shovel's scoop removed six to eight corpses with each dip into the pit and dumped them on the edge of the pit. A special team of prisoners, working in twos, transferred the corpses to the crematorium on stretchers. There, another special team, called the "burning group" (*Feuerkolonne*), removed the corpses from the stretchers and arranged them in layers on the roaster to a height of two meters. Between two thousand and twenty-five hundred bodies— sometimes up to three thousand—would be piled on the roaster. When all was ready, dry wood and branches, which had been laid under the roaster, were ignited. The entire construction, with the bodies, was quickly engulfed in fire. The railings would glow from the heat, and the flames would reach a height of up to ten meters.

At first an inflammable liquid was poured onto the bodies to help them burn, but later this was considered unnecessary; the SS men in charge of the cremation became convinced that the corpses burned well enough without extra fuel.

Yechiel Reichman, a member of the "burning group," wrote:

> The SS "expert" on body-burning ordered us to put women, particularly fat women, on the first layer on the grill, face down. The second layer could consist of whatever was brought—men, women, or children—and so on, layer on top of layer. . . . Then the "expert" ordered us to lay dry branches under the grill and to light them. Within a few minutes the fire would take so it was difficult to approach the crematorium from as far as 50 meters away. . . . The work was extremely difficult. The stench was awful. Liquid excretions from the corpses squirted all over the prisoner-workers. The SS man operating the excavator often dumped the corpses directly onto the prisoners working nearby, wounding them seriously.[13]

Jacob Wiernik, who was in the "extermination area," described the fire itself: "It was genuine hell. From a distance it looked like a volcanic eruption boiling up through the earth's surface and spreading flames and lava. Everything around was caught up in the noise and turmoil. At night the smoke, fire, and heat were unbearable."[14]

The body-burning took on a rapid pace. To further streamline the operation, a new work team was set up to place the bodies on the stretchers. The idea was to keep the stretcher-bearers from having to place the stretchers on the ground and load the bodies themselves; during this time they could rest for a second. Under the new system the men who transferred the bodies did not set the stretchers down throughout the day. Other efficiency measures introduced included increasing the number of cremation sites to six—thus enabling the workers to burn up to twelve thousand corpses simultaneously—and placing the cremating roasters nearer the mass graves to save time in transferring the bodies. The roasters occupied a good portion of the area east of the gas chambers, which was dear of mass graves and buildings.

The bodies of victims brought to Treblinka in transports arriving after the body-burning began were taken directly from the gas chambers to the roasters and were not buried in the ditches. These bodies did not burn as well as those removed from the ditches and had to be sprayed with fuel before they would burn.

The body-burning went on day and night. The corpses were transferred and arranged on the roasters during the day; at nightfall they were lit, and they burned throughout the night. When the fire went out, there were only skeletons or scattered bones on the roasters, and piles of ash underneath. Another special prisoner team, known as the "ash group" (*Aschkolonne*), had the task of collecting the ash and removing the remains of the charred bones from the grill and placing them on tin sheets. Round wooden sticks were then used to break the bones into small fragments. These were then run through a tightly woven screen made of metal wire; those bone fragments that did not pass through the screen were returned for further smashing. Unburned bones that proved difficult to fragment were returned to the roaster and reignited with a new pile of bodies.

The camp command was confronted with the problem of disposing of the large piles of ash and bits of bone that remained after the process was completed. Attempts to mix the ash with dirt and dust proved unsuccessful as a means of concealing the ash. Ultimately it was decided to dump the ash and bits of bone into the ditches that had previously held the bodies and to cover them with a thick layer of sand and dirt. The ash was scattered in the pits in several layers, interspersed with layers of sand. The top two meters of the pit were filled with earth.

A few prisoners who worked inside the pits from which the corpses were removed and who were engaged in cleaning the pits of solid human remains and scattering the ashes decided to leave some evidence of the Germans' mass murders. Abraham Goldfarb related: "We secretly placed in the walls of the graves whole skeletons and we wrote on scraps of paper what the Germans were doing at Treblinka. We put the scraps of paper into bottles which we placed next to the skeletons. Our intention was that if one day someone looked for traces of the Nazis' crimes, they could indeed be found."[15]

In the Lower Camp the body-burning could be both seen and felt. Occasionally the prisoners there would see the shovel scoop raised high with corpses inside. Smoke from the roasters often blanketed the Lower Camp; the smoke, and the smell of charred flesh, caused the prisoners breathing difficulties. Moreover, the fire and billowing smoke from the roaster could be seen for miles around. They were evident even at Treblinka Penal Camp 1, located three kilometers away. A prisoner at "Treblinka 1" described what he saw: "The spring winds brought with them the smell of burning bodies from the nearby extermination camp. We breathed in the stench of smoldering corpses. . . . We heard the clatter of the excavators for days and nights on end. . . . At night we gazed at skies red from the flames. Sometimes you could also see tongues of flame rising into the night.[16]

The burning of the bodies, the scattering of ashes, and the refilling of the ditches went on for months. The mass graves, emptied of the victims' bodies and refilled with the victims' ashes and bits of their bones, were covered with a thick layer of earth. The cremation of the corpses in the death camps of Operation Reinhard continued until the last days of activity there.

In Sobibor, which was the first Operation Reinhard camp to go ahead with the cremating, the number of corpses that had to be unearthed was much smaller than in Belzec and Treblinka. Only one-third of the two hundred fifty thousand victims in this camp had been killed and buried there before the cremating began. Those who were gassed there afterward, in the period between October 1942 and October 1943, were taken directly from the gas chambers to the cremating sites. The ample time allowed for the cremation and the relatively small number of victims enabled the cover-up in Sobibor to be carried out without haste.

In Belzec and Treblinka the situation was different. In Belzec, all the victims had been buried already when the cremation started. During a period of four to five months they had to be unearthed and burned. This was the sole reason for the continued existence of the camp, along with its entire personnel, until the spring of 1943, in spite of the fact that the last transports with Jews had arrived and were liquidated there at the end of November 1942. The fact that during the cremation operation no transports arrived made it easier for camp authorities to accomplish their task.

One of the excavators used at the Treblinka death camp. From Kurt Franz's personal album. YVA, FA 200/47

In Treblinka, the camp command faced the most difficult task—unearthing over 700,000 corpses and cremating them while at the same time continuing to receive new transports with Jews for extermination. In this camp the entire cremation operation lasted about four months, from April to the end of July 1943. To accomplish the task, the cremating took place simultaneously in a number of sites and the largest number of Jewish prisoner-workers were put to work in the various required stages.

The vast number of corpses and the limited available time were the main reasons that open space "simple" crematoria were used in the Operation Reinhard death camps. The type of enclosed crematorium used in Auschwitz, for example, would have been totally inadequate for the task that the commanders of Operation Reinhard faced. Constructing crematoria with large ovens in permanent structures required months of labor, special equipment, and skilled craftsmen—none of which were available in Operation Reinhard camps. Moreover, the system of burning corpses in ovens inside buildings was comparatively slow. Auschwitz's modern crematorium, with eight furnaces, could burn approximately 1,750 bodies in a day. To speed things up, four such crematoria were put into operation there. At Belzec and Treblinka, in contrast, a system had to be found to cremate 150,000 to 200,000 corpses within one month and 5,000 to 7,000 in one day. By using excavators to unearth the corpses of the victims, employing Jewish prisoners in large numbers, and operating simply built, huge, open-space crematoria, which were activated in the shortest possible time, the Operation Reinhard staff was able to complete its mission of cremation and the erasure of their despicable crimes.

DEPORTATIONS TO THE DEATH CAMPS OF
OPERATION REINHARD, 1942–1943

Poland, Jews boarding a transport train under the supervision of a German Policeman.
YVA, FA 16/29

Deportation of the Jews of the Lublin ghetto to the Belzec death camp, March (?) 1942. YVA, FA 16/9

Deportation of the Jews of the Cracow ghetto to Belzec, June or October 1942. YVA, 3939/29

Deportation of the Jews of the Szydłowiec ghetto to Treblinka, August–September 1942.
YVA, FA 76/68

Deportation of the Jews of the Losice ghetto to adjacent Siedlice. From there they were transported to the Treblinka death camp, August 1942. YVA, 4613/592

Deportation of the Jews of the Rzeszow ghetto to Belzec, July 1942. YVA, 73FO4.

Deportation of the remaining residents of the Warsaw ghetto after the Jewish uprising was put down, April–May, 1943. The Stroop Collection, YVA, 2807/115

Deportation of the Jews of Eisenach, Germany, to the Bełzyce transit ghetto in the Lublin district, May 1942. YVA, 1567/32; YVA, 1567/37

Deportation of the Jews of Bardejov, Slovakia, to transit ghettos in the Lublin district, May 1942. YVA, 2986/73

Deportation of the Jews of Stropkov, Slovakia, to the Rejowiec transit ghetto in the Lublin district, May 1942. YVA, 3131/1

Deportation to Treblinka of the Jews of Yugoslavian Macedonia (annexed to Bulgaria), Skopje (?), March 1943. YVA, FA 213/6

The Jews of Macedonia awaiting deportation to Treblinka at the gathering point at the "Monopol" tobacco depot, Skopje, March 1943. YVA, FA 213/67

PART II

LIFE IN THE SHADOW OF DEATH

CHAPTER TWENTY-FIVE

PORTRAITS OF THE PERPETRATORS

THE GERMAN EXTERMINATION MACHINE, WHICH geared itself to the concentration and transport of the Jews of Poland and other European countries to Belzec, Sobibor, and Treblinka, included in its ranks thousands of people—government officials and SS personnel of the highest ranks in the Third Reich, who made the decisions and published the orders to transport the Jews to the extermination camps; local administrative and police personnel, whose job was to round up the people and have them brought to the trains; the executives and workers of the Reich railway; and the security personnel who accompanied the deportees to the camps.

The suffering and hardships that the hundreds of thousands of Jewish deportees experienced while still on their journey to the camps were the direct result of the attitude and treatment that was meted out to them by the Germans and the collaborators of other nationalities, who were all part of this very complicated network. But the most excruciating experiences that the deportees went through, in the final hours of their lives, when they finally reached their destination, were determined above all by the local SS personnel, and especially by the commanders. This was likewise true with regard to the daily routine set for the prisoners who were kept on in these camps.

Sources and pertinent material on the daily lives of the SS men in the Operation Reinhard camps, on their personal feelings about the tasks that they carried out—the murder of hundreds of thousands of men, women, and children—and on their relationship to their innocent victims are almost nonexistent. SS men, who were more than anxious to cover up their past, were not about to sit down and record their memoirs. Even at the trials at which some of them were forced to attest to their deeds, very little was brought out about their personal feelings and experiences. A notable exception in this regard is Franz Stangl. As a result of the conversations that Gita Sereny conducted with him while he was under arrest, Stangl also exposed his thoughts to her, and Sereny has recorded them in her book *Into That Darkness*. Otherwise, the primary sources on the behavior of the

SS men in the camps and their actual relationship to their victims are the testimonies of those who survived the camps, as well as some material and testimonies that were exposed during the trials of the war criminals who served in these camps.

Among themselves, the prisoners used to nickname the various SS men, and these names were also indicative of their reputations and activities in the camp. These nicknames were also a type of code to be used as a warning when a particular SS man happened into the area.

CHRISTIAN WIRTH, INSPECTOR OF THE OPERATION REINHARD DEATH CAMPS

Christian Wirth was born in Oberbalzheim, Württemberg, in November 1885. During World War I he served as a noncommissioned officer on the western front, distinguished himself in battle, and was highly decorated. After the Nazi Party came to power in Germany, he served in the Württemberg police force, and in 1939 he attained the rank of commissar in the Stuttgart criminal police. At the end of 1939, along with other police officers, he was appointed to the euthanasia program at the Grafeneck Psychiatric Clinic in Württemberg. Shortly afterward, he was transferred to the euthanasia institution at Brandenburg an der Havel in Prussia as administrative director. (The medical director was Dr. Irmfried Eberl, the first commander of Treblinka.) In December 1939 or January 1940, the first known gassing experiment using carbon monoxide was carried out in this institution. The victims were twenty or thirty German mental patients. It was there also that the idea of disguising the gas chambers as shower rooms was introduced.

Wirth's involvement with killing Jews can be traced to September 1940, when crippled and insane Jews were brought to the Brandenburg euthanasia institution to be gassed.[1]

In mid-1940, Wirth was appointed as a kind of roving director or inspector of a dozen euthanasia institutions throughout the Third Reich. In this capacity he often visited the euthanasia institution in Hartheim, where some discipline problems had arisen. Stangl, who was in Hartheim at that time, said: "Wirth was a gross and florid man. My heart sank when I met him. He stayed at Hartheim for several days that time and often came back. Whenever he was there he addressed us daily at lunch. And here it was again this awful verbal crudity: when he spoke about the necessity for this euthanasia operation he was not speaking in humane or scientific terms . . . he laughed. He spoke of doing away with useless mouths, and that sentimental slobber about such people made him 'puke.'"[2]

In the middle of 1941, Wirth was active in the euthanasia *Aktionen* carried out in the western areas of Poland annexed to the Third Reich. His activities during this period are obscure until his appearance in Belzec at the end of 1941.

The experience gained by Wirth in the euthanasia institutions, his enthusiasm for National Socialism, as well as his innate cruelty were all put to use when he assumed command of Belzec and later was appointed inspector of the Operation Reinhard death camps. Not only was he the inspector of the death camps and, in this capacity, the actual commander, but it was he who also developed the entire system of the extermination machine in these camps.

SS *Scharführer* Franz Suchomel, who served under Wirth's command, testified: "From my activity in the camps of Treblinka and Sobibor, I remember that Wirth in brutality, meanness, and ruthlessness could not be surpassed. We therefore called him 'Christian the Terrible' or 'The Wild Christian.' The Ukrainian guardsmen called him 'Stuka' [a kind of dive-bomber]. The brutality of Wirth was so great that I personally see it as a perversity. I remember particularly that on each occasion, Wirth lashed Ukrainian guardsmen with the whip he always kept."[3]

Human lives, and particularly those of Jews, had no value in Wirth's eyes. He called the Jews "garbage." Stangl described Wirth's arrival in Sobibor during the final construction stage and the gassing experiment carried out there: "Wirth stood in front of the building [of the gas chamber] wiping his sweat off his cap and fuming. [Hermann] Michel [the sergeant major of the camp] told me later that [Wirth] had suddenly appeared, looked around the gas chambers on which they were still working, and said: 'Right, we'll try it out right now with those twenty-five working Jews. Get them up here.' They marched our twenty-five Jews up there and just pushed them in and gassed them. Michel said Wirth behaved like a lunatic, hit out at his own staff with his whip to drive them on."[4]

It was Wirth who introduced the regime of terror and death in the Operation Reinhard camps and influenced the daily life—and sufferings— of the Jewish prisoners there more than any other commander. The day-to-day selections among the prisoners and the decision of who among them would be sent to death were based mainly on his guidelines. Stangl testified: "In relation to the working Jews, Wirth constantly stressed that those who do no work had to be taken away. Each leader of a working group and each camp commander could send to the *Lazarett* every prisoner who did not work or behave satisfactorily."[5]

Wirth's guidelines and policy toward the prisoners gave each SS man in the camps the right to do anything he wanted to the Jews there. It allowed a free hand to the wild and sadistic character of many of the SS men in the Operation Reinhard camps.

The survivors mention Wirth very little. This is explained by the fact that no prisoners survived from the period when Wirth commanded Belzec, and his presence in Sobibor and Treblinka was very infrequent. As officially announced by SS authorities, he did not survive the war. He was killed in Italy by partisans in the Trieste area.

FRANZ STANGL, COMMANDER OF TREBLINKA

Franz Stangl was born on March 26, 1908, in Altminster, Austria. He joined the police in 1931, working in the criminal police force's political wing. He enthusiastically welcomed Austria's incorporation into the Third Reich—the Anschluss. In 1940, he was transferred to the euthanasia program and was transferred to Operation Reinhard in late 1941.

Although he was the commander of Treblinka, he had very little direct contact with the people he had sent to their death or with the Jewish prisoners; he was seen only on rare occasions. He ran the camp and supervised the extermination actions that were carried out through his assistant, Kurt Franz, and the other SS men under his command. In his testimony, Jacob Wiernik mentions several times that while the various structures were being built in Treblinka, Stangl would come and inquire about the work that was being done. Wiernik wrote: "When the new gas chambers were completed, the *Hauptsturmführer* [Stangl] came and remarked to the SS men who were with him: 'Endlich is der Judenstadt fertig' (Finally the Jewish city is ready)."

Stangl regarded his job as commander of a death camp as he would have viewed any other job. He wanted to succeed at the task and mission that had been assigned to him, that is, to eliminate the people who had been sent to the camp and to dispose of their property in accordance with the directives that he had received from his commanders, and to make certain that this be carried out quickly and efficiently. "That was my profession. I enjoyed it. It fulfilled me. And yes, I was ambitious about that, I won't deny it."[6] He wanted the camp that he commanded to look attractive, so he ordered the paths paved and flowers planted along the sides of Seidel Street, near headquarters, and near the SS living quarters.

He accepted the extermination of the Jews as a fact. About his attitude to the extermination activities and the victims, he said:

> To tell the truth, one did become used to it . . . they were cargo. I think it started the day I first saw the *Totenlager* [extermination area] in Treblinka. I remember Wirth standing there, next to the pits full of blue-black corpses. It had nothing to do with humanity—it could not have. It was a mass—a mass of rotting flesh. Wirth said, "What shall we do with this garbage?" I think unconsciously that started me thinking of them as cargo. . . . I rarely saw them

as individuals. It was always a huge mass. I sometimes stood on the wall and saw them in the "tube"—they were naked, packed together, running, being driven with whips.[7]

This attitude toward the victims—absolute apathy toward them, seeing them as inhuman, seeing them as a cargo that must be destroyed—was what characterized Stangl's image and activity in the camp. This apathetic attitude also expressed itself in Stangl's noninterference in what happened in the camp and his withdrawal from any contact with the prisoners, even with regard to the most cruel acts that were perpetrated upon them. This outlook, that the Jews are not within the realm of humanity, was a complete identification with the Nazi racial ideology and in this respect Stangl was the perfect embodiment of and instrument for the German extermination machine. In justification of his activities in Treblinka, he said:

> What I had to do while I continued my efforts to get out was to limit my own actions to what I—in my own conscience—could answer for. At police training school they taught us that the definition of a crime must meet four requirements: there has to be a subject, an object, an action, and intent. If any of these four elements is missing, then we are not dealing with a punishable offense. . . . I could apply this to my own situation—if the subject was the government, the "object" the Jews, and the action the gassing, I could tell myself that for me, the fourth element, "intent," (I called it free will) was missing.[8]

The motive to murder did not originate with him. He "only" carried out the order he had received in the best possible way. Looking at the situation in this way relieved his conscience and enabled him to oversee the death factory in which hundreds of thousands of people were murdered. To him they were only "a mass of rotting flesh."

In 1967, Stangl was caught in Brazil, extradited, and stood trial in 1970 in Düsseldorf, Germany. He was sentenced to life imprisonment and died in prison a few months later.

SS OBERSTURMFÜHRER IRMFRIED EBERL

Irmfried Eberl was born in Austria in 1910. He studied medicine, and practiced as a doctor in Vienna and in other locations. He was forced to leave Austria after joining the Nazi Party and relocated to Germany. In January 1940, he joined the euthanasia program, managing the euthanasia institutes in Brandenburg and Bernburg. In February 1942, he supervised the establishment of Treblinka and served as its first commandant. He was one of the few commandants of Operation Reinhard extermination camps who was also a medical doctor. Failing in his position as Treblinka's commandant, he was dismissed from this role and returned to working in Germany's euthanasia institutes. After the war he continued working as a doctor until his arrest in 1948. Shortly thereafter he committed suicide.[9] Due to his brief time at Treblinka there are no testimonies about Eberl's relationship to his position and his victims. As an enthusiastic Nazi and euthanasia advocate, his approach to his position and to the Jews was presumably similar to Stangl's.

SS *HAUPTSTURMFÜHRER* GOTTLIEB HERING

Gottlieb Hering replaced Wirth as commander of Belzec at the end of August 1942. Like his predecessor, Hering was an officer in the criminal police and had been attached to the euthanasia program. He was an old acquaintance of Wirth, as they had served together in the criminal police of Stuttgart. SS *Scharführer* Heinrich Unverhau, who served in Belzec, testified that "Hering and Wirth were definitely wicked people, and the whole staff of the camp was afraid of them. . . . I heard that Hering shot two Ukrainian guards who expressed their dissatisfaction with what was going on in Belzec."[10]

Rudolf Reder wrote about Hering:

We knew that in the most beautiful house close to the station of Belzec lived the commander of the camp. He was an *Obersturmführer* [sic]. . . . He seldom was present in the camp and came only in connection with some event. He was a tall bully, broad shouldered, age around forty, with an expressionless face. He seemed to me as if he were a born bandit. Once the gassing engine stopped working. When he was informed, he arrived astride a horse, ordered the engine to be repaired and did not allow the people in the gas chambers to be removed. He let them strangle and die slowly for a few hours more. He yelled and shook with rage. In spite of the fact that he came only on rare occasions, the SS men feared him greatly. He lived alone with his Ukrainian orderly, who served him. This Ukrainian submitted to him the daily reports.[11]

Tadeusz Miziewicz, a Pole who lived in Belzec and worked at the train station, testified about Hering: "Once the major [sic], the commander of Belzec death camp, invented a new type of entertainment: he tied a Jew with a rope to his car; the Jew was forced to run behind the car and behind them ran the major's dog and bit the Jew. The major rode from the camp to the water pump, which was in Belzec on Tomaszowska Street, and back. What happened with this Jew I do not know. This event was witnessed by the people of Belzec."[12]

Regarding the other members of the SS staff in Belzec and their relationship and treatment of the Jews there, almost no evidence exists. Except for Reder, there were no survivors among the prisoners there.

Franz Reichleitner was the commander of the euthanasia institution in Hartheim, and he knew Wirth from that period. He replaced Stangl as commander of Sobibor when Stangl was transferred to Treblinka. Reichleitner had little contact with the prisoners, and they saw him seldom. Even in the survivors' testimonies he was rarely mentioned. Moshe Bahir, one of the camp inmates, wrote about him: "Reichleitner, a man in his late forties, with an Austrian accent, was dressed always with great elegance and wore gloves. He did not have direct contact with the Jews and the transports. He knew that he could rely on his subordinates, who were very frightened of him. He ran the camp with German precision. During his time the *Aktionen* went smoothly, and all the transports that arrived on a certain day were liquidated. He never left them for the following day."[13]

Once there was an old Jew who was brought in a transport of thousands and who did not allow the SS to drag him forcibly, so they threw him into the freight car. By chance, Franz Reichleitner was present. The Jew declared that he did not believe the lies that had been told to the arrivals about a "hospital, light work, and good living conditions." By his own effort he got out of the car, bent down, and in his trembling hands scooped up two fistfuls of sand. He turned to Karl Frenzel, the SS man, and said, "You see how I'm scattering this sand slowly, grain by grain, and it's carried away by the breeze? That's what will happen to you: this whole great Reich of yours will vanish like flying dust and passing smoke." The old man went along with the whole convoy, reciting "Hear, O Israel," and when he said the words, "the Lord is One," he again turned to Frenzel and slapped him with all his might. The German (Frenzel) was about to attack him, but Reichleitner, who was standing by enjoying the whole performance, said to Frenzel, "I'll settle the account with him. You go on with your job." The camp commander took the old man aside and killed him on the spot, in front of his family and all the people in the convoy.[14]

As officially announced by the SS authorities, Reichleitner was killed by partisans in the Trieste area.

SS *UNTERSTURMFÜHRER* KURT FRANZ

Kurt Franz was born in 1914 in Dusseldorf. He completed elementary school and from the age of fifteen began working as a cook. In 1935 he was drafted into the army and served as a cook in an artillery regiment. After the completion of his military service, he joined the SS and served for a time in Buchenwald. At the end of 1939, he was transferred to the euthanasia program. In April 1942, having attained the rank of SS *Oberscharführer*, he was sent to Belzec and served there until the end of August or beginning of September 1942, when, with the change of command at Treblinka, he was transferred to Treblinka and appointed deputy commander of the camp.

Kurt Franz was the dominant personality in Treblinka when it came to the day-to-day running of the camp, and especially with regard to the prisoners. To the prisoners Franz was the most cruel and most frightening among the SS personnel in the camp. His physical appearance was extremely deceiving: he was nice-looking; he had a round, almost baby, face; and he was younger than most of the other SS men. He was therefore nicknamed *Lalke* ("doll" in Yiddish) by the prisoners. Franz, however, was a murderer and a sadist who made the prisoners' lives a nightmare.

As he would make his rounds of the camp, often riding a horse, he would take his enormous, frightening dog Barry along with him. Barry had been trained to obey Franz's command. And the command was usually to attack Jews—to snap at their bodies and, especially, to bite their genitals.

Kurt Franz frequently toured the camp, visiting the work sites in the Lower Camp and the extermination area. It was he who reviewed the prisoner roll call and took part in meting out the punishments. He especially enjoyed shooting at the prisoners or the people in the transports with his pistol or a hunting rifle. He would usually remove bearded men from the transports and ask them whether they believed in God. After he received the expected affirmative answer, he would tell each man to hold up a bottle as a target and said: "If your God indeed exists then I will hit the bottle, and if he does not exist then I will hit you."

Before coming to Treblinka, Kurt Franz had been a boxer, and in the camp he used his knowledge of the sport for sadistic torture of the prisoners. He would choose prisoners, give them boxing gloves, and force them to box him. But heaven help the prisoner who took Franz seriously; his real intention was to set up the prisoner as a punching bag. One Sunday, toward the end of 1942, Franz "asked" a young Jew from Cracow who had been a boxer to compete with him. He gave him two boxing gloves, but for himself took only one, the right one. Inside he had hidden a small pistol. As the two squared off in the starting position, Franz shot his opponent through the glove and killed him.

When Franz and his dog Barry would approach a group of prisoners, they would all instantly be on their guard, for they knew his tours always ended with someone being victimized. Oscar Strawczinski wrote:

> He walked through the camp with great pleasure and self-confidence. Barry, his big, curly-haired dog, would lazily drag along behind. . . . "Lalke" would

never leave the place without leaving some memento for somebody. There was always some reason to be found. And even if there were no reason—it made no difference. He was an expert at whipping, twenty-five or fifty lashes. He did it with pleasure, without hurrying. He had his own technique for raising the whip and striking it down. To practice boxing, he would use the heads of Jews, and naturally there was no scarcity of those around. He would grab his victim's lapel and strike with the other hand. The victim would have to hold his head straight so that Franz could aim well. And indeed he did this expertly. The sight of the Jew's head after a "training session" of this sort is not difficult to imagine. Once "Lalke" was strolling along the platform with a double-barreled shotgun in his hand and Barry in his wake. He discovered a Jew in front of him, a neighbor of mine from Czestochowa, by the name of Steiner. Without a second thought, he aimed the gun at the man's buttocks and fired. Steiner fell amidst cries of pain. "Lalke" laughed. He approached him, commanded him to get up, pull down his pants, and then glanced at the wound. The Jew was beside himself with pain. His buttocks were oozing blood from the gashes caused by the lead bullets. But "Lalke" was not satisfied. He waved his hand and said: "Damn it, the balls haven't been harmed!" He continued his stroll to look for a new victim.[15]

On the platform where the women undressed, three babies were discovered after one of the transports had arrived in the beginning of 1943. Their mothers had lost them in the mayhem as they were made to run to the gas chambers. Franz, who was on that platform, picked up one of the babies, tossed him up with his foot, hurled him through the air and watched as the baby's head shattered against a wall. Another time, on that same platform, underneath the pile of clothing that the women had left behind were two babies, one six months and the other a year old. Franz and another SS man kicked and killed them in the same way.[16]

In 1965 Kurt Franz was put on trial and sentenced to life imprisonment.

SS *OBERSCHARFÜHRER* KURT KÜTTNER

Kurt Küttner was in charge of the Lower Camp in Treblinka. His nickname in the camp was "Kiva." He had served for many years in the German police, and in Treblinka he was one of the most hated and feared of the SS men. He would follow people around, stop them, and search them for money, pictures, or any family mementos that the prisoners would try to hide on their person. If he caught someone carrying anything, he would beat him cruelly and send him to the *Lazarett*. In his capacity as commander of the Lower Camp and over the Jewish prisoners, he wanted to know exactly what was going on throughout his jurisdiction. He therefore exploited the weakness or baseness of some of the prisoners and turned them into informers.

From one of the transports that arrived in October 1942, Küttner removed ten or twelve young boys and put them to work at various service tasks in the camp. One of the boys he appointed capo of the group. After about three weeks, the boy was caught giving gold coins to one of the Ukrainians, and Küttner had him, along with all the other boys in the group, taken to the gas chambers. Küttner was also in charge of punishing the prisoners at the evening roll call and at "sports," which were a never-ending nightmare for the Jews in the camp.[17]

Küttner's fate after the war is unknown.

OBERSCHARFÜHRER GUSTAV WAGNER

The man who actually supervised the routine and daily life at Sobibor was Gustav Wagner. He was the quartermaster sergeant of the camp. Moshe Bahir described him:

> He was a handsome man, tall and blond—a pure Aryan. In civilian life he was, no doubt, a well-mannered man; at Sobibor he was a wild beast. His lust to kill knew no bounds. I saw such terrible scenes that they give me nightmares to this day. He would snatch babies from their mothers' arms and tear them to pieces in his hands. I saw him beat two men to death with a rifle, because they did not carry out his instructions properly, since they did not understand German. I remember that one night a group of youths aged fifteen or sixteen arrived in the camp. The head of this group was one Abraham. After a long and arduous work day, this young man collapsed on his pallet and fell asleep. Suddenly Wagner came into our barrack, and Abraham did not hear him call to stand up at once before him. Furious, he pulled Abraham naked off his bed and began to beat him all over his body. When Wagner grew weary of the blows, he took out his revolver and killed him on the spot. This atrocious spectacle was carried out before all of us, including Abraham's younger brother.[18]

Wagner's ruthless behavior toward the Jews is mentioned in some other testimonies of Sobibor survivors. Ada Lichtman wrote that on the fast day of Yom Kippur, Wagner appeared at the roll call, took out some prisoners, gave them bread, and ordered them to eat. As the prisoners ate the bread, he laughed loudly; he enjoyed his joke because he knew that the Jews he had forced to eat were pious.[19]

Gustav Wagner escaped after the war to Brazil, where he lived openly. The Brazilian Supreme Court refused to extradite him. In October 1980 his attorney announced that Wagner had committed suicide.

OBERSCHARFÜHRER KARL FRENZEL

Karl Frenzel was born in 1911, in Zehdenick, Templin district. He finished primary school and by profession was a carpenter. In 1930 he became a member of the Nazi Party and the SA, and from the end of 1939 he served in the euthanasia program. In the spring of 1942, he was assigned to Operation Reinhard and sent to Sobibor.

Frenzel was in charge of Camp I in Sobibor and replaced Wagner as quartermaster sergeant of the camp when the latter was out of the camp or on vacation. SS *Scharführer* Erich Bauer, who served with him in Sobibor, said that "he [Frenzel] was one of the most brutal members of the permanent staff in the camp. His whip was very loose."[20]

Frenzel himself testified that he tried to avoid personal participation in the dreadful actions that took place in the camp. Regarding his appointment as the SS man in charge of the trolley that took the Jews to the gas chambers, he said: "After the disembarking of the train, the children and the feeble Jews were forcibly thrown onto the trolley. Terrible scenes happened then. The people were separated from their families, pushed with rifle butts, lashed with whips. They cried dreadfully, so I could not cope with this task. Reichleitner complied with my request, and he appointed [Paul] Bredow to escort the trolley."[21]

Frenzel justified his activity in Sobibor by claiming: "As I already pointed out, under the prevailing war conditions, which are now difficult to comprehend, I unfortunately believed that what was going on in Sobibor was lawful. To my regret, I was then convinced of its necessity. I was shocked that just during the war, when I wanted to serve my homeland, I had to be in such a terrible extermination camp. But then I thought very often about the enemy bomber pilots, who surely were not asked whether they wanted to carry out their murderous flights against German people in their homes in such a manner."[22]

In 1966 Frenzel was put on trial and was sentenced to life imprisonment.

SS Oberscharführer Kurt Bolender

Kurt Bolender was born in 1912 in Duisburg-Beeck. He remained in school until the age of sixteen. In 1939 he joined the SS *Totenkopfstandarte* "Death's Head" unit and was assigned to the euthanasia program. He served in Brandenburg and other euthanasia institutions. In the winter of 1941–1942, he was sent to the eastern front in Russia with other euthanasia members and was attached to an ambulance unit. In the spring of 1942 he was appointed to Operation Reinhard and posted to Sobibor.

SS *Scharführer* Erich Bauer, who served with Bolender in Sobibor, testified about him: "Bolender was in charge of Camp III. In Sobibor there was a working Jew whom Bolender ordered to box with another working Jew, and for his pleasure they hit each other almost until death. Bolender had a big dog, and when he was in charge of the platform workers he set the dog at the Jews who did not work quickly enough."[23]

Moshe Bahir wrote about him:

> It is hard to forget *Oberscharführer* Kurt Bolender, with his athletic body and long hair, who used to go walking half naked, clad only in training breeches, carrying a long whip with which he brutally lashed the camp prisoners whom he came upon on his way. He also "worked" in Camp III in the gas chambers. On his way to lunch he was in the habit of passing by the main gate and swinging a whip with all his strength upon the heads of the Jews who went through—this to increase his appetite for the meal which awaited him. Once, when I was still working in the platform commando, the group was accused of carelessness because we had left a window open on one of the train cars. Each one of us was punished with 100 lashes. Bolender was very active in this task. More than once I saw him throwing babies, children, and the sick straight from the freight cars into the trolley with the load that went to the *Lazarett*. He was the one who chose the ten men to deliver the food to the workers in Camp III. When he had a yen to accompany the group, not one of them would return to us when the task was done.[24]

In December 1965, a trial of the Sobibor criminals was held in Hagen, West Germany, and among them was Kurt Bolender. Bolender committed suicide by hanging himself in his detention cell.

SS *SCHARFÜHRER* HEINRICH MATTHES

Heinrich Matthes was born in 1902 near Leipzig. He attended elementary school and then became a tailor. When he was older, he worked as a male nurse in various hospitals. He was married and had one daughter. At the beginning of 1934, he joined the Nazi Party and became a member of the SA. When war broke out, he was drafted into the army but was released after about two years. In August 1942 he was drafted into the SS, dispatched to Operation Reinhard, and sent to Treblinka. There he was appointed commander of the extermination area with the rank of *Scharführer* (sergeant).

In the winter of 1942–1943, with the outbreak of a typhus epidemic, Matthes took eight patients to the *Lazarett* and had them shot. During that same winter he shot the prisoner Ilik Weintraub because, while transferring bodies from the gas chambers to the pits, Weintraub had stopped for a moment to drink some water from the well.

Matthes's particular fetish had to do with cleanliness: in the autumn of 1942 he shot two prisoners because at the end of the workday they did not clean to his satisfaction the stretcher on which they had carried the bodies.

Jerzy Rajgrodzki, a prisoner in the extermination area, wrote about Matthes: "He used to beat the prisoners with a completely expressionless, apathetic look on his face, as if the beatings were part of his daily routine.

He always saw to it that the roll-call area would always be extremely clean. One of the prisoners had to rake the sand in the square all day long, and he had to do it with Prussian exactness."[25]

In the autumn of 1943 Matthes was transferred to Sobibor. He was put on trial in 1962 and sentenced to life imprisonment.

SS SCHARFÜHRER AUGUST MIETE

August Miete was born in 1908 in Westphalia. He completed elementary school and worked as a grinder in a flour mill. At the beginning of 1940, he was attached to the euthanasia program and at the end of June 1942 was transferred to Operation Reinhard and sent to Treblinka. He was one of the cruelest SS men; the prisoners nicknamed him the "Angel of Death." Miete was in charge of the *Lazarett*, and it was he who carried out most of the killings. The old, the sick, and the children were taken directly from the transports to the *Lazarett*, and most were shot by him. As the *Lazarett* was close to the selection square, where most of the Jewish prisoners worked, Miete also supervised the work there. He would walk around, check the prisoners, and those who seemed to him too sick or too weak to work at the required pace would be taken straight from the selection area to the *Lazarett*. Miete would have each man stand near a pit in which a fire was always going, then he would calmly take out his gun and shoot. Sometimes he would tell his victim to undress first.

He would also stop prisoners, search them and, if he found money, food, or anything at all, would brutally beat them and march them to the *Lazarett*. If a victim was stopped, even if nothing incriminating was found on him, Miete would still invent some reason to beat him and bring him to the *Lazarett* for extermination. He also used to visit the living barracks and hospital room of the prisoners, remove the sick, and shoot them.[26]

Miete would also look for Franz's victims who had been injured by the hunting rifle or whose faces had been bashed in by his boxing and remove them to the *Lazarett* as well. He would find additional victims among the prisoners who had been whipped for one reason or another or for various "crimes"; after they had been weakened by the blows and injuries they had sustained, Miete would decide that they were no longer fit for work and shoot them, too.

Miete was tried in 1960 and sentenced to life imprisonment.

SS SCHARFÜHRER PAUL GROTH

One of the most dreadful SS men in Sobibor was Paul Groth. His name and deeds are mentioned time and again in testimonies of survivors. When he was in charge of the working group that cleaned the freight cars, after the work was done he used to ask the Jews who among them was tired, felt bad, or required medical attention. On occasion, when the working group was composed of Jews taken from the transport that had arrived that day, some responded to Groth's "polite" question. He took them aside, hit them, and marched them to the *Lazarett*, where they were shot. In some cases he organized a flogging party and forced the Jews to run past Ukrainians with whips. Once he ordered a prisoner to gulp down vodka, and when he became drunk, Groth forced him to open his mouth and he urinated in it, roaring with laughter.[27]

But something happened to change Groth's behavior toward the Jews. Three Jewish girls were taken from one of the transports, and among them was Ruth, aged sixteen or seventeen, from Vienna. Ada Lichtman testified: "After a short period Paul Groth fell in love with Ruth. She was a beautiful brunette. The love affair became serious, and Ruth influenced Groth's behavior. He changed for the better. . . . Once Groth was sent out of the camp for three days. . . . That night Ruth was killed by Groth's fellow SS men together with the two other girls, Berta and Lena. When Paul returned and found out what had happened, he changed. During work he did not beat and maltreat the prisoners. It was not the same Paul."[28]

A short time later Groth was transferred to another camp. His love for a Jewess had been an insult to the Aryan race and in violation of Nazi regulations.

SS Personnel of a Different Nature

The overwhelming majority of SS men in the camps were accessories to the murder of hundreds of thousands of Jews and perpetrated acts of inhuman torture and cruelty on the Jews who were brought to the camps and exterminated there. An untold number of atrocities will never be known, because none of the victims lived to tell the tale and naturally the murderers themselves would not volunteer that sort of information.

Yet it should be noted that even in the hellhole of the camps there were isolated incidents of humane behavior toward the prisoners. Wiernik writes about one such SS man, Erwin Herman Lambert, who was in charge of a group of builders in Treblinka:

> *Urterscharführer* Herman was humane and likeable. He understood us and was considerate of us. When he first entered Camp II and saw the piles [of bodies] that had been suffocated by the gas, he was stunned. He turned pale and a frightened look of suffering fell over his face. He quickly took me from the place so as not to see what was going on. With regard to us, the workers, he treated us very well. Frequently he would bring us food on the side from the German kitchen. In his eyes one could see his good-heartedness . . . but he feared his friends. All his deeds and movements expressed his gentle soul.[29]

Joe Siedlecki testified about another SS man in Treblinka who treated Jewish prisoners humanely: "There was a[n] SS man, Karl Ludwig. He was a good man. If I would meet him today, I would give him everything he might need. I cannot even count the times he brought me all kinds of things and helped me, or the number of people he saved."[30]

Scharführer Karl Ludwig also served for a time in Sobibor. Ada Lichtman testified: "When the German Jews were selected for work, *Scharführer* Ludwig was present. More than once he took people from the lines. In this way he saved two doctors. He brought bread to the shoe repair barrack and divided it among those there. It was said that he also helped people escape from Ossowa."[31] Karl Ludwig was among those from the euthanasia program who remained alive at the end of the war.[32]

Another SS man in Sobibor who is favorably remembered in various testimonies is J. Kliehr, who was in charge of the bakery. He would try to cheer up the prisoners and brought them bread on the side.[33] At his trial in Berlin in 1950, Kliehr was acquitted as a result of testimonies by survivors in his favor.

UKRAINIANS

The direct contact that the prisoners had with the Ukrainians in the camps was considerably less than the contact between prisoners and the SS. The Germans generally assigned the Ukrainians to guard duties and retained the supervision over the prisoners for themselves. There are few survivors' testimonies that mention Ukrainians by name.

Ivan Demianiuk

The Ukrainian Ivan Demianiuk and his deputy Nikolai, who were put to work near the gas chambers in Treblinka, supervised the Jews entering the gas chambers and worked the motor that supplied the gas to the gas chambers. These two Ukrainians were exceptional in that they did maintain daily contact with Jewish prisoners who worked in the extermination area. Eli Rozenberg wrote about Ivan Demianiuk and his behavior:

> This Ukrainian took special pleasure in harming other people, especially women. He stabbed the women's naked thighs and genitals with a sword before they entered the gas chambers and also raped young women and girls. The ears and noses of old Jews which weren't to his liking he used to cut off. When someone's work wasn't to his satisfaction, he used to beat the poor man with a metal pipe and break his skull. Or he would stab him with his knife. He especially enjoyed entwining people's heads between two strands of barbed wire and then beating the head while it was caught between the wires. As the prisoner squirmed and jumped from the blows, he became strangled between the wires.[34]

In prisoners' testimonies a Ukrainian by the name of Rogosa also appears. He is accused of beating Jews during roll call. Wiernik also writes of other Ukrainians' cruel behavior, but does not cite specific names: "Between Camp I and II were the living quarters of the Ukrainians, who were always drunk. Everything they could get their hands on they stole from the camp and sold in exchange for vodka.... They would pick out the prettiest Jewish girls, drag them to their rooms, rape them, and then lead their victims to the gas chambers."[35]

AND MORE

The SS personnel and others who have been described here were part of the upper command echelon in the Operation Reinhard camps and, as such, are mentioned repeatedly in survivors' testimonies. They certainly were not the only ones involved, however. SS men like *Untersturmführer* Josef Niemann, the last commander of Sobibor; *Oberscharführer* Hubert Gomerski, who supervised the forest group there; and *Oberscharführer* Paul Bredow, in charge of the *Lazarett*, have also been singled out for their cruelty. The first commander of Treblinka, *Untersturmführer* Irmfried Eberl; *Oberscharführer* Otto Stadie, the sergeant major of the camp; *Scharführer* Franz Suchomel, in charge of the "gold Jews"; and *Scharführer* Josef Hirtreiter are also names that survivors of Treblinka vividly recall for their beastly manner. Although we have not elaborated on them here, these SS men—and many others—were all part of the group that determined life—and death—in the camps. As SS *Scharführer* Erich Bauer, who served in Sobibor, testified: "I cannot exclude any member of the Sobibor camp staff of taking part in the extermination operation. We were a 'blood brotherhood gang' in a foreign land."[36]

In recent decades, research has been conducted on the social background of the German staff in the death camps of Operation Reinhard.[37] The following brief analysis is based on data related at the trials of those SS men who served in Belzec, Sobibor, and Treblinka camps who were brought to trial as war criminals.

Almost all of them came from the lower middle class; their fathers were factory workers, craftsmen, salesmen, or shopworkers. Most of them had finished primary school, some lower high school, and a few had attended a secondary school. Some had gone to commercial schools or had received vocational training. Those who were former euthanasia program employees were mostly former nurses, craftsmen, farmworkers, or salesmen. Almost all of the accused were members of either the Nazi Party, the SS, or the SA. Some had joined these organizations before Hitler came to power, and others joined the party later. Their average age was between thirty and forty at the time they served in Belzec, Sobibor, or Treblinka. This applies to twenty-seven Germans who served in the death camps and who were brought to trial, but we may assume that the others were of a similar social background.

The SS personnel who ran the camps and supervised the extermination activities were absolutely "ordinary" people. They were not assigned their tasks because of any exceptional qualities or characteristics. The anti-Semitism that festered within them was no doubt part of their origin and was an accepted phenomenon among large segments of German society. Most were married, and most held no criminal record. They had either volunteered to serve in the SS or had been drafted to its ranks after having served in the euthanasia program. It was they who were to carry out the murder of hundreds of thousands of men, women, children, and old people. These SS men and Ukrainian guards carried out their duties loyally and unquestioningly. What is more, they constantly displayed initiative in trying to improve the extermination process. An integral aspect of their duties was that they were also to exhibit cruelty toward their victims, and many of them contributed their own "ideas" and innovations for various forms of torture that would "entertain" them all. Under the regime of Nazi Germany, these perfectly "ordinary" people were turned into something extraordinarily inhuman.

THE PRISONERS' DAILY LIFE

THE ROUTINE OF THE PRISONERS' daily life began early in the morning, usually at four o'clock. In the summer at this time it was already light, but in the winter it was still pitch dark. Rudolf Reder described the start of the day in Belzec: "At 3:30 in the morning the Askar [Ukrainian] who guarded the barrack during the night knocked on the door and shouted: 'Get up! Get up!' Before we could even rise, the bully Schmidt burst in and rushed us out with a whip. We ran out with one shoe in our hand, and sometimes even barefoot. Usually we slept in our clothes and shoes because we had no time to get dressed in the morning. . . . We got up feeling miserable and tired. The same feeling we had gone to sleep with."[1]

As the prisoners got up, the entire area of the Jews' living barracks came alive. The doors of huts were opened from the outside by the Ukrainians and the urination and excrement bowls were taken to the toilets. The huts were cleaned, the blankets were folded, and the prisoners were allowed to leave for their meager breakfast, which was followed by roll call.

During the roll call the prisoners were lined up in several rows in front of the huts. The "barrack elders" reviewed their people and reported the number to the "camp elder." He, in turn, added up the total number of prisoners and submitted his report to the SS man who was reviewing the roll call. These statistics were then reported to the camp commander or his deputy.

After the morning roll call, the prisoners were divided into work groups. The capos escorted the work groups to the work sites and supervised the prisoners throughout the day. Throughout the workday the prisoners were exposed to the harsh treatment of the SS supervisors. Dov Freiberg testified about these cruelties in Sobibor:

I shall tell the story of one day, an ordinary day, much like any other. That day I worked at cleaning a shed full of belongings and transferring them to the sorting shed. An umbrella had gotten stuck in a roof beam, and the SS man Paul Groth ordered a boy to get it down. The boy climbed up, fell from the roof and was injured. Groth punished him with twenty-five lashes. Groth was pleased with what had happened and called over another German and told him he had found "parachutists" among the Jews. We were ordered to climb up to the roof, one after another. The agile—and I was one of them—succeeded in climbing up without falling. But the majority did not succeed; they fell down, broke legs, were whipped, bitten by Barry, and shot.

This game was not enough for Groth. There were many mice around, and each of us was ordered to catch two mice. He selected five prisoners, ordered them to pull down their trousers, and we dropped the mice inside. The people were ordered to remain at attention, but they could not without moving. They were whipped.

But this was not enough for Groth. He called over a Jew, forced him to drink alcohol until he fell dead. When the work was finished, we were ordered to lay the man on a board, pick him up and slowly march while singing a funeral march.

This is the description of one ordinary day. And many of them were even worse.[2]

The workday usually lasted from six in the morning until six in the evening, with a short break for lunch. At twelve noon the signal for lunch would be given, and the prisoners, work group by work group, led by the capos, were taken in the direction of the kitchen, where they received their meal. Shortly after, the signal for the end of the lunch break was sounded, and the prisoners were returned to their work sites. On the way to and from work, the prisoners were made to sing, and whoever dared sing without "enthusiasm" was whipped. During periods when there was not much activity going on in the camps, work on Sunday would last only until the afternoon, and the rest of the day would be spent cleaning the living barracks, airing out the blankets, and performing various other cleaning jobs. At six in the evening, the signal for the end of the workday was given, and the prisoners were returned to Roll-Call Square for the evening roll call. This roll call took much longer than the morning roll call and sometimes lasted as much as a few hours. After attendance was taken, the sick or weak-looking prisoners were taken from the ranks, brought to the *Lazarett*, and shot. Reder described a scene of this sort in Belzec: "Usually the doctor prepared the list of the feeble, or the *Oberzugführer* who was in charge of the prisoners prepared the list of the 'transgressors' in order to execute thirty to forty prisoners. They were taken to the pit and shot. They were replaced by the same number of people, taken from the arriving transports."[3]

At the evening roll call, punishment was meted out to those prisoners who had committed some "crime" during the workday. Any small infringement was an excuse for punishing a prisoner: if he did not work fast enough, or energetically enough; if he did not respond properly when an SS man passed him; or if, in a search of his belongings, food, money, a cigarette, or a picture or memento—the only tangible thing left him from his past—was found. Even those prisoners who had already received "treatment" during the workday and who still bore fresh whip lashes on their bodies were given additional "treatment" at the evening roll call.

The punishment at the evening roll call was generally whipping. In Treblinka, at Roll-Call Square, there was a special bench cemented into the ground for this purpose. The prisoner was tied to the bench with straps in a way that his torso rested on the bench while his feet dangled on the floor at a ninety-degree angle to his body and his buttocks protruded exactly at the corner of the bench.

In the first months of the camp's existence, they would whip the prisoners while they were dressed. But at one of the whipping sessions it seemed to Kurt Franz, who happened to be present, that there was something suspicious. He ordered the prisoner to take off his pants, and then they saw that the prisoner had stuck a towel in the seat of his pants to soften the blows. From then on the prisoners were ordered to lower their pants before they were strapped to the bench, and the blows were inflicted on the bare skin.

Prisoners were usually given between twenty-five and fifty lashes with a special leather strap. The SS usually did the whipping; sometimes a Ukrainian was given the assignment. Frequently the prisoner had to count the number of lashes out loud, and if he made a mistake, or if he had no more strength to count, they would start over—from the beginning. There were prisoners who, gritting their teeth, took their lashes without a sound; others screamed to high heaven. There were instances of beatings of twelve- or fourteen-year-olds, and their screams shocked and terrified the prisoners standing on the sides. But the SS enjoyed it. As the screams grew louder and louder, Franz and Kurt Küttner—when they attended the roll call—enjoyed themselves all the more. When the whipping was over, the prisoner's buttocks were a piece of bleeding meat. The prisoners who had no strength to return to the ranks after the whipping were taken straight to the *Lazarett*. Those who were still able to return to the ranks but who had no strength to go out to work the next morning were also taken to the *Lazarett*.

SS *Oberscharführer* Karl Frenzel testified about the whipping of prisoners in Sobibor: "During my year and a half stay in Sobibor, I frequently saw that the working Jews were whipped. The Jews had to bow down, and the *Unterführers* [SS men] ordered the Jewish capos to whip them. Usually they received between ten and twenty-five lashes. The working Jews attended the punishments in order to maintain camp discipline and as a deterrent. In most cases the Jews who were whipped were dressed."[4] Rudolf Reder, from Belzec, wrote about the lashes: "Our overseer was SS man—Schmidt. If he was dissatisfied with a prisoner's pace of work, he beat and kicked without mercy. If Schmidt thought a prisoner was shirking he forced him to lie down and gave him 25 lashes of the whip. The prisoner had to count aloud each stroke, and if he counted incorrectly he got another 25–50 lashes. The victim usually could not sustain fifty lashes; he would just barely make it back to the barracks, and pass away by the next day. This scene repeated itself several times a day."[5]

Another form of punishment was "sports activities." In Treblinka the prisoners who received punishments of this kind had to run in a circle and alternately drop to the floor and get up, and all the while the SS and the Ukrainians would whip them. The prisoners who had no strength to continue with this "exercise" were taken to the side. The "sports" would continue until all the weak had collapsed and had been removed from the circle of runners. With the completion of the "sports activities," all those who had not been able to go on were taken to the *Lazarett* and put to death. The "activity" itself was a selection in which the strong survived and the weak were finished off. Frequently the Germans forced whole groups of prisoners to take part in these "sports activities" in order to weed out the weak and have them taken to the *Lazarett*. Young, strong workers from recent transports replaced those who had been killed. Usually Franz or Küttner were present at the "sports activities" and observed with obvious pleasure.

Shmuel Wilenberg wrote about the whipping and "exercises" that he and a building team foreman endured after a barrack wall on which they had been working collapsed:

At the evening roll call we were called out of the ranks. My punishment was fifty lashes and the foreman was ordered to run around the square. The poor man had to run, lie down, and then get up at the order. All the while he was given kicks and lashes. After a quarter of an hour of this "pleasure" he was returned to the ranks. Then the hangmen turned to me, they tied me to a wooden horse and gave me fifty strong blows. They made me count them. I writhed with pain because they struck me in the area of my kidneys and spine, where I had suffered wounds previously which hadn't healed for many months. The next day I felt the results. During the day my fever reached 40 degrees [centigrade]. Horrible pains in my hips prevented me from making any movement. I couldn't even think about going out to work. . . . My friend found me a corner in the infirmary. He camouflaged me nicely with blankets and covered me. That's how I remained until the evening. From time to time Germans came into the hut, but, my luck, no one spotted me. If they had discovered me I wouldn't have escaped them, and no doubt they would have finished me off with a bullet.[6]

The whipping, the "sports," and the killing were all part of the routine of the evening roll call. The prisoners had to stand and watch the selections, the whipping, and the "sports" until the end. After the orchestra, under the direction of Artur Gold, was established, when the whipping was finished they would play marches and the choir would sing. At the end of the roll call, all the prisoners had to sing the "Treblinka Anthem," and only then was the "Dismissed!" order given. The prisoners finally could return to their quarters. The "barracks elder" would then assign sleeping places to prisoners who had just arrived.

There was no shower in the area of the living quarters, and the prisoners had no opportunity to wash or shower for months at a time. The limited amount of water that they were rationed was hardly enough to quench their thirst, let alone for washing. In the routine and daily life of the prisoners, no time was even set aside for washing. In testimonies that prisoners gave in great detail about the routine and life in the camps, there is barely a mention of cleanliness and washing. Conditions such as these all but invited disease and epidemics.

FOOD IN THE CAMPS

The food that was distributed to the prisoners in the camps was very meager, and it was difficult to live on it for an extended period of time—especially since we are talking about people who were put to work at hard labor for many hours of the day. For breakfast the prisoners received a cup of warm water, which was supposed to be coffee, with 150 to 200 grams of frequently stale bread. For lunch they were given soup with some unpeeled potatoes; sometimes this meal also included horse meat. In the evening they got only coffee.

In Treblinka during the period of almost daily transports, until December 1942, the prisoners were able to help themselves to the food that the transportees had brought with them. In the parcels of those who were taken to the gas chambers were substantial quantities of food, since the deportees thought they were being taken to work camps in the East. The packages usually included bread, potatoes, meat, butter, and other foodstuffs. Although the prisoners were ordered to transfer everything to the camp authorities, the SS became resigned to the fact that some of the large quantity of food that was brought into the camp by the deportees remained for the prisoners. There was therefore never a scarcity of food during the period of the transports, and the prisoners were not hungry. In December, however, as the frequency of the transports subsided, the SS men and Ukrainians took for themselves all the food that was brought into the camp, and the prisoners were forbidden to take any of it. Prisoners caught with a single piece of bread were executed. When the transports for extermination stopped, the Jewish prisoners began starving and had to make do with the meager portions that the Germans distributed. One of the prisoners described the hunger:

> From day to day our meager rations were reduced. Food was distributed only once a day, in the evening. Every man received six cooked potatoes with the peels still on them. In addition, they distributed a slice of bread which was for the morning and which we were not allowed to eat until then. As we twisted and turned on the bunks at night, our insides were so empty that we couldn't stop thinking about that slice of bread until we broke off a piece of the bread that tasted like clay and smelled like a sick animal. There were those who gobbled up the entire piece but who were still hungry afterward. What's more, in the morning they could expect harsh punishment as well.[7]

The hunger brought on trade and speculation in food. Money, gold, and other valuables that the prisoners took from the clothes and belongings of the murdered were used to buy food. Trade in food, on a limited scale, went on in the camps during the entire time, even when food was relatively plentiful. During those times the prisoners would buy special foods like salami, canned goods, alcoholic drinks, and cigarettes. But when the hunger set in, they bought anything they could get their hands on: bread, potatoes, fat, sugar, and so on. Then the prices soared: they would have to pay gold rubles for a loaf of bread or tens of dollars for a half pint of vodka. The middlemen in the food trade were the Ukrainian guards: the Jewish prisoners paid, and the Ukrainians brought in food from the villages around Treblinka. Sometimes food smuggling was done with the cooperation of the Ukrainians and the prisoners in the forest group or camouflage group who worked outside the camp.

A prisoner who was caught with smuggled food, or with money or valuables that he intended to trade for food, paid with his life. The SS men kept a close watch over the buyers and sellers of food. In testimonies about Treblinka, there are even stories of Jews who for the slightest favors or for additional food would be willing to inform on their friends. Informers of this kind were known to all the prisoners. One of them, (Ye)Chezkel, had the position of "official informer," and that was his job in the camp. He would go through the camp following the prisoners, who were as wary of him as of a German. Another informer was Kuba, who officially was a "barrack elder." Shmuel Wilenberg wrote: "Certain informers were executed by the prisoners. It was done at night when the entire camp was deep in sleep. Four men would approach the informer, throw a blanket over his head, tie a rope to one of the roof beams and hang the accused. In the morning, when the SS men would see the hanging man, they would not be surprised, for it was a frequent sight—many people would commit suicide by hanging or by swallowing poison."[8]

Other testimonies of prisoners in Treblinka contain no mention of the killing of informers.

Despite the efforts of the SS personnel and despite the executions that were carried out, the trade in and smuggling of food in Treblinka never stopped; it continued during the entire period that the camps functioned.

In testimonies from Belzec and Sobibor there is no mention about food smuggling.

Reder wrote about the food in Belzec:

> At 12 o'clock midday we assembled for our "meal." We lined up in front of two small windows; at the first window we were given a tin mug, at the next window we were given half a liter of soup made of coarse grains, meaning water, and sometimes a small potato. Before our midday "meal" and before our coffee in the evening, we were forced to listen to the orchestra and to sing. And all the while, [amid the singing and music], we could hear the cries of anguish from the gas chambers of those suffocating. Opposite our kitchen [was positioned] a high gallows [pole].[9]

LAVATORIES AND *SCHEISSMEISTER*

Throughout the day the prisoners were under the careful watch of the SS, the Ukrainians, and the capos. Theirs was a day of perpetual work and motion, and woe to anyone who stopped to rest. Anyone who slowed down would be whipped on the spot or recorded by the capo or the SS man in charge for "treatment" at the evening roll call. The only place the prisoners were able to sit quietly for any amount of time without being watched was in the lavatories. There were only a few toilets in the camps, but the prisoners—and especially the weak and sick among them who continued working only out of fear that if they stopped working they faced certain death—found the only place for a short rest was in the lavatories. In general the Jewish capos were considerate of the sick and looked the other way during their frequent visits and long stays in the lavatories. During the winter that the typhus epidemic spread through Treblinka, the toilets became the main rest area.

In Treblinka, Küttner began noticing the "exaggerated" use of the toilets by the prisoners and, to put a stop to it, he appointed a Jewish supervisor over every toilet; these supervisors were given the title *Scheissmeister* ("shit master"). For their entertainment, the Germans dressed the *Scheissmeister* in a special outfit: the clothes of a rabbi and an eight-cornered cantor's turban. He had to wear a large alarm clock around his neck and carry a whip. He was also ordered to grow a Vandyke beard. He would have to make certain that the prisoners did not stay in the toilet for more than two minutes and that there should be no more than five people in the lavatory at a time. It was the duty of the *Scheissmeister* to chase out those who dallied. A prisoner who did not obey the *Scheissmeister* was registered and his number was submitted to Küttner.

Thus the lavatories, which had been the only place where the prisoners had found some semblance of peace, turned into yet another place of hardship and torture.

Night in the Camp: A Time of Rest and Reflection

At nine in the evening, the prisoners were locked into their barracks. Shortly thereafter, the lights were turned out and night fell on the camp. In Belzec the lights were turned out half an hour after nightfall, and the prisoners were not even allowed to talk with one another. In Treblinka lights-out was usually at 21:00 and in Sobibor at 22:00.[10]

The night hours in the huts were the only time that the prisoners were able to rest, relax a bit, collect themselves and their thoughts, with no Germans or Ukrainians spying on them. Wilenberg described night in Treblinka:

> We would welcome the night and the few hours of relative quiet that we had for sleeping. Sleep allowed us to forget the harsh life in the camp, dulled our suffering and sometimes transported us to a dreamland where everything was fantasy. But usually nightmares came to haunt us, actually they were the impressions of what we had seen during the day. Because we were suffering from sickness and weakness from hunger and hard labor, into our sleep came all kinds of weird thoughts, extraordinary notions that, combined with the hallucinations that ruled our subconscious, expressed themselves in nightmares and horrible dreams. Sometimes the stillness of night was broken by a sigh or scream; sometimes by the muffled cough of someone suffering from tuberculosis, or someone snoring loudly. Here and there someone would wake up, let out a juicy curse, punch his noisy neighbor, and then fall back to sleep—which was more of a snatched nap. But there were also nights with no sleep, full of work, beatings, and endless running.[11]

For the new prisoners who had just arrived in the latest transports, the first night in the camp was a time for reflection and a bit of unwinding from the shock they had experienced from the moment they had arrived in the camp. Yechiel Reichman told of such a night in Treblinka:

> We came into the hut, which was so full to capacity that people were lying on the floor. I looked at my friend Leibel, and he looked at me, and our tears poured down like rain. We asked each other: "Why the tears?" I couldn't answer. I wasn't able to talk. We tried to encourage and calm each other. "Leibel," I said to him, "yesterday at this time my little sister was still alive." And he answered, "And my whole family, my relatives, and 12,000 poor Jews from

our city." And we were alive, spectators to this great calamity, and we became like stone, so that we could eat and carry with us this great pain. Where did this unnatural strength to keep going come from? Among the people in the hut we suddenly saw Moshe Ettinger from our city. He embraced us with bitter tears. After he calmed down somewhat, he told us how he had been saved. . . . Now he was crying and could not forgive himself for remaining alive while his wife and son had died. We were like drunkards. Yesterday all who were close to me were still alive, and today—everyone was dead. I was crying over my fate, what had become of me. At that moment I saw in the corner of the hut the poor people who had remained alive standing and praying the Afternoon and Evening Services, and then, with tears in everyone's eyes, reciting the Kaddish. . . . The time is nine o'clock. The hut is locked. The lights are put out. We lie down with our pain. . . . At five in the morning we are awoken by the signal to get up and we are torn from the night and sleep.[12]

The morning had ushered in another routine day, another day of suffering.

In their testimonies, the former prisoners do not speak too much about the nights in the camps. The difficult and unending experiences that occurred during the day completely overshadowed the nights, which usually passed uneventfully.

In spite of the hell they lived in, which became their daily existence, those who survived continued to go through this routine and, to a certain extent, even got used to it. Dov Freiberg said:

It is difficult for me to explain what happened to us—how we could continue to live. I remember in the beginning, when a transport arrived, we wanted to die. But later, after some time, transports arrived, and we were sitting and eating. Even the suicides stopped, and those who did commit suicide were the newcomers who were not yet used to living in this inferno. All this in spite of the fact that we knew that our end would also be cremation in Camp III. If someone among us looked a little better than the others, we used to tell him jokingly, "You'll burn better because of your fat."[13]

DAILY LIFE

The conditions under which the prisoners were kept in the camps—the daily selections, the torture and punishment, the hunger and disease—all contributed to the fact that the average time that a Jewish prisoner remained alive in the camps was a few months at most. Only a few survived for longer periods. Those who entered the camp around the time of its establishment and lasted until the final stages of the camp's existence can be counted on one hand.

The constant turnover in the prisoner ranks, the daily executions and replacement with new arrivals from transports that came from different cities and countries, retarded the growth of personal contact and deeper ties among the prisoners. That hardly anyone knew anyone else was a deterrent to establishing close relationships. It also protected the prisoners from future emotional hurt in the event of a death of a friend. Reder wrote about this: "We were one mass. I knew a few names, very few. It was meaningless for me to know who a man was or what his name was. I know that the doctor was a young man from the Przemysl area; his name was Jakubowitz. I knew a tradesman from Cracow; his name was Schlussel, and his son. Another Jew from Czechoslovakia, Ellbogen, and the cook Goldschmidt from the famous restaurant in Karlsbad, 'The Hanicka Brothers.' No one was interested in the other. We went on with our horrible lives in a purely mechanical way."[14]

This description relates to Belzec, but the situation was similar in the other camps, especially until a permanent prisoner work staff was maintained. During a later period, in 1943, in Sobibor and Treblinka, when the frequency of the transports lessened, despite the problem of food, some aspects improved, some of the previous tension subsided, and the prisoner population became more stabilized. Then personal ties and meetings between the prisoners became a more natural occurrence.

THE PRISONERS AND THE DEPORTEES

AS A RESULT OF THE duties that were assigned to them, the Jewish prisoners, who themselves were destined to die and many of whom were killed every day, became elements in the camp staff and were exploited in the extermination process. All the physical work that was part of the extermination process, from the disembarking of the deportees from the trains onto the platform to the burial and cremation of the bodies, was carried out by Jewish prisoners. With their own eyes they saw how their families and friends were taken to the gas chambers, and there were those who had to bury and burn those dearest to them. The various work groups—the "blues," the "reds," the barbers, the "gold Jews," and those who worked in the selection area—had direct contact with the Jews who were brought to the camp and taken directly to the gas chambers. The prisoners who worked in the extermination area, however, did not have contact with the transports while the people were still alive—they only saw the bodies after suffocation.

Most of the Jews who were brought to the camps did not know where they had come, nor what awaited them in this new place. They therefore asked the prisoners that they met on the platform, in the transport yard, and at the sorting square what was going to happen to them. In Treblinka, after the men undressed they were told to take their clothes, as well as those of the women, to the sorting area and to throw them all onto the large piles that were being sorted by the prisoners who worked there. As the deportees ran by the working prisoners on their way to the gas chambers, the condemned asked what awaited them and asked for help. Yechiel Reichman wrote about this: "Near the piles stand people who are busy sorting belongings. I see that everyone is Jewish. As I run past, I try to ask them: 'Brothers, tell me, what is it here?' To my disappointment, I do not receive an answer. Each one tries to turn his head away so as not to answer me. I ask again: 'Tell me, what happens here?' One answers me: 'My brother, do not ask questions. We are lost!' The running with the packages goes on at such a pace that I don't know what's happening to me."[1]

Reichman was not sent to the gas chambers that day. The camp authorities needed barbers, and so he was saved.

At Sorting Square in Treblinka, among the huge piles of clothes, it was sometimes possible for some of the naked men to sneak away from the watchful eyes of the SS guards and Ukrainians and join the working prisoners. This escape route depended on their immediate realization that this was a way to be saved and on finding a hiding place for a few minutes in order to grab some clothes from a pile and get dressed. This was possible in the summer and autumn of 1942, before the working prisoners were given numbers, and was in part due to the help extended by the working prisoners who sorted the piles of clothing. One of the deportees to Treblinka relates that as he was running naked to throw his clothes on the piles, he asked one of the Jews standing on the side in a line what was happening and what to do to escape, but the prisoner did not answer him. Finally a man whispered to him that he had to get dressed again. He tried to push his way into the line of Jews standing on the sides, but they did not let him, as they feared the consequences if one of the SS men in the vicinity were to see. Finally he somehow succeeded in getting into the line, and he was saved. Another deportee hid under a pile of clothes, took out a coat and pants, and got dressed. Prisoners who were working in the area gave him a pair of shoes and let him join them as if he were one of them.[2]

Aron Gelbard writes about how a group of Jews from Czestochowa was saved by prisoners from the same city who happened to be working at Sorting Square in October 1942. Gelbard himself succeeded in escaping from Treblinka nineteen days after he was taken prisoner:

> During the nineteen days that I spent in Treblinka we tried to save whomever we could. How? As they would run naked with clothes in their hands, we would push them into a pile of belongings and cover them with packages. Later we slipped them a pair of pants and a shirt, and they emerged from the pile and stood near us sorting out the belongings. The Germans did not know exactly how many people were supposed to be working at any one time, because every day they murdered tens of prisoners. Unfortunately, many of the Jews did not understand what we were trying to do when we pushed them under the piles of clothing, and so they got up and out and continued to run. . . . Despite this we were still able to save a few Jews from Czestochowa, among them Jacob Eisner, Rappaport, Yitzchak Zeidman. I would like to mention the people that we were not able to save.[3]

The tumultuous situation in Sorting Square when a new transport arrived, the many piles of belongings scattered all around, the prisoners working there, the thousands of men from the transports running with bundles of clothing in their hands, provided a limited opportunity to a few of those who were being sent to their death to save themselves, even though the SS men and Ukrainians were in the vicinity and were observing the scene. But this method, by its very nature, was extremely limited, because the number of workers in the yard ranged from a few dozen to a hundred, and so only a few could be absorbed in this way into the workforce. The prisoners generally tried to assist acquaintances, people from the same city, or relatives they identified among the victims. In Treblinka, Sorting Square was the only place in the camp that the prisoners, despite the danger to which they exposed themselves, were able to assist some people from the transports to save themselves. However, in other areas of the camp, and especially along the route to the gas chambers, the conditions were such that no one was able to help the victims; there were no hiding places, and the Germans and Ukrainians kept a constant watch over the victims.

The women and children, who had been separated from the men, were collected in a hut and undressed there. They did not usually go through Sorting Square. The only direct contact between the women deportees and the prisoners was in that hut, when the "gold Jews" searched their bodies for money and valuables, and finally when the barbers cut off their hair. Jakub (Abraham) Krzepicki, who worked in this hut in Treblinka, wrote:

> It is difficult to describe the scene in the hut—the embarrassment of the women, the fear of the children, the confusion, the crying. . . . As I stood near the open door looking at the wild scene before me, a blond girl, as pretty as a flower, asked me quickly: "Jew, what are they going to do with us?" It was difficult for me to tell her the truth. I shrugged my shoulders and tried to answer her with a look that would calm her fears. But my behavior frightened the girl even more, and she shouted: "Tell me the truth now! What are they going to do with us? Maybe I can still get out of here!" I had no choice but to say something, so I answered her with one short word: garbage. The girl began to run around the hut like a mouse in a trap looking for the doors and windows, until an SS man came, beat her with a whip, and ordered her to undress.[4]

Alexander Pechersky, a prisoner of war from a transport from Minsk, wrote about Luka, his girlfriend in Sobibor, who told him about her feelings and thoughts:

> Do you know where I work? In the yard where the rabbits are. It is fenced off with a wooden fence. Through the cracks you can see the naked men, women, and children as they are led to Camp III. I look and shake as if in a fever, but I cannot turn my eyes from the sight. At times some call out, "Where are they taking us?" As though they knew that someone was listening and could answer their question. I tremble and remain silent. Cry out? Tell them they are being led to their death? Will it be of any help to them? On the contrary, like this, at least, they go without crying, without screaming, without humiliating themselves before their murderers. But it is so horrible, Sasha, so horrible![5]

During the few minutes that the women spent with the barbers who cut their hair, they asked about their imminent fate and why their hair was being cut. They wanted to believe that it was being done for hygienic purposes, before they were taken to the showers. Usually the women were answered with silence or with words of comfort. Yechiel Reichman, who worked as a barber in Treblinka, wrote:

> I look at the victims—and I cannot believe my eyes. Every woman sits near a barber. In front of me a young woman sits down. My hands become frozen, and I cannot move my fingers. . . . My friend next to me yells at me: "Remember, you'll be finished—the murderer is looking at you, and you're working slowly!" I move the fingers of my dirty hand, cut the woman's hair, and throw it into the suitcase. The woman stands up. . . . Another woman sits down. She takes hold of my hand, wants to kiss it, and says: "I beg of you—tell me, what will they do with us? Is this the end of us?" She is crying and asks me to tell her whether the death is long and difficult. Will they die of gas, or electric shock? I do not answer her. . . . I cannot tell her the truth and comfort her. The entire conversation lasts only a few seconds, the time it takes to cut her hair. I turn my head away, because I am ashamed to look her in the eye. The murderer standing near us yells: "Cut faster!" Thus the victims come one after the other, and the scissors cut the hair without stopping. All around there is crying and yelling, and we must see all this and remain silent.[6]

A different sort of reaction was recorded by Shmuel Wilenberg, who also worked in Treblinka as a barber:

> At a certain point a young girl of about twenty, unbelievably beautiful, came close to me. Our acquaintance lasted only a few minutes, but this short time was enough to fill my memory for many years. She told me that her name was Ruth Dorfman. . . . I saw no fear in her lovely eyes. There was just deep sorrow. In a muffled voice she asked me how long she would have to suffer. I answered her only a few minutes. It was as if a burden had been lifted from us, and our eyes became damp with tears. An SS man passed near us, and I was forced to cut the girl's long, silken hair. Finally she got up, gave me a long strange look, as if she were taking her leave of me and of the entire unmerciful world, and slowly made her way to the place of no return. After a short time I heard the tremor of the motor expelling the gas, and in my inner eye I saw Ruth among the unclad bodies, lifeless.[7]

Richard Rashke described the tragedy that took place in the haircutting barrack in Sobibor, based on Tovia Blatt's testimony, who, at the age of fifteen, worked there as a barber:

> Naked women and girls would come into the shed. . . . It took Tuvia less than a minute to cut their pigtails or flowing locks. . . . The Dutch women did not resist, and in a way, it was merciful. They had been told that their hair would be cut to prevent lice from spreading. Some wept. Others, in the presence

of men and boys, covered their breasts and squeezed their thighs together. They rarely talked, filing into the shed, their bare feet stepping over the piles of pigtails and black hair on the floor, sitting on the stools, hunched forward, eyes cast down in modesty. Then they filed out through the other door. Tuvia had never seen a naked woman before and, like every fifteen-year-old, he wanted to. But as the women walked tentatively through the door, he cast his eyes down out of shame for them, for seeing them, for snipping their last shred of feminine dignity. The Polish Jews were not fooled, and they tried to defend their nakedness with their tongues. They would curse the Nazis and shout at Tuvia and the other barbers—mostly boys—"We're going to be murdered. Why don't you say something? Don't just stand there! Do something!" Tuvia would ignore their remarks, avoid their eyes filled with hatred and fear, and concentrate on clipping their hair as fast as he could.[8]

In some survivors' testimonies there is some criticism of the prisoners who were put to work in the transport area. Oscar Strawczinski from Treblinka wrote:

> The yard is full of people. On one side women and small children, and on the other side, kneeling men. In the center armed SS men and Ukrainians and a group of about forty men with red bands on their sleeves. These were the Jews from the "red" group. In the jargon of Treblinka they were called the "burial society." At the head of the group was Jurek, in the past a crude wagon driver from Warsaw for whom the most despicable thing was not despicable at all . . . dressed elegantly—something which was not a special problem in Treblinka—with a whip in his hand, which he frequently used on the Jews.[9]

The prisoners in Sorting Square, those put to work in the transport yard, the "gold Jews," and the barbers, who all had contact with the people from the transport as they made their way to the gas chambers, did not generally warn them as to what awaited them, nor did they answer their questions when they were asked. There were several reasons for this behavior. The prisoners were convinced that there was no way they could secure freedom for the deportees and that the masses of Jews being brought in the transports would in any case be taken to the gas chambers. It would therefore be better if they believed they were going to showers, as this would ease their final minutes. If they had known the truth, it could in no way change the tragic reality of the fate that awaited them. Resistance, escape, or deeds out of despair on the part of individuals or groups among the victims, which could occur as a result of the knowledge that they were being led to the gas chambers, could not, in the opinion of the prisoners in the camp, ensure their survival. What's more, acts of this kind could also jeopardize the lives of the prisoners. Especially in Treblinka the Jewish prisoners were well aware of the consequences of such actions. The killing of the SS man Max Bialas had provoked serious retaliatory measures by the camp authorities against the prisoners. "Quiet" behavior on the part of the people in the transports was essential to ensure the continuation of the prisoners' routine. The prisoners came to the conclusion that for the good of all involved—the deportees and the working prisoners—it would be better if the prisoners would not answer the deportees' questions; they should not be told that they were on their way to their death. This was the overriding factor in the prisoners' silence.

FAITH AND RELIGION

IN THE HELL OF THE death camps, there were people who still believed in God, recited prayers, and kept the Commandments as best they could. The face-to-face encounter with death, the trauma of the murder of loved ones and close friends and relatives, the feeling of impotence, the incomprehensibility of what was happening around them and to them, the feeling that in a matter of minutes or days they, too, would no longer be among the living, produced varying reactions; one of them was turning to God. Cries of the *Shema* could be heard from people who were being pushed into the gas chambers. After the doors had been closed, the cries weakened gradually and finally ceased completely. In their last moments of life, many of those who were taken directly from the transports to the gas chambers turned in faith and hope to their Father in heaven.

In Treblinka, one of the prisoners from the "red" group, who worked in the area where the women undressed as they began their march to the gas chambers, wrote:

> There were women who, in the last moments of their lives, tried to find solace in God and died with the name *Adonai* on their lips. Others prayed for a miracle from heaven, for salvation at the last minute. I saw a tall woman with a wig on her head standing with arms upraised to heaven, like a cantor before the Ark, and behind her a group of women—they, too, with their arms raised—reciting after her word for word: "Hear, O Israel, the Lord our God, the Lord is One. We sacrifice our lives for *Kiddush HaShem*. Avenge us on our enemies for their crimes, avenge our blood and the blood of our children, and let us say: Amen."[1]

Richard Rashke wrote of an old man who was brought to Sobibor and on the way to the gas chambers said out loud: "Hear, O Israel. . . ." As he completed the verse, the old man slapped the face of *Oberscharführer* Karl Frenzel. The commander of the camp, Franz Reichleitner, who happened to be nearby, pulled the old man over to the side and killed him.[2]

Abraham Krzepicki, a prisoner in Treblinka, wrote about the feelings of uncertainty, of absolute astonishment, as to the tragedy that had befallen them, but also of some expressions of the justice of the verdict:

> Was this our last night or last hour? No one knew, but it was clear that the end was near. Different people reacted in different ways. Young people who had not been religious before joined the young *Hasidim* and together with them said the *Kaddish*. There was no shortage of moral people who were of the opinion that the tragedy was our punishment from heaven on the sins of the Jewish people. As a result of this kind of talk, there were people who felt guilty like sinners. They confessed, prayed, bowed, and expressed their fear with crying and chanting psalms.[3]

Religious expressions and what might even be taken as justification of the mass killings also caused antagonistic reactions, protests and demands of "Where is God?" Yechiel Reichman wrote:

> I hear from the left side of the hut how the poor miserable people are standing there, praying the Afternoon and Evening services, and after the prayers, with tears in their eyes, they say *Kaddish*. The *Kaddish* wakes me. . . . I was almost out of my mind, and I yelled at them: "To whom are you saying *Kaddish*?! Do you still believe?! In what do you believe and whom are you thanking?! You are thanking the Master of the Universe for His righteousness, Who took our brothers and sisters, our fathers and mothers—you are thanking Him?! No, no! It is not true that there is a God in Heaven. If there were a God, He would not be able to look at this great tragedy, at this great injustice, as they murder newborn children innocent of any crime, as they murder people who wanted to live in honesty and benefit humanity, and you, the living witnesses to this great tragedy, you are still thanking?! Whom are you thanking?!"[4]

But both justification of and protest against God were extreme expressions of only a few prisoners. Most of the believers among the prisoners accepted what was going on around them, the mass extermination that was being perpetrated in front of their eyes—and with their forced participation—as something beyond their grasp and expressed neither justification nor protest. Their prayers were above all a plea for mercy from God in heaven, and the recitation of the *Kaddish* in memory of their dear ones.

Organized religious activity was carried out under the leadership of a few prisoners. The central figure in the religious life in Treblinka, for example, was Meir Grinberg, the capo of the "blue" group, the son of a scribe. Each evening, at the end of the workday, when all were locked into the barracks, he would stand and pray the Evening Service and end with *El Male Rachamim* for those who had been killed that day. Then the Jews in the hut would say *Kaddish*. The SS men would come and stand near the hut and listen to the pleasant voice of Meir and his prayers to the memory of those whom they had killed.

Rudolf Reder wrote about Belzec: "The prisoner staff was made up mostly of people who had lost their wives, children, and parents. Many of us acquired prayer shawls and *tefillin* from the storage shed, and at night, when they locked us into the barracks, we heard from the pallets whispers of the *Kaddish*. We prayed in memory of the dead."[5]

Ada Lichtman from Sobibor wrote that "when they found out that in Camp III they were murdering the Jews, the prisoners assembled in the carpentry workshops and said *Kaddish*."[6]

In the Lower Camp of Treblinka, camp authorities allowed prayers to be conducted in the living barracks in the evenings and prayer and a *minyan* in the carpentry workshop in the early hours of the morning immediately upon waking and also toward evening. There was no shortage of prayer books, prayer shawls, and *tefillin*, because so many had been brought by the Jews in the transports.

In the extermination area of Treblinka, there was a relatively large number of religious prisoners, and public prayers were held in the living barracks with the authorization of the SS men. Jacob Wiernik wrote about a German by the name of Carol who brought the worshipers prayer shawls and *tefillin* and, as a joke, in certain instances allowed funerals for the prisoners who had died and even the erection of headstones. A few weddings were also performed in the extermination area. Eli Rozenberg related: "In the extermination area, the prisoners who wanted could observe tradition. An *Unterscharführer* whose nickname was 'Rosha' once looked at the worshipers and said: 'Why are you praying? Your God won't help you—you see what's going on here.' The weddings in the extermination area were performed according to Jewish law . . . under the direction of the prisoner Zalman Lenge, a porter from Warsaw, who at these ceremonies assumed the duties of the cantor and the rabbi. At his initiative authorization was given to bake a few *matzot* for Passover in the kitchen in the extermination area."[7]

On Yom Kippur that fell on October 9–10, 1943, the prisoners in Sobibor were allowed to assemble in one of the huts in the living area and pray. Mordechai Goldfarb testified: "When *Kol Nidre* night came, we all assembled in the hut, even though we had not spoken about it before. I am not sure how we knew the correct date. We prayed the *Kol Nidre* service together and wished one another a good year."[8]

With a few isolated exceptions, faith in God did not suddenly burst forth in the hearts of those who were brought to the death camps, nor did it stop at the entrance, at the gates. Religious people usually continued in their faith, even in light of the situation in which they found themselves; they found solace in God. And among the nonreligious prisoners, there was no noticeable religious awakening or repentance, save for a few. In general, thoughts about faith and religion in the camps take up a small place in the testimonies of the survivors.

The tolerance of the SS men to religious events and expressions on the part of the prisoners was especially apparent in the second half of the period that the camps were in operation. Although freedom of this sort had not been allowed in the ghettos and other camps, in the death camps it was the result of the Nazis' calculation that it would not thwart their aims nor their use of these people for work. On the contrary, in their estimation, the prayers would be an outlet for the prisoners' feelings and something to do after work—much like the sports and entertainment activities that were organized in the camps. For the Nazis the religious ceremonies were also a matter of curiosity, entertainment, and ridicule. This cynical attitude of the Germans to the Jewish faith was evident in the fact that they hung a Torah curtain at the entrance of the gas chambers in Treblinka and above it inscribed: "This is the gate of the Lord, the righteous will pass through it."

DISEASES, EPIDEMICS, AND SUICIDE

IN THE CAMPS THERE WAS no room for the sick. Those who fell ill and were not able to continue working and thus hide the fact from the Germans and Ukrainians were shot or sent to the gas chambers. The SS followed the prisoners around while they were working, checked them at roll call, searched them in the barracks; and those who seemed sick were taken directly to the *Lazarett*.

Among the prisoners in Treblinka were two doctors who were allowed to practice: Dr. Julian Chorazycki, who treated the German patients; and Dr. Irka, who treated the Ukrainians. It was forbidden for either of them to treat sick Jews. Despite this absolute prohibition, however, in the evenings, inside the barracks, these doctors did try to aid the sick prisoners and even administered whatever medicine they could filch from the infirmary. But this help was of small consequence, considering the large numbers of prisoners who fell sick.

In 1942, the "camp elder," Galewski, was able to obtain permission from the camp administration for fifteen sick prisoners a day to remain in the lower camp and not go out to work. These prisoners were given numbers in the morning, which was authorization to remain in the barracks. In the autumn of 1942, even an infirmary was established in the living barracks. At first Dr. Chorazycki treated the sick in the evening, but, later, two prisoner doctors, Dr. Beck and Dr. Reisman, were assigned to this infirmary. But even this new arrangement did not solve the problem, because the number of sick per day greatly exceeded the number fifteen.[1] In the other camps, Belzec and Sobibor, even this type of arrangement did not exist.

In the extermination area of Treblinka there was no facility for the treatment of the sick, and those who could not continue working were taken directly to the *Lazarett*. However, when Jacob Wiernik, an outstanding carpenter whom the Germans needed to build the new watchtowers, fell ill with pneumonia, the Germans found a Jewish doctor among the prisoners in the extermination area to treat him, and the SS man responsible for his work even brought him food.[2] But this was a notable exception.

There were also instances of sick prisoners being killed by injection. These deaths were inflicted on those who were not able to walk on their own to the place where they were to be shot. The injections were given by prisoner doctors according to the decision of the SS.[3] Death injections were also given to prisoners who had gone mad in the camp. Shmuel Wilenberg, from Treblinka, wrote about this:

> One night, when most of the prisoners had already fallen asleep and a small group wrapped in prayer shawls was praying by the light of small candles, the stillness of the night was pierced with a laugh that could freeze the blood in the veins. Everyone who heard the laugh felt a chill go through his spine. It was like the screech of a crow or the howl of a jackal. . . . I felt that in another minute I would also break out in that kind of laughter. . . . I covered my head with the blanket and with my fingers I shut my ears so that I would not hear that crazed laughter. The next day the doctors gave him a death injection. The poor man did not know what they had done to him, and perhaps it was better that way.[4]

The death of prisoners from sickness and the executions of those who could no longer work were a daily occurrence in Treblinka during typhus epidemics.

The hygienic conditions in the camps until the beginning of 1943 were the worst and most inhumane that could be imagined. There were no showers, and even the water was rationed. The prisoners, except for those who worked in the extermination area, had no problem in taking clothing from the piles of belongings left by the Jews in the transports, and from time to time they were able to change their clothes. It was not that easy, however, to get clean clothes, and there was a serious problem with lice. Yitzhak Lichtman from Sobibor testified: "The filth took its toll. Lice and bedbugs ate our bodies. It is true that there was no shortage of clothes, and when we took them out of the packages they were sometimes even clean, but they were also sometimes full of lice. Almost all of us broke out in a rash from the itching, but we had to hide the fact, because if not we would be taken to the *Lazarett*."[5]

In the extermination area, however, the prisoners worked and slept in the same clothes for weeks at a time, and only infrequently were they brought a change of clothes from the other part of the camp. Under these conditions, and with the horrible overcrowding in the living barracks, the lice and bedbugs became an unavoidable part of camp life.

At the beginning of winter 1942, in the middle of December, the transports to Treblinka became less frequent. Also at that time, however, bright spots on the skin and high fever, characterizing typhus, began afflicting all the prisoners in the camp, both in the lower camp and in the extermination area. At first the prisoners attempted to conceal this from the SS men and the Ukrainians, but because there was absolutely no way of isolating the sick from the healthy prisoners, the disease spread quickly, and hundreds of prisoners became infected. At that point it was no longer possible to hide what was happening from the Germans.

The infirmary in the Lower Camp quickly became filled, and the number of "official" sick was increased—with the authorization of camp authorities—to twenty. Those given first preference to be taken to the infirmary were the capos and those close to them. Among them was the "camp elder," Galewski, who came down with typhus, and some other capos. Also the informers Chezkel and Kuba became ill, and, out of fear for their health, the authorities ordered that they be brought to the infirmary and treated. Therefore, there was hardly any room in the infirmary for the "plain" sick, and every day tens of people were taken to the *Lazarett* and shot.[6]

The prisoners did all they could to continue working. They went to the roll calls and to work even with a fever of 40 degrees (Celsius) and more, because they knew that the moment they remained to rest in the hut their fate was sealed. The healthy helped their sick friends by trying to do some of their work for them. The capos also tried to help and allowed the sick to rest whenever the Germans and Ukrainians were not in the vicinity. The sick used the toilets to rest, but the Germans made the *Scheissmeisters* chase them out of there at the end of the allotted two minutes. Rakowski, who was appointed "camp elder" in place of Galewski while he was sick, was able to appoint some of the weak to easier work details and in this way help some of them overcome the disease. This was the situation in the Lower Camp.

In the extermination area the situation was more acute. There was no medical treatment whatsoever, and every day dozens were shot. Here also the prisoners tried every possible way to hide their sickness and continue working as long as they could. One day, at the morning roll call, an SS man announced that at the far end of the living barracks, an infirmary had been set up, and every sick man should report there for rest and treatment. The prisoners were not sure whether or not to admit they were sick. They were hesitant about relying on the promises of the SS men. But the disease overpowered them. Reichman wrote:

> The fear is great. Despite this, many sick are reporting because they cannot hold out any longer. Within a few days the infirmary is filled, and the number of sick reaches a hundred. I am among the sick in the room, and all of us have high fever. We do not receive any medical help, but it is good that they let us

rest a few days. But the murderers do not keep their word, just like all the false promises of the Germans. A few days later, at five in the evening, a few SS come to us and order ninety sick people out. The Ukrainians burst in and drag the sick from their pallets by their feet.... In a matter of fifteen minutes, more than eighty sick are taken out. They are not permitted to dress, and they are ordered to take their blankets with them. From the hundred, thirteen of us are left. The rest are taken to the yard, and after a few minutes we hear the bullets begin whistling.[7]

Camp authorities were afraid that the disease would spread also to the SS men and Ukrainians, and in February 1943 they instituted widespread cleaning and disinfection actions in the camp. For this purpose they brought an expert to the camp along with disinfection equipment from Majdanek, and they organized a special disinfection group from among the prisoners, which sprayed all the barracks and buildings in the camp. In the extermination area, a laundry was established, and a group of women from one of the transports that arrived during that period in Treblinka was transferred to work there. These measures and the change in the weather with the coming of spring gradually weakened the epidemic.

Typhus continued to appear in the camp until the end of March 1943. A great number of the prisoners had been taken ill with the disease, but most had been able to overcome it. Out of more than eight hundred prisoners who were in the Lower Camp when the disease broke out, about three hundred people had died or been shot. In the extermination area, more than one hundred prisoners, more than half the total number of prisoners working there, died or were shot.[8]

The places of those who had been killed were filled with people taken from the transports that arrived from the Bialystok-Grodno area in the winter of 1942 and from the Warsaw ghetto in January and April 1943.

Disease was also widespread in Sobibor. The sick who remained lying in the barracks were usually taken to the *Lazarett* and shot. Ada Lichtman wrote:

> The Germans would come to the barracks during the work hours, drag the sick from the pallets, and take them to the *Lazarett*. The death of these sick people was most cruel. They were made to stand near the stairs of the watchtower. On the steps themselves were bottles, cups, and pots. A few SS men made a firing range out of these utensils, and the bullets frequently hit the sick people and wounded them. With the blood running, the sick people lay on the spot until the "game" was over. At the end the Ukrainians took those who were left to Camp III. [9]

In Sobibor there was also a typhus epidemic, but on a much smaller scale than in Treblinka. Ada Lichtman mentioned a prisoner, Shimon

Rabinowitz, who cooked during that time and saw to it that the sick received food. SS *Oberscharführer* Karl Frenzel almost discovered this, and it was a miracle that Rabinowitz did not pay for this act of mercy with his life.[10]

To improve the cleanliness in the camp, a laundry was established for the prisoners. Three Jewish women, who had been removed from one of the transports, worked in this laundry.[11]

The situation in Belzec was certainly no different from that in Treblinka or Sobibor, but no testimonies about disease in the camp have been left to us.

The horrifying conditions in which the prisoners lived and the type of work the camp authorities demanded of them required an infinite amount of spiritual and physical strength to survive. Not all the prisoners were endowed with the type of strength needed to see them through this sort of work, to be able to cope with it, and to become part of the human system that made the operation of the camp possible. It was difficult enough for the prisoners who came in contact with the people from the transports, but it was even more difficult for the prisoners who were put to work in the extermination area. Their main problem was how to cope physically and mentally with the difficult and shocking work, the unending physical contact with the corpses of so many people, among them acquaintances, relatives, and family, from morning until night, for days, weeks, and months. How could anyone stand all this without breaking down? Indeed, there were many who could not keep it up, and dozens, perhaps hundreds, committed suicide. Many of those who did commit suicide were part of the intelligentsia. Yechiel Reichman from Treblinka wrote of his first wake-up in the extermination area: "I awake with a headache. . . . I see opposite me a man hanging, one who had hanged himself. I point this out to my neighbor, and he points in another direction; there two more men are hanging. Here it is nothing new. He tells me that today less people than usual hanged themselves, and every morning they remove from the hut those who hanged themselves during the night. Here they don't bother with little things like that. I look at those hanging and am jealous of the peace they now know."[12]

The people would hang themselves at night, when the other prisoners slept. There were nights in Treblinka when the number of suicides was two or three, and nights that it reached fifteen to twenty. The people would hang themselves with their belts, which they tied to the roof beams in the hut. There was one instance of a father and son who hanged themselves after having been in the extermination area for only a few days. First the father killed himself and then the son.[13]

In his testimony at the Eichmann trial, Abraham Lindwaser described how he was put to work at extracting gold teeth from the mouths of the dead, his attempted suicide, and how he was prevented from going through with it:

> After I was informed of my job, I couldn't stand it. I tried to commit suicide. I was already hanging from the belt. A bearded Jew took me down. I don't know his name. He began lecturing me and said that although the work that we were doing was despicable work, not only would we have to do it, but we would have to cope with it. We would have to make an effort so that at least someone would remain who could tell what was going on there, and that was my job, and because I had easy work I could endure and be of help to others.[14]

The camp authorities in Treblinka decided to prevent suicides. They did not like the fact that Jews could rule over their own lives and decide the time of their deaths; this authority was supposed to be solely in the hands of the Germans. At the beginning of the winter, two Jews were therefore picked to be on duty during the night. Part of their job was to prevent prisoners from committing suicide. These men were exempted from all other work during the day. After the night watch was instituted, at the beginning of 1943, the number of suicides lessened. But when, after the appointment of the guards, Jews were still found committing suicide, the night watchmen were whipped and removed from their jobs and, in one instance, even hanged.[15]

Most suicides in Treblinka occurred in the extermination area. In the testimonies of the survivors, there is no mention of suicides in the Lower Camp. It seems that instances of this sort were few. The type of work in the extermination area, the constant handling of corpses and the direct contact with the gas chambers and the mass pits with no possibility of getting away or changing the type of work, turned life in that area into unbearable existence for normal people and pushed many of them over the edge of despair. Some prisoners turned to religious belief; others became convinced that the only way left to them was taking their own lives, and they followed through on this. But some clung to life at any cost. In the extermination area in Treblinka, life had a different meaning and value than in any other place on earth.

In Sobibor there are no testimonies about what went on in the extermination area, as there are no survivors. On the other hand, there were some instances of suicide among the prisoners in the central section of the camp. Dov Freiberg testified: "It is difficult to describe how we lived in hell. I can say that during the first month of my stay in the camp, out of 150 people, only 50 were left. The others were tortured and killed by the

Germans. Suicide was a daily occurrence. . . . I personally tried to commit suicide but was unsuccessful. At the last minute all kinds of hopes came into my head, and I gave up this idea, even though pure logic instructed me to kill myself. Once I volunteered to be taken to the *Lazarett* but I was sent back."[16] Other sources on Sobibor mention that at least ten male prisoners committed suicide in Sobibor in the winter of 1942–1943.[17]

Rudolf Reder does not mention suicide in his testimony on Belzec, but in light of what happened in Treblinka and Sobibor, there were almost certainly instances of this sort. The absence of hope, the terror and torture, not knowing what was going to happen at any given moment, and the fear of the next day in the camp pushed people into taking their own lives. In addition, the shock and the certainty that relatives and friends had been killed, the daily scene of the Jews being led to their death, and the sorting of their clothes, belongings, and bodies influenced the wave of suicides in the camps. The inclination to commit suicide was usually in the initial period of incarceration in the camp. This was a traumatic period of crisis for every prisoner. As one's stay in the camp lengthened, the desire to commit suicide lessened. Instances of suicide were rarest during the last months of the camps' existence.

CHAPTER THIRTY

SOCIAL LIFE

IN THE SHADOW OF THE gas chambers and the mass burial pits of the camps in which thousands of people were buried almost every day, orchestras of Jewish prisoners made the lives of the SS in the camps more pleasant—and their melodies accompanied those on their way to the gas chambers. In the same small section of the camp, a few meters from the place where the women undressed on their way to their death, only a few meters from the gas chambers, the orchestra rehearsed, plays were produced, arts and sports events were held, and love affairs blossomed. All this was at the initiative of camp authorities and with their encouragement. This was perhaps the most horrible paradox of the extermination camps, the ultimate combination of the Nazi character: cruelty, tragic irony, and torture.

In the last months of the camp's existence, when camp authorities were already aware that Operation Reinhard was almost over, that in a short time all the prisoners in the camps would be killed, the Germans attempted to delude the prisoners, to prevent them from thinking about their end, which was near, about escape, or about any kind of resistance. They therefore encouraged activities such as the orchestra, "entertainment," and love affairs between the prisoners. This was the general policy instituted in all the Operation Reinhard camps and was not merely a local initiative of the SS in a specific place.

Leon Feldhendler, who was one of the leaders of the revolt in Sobibor, wrote: "The music, the dancing, and the women all had one purpose—to kill any thought of liberation that the prisoners might have; they [the Germans] wanted to turn them into unthinking instruments. Those who looked to them as if they were thinking too much and talking among themselves were taken to Camp III or were whipped. The absence of worry [among the prisoners] was forced; they [the Germans] encouraged love affairs, they allowed meeting with the women, and they allowed card and chess games."[1]

In effect, however, this attempt at deception on the part of camp authorities was to a certain extent in line with the simply human nature of the prisoners and their desire to live and make use of every minute of life until the last. The prisoners in the camps had lost their families—their parents and children, their husbands and wives. Being alone with the knowledge that their days were also numbered, these people sought the closeness of the opposite sex. The relationship that sprang up between men and women was sometimes purely emotional; sometimes it assumed the more practical purpose of mutual aid in acquiring food, with work and in time of illness. Among the young people, these relationships between the sexes were sometimes the first—and perhaps the last—opportunity for any sort of sex life. The crowded conditions and the absence of minimal privacy among the prisoners did not prevent intimate relationships; accepted norms of what was allowed or prohibited in public took on a very different reality in the extermination camps.

BELZEC

In Belzec there was a small orchestra, which was used primarily during the extermination of the transports and to entertain the SS men during their nights of drunkenness and debauchery. The orchestra was made up of six musicians and usually played in the area between the gas chambers and the burial pits. The transfer of the corpses from the gas chambers to the graves was done to the accompaniment of the orchestra.

Rudolf Reder describes the extermination of a transport with Jews from Zamosc and the torment of the chairman of the *Judenrat* from this city to the accompaniment of the orchestra:

> It was the middle of November. It was cold and all around was mud and snow. . . . The transport from Zamosc also included the *Judenrat* from there. When everyone was already naked, the men were taken to the gas chambers, and the women to the hut to have their hair cut. The chairman of the *Judenrat* was ordered to remain in the square. . . . The SS men ordered the orchestra to the square. . . . I worked near there, so I saw the whole thing. The SS ordered the orchestra to play "*es geht alles voritber, es geht alles vorbei*" ("Everything passes, everything goes by") and "*drei Lilien, kommt ein Reiter, bringt die Lilien*" ("Three lilies, a rider arrived and brought the lilies"). The orchestra was made up of a violinist, a flutist, and an accordionist. The playing lasted a long time. Afterward the SS men put the chairman of the *Judenrat* against the wall and hit him until he bled profusely. . . . Only at six in the evening did the SS man Schmidt take him to the pit and shoot him.[2]

Before receiving their food in the afternoon and evening, the prisoners were forced to sing, and the orchestra played. The background to these "concerts" were the high gallows near the kitchen and the screams of the murdered from the direction of the gas chambers.

On Sundays, toward evening, the SS men would have the prisoner orchestra brought to the SS living area near the railroad station, and while the Germans were flaming drunk, the orchestra was made to play for them.[3]

Reder does not mention any love affairs among the prisoners in Belzec.

From the beginning, in Sobibor, a prisoner orchestra was organized. It was first used to create an illusion about the place, and the music accompanied the entire extermination process. Dov Freiberg described his arrival in Sobibor in May 1942, the harsh treatment, the panic that grasped the people. Looking around he heard "cries of women and children, shouts and wild laughter of the SS men, the noise of a working engine, and music played by an orchestra."[4]

In Sobibor the Germans encouraged, even forced the prisoners to take part in entertainment. When the camp authorities decided to organize a choir, and there were no volunteers for it, except the conductor, they ordered a group of men and women to become the choir and, under threat, forced them to sing. Moniek, the conductor of the choir, was "promoted" to the rank of capo.[5]

In the summer of 1943—when a transport with Jews arrived every week from Holland—the same day that the people of the transports were exterminated, dances were organized in the evenings. Richard Rashke wrote about a young woman, Selma Wijnberg, who was selected from such a transport:

That evening after the roll call, the Nazis made the Jews sing and dance in the yard of Camp I. For Selma, it was almost like old times, except there were fences, and she was in Poland. Although the fiddle, bugle, and accordion made happy sounds, the Polish Jews were not smiling. One of them, a twenty-eight-year-old man, could not take his eyes off Selma as she lightly stepped to the music, hips swaying. He asked her to dance. . . . They polka-ed and waltzed in the yard. She was light on her feet and gracefully followed his lead. Somehow she felt less afraid with the music and with his hand on her waist. . . . After the Germans grew tired of watching the Jews dance, they locked the gate between Camp I and Camp II. A boy whom Selma had known from Holland came up to her. . . . "You know what that is?" He pointed to the north, where the orange sky silhouetted the tips of the pine trees on the horizon. "No. What?" He told her, and she felt as though someone had jumped on her stomach. . . . Selma walked to her bunk in a daze. She could not talk. . . . Then she began to weep, first one tear at a time, then a quiet flood, late into her first night in Sobibor.[6]

Tovia Blatt testified about his first few days in Sobibor, in the spring of 1943:

We were ordered to take away the baggage left by the people from our transport. . . . I looked after somebody whom I knew. Somebody caught my hand. I turned around . . . Jozek! We embraced. . . . He asked me to go with him to meet his girl. We entered the women's barrack. He introduced me to a seventeen-year-old girl. After half an hour we went outside. Music was heard from the tailor's shop. I could not believe it. A small orchestra was playing, a couple was dancing, a Jewish man with a woman from Holland. I asked my friend: "What's going on here? How can you laugh, dance, speak freely, and think about women? Look around, there is barbed wire everywhere; we shall not get out of this place. How can you behave like this?" "Tovia," he answered, "don't be surprised. You will get used to it. We know what awaits us. You see the fire? There your family is turned into ash, the same as my family a few months ago. You look at that and don't cry. You say that you don't have any more tears— what can we, who see it for months, say? We remain indifferent, and we live like animals, for the present day." A signal for night silence stopped our talk....

In the evening [a few days later], a young, beautiful girl from Holland entered the barrack. She started to sing the well-known song "Mother." She had a strong, pleasant voice, and the word "mother" was expressed sadly and movingly. This was the only word that I understood.... I wanted to cry. I had lost my parents only a few days before. Nearby, music was playing. In the corner of the barrack, a group of people were drinking smuggled vodka and eating sausages. The moon was above the camp, and large tongues of fire were rising to the sky....

When we marched to work, we had to sing. Usually we sang military marches: German, Polish, Ukrainian, and Russian. About 300 meters from us, people were seeing the world for the last time, and we had to sing—loudly and as best we could—a real inferno.[7]

Love affairs among the prisoners in Sobibor are mentioned in some of the testimonies. The men were permitted by the German camp authorities to enter the barrack where the women lived during the evening hours, and this was the time and place where most of the intimate relationships developed. A known love affair grew between Ada and Yitzhak Lichtman and between some other prisoners. There were love affairs that ended tragically. A love affair between a young man from France and a girl from Holland ended when the young man was taken to Camp III; the girl joined him so that they could die together. The same happened with a woman from France who decided to share the fate of her lover, a prisoner from Poland.[8]

Sasha Pechersky, who led the uprising in the camp, wrote in his memoirs about close relations that developed between him and Luka, a girl from Holland. They usually met in the women's barrack.[9]

Sometimes the roll calls of the prisoners were used by the SS men for their entertainment and for mocking the Jews. *Oberscharführer* Weiss used to dress one of the prisoners in a long robe and Jewish cape and give him a broomstick in his hand. The prisoner had to stand on a table and sing the following song in Yiddish, composed by one of the camp inmates:

Moses, Moses! Wi hos du deine bruder in di shmole rine
Wi di yuden sinen shoin derinen

Macht men die klape zu
Weln ale felker hobn ruh.

("Moses, Moses!
How you have your brothers in the narrow gutter
When the Jews are already in,
The cover [or valve] is closed, then
And all the nations will have rest.") (free translation)

At the end of this song the prisoners had to fall down on the floor and say "Amen."[10]

As the prisoners marched to and from work, they were ordered to sing. One of the prisoners, nicknamed "*der Neger*" (the Negro), improvised a song, which described ironically their life in the camp:

Wie Iustig ist da unser Leben
Man tut uns zu essen geben
Wie Iustig ist im grunen Wald
Wo ich mir aufhalt

(Our life is happy here,
We receive good food,
How happy we are in the green forest,
Where I stay.) (free translation)

SS *Oberscharführer* Gustav Wagner enjoyed the song, and he forced the prisoners to sing it frequently.[11]

A favorite SS game was to gather a group of Jews around a coffin in which the Nazis would lay out a prisoner dressed like a Hasid. Then the Germans would sing, "I am a Jew with a long nose." The prisoner would pop up from the dead and repeat the phrase. Next the Nazis would chant:

O God we pray to Thee,
Listen to our plea,
To the Jews put an end,
To the rest peace send.[12]

When a group of Jewish prisoners who were former soldiers in the Soviet army arrived in camp, they sang Russian songs in the evenings.[13] In Sobibor the prisoners also played chess.

The camp authorities in Sobibor tried to mislead the prisoners about their fate and gave them even more opportunities for relaxation than in Treblinka and Belzec. The motive was explained by Philip Bialowicz, a

Sobibor survivor: "The [SS men] were interested in keeping up our spirit, so that we should not be depressed and would work better. They organized concerts for us, music was played, and we were entertained.... Their purpose was that we should not feel that we were doomed for extermination and think about an uprising."[14]

TREBLINKA

In the first days of the camp's existence, the SS men organized a "musical trio" that would play for them during meals, in the evenings, and whenever they had free time, at parties and for guests. The musicians were three Jews from Stock who had been brought to Treblinka originally to build the camp. They were amateur musicians who had played at Jewish weddings in their town. The SS men also ordered the trio to play near the gas chambers so that the music would drum out the screams of the people within the "tube" as they were being raced through it on their way to the gas chambers.

During the same period that hundreds of Jewish prisoners were put to work at the difficult and depressing task of vacating the reception area of the thousands of corpses that had accumulated there, the third anniversary of the outbreak of World War II was marked. On the eve of September 1, the SS men in the camp decided that the event should be celebrated, and so that they could torture the prisoners as well, they decided to include them in the festivities. That same evening the Jews were made to stand at attention, and the "musical trio," which at that time was playing near the gas chambers, was brought to the yard to play Jewish songs and melodies. A few young people were ordered to get out of line and dance. A Ukrainian corporal was in charge of the whole event and the Germans stood on the side watching, clapping, and laughing at the scene. The Jews stood at attention and wiped away their tears. It is difficult to describe their suffering at the fact that they were made to participate in this nightmarish event while strewn all around them were the corpses of their families, their friends, and innumerable other people.[15]

But the standard of the trio's playing was not good enough for the SS men. From the transports that came from Warsaw they removed professional musicians and organized a small orchestra. In the winter, conductor Artur Gold arrived in one of the transports. Before the war he had conducted one of the best orchestras in Warsaw, in the fanciest cafes and dubs. He was removed from the transport when he was already naked and on his way to the "tube." After the SS men found out that he was a famous conductor, they gave him the task of organizing the orchestra in the Lower Camp.

The orchestra consisted of ten musicians. The rehearsals were held at specified times, and the musicians, who were detailed to various work groups, were excused from them in order to rehearse. Singers performed together with the orchestra. Oscar Strawczinski tells about the orchestra, its performances, and its conductor:

> Gold assumed his work energetically. The Germans helped him. Quite a large amount of musical instruments was left in the yard by the Jews when they went to the showers. . . . Only jazz was missing. To rectify this, the *Hauptsturmführer* [Franz Stangl] brought back cymbals with him from his vacation . . . the drum was made in the camp. And in good time we also had ourselves a jazz band. One of the musicians who had come with Gold was an excellent jazz musician. A mixed choir of men and women was also formed. A Jew from Czechoslovakia wrote the texts and Gold the melodies. He wrote wonderful compositions for his orchestra. To round it off, Jazik, who was a soloist and cabaret dancer, was also added to the orchestra.
>
> By the order of Kurt Franz, white suits with blue collars and lapels were sewn for the people in the orchestra in the tailor shop. Gold appeared in a white frock coat with the same decoration, patent leather shoes, pressed pants, and a white shirt.[16]

Gold was liked by the SS, and for his fortieth birthday a party was held for him in the tailor shop. Drinks and baked goods were brought from the German kitchen, the orchestra performed in its gala clothes, and for the occasion a special repertoire was prepared. The SS men and prisoner capos were invited to this show. But Gold's groveling in front of the SS men and the special food rations he received—even though he sometimes shared them with the members of the orchestra—did not endear him to the prisoners. Many prisoners were even very critical and revolted by what was going on, but sometimes they were forced to participate in the very events that they so detested. Strawczinski wrote:

> After supper [the orchestra] plays music in the tailor shop, the largest and nicest hall in the "ghetto." The sky over and around the camp is red from the fire burning in the tremendous oven that was built lately, and the wind brings the smells of flesh and charred bones. It is almost impossible to breathe outside. In the tailor shop, our "aristocracy" has gathered [capos and prisoners with position of authority] with their girls. Germans and Ukrainians also appear. The girls and our "cavaliers" dance to the rhythm of the wonderful sounds of Gold's orchestra. They spend almost every evening this way. Later, when it grows warmer, the orchestra plays outdoors, near the closed gate. On the other side of the gate, groups of Ukrainians gather and perform their dances. This is a daily event in Treblinka. And as has been said before, we lacked only bread, lashes, death, and music.[17]

In accordance with Kurt Franz's orders, a song in German was composed, and the prisoners were forced to memorize it and sing it during roll call and on their way to and from work. The melody was written by Artur Gold, and the song was nicknamed "The Anthem of Treblinka":

We look straight out at the world,
The columns are marching off to their work.
All we have left is Treblinka,
It is our destiny.

We heed the commandant's voice,
Obeying his every nod and sign.
We march along together
To do what duty demands.

Work, obedience, and duty
Must be our whole existence.
Until we, too, will catch a glimpse at last
Of a modest bit of luck. (free translation)

A most macabre phenomenon was the playing of the orchestra at the evening roll call, when the selections of the sick took place or while prisoners were being whipped or ordered to engage in "sports activities." The orchestra's playing accompanied the yells of the beaten and the silence of the sick and weak who were removed from the rows and taken to the *Lazarett*. At the end of the roll call, the prisoners sang the "Treblinka Anthem" to the accompaniment of the orchestra.[18]

In the last months of Treblinka's existence, in the spring and summer of 1943, boxing matches were instituted among the prisoners. Kurt Franz, who was an amateur boxer and who used to keep in shape by hitting prisoners, was the initiator of these matches (see chapter 25). In the same period the number of transports decreased, and, as a result, the work pace had slackened a bit. Kurt Franz thought the mock performance of one Jew hitting another would be a pleasant way for the SS men and Ukrainians to pass the time. A few boxers were found in the transports from the Warsaw ghetto that arrived in the spring of 1943, and they became the nucleus of this sport in the camp. Franz also saw to it that there were boxing gloves in the camp. In the evenings one could see prisoners practicing boxing, holding contests, and hitting one another, while around them a group of observers enjoyed the scene. The pinnacle of these training sessions was the matches.

In roll-call square in the prisoners' living area, a ring was set up for the matches held every two weeks on Saturday afternoon. At the front of the ring, chairs were arranged for the SS men, and on the side were benches for the capos, the work managers, and the women. On the other side of the ring was the section for the rest of the prisoners, who were forced to attend the matches. The matches were opened by Gold's orchestra, which performed operas and operettas with the singers and choir. The "artistic" part of the program also included some humorous sketches, among them some jokes about the "Treblinka Rest Home."

The first matches boasted professional boxers of a high standard, but Kurt Franz was not satisfied with this. He forced into the ring barbers, tailors, *Scheissmeisters*, and prisoners who did not have any idea about boxing; he stuck gloves on their hands and made them start hitting each other, to the yells and cries of encouragement of the SS men. The sports event would then be concluded by another performance by the orchestra and choir.[19]

The establishment of a small orchestra in the extermination area was the result of the initiative of the capos after they found out about the existence of an orchestra in the Lower Camp. Authorization was granted by the SS men in charge of the extermination area. Jerzy Rajgrodzki, a member of the orchestra in the extermination area, wrote:

> In the month of October, while I was put to work at removing corpses from the new gas chambers, a capo came and in his hand was a violin. He asked who knew how to play and I said that I knew. He excused me from transferring the bodies and ordered me to play in the yard, near the corpses. After a while the "camp elder" arrived and took me into the kitchen. There I played a number of works as he requested. From then on they put me to work in the kitchen at peeling potatoes. There were six prisoners doing this work. One was Fuchs, who played the clarinet and who had worked in the past for the Polish radio.... At first I played only with Fuchs—violin and clarinet—with no accompaniment. We played from time to time during the roll calls.... On New Year's Eve we played in the kitchen. The "camp elder," the capos, and others came. There were only men. They brought some vodka and danced. It was a sad New Year....
>
> We heard that in Camp I there was an orchestra under the direction of Artur Gold. Camp II [extermination area] demanded an orchestra of its own. There was a need for a harmonica player, and we looked for one among the people in the transports. Who could count the number of harmonica players who were already in the pits! The "camp elder" was especially worried about the missing harmonica player, and he turned to the SS with this problem. Finally they found one in one of the transports; he was also a pianist and a well-known composer from Warsaw. From that time we were a trio. It became the custom during the roll calls. As the people fell into [rows of] fives for the roll calls, we stood at the side and played the Polish army march "We, the First Brigade" ("*My Pierwsza Brygada*"). After a while we substituted the

march from the movie *The World Laughs* for the march "We, the First Brigade." Sometimes we accompanied with melody the singing of the prisoners. The most popular song was "Tumbalalaika." One of the prisoners would sing a verse, and the others would join in the chorus with "Tumbalalaika." The words of the song reflected the lives of the prisoners in the camp with humor and criticism. The words of the song changed with time. In 1943 they stopped singing "Tumbalalaika" and more cultured songs were included in the repertoire. One of the prisoners composed a song in words of the song spoke about a different world that existed outside of Camp II . . . .

The songs served a revolutionary purpose for us. They encouraged us to continue our struggle to live and find ways to salvation. For the SS men and in order to note where we were living, a composition of Treblinka, *"Lager zwei is unzer Ieben, ay, ay, ay"* ("Camp II is our life, ay, ay, ay"), was composed. The chorus was sung by a professional singer, Spiegel, who had appeared in the Prague theater. . . .

In the spring, when the warm days came, the SS men would come to our camp early. The one who stuck out the most was the one whose nickname was "the black one" (*der Schwartzer*). He would sit himself down on a chair near the well and order us to play for him. While the other prisoners were still dressing or eating their breakfast and preparing for work, we would put the chairs in front of the hut, sit down, and begin the morning concert. Sometimes they would bring us cigarettes, chocolate, or other valuable items. We also performed concerts as per the wishes of the Ukrainian guards—in the afternoon, after work, when the prisoners were locked up. We would stand near the fence and play for the Ukrainians dozens of Soviet songs. Ivan [Demaniuk] and Nikolai loved these songs, and they made a big impression on them. During that time they did not beat or torture the prisoners, except when they committed some unusual crime.[20]

In the summer of 1943, in June and July, the work of burning the bodies commenced at four in the morning and continued until twelve noon. In the afternoon, the prisoners were locked in their huts with nothing to do. To keep the prisoners busy, the SS decided that the prisoners would prepare a play. Preparations got underway, and even actors were located. One of them, Spiegel, was a professional actor. The orchestra and women also took part in the play. The "camp elder" was the director; the tailors in the extermination area sewed costumes for the players. Rehearsals were held in the corridors of the gas chambers. The participants learned how to dance the minuet and the czardas. Preparations for the performance went on for a few weeks. In the square where the roll calls were held, a stage was built and seats were set up in preparation for the play, which was to be held one Sunday. In the front row sat a few SS men, and all around were Ukrainian guard units, which had been enlarged for the event. But the play went on without any hitches. Jerzy Rajgrodzki wrote about the prisoners' feelings during the performance, with the SS men sitting in front of them: "Most of us felt that we had had enough of this disgrace and we were ready to get even with the murderers. If only to throw a knife at one of them and kill him. Many of us had feelings of this sort. But we did not plan anything— an act of this sort would have ended in disaster. The guards outside had been strengthened then, even though they [the Germans] did not even suspect that this 'garbage' could even think of such a thing."[21]

In the tragic reality of Treblinka, there were also love affairs between the men and women prisoners. Usually the people in the more privileged group of prisoners were the ones involved in these affairs—for example, the capos, the "barrack elders," and those with other special positions in the camp. The living conditions of the more privileged prisoners allowed them to come into contact with the women, and their work, which was relatively easier than that of the others, allowed them greater freedom of movement about the camp. The SS men usually were inclined to allow this phenomenon, especially in the last months of the camp's existence, and they permitted visits in the evening hours to the women's living quarters.

The women, most of whom were young girls with little experience and whose physical and spiritual ability to survive in the camp was to no small degree conditional on any help with food or aid in time of illness, were in part amenable to the flirting of prisoners from this group. These were the people in a position to provide them with more food, medicine, or clothing.

But besides these relationships of convenience, there were also true love affairs that developed into deep emotional attachments between two people who knew their days were numbered. Despite the horribly over-crowded conditions in the living barracks, despite the nonavailability of any private place, and despite the prohibition of sleeping in any but one's assigned place, couples in love found a way and places to be together secretly in order to carry on intimate relationships.

In the Lower Camp, the known love affairs were between Rakowski, the "camp elder" during the typhus epidemic, and a young girl, and between the "barrack elder" Kuba and another young girl. In the extermination area an affair between the one in charge of the kitchen, Heller, and a girl whose name is unknown was common knowledge. Rajgrodzki writes about a wedding that took place in the extermination area:

> The groom was a mechanic who worked near the motors that provided the gas, and the bride was one of the young girls. They made them a nice wedding, according to the Law of Moses and Israel. Even some SS men came to the reception that was in the evening in the kitchen. . . . We played at the wedding, and the young people were escorted to the bridal canopy. There was

one who knew how to write the *tnaim* [terms of the marriage contract] and to read the prayers. The guests in uniform left. Those invited from the prisoners had a bit of fun. Then they left and the young couple remained alone. A double bed had been prepared for them on a pallet in the kitchen.[22]

In addition to these known incidents, in the camp there were love affairs and amorous relationships between anonymous men and women prisoners who did not receive mention in the testimonies. Their secret was kept during their affairs, and their secret went with them to the grave. In the shadow of death, love thrived.

CREATIVE WRITING

Among the prisoners there were quite a few who decided to put into writing all the horrible things they had witnessed, in the hope that the description of the events in writing would be preserved even after the writers were no longer alive.

In Treblinka, the capo of the *Lazarett*, Ze'ev Korland, a Jew of about fifty from Warsaw, who saw the killings that were carried out in the *Lazarett* every day and helped the sick undress and comforted them in their final minutes, recorded these tragic experiences. Korland used to read aloud from his work to his friends at night—poetry, parts of a play, descriptions of things that had happened—but everything referred to the *Lazarett*.

In the extermination area of Treblinka, there was a dentist (whose name is not known) who used to write down what had happened there every day. He also wrote poetry and read some of his works aloud to his friends. The works that were written in Treblinka were not found; they were either lost or destroyed when the camp was demolished.[23]

There were probably other prisoners who wrote in the various camps, but their work has not been mentioned in the testimonies, nor has it been recovered.

PART III

ESCAPE AND RESISTANCE

THE COGNIZANCE AND REACTION OF THE VICTIMS IN OCCUPIED POLAND

THE SMOOTH EXECUTION OF THE deportations from the ghettos depended on the passive behavior of the Jews. The Germans employed ruse and deception as far as the aim and destination of the deportations were concerned and kept the very existence of the death camps top secret. And, indeed, during the first six months of the deportations, until August or September 1942, there was an almost total unawareness of the true aim of the deportations among the large majority of Jews in the ghettos of occupied Poland.

FIRST PHASE: MARCH–AUGUST 1942

On the eve of a deportation, the Jews in the ghettos were told that they were being sent to the East, to labor camps somewhere in the occupied territories of the Soviet Union, mainly the Ukraine. The fact that many of the weak and sick who were unable to walk to the railway station were shot on the spot merely encouraged the belief that the others would be sent to work. The deception was further strengthened by rumors spread in the ghettos that deported Jews had been seen by some non-Jews somewhere in the East and that letters had even arrived from them.

The extent to which the fabrication was successful can be seen in the example of Lublin. Although the Jewish council had itself cooperated with the German authorities in the deportations, it was no more privy to the true situation than was anyone else. Twelve of its twenty-four members, along with thirty-five Jewish ghetto policemen, were deported to Belzec at the beginning of April 1942.[1] They did not know, of course, that they were being sent to their deaths. The Jews of Lvov did not know that fifteen thousand from their city who had been deported in March 1942 had been sent to Belzec and murdered there. Rabbi David Kahane, who witnessed this *Aktion*, wrote in his wartime diary: "With the liquidation of the assembly point at the Sobieski school building several days afterward, the Jews began inquiring about the destination of the victims of the last *Aktion*.

As before, rumors and speculations abounded. . . . Railroad workers who worked on the trains revealed to us that the victims had been transported to Belzec. . . . What befell the Jews taken there? Not one Jew managed to escape from Belzec at that time. Nor had an Aryan inhabitant of the area visited the place."[2] A Pole, Tadeusz Pankiewicz, who was permitted by the Germans to keep his pharmacy inside the Cracow ghetto, witnessed the deportations at the beginning of June 1942, and wrote in his memoirs: "There are rumors that the deported were sent to the Ukraine, where they will work in agriculture. Some German railway workers told us that they personally saw there a large number of barracks with Jews from all over Europe. The Jews are kept there in good conditions; they work hard, but have everything they need, and receive food and clothes. Naturally they are under a strong guard. Surrounded with barbed wire and nobody can come close to them. They are forbidden to write letters, therefore there is no news from them."[3]

But even during that first period, the Germans were unable to shroud Belzec in total secrecy. Two Jewish women who had been deported to Belzec at the end of March 1942, from Zolkiew in the Lvov district, a town close to the camp, escaped and returned to their hometown. An eyewitness from Zolkiew wrote: "After a few days, two Jewish women, Mina Astman and Malka Talenfeld, came back from the *Aktion*. After they had calmed down from their terrible experience, they secretly told some of their friends what they had been through."[4] But in spite of such stories, the truth about what was going on in Belzec and the real purpose of the deportations reached only a limited number of Jews, even in Zolkiew.

People sent to Sobibor during the first months of its operation had not heard of the place. Yitzhak Lichtman, who was expelled in the middle of May 1942 from Zolkiewka (Lublin district) to Sobibor, testified that he had never heard of Sobibor and that "the Germans had succeeded in concealing the existence of this camp. On the train to Sobibor, we were told by some Poles that we were being taken to be burned. We didn't believe them. We thought that the Poles, who were anti-Semites, wanted to scare us."[5]

Whereas the deported Jews from the Lublin, Lvov, and Cracow districts knew nothing about the real purpose of the evacuation, some news about Belzec did reach the Jewish Underground organization in the Warsaw ghetto. The first Jewish Underground newspaper that wrote about the deportations to Belzec was *Nowe Tory* ("New Tracks"), of the Bund organization, in April 1942:

> New facts about the evacuation of Jews from Lublin are arriving all the time and continue without interruption. . . . Until now two transports of deported left already—about 6,000 people. Now are awaiting the deportation of

additional 20,000 Jews. It was possible to ascertain definitely that the evacuated were deported to the famous camp of Belzec, where hundreds of young Jews were murdered in an inhuman way. . . . Among the [local] population rumors are being spread that in this camp extermination is being carried out like in Chelmno, by poisoning with gas. The Jewish population of Lublin is so terrorized that they are going to the collection points without trying to resist. On the way to the collection points, masses of Ukrainians are waiting and are beating the deportees and robbing them of the rest of their property. The Germans are telling the unfortunates that they are being deported to Jekaterynoslav (East Ukraine).

From Izbica (Lublin) district 1,000 Jews were deported in an unknown direction on March 19. A week later, on March 26, the remaining 7,000 people were deported. There is no doubt that they were deported to Belzec, where they are murdered with poisonous gas. Such news arrived also from Rava-Russkaya, Bilgoraj, Okuniew, Wawer, and other places.

Horrible news arrived from Lvov. Recently, the Germans published an order about the evacuation of 33,000 Jews from the city. The evacuation had to be carried out according to the plan—1,000 people per day. But in the middle of March, two transports left with 13,500 people in both of them. It was impossible to find out about their direction or destination. Their fate arouses the greatest anxiety.[6]

The Dror (Zionists) Underground newspaper *Yediot* ("News"), June 9, 1942, stated: "Turobin (Lublin district). On May 31 all the Jews from this township, numbering 1,500 souls, were deported in unknown directions, very few remained on the spot. . . ."[7] The information about Belzec came mainly from Poles who lived close to the camp and from Polish railway workers, and it reached the Polish underground. From their underground publication, it reached the Jewish underground (see chapter 33).

The news about the deportations and the mass killings carried out in Belzec that reached the Jewish Underground in the Warsaw ghetto did not reach the majority of the people and did not heighten the awareness of the Jewish population there about the dangers they were facing. When the deportations actually started there, on July 22, 1942, the Warsaw Jews did not know what awaited them at the end of the journey.

Jacob Wiernik, who was sent from Warsaw to Treblinka on August 3, 1942, wrote: "Rumors abounded that they were sending us to work in the Ukraine. . . . I knew it was our lot to suffer, to wander, to starve . . . but I honestly did not believe that the hangman's noose was hovering mercilessly over our heads, over that of our children, and that our very existence was at stake."[8] And Marian Platkiewicz, also bound for Treblinka, wrote: "At that time the general opinion in the Warsaw ghetto was that Treblinka was no more than a forced labor camp. . . . According to another version, a transit and selection station had been built there for those sent to do agricultural work in the Ukraine."[9] Even the testimonies of those sent to Treblinka in September 1942 reflect their ignorance of their true destination and fate.[10]

Rumors made the rounds in the Warsaw ghetto concerning letters and messages arriving from the deportees, which indicated that they were in Bialystok, Brest-Litovsk, Pinsk, and even Smolensk, and that they were working. If such letters did arrive, at least some of them had been forged by the Germans to fool the Jews in the ghetto. However, a small proportion of those expelled from the *Umschlagplatz* were indeed sent to labor camps, and messages from them, or from people who had seen them, contributed to the general ignorance and illusion concerning the fate awaiting the vast majority of the ghetto Jews.

SECOND PHASE: SEPTEMBER 1942 UNTIL THE END OF THE DEPORTATIONS

The Germans did not succeed in preventing information from leaking out about the existence of the death camps of Belzec and Treblinka for a prolonged time. From August/September 1942, rumors and information about these camps and the actual fate of the deportees spread gradually among the remaining Jews in the ghettos and labor camps of the General Government.

Pankiewicz wrote about the news that reached the Cracow ghetto:

A few months later [after the deportations of June 1942], some information started to reach the ghetto. This was the first time names like Belzec, Majdanek, Treblinka were heard, camps with high smoking chimneys of crematoria. But even then, there were not yet any thoughts of mass murder.... One day, with the speed of lightning, a story spread that a man escaped from a transport in Belzec. This courageous man was the dentist Bachner.... From him, the escapee from the extermination transport, it became known in the ghetto the truth about the existence of camps where Germans are killing, gassing, and cremating the arriving prisoners.[11]

The underground newspaper of the Bund, *Oif der Vach* ("On Guard"), which appeared in Warsaw on September 20, 1942, wrote about Treblinka:

The Jews of Warsaw Are Killed in Treblinka
During the first week of the "deportation *Aktion*" Warsaw was flooded with greetings from the deported Jews. The greetings arrived from Bialystok, Brest-Litovsk, Kosov, Malkinia, Pinsk, Smolensk. All this was a lie. All the trains with the Warsaw Jews went to Treplinka, where the Jews were murdered in the most cruel way. The letters and greetings came from people who succeeded in escaping from the trains or from the camp. It is possible that in the beginning, from the first transports, some of the Warsaw Jews were

sent to Brest-Litovsk or Pinsk, in order that their greetings would mislead, deceive, and provoke false illusions among the Jews in Warsaw. Actually, what was the fate of the deported Jews? We know it from the stories of the Poles and of those Jews who succeeded in escaping from the trains or from Treblinka. . . .

The size of Treblinka was one-half square kilometer. It was surrounded by three fences of barbed wire. . . . After unloading the train of the living and the dead, the Jews were led into the camp. . . . During the descent from the train, shots were fired on those who were slow or even for no reason. Those who died en route or were shot on the spot were buried between the first and second fence. . . .

The women and children from the arriving transport were divided into groups of 200 each and were taken to the "baths." They had to take off their clothes, which remained on the spot, and were taken naked to a small barrack called the "bath," which was located close to the digging machine. From the bath nobody returned, and new groups were entering there constantly. The bath was actually a house of murder. The floor in this barrack opened up and the people fell into a machine. According to the opinion of some of those who escaped, the people in the barrack were gassed. According to another opinion, they were killed by electrical current. From the small tower over the bath, there were constant shots. There was talk that the shots were aimed at the people inside the barrack and those who survived the gas. The bath absorbs 200 people every fifteen minutes, so in twenty-four hours the killing capacity is 20,000 people. That was the explanation for the incessant arrival of people in the camp, from where there was no return, except a few hundred who succeeded in escaping during the whole time. . . . During the daytime women and children were liquidated and during the nights, the men. . . .

The escape from the camp was difficult and dangerous, but there were people who tried to do it, in spite of the fact that the camp was strongly illuminated during the night. . . . Why wasn't a mass escape organized? There were rumors in the camp that it was surrounded by a strong guard and the fences were electrified. The people were broken from their terrible experiences at the *Umschlagplatz*, on the train and in the camp. The general depression influenced also those who were, by nature, more active. . . .

An SS man gave a speech before each of the arriving transports and promised that all of them would be sent for work in Smolensk or Kiev.

The night between August 19 and 20, when Warsaw was bombarded, there was a blackout in the camp for the first time. An SS man addressed the assembled Jews. He told them that an agreement had been reached between the German government and Roosevelt about the transfer of European Jews to Madagascar. In the morning they would leave Treblinka with the first transport. This announcement aroused a great joy among the Jews. As soon as the all-clear signal was given, the extermination machine started its "normal" activity. Even inside the camp, the Nazis continued to mislead the Jews until the last moment. . . .

There were three such camps: one in the vicinity of Pinsk for the eastern areas, another in the area of Lublin at Belzec, and the third, the largest, was Treblinka near Malkinia.[12]

It took several months from the time that the first shreds of information about Belzec and Treblinka reached the ghettos until the remainder of the Jewish population realized that when they were deported they were being sent to their deaths.

The secrecy surrounding Sobibor and the activities there was preserved for a much longer period. The camp was in a more remote and desolate area. Fewer transports arrived there, and very few people succeeded in escaping. Sobibor was the camp "in the vicinity of Pinsk" mentioned in the Underground newspaper *Oif der Vach*. Even as late as the end of 1942, Sobibor was unknown to the Jews in the ghettos. Abraham Wang, who was deported there at the beginning of 1943 from Izbica, which was close to Sobibor, testified that when the people arrived at Sobibor, they did not know what place they had come to, what Sobibor was, and what happened there.[13]

When the information about Belzec and Treblinka finally reached the Jewish population in the ghettos of Poland, the deportations did not continue as smoothly as before. Jews went into hiding inside the ghettos, and bringing them to the collection points and trains was no longer as easy as it had been before. In the east and northeast of Poland, in the area of the forests, groups of youngsters tried to escape and join or form partisan units. In other places Jews resisted. Yet these limited responses could not and did not bring about any substantial change in the fate of the majority of Jews, who were doomed to deportation and extermination. For them there was no escape, and hiding in the ghetto was only a temporary rescue.

Rudolf Reder, one of the two survivors of Belzec, wrote about the deportation from Lvov:

> Two weeks before the deportation, people spoke everywhere of the approaching disaster. We were in despair. This time we knew the meaning of "deportation." . . . The Legend of Belzec became a truth we knew about, and we trembled with fear. Days before August 10, people ran around the streets of the Jewish quarter, full of despair, but powerless, asking one another what to do. Early in the morning of August 10, the Jewish quarter was surrounded by Gestapo men, SS, Sonderdienst, who, in teams of four or six, patrolled the streets. The Ukrainian police were very helpful to them. . . .
>
> For several days these patrols carried out house-to-house searches. People who did not have stamped work permits or people whose work permits were not valid were expelled from the houses. Those who resisted got a bullet in the head. . . . I was caught in a hiding place, beaten, and taken. We were packed densely inside a tram where it was impossible to move or breath,

and taken to the Janowski camp. It was evening. We were kept in a closed ring on a big lawn. There were 6,000 of us. We were ordered to sit, forbidden to get up, to smoke. We were illuminated by a searchlight from a watchtower. It was bright as day. Surrounded by armed beasts, we were sitting tightly squeezed, young and old, women and children of all ages. There were some shots, somebody got up, maybe he wanted to be killed. We sat during the whole night in deathly silence. Neither children nor women cried. At six o'clock in the morning, we were ordered to get up from the wet grass, and a long column of the doomed marched to the Kleparow railway station. We were surrounded by Gestapo men and Ukrainians. Nobody could escape.[14]

On the eve of the deportation from the Grodno ghetto, in January–February 1943, Tzipora Birman, a member of the Zionist anti-Nazi Underground movement there, wrote about hope for a miracle and the frustrating facts about the forest as a way of rescue for the Jews:

No tranquility was in the ghetto . . . there was again talk about an *Aktion*. Almost all of the people knew already that the deportations were to Treblinka. Many responded: We shall not go, let them kill us on the spot. But this was only talk. All the people packed their bundles. They still hoped, perhaps some miracle would happen on the train; they put their trust in a miracle and went silently to the cruel death. We sent a group into the forests . . . it was hard to get arms in the ghetto. We believed that they would purchase arms there. We sent them to find a way for us also. They left, but did not reach the forest. One returned, four were killed. Leizer Reizner (the one who returned) told us the terrible things he had seen. Hundreds of killed Jews were lying in the forests of Marcikance; dozens were still alive asking for death. Better to die than to live such a life. Our hopes about the forests vanished. It is impossible with no arms . . . the failure with the forest depressed us. We were left with no way out. There was no choice but to die honorably in the ghetto. We started to prepare a counter-action.[15]

The deportations carried out in January–February 1943 were fraught with difficulties and resistance, which caused casualties even to the Germans. When on January 18 the Germans tried to expel from the Warsaw ghetto eight thousand Jews who did not have work permits, they could not find them—despite this particular *Aktion* coming as a surprise. To carry out the deportation, they caught three thousand Jews who worked in the German enterprises, although the Nazi authorities had not intended to deport them. On the day of the deportation, there was armed resistance by the Jewish Underground, and the Germans suffered casualties—dead and wounded. The deportation continued for four days. The Germans succeeded in deporting five thousand to sixty-five hundred Jews to Treblinka, a few thousand less than the fixed goal. About a thousand Jews were shot in the houses and while trying to evade deportation.

During the deportations from Bialystok, February 9–13, 1943, tens of thousands of Jews went into hiding. Houses were burned and blown up to force the people to leave the hiding places. There were acts of resistance, and Germans were killed and wounded. Close to ten thousand people were taken to Treblinka, and about nine hundred were killed on the spot. The planned deportations met with more and more difficulties. When the Germans decided to liquidate the remnants of the Warsaw ghetto on April 19, 1943, there was an uprising that lasted weeks and months. An uprising also took place in August 1943, when they decided to liquidate the Bialystok ghetto.

Hundreds of thousands of Jews, including the heads of the *Judenrat*, who were deported from their hometowns in the spring or summer of 1942 did not know their destination or fate, and even if rumors reached them about the existence of death camps, they did not believe them. When these Jews were expelled from their homes and told that they were being sent to labor camps somewhere in the East, they accepted this and were unaware of the true meaning of deportation.

The surprise, brutality, and swiftness of execution of the deportations, the shootings and killings inside the houses and on the streets, generated panic and shock and indeed may be said to have mesmerized the Jews. The belief and hope of the victims that they were being sent to work, the unawareness of their true destination, enabled the Nazis to carry out the deportations at this stage with relative ease. However, at the end of that summer and in the autumn of 1942, when information about the death camps began seeping back into the ghettos and the Jews realized what it meant to be deported, they tried to find ways to survive. They went into hiding and to the forests and tried to escape; they resisted and fought, but the odds were against them.

To find rescue and to survive, they needed the active help of large segments of the local populations, but this was not forthcoming. Instead, those who did try to escape encountered indifference, sometimes even hostility, and very little help (see chapter 43). Under those conditions, even the knowledge of the true aim of the deportations did not leave the victims any viable alternatives. At that stage, the deportations became more difficult for the Nazis. They were in need of larger security forces, they met with resistance, and they suffered some losses, but on the whole they carried out and accomplished the extermination actions according to their basic plans.

ESCAPES FROM THE TRAINS AND SPONTANEOUS ACTS OF RESISTANCE

As TIME PASSED AND MORE information reached the Jews in the ghettos of the General Government about what was happening in the camps, more and more people attempted escape. The terrible conditions inside the densely packed deportation trains and the resulting death toll also encouraged attempts at escape. The doors of the freight cars were closed from the outside at the embarkation station, so the escapes were usually carried out through the small windows of the freight cars, which were covered with barbed wire, or by breaking some wooden board through the door, wall, or floor. For the most part, the escapes occurred while the train was moving; only sometimes were escapes attempted when it stopped at a station.

The odds for a successful escape were extremely low. The train guards, armed with rifles and machine guns, were dispersed throughout the train and fired on any escapee they spotted. Moreover, military or police patrols were stationed along the railway routes, on the bridges, and at other crucial points. Many who tried to escape were killed or wounded by the guards or patrols; others were killed or injured in an unsuccessful jump from the speeding train. In most cases, the wounded were immediately caught and shot.

Jerzy Królikowski, a Polish engineer who was engaged at repairing a bridge close to Treblinka along which the deportation trains passed, wrote:

> More often than in the past, people tried to escape from the transports by breaking boards from the freight cars. Most of these experiments ended in the shooting of the escapee by the guards. The passing trains were usually accompanied by intense rifle fire. . . . Sometimes we could see naked people running through the fields. Most of them were shot by the guards, and only a few succeeded in escaping. . . .
>
> For many of the prisoners, the Treblinka station was the last station in their life. The drunken guards "played" with them, proposing escape to them in return for money and valuables, and then shot them when they were running. . . . In the few cases where prisoners succeeded in escaping, it was because the drunken guards did not aim well.[1]

Melech Helber testified about a successful escape from a train:

The liquidation of the last Jews at Siedlce was on November 30, 1942. . . .
Feeling that I might need them, I took with me on the train some tools: pliers, a saw, and a drill. When the train moved, I tried to break the door with
my tools. Finally, I succeeded. I jumped from the fast-moving train into the
darkness of the night. Full of bruises and bleeding wounds, I lay half-fainting
close to the railway track. I saw that others had jumped from the train. Some
of them were caught by peasants armed with axes who waited near the track,
robbed and killed them. After I had recovered a bit, I quietly left the place.[2]

A report of a German company commander of Police Battalion No.
133 to the commander of the Order Police in the Lvov district, dated September 14, 1942, described the whole process of the deportation of Jews
from the city and area of Kolomyya in the Lvov district to Belzec, and the
escapes from the train.

Subject: Deportation of Jews
After carrying out the deportation of Jews in Skole, Stryj, and Khodorov on
3–5/9/42 . . . we were in Kolomyya according to the order, on the evening of
6/9/42.
    The action in Kolomyya, carried out on 7/9/42, was, for all the forces
that took part, easy and well prepared, contrary to the experience in Stryj. . . .
    The loading of the transport train was completed at 17:00 hours. About
1,000 of the assembled Jews were released by the Security Police, 4,769 Jews
were deported. . . . After we had nailed and sealed all the freight cars according to orders, the train left in the direction of Belzec at 21:00 hours accompanied by a guard of ten men.
    In the darkness of the night, many Jews escaped, after removing the
barbed wire from the air holes. Some of them were shot by the guards, but
the majority were liquidated that night or the next day by the railway guards
or by other police forces. . . .
    . . . The total number of Jews was 8,205. During the *Aktionen* in the vicinity
of Kolomyya on September 8 and 10, 400 Jews were shot, for unknown reasons. As I remember, during the big drive of the deported Jews in Kolomyya on
September 10, the Security Police loaded all the Jews onto the thirty available
freight cars. Considering the oppressive heat that prevailed that day, the stress
of the Jews from the long foot marches or the day-long waiting, without the
supply of any food worth mentioning, with the excessive overloading of most
of the freight cars, with 180–200 Jews in each, the effect was catastrophic. . . .
    Because of the strain on the Jews already described, the unfavorable influence of the heat, and the heavily overloaded freight cars, the Jews tried to
break out from the standing train, again and again, using the darkness which
fell at 19:30 hours. . . . The break-out attempts from the standing train, in the
darkness, were prevented or the fleeing Jews were shot during the escape. Because of the heat, the Jews in all the freight cars were completely undressed.

The train left Kolomyya at 20:50 according to plan. . . . After a short period of travel, Jews in some of the freight cars tried to break the boards of the train. In part they succeeded. When the train arrived at Stanislavov station, the necessary repairs were carried out by local craftsmen. . . . After the train traveled further and stopped at some station, big holes made by the Jews were again discovered in freight cars, and most of the barbed wire on the air windows had been torn down. In one of the freight cars, the Jews used a hammer and pliers. . . . We were forced at each stop at a station to nail the freight cars provisionally, otherwise we could not continue the journey. . . .

At 11:15, the train arrived at Lvov. . . . In Lvov, the locomotive was changed—we got an old one—so that the continuation of the journey was possible only with prolonged interruptions. The slow journey was exploited by those Jews who still had strength to slip through the openings and find rescue in escape, which was not dangerous on the slow-moving train. . . . Beyond Lvov, the guards ran out of the ammunition they had taken with them and the additional 200 bullets they had received from the army people. So, during the rest of the journey they used stones when the train was traveling, or their side-arms [bayonet] when the train stopped. . . . At 18:45, the train arrived at Belzec.[3]

Iesaja Feder, who lived in Kolomyya and was among the deportees to Belzec, testified about his escape from the train on the way to Belzec:

We were told that we were traveling to work in the Ukraine, but somehow, while closed in the freight car, the word "Belzec" came up. After traveling some time, I decided to escape. We were a few youngsters, and we tore down the barbed wire from the small window. I climbed to the window, squeezed myself through and jumped. It was dark, and the SS guards were shooting all the time, even without seeing any escapee, just to frighten. I fell on the earth, the train passed by . . . . I was marching on a path, suddenly in front of me appeared a Ukrainian who shouted at me: "Where are you going?" I answered that I was on the way to Kolomyya. "So you escaped from the train. Let's go to the police," he said, and caught my hand. He was a strong peasant, and I was weakened from life in the ghetto, so I could not resist him. After marching a while, I asked him to let me urinate, and then I started to run. I ran as if Death were behind me, and succeeded in escaping. During daylight I continued to march. Passing a forest, I met a girl from Kolomyya with a broken leg. She had escaped from the same train as I had. She decided to stay for a while in the forest. I continued on my way when I found myself surrounded by three Ukrainians. They led me to a small barrack at a train stop, where I met some other Jews who had escaped the transport and had been caught. We were beaten up and taken to Kolomyya. Along the railway, many victims were lying who, like myself, had jumped from the train. Some were dead; others were still alive, but with broken hands and legs. In Kolomyya the Ukrainians handed us over to the railway police guards. We were again beaten up and then taken to the Gestapo and to prison.

For a few days we were kept in prison with no food, and afterwards we were taken to the railway station. We were packed, 160 people into a freight car. . . . The train moved. I decided to escape again. We again cut the barbed wire and, with help from other people, climbed through the small window and jumped from the train. I found some corn in the field and quelled my hunger. Two Ukrainians approached me. I had some money and offered it to them. They let me go. Having no place to hide myself, I went back to Kolomyya, where some Jews were still kept in a labor camp. On the way I met a Polish woman. She took me, the stranger, to her house, kept me there for two days. She fed me, prepared me an armband with a Star of David that the Jews were wearing. She led me to a group of Jews who worked in the neighborhood, and with them I returned to the ghetto.[4]

Another survivor, Giza Petranker, testified about her escape from a train on the way from Lvov to Belzec. While jumping from the train, she was wounded by a bullet in her hand. Barefoot and almost nude, she and a little girl who had also escaped from the train succeeded in reaching the ghetto in Zolkiew. This after wandering and hiding for four days. But her repose was short. When Jews from Zolkiew were deported to Belzec, she was caught and sent with them. She succeeded again in jumping from the train and returned to Zolkiew, where a ghetto still existed. Many Jews who escaped the trains were gathered in this ghetto and the ghetto inhabitants, who gave them refuge, nicknamed them "jumpers" or "parachutists." When the Zolkiew ghetto was finally liquidated, all the escapees from the transports to Belzec shared the fate of the local Jews.[5]

There were also escapes from the deportation trains to Sobibor, but to a lesser extent than to the other two camps. Sobibor, as a death camp, was almost unknown to the Jews in the ghettos until the late autumn of 1942. Therefore, only a few Jews escaped from the trains in the first six months of Sobibor's existence. Even after this period, by the fall of 1942, the information about Sobibor reached only the ghettos in the vicinity of this camp. Shlomo Alster, who was deported at the end of October or beginning of November 1942 from the ghetto of Chelm, which was not far from Sobibor, testified: "When on the way it became known to us that we were being taken to Sobibor, which meant for us death, people started to jump from the freight cars. The guards were shooting at the escapees, and most of them were hit by the bullets."[6] Israel Trager, who was also on a train from Chelm to Sobibor, said: "When the Germans saw that the Jews were jumping, they stopped the train and opened up with intense fire on the fleeing Jews. Most of them were hit. The dead Jews were loaded onto the freight cars and the train moved again, increasing its speed to make it more dangerous to jump."[7]

Another ghetto close to Sobibor was in Wlodawa. Hella Fellenbaum-Weiss testified about the deportation that took place in November 1942: "We left for Sobibor in carts. One might wonder why so few tried to escape, since we knew the fate awaiting us. . . . Our cart was guarded by an armed Ukrainian who watched us [constantly]. German soldiers with machine guns rode alongside us on horseback. At the border of a wood, my young brother gave a farewell sign, left the cart, and started to run, followed by my older brother. My little brother fell; the other escaped. I learned later that he, too, was murdered."[8]

All the known, available testimonies about the escapes from the transports to Sobibor are not of people who escaped themselves, but only of people who witnessed the escapes. Very few, perhaps none, of those who were deported to Sobibor and tried to escape or succeeded in escaping survived the war. The small number of those who tried to escape and the remoteness and isolation of Sobibor made it easier for German security forces to catch and kill these escapees.

Very few attempts were made to escape from trains deported to Operation Reinhard camps from other European countries. Those who wanted to evade the "deportation to labor camps in the East," as the Jews were told, tried to find refuge before they were taken to the trains. All the others believed that they were really going for work "somewhere in the East." Only in one testimony about a deportation from France to Sobibor is there mention of people having escaped from the train (see chapter 20).

The scale of the escape attempts from the deportation trains to the death camps of Operation Reinhard was influenced by the knowledge and awareness of the Jews as to the destination of the transports and what awaited them after arrival.

The chances for survival after the escape and of finding a refuge also influenced the decision to jump from the train. Most of those who escaped the transports faced a hostile or indifferent population with little help forthcoming. Therefore, almost all of the escapees tried to reach the ghettos that still existed and find shelter there. But those who succeeded in reaching the ghettos had only a short respite. When the ghettos were liquidated, the escapees were again deported to the death camps. Thousands of Jews who tried to escape the transports found their death while jumping or from the bullets of the guards. Some were caught by local people and handed over to the police or to the Germans. Hundreds who succeeded were unable to find refuge; they were caught, killed, or deported once more to the death camps. Yet despite all the factors working against them, some of the escapees managed to survive the war, in part with the help of local people.

The overwhelming majority of the Jews did not try to escape, however. They arrived in the camps and disembarked from the trains, completely unsuspecting. They obeyed the orders of the SS men and went quietly to the gas chambers. There were, however, some individuals or groups of deportees who grasped what was happening and staged spontaneous acts of resistance and mass flights. Cases of group resistance usually occurred with transports that arrived from ghettos where some information about extermination had reached the Jews prior to deportation, and therefore they were more suspicious about the place to which they had come.

After Max Bialas's murder in Treblinka and the collective punishment that followed, during which about 150 Jews were killed in September 1942, there were no attempts at resistance for approximately three months. The next act of resistance witnessed by prisoners in the camp, and testified by them later, occurred in the first half of December 1942. At the time the transports to Treblinka, which were originating in the ghettos and collection camps in the area of Bialystok-Grodno, increased. The directorate of the German railway announced to Operation Reinhard headquarters that from December 15 there would be a hiatus in the appropriation of railroad cars for the transport of Jews because of the military priority on the eastern front; Operation Reinhard headquarters therefore decided to increase the transports to Treblinka until the train allotment ceased. The commanders of the camp agreed that some transports could arrive in the evening and after dark, even though until that time transports were received only during the day.

In the second week of December 1942, in the evening hours, a transport of about two thousand Jews was brought to Treblinka from the Kelbasin camp near Grodno and included people from Grodno and the surrounding area. When the transport entered the camp, most of the prisoners had already been locked into their barracks. Only the "blues" and "reds," along with SS men and Ukrainians, waited on the platform and in the transport yard, ready to receive the deportees. When the people from the transport disembarked, they had no idea where they were. They asked the Jewish prisoners if they were in Treblinka, but their questions were left unanswered.[9] The deportees were brought to the transport yard and were ordered to undress and go to the "baths." Some obeyed the order and were taken through the "tube" to the gas chambers. Among the last who remained in the transport yard and who had not yet undressed were a few dozen youths. The intertwined barbed wire all around, the flames rising from the direction of the *Lazarett*, the confusion of the naked as they were pushed into the "tube" were enough for them to realize the truth about the place. What happened then is related by Kalman Taigman, one of the prisoners who received the transport:

> There were still many youths there. Some of them began calling out not to listen to the Germans and not to undress. A great riot began. The Germans opened fire on the crowd. The SS men, with Kurt Franz at the head, cruelly beat the men, women, and elderly indiscriminately. We stood at the side and witnessed the scene. Germans and Ukrainians were [stationed] on the roofs, and they also began firing into the crowd. We heard an explosion. It seems that a Jew threw a grenade in the direction of the shooting, and we saw how a seriously wounded Ukrainian was evacuated from the yard."[10]

Dozens of youths who were still in the transport yard began beating the Ukrainians and Germans with their fists and, with knives they had brought with them, tried to break through the fences and escape. Other people from the transport joined them, and many dispersed throughout the various sections of the camp. Some succeeded in breaking through into the living barracks of the Jewish prisoners and sought cover. The Germans and Ukrainians, with the help of the capos and the prisoners themselves—who were afraid to hide the resisters—removed them from the barracks and escorted them to the extermination area. The rest of the escapees were also caught throughout the camp. Dozens were shot on the spot as they resisted capture, and the others were taken to the gas chambers. In the corridor at the entrance to the gas chambers, the people continued to resist and absolutely refused to enter the gas chambers. The Germans and Ukrainians shot into the corridor. Many were killed, and the rest were finally forcibly pushed into the gas chambers.

The prisoners in the extermination area heard the shots, but had no idea what was going on outside. Wiernik wrote:

> We were locked into the barracks. The Germans and Ukrainians handled the victims without us. Suddenly we heard noise, yells and shots. Many shots. We didn't move from our places. We waited impatiently for the morning light. We wanted to know what happened. The next day the area was full of murdered people. During work, the Ukrainians told us that the people from the transport had refused to be taken to the gas chambers. A tragic struggle had developed. They destroyed everything in sight and broke the crates with gold that stood in the corridor of the gas chambers. They grabbed sticks and anything they could get their hands on and began resisting. But the bullets cut them down. In the morning the yard was still full of the dead and the instruments they had used to defend themselves. They fell in battle. The rest were thrown into the gas chambers . . . by dawn the whole thing was over.[11]

The prisoners removed the bodies from the gas chambers and corridor and transferred them to the burial pits. The floors were cleaned and the walls were painted so that no trace of blood would remain. The gas chambers had to be ready to receive new victims. The murdered who were scattered throughout the various areas of the camp were also removed. The "tube" was cleaned, and the barbed wire that had been damaged during the attempted escape was repaired. The Germans learned a lesson from this mass resistance incident, and subsequent transports to Treblinka were not received after dark.

The fact that the transport that had resisted was from the area of Bialystok-Grodno is not incidental. In the ghettos and camps in this area there was an organized youth underground. They hoarded arms, and quite a few young people left for the forests and the partisans. The youths who resisted evidently were organized; they had knives and, according to one testimony, a grenade. When their situation became clear, they began their revolt.

In yet another transport a group of young women resisted entering the gas chambers. An eyewitness to this event stated: "I shall not forget the construction work of the stores. While on the roof I could see a terrible picture: a group of naked women were standing near the gas chambers and refused to enter. The SS men and Ukrainians were beating them brutally with sticks and butts. Some of them were killed on the spot."[12]

In Sobibor also there were some attempts at resistance, among the transports that arrived from the Wlodawa ghetto. The people in this ghetto, which was only eight kilometers from Sobibor, had received some information as to what was going on in the nearby camp. A transport with the last two thousand Jews from Wlodawa arrived in Sobibor on April 30, 1943. When they disembarked from the train and were driven to the gas chambers, they attacked the Germans and Ukrainians and started running. A prisoner from the *Bahnhofkommando* testified: "When I was working in the *Bahnhofkommando*, I witnessed two resistance attempts by two transports from Wlodawa. To the second transport we said quietly to the people: 'You are being taken to your death, attack the Germans.' Indeed, they wounded a few Germans."[13] Another prisoner testified that he saw the people of Wlodawa running from the direction of Camp III and that they destroyed a wall close to the gas chambers. They were caught and killed.[14]

Another case of resistance happened in a transport that was brought to Sobibor on October 11, 1943. During these last days of Sobibor's existence, some transports arrived from Minsk. Alexander Pechersky, the commander of the uprising in Sobibor, wrote about this:

In the morning we suddenly heard horrible screams and shooting from automatic rifles. Soon thereafter came a command that no one was to leave the workshops. The gates of Camp I were shut. The number of guards was increased everywhere. The screaming and the shooting were heard more frequently . . . . It lasted for some time. Then it grew quiet. It was not until five in the evening that we learned what had happened. A new transport had arrived. When the people were already undressed, they realized where they were being taken and began to run, naked. But where was there to run? They were already in the camp and fenced in on all sides. So they ran toward the barbed wire fence. There they were met by a hail of bullets from automatic rifles. Many fell dead on the spot. The rest were led away to the gas chambers.[15]

There were additional attempts of resistance in Sobibor, but no detailed testimonies are left.

The authorities in command in Treblinka and Sobibor were aware that the transports arriving from the General Government or from Ostland in the last months of the camps' activities may stage acts of resistance. Therefore stronger security measures and precautions were taken in anticipation of their arrival. More SS men and Ukrainian guards were at the station and along the route to the gas chambers. In some cases not all the freight cars were opened simultaneously, and the transport was liquidated in groups. On other occasions, the young men were taken first to the gas chambers, before they realized what was going on.

All these acts of spontaneous resistance were carried out by small groups of victims and had no chance of success. Since they were already in the closed, heavily guarded camp, the Jews of the transports were doomed to extermination, and these unorganized acts could in no way change that situation at the very last moment.

A spontaneous act of resistance and escape was staged in Belzec by a group of prisoners who worked in the removal of corpses from the gas chambers, on June 13, 1942. The Polish underground reported: "The revolt in the camp, probably the first one, took place on June 13th, when Jews were summoned to remove the corpses of murdered women and children: at the horrible sight (they were standing in the gas chamber holding each other's waists and necks, presumably in the prenatal reflexes), they attacked the 'Wachmannschaft' [the guards], which resulted in a struggle in which 4–6 Germans and nearly all the Jews died; several Jews managed to escape."[16] This event is not mentioned in any other source. The transports liquidated in Belzec in those days came from the Cracow district. A few days after this event the killing operations in Belzec stopped for about a month; they were resumed in the middle of July 1942 (see chapter 10). It may well be that the month's pause in the killing was caused not only by the need for the construction of larger gas chambers but also by this act of resistance.

ESCAPES FROM THE CAMPS

THE PRISONERS IN THE DEATH camps understood that they were being kept alive only as long as they were able to work and be of use in the extermination process. Every day they faced a selection and possible death in the *Lazarett* or gas chambers as punishment or in retaliation by any SS man in the camp. Almost all of them knew that as soon as the purpose for which the camp had been built—annihilation—had been achieved, they would all be killed. Their fate was sealed both because they were Jews and because the Germans had no desire to leave witnesses to their crimes. Most of the prisoners were convinced that the only way to survive was by escape. However, while the thought and the desire to implement this conviction were widespread among the prisoners, the obstacles and dangers involved in any attempt to escape were overwhelming. Among these were the security measures and precautions taken by the camp authorities and guards; the limited opportunities to find help and hiding places among the local population after the escape; and the severe retaliation against the prisoners who remained in the camp. In reality there was little chance for a successful escape. Nevertheless, attempts by individuals or groups of prisoners to get away from the camps continued during the entire period.

ESCAPES FROM TREBLINKA

In the disorder and confusion that prevailed in Treblinka in the first month of its existence, there were many attempted escapes from the camp—some of which were successful. The first escapes were individual initiatives and were carried out by using the freight cars in which the victims' belongings were shipped out of the camp. Jews were taken from the transports and employed at loading the belongings on the cars; after a few days they were killed. The escapees hid in the piles of clothes and sometimes were helped by their fellow workers, who piled more belongings over their hiding places. After the train left the camp and was already some distance away, the escapees jumped from the train. Many were shot at the moment of their escape by the train guards, but others succeeded in getting away. Simcha

Laski, who was taken from Warsaw to Treblinka at the end of July, escaped after four days. He told of his escape:

> After about three days in the camp, only 17 men out of the 800 were left of those picked for work. . . . On the fourth day a train came with empty cars. We loaded the cars with packages of clothes and underwear. I decided to hide in one of the cars. As I stepped into the car with a package of clothing, I burrowed under a pile of clothes. I heard how they closed and locked the cars. . . . I took a chance and stuck my head out of the pile so that I could breathe a little air. To my great surprise, I saw another head stick out from the piles of clothes. We exchanged a few words. It was a boy from the provinces. Later we discovered another two boys in the car. One was my friend Moshe Boorstein. They had all chosen this particular car because the small aperture was not barred. . . . We traveled for a few hours without even knowing in which direction. Only as we neared Lublin did we realize in which direction we were traveling. We decided to jump from the speeding train because if we reached Lublin or Warsaw they would catch us as they unloaded and would shoot us.
>
> Near Lukov two of the friends jumped . . . and immediately after we heard shots. I was already apathetic to the idea of being shot. . . . I left the car and hung on the window sill. I pushed off from the train and jumped. As a result of the fall I fractured my leg and scratched my face. Again a machine-gun round was heard. On the roof of the last car I saw a machine gun and the shots were coming from there. I was not wounded from the bullets. I went to look for my friends who had jumped before me. After a short time I met Boorstein and, after continuing a bit more near the track, we found the other two, who were no longer alive. After two weeks of wandering we reached Warsaw. It was the day of the "Children's *Aktion*."[1]

In a similar way, Abraham Krzepicki also escaped from the camp. He ran away after eighteen days in Treblinka, in the middle of September 1942. He hid in a freight car full of clothing, together with three other people, but alone succeeded in reaching the Warsaw ghetto.

Oskar Berger testified to an escape in a freight car of belongings. Berger succeeded in escaping from Treblinka with a young boy in September 1942.[2]

People also escaped under cover of darkness through the camp fences, which were not electrified and did not contain any special alarm system. The sorting group workers found a unique way of escaping. Throughout the day, as they sorted the clothes and prepared the piles of belongings for transport, the ones who were planning escape also prepared hiding places for themselves in the tremendous piles of clothing. Toward the end of the workday, before the scheduled return to the barrack and the lockup for the night, the escapees crept into their hiding places. Friends who were not among those planning to escape covered the entrance to the hiding place with additional piles of belongings. At night, the escapees crawled out from under the piles of clothing, crept over the fence at the end of the sorting yard, and ran away.

Abraham Bomba told about the plan and implementation of such an escape:

> On Saturday, during the entire workday, Yechiel Berkowicz, Yechezkel Cooperman, and I prepared a "bunker" [a nickname for a hiding place under the piles of clothing] in a way that by the evening roll call it would be ready. Before the roll call, we noticed that someone was loitering in the vicinity of our "bunker." . . . We decided to put off hiding in the "bunker" till the next day. On Sunday we worked all day and at night we hid in the "bunker." After the roll call the Ukrainians and the SS began searching for prisoners and, from our hiding place, we could see how they stabbed at the piles of clothing with their bayonets to see whether anyone was hiding there. After a while they left the yard, and we breathed a small sigh of relief. We lay in the hiding place another few hours until we decided to get out. The direction of escape was through the *Lazarett*; the fire in the pit lit up everything around it. On the other side was the watchtower with the searchlight. We reached the barbed wire. The first to go over was Berkowicz. I went after him, and Cooperman last. We crawled several hundred meters and then we got up and started running. After a few hours of running, we suddenly heard a conversation in Ukrainian. We realized that we were still near the camp, near the Ukrainian barracks.
>
> It seems that for hours we had run in a semicircle and had made no distance from the camp. We began running in the opposite direction and after a while we reached the Bug River. We were about six kilometers from the camp. The time was five in the morning and soon the day would begin.[3]

Bomba received help from a few farmers, reached Warsaw, from there went to Czestochowa, and was able to remain hidden until the liberation.

Among those who escaped from Treblinka were other people from Czestochowa. One was Aron Gelberd, who escaped from the camp on October 21. When he was eight kilometers from Treblinka, he was caught by Ukrainian farmers. They stripped him of his outer clothing and left him, but somehow he got back to Czestochowa and remained there until the liquidation of the "small ghetto."[4]

There is an anonymous testimony on the escape from Treblinka of a Jew from Czestochowa who was brought to the camp on September 24 and escaped after six days. He was taken to work under guard outside the camp with five other men to gather branches. The Ukrainian guard got drunk and fell asleep and the Jew from Czestochowa was able to escape. There are no further details as to his identity or what happened to him afterward.

Another testimony tells of an escapee from Treblinka whose name was Richter. This man returned to the "small ghetto" in Czestochowa and told of what was happening in Treblinka. On the day that the ghetto was liquidated, at the beginning of October 1942, Richter tried to kill the German officer Rohn, who commanded the expulsion *Aktion*.[5]

A few escapees from Treblinka reached the "small ghetto" that continued to exist in Siedlce until the end of November 1942. They related what was happening in Treblinka, but with the final liquidation of the ghetto they, too, were taken once again to the camp for extermination.

The Treblinka escapees who reached the Warsaw ghetto are mentioned in various sources. Among them were David Novodvorski, who returned to the Warsaw ghetto in August 1942, and the journalist Jacob Rabinowicz. As a result of Rabinowicz's report on the extermination in Treblinka, the Jewish Labor Party Bund, which was active in the Underground in the Warsaw ghetto, sent a few emissaries to Kosov and to Sokolow-Podlaski in the area of Treblinka to test the veracity of the report. In Sokolow-Podlaski the Bund emissaries met with another escapee from Treblinka by the name of Azriel Wallach and from him they received verification of Rabinowicz's report. Following the reports of the escapees who reached Warsaw, there was no longer any doubt among the organizations and parties in the ghetto that the Jews who were sent to Treblinka were killed there. This information was one of the decisive factors in establishing the "Jewish Fighting Organization" in the Warsaw ghetto and in preparing for resistance and revolt.[6]

A great number of people escaped from Treblinka in the summer of 1942. Most reached the nearby ghettos that still had Jews living in them, but were later sent again to extermination when these ghettos were liquidated. When they came to Treblinka for the second time, a small number were able to join the prisoners and in this way save themselves from the gas chambers.[7]

The prisoners in the camp covered up for the escapees. So as not to arouse the attention of the SS men to the escapes, during the daily roll calls the "camp elder" Galewski, with the help of other prisoners, succeeded in removing a few people from the latest transports and have them join the workers. This was done in such a way that the absence of the escapees was not noticeable during the roll call. In spite of this, the escapes could not be hidden from the Germans and Ukrainians for long, as they discovered the holes in the camp fences. That the Jews escaped from the camp did not bother the Germans to any great extent, because they were certain that sooner or later most of them would be recaptured. However, they did want to ensure that the fate of the Jews who were brought to Treblinka would not be made public knowledge, and therefore they employed sundry ways and means of persuasion and threats. Oscar Strawczinski related:

> At first they wanted to persuade us with nice words. An important person from Lublin came to the camp, gathered us together and spoke to us. We were told that a "Jewish city" was being established and that the Jews would be granted full autonomy there, and if we would work with dedication and earn their trust we would receive leadership positions in the Jewish city. When the nice words did not help, they began to threaten us. They announced that if the escape attempts continued, they would strip us and we would have to work naked, and that attempted escape would be punished by death by torture, because we had violated the trust that had been placed in us. To demonstrate that these were not idle threats, the next day two young boys were stopped and accused of having planned an escape from the camp. In the center of the roll-call square, a gallows was built and all the prisoners were gathered around it. The commander gave a short speech on the punishment of the escapees, and the two boys were hung naked by their feet. The Germans whipped their swinging bodies for about half an hour, until one of the Germans pulled a gun and shot them.[8]

Another witness wrote that while they were still alive, hanging by their feet and repeatedly beaten, the boys called out to the prisoners: "Jews, escape, because death awaits you also. Pay no attention to the fact that meanwhile you have something to eat. Our fate today is your fate tomorrow." The two youngsters were shot by SS *Scharführer* Josef Hirtreiter.[9]

Despite the severe punishments, escapes from the camp did not cease as long as the killing of the prisoner work staff continued. The prisoners were aware of what was going on in Treblinka and knew that they were marked for death within a few days. In the second half of September 1942, with the cessation of the murder of the prisoner work staff and the institution of a cadre of working prisoners in the camp, the number of escapes decreased. The concentration of the Jews in the living area and the intensification of the supervision and security also resulted in a reduction in the number of escapees.

Yet improvements in the living conditions of the prisoners, stricter supervision in the camp, and the inauguration of severe punishments did not completely eliminate further attempts at escape. At the end of November or beginning of December, seven "blues," who worked on the platform, attempted escape. They were caught, taken by the deputy commander, Kurt Franz, to the *Lazarett*, and shot there. Franz ordered a roll call and announced that if there were further attempted escapes, and especially if prisoners succeeded in escaping, ten prisoners would be shot for every escapee.[10]

At the beginning of the winter of 1942, four prisoners escaped from Treblinka by using a breach in the security arrangements in the camp. Throughout the night, the Jews were locked into their barracks and the Ukrainians guarded the prisoners' living area. As a result the security around the fences was more lax during the night. In the winter the prisoners rose while it was still dark; the doors to the barracks were opened so that they could go to the latrines, which were located outside the barracks, on the edge of the living area. At the same time, the night guard around the living area went off duty and was replaced by an enlarged guard in the watchtowers around the camp fences. The rule was that these two changes were to be carried out simultaneously, but frequently the guard posts in the living area were vacated before the guard in the watchtowers around the camp was strengthened. This gap in the guard system was used by the escapees, who were aware of it.

Before dawn, when it was still dark and the living barrack was opened, four prisoners left the barrack. When they saw that the Ukrainians who had guarded them during the night had left the area, they cut the fences around the barracks, crossed the selection square, crawled beneath the outer barbed wire of the camp, and escaped before the guards who manned the watchtowers came on duty. In the morning, the camp guards discovered the gaps in the fences, and when they counted the people in the barrack they saw that four were missing. The prisoners were lined up for roll call and, after threats, an SS man announced to them that in the future for every escapee every tenth prisoner would be put to death. While the roll call was going on, twenty sick prisoners who had not gone out to the roll call were taken to the *Lazarett* and were shot in reprisal.[11]

Escapes were also attempted in the extermination area. A group of twenty-four prisoners planned an escape, but as a result of an informer they were all arrested and shot. Another attempt also ended in failure. A group of seven people planned to escape through a tunnel that they would dig under the living barrack that bordered on the camp fence. The distance from the edge of the barrack to the first fence was only about five meters. At the beginning of the digging, the people in the group changed sleeping places with other prisoners so that their pallets were all concentrated in the corner of the barrack from which the entrance to the tunnel was planned. The digging was done at night, throughout the entire month of December 1942. The men in the group exhibited considerable initiative and cleverness in that they succeeded in digging in absolute secrecy, without the SS men or Ukrainians finding out, and also in improvising a method to hide all the earth that they dug out of the tunnel. It should be noted that most of the people in the barrack—about 250 men—knew about the tunnel and despite the absolute certainty that the escape would endanger all the prisoners, nothing was leaked to the camp authorities.

The escape was carried out on the night of December 31, 1942, New Year's Eve. Five men succeeded in getting out through the tunnel and crossing the fences, but then a Ukrainian noticed the escapees and opened fire. Two of the group remained in the barrack, as they had not had time to get out through the tunnel. The entire extermination area was ordered to a roll call. The prisoners were taken out of the barrack and, after counting, five prisoners were found missing. That same night snow fell. The Germans and Ukrainians followed the tracks and reached a neighboring village. There they caught up with the escapees, who had gone into the village to rent a wagon. One of the prisoners got away, but the other four were caught, despite resisting capture. One was shot on the spot as he attacked an SS man. The other three were returned to the camp and after being tortured were hanged in front of all the prisoners in the extermination area, who were called to a special roll call to view the hanging. One of the escapees, called Mechele, who came from Warsaw, was hanged last, and as he stood under the hanging post he called out: "Down with Hitler! Long live the Jewish people!"[12]

The only one to escape was Lazar Sharson, who returned to the Warsaw ghetto, joined the Underground, and at the time of the revolt commanded a group of combatants and fought among the ruins of the ghetto until the end of September 1943.[13] He was the only one during those months who succeeded in escaping from the extermination area of Treblinka.

ESCAPES FROM BELZEC

There were few escapes from Belzec. The first escape was of two women, Mina Astrnan and Maika Talenfeld, from Zolkiew, who succeeded in escaping and returning home after only a few hours in the camp. This was at the end of March 1942. Back in Zolkiew they told the story of their escape, which was later recorded:

> In closed wagons they were brought into the Belzec camp. They were ordered to undress. The people became scared. One of them asked the SS man who was close to him: "What's the reason that we should undress?" Afterward the women were ordered to enter the barrack. . . . Exploiting the disorder and noise and lack of experience of the Germans [these were the first transports to arrive in Belzec], Astman and Talenfeld jumped into a nearby ditch and sat there undiscovered until dark. Under cover of darkness, they escaped from the camp and after a few days returned home.[14]

Another escape from Belzec was of the dentist Bachner from Cracow. He arrived in the camp with the last transports from Cracow at the beginning of October 1942. When the transport reached the camp, he succeeded somehow in entering a latrine and found a hiding place in the pit with excrement. He stayed there a few days. One night he was able to leave the pit, escape, and return to Cracow.[15]

The most famous escape from Belzec was carried out by Rudolf Reder, who wrote about it:

> At the end of November, I had already been confined to the hell of Belzec for a few months. One morning I was told by the bully Irman that there was a need for tin in the camp.... I went with a truck, accompanied by four SS men and a guard to Lvov. After a whole day of loading the tin sheets, I remained in the car, under the guard of one of the bullies, while all the others went for entertainment. For hours I sat without moving. Then I saw that my guard had fallen asleep and was snoring. Without thinking, instinctively, I slid down the car. The bully continued sleeping. I stood on the sidewalk, appearing as if I were arranging the tin sheets, but slowly moving toward Legionow Street, where the traffic was quite heavy. I pulled my hat over my eyes; the streets were dark and nobody saw me. I remembered where a Polish woman, my landlady lived. I went there, and she hid me.[16]

Rudolf Reder survived the war.

A Jew from Czechoslovakia was planning to escape from Belzec, but the camp authorities found out about his intentions. He was arrested and hanged. Jewish prisoners had to carry out the hanging of their fellow prisoner.[17]

The last escapee from among the prisoners of Belzec was Chaim Hirszman. He escaped from the last train out of Belzec after the camp was dismantled. The remaining Jews were being taken to Sobibor, where they were liquidated in July 1943. Hirszman and two other prisoners decided to escape from the train by removing a plank from the car's floor. He jumped first; the other two were to jump after him. Hirszman succeeded in escaping and later joined the partisans. Whether or not the other two jumped and their subsequent fate remain unknown. Chaim Hirszman survived the war but was killed in 1946 by Polish anti-Semites.[18]

There is no information about other successful escapes from Belzec. The fate of Bachner from Cracow and of Astman and Talenfeld from Zolkiew after their return to their native towns is unknown. They did not survive the war.

ESCAPES FROM SOBIBOR

The escapes from Sobibor were on a much smaller scale than those from Treblinka. The few known escapes took place at the end of 1942 and in the first half of 1943. There were several reasons for this. In contrast to

Treblinka, in Sobibor order and tight security arrangements, introduced by Franz Stangl, reigned from the beginning of the camp's operation and made successful escapes more difficult. The number of transports to Sobibor were fewer than to the other two camps, and therefore the supervision of the prisoners was easier and a deterrent to escapes. There is no information about escapes from Sobibor until the end of 1942. Even the available evidence about escapes carried out in 1943 is not based on direct testimonies of the escapees, nor on the testimony of people who met them. There were no survivors among the escapees from Sobibor except for those who escaped during the uprising of October 1943.

The first escape mentioned briefly in some testimonies was of a young man who was working at loading a train and who hid himself in a freight car among piles of clothing being sent out of Sobibor. This man reached the ghetto of Chelm and told the people what was going on in Sobibor.[19] The exact date of this escape is unknown, but it must have been some time at the end of 1942 and not later than February 1943, when the Chelm ghetto was finally liquidated.

An escape of five Jewish prisoners, two of them women, together with two Ukrainian guardsmen was set for Christmas night, December 25–26, 1942. The escape was from Camp III, the extermination area. This was a well-planned and well-organized escape, but the details are unknown. Their choice of Christmas night was not accidental—that night the Germans and Ukrainians were celebrating and drunk. After the escape the whole group separated into at least two groups. The two Ukrainians, Victor Kisiliev and Vasyl Zischer, together with one of the young women, Pesia Lieberman, found refuge in the home of a Polish farmer near the big village of Olchowiec, forty-five kilometers southwest of Sobibor, on the night of December 31–January 1. But the farmer informed the nearby police station of Wierzbicy about the arrival of the escapees, and a group of the Polish-manned "Blue Police," under the command of Police Officer Meisnerowicz, surrounded the farm and killed the three of them while they tried to escape. The names and fate of the other four escapees remain unknown, but they did not survive the war. In reprisal for this escape, a few dozen prisoners in Camp III were murdered.[20]

In the spring of 1943, on a stormy night, two Jews from Chelm escaped from the camp. Under cover of the darkness and rain, they cut the barbed-wire fences and crawled out. In the morning, the guards discovered the breach. Tovia Blatt testified about what happened at the morning roll call: "The Germans consulted among themselves, and *Scharführer* Frenzel announced this verdict: each tenth prisoner in the rows of the roll call would be executed. He approached my group. I was seized with fear. . . . He is in the row behind me. My God, only not me—a man is an egoist. The third from me became the victim. After the selection, the doomed were taken to Camp III, and we went to work. Afterward we heard shots, and later the clothes of those who had been killed were brought for sorting."[21] Twenty prisoners were shot as a reprisal for this escape of two prisoners.

After these escapes, the camp commander decided to lay mines around the camp. A group of soldiers from the Wehrmacht, under the guidance of *Oberscharführer* Gustav Wagner, carried out the work. The camp was surrounded with rings of mines. To make the escapes even more difficult, a ditch filled with water was dug between the barracks where the Jewish prisoners lived in Camp I and the nearby fences of the camp. Work was completed by the beginning of July 1943.[22]

The mining of the camp also was to serve as a defense against the partisans who operated during that time in the forests in the vicinity of Sobibor. One night during the summer of 1943, the Jewish prisoners were driven out of their barracks for a roll call and were surrounded by a strong force of Ukrainians. The prisoners could hear sounds of shooting coming from outside the camp. After some time calm was restored, and the prisoners were driven back to their barracks. The next day, the Ukrainians told them that partisans had approached the camp. Whether there really had been partisans or it had been a false alarm remained unclear. In no war reports of partisan activity in areas close to Sobibor is there mention of partisans intending to attack the camp or being active close to the camp. But the rumors about partisan activity in the forests served as an incentive for the prisoners; it gave them hope and encouraged escapes. It provided them with a target for escape.[23]

The minefield that had been set around the camp greatly limited the possibilities of escape from inside the camp. The *Waldkommando*, which worked outside the camp, afforded a better opportunity. On July 20, 1943, the *Waldkommando* consisted of twenty Polish Jews and twenty Dutch Jews cutting wood in the forest for the construction of new barracks and arms stores in Camp IV. The *Waldkommando* left the camp in the morning escorted by Ukrainian guards under the command of *Scharführer* Werner Dubois. Before the lunch break, two prisoners, Shlomo Podchlebnik and Yosef Kopf, escorted by a Ukrainian, went to bring drinking water from the nearby village of Ztobek. The two prisoners seized this opportunity. On the way back, they attacked and killed the Ukrainian, took his rifle, and escaped. *Scharführer* Werner Dubois testified about this escape:

> For about three weeks, I was a leader of a Jewish group which worked outside the camp. I can remember the following event. During the time of my

command, a Ukrainian guardsman was killed by two Jews when they went to bring water at a distance of 400–500 meters from the working place. These two Jews escaped. When I saw that the water-bearers did not return for a long time, I sent another guardsman to see what was going on. He returned and reported to me that he had found the guardsman—dead—and no sign of the two Jews. After that I ordered all the Jews to lie on the ground to prevent further incidents. I sent a guardsman to the camp to inform camp commander Reichleitner what had happened. [24]

When the remaining prisoners from Poland became aware of what had happened, they knew what the retaliation would be and so some of them decided to escape. Using the confusion among the guards, one of the prisoners shouted "Hurrah" and the Polish Jews started to run. The prisoners from Holland remained in their places and did not join the escape. The guards opened fire on the escaping prisoners. Two of them were killed, three got away, and thirteen were caught. According to another source, four of them succeeded in escaping, but one of them was caught the next day and brought back to the camp.[25] All the Polish Jews from the *Waldkommando* were shot in front of all the camp prisoners; the Dutch Jews were left alive. Ada Lichtman testified about the shooting action in the camp:

> When we were called for a roll call, we knew already what had happened. We trembled, thinking about what would happen to us. As we stood in the roll call, we decided among ourselves that we would not go to the gas chambers alive. We would defend ourselves by all means. Time passed, and our tension rose. We bid farewell to one another and to life. Some Germans arrived, opened the gate, and we were ordered to march to Camp II. There we stopped and were arranged in a semicircle. On the square lay, tied, the remaining members of the *Waldkommando*. One by one they were lashed and, at an order of a German, shot by a guardsman. The Germans were strolling among us. We had to watch all these cruelties without moving our eyes or turning our heads. After the execution we were taken back to Camp I. Wagner and Frenzel announced to us that next time all of us would be responsible for one escapee.[26]

After this escape, Polish Jews were no longer included in the *Waldkommando*. They would no longer be among those taken for work in the forest, outside the camp. Now only Dutch Jews were included in this group. They, as strangers in Poland, without knowledge of the local language and people, unfamiliar with the country and countryside, did not regard escape as potentially successful. For this reason, the commanding authorities of the camp saw them as a more reliable element, as was proven during the *Waldkommando* escape.

SUMMARY

Escapes were attempted from all three camps, but the outcome differed as a result of the specific conditions prevailing in each camp. The number of escapes was the largest in Treblinka and, after that, in Sobibor. In Belzec, the relatively small number of escapes might have been because of stricter supervision and security: it is safe to assume that the number of escapees was larger than what is known, but because of the small number of survivors from Belzec we have no further details.

One of the basic problems that the escapees faced was a viable destination. While the ghettos still existed, most escapees made for these ghettos. But as time passed, more and more ghettos were liquidated—most by the end of October 1942. Very few prisoners had Gentile acquaintances whom they could hope would shelter them. The absence of a refuge or hiding place after escape made many give up any thought of escaping from the camp.

Hundreds of people escaped or attempted to escape from the camps. Most were caught, tortured, and killed. In the first month of the camps' existence, the opportunities for escape were easier and, indeed, during that time most of the successful escapes were carried out. As time passed, escape became more and more difficult. The security measures were improved; barbed-wire fences were added around the camps, each made up of two or three separate fences. In the same way, the inner sections of the camps, including the living barracks of the prisoners, were also cordoned off. Additional watchtowers were built. Considering the relatively small area of the entire camp, the guards in the watchtowers had an excellent and constant view over everything that was going on in the camp during the entire day. At night the prisoners were locked into their barracks and Ukrainians stood guard outside. In addition, the severe punishments— torture and hanging—that were the fate of the escapees and the assurance that for every prisoner who escaped ten or the tenth prisoner would be executed were further deterrents. In the winter, the snow and the tracks left in the snow also made escape more difficult. At the beginning of the winter, in December 1942, the last escapes were attempted in Treblinka and, for the most part, ended in failure. In Sobibor, the escapes were carried out mostly from the end of 1942 until the summer of 1943, when the mining of the camp made escape almost impossible.

Those prisoners in Treblinka and Sobibor who sought a way out of the extermination and had planned quiet, simple escapes soon learned that that way was no longer open to them and that they would have to go about it with unconventional, organized, and very complicated plans. And so at the beginning of 1943 in Treblinka and in the summer of 1943 in Sobibor, the first ideas in these camps about organized resistance and escape began to take shape.

THE UNDERGROUND IN TREBLINKA

DURING THE EARLY MONTHS OF 1943, the level of activity in Treblinka underwent a drastic change. A few transports still arrived from Bialystok and Warsaw in January, but by the end of the month and during February and March they ceased almost entirely. The extermination of the Jews in the General Government and Bialystok General District had been completed with the exception of a small number of Jews left in some of the ghettos and in a few labor camps. The huge piles of belongings stacked in Treblinka's Sorting Square, which had become part of the camp's routine appearance, now disappeared; the storage barracks emptied out, too. Everything was packed and sent by train to Germany and elsewhere. Without transports, the prisoners' workload dropped, particularly in the Lower Camp, where they had been involved in handling the deportees and their belongings. The prisoners were aware of the new situation, and harbored suspicions that without transports and work for them, the camp would be eliminated. Rumors of an impending selection made the rounds of the prisoners in the Lower Camp.

A typhus epidemic in the camp, which claimed dozens of victims every day, also darkened the prisoners' spirits. And news of German losses at the various fronts, and reports from the battle at Stalingrad, which reached the prisoners through those who worked in jobs where they managed to steal an occasional look at a newspaper, increased their fears that, with the end of the Third Reich, they, too—eyewitnesses to Nazi Germany's crimes—would be eliminated.[1] This new sense of an impending end was particularly acute in the Lower Camp, where the prisoners lacked full employment. The situation was different in the extermination area, since at about this time, following Heinrich Himmler's visit to the camp, the prisoners there were employed in opening the mass graves and burning the corpses.

Against this new situation, the prisoners began to discuss both possible ways of rescuing themselves and the need to bring Treblinka and its horrors to the world's attention before it was too late. They sat in their closed barracks during the long winter evenings and analyzed their situation over and over, discussing the instances of escape and resistance that had occurred until then. It was clear that quiet escapes by individuals or small groups of prisoners were no longer viable; the most recent attempts had failed, night lighting and security in the camp had both been enhanced, and the reprisals and punishments inflicted on the prisoners for escape attempts worked against this option.

These conversations and appraisals of the situation prompted several prisoner groups to come to the conclusion that the only way to save themselves was through a large-scale organization aimed at overpowering the camp security guards and allowing a subsequent mass escape. These prisoners estimated that since they were superior in numbers to the Germans and Ukrainians in the camp—close to 1,000 against some 150—and since for extended periods during the day the guards mixed with the prisoners, they could, with the proper planning and organization, stage a revolt, overcome the guards, and escape. Such a plan had a chance for success. Oscar Strawczinski wrote:

> In the first months of winter, while we were a small group in the carpentry shop, Mordechai came up with the idea of resistance and escape. There were Germans who came nearly every evening to the tailor shop to listen to [the prisoner orchestra's] music, and the idea was that a combat team would ambush these Germans, kill them quietly and take their weapons. One of the team would then put on a German uniform and call the Ukrainian guards who were near the Jewish barracks, one by one. As they entered the hut they, too, would be killed silently. With the guards eliminated, the prisoners would be summoned to leave their huts and escape from the camp. . . . The plan sounded altogether too fantastic and gained few supporters, but within a short time the idea of revolt had taken root.[2]

As a result of these conversations and brainstorming sessions, by late February or early March a small group had formed that took upon itself the initiative of establishing an underground, acquiring weapons, and organizing a revolt and escape from the camp. The group, called the "Organizing Committee," included the following men: Dr. Julian (Ilya) Chorazycki from Warsaw, about age fifty-seven, a former captain in the Polish army, who, as a physician, treated the SS and worked in their clinic; Ze'ev Korland, about fifty, the capo of the *Lazarett*; Zialo Bloch from Czechoslovakia, who had come to Treblinka from Theresienstadt, was a former lieutenant in the Czech army and at Treblinka headed the work team at Sorting Square; the agronomist Sadovits from Warsaw; and Salzberg from Kielce, who worked in the camp as a tailor. Shortly after the underground was established, Adolf Freidman, in his thirties, from Lodz, also joined.

Several testimonies place him in Palestine and the Foreign Legion before the war. In Treblinka he headed a work team at Sorting Square.[3] The Organizing Committee had several additional members whose identities are clouded by conflicting accounts.

All of the Organizing Committee members came from the "court Jews," held central jobs among the prisoners, and were of the camp's "elite." Most were among the intelligentsia and were relatively old. The central figure in the Organizing Committee was Dr. Chorazycki. Lieutenant Zialo Bloch, an energetic man with leadership qualities, was to handle the military aspects of the organization.

But as soon as the underground began its work, in the second half of March 1943, it suffered a serious loss. Zialo Bloch and Adolf Freidman were transferred to the extermination area. They and other prisoners were transferred from the Lower Camp because the workload there had dropped due to the lack of transports, while in the extermination area, the cremating of the corpses required additional manpower.[4]

In the beginning, the camp underground comprised the members of the Organizing Committee and a group of their close friends—a total of ten to fifteen persons. For conspiratorial reasons, the Organizing Committee did not attach great importance to the task of enlarging the underground, and preferred to concern itself with the problem of acquiring weapons. The first thoughts about how to secure arms focused on purchasing them outside the camp.

The coordination of the weapons procurement activity was taken on by Dr. Chorazycki. Money for purchasing weapons was no problem. While sorting the victims' clothing and belongings, the prisoners would often find quantities of money, gold, and valuables; a portion of this they turned in to the camp authorities in accordance with regulations, while another portion would be sequestered and hidden in the barracks and workshops, or else buried. Another source of money was the "gold Jews," through whose hands passed the money, gold, and valuables that were turned over to the camp authorities.

Attempts to purchase arms were made through the Camouflage Team, whose members would go outside the camp to the nearby forests to cut branches for camouflaging the barbed-wire fences. Occasionally they would come into contact with farmers from the neighborhood and purchase food to smuggle back into the camp. They hoped the same could be done with arms. But these efforts did not bear results.

Simultaneously, attempts were made to procure weapons from outside the camp through the Ukrainian guards. Some of the capos and other Jewish prisoners had cultivated ties with Ukrainians who were prepared, for suitable remuneration, to bring food into the camp from the outside. Several attempts were made to obtain weapons in this way. The Ukrainians, however, while prepared to take the money, did not produce guns; still, they refrained from informing on these activities. All they were interested in was keeping the money for themselves.[5]

During one of these attempts to procure weapons, Dr. Chorazycki paid with his life. He was in contact with a Ukrainian through whom an attempt was made to buy guns, and this required that he handle large sums of money. One day in the first half of April 1943, in the infirmary where he worked, Chorazycki received a considerable sum for arms purchases from the "gold Jews" who worked in a nearby hut. Unexpectedly, Deputy Camp Commander Kurt Franz entered the infirmary shortly afterward. Chorazycki quickly tried to stuff the money into the pocket of his coat, which was hanging on the wall, but Franz noticed the money sticking out of the pocket and removed it. Chorazycki, realizing that he now had nothing to lose, grabbed a surgical knife and rushed Franz. The two struggled and fell to the floor. The younger and stronger Franz quickly gained the upper hand, but Chorazycki was able to free himself long enough to jump out of the window. As he did so, he removed a small vial from his pocket, drank the contents, and fell, unconscious. Other accounts have Franz escaping or being pushed outside the infirmary, and Chorazycki swallowing the poison while still inside the barrack.[6]

SS men and Ukrainian guards were called to the scene. They tried to revive Chorazycki so they could interrogate him concerning the source and purpose of the money. They suspected Chorazycki of planning an escape from the camp together with other prisoners, and assumed the money was intended for use after the escape. The physician-prisoner Dr. Irena Levkovski, who worked with Chorazycki in the infirmary, was brought in. SS *Scharführer* Franz Suchomel, who accompanied her, related: "The old witch [the doctor] pretended she couldn't walk fast. When we did arrive, Chorazycki's eyes were open; he was still alive. The doctor pumped out his stomach, but Chorazycki did not recover. Franz was seething with anger."[7] Chorazycki's body, after being abused, was taken to the *Lazarett* and thrown into the cremation ditch.

The Germans suspected the "gold Jews" of being the source of the illicit money and searched their barrack for more, but to no avail. The "gold Jews" were assembled near the *Lazarett*, beaten, and interrogated concerning their ties with Chorazycki, but they denied everything. The SS men selected eight "gold Jews" and ordered them to undress. Franz took one of them to the *Lazarett*, forcing him to jump like a frog. At the *Lazarett*, Franz stood the man beside the ditch and threatened to shoot him unless he revealed the truth. The man claimed he knew nothing. Franz left him at the *Lazarett* and forced the others through a similar routine. All denied any connection with Chorazycki and the money he had. Ultimately they were all freed.[8] The SS still required their services.

Chorazycki's death was a hard blow to the underground. By virtue of his character and his stature in the camp as the SS personnel's physician, he had been the central figure in the Organizing Committee. Despite the fact that in the daily life of the camp he had been detached from the main body of prisoners, they had respected him highly. He had been capable of influencing other figures from the prisoner "elite" to join the underground and contribute money for purchasing arms. His bravery in dying, not without a struggle, also won the prisoners' respect.

In spite of Chorazycki's death and Zialo Bloch's transfer to the other part of the camp, the Organizing Committee continued with preparations for the uprising. The "camp elder," Rakowski, was now brought in on the secret underground activity. The members of the underground, who numbered several score, were organized into a number of groups.[9]

The efforts to procure weapons continued, and this time the underground was luckier. One day, a lock broke on the door of the arms store-room located between the two SS barracks. One of the prisoners, a lock-smith, who was in touch with the Organizing Committee, was ordered by the Germans to repair the lock. The door (or possibly only the lock) was brought to the locksmith's shop, and in the course of repairing it, a spare key was made and passed on to the Organizing Committee.[10]

In the latter part of April 1943, the Organizing Committee decided to remove weapons from the storeroom. If the operation succeeded, they would initiate a revolt.

The firearms in the storeroom could be removed only during those daylight hours when the SS men were not in their barracks and the Ukrainian guards were not stationed in the vicinity. During the day these barracks were also visited occasionally by Polish and Ukrainian girls who worked in the SS mess hall and were sent to clean the rooms, and by a group of Jewish boys called *putzers* (cleaners) who shined the boots and cleaned the uniforms of the SS. It was this group of four boys, led by a youth named Marcus from Warsaw, that was assigned the task of removing the weapons from the storeroom.

On the designated day, the underground members were alerted at their work stations, and they awaited developments anxiously. The action was carried out successfully; two boxes of hand grenades were brought to the shoemaker's shop near the prisoners' barracks and were received by members of the Organizing Committee. But when they were opened, it was discovered that the grenades lacked detonators. The boys had not been aware that the Germans stored the detonators separately. The entire dangerous operation had been in vain. It was decided to return the grenades to the storeroom immediately, before the Germans could discover that they were missing. The boys succeeded in returning them.[11]

The various bits of evidence available offer no details as to how the grenades were removed and returned, or the identity of the Organizing Committee members who handled the operation. Nor are any details known concerning the revolt plan; it appears as if the entire affair of the removal of the arms and the uprising was an improvisation and had neither a proper plan nor suitable preparations.[12]

The underground activists, whose expectations had risen as preparations progressed, were deeply disappointed. Although there were informers in the camp who must have "smelled" something going on, the entire affair of the smuggled grenades never became known to camp authorities. Following the postponement of the uprising, there was a short period of inactivity. Then, again, thoughts of individual or small-group escapes began to take form. The "camp elder," Rakowski, decided to organize a group of some fifteen prisoners, among them Chesia Mendel, who was known to be his mistress, to escape from the camp in late April or early May 1943. Rakowski had developed ties with two Ukrainians who brought him food from outside the camp for a suitable payment. For the right bribe, these Ukrainians had agreed to help him escape.

In the course of his preparations, Rakowski collected a large sum of money and gold and hid it in the wall of the capos' barracks. The plan called for the preparation in advance of a camouflaged exit through the outer wall of the tailor shop, and the escape was fixed for a night when the two bribed Ukrainians were scheduled to stand guard. The escapees were to hide in the tailor shop before the prisoners were locked in their barracks. During the night, the two Ukrainians would approach the shop's outer wall and signal the prisoners to escape through the opening they had prepared. The Ukrainians would lead the escapees through the camp's east fence and possibly supply them with arms.

Before these preparations had been completed, however, an incident occurred that upset the entire plan. One morning, *Scharführer* August Miete entered the capos' barracks and found Rakowski with his friend Chesia, eating a breakfast of vodka, white bread, and bacon. Miete remarked mockingly, "So, Rakowski, you, too, are black marketeering?" and left the room. Rakowski finished his breakfast and went out to tour the camp. A short while later, Miete returned to Rakowski's barrack with two Ukrainians and, after a thorough search, found money, gold, and valuables hidden in the walls. Rakowski, confronted with the evidence, denied any connection to the hoard and claimed that Dr. Chorazycki, who had died a few weeks previously and who had also lived in the room, must have hidden the money. Rakowski was arrested and, at dusk, taken to the *Lazarett* and murdered. Galewski replaced him as "camp elder," as he had preceded Rakowski in this post and had been replaced by him when he came down with typhus, from which he had since recovered.[13]

In early May 1943, transports began to arrive at Treblinka from the Warsaw ghetto, after the revolt against the Germans there. The transports were sent directly to the gas chambers, but a few hundred men and women were selected to remain and work in the Lower Camp and the extermination area, to replace those who had died in the typhus epidemic.

One of the last transports from the Warsaw ghetto included several captured rebels who managed to smuggle in a hand grenade concealed in their clothing. When they were brought to Transport Square and ordered to undress, one of them removed the grenade and threw it into the square. What ensued is clouded in conflicting versions. One testimony claims that the grenade killed one Ukrainian and wounded two Ukrainians, a German, and three Jews from the "reds." Several Jews who had just arrived in the transport and were still in the square were also wounded. For a few minutes confusion reigned, with SS men and Ukrainians running in every direction. Then they regained control over the situation and killed the grenade throwers on the spot with blows from their rifle butts. According to another version, only three Jews from the "reds" and several Jews from the transport were wounded. The wounded "reds" were taken to the prisoners' infirmary—which had been established during the typhus epidemic—and were treated until they recovered from their wounds. They even received a visit from Kurt Franz and Küttner.[14]

News of the Warsaw ghetto uprising was a boost to the morale of many in the camp and strengthened their will to revolt. Yet others, in contrast, felt deflated by the descriptions of the repression of the uprising, the thousands of victims, and the fact that no help came from outside. Some Jews who had fled the ghetto during the uprising and sought shelter in the Aryan quarters of Warsaw were caught and brought to Treblinka. Their tales of the enmity they encountered outside the ghetto, of the Poles who informed on them to the police, only added to the general depression. Many asked themselves what would happen if and when they rose up and succeeded in escaping from the camp—where would they turn, and how would they find shelter?[15]

After the last transports from the Warsaw ghetto, in May 1943, there was another extended cessation of transports to Treblinka. In the Lower

Camp there remained little to do by way of sorting and packing, and most of the prisoners were employed in general utility work and in construction and camp maintenance—paving roads, reinforcing fences, gardening, and so on. Shmuel Wilenberg described the situation in Treblinka: "The workload in the camp was dwindling. Often we were idle. We were ordered to flatten a lot of dirt, hundreds of pits and mounds that had hitherto not bothered a soul. We dug up the hard-packed earth, transferred dirt from one spot to another, and slowly smoothed out the rolling terrain. For some time we had been receiving better and more satisfying portions of food. We got the impression that the Germans wanted to kill us all and were trying to dull our senses and deceive us with their behavior."[16]

June passed without anything out of the ordinary happening in the Lower Camp. In the extermination area, the cremations continued at full speed. The smoke and stench of burning flesh reached the Lower Camp. From the newspapers that Marcus, the head of the *putzers*, managed to remove from the SS barracks, the prisoners learned of the extensive German setbacks in North Africa and on the eastern front. In July, news arrived of the Allied invasion of Italy. The general feeling was that Nazi Germany was on the way to eventual collapse. However, the prisoners' assessment that the Germans would not let them leave Treblinka alive brought about a renewal of underground activity.

Galewski, the "camp elder," now joined the Organizing Committee and became its central figure. Other new recruits were Moniek, a young, dynamic fellow from Warsaw who served as capo of the "court Jews." A single testimony also places Rudolf Masarek, a twenty-eight-year-old half-Jew who had served as a lieutenant in the Czech army, in the Organizing Committee. He had been married to a Jewess and chose to accompany her when she was deported to Theresienstadt and then to Treblinka. She was taken to the gas chambers, but he was left alive to work.[17]

The Organizing Committee, led by Galewski, now contained about ten members, most of them capos and work-team leaders. From the original Organizing Committee remained Ze'ev Korland, the *Lazarett* capo, who was second to Galewski in the underground, and Sadovitz and Salzberg. It was largely because of them that the idea of revolt remained alive during the period of underground inactivity. The new Organizing Committee now intensively renewed activity, but as clandestinely as possible. That the head of the committee was the "camp elder" and most of its members capos facilitated meetings; these could be camouflaged as work conferences. Generally the meetings were held in the tailor shop.

Since the underground had previously failed to procure weapons through the Ukrainians, it was decided that the uprising would rely on those arms that could be removed from the camp's weapons storeroom by using the key that the Organizing Committee had already obtained. That this was possible had already been proven: the *putzers'* first and only attempt to remove hand grenades from the storeroom, and even to return them, had gone unnoticed by the camp authorities. This time, it was clear, the boys would have to be briefed more thoroughly and professionally if they were to remove combat-ready weapons and grenades.

Weapons could be removed from the storeroom only during the day, when the SS men were not in their barracks. This factor in effect determined the timing of the uprising—it had to take place during daylight hours, before the SS men could return from their daily tasks and discover that the weapons were missing.

This fundamental conception of the uprising as a daytime operation, when the prisoners were scattered among their work teams, also dictated the underground's organizational system. The underground members were divided into squads of five to ten men, according to the work teams in which they would be located when the uprising began. Every work team would include underground cells. Since there were informers among the prisoners, the organizers were careful when recruiting new underground members and chose only trustworthy and capable people. By July 1943, the underground numbered about sixty members, subdivided into smaller groups.[18]

Despite this progress in planning the uprising and organizing the underground, the timing of the revolt remained a subject of indecision, for a number of reasons. For one, it was clear that most of the prisoners would die in the course of the uprising and escape. The prisoners also were well aware that the possibilities for finding shelter or aid after the escape were extremely limited. Then, too, during these months of June and July 1943, life in the Lower Camp had become easier than before; transports did not arrive, and this made life physically and emotionally more tolerable for the prisoners. Moreover, the disciplinary regime was somewhat relaxed. While fears about the future—the knowledge that one day they would all be eliminated—were constantly in the prisoners' thoughts, the present was at least tolerable. The leaders of the Organizing Committee therefore would, from time to time, postpone the day for the uprising. What ultimately brought on the revolt were the developments and reports passed on by the underground that had been organized in the extermination area. The underground in the extermination area began organizing in late April or early May 1943, a few weeks after the transfer of Zialo Bloch and Adolf Freidman. At that time the principal task of the extermination-area prisoners was to open the mass graves and burn the bodies. Bloch and

Freidman were appointed heads of work teams. Some evidence even places Zialo Bloch as capo shortly thereafter.[19]

Bloch and Freidman, after studying conditions in the extermination area and meeting with the prisoners, held exploratory conversations about the idea of resistance and then began to form an underground and establish an Organizing Committee similar to the one in the Lower Camp. This was in late May or early June 1943.

Aside from Bloch and Freidman, the names of Organizing Committee members in the extermination area cannot be determined with any certainty. One of those connected to underground activity there was Jacob Wiernik, an expert builder who enjoyed special status in the extermination area due to the SS camp command's respect for his construction skills. Other underground members from the Lower Camp were also transferred to the extermination area at this time, and they joined the underground in their new location.

The extermination area was much smaller than the Lower Camp. The work was carried out in the open, near the mass graves and the cremation grills, and at the end of the workday the prisoners were closed into a barrack and an adjacent fenced-in compound. Under these conditions, it was extremely difficult to hide underground activity. Moreover, the underground members had to keep their distance from the "camp elder," Singer, and several others who were suspected of informing to the Germans.

Bloch and Freidman, with their background in the Lower Camp underground, based their plans from the beginning on close coordination of the uprising with their comrades there, and on any further progress with regard to arms procurement. They were well aware that the underground's main numerical strength was in the Lower Camp and that only there could arms be purchased from the Ukrainians or stolen from the weapons storeroom. They also realized that the overriding condition for a successful uprising in the extermination area was for it to be synchronized with the revolt in the Lower Camp and, in fact, be part of a general uprising throughout the entire camp. One problem, therefore, was to establish reliable communications with the underground in the Lower Camp. An opportunity soon presented itself.

Wiernik was ordered by the camp commander to build a log guardroom in the Lower Camp. With the help of eight other prisoners, Wiernik first built the structure in the extermination area, then dismantled it and rebuilt it in the Lower Camp. During his stay in the Lower Camp, Wiernik established contact with the underground leaders there. He told them about the underground in the extermination area and requested instructions regarding the date of the uprising, but did not receive a clear reply.

Wiernik, later wrote of the event: "We returned to our camp filled with hope of liberation, but with nothing concrete." Wiernik does not mention with whom he met in the Lower Camp.[20] Even though they had received no firm commitment about a date for the uprising, these contacts with the Lower Camp underground gave impetus to the organizational preparations and operational planning in the extermination area. The Organizing Committee meetings were held in the evenings, after the prisoners had been locked in their barracks. Wiernik wrote: "When all the prisoners who were tired from work and from suffering would fall asleep, we would gather in the corner of the barrack on an upper bunk and take counsel. The younger ones among us, who pressured for immediate action, even without a detailed plan, nearly had to be restrained by chaining them down. We decided not to act without the Lower Camp, because to do so would have been suicidal. In our camp we were a small group, and not all were in any sort of combat condition."[21]

The underground members were now organized in teams of five, each with an appointed leader. These teams were drawn from the various work stations: grave openers were on the same team, body burners were together, and so on. While there are no precise data available on the number of extermination area prisoners organized into teams of five, the total can be assumed to include several dozen.

The principal element of their operational plan called for the SS men and Ukrainians to be attacked at their posts by the nearest team of five the moment the uprising broke out. The weapons would consist of the tools already in the prisoners' possession, depending on their work—for example, axes, pitchforks, and shovels. To these the weapons taken from the Germans and Ukrainians would quickly be added. Usually there were between four and six Germans in the extermination area during work hours. One of them was in charge of the cremation operation and was known as the *Brennmeister* (literally, "burn master"). Two or three operated the excavators and another one or two SS men were posted for supervision. About eight Ukrainians manned the watchtowers and other guard posts and were in charge of the gas chambers. The center of activity for the SS men and Ukrainians was the guardroom, which was adjacent to the old gas chamber structure. An SS man was always present there.[22]

During the second half of July, work in the extermination area was close to termination. There were no new transports, with the exception of a group of Gypsies and a transport of Jewish prisoners from Treblinka labor camp, both of which were taken straight to the gas chambers. More than three-quarters of the burial pits in the camp had been opened, and the corpses extracted and cremated. Part of the prisoners began filling the empty pits with earth and planting trees to erase traces of the murder. The prisoners sensed that the end was very near—a matter of weeks before their work was finished. A verbal message to that effect was passed on to the Lower Camp underground by Wiernik. The message included a demand to launch the uprising soon and to set a date for it immediately. The replies brought back by Wiernik placated the extermination area underground. Galewski, with whom Wiernik had spoken, told him that the day of liberation was near and called upon the extermination area underground to be patient.[23]

Wiernik continued to relay demands to launch the rebellion soon, but the responses received from the Lower Camp were ambiguous. The Lower Camp Organizing Committee—not confronted with the same sense of a rapidly approaching end to the camp's usefulness as were the extermination area prisoners—still hesitated to fix a final date for the uprising, although in the Lower Camp, too, it was obvious that the end could not be far away.

In the extermination area underground leadership meetings, demands were now made to launch the uprising even without coordination with the Lower Camp. Others argued that such a move would meet with total failure. Thus the tension among the extermination area underground members reached a peak. Moreover, the number of prisoners privy to the secret of preparations for an uprising also had risen, and this, too, added to the tension. The general feeling was that within a few days the work would be completed and the prisoners would be eliminated, while the Lower Camp continued to delude itself.

The SS men in the extermination area even held a celebration to mark the approaching completion of their task. Wiernik wrote: "The party began as the excavator that had been removing our brothers from their graves moved to a resting position. The arm and shovel were raised high, like a turret gazing proudly into the sky. Guns were fired into the air to celebrate. Then there was a feast: they drank, joked, and enjoyed themselves."[24]

The extermination area Organizing Committee met and decided to send the Lower Camp an ultimatum: if they did not immediately fix a date for the uprising, and if it did not take place by early August, the extermination area underground would take action independently. Wiernik delivered the ultimatum to the Lower Camp.[25]

THE PLAN FOR THE UPRISING IN TREBLINKA

THE ULTIMATUM, COMING AFTER THE reports from the extermination area of the near completion of the body burning, finally put Galewski and his comrades in a position where they had to make an immediate decision. They, too, realized that the end was near. The prisoner population in the Lower Camp was gradually being reduced; some were transferred to work in the extermination area, while others had died or had been murdered in the *Lazarett*. The total number of Lower Camp prisoners had dropped from about eight hundred to between five hundred and six hundred. This factor also strengthened the sense of a rapidly approaching end. Then, too, the ultimatum from the extermination area was clear and unequivocal. The Organizing Committee members were well aware that if a rebellion were to break out in the extermination area alone, all the prisoners in the camp would be killed—including those in the areas not involved in the uprising. With these considerations in mind, the Organizing Committee decided on Friday, July 30, or on Saturday, July 31, that the uprising would take place on Monday, August 2, in the afternoon. Jacob Wiernik brought the announcement to the extermination area underground, but the hour of the uprising was not specified.[1]

With the date decided on, the Organizing Committee now worked out the operational details. It had already been determined in principle that the rebellion would take place during the day. The timing constraint also fit in with another assumption—that it was more convenient to attack the SS men and Ukrainians during the day, when they were scattered throughout the camp, interspersed with prisoner work teams, and not grouped together. With the proper planning and organization, they could all be overcome at the same time, and it might even be possible to do it quietly. The night hours were not suitable for yet another reason—at night the prisoners were locked into their barracks and were under tight Ukrainian and SS guard. The underground leaders assumed that within a short time after the uprising and escape, German security forces in the region would be called in to pursue them. The chances for eluding the German pursuers would be better at night. These two factors—the necessity of initiating the rebellion during work hours and the preference for eluding pursuing forces under cover of darkness—determined fixing the hour for 4:30 p.m., about thirty minutes before work normally came to a stop in the camp.

The need to begin the uprising in the afternoon hours of a regular workday explains the choice of Monday, August 2. The decision was reached on Friday or on Saturday, and on Sunday the prisoners did not work in the afternoon, so the first practical day for the rebellion was Monday. When zero-hour was fixed at 4:30 p.m., the passage of a trainload of four hundred to five hundred Polish and Jewish prisoners from Treblinka penal camp, who were returned daily from work at Malkinia at 4:45 p.m., was also considered. The underground planners hoped to stop this train and free its passengers, who, they hoped, would join the uprising.[2]

The final plan called for taking control of the camp, setting it on fire, and only then abandoning it. The planners believed that their numerical superiority, the weapons they would have, and the element of surprise would give them a good chance of succeeding. They also hoped that after they had eliminated most of the SS men, the Ukrainians would cease to resist. The German setbacks at the front had on several occasions provoked the Ukrainians into criticizing the Germans openly in conversations with Jewish prisoners. There had also been a few instances of Ukrainians fleeing Treblinka into the nearby forests.[3]

According to the plan, SS personnel would be attacked and eliminated quietly at the beginning of the uprising. They would be approached at their workplaces. Alternatively, an attempt would be made to lure them into the various workshops just before zero-hour—using some excuse such as measurements for a suit at the tailor's or a new pair of shoes at the shoemaker's—where a group of rebels would be waiting to eliminate them. In this way, it was hoped, the rebels could obtain additional weapons from the SS, besides those removed from the storeroom.

The Ukrainians would be handled differently. Those at guard posts had to be killed and their weapons taken. But regarding the others, who would be at the Max Bialas Barracks, the plan was to capture them alive, take their weapons, and hold them under guard until the camp had been abandoned.[4]

The majority of the prisoners were not members of the underground, and it was decided not to tell them of the planned uprising until it actually took place. The presence of informers among the prisoners, some of whom, such as Chezkel and Kuba, were known to the underground, required that the utmost caution be exercised at all phases of preparation. According to the plan, after the takeover of the camp, all the prisoners would be assembled, captured weapons would be distributed, and all would leave the camp for the forests together. The general direction of flight would be north and east, crossing the Bug River and heading toward Puszcza Bialowiezska.

The operational plan that had been formalized at the meetings of the Lower Camp Organizing Committee included the following phases:

- Phase I: *Acquiring weapons through covert and quiet action; 2:30–4:30 p.m.* The *putzer* boys would remove the weapons from the storeroom and distribute them among the fighting squads at their workplaces. Those Germans who came or were lured into the workshops would be quietly eliminated.
- Phase II: *Takeover by force and destruction of the camp; 4:30–5:30 (approximate).* An exploding grenade would signal the start of the uprising. Camp headquarters would be attacked, as would the SS men and Ukrainians scattered about the camp at their workplaces; the camp telephone line would be cut, and the buildings set on fire. In the extermination area the SS men and Ukrainians there would be eliminated and the gas chambers destroyed.
- Phase III: *Abandoning the camp and departure for the forests.* This phase was not planned in detail, but the main idea was that after the camp was destroyed and the prisoners were armed with the captured weapons, an organized departure to the forests, mainly under cover of night, would follow.

A final meeting of the Organizing Committee was held on August 1 and the plan for the next day's uprising was approved. Shmuel Rajzman, who was present, wrote:

At the Organizing Committee meeting, held late at night by the light of fires burning the bodies of hundreds of thousands of those dearest to us, we unanimously approved the decision to launch the uprising the next day, August 2. I will never forget white-haired Ze'ev Korland, the eldest among us all, who, with tears in his eyes, administered to us the oath to fight to our last drop of blood for the honor of the Jewish people. Every man present sensed the tremendous responsibility involved in our decision to eliminate this creation of mad German sadism and bring an end to Treblinka.[5]

That same night the decision was passed on to all the members of the Lower Camp underground—sixty men.[6] In the extermination area, the announcement of the August 2 date brought by Wiernik aroused extreme excitement. In this part of Treblinka, most of the prisoners, while not underground members, knew of the approaching uprising and supported it.

Because of the summer heat, work in the extermination area went on from four o'clock in the morning until twelve noon. From then on the prisoners were locked into a fenced-in compound, which included their barracks and a courtyard, near the camp's southern fence. A Ukrainian guard stood near the entrance gate to the yard, while two others manned the guard towers. The extermination area underground leaders realized that when the uprising began, in the afternoon, all the prisoners were liable to be locked up in this single area, making it difficult for them to fight. The problem was how to create a situation whereby at the moment the uprising began in the Lower Camp, a group of prisoners, all underground members, would be outside the fenced-in compound in the extermination area. The underground leaders decided that on the appointed day, when work stopped at noon, they would leave a large quantity of corpses near the cremation grills, and would claim that they had not had time to burn them; it would then be necessary to detail a group of prisoners to work in the afternoon, too. It was also decided to initiate additional jobs in order to create as large a group of prisoners as possible outside the barracks that afternoon.[7]

Another problem was the method of overcoming the Ukrainians who would be perched on the two watchtowers—one in the center of the extermination area, the other near the southeastern corner of the camp. Particularly threatening was the centrally located watchtower; it afforded unimpeded observation and control over all activity at the prisoners' barracks and near the grills. It was decided that before the uprising began, one of the underground activists would approach this tower and, offering the guard gold and dollars as payment for food, ask him to descend. In view of the Ukrainians' eagerness for money and valuables, the guard could be expected to take the bait; when the uprising broke out, he would be on the ground and could be eliminated.[8]

Details of the operational plan for the extermination area were based on the Lower Camp's plan. Once the uprising had begun in the Lower Camp, the extermination area underground would attack their Ukrainians and SS men and eliminate them. Then they would set fire to the buildings, including the gas chambers, join up with the Lower Camp fighters, and together leave for the forests.

On the eve of the rebellion, the extermination area underground leaders still did not know the exact zero-hour. They decided that Wiernik would try to find an excuse to go to work in the Lower Camp the next morning in order to obtain this information.[9]

Meanwhile, last-minute deliberations and briefings went on in both parts of the camp until late into the night of August 1–2, while the other prisoners slept. Few of those who knew what would happen the next day slept that night.

AUGUST 2, 1943: THE UPRISING IN TREBLINKA

AUGUST 2 BEGAN LIKE ANY other day in the Lower Camp and the extermination area: reveille, roll call, a meager breakfast, and report to work detail. Ostensibly a routine morning, one of many; however, the prisoners felt different. The underground members barely succeeded in concealing their excitement. In the workshops they were sharpening knives and axes; the storeroom workers prepared tins of gasoline to burn down the warehouses. Many other prisoners noted the unusual attitude of their fellow workers and understood that something was about to happen. Indeed, many prisoners knew of the underground's existence, as well as of the general idea of an uprising and escape, and rumors abounded that the fateful day was near.

Sonia Lewkowicz stated: "The truth is that I didn't know when the uprising would break out. . . . For the past weeks they were saying every day that there would be a rebellion. But the day before it occurred, and especially on the actual day, we felt it had to be, it had to break out, because the entire camp seemed to be electrified. We could feel it. . . . Everyone prepared bundles of clothing for the way."[1]

Thus, tension among all the prisoners was high that day. Many secretly packed a bundle of clothing for the road, removed money and valuables from hiding places where they had been kept for the day of flight, and prepared themselves to buy their way to shelter and safety outside if possible. A careful eye would have noticed the prisoners' unusual behavior and preparations. Galewski and the capos who belonged to the Organizing Committee made the rounds of the camp, calmed their comrades as best they could, and made sure that the work routine was maintained.

That morning, Jacob Wiernik and three other prisoners from the extermination area came to the Lower Camp. Wiernik had persuaded the SS official in charge of construction that he needed some boards from the building materials storeroom in the Lower Camp. While they were in the storeroom, Organizing Committee members managed to get word to Wiernik that zero-hour was set for 4:30 p.m. Wiernik and his comrades returned to the extermination area and confirmed to the underground leaders there the go-ahead for the uprising.[2]

At 1:00 p.m., Galewski held the usual noon roll call, after which the prisoners dispersed to their work stations. This time, however, the work teams had been altered in composition: several of them now received reinforcements from other teams. This was not an unusual step; work requirements had dictated such changes in the past. Galewski, as "camp elder," along with the capos and work foremen, had the authority to transfer men from one routine task to another. In this case the "potato-workers" team and the working group that tended the vegetable garden and the animals were strengthened with underground members. They would have to attack camp headquarters and deal with the Ukrainians' barracks.

The Organizing Committee members scattered themselves at different workplaces in order to take charge of the actions to be carried out nearby. The agronomist Sadovits was responsible for the vegetable garden, which was near camp headquarters and the arms storeroom, and was therefore appointed to supervise the removal of weapons. In the "ghetto" area, Salzberg, the head of the tailor shop and a member of the Organizing Committee, was put in charge of operations. Korland, the *Lazarett* capo, took command of the underground members who worked in Sorting Square.

Galewski took up a position with Korland. As commander, he probably felt that he should be in the southern part of the camp, near the most convenient spot for breaking out—due to the relatively few SS men and Ukrainians stationed there—just in case the takeover operation failed and plans had to be changed. Another advantage of Galewski's position was its proximity to the extermination area, thus facilitating contact with the underground there. However, this position also had its limitations: as chief commander, Galewski was now too far from the two main actions planned for the entire operation—the removal of arms and the attack on camp headquarters and the main concentration of SS men and Ukrainians.

Early in the afternoon of that hot summer day, a group of four SS men and sixteen Ukrainians, headed by Kurt Franz, left the camp for a swim in the Bug River. This depleted the ranks of the camp's security force considerably and worked in the rebels' favor.[3]

Phase I of the uprising, which included the "quiet" preparatory actions, began with the renewal of work after the noon break. Rudek Lubrenitski, who was in charge of the garage and gasoline stores, sabotaged the engine of the armored car which was normally parked near the garage and the SS barracks, so that at the outbreak of the rebellion it would be out of commission.[4] Axes and wire cutters were removed from the tool shed and distributed to underground members.

Removal of the weapons was to begin at 2:00 p.m. As the hour approached, however, it was discovered that the SS man Müller, who was in charge of the camp ordinance and had been camp duty officer that night, had remained throughout the afternoon in the barrack next to the weapons storeroom. His presence there could disrupt the weapons-removal operation and endanger the entire uprising. The *putzer* boys, whose job it would be to remove the weapons, reported to Sadovits on the situation. Sadovits resorted to a trick to get Müller out of his hut. He told Müller that certain problems had arisen in the potato-workers team and that Müller was needed there. Müller left the barrack with Sadovits. Now two boys, led by Marcus, could begin removing the weapons. But due to the Müller incident, they were now slightly behind schedule.[5]

The weapons kept in the storeroom consisted of several dozen hand grenades, a few pistols, and over a dozen rifles. The boys wrapped the weapons in sacking, in small bundles. They removed a bar from the back window of the storeroom, facing the western fence, and passed the weapons out. From there they were taken to a lean-to at the nearby garage and delivered to Lubrenitski, who took charge of their distribution. The operation was slow: each sack had to be passed through separately and with utmost care. At the garage, the weapons were loaded onto a handcart used for moving building materials. A small group of construction workers had been especially assigned that day to the task of collecting odd building materials scattered over the northwest section of the camp. The sacks of weapons were hidden among whitened old boards and tins of whitewash on the cart and delivered to the underground members at their workplaces. Marian Platkiewicz, who was with the potato group, testified: "Like every day, we were working at a pile of potatoes. Then, a handcart, pushed by two men from the construction group, passed by. Swiftly, they handed over to us some grenades and detonators. We put them into the buckets we used for potatoes."[6]

While the weapons were being removed, preparations were in progress for setting fire to the camp. One of the underground members worked at decontaminating the buildings throughout the camp. This prisoner would move about the camp spraying disinfectant on the buildings. That afternoon, as he set off to work, he filled his spray tanks with gasoline instead of disinfectant. Then he sprayed the barracks, the storerooms, and the workshops. These structures were all made of wood, and the gasoline ensured that they would burn well.[7] Preparations during the morning in the extermination area included several activities. The prisoners employed at removing the bodies from the last ditches worked particularly hard that day so that the number of bodies they brought to the grills was far greater than that morning's cremation capacity. The excess corpses remained lying near the grills. Prior to work's end, Adolf Freidman, who was the foreman of the body-burning group, turned to the SS man Karol Petsinger, who was in charge of the cremation, and informed him that he and his team were ready to work in the afternoon to complete the burning of the remaining bodies. So that his willingness to volunteer would not arouse suspicion, Freidman asked in return for a double bread ration for the thirty men in his team. Petsinger agreed.[8]

Wiernik returned from the Lower Camp at about noon and confirmed that the uprising would begin at 4:30 p.m. The extermination area plotters received a second announcement concerning zero-hour from Ya'akov Domb, who drove a wagon to collect trash in the Lower Camp. While driving near the extermination area, Domb shouted out in Hebrew to prisoners working across the fence, "End of the world today, the day of judgment at four o'clock."[9]

When work ended at noon, all the prisoners were returned to the fenced-in compound around their barracks. Throughout the extermination area, no SS men were to be seen, including the excavator operators. They, too, had finished work at noon and had gone to their mess hall in the Lower Camp. Only Ukrainian guards remained. That afternoon, thirty men, led by Adolf Freidman, went out to work by the grills. This group had been specially composed of young and fit men because they would have to overcome the Ukrainians guarding them. All members of this group were volunteers. Their work near the grills required them to be equipped with axes, shovels, and pitchforks. These tools would have to do as weapons.

Every afternoon, two or three prisoners would be allowed out of the barracks area to the well, some twenty meters from the gate in the barracks fence, to fetch water for the barracks kitchen for preparing supper and washing dishes. That day the water-fetchers were reinforced to five men, to further enlarge the number of prisoners outside the fenced-in barrack when zero-hour arrived. Zialo Bloch, the extermination area uprising commander, had decided that he had to be outside the barracks compound, so he and four other underground members went out to draw water. The work of carrying the water was executed slowly that day, and the quantity of water brought to the kitchen was greater than usual—all in order that the work continue until zero-hour. The rest of the prisoners sat in the barracks or the yard of the compound in tense silence, waiting for the signal from the Lower Camp. A Ukrainian guard accompanied the water-fetchers, and another stood at the compound gate. The other Ukrainian guards were stationed near the body-burners and in the two guard towers—one in the center of the extermination area, the other near the fence.[10]

As these activities were going on, an unexpected event upset the plans. At about 3:30 p.m., *Oberscharführer* Kurt Küttner, commander of the Lower Camp, appeared at the Jewish prisoners' barracks in the "ghetto." The living quarters were empty, as no prisoners were allowed there during working hours, but there were many prisoners in the workshops. Küttner's appearance on a normal day would not have aroused unusual suspicion, but his arrival at a time when preparations for rebellion were at their height caused considerable unrest among the underground members in the workshops.

Kuba, who was "barrack elder" of barrack no. 2, invited Küttner into the barrack. No one knew what the two were discussing, but a suspicion arose that Kuba, who was known as an informer, had sensed that something was about to happen and was telling Küttner. Salzberg, appointed by the Organizing Committee to be in charge of the "ghetto" area, thought it best to eliminate Küttner on the spot and start the uprising then and there, even though the weapons had not yet been entirely removed and distributed and the workshop area underground members had not received firearms. He sent a messenger to Galewski and Korland to report on the event and asked for an armed man to be sent to kill Küttner.

Meanwhile, Küttner, on his way out of the barracks, met a young prisoner who was not supposed to be there during work hours. Küttner searched the man and found packs of money, which the prisoner had prepared for his escape. Küttner hit the man and led him toward the "ghetto" gate. Salzberg and the other underground members present now feared that if Kuba had not in fact informed about the rebellion, the young prisoner might break under the anticipated beatings and tell all. Immediate action was obviously necessary. At that moment the messenger returned from Galewski, accompanied by an underground member named Wallabanczik, a young man from Warsaw who had been sent to shoot Küttner. Seeing Küttner leading the young prisoner toward the gate, Wallabanczik drew a pistol and shot him. Küttner fell, bleeding.[11]

The shot fired at Küttner at about 4:00 p.m. served as the signal to launch the rebellion. It was followed by more shots, and several minutes later by the sound of grenades exploding in different parts of the camp. Flames rose from several buildings and from the gasoline store.

The uprising had begun before all the weapons had been removed from the storeroom and while those removed were still being distributed. From the testimony of survivors, it is impossible to determine how many arms had been removed and to whom they had been distributed. Clearly, a few dozen grenades and a few pistols and rifles, with a small quantity of ammunition, had, in fact, been removed. Most of these, and particularly the grenades, had been delivered to the potato-workers team, who were to attack camp headquarters, and to an underground team at Sorting Square, which included Galewski and Korland. No weapons had been delivered to the large group of underground members in the "ghetto" workshops nor, apparently, to the team assigned to attack the Ukrainians' barracks.

The shot fired at Küttner, and the shots that followed, surprised most of the underground members who were scattered about the camp. They had no way of knowing of the incident with Küttner in the ghetto. After this first shot, the commander of the uprising, Galewski, no longer had contact with those underground teams positioned far from Sorting Square. No orders were given. Centralized control over the uprising had been lost.

In the absence of orders from the Organizing Committee, and despite the sudden change in the timetable, several groups of underground members commenced operations against their predetermined objectives. The potato-workers team approached camp headquarters and threw several grenades at it. These caused no casualties among the SS personnel in the building. Lubrenitski and a comrade set fire to the gasoline store, causing explosions and a huge blaze, which spread to the surrounding area. They were both shot and killed by Ukrainian guards.[12] The Sorting Square team opened fire on nearby Ukrainians and in the direction of the guard towers of the southern perimeter fence; the latter returned fire from automatic weapons and caused the team many casualties. The prisoners in the "ghetto" workshop area killed the informer Kuba and set fire to the workshops.

One of the underground members, whose task was to overcome the Ukrainian posted on the watchtower at the camp's eastern fence, described the mission: "[The Ukrainian] sat on the tower sunning himself. When he heard the first shots from the Lower Camp and realized there was trouble, he jumped down. I ran up to him and said: 'Hey, the Russians are coming.' I grabbed his rifle; he offered no resistance. 'Get out of here,' I told him, and he took off."[13]

The rebels' limited ammunition and grenades ran out quickly. In the general confusion, the camp's telephone line to the outside world was not cut as planned. After their initial surprise, the Germans and Ukrainians began firing from the towers and other positions at the rebels and the other prisoners. Hundreds of prisoners who were not in the underground and did not understand exactly what was happening heard the shots and explosions from every direction, saw the flames rising and spreading among the buildings, and began to run about the camp in a state of panic. Many ran toward their barracks; a group of some three hundred Jews collected in the "ghetto" area. A large group of these broke the bars of the carpentry shop and ran eastward, cutting the "ghetto" perimeter fence with wire cutters. Some continued east toward the outer fence, while others headed south toward the extermination area. Those underground members who were armed and still had ammunition continued to fire sporadically at the Ukrainians in the watchtowers and at other positions. In their flight, some of the prisoners ran into lone Ukrainians and took their rifles.[14] Shmuel Wilenberg related:

> Upon hearing the shot, I took off at a run for the barracks to grab the jacket in which I had hidden gold for the escape. . . . Shots were being fired at the tower guards. The air shook from an explosion, then a second and a third. . . . Prisoners were running in every direction. . . . The confusion was indescribable. One of the wooden huts, well dried by the sun and wind, went up in flames. Among the crowd I saw several panic-stricken Germans running about the square, hiding behind trees. . . . Black clouds of smoke covered the sky. Rifles and machine guns cracked from the six guard towers. Scattered single shots from our side replied. . . .
>
> From the nearby tower, a machine gun spit out bursts of fire. They hit their mark, thinning out our ranks. The situation in this sector had become critical. Near me a man was holding a rifle but not firing. I grabbed it, aimed it long and carefully, then pulled the trigger once, twice, a third time. The dark silhouette on the tower slumped over the railing, the machine gun was silenced. . . . then again firing commenced. We dodged from tree to tree toward the fence. . . . I reached the fence. The severed wire dangled lazily. Now we had to run across an open area of 50 meters to the next barbed wire and the anti-tank barriers. The machine gun stepped up its bursts. Behind me, at the outer fence, tragedy. The brave ones climbed up the iron and wire complex only to be hit there by a bullet. They fell with screams of despair. Their bodies remained hanging on the wires, spraying blood on the ground. No one paid any attention to them. More prisoners climbed over the still-quivering bodies, and they, too, were cut down and fell, their crazed eyes staring at the camp, which now looked like a giant torch. . . . I crawled through the open area and reached the barriers. I looked around. The dead had created a sort of bridge over the barbed-wire complex across which another escapee moved every moment. Past the barriers began the forest, rescue, freedom. . . . With a leap, I climbed the bridge of bodies. I heard a shot, felt a blow—but another jump, and I was in the forest. Ahead, to the sides and behind me, men were running.[15]

In the extermination area, a few minutes before 4:00 p.m., a shot was heard from the Lower Camp; shortly after, more shots were heard, together with exploding grenades. After the first shot (aimed at Küttner), Zialo Bloch hesitated, uncertain whether zero-hour had been moved half an hour ahead of schedule. But when more shots and explosions were heard, he decided to commence operations. One of the water carriers was dispatched by him to the compound, where he yelled, "Revolution in Berlin." This was the code signal to begin the uprising. Zialo Bloch and his comrades near the well attacked their Ukrainian guard, took his rifle, and threw him into the well. Bloch took the rifle and fired at the guard on the tower, who fired back. The prisoners near the barracks, armed only with shovels and pitchforks, broke out through the compound gate, killed the Ukrainian guard, and took his weapon. Several underground members broke into the guardroom and removed weapons. The rebels succeeded in injuring the Ukrainian on the guard tower. The prisoners of the cremating site eliminated their Ukrainian guard, too.[16]

The rebels had, in fact, taken over the extermination area. Now they set fire to several wooden buildings. During the shooting, most of the prisoners headed for the southern fence near their barracks, cut it with axes, threw blankets on the barbed wire, and began to flee from the camp. On their way to the second fence, which consisted of antitank obstacles tangled with barbed wire, they were shot at from the towers on the southern side of the camp and at the corners of the perimeter fence. At the same time, several groups of Lower Camp prisoners arrived at a run; they had fled the "ghetto" area and passed through the extermination area entrance gate. Now they joined the fleeing extermination area prisoners. Many of the escapees were hit by the Ukrainians' bullets when they got caught up in the barbed wire of the second fence. Jerzy Rajgrodzki described the escape:

> A large group of prisoners had assembled in the square in front of the compound, where roll call was usually held. A few had rifles. We waited for more to come, since many had run to the barracks to take the clothes they had prepared for the way. We began to run toward the fence. I saw some who hesitated whether or not to flee, and when I looked back I saw that several of these had remained standing by the barracks. What their fate was I don't know. We went through the fence, southward. Bullets whizzed overhead— the guard on the tower was shooting a machine gun. The running prisoners spread out over the field. To my right, across an expanse about 1 kilometer long, I saw the escapees from the Lower Camp. I would estimate the total number fleeing at about 600, most from the Lower Camp. They fled across Sorting Square southward. They were armed with clubs, knives, pitchforks, and a few had rifles.[17]

Zialo Bloch, Adolf Freidman, and some of the others continued firing their rifles and covering the escape until they either fell or ran out of ammunition.

The uprising plan for the extermination area had not been executed in full, but it had achieved a great many of its objectives. Despite the surprise that zero-hour had been moved up, the rebels acted quickly. They succeeded in eliminating the Ukrainians who were nearby, taking their

Pillars of smoke rising from the Treblinka death camp. YVA, 2BO8

weapons and opening fire at the guard towers, and setting fire to some of the buildings. They did not manage to destroy the gas chambers or to eliminate the guards on the towers, and this was to cost them many lives when the victims tried to cross the fences and flee. Still, most of the extermination area prisoners succeeded in bridging the fence complex and escaping.

Camp Commander *Hauptsturmführer* Franz Stangl described what happened that afternoon:

> Looking out of my window I could see some Jews on the other side of the inner fence—they of the SS billets and they were shooting. . . .
>
> In an emergency like that my first duty was to inform the chief of the external security police. By the time I'd done that, our petrol station blew up. That, too, had been built just like a real service station, with flower beds round it. Next thing the whole ghetto camp was burning and then Matthes, the German in charge of the *Totenlager*, arrived at a run and said everything was burning up there too."[18]

German and Ukrainian losses during the uprising were minimal, because Phase II—the attack on the Germans and Ukrainians and the takeover of the camp—was never carried out. Another contributing factor to the relatively small number of losses was that the underground succeeded in procuring only a few arms and a small amount of ammunition.

From existing documentation, we can conclude that the losses suffered by the camp's security forces were one German wounded—*Hauptscharführer* Küttner—five or six Ukrainians killed or wounded. There are no official German reports on the revolt in Treblinka and the casualties they suffered.

By late afternoon, the uprising was no longer an organized and coordinated operation—but it continued. Hundreds of prisoners—individually and in small groups—continued to run and break through the fences. Those who were still armed and had ammunition returned the guards' fire. The entire camp was in turmoil and the flames continued to burn.

PURSUIT AND ESCAPE FROM TREBLINKA

SHORTLY AFTER MOST OF THE prisoners had escaped through the fences, under the guards' fire, the camp command succeeded in organizing a force of Ukrainians and some SS men to begin a pursuit. At the same time, German security forces in the surrounding area were also alerted.

German reinforcements from the Treblinka area arrived quickly. The shots, grenade explosions, and billowing smoke rising from the camp could be heard and seen easily from Treblinka penal camp and other locations in the region. Stangl's telephone call clarified the nature of the event. The first reinforcements arrived from Treblinka penal camp. The twenty Germans and Ukrainians who had been swimming in the Bug River with Kurt Franz also returned to the camp immediately. A Polish engineer working on the rail line from Malkinia wrote: "Suddenly rifle fire could be heard from the vicinity of the camp [Treblinka]. . . . All the Germans from Malkinia hurried to help the camp contingent. They traveled to the camp in cars and a special train, armed with rifles and pistols. Not only the gendarmerie, the Gestapo, and police went, but even simple German rail workers. Afterward, Ukrainian horsemen appeared in the fields around the camp, looking for fugitives."[1]

The forces coming to the camp's aid were from Malkinia, Sokolow-Podlaski, Kosov-Laski, and Ostrow-Mazowiecka, and included police, gendarmerie, railroad guards (*Bahnschütze*), and Ukrainians. Firemen were called in from Malkinia to put out the fire that had swept the camp. Together, these forces, totaling hundreds of men, took up the pursuit. Some of them surrounded the entire area at a distance of several kilometers from the camp to block the fugitives' escape routes. Franz Stangl described the pursuit:

> The security troops had surrounded the camp at a distance of 5 kilometers. And of course they caught most of them . . . they shot them. Toward the end of the afternoon the figures began coming in.
>
> By five or six o'clock it looked as if they had already caught forty more than had ever escaped. I thought, "My God, they are going to start shooting down Poles next"—they were shooting at anything that moved."[2]

Stangl's implication that all the escaping prisoners were caught and shot is incorrect. True, the rebels were impeded by the quick alert to the German forces and their rapid appearance, as well as by the fact that the uprising's premature start gave the pursuing forces more daylight time. Nevertheless, some of the prisoners did succeed in escaping both from the camp and from the pursuing forces.

The fugitives' initial goal was to get as far away from Treblinka as possible. At first they ran in large groups; these scattered and shrank in size the farther they ran. Some were physically able to run fast without stopping, while others gradually fell back, despite the obvious danger involved, and even collapsed from exhaustion. Jerzy Rajgrodzki described the flight:

We ran through the wheat fields. The sun was dipping to the west. To our left we saw country houses and dirt roads. I saw a Ukrainian guard galloping on a horse. The farmers fled their fields. The pace was exhausting. The others began to overtake me. It took all my strength not to fall back. Others were running near me. Among them I saw people I did not know, from the Lower Camp. I knew all of our people. Near me a young couple were running, a dark girl with her boyfriend from the camp. In my hands I was holding a club and a razor, ready for use against anyone and, if need be, against myself. The running went on for about two hours. We reached the forest. To my left was a large group of fugitives. They said they would walk eastward, toward Puszcza Bialowiezska. We stopped to rest in the forest.

There were eight of us. Moishele the tailor was with us. He had a rifle without bullets. He was wounded near the heart. I took a shirt out of my knapsack and cut it up as a bandage. One of the others dressed Moishele's wound, but it continued to bleed. A short while later he lost consciousness and died. May he rest in peace. One of those with us was a former sergeant in the Polish army, named Adas, and he took the rifle. We held a consultation. Most of the comrades decided to head east, which is where the majority of the fugitives were going. Adas and I decided to head south. Anyone going north or east would have to cross the River Bug, which was not easy; also, we estimated that the main German pursuit effort would be made in these directions. We also hoped a small, two-man team would have an easier time.

We decided to walk at night. We had to cross a road. From a distance we could see traffic heading for the camp. We lay near the road until a convoy had passed. We were hungry and decided to enter a nearby farmhouse. We approached it. My companion stayed at a distance, his rifle at the ready, while I knocked at the door. They opened—an old man, a woman, and a boy. We asked for and received food. As we went on, we met Jews who had fled the camp, now going in the opposite direction. At dawn we stopped in a forest, and there we remained throughout the day, hiding in the bushes. We were about a dozen kilometers from the camp. We heard screams from far away. They must have been the screams of Jews caught by the Germans. The day passed, and at nightfall we resumed our march. . . . After several days' walk we passed near Siedlce and finally reached Warsaw.[3]

The fate of another group of fugitives was described by Yechiel Reichman:

> The murderers were chasing us with their machine-gun fire. Simultaneously a car was pursuing us, a machine-gun firing from its roof. Many of us fell. The dead were scattered everywhere. I ran to the left, while the car stayed on the road, firing. They were chasing us from every direction. . . . After a 3-kilometer run we reached a grove of young trees. We decided that it was senseless to keep running, and we took cover among the dense trees. We numbered twenty people—too large a group to hide—so we split up into two teams of ten. We hid 150 meters apart.
> After a short while we saw Ukrainians, led by a few SS men, surrounding the grove, then entering it. They discovered the other group and killed them all. We lay quietly, and to our good fortune they didn't discover us, and eventually left the grove. . . . We marched all night, and at dawn entered a large forest where we remained all day. We were tired and hungry. The second night we left the forest and kept going. It was clear, and after walking a few hours we suddenly discovered that we were not far from Treblinka. We had taken the wrong route and returned to the forest from which we came. . . .
> After three days, tired and hungry, we decided to risk entering a farmhouse and ask for a little food and details as to our whereabouts. . . . The farmer opened the door, but would not let us enter. He told us that throughout the day the Germans were coming in cars and searching for us. The head of the village had told them that any farmer delivering a Jew to the gendarmerie would receive a large prize. The farmer gave us bread and a little milk and demanded payment in gold. We gave him two watches. It turned out we were 15 kilometers from Treblinka.[4]

All the Underground commanders and members of the Lower Camp and extermination area Organizing Committees fell either during the uprising or in the course of the escape. Galewski managed to get out of the camp but died in the subsequent chase. Marian Platkiewicz wrote that once they had reached the forest, Galewski crawled from one fugitive to another, urging them to break away from the surrounding Germans while it was dark, because in the morning they would all die. At night, he said, there was still a slim chance of escape.[5] Another prisoner who was with Galewski during the escape related that after they had covered a few kilometers Galewski felt unable to go on. He took a vial of poison from his pocket, swallowed the contents, and died on the spot.[6]

The only testimony regarding Zialo Bloch's death indicates that he was last seen during the uprising firing a rifle from a kneeling position at the

Ukrainians. Apparently that is where he fell, covering the others' escape.[7] No details are extant regarding the deaths of the other Underground leaders.

Out of approximately 850 prisoners in the camp that day, more than 100 were captured alive inside the camp. They had either not tried or simply not succeeded in escaping; some were sick or weak and lacked the strength to try to escape. There were also those who had decided in advance that they had nowhere to run to, or that they would be caught or killed in the pursuit, and that they were thus better off staying put and leaving their fate in the hands of the Germans.

A large number of rebels was killed inside the camp or near the fences; the estimate is around 350 to 400 people, nearly half the prisoners who participated in the uprising and escape. About the same number succeeded in breaking out of the camp, crossing the fences, and escaping. Approximately half of these fell in the course of the first day and night after the uprising as the Germans and Ukrainians blocked roads, combed the countryside, and ran down those they discovered. This left some 200 prisoners who managed to survive the extensive dragnet of the first twenty-four hours. About half of these were caught in the larger German combing operation, which for days covered the forests and villages at a radius of several dozen kilometers from the camp. Some were caught and murdered by local peasants or handed over by them to the Nazis. Yet it can be assumed that about 100 fugitives managed to get clear of the Treblinka region and scatter throughout occupied Poland, or even beyond its borders.

IDEAS AND ORGANIZATION FOR RESISTANCE IN SOBIBOR

THE FIRST IDEAS CONCERNING ORGANIZED resistance and mass escape were raised by prisoners in Sobibor at the beginning of 1943, and for the same reasons as in Treblinka: the feeling that the camp had almost accomplished its task and that therefore the liquidation of the prisoners was close. However, it was not until the late spring or the summer of 1943 that the ideas of resistance and escape began taking on some organizational form.

The leading figure in the circle of those with ideas for resistance was Leon Feldhendler, in his early thirties, the son of a rabbi, and a former head of the *Judenrat* in the Zolkiewka ghetto. The group also included some heads of the workshops in Sobibor: among them, Josef (family unknown), a tailor; Jakub (family unknown), a shoemaker; Yanek (family unknown), a carpenter; and several others.[1]

The event that prompted the operational decision to form an underground organization was the killing of Jewish prisoners from Belzec death camp. After the liquidation of the camp at Belzec, the six hundred prisoners who still remained in the camp were brought to Sobibor in late June 1943. They were told that they were being taken to Germany to work, but when they arrived at Sobibor they were removed from the train in groups of ten and shot. From a note found among the clothing of the murdered, the Sobibor prisoners learned that those who had been killed were, like themselves, prisoners. The note said: "We worked for a year in Belzec. I don't know where they are taking us now. They say to Germany. In the freight cars there are dining tables. We received bread for three days, and tins and liquor. If all this is a lie, then know that death awaits you, too. Don't trust the Germans. Avenge our blood!"[2]

The Sobibor prisoners were suddenly confronted with the almost certain fate that awaited them. The slowdown in the transports at the end of July as a result of the cessation of transports from Holland contributed to the general feeling that the end was approaching.

The main work at which many of the prisoners were engaged during that period was the construction of barracks and bunkers for storing ammunition in Camp IV, but the prisoners realized that this work would not save them. The minefield laid around the fences of the camp at that time—June 1943—and the retaliation killings of prisoners after the escapes (see chapter 33) emphasized to Feldhendler and his friends that only a large-scale, organized escape might have a chance of success.

To carry out a successful escape, a way had to be found to eliminate the SS men. The underground hoped that if the Germans were eliminated, the Ukrainians, or at least some of them, would not act against a prisoners' uprising and that some of them would even join the escape. These hopes were based on the fact that after the German defeats on the eastern front the Ukrainian guardsmen began having second thoughts about their involvement in the camps. Some of them expressed these feelings in talks with prisoners, and some of them even escaped from the camp and joined the partisans.[3]

In the summer of 1943, the organizational framework of the underground was still vague. In the testimonies of the survivors, there are only passing remarks concerning the activity of the underground and their plans for uprising and escape in this period. Some details are even contradictory. The only plan about which we have more complete data is the plan to poison the SS men and stage a mass escape from the camp with the help of partisans. The initiators of this plan were Herszl Cukerman, a prisoner who worked as a cook in the prisoners' kitchen, and Koszewadski, a Ukrainian from Kiev, who was in charge of this kitchen. Cukerman and Koszewadski had become friendly, and Koszewadski told Cukerman that he had contacts with partisans who would be able to help an escape of prisoners from the camp, but that money was needed to keep up these contacts. Cukerman gave Koszewadski hundreds of dollars on several occasions. He testified:

> Koszewadski used to say that a day would come and he would open the gates of the camp for us. Whether his intention was that he would do it for money or for moral reasons I did not know. . . . I had full confidence in him. He told me that he was going to the "friends" in the forest and he needed money to get weapons. I spoke about him to Leon Feldhendler. . . . Koszewadski told me about a talk [he had had] with a certain doctor in Chelm who was in contact with the partisans. According to him, an attack on the camp was impossible because the camp was heavily guarded. In addition, he said such an attack would cause the death of the prisoners in the camp because the Germans would kill them. Koszewadski and the doctor proposed to poison the Germans and the Ukrainians who collaborated with them. The poisoning had to

be carried out by two Jewish boys who worked in the German kitchen.... The poison was to take effect after six hours. The partisans would arrive that evening and liberate us. But this plan failed. An officer arrived from Majdanek (Lublin) who ordered that no Jews were to work in the German kitchen. The prisoners who worked in the German and Ukrainian kitchens were transferred to another working place.[4]

The poison that was to be used in this operation was taken from the camp pharmacy. Simha Bialowicz, who worked in the pharmacy, gave his version of the plan: "We were obsessed with the idea of avenging our dead and killing the SS. Hersz Cukerman, a young prisoner from Zamosc, suggested poison. He told me: 'Try to find three bottles with 200 grams of morphine.' I got the morphine and gave it to him, but Wagner found one of the bottles. Four men and one girl were arrested. Wagner showed me the bottle, and I said: 'I have never seen it before. Our bottles are labeled.' The SS man in charge of the pharmacy confirmed my words. I was lucky, but the five others were executed."[5]

Which of the two versions for abolishing the poisoning plan—the transfer of the Jews who worked in the kitchen, or the discovery of the morphine—was the true one, or if perhaps both of them took place, remains unclear. Koszewadski himself escaped from the camp. Whether he actually had contacts with partisans and intended to help organize an escape of the prisoners, or if his aim was merely to get money by using different excuses, is also an open question. In the testimonies concerning the plan no dates were mentioned. But if we consider that at that time there were partisans in the area of Sobibor, it had to be in the summer of 1943.

Cukerman also mentions a contact that he, Feldhendler, and his group had established with some other Ukrainians. In the summer of 1943 these Ukrainians presented themselves as Communist party members. They promised that for a substantial sum of money they could hire trucks to drive close by the camp on the night that they would be on guard duty and thus take out the prisoners. The Ukrainians with the lorries were to take the prisoners across the Bug River, where they would organize a partisan unit. The Ukrainians requested the money in advance to pay for the trucks. In the underground there were differing opinions whether or not to trust the Ukrainians and give them the money in advance or to give them the money only after the prisoners were taken out of the camp. The compromise was that $700 would be given in advance and the rest would be handed over after the prisoners left the camp in the trucks. One day a Ukrainian approached a member of the underground group and informed him that they could remove only fifteen members of the underground group from the camp. This proposal was refused. The underground members suspected that the Ukrainians wanted to lure them out of the camp, take the money, and kill them.[6] The entire proposition of the escape by truck was merely an invention of some of the Ukrainian guardsmen to get money from the prisoners.

Another plan that was discussed in Feldhendler's group was to kill the SS men while they were sleeping. The killing had to be carried out by the youngsters, the so-called *putzers*, who worked daily, from the early hours, in the SS living quarters. On the day this plan would be carried out, these youngsters would be accompanied by some older prisoners and together they would kill the sleeping SS men with the axes that they used for their work. But this plan was eventually dropped. There were doubts as to whether the youngsters, boys between the ages of fourteen and sixteen, even with the help of some older prisoners, would be able to kill a dozen or so SS men. The other drawback to this plan was that the killing could be carried out only in the early morning; therefore the escape from the camp would have to take place during the day. This would leave the pursuing forces the entire day for rounding up the escapees.[7]

In August 1943, an idea was raised in the underground to set the clothing stores on fire. In the ensuing commotion, while the SS men and Ukrainians would be engaged in extinguishing the fire, the prisoners would burst through the gates and flee. This would have to take place either at noon, when the prisoners who were working in the stores would be out for lunch, or in the middle of the night. Two youngsters volunteered to hide inside the stores and remain there after all the others left; they would then set the fire, although they realized that they would not be able to escape the closed burning stores. Some bottles of gasoline were even prepared for this purpose. According to one of the survivors, Dov Freiberg, the plan was not realized because two of the prisoners who were supposed to participate in the escape opposed it and threatened to inform the Germans if the plan were not dropped. They did not believe in the possible success of the plan and claimed that "if we can live two or three weeks more, don't kill us now."[8]

Leon Feldhendler's wife gave another version of what happened and why this plan was canceled. Based on what her husband told her, she wrote:

A young boy agreed to remain in the clothing store and set it on fire. This was to draw the attention of the Germans and be the sign for mass escape. He was closed inside the store. As he bid farewell, he wished all the others luck and expressed his happiness for his sacrifice. But at the last moment, before the fire could be set, some Germans appeared, and, being either drunk or suspecting that something was wrong, they went round the storage barrack. And then, he [Feldhendler], seeing that this time the plan could not succeed, opened the store with the key he had and pulled out the boy, who was in despair because the plan had failed.[9]

Another plan was to dig a tunnel that would lead from Camp I outside the fences and minefield. It had to start in the barrack where the prisoners were living and its length had to be 120 to 130 meters. The work on this tunnel continued for two months and part of it had been completed. But after the Germans discovered a tunnel in Camp III they began searching for more tunnels and the idea was abandoned.[10]

All these plans lacked thorough detailed planning and can be considered more as general ideas than actual plans for action. One of the major shortcomings of the underground group was the absence of someone with leadership ability and military training who would be able to work out a complex escape plan and inspire the prisoners to believe that it could be carried out successfully. Feldhendler was more an idealist than a man to command such an action. He realized this and began looking for such a person among the prisoners.

Feldhendler finally found a Dutch Jew, Joseph Jacobs, who was a former naval officer and who had been brought to Sobibor on May 21, 1943. According to some testimonies, Jacobs was a journalist and had fought in the International Brigade in Spain. Jacobs took it upon himself to organize the uprising together with his Dutch friends, in conjunction with the underground group. According to the new plan that was formulated in August, the insurgents, assisted by several Ukrainian guards who had agreed to collaborate, would steal into the arms shed in the afternoon when the SS men were in the dining hall. The insurgents would arm themselves, burst through the main gate, and escape to the forests. One of the Ukrainians informed, however, and the escape plan became known. Jacobs was seized and interrogated about his partners in the plot. In spite of continued blows and torture, Jacobs did not break; he adhered to his claim that he alone planned the escape. In reprisal for the escape attempt, Jacobs and seventy-two Dutch Jews were shot.[11] Ada Lichtman testified about what happened at the roll call: "Wagner appeared at the square and ordered all seventy-two Dutch men to march out. They were taken to Camp III. After a short while we could hear salvos of shots aimed at our comrades. We had to remain [at the roll call] during the entire time. The execution lasted half an hour. In the meantime, Frenzel arrived and ordered the Dutch women to sing Dutch songs. The salvos of the shooting mixed with the tunes of the forced songs."[12]

According to some testimonies a prisoner afraid of retaliation if the escape were to be carried out informed the Ukrainians with whom he was friendly about the planned escape. In some testimonies given about this escape plan, neither Feldhendler nor other Polish Jews are mentioned as having had any contact with Jacobs, and the initiative for this escape is credited exclusively to Dutch Jews.[13]

While the resistance and escape plans were being discussed by Feldhendler's group, another escape was planned in the first half of September 1943 by six capos headed by *Oberkapo* Moshe Sturm, nicknamed "Moses the Governor." The details of this plan and how the capos intended to escape are unknown. One of the prisoners, a man called "Berliner" (from Berlin), informed the camp authorities about the planned escape and the six capos were arrested and executed in front of all the prisoners. As a reward, Berliner was appointed *Oberkapo* instead of Moshe Sturm. Shortly thereafter, Berliner was poisoned by the prisoners. Or, according to another version, some of the prisoners, headed by a capo named Pozyczka, under cover of night threw a sack over Berliner's head and beat him badly. Berliner was forced to remain in bed the next day and eventually died. Before Berliner's death, *Oberscharführer* Karl Frenzel brought him coffee and bread from the SS kitchen, so rumors spread in the camp that it was Frenzel who poisoned Berliner. Frenzel had received many precious objects from Berliner in the past and he was afraid that someday Berliner might reveal this to his superiors.[14]

Very little is known about what was going on in Camp III. Unlike in Treblinka, where clandestine contacts existed between the undergrounds in both sections of the camp, in Sobibor there were no such connections. And since no prisoners survived from Camp III, there is no eyewitness evidence about what happened there.

In the summer of 1943, the prisoners in Camp III were almost idle. Only a limited number of transports arrived, and no doubt they felt—even more than in the other part of the camp—that they were no longer needed and that their end was near. This feeling prompted the initiation of underground activity and preparation for a mass escape.

An underground group in Camp III decided to dig an escape tunnel from the living barrack, beneath the fences, and through the minefield. The digging of such a tunnel was a complicated action; it had to be carried out in strictest secrecy and required leadership and organization. Most of the prisoners who lived in the barrack had to know about the work and were involved in digging, removing the surplus earth, and concealing the tunnel. The camp authorities discovered the tunnel before the work was accomplished, in mid-September 1943. The punishment was very severe: 150 prisoners, the majority in Camp III, were shot. The executions were carried out by Kurt Bolender, the commander of the extermination area. This was the last attempt of the Jews in Camp III to escape.

The way in which news of the events in Camp III reached the prisoners in the other parts of the camp was described by Tovia Blatt:

> We had to go back to work already [from the noon roll call], but we were still standing in Roll Call Square. Something unusual was happening. Behind the fences which surrounded the square, Ukrainians were posted with rifles ready to shoot. On the watchtowers, there were machine guns. We did not know what happened. At about 15:30, we heard shooting coming from Camp III. Our first thought was, they are liquidating the "hell" [Camp III]. After some time the guards were removed, and we went to work. That evening, the clothes of the workers in Camp III were brought for sorting. The Germans told us that the prisoners in the "hell" wanted to escape and therefore all of them were shot. Some people from our camp were sent to Camp III.[15]

In spite of the repeated failures at organizing an escape and in spite of the heavy collective punishments that caused a drop in the morale and self-confidence of the prisoners, the underground group headed by Feldhendler did not give up its idea of resistance and escape. The lesson learned from the unsuccessful attempts was that plans for escape could not be based on the help of partisans or Ukrainians. The prisoners had to rely on their own ability and strength to get out of the camp.

THE UNDERGROUND IN SOBIBOR

THE ARRIVAL OF A TRANSPORT with two thousand Jews from Minsk, including about one hundred Soviet prisoners of war, on September 23, 1943, was a turning point in the underground activity in Sobibor. From this transport, eighty men were selected for construction work in Camp IV. Most of these men were prisoners of war. Among them was Lieutenant Alexander "Sasha" Pechersky.

Pechersky was about thirty-four, married with one daughter; until the war he had lived in the city of Rostov-on-Don and had worked as a bookkeeper. He had been called up into the army when the Germans invaded the Soviet Union and was sent to the front in October 1941. Near the city of Viazma he was taken prisoner, and in the prisoner of war camp he contracted typhus. He succeeded in concealing his illness, however, and summoned up all his strength to stand at roll calls. Had he not been able to do this, he would have been shot, as the Germans executed the sick prisoners. In May 1942 he and four other prisoners attempted to escape, but they were caught. They were lucky not to be shot on the spot, as usually happened to Soviet prisoners of war caught escaping; instead, they were sent to a penal camp in Borisov. There Pechersky was stripped, and the Germans discovered that he was circumcised and was a Jew. He was sent to the SS labor camp on Sheroka Street in Minsk, where about one hundred Jewish prisoners of war, a few hundred Jews from the Minsk ghetto, and some non-Jews arrested for petty crimes were held. In this camp he met and became very friendly with a carpenter, a Polish Jew, Shlomo Leitman, who had been brought there from the Minsk ghetto. From this camp they were sent to Sobibor.

The arrival of the prisoners of war, a cohesive group with battle experience and bearing the glory of the Soviet army, raised the morale of the Sobibor prisoners. Lieutenant Pechersky drew the attention of the other prisoners by his behavior and courage in an event that occurred on September 26. Pechersky wrote about it:

> An ordinary day.... About twenty-five men received twenty-five lashes for various infractions. I was almost one of them. This is how it happened: forty

of our men were busy chopping wood. Hungry, emaciated, exhausted, they raised the heavy axes with great effort and dropped them on the chunky stumps. Frenzel [Pechersky called him "Franz" by mistake] kept hurrying them on: "*Schnell, schnell.*" Quietly he walked over to one of the Dutch Jews. . . . Frenz[el] let him have one with his whip. . . . Frenz[el] noticed that I had stopped chopping. He called out to me: "*Komm.*" He pushed aside the Dutch Jew and said to me in broken Russian: "Russian soldier, you don't like the way I punish this fool? I give you exactly five minutes to split this stump. If you make it, you get a pack of cigarettes. If you miss by as much as one second, you get twenty-five lashes. . . ." Frenz[el) gave the command: "Begin." . . . With all my strength and with genuine hatred, I hit it time and again until I smashed it into pieces. . . . Frenz[el] handed me a pack of cigarettes. "Four and a half minutes," I heard him say. . . . But I literally could not take the gift from the scoundrel's hand. "Thanks, I don't smoke," I said and resumed working. Frenz[el] went away quietly and returned in about twenty minutes holding half a roll and a slice of margarine in his hand. . . . "Russian soldier, take it," he said. . . . "Thank you, the rations we are getting satisfy me fully." Naturally, the German could not let the irony of my reply pass unnoticed. . . . I saw Frenz[el) clench the whip in his hand, but he restrained himself, turned abruptly and left the yard.[1]

Pechersky's proud, bold behavior was something unusual in the camp. The story spread quickly among the prisoners, and Pechersky became the object of considerable admiration. His fellow war prisoners accepted him as their natural leader because of his officer's rank and his personal qualities and behavior. There was a second officer, a major in the signal corps, among the prisoners of war in Sobibor who arrived from Minsk, but although his rank was higher than Pechersky's, he was always depressed and it was clear that he was not the man to take initiative and assume leadership. The more active prisoners of war expected Pechersky to outline an escape after they learned what Sobibor was and the fate that awaited them there.

On September 27, four days after their arrival in Sobibor, Pechersky was approached by two of his friends while a large group, part of them war prisoners, were working on construction in Camp IV. At that time a transport with Jews arrived, and the screams of the women and children on their way to the gas chambers reached them. Pechersky wrote:

Shlomo Leitman and Boris Tsibulsky came up to me. Both were shaken and pale. Tsibulsky said: "Sasha, we must run from here. It is about 200 meters to the wood. The Germans are now occupied. We can waylay the guards at the fence with our axes." I replied: "We, perhaps, may succeed in running away, but what will happen to the others? They will all be finished at once. If the plan is to run away, then we must all run together. . . . "You are right,"

Tsibulsky said, "but we must not delay too long. Winter is approaching. Footsteps leave marks in the snow. Generally it is more difficult to remain in the woods in wintertime."[2]

Two days later, on September 29, while eighty prisoners were working in Camp IV, Pechersky was again approached by some prisoners of war who urged him to join them in an immediate escape. "There are only five guards now," they said to him. "We will waylay them and make for the woods." Pechersky convinced them that a thoroughly unprepared escape had no chance to succeed. The few of them would be unable to kill all the guards, and there would still remain the problem of crossing the minefield and eluding the ensuing German pursuit in the daytime. In addition, all the other prisoners who were working with them would certainly be shot. Pechersky made them understand that more preparations were needed for a successful escape. His words had the desired effect.[3]

There were other plans of escape by war prisoners. On October 9, Grisha, a prisoner of war who had received twenty-five lashes for chopping wood in a sitting position, decided to escape the same night with some other prisoners of war. Pechersky was informed by his fellow prisoner Shubayev about Grisha's intentions. He warned Grisha not to go through with his plan, because it would spoil the mass escape that was to be carried out soon. However, Pechersky did not succeed in persuading Grisha to give up his plan. Therefore, Pechersky posted some members of his group on alert close to the fence near the latrine where Grisha's group planned to cross and forcibly prevented Grisha's escape. This indeed foiled the escape.[4]

Pechersky's closest friends in the camp were Shlomo Leitman, Boris Tsibulsky, and Alexander Shubayev from Baku (nicknamed Kalimali). With them he discussed the different options and ways for organizing the escape. Pechersky's personality and prominent position among the prisoners of war drew the attention of Leon Feldhendler, who still sought an organizer and leader for a mass escape. Feldhendler knew about the talks of escape among the prisoners of war and that Pechersky was involved in these plans. On September 28, at lunchtime, Feldhendler approached Shlomo Leitman and asked him to bring his friend Pechersky to the women's barrack for a talk in the evening. The women's barrack served as a place for social meetings, but Leitman understood that this invitation was not just for a social talk. Pechersky and Leitman came as requested, but Feldhendler was not yet there. The women surrounded the Soviet officer and asked many questions about the war, about partisans, and about the Soviet army. Pechersky spoke in Russian, and Leitman translated his answers. One of the women asked why the partisans did not attack and liberate the prisoners in Sobibor. Pechersky replied that the "partisans have their tasks, and no one can do our work for us." During the talk, capo Pozyczka appeared in the barrack and listened to Pechersky's answers. Feldhendler did not arrive that evening. Pozyczka's attendance prevented him from having an intimate talk with Pechersky, and he preferred not to be seen discussing anything with the Soviet officer.[5]

The meeting between Feldhendler and Pechersky took place the next day, on September 29, in the evening. Feldhendler told Pechersky about the underground group that existed in the camp, and proposed that he, Pechersky, take command and organize a mass escape. As Pechersky did not know Feldhendler too well, he was prudent in his answers. He neither rejected nor agreed to the proposal, but he did leave the door open for further talks. Pechersky, who in his records mistakenly called Leon Feldhendler "Baruch," wrote about this meeting:

> In the evening I met with Baruch [Leon]. He began by saying that what I had said in the women's barracks the other night—no one can do our work for us—had made a deep impression on the women and that they understood the meaning of those words. But that nearby there had been standing a tall, skinny man, one eye always slightly closed, perhaps I had noticed him. "He is the capo Pozyczka, a vile creature. One has to be on guard against him."
>
> "I have no reason to be on guard," I said, "because I do not intend to do anything other than what I am told."
>
> "I understand, you have to answer me that way," Baruch [Leon] said. "We must, nevertheless, have a talk. . . . I understand you are up to something, but did you stop to consider what might happen to all of us if you should escape? The Germans cannot afford to have the secret of this extermination camp broadcast. As soon as one demonstrates that escape is possible, they will liquidate all of us at once. That is clear."
>
> "Tell me," I asked, "have you been in this camp long?"
>
> "Close to a year."
>
> "So you, too, believe the Germans will not kill you. And I believe it as much as you do. What makes you think I am planning to escape?"
>
> "Don't run off," Baruch [Leon] held my arm. "Wait a minute. You wonder why we haven't escaped till now. So I'll tell you. We had thought about it more than once, but we didn't know how. You are a Soviet man, a military man. Take over. Tell us what to do and we'll do it. I can understand your misgivings. We hardly know each other. But be that as it may, we must talk it over. In the name of a group I come to tell you: we trust you. Act."
>
> I looked at him as he stood before me. He was not a tall man, but compact, with a clever, open face. I liked him.
>
> "Anyway," I said, "thank you for warning me against Pozyczka. You are long in this camp. Would you perhaps know how the field behind the fence is mined? How thick and in what order?"

As it turned out, the camp inmates had dug the holes [for the mines] and Baruch [Leon] was able to supply some valuable information about the mine fields. We arranged that future contact between us would be made through Shlomo [Leitman].

After that I went to see the women.[6]

Although Pechersky did not mention any contacts or developments between him and Feldhendler for about nine days, between September 29 and October 7—he did write about a close friendship that developed between him and Luka, an eighteen-year-old girl from Holland with whom he used to sit for hours in the evenings in the women's barrack—the contacts between Pechersky and Feldhendler did continue during this entire period. The liaison man was Shlomo Leitman, who enjoyed the confidence of both men. It was with his help that Pechersky dropped his suspicions and began trusting Feldhendler and his group. As a result of these contacts and talks, a united leadership of the underground in Sobibor, called the "Underground Committee" came into being. Pechersky was the leader, and Feldhendler was his deputy. The other members were Yanek the carpenter, Josef the tailor, Jakub the shoemaker—all of them heads of their respective shops—and Moniek, who headed the youngsters, the *putzers*. The prisoners of war were represented by Tsibulsky, Shubayev, and Leitman.[7]

Cooperation between and unification of these two groups were very important and decisive for the underground in Sobibor. Feldhendler's group contributed its experience in the camp and familiarity with its conditions, and Pechersky's people had the military know-how, fighting experience, and leadership. Each side contributed what the other side lacked and needed. The evening visits in the women's barrack, where Pechersky used to meet Luka and where social meetings of men and women were common, served also for meetings of members of the Underground Committee. One of the prisoners of war testified about these meetings of Pechersky, Feldhendler, and the Underground Committee and the security measures taken to conceal them. Semion Rosenfeld related: "In the evenings Pechersky's group used to meet in the women's barrack. I, Sasha Kuptshin, and three others were appointed as a 'security team' to safeguard these meetings. During the time that the consultations were going on, we organized games, dancing, and group singing to draw the attention of the other prisoners to our activity. Simultaneously we were on guard. If somebody suspicious approached the barrack, we warned the Underground Committee. The women in the barrack did not suspect that in this barrack their fate and freedom was decided."[8]

From the talks with Feldhendler, and from his own observations, Pechersky learned about everything he needed for planning a mass escape.

He gathered information about the camp and its occupants, about the security arrangements, the fences, and the minefields, and about the routine of life in the camp. He also learned about the successes and failures of past escape attempts from the camp and about the recently discovered tunnel in Camp III.

The first result of this research was Pechersky's plan to dig a tunnel for a mass escape from the camp. According to another source, the idea for the tunnel was Leitman's and he came up with it when Feldhendler told him and Pechersky about the tunnel in Camp III.[9]

The digging had to be conducted by Boris Tsibulsky, who was by profession a miner from Donbas. The tunnel had to start at the carpentry, which was the closest barrack to the fences where prisoners were working, and it had to run beneath the fences and minefields. The tunnel had to originate at the stove in the carpentry and exit behind the minefield, a distance of about thirty-five meters. According to the plan, its height and width would have to be seventy-five by seventy-five centimeters, and it would need to be eighty centimeters beneath the earth's surface, so that it would not touch the mine holes. It could not go any deeper, because there was a danger that it might strike water. About twenty cubic meters of soil had to be shoveled out. Part of the dug-out earth had to be hidden beneath the floor of the shop and, in the course of the work, some other places for the surplus earth had to be prepared somewhere along the wooden walls of the barrack. The plan called for the digging to be done during the night and to last from twelve to fifteen days.[10]

The digging of the tunnel started at the beginning of October. The main work was done at night, but some work was done also during daytime. A digging shift included four people: while two were digging, the other two disposed of the earth and rested. They remained in the carpentry during the entire night. About fifteen prisoners, some of them Polish Jews, knew of and were involved in the digging work. The digging progressed smoothly for a few days, but on October 8 and 9, heavy rains fell on the camp and water penetrated the tunnel and flooded it completely. When Tsibulsky entered the tunnel on the night of October 9, he found it utterly wrecked. The tunnel escape plan had to be abandoned. An alternative plan for escape had to be found.[11]

Pechersky was aware of the difficulties of the tunnel escape plan even before its failure. He did not foresee the flooding, but he was worried about other drawbacks. On October 7, two days before the tunnel plan had to be abandoned, he said to Feldhendler and Leitman: "What are the drawbacks of this plan? I am afraid that from eleven at night till dawn will not be sufficient time for 600 people to crawl, one behind the other, a distance of 35 meters. Because it is not a matter of just these 35 meters. It is important to get as far beyond them as possible, unnoticed. We must also bear in mind that in the course of the hours it will take to cover this distance, fights may flare up. Everyone will want to be the first in line."[12]

So, even as the digging was going on, another plan was taking shape in Pechersky's mind. The main idea of this plan was to eliminate the SS men in the camp by force and then to carry out the escape. For this purpose, he asked Feldhendler to prepare in the workshops about seventy sharp knives to be distributed to the underground members in time for action. "In case the plan fails," Pechersky said to Feldhendler, "we should at least have some weapons in our hands." Pechersky also asked Feldhendler to find a way for him and Leitman to be transferred from their work in Camp IV, which was in the remote part of Sobibor, to work in the carpentry workshop, which was in Camp I. From this working place, which was located in the center of the camp, it would be easier for them to control the preparations and to command the operation when it began. The next day, October 8, Yanek, the head of the carpentry and an underground member, requested three more workers from the SS man in charge. He received permission, and during the morning roll call he took out three prisoners, including Pechersky and Leitman.[13]

October 9 was Yom Kippur. The prisoners were permitted to gather for *Kol Nidrei* prayers in one of the barracks. This prayer gathering was used by members of the Underground Committee to discuss further plans. It was already clear that the tunnel escape plan had failed. What remained was the plan for escape by using force and arms. All efforts had to be directed to preparing an underground cadre divided into combat groups; to arm them with knives, axes, and shovels; and to be ready for the uprising. This was the outcome of the Yom Kippur talks.[14]

The uprising plan had to take many details into consideration. Pechersky, in his talks with Feldhendler, had gathered information and studied the routine of the German staff in the camp—where they were during the day, in which places they were working, when they came for inspections, whether they could be summoned for some reason to the workshops. He learned when the SS men were going on vacation to Germany, for before they left they used to come to the workshops of the tailors, shoemakers, and goldsmiths, or to the stores, to ask the Jewish prisoners to prepare clothing and other presents to take to their families. He also learned a very important fact: only the Ukrainians who were on guard duty received ammunition for their weapons, and this only in small numbers—in some cases no more than five bullets. All the others carried no ammunition in their rifles.[15] The reason for this procedure was that a short time before, some

Ukrainians had escaped from the camp to join the partisans and had taken their arms with them. Rifles with no bullets made it more difficult for the Ukrainians to escape and fight their way to the partisans.

From the information Pechersky collected and during the night talks with Leitman in the barrack, as they lay side by side on the wooden bunks, the general plan of the uprising started to take shape. The main idea was to kill the SS men within a short time while they were dispersed in different work sites or when they would be summoned to the workshops under different pretexts. The next stage would be the organized escape from the camp.

There were still many unsolved problems. One was how to place prisoners of war, who had to be the backbone of combat groups, in the different workshops and stores where the SS men had to be liquidated. Another problem was how to organize the six hundred prisoners who knew nothing about the uprising for a mass escape after the SS men would be eliminated. All this had to be carried out in a very short time and unnoticed by the Ukrainians on the watchtowers. The whole problem of the Ukrainian guards and their reaction after they discovered what was going on had to be considered. As Pechersky began working on the details of the plan, an unforeseen development, connected with some of the capos, opened new possibilities for Pechersky and his friends.

The underground activity did not pass unnoticed by two of the capos in the camp, Czepik and Pozyczka. Indeed, it was very hard in such a small camp, where the life of the prisoners was limited to a few workshops and living barracks, to conceal any unusual talks and movements. The intimate talks between Pechersky, Leitman, and Feldhendler in the women's barrack, as well as the tunnel digging, had drawn their attention. In the first days of October, Czepik, who was the capo in charge of the *putzers*, approached Moniek, the *putzer* foreman and a member of the Underground Committee. Czepik told Moniek that he knew some clandestine activity was going on and that he would like to participate and help in the escape from the camp. Moniek denied any knowledge of such activity or preparations for an escape. On October 7, Feldhendler told Pechersky and Leitman about Czepik's request and Moniek's opinion that it would be worthwhile to include the capos in the escape plot. The decision was to postpone the resolution about including the capos in the activity of the underground.[16]

On October 10, Pechersky and Leitman were invited to the smithy to listen to a record player that had been brought by the Ukrainian guards for repair. Someone had found several Soviet records among the belongings left by the victims in Camp II and brought them along. Capo Pozyczka was there also, listening to the records and taking part in the conversation.

Alexander Pechersky, leader of the
Sobibor uprising. YVA, 4216/2

Later, some of the prisoners, including Pozyczka and Pechersky, went over
to the locksmith's shop, which was in a nearby room. There, Pozyczka
found an opportunity to speak to Pechersky and asked him to include him
and Czepik in the escape plan. In his opinion, the third capo, Schmidt,
could not be trusted. Pozyczka said to Pechersky:

> You need not tell me anything. I know all. . . . You yourself are not talking
> about it to anybody but that little one Shlomo I believe his name is, that clev-
> er fellow, does all the talking for you. You are sleeping next to one another
> and you have the opportunity to talk things over. I know but I'm not inform-
> ing on you and I don't intend to. . . . I propose that you make me a partner
> in the undertaking. Together we'll carry it through much easier and more
> efficiently. We, the capos, have the possibility, during work time, to move
> about freely through all the camps except Camp III. We can talk with whom-
> ever we have to without arousing suspicion. Just think how useful we could
> be to you. You may ask why do I propose this to you? Very simple. Because
> I don't believe the Germans. Frenzel makes all kinds of rosy promises to us.
> We have privileges, but when the time comes to liquidate the camp, we'll find
> ourselves standing next to you. They'll kill us too. That is clear.[17]

Pechersky did not give Pozyczka a definite answer. He neither confirmed
nor denied the existence of an underground group and the preparations for

an escape. He faced a dilemma. He understood the advantages of having the capos with them and the important help they could extend in the preparation and implementation of the escape. On the other hand, to put their trust in the capos, to believe in their honesty, to be dependent on their loyalty, was not an easy decision. He decided to discuss the whole matter with the other members of the Underground Committee.[18]

Time was running out. Winter was approaching, and in November there could be snow. The trails left in the snow would make a successful escape almost impossible. The time for action was limited to the end of October, no more than two weeks away. It was also becoming more and more difficult to preserve the secrecy of the existence of an underground organization and the preparations for a mass escape from the prisoners in the camp. The talk with Pozyczka convinced Pechersky that their clandestine activity was known among the prisoners. This created a very dangerous situation, because in some way their activity and preparations could reach the camp authorities. There was no time to postpone the action; decisions had to be taken promptly.

CHAPTER FORTY

THE PLAN FOR THE UPRISING IN SOBIBOR

ON THE MORNING OF OCTOBER 11, when the prisoners were already at their workplaces, horrible screams and rifle shootings came from the direction of Camp II. A new transport of victims had arrived and was taken to Camp III. The people of this transport resisted. Some who were already undressed realized what was going on and started to run to the barbed wire; they were shot down by the guards. It took some hours of turmoil in the camp until this transport was liquidated.

October 12 was also an unforgettable day for the prisoners. In the morning a group of SS men led by Frenzel entered the living barracks. At that time, eighteen camp inmates, who had been sick for several days, were lying on the bunks inside. Karl Frenzel ordered the sick to rise at once and march to Camp III. One of the sick was a young man from Holland who could hardly stand on his feet. His wife, who was in the women's barrack, found out where her husband was being taken. She threw herself at the Germans, screaming, "Murderers! I know where you are taking my husband. Take me with him. I will not, you hear, I will not live without him. Murderers! Scum!" She took her husband's arm, supporting him, and marched off with the others to her death.[1]

Alexander Pechersky and his fellow prisoners from Minsk were not used to such tragic events, and they were shocked at the liquidation of the transport and at the way prisoners like themselves, with whom they worked and slept side by side, were taken to the gas chambers. They faced the fact that they, too, could at any moment be taken to their death. They became eager to act.

Another important factor influenced the decision for not delaying the uprising. The underground leadership learned that Franz Reichleitner, the camp commander; Gustav Wagner; the sergeant major of the camp; and Hubert Gomerski, one of the cruelest in Sobibor, as well as some other SS men had left the camp for vacations in Germany. This considerably weakened the German staff in the camp; especially important was the absence of Wagner, who was very shrewd and suspicious and was the man who kept the strictest supervision over the prisoners. It followed that the uprising and escape would have to be carried out before these key persons returned.[2]

The Underground Committee held meetings on the evenings of October 11 and 12, at which time the plan for the uprising was presented by Pechersky and discussed in detail. These meetings were held in the carpentry, and some members of the underground were posted in the yard and at the gate of Camp I to warn if Germans or Ukrainians were approaching. In that event the Underground Committee would have time to scatter.

The first subject discussed at the meeting on October 11 was the request of the two capos, Pozyczka and Czepik, to join the underground. In Pechersky's plan for the uprising and escape, the two capos would play an important role. They would place members of the underground in the stores and workshops where the killing of the SS men had to be carried out. They also would be indispensable in organizing all the prisoners of the camp for the escape. Of particular importance was Pozyczka, because he could move freely through the whole camp, while Czepik was limited mainly to Camp I. After a short discussion, it was agreed to accept them into the underground, and Pozyczka was called to join the meeting. When Pozyczka walked into the carpentry workshop, Pechersky told him: "Pozyczka, we have decided to invite you to this consultation. I think you understand what kind of responsibility you are assuming by coming here. If we fail, you will be one of the first to be executed." Pozyczka replied that he understood and that they should not worry about him.[3]

After Pozyczka joined them, Pechersky presented his plan. The first stage of the action would be the liquidation of the SS men. They had to be eliminated one by one, without the slightest sound and within no more than one hour. Less time was impossible, but it could take no longer. If one of the SS men became aware that another SS man was missing, he might sound the alarm. The task of killing the SS men would be assigned to people selected mainly from among the prisoners of war, those who were known for their courage and resolution, who had battle experience, and who would be firm and unwavering at the decisive moment. One moment of vacillation, one failure, could spoil the whole action. It would be the duty of Pozyczka to transfer some prisoners of war to Camp II, where none of them were working, to kill the SS men there.[4]

The details of the uprising and escape were discussed also on the following evening, October 12, at a meeting attended by all the members of the Underground Committee, and by Capo Pozyczka. This meeting was held a few hours after the eighteen sick prisoners were taken to the gas chambers, and this selection overshadowed the deliberations.

A detailed plan for the uprising was discussed at this meeting. It was decided where the battle teams would be stationed; an exact timetable was fixed for the uprising; and members of the Underground Committee received their assignments. The time of the action was influenced by two factors, similar to those in Treblinka. First, it had to be carried out during working hours, when the SS men who had to be liquidated were still dispersed in the different areas of the camp and the prisoners were working in their vicinity. Second, it had to be close to nightfall, so the escape of the prisoners and the ensuing pursuit by German forces would be in darkness.

The plan of escape was based on the assumption that the Ukrainians, except for those ten or so on guard duty, had no ammunition for their rifles. According to this plan, the prisoners would escape through the main gate, where it was known that there were no mines, but this would mean they would pass right by the Ukrainians' barracks. It would therefore be disastrous for the whole plan if the Ukrainians in the barracks had ammunition and dozens of them, in addition to those who were on guard duty, could open fire on the prisoners. Pechersky decided to check this personally. He asked Pozyczka to send him to the Ukrainians' barracks for some repairs. The next day a request came to Yanek, the head of the carpentry shop, to send somebody to repair the doors in these barracks. Yanek, a member of the Underground Committee, sent Pechersky to carry out the work. The barrack was empty when Pechersky came in, and he was able to check some closets where rifles were kept. There was no trace of ammunition in the barracks. Pechersky returned to the camp carpentry satisfied with the results of his search.[5]

The quiet liquidation of the SS men had to be carried out in the workshops of Camp I and in the warehouses of Camp II. Pechersky was in charge of the operation in Camp I. Feldhendler had to command the killing of the SS men who were in Camp II at that time and to cut the phone line that connected the administration building in the forester's house to Wlodawa and Lublin. The cutting of the phone line was essential to prevent a call for help from these places and postpone the pursuit. For these actions, Feldhendler would have under his command a group of Polish Jews and some prisoners of war.

The plan did not take into consideration the prisoners in Camp III. There were still Jewish prisoners there to clean the gas chambers and cremate the corpses from the transports that continued to arrive from time to time. The last of these had been the transport of October 11. The number of Jews in Camp III was unknown: it may have been several dozen or as many as 150. The prisoners in Camp III were totally unaware of the preparations for the uprising in the other parts of the camp and did not participate in them.

The detailed plan that was crystallized during the consultations held on the evenings of October 11 and 12 was divided into two main stages:

- Stage A: The quiet liquidation of the leading SS staff: 15:30–16:30 hours.
- Stage B: The escape from the camp: 16:30–17:30 hours.

In Stage A the leading SS men would be asked, for various reasons, to come to the workshops in Camp I or to the warehouses in Camp II. They would be asked to these places by the heads of the workshops or warehouses, for clothing or shoe measurements, for inspecting some work in the carpentry workshop, or for similar excuses. In each of these places, a battle team of two or three underground members, armed with knives and axes, would be hiding; they were to kill the SS men. Six battle teams were assigned to carry out this action.[6] It was to take place inside the barracks, in absolute silence, so that the Ukrainian guards on the towers or in other places would neither see nor hear what was going on.

The underground members in Camp II would be reinforced by a battle team of prisoners of war whom Capo Pozyczka would transfer from Camp I at 15:30 hours. They would be received there by Feldhendler, who was working in Camp II. The liquidation of the SS men in Camp II was to begin at 15:30. At 16:00, the phone line, which was the only means of communication from the camp to the outside world—there was no wireless equipment in the camp—was to be cut. The electric lines had to be cut later in order not to raise unnecessary suspicion at this early stage of action. The trucks had to be sabotaged by the prisoners working in the garage. The underground members had to prevent, even by force, any prisoners who had witnessed the killings in the workshops and stores from leaving the barracks in case they might panic and reveal what was going on and thereby jeopardize the entire action. The liquidation of the SS men in Camp I had to begin at 16:00, after or close to completing the elimination of the SS men in Camp II.

An underground member, Shlomo (Stanislaw) Szmajzner, a Polish Jew who was in those days in charge of repairing the stoves in the Ukrainian barracks, undertook to smuggle out some rifles from there and bring them to Camp I at the start of the action. According to the plan, the firearms that would be at the disposal of the underground at the end of Stage A would include a dozen revolvers taken from the killed SS men and some rifles that Szmajzner was supposed to seize. Some youngsters and women who worked in the SS barracks were to smuggle out any ammunition that they might find there. For crossing the fences between the sections within the camp and the outside fences, wire cutters also had to be prepared in the workshops. The main goal of Stage A was to quietly eliminate most of the SS men in the camp, among them all the key personnel, so that no authority would remain capable of organizing the Ukrainians for suppression of the uprising and for immediate pursuit.

During Stage B, all six hundred prisoners in the camp had to be assembled and, in an organized way, leave the camp through the main gate, the only exit from the camp without mines. The idea behind this plan was that after Stage A was quietly accomplished, the Ukrainians at the guard positions would still be unaware of what was going on. Then, by sticking to camp routine, the prisoners would be called to the daily evening roll call by Capos Pozyczka and Czepik. In the autumn, when night fell early, the evening roll call was around five o'clock. At the roll call, those prisoners who were still unaware of what was happening would be informed about the action. They would be warned not to panic and told that, since there was no possible penance after the SS men had already been killed, the only chance of survival was to proceed with the plan. Then the entire prisoner body in the roll call, lined up four abreast, headed by the prisoners of war, armed with pistols taken from the SS men and led by Pozyczka, would march to the camp gate—just like the *Waldkommando* used to go to work in the woods. Until the march toward the gate, nothing of the daily routine would have been altered. The assumption was that without the key SS personnel in the camp, it would take some time for the Ukrainian guards or some of the surviving Germans to grasp that something unusual was happening. With some luck, the prisoners might march right out the gate—or at least be close to it—before their ruse was discovered.

While marching toward the camp exit, some of the underground members would try to penetrate the arms store of the SS, which was close to the gate—but only after the main body of prisoners would be near the gate, or even outside it. It was assumed that at this stage the guards would certainly catch on to what was happening and open fire. But, being close to the gate and armed with the weapons, the prisoners would continue the breakthrough from the camp by force and fighting.

The plan did not detail what the prisoners would do after they left the camp. Once outside the camp, everyone was on his own. They would try to escape to the woods and later attempt to find the partisans or some other shelter.

During the discussion about the uprising plan held by the Underground Committee at the meeting in the carpentry workshop on the evening of October 11, Pechersky was asked by Yanek what would happen if the Germans were to cut off the gate and the approach to it with machine-gun fire. This might even happen before they had a chance to get enough weapons to arm themselves. Pechersky replied:

> It's quite possible that the guards will become aware of this before the anticipated time, cut off our path to the gate and open fire on us from the two machine guns they have there. In that case, if we have succeeded in arming ourselves, we'll engage them in battle. But just in case this doesn't come off, we must be ready with an alternate plan.
>
> Not far from the carpentry workshop, very close to the wire fence, stands the officers' house. We must assume that even if the strip of field nearby is mined, it is mined with signal mines which are not dangerous. Right there, behind the officers' house, the wire fence must be hacked through. Those in the front lines will hurl stones as they advance. Where the stones fall, the mines will explode. Thus the way will be at least partially cleared of mines.
>
> This is the plan. Shlomo [Leitman] and I have thought it through more than once. We see no other alternatives. Now let each of you consider carefully whether you'll be able to carry through the task assigned to you. Tomorrow evening we will meet again. And remember, comrades, not a word to anyone. Neither to wife, brother, nor friend may you utter a single word of what was decided here.[7]

The possibility that gunfire might be opened on the prisoners while they were still in Camp I at the roll call was taken into account and the carpenters prepared planks and a ladder to be used to cross the water ditch west of Camp I in front of the fences and to climb over the fences. The planks and ladder were hidden in the weeds behind the carpentry workshop.[8]

At the meeting held on October 11, the date for the uprising was fixed for October 13, and this was confirmed at the meeting on October 12. The secret of the uprising was known to the members of the Underground Committee and to some prisoners of war who had to take part in eliminating the SS men, a total of about thirty to forty members of the underground. The details were known only to the Underground Committee. The axes and knives were distributed at the last moment to those assigned for action.[9]

In Sobibor, as in Treblinka, it was a sleepless night for the prisoners who knew what was going to happen the next day.

On October 13, the day that had been set for the uprising, a group of SS men from the Ossowa labor camp came to Sobibor. The reason for their visit was unknown, but their arrival changed the whole situation. It strengthened the SS force in the camp and raised the question of whether the SS men from the camp staff would be at their usual working places or would respond to the invitations to the workshops and stores where, according to the plan, they were to be liquidated. When at noontime the SS men from Ossowa had not yet left the camp, the underground leadership decided to postpone the uprising, and in the late afternoon, when the SS men from Ossowa did finally leave, it was too late to rescind the postponement. That evening the underground leadership met again and decided that the uprising would be carried out the following day, according to the existing plan.[10]

As he closed the last meeting of the Underground Committee, Pechersky said, "Friends, you should remember that we cannot hope for any outside help. The front line is still far away, somewhere in the area of Kiev. We have no contact with the partisans. Therefore we can rely only on our own strength."[11]

During the night the knives and small hatchets that had been prepared and specially sharpened in the smithy were distributed to members of the battle teams. There was a hidden tension among those who were privy to the secret of the uprising. In spite of Pechersky's warning not to reveal anything to the prisoners and even to underground members that were not assigned to the killing operation, the information leaked out to a circle of prisoners during the late evening and night. Some of those who knew about the plan warned their relatives and close friends to be ready for escape the next day. This information cause excitement, fear, and hope. Ada Lichtmen described the talks and feelings of a group of women late that evening:

> When it became known to our small group that the next day, October 14, the uprising would finally happen, it caused excitement and nervousness among us. Esther Grinbaum, a very sentimental and intelligent young woman, wiped away her tears and said: "It's not yet the time for an uprising. Tomorrow none of us will be alive. Everything will remain as it was—the barracks, the sun will rise and set, the flowers will bloom and wilt, but we will be no more." Her closest friend, Helka Lubartowska, a beautiful dark-eyed brunette, tried to encourage her: "There is no other way. Nobody knows what the results will be, but one thing is sure, we will not be led to slaughter." The little Ruzka interrupted the conversation: "What silly talk. What have we to lose—one day more of a life of suffering? Whatever will be, let it be." Esther Turner approached the group and said enthusiastically, "Girls, at least something is going to happen. I have a feeling that everything will go smoothly and will succeed." Sala, a blond with blue eyes, who was always quiet, interfered: "Stop chattering like old women. We have to prepare ourselves, and that's that." It was wise advice. The talk stopped, but the whispers continued during the night. We made preparations for the escape. We could not fall asleep, and the night was a nightmare. Sala was singing quietly, sentimental songs; others were crying silently.[12]

Many did not sleep that night. The leaders of the underground also could not fall sleep. Pechersky wrote: "That night I and Leitman did not sleep. Lying side by side on the wooden bank we discussed details of the uprising plan. We were thinking whom to send to Camp II. I remembered the face of Boris Tsibulsky while working in Camp IV when we heard the children's scream [on their way to the gas chambers]. . . . I decided that he was the man to be sent there. As we knew him, his hands would not tremble in time of action. We also discussed different alternatives in case something unexpected would occur.[13]

But for the majority of the prisoners, and for the German and Ukrainian staff, who did not suspect anything about the imminent events, that night was a perfectly ordinary one.

OCTOBER 14, 1943: THE UPRISING IN SOBIBOR

OCTOBER 14 WAS A CLEAR, sunny autumn day. It began as any routine day—with the morning roll call and the prisoners dispersing to their workplaces. The atmosphere was tense, however. Many felt that something unusual was going on that day. A sharp eye would have noticed that some of the prisoners had put on their best clothes and boots. Those who were privy to the secret of the impending uprising removed money and valuables from their hiding places in the hope that this would increase their chances for survival once they were outside the camp. The Underground Committee even directed the members of the underground to remove any valuables in the workshops or warehouses and distribute them among the trustworthy prisoners.[1]

Alexander Pechersky was at his command post in the carpentry workshop from the morning hours. Through the window he had a good view of the square in Camp I. With him was another prisoner of war, Semion Rosenfeld. The main group of about twenty underground members, mainly prisoners of war, were working in the nearby barrack, under the command of Shlomo Leitman, preparing wooden bunks. These prisoners had been selected by Pechersky, Leitman, and Yanek to carry out the liquidation of the SS men and the breakout from the camp. Among them were Boris Tsibulsky, Alexander Shubayev, and Arkady Vaispapir. Leon Feldhendler, who was to command the action in Camp II, had taken up his position in the warehouse in that part of the camp from the morning hours. Communications between Pechersky and Feldhendler were handled by some young *putzers* who were able to move freely between Camps I and II. Yanek was in charge of coordinating the "invitations" of the SS men to the workshops in Camp I. According to the plan, this was scheduled to occur between 16:00 and 16:30 hours.

At ten o'clock in the morning, at a short meeting of Pechersky, Yanek, and Leitman, Yanek informed the others that the SS men had been asked to the workshops. *Untersturmführer* Josef Niemann, the acting commander of the camp, was scheduled to come to the tailor workshop at four o'clock to be measured for a suit. At the same time, *Oberscharführer* Goettinger, the commander of Camp III, was to come to the shoemaker shop. Karl Frenzel would be coming to the carpentry between 16:00 and 16:30 to check on a new cupboard. Other SS men were asked to come to the workshops at intervals of fifteen to thirty minutes later.

Pechersky was satisfied; everything seemed to be under control. He asked Leitman to send him the commanders of the battle teams one by one so that he could brief them about their assignments.[2] The first to arrive was Shubayev. Pechersky told him that at three o'clock he, together with another prisoner of war called Senia, would go to the tailor shop, armed with axes. Their task was to kill the Germans who would come there. When Tsibulsky came, Pechersky explained to him that his task was the most important. He, together with two other prisoners of war, would be taken by Capo Pozyczka to Feldhendler in Camp II. They were to kill the Germans there. Pechersky stressed that Tsibulsky would be the first to start the whole operation. The first blow that he would inflict, the first murder of an SS man, would raise the prisoners' spirits and symbolize the point of no return. Once the killing of the SS men began, only one way remained for the prisoners—to go ahead with the uprising and escape. The alternative was death in immediate reprisal for the killings. Tsibulsky assured Pechersky that he would carry out his assignment.

Arkady Vaispapir was next. Pechersky told him that he and Yehuda Lerner, a Polish Jew who had come to Sobibor with the Minsk transport, would take up a position inside the shoemaker shop. They had to eliminate the three SS men who had been asked to the workshop. Nachum Plotnicky and Alexey Vaitsen's assignment was to command a group of underground members at the head of the prisoners' columns while they were marching from the evening roll call toward the gate at the last stage of the uprising. They also had to command the takeover of the SS arms store, distribute the captured weapons to the underground members, and fight the camp guards until the unarmed prisoners could reach the forest. Only then would they, too, retreat to the forest. Two other prisoners of war, Jefim Litwinov and Boris Tabarinsky, were put in charge of a battle team that was to cut the barbed-wire fence near the camp commander's house, in case the escape through the gate would be impossible and prisoners would have to use this route from the camp.[3]

All the briefings were completed by noon. Zero-hour was approaching. Everything seemed to be ready.

In the afternoon there was an unexpected development. At two o'clock, *Unterscharführer* Walter Ryba came to Camp I and took Capo Pozyczka and three other prisoners and led them away. Ryba was armed with a submachine gun, which was peculiar because usually the SS men carried only pistols. This raised Pechersky's suspicion that the Germans suspected that something was going on in the camp. He connected this with Frenzel's visit to the carpentry workshop at noontime, when his attention was drawn to Yanek's new clothes. Frenzel mockingly asked Yanek whether he was preparing for a wedding. He left without asking further questions. The fact that Pozyczka was taken away also endangered an important part of the uprising plan. It was he that had to take Tsibulsky's battle team to Camp II. Extremely disturbed about the whole matter, Pechersky asked Yanek to find out where Pozyczka had been taken. Pechersky passed an hour of nerve-wracking tension until Capo Czepik came and informed him that Pozyczka and the other prisoners with him had been taken to Camp IV to pile up wood. Since Ryba was not accompanied by a Ukrainian guard, he had taken a submachine gun. This calmed Pechersky's suspicions, but the problem of who would take Tsibulsky's team to Camp II remained.

Pechersky asked Czepik to take Tsibulsky and his men to Camp II. Czepik answered that he was not authorized to leave Camp I and proposed that the uprising be postponed until the next day, when Pozyczka would return to his usual post. Pechersky rejected this proposal; things had already gone too far and any delay would gravely endanger the entire plan. Too many prisoners already knew about the planned uprising and about its leaders, and it could leak out to the German camp authorities at any moment. Pechersky insisted on carrying out the plan and ordered Czepik to take Tsibulsky and his men to Camp II using any excuse he could muster. At twenty past three, Czepik entered the barrack where Leitman was working and took Tsibulsky and two other men with him to Camp II.[4] Upon their arrival in the warehouse in Camp II, Feldhendler briefed them and gave his final directions.

The quiet liquidation of the SS staff in the camp started around 15:30. There are many contradictions in the testimonies about who killed whom, as well as about the sites and sequence of the liquidation action. The four SS men who usually worked in Camp II had to be killed between 15:30 and 16:00. Feldhendler, who was in charge of the operation in Camp II, had based his plan on the greed of the SS men for goods in the warehouse where the property of the victims was sorted and prepared for transport. The SS men frequently visited these storerooms and selected clothes and valuables for themselves or for their families. They asked prisoners who worked there to find them special items and to call them when something of value turned up.

According to Feldhendler's plan, Tsibulsky and his team would take up their hidden positions inside the storeroom and then the SS men would be invited, one by one, by one of the *putzers* to try on a new leather coat.

The first SS man invited into the storeroom was *Unterscharführer* Josef Wulf. He did not suspect a thing. When he entered the storeroom, everything looked normal. There were some prisoners piling the clothes in bins. One of them approached Wulf with a coat, another prisoner stood behind him to help him into it. At that moment, Tsibulsky and another prisoner of war stepped out of their hiding place behind a bin and cracked Wulf's head with their axes. Wulf fell without a sound. The dead body was dragged into a bin and covered with clothes. The blood on the floor was covered with sand. Wulf's pistol was taken by Tsibulsky.

The die was cast, the first SS man had been killed—the underground had crossed the point of no return. The prisoners in the barrack who were not members of the underground only then became aware of what was happening. To prevent any leaks about the killing, Feldhendler forbade any of the prisoners to leave the barrack. An underground member was posted as guard at the entrance to the warehouse.[5]

Another prisoner, Tovia Blatt, who knew about the uprising, was sent to guard the entrance gate to Camp II. That gate was usually guarded by prisoners, whose duty it was to prevent free movement of other prisoners and removal of clothes and other goods from the warehouse to Camp I. That afternoon a Dutch Jew was guarding the gate. It was Blatt's duty to ensure that this Dutch Jew would not find out what was going on in the nearby storeroom and sound an alarm.

A few minutes after Wulf's death, *Scharführer* Kurt Beckman, who was in charge of the camp office located in the administration building in Camp II, passed close to the warehouse. A young *putzer* approached him and asked whether he wanted a new leather jacket that seemed to be made just for him. He was asked to come to the warehouse to try it on. For a moment the SS man seemed to hesitate. He started to walk in the direction of the storeroom but then suddenly turned and walked to his office.[6]

Feldhendler sent the *putzer* Drescher, who could move freely between Camp I and Camp II, to report to Pechersky. Drescher came to the carpentry workshop and told Pechersky about the killing of Wulf and the unsuccessful attempt with Beckman. The time was close to four o'clock, and Pechersky had waited for this report before starting the action in Camp I. He told Drescher to go back and tell Feldhendler to handle Beckman as he saw fit and wished him success.[7]

The operation in Camp I started as planned at four o'clock. Exactly at that time the deputy commander of the camp, *Untersturmführer* Josef Niemann, rode his mare into Camp I and reined up in front of the bakery. He dismounted, left the horse to one of the prisoners, and entered the tailor shop. There Josef, the head of the tailor shop and a member of the Underground Committee, brought him his new uniform and began to take the fitting. At that moment, Shubayev approached from behind and hit Niemann on the head with an axe. Niemann died on the spot. His body was dragged into the back room and stuffed under a bunk, and the bloodstains on the floor were wiped away and covered. The presence of Niemann's horse close to the tailor shop for longer than the time needed for a uniform measurement could arouse suspicion, so one of the underground members took it to the stables.[8]

Shubayev came running to the carpentry and handed over Niemann's pistol to Pechersky. They embraced and kissed each other. Pechersky thanked him and said, "Even if someone would want to turn back, it would be impossible for him." Shubayev returned to the tailor shop, where other SS men were scheduled to arrive.[9]

After Shubayev's departure, Pechersky's girlfriend Luka came to the carpentry workshop. Pechersky told her what was happening, to be ready for escape within half an hour, and to change into men's clothes. Although she had been very close to Pechersky, he had never revealed to her the preparations until that very last minute. Luka was surprised about the uprising and expressed her fears for the outcome. She embraced Pechersky, burst into tears, and left. After a short time, she returned dressed in men's clothes.[10]

The liquidation of the SS men was gaining momentum. *Oberscharführer* Goettinger, who was in charge of Camp III, came into the shoemaker's shop. Jakub, the head of the shop and a member of the Underground Committee, handed him a pair of boots and asked him to try them on. Goettinger asked Jakub to prepare a pair of slippers for his wife, which he would take with him when he left for leave to Germany within the next five days. While the conversation was going on, Arkady Vaispapir approached from behind and smashed Goettinger's head with an axe.[11]

The next one to be killed in the tailor shop was *Scharführer* Greischutz, the commander of the Ukrainian guard in the entire camp. Even though he was an SS man, he used the Ukrainian tailor shop, where he got high priority from the Jewish tailors. Yehuda Lerner testified:

My assignment was to liquidate *Scharführer* Greischutz, who was in charge of the Ukrainian guard. I was happy for the opportunity given to me to kill a

German. We had prepared axes, which we had sharpened in the smithy. We took up our position an hour earlier. At four o'clock we were sitting in the rooms and waited. According to the plan the first one to arrive was Niemann. He came in time and entered the room where the tailors working for the Germans were sitting. . . . Five minutes later the German entered that I and my friend awaited. He said that he hoped his winter overcoat was ready. The tailor brought the coat and started to fit it on him. It turned out that the German was closer to me than to my friend. I was sitting and sewing a button on a coat for a Ukrainian and the axe was between my legs. I got up, keeping the coat over the axe, approached the SS man from behind and split his head. . . . We put the body beneath the table the tailors were working at.[12]

Shortly afterward, the Ukrainian Klat was killed.[13] In Camp II, the action continued. Two more SS men came into the warehouse and were killed there. One of them was Steubel.[14] In this part of the camp, only *Scharführer* Beckman, who was in his office in the forester's house, still remained. Time was running out; it was close to roll call. Feldhendler decided that they could wait no longer. If Beckman would not come to the warehouse, he had to be killed in his own office. Capo Pozyczka's younger brother and two other underground members were sent by Feldhendler to carry out this mission. The young Pozyczka knocked on the office door and asked Beckman's permission to enter to discuss some problem that had come up in the warehouse. Beckman, who knew Pozyczka, told him to enter. He was quite surprised to find that, in addition to Pozyczka, two more Jews entered the room. But it was too late. They caught him and stabbed him to death with daggers. Beckman's body remained behind the desk, as there was no time to hide it.[15]

The next task imposed on Feldhendler was to cut the telephone wires leading from the administration building to outside the camp and to disconnect the electricity of the camp. This was carried out by Schwartz, an electrician from Czechoslovakia.[16] With this, the operation in Camp II was completed. To keep the action secret, Feldhendler and his men had not permitted any prisoners to leave either the warehouse or the area of Camp II. He waited for the sound of the bugle from the forester's tower, the signal for the end of work and the evening roll call.

At a quarter to five Tsibulsky returned to Camp I. He excitedly reported to Pechersky that all four SS men in Camp II had been finished off, the telephone wires had been cut, and the electricity was off permanently.[17]

Capo Pozyczka, who was in Camp IV, returned with the prisoners who had been chopping wood there. He was heading for the carpentry workshop, followed by *Scharführer* Friedrich Gaulstich. Leitman, who was in the vicinity, turned to Gaulstich and asked him to come in the barrack where he and his men were working, because he needed his advice to continue the work. Gaulstich went into the barrack. Capo Schmidt, who was also there, wanted to enter the barrack in case Gaulstich needed him. But Pechersky, who had observed the scene from the carpentry workshop, ran over to Pozyczka and told him to prevent Schmidt from entering the barrack. Pozyczka took Schmidt by the arm, told him what was going on and that if he wanted to remain alive, not to go inside. Schmidt was struck speechless by the news but remained outside. In the meantime, inside the barrack, Leitman axed Gaulstich to death.[18]

Around five o'clock Shlomo Szmajzner, with the help of two *putzers*, removed from the Ukrainian barracks six rifles inside a pipe, wrapped in a blanket. No Ukrainians or Germans were around. He marched through the gate of Camp II toward the kitchen, where he delivered the rifles to the underground members. One rifle he left for himself. He also brought some cartridges with him.[19]

Pechersky was informed that Engel, a locksmith, had killed *Unterscharführer* Walter Ryba when he came into the garage where Engel was working that day. The killing in the garage had not been planned by the underground. It was a private, impulsive action by Engel, and Pechersky was worried that the body of Walter Ryba in the garage close to the living quarters of the SS men and Ukrainians had not been camouflaged and at any moment it could be discovered.[20]

For about an hour and a half, from 15:30 to 17:00, the uprising action had been carried out according to plan. Most of the SS men had been liquidated, among them three key persons: Niemann, the acting commander of the camp; Greischutz, the commander of the Ukrainian guard; and Goettinger, the commander of Camp III. The prisoners had armed themselves with pistols taken from the killed SS men and the rifles brought by Szmajzner. Up to that moment, the Ukrainians who were in guard positions and those on the watchtowers, from where they had complete visibility of all corners of the camp, had not discovered or suspected any unusual activity in the camp. In fact, the German and Ukrainian staff was now leaderless—with the exception of Frenzel, who was still somewhere in the camp. According to the plan, Frenzel was to come to the carpentry to check on a new cupboard. Semion Rosenfeld was waiting for him there, but Frenzel did not arrive. Rosenfeld testified: "On the day of the uprising, Pechersky called me and gave me an assignment. I had to kill Frenzel when he came to the carpentry workshop at 4:00 or 4:30 to receive new cupboards. I prepared myself thoroughly for this task: I sharpened the axe and selected the proper place to carry out the mortal blow. But the scoundrel did not come. Until today I am sorry for that."[21]

At five o'clock in the afternoon, as the time for the evening roll call approached, Pechersky faced a dilemma: whether to wait for Frenzel, the last remaining SS man who could organize the Ukrainians for an action against the prisoners and an immediate pursuit after their escape or to go ahead with the plan, leaving Frenzel alive. By that time it was difficult to keep the prisoners quiet as the tension was so high. Most of them already knew about the killings, and at any moment the underground could lose control over the events. Capo Pozyczka was now with Pechersky and could sound the signal for the end of work and assembly for the roll call. The killing of Walter Ryba in the garage disturbed Pechersky because it was clear that it would become known very soon. Leitman, who was with Pechersky, urged him not to wait any longer for Frenzel but to immediately begin the next stage of the uprising—the roll call and march toward the gate. It was already after five, and Pechersky decided not to wait any longer. Leitman sent a messenger to Feldhendler in Camp II to inform him of the decision, and Pechersky ordered Pozyczka to carry out his part of the plan. Yehuda the barber climbed the forester tower and blew the bugle—the signal for the whole camp to stop work and gather for roll call.[22]

Feldhendler lined up the prisoners in Camp II. It was difficult to organize them into an orderly column similar to the everyday routine march at the end of work because of the tension. But slowly they started to move in the direction of Camp I. Dov Freiberg, who was among the prisoners in Camp II, described the march: "When we marched to Camp I we were singing a German song in order not to provoke any suspicion. . . . We arrived there after all the other groups had already gathered. There was great excitement. Some of the Jews were armed with rifles and pistolets. . . . A Jewish boy climbed the Forester Tower and trumpeted for the roll call.[23]

Pechersky described what happened in Camp I after the signal for roll call was given:

> People came streaming from all sides. We had previously selected seventy men, nearly all of them Soviet prisoners of war, whose task it was to attack the armory. That was why they were in the forefront of the column. But all the others, who had only suspected that something was being arranged but didn't know when and how, now found out at the last minute. They began to push and jostle forward, fearing they might be left behind. In this disorderly fashion we reached the gate of Camp I.
>
> A squad commander, a German from Near-Volga, approached us. "Hey, you sons-of-bitches," he shouted, "didn't you hear the whistle? So why are you pushing like a bunch of cattle? Get in line, three in a row!"
>
> As though in response to a command, several hatchets suddenly appeared from under coats and came down on his head.

At that moment, the column from Camp II was advancing toward us. Several women, shaken by the unexpected scene, began to scream. One prisoner was on the verge of fainting. Another began to run blindly, without any direction. It was clear that under these circumstances it would be impossible to line up the people in an orderly column.

"Comrades, forward!" I called out loud.

"Forward!" Someone on my right picked up the slogans.

"For our Fatherland, forward!"

The slogans reverberated like thunder in the death camp, and united Jews from Russia, Poland, Holland, France, Czechoslovakia, and Germany. Six hundred pain-wracked, tormented people, surged forward with a wild "hurrah" to life and freedom.[24]

According to the plan, a group of prisoners under the command of Nachum Plotnicky and Alexey Vaitsen were supposed to penetrate the armory and take control of the arms there. This attack prompted some controversial testimonies. According to Pechersky, "The attack on the armory did not succeed; a barrage of automatic fire cut us off."[25] In truth, the initial stage of the attack did succeed, and the prisoners penetrated the armory. *Scharführer* Werner Dubois, who was in charge of the armory, testified:

> On the day of the uprising, in the afternoon, I was in the armory together with some Ukrainian guardsmen. The door was open. I saw a group of Jewish prisoners with axes approaching the armory. I thought that this was an ordinary working group. This group of five or six men passed by the armory. They went around the armory, crashed into the room, and hit me with axes. My skull was fractured with an axe. Other axe blows wounded my hands. In spite of it, I succeeded in extricating myself and escaping outside the armory. After running about 10 meters, I was shot in the lung and lost consciousness. Some Ukrainian guards treated me with vodka and I returned to consciousness. Then I learned that an uprising had broken out.[26]

Mordechai Goldfarb, who was with the attacking group, described what was happening in the armory: "Four of us ran to the armory. . . . There was an SS man. . . . He wanted to shoot at us, but Boris threw sand into his eyes, we jumped at him and killed him. We grabbed some rifles and ran to the fence."[27]

A short time before the sound of the bugle announced the end of work, a truck with provisions and liquor driven by *Scharführer* Erich Bauer returned to camp and drove in the direction of the forester's house. Crossing close to Camp I, Bauer came across two prisoners, Jakub Biskubicz and David, who were repairing the gate of Camp I. He ordered them to follow the truck to unload it. The truck stopped in front of the forester's house in Camp II. Biskubicz testified: "As we were unloading the first box from the truck, we saw inside the forester house a German whom we stabbed in the back. As we were taking the second box, a Ukrainian came running and called to Bauer, 'A German is dead.' Bauer did not immediately understand what he meant. But David, who had heard it, started to run in the direction of Camp I. Bauer shot at him twice and ran after him. I remained alone. Then I heard a cry, 'Hurrah!' from Camp I and shooting."[28]

At that point, the "quiet" part of the uprising came to an end. The killing of the *Volksdeutsche*, a squad commander of the Ukrainians, which took place in the open, close to the gate of Camp I, was spotted by the guards. When the attack on the armory was carried out, in addition to the SS man Werner Dubois, who was badly wounded, there were some Ukrainians present. Automatic fire from a watchtower and some other directions was opened on the prisoners running toward the camp's main gate. *Scharführer* Frenzel, who until then had not been seen, came out from a barrack close to the main gate and opened automatic fire on the escaping prisoners.[29] The prisoners who had run through the gate killed the Ukrainian guard posted there, but further escape through the camp's main gate was cut off by the fire of Frenzel and some guards. The prisoners ran toward the fences and minefields. Pechersky and the other leaders of the uprising had lost all control over the events and the mass of prisoners, who were running in all directions. This was around 17:15.

With the escape through the main gate cut off by gunfire, the prisoners who were still in Camp I, which constituted the majority, ran toward the fences and minefields, south and southwest of the camp. The prisoners who were first to cross the minefields were killed or wounded. They remained lying in the field, just behind the fences. Those who followed them had clear passage through the minefields, because the mines had blown up with the first wave of escapees. Ada Lichtman wrote:

> Suddenly we heard shots. In the beginning only a few shots, and then it turned into heavy shooting, including machine-gun fire. We heard shouting, and I could see a group of prisoners running with axes, knives, scissors, cutting the fences and crossing them. Mines started to explode. Riot and confusion prevailed, everything was thundering around. The doors of the workshop were opened, and everyone rushed through. . . . We ran out of the workshop. All around were the bodies of the killed and wounded. Near the armory were some of our boys with weapons. Some of them were exchanging fire with the Ukrainians, others were running toward the gate or through the fences. My coat was caught on the fence. I took off the coat, freed myself and ran further behind the fences into the minefield. A mine exploded nearby, and I could see a body being lifted into the air and then falling down. I did not recognize who it was. Many were shot on the fences.

Behind the mines was a ditch, luckily without water. With the help of two other women, I crossed the ditch and reached the forest.[30]

Unterscharführer Franz Wulf, whose brother Josef had been the first one killed in the storeroom in Camp II, was also in the camp at the time. When the shooting started, he was accompanying a group of Jewish women who worked in the garden to Camp I. He testified: "I went into the garden between Camp I and Camp II. On the way back with the Jewish women, I suddenly heard shots. I ran to the office which was in the forester's house. I found Beckman and another member of the permanent staff there; both had been shot. I ran back to Camp II to the sorting barrack to find my brother. Later, when the shooting stopped, I ran to the guard in the Forward Camp. There were more dead and Werner Dubois, who was badly wounded."[31]

When the shooting started it was already dusk. At least two SS men, Frenzel and Bauer, and about a dozen Ukrainians who were on guard duty opened fire from machine guns, rifles, and pistols on the escaping prisoners. The most dangerous gunfire was from the two watchtowers in the southern corners of the camp. From these towers the Ukrainians had full control of gunfire on Camp I, on the Forward Camp, and on the southern fences and camp's gate—all the places through which the prisoners tried to escape. Those underground members who were armed returned fire, trying to silence the guards on the watchtowers and cover the escape of the prisoners. Pechersky described the situation at this stage:

The guards on the watchtower opened intensive machine-gun fire on the escaping prisoners. The guards who were at and between the barbed-wire fences joined them. Yanek the carpenter aimed and shot at the guards on the watchtower. The machine gun fell silent. The locksmith Henrick used the captured submachine gun to silence the gunner from the second watchtower. But this machine gun continued to fire incessantly. The remaining SS men tried with automatic fire to cut off the way of the crowd of prisoners. . . . The main body of the prisoners turned toward the fences of Camp I. Some ran directly over to the minefields. According to the plan, stones and planks had to be thrown on the mines to explode them, but in the confusion nobody did it. Many found their death there, but they paved the way to freedom for the prisoners who followed them. A special group started to cut the fences close to the house where the commander of the camp lived. . . . When I passed by this house, I saw Frenzel crouching behind another house and shooting with a submachine gun. I shot at him twice with my pistol but missed him. I did not stop. A large group of prisoners under the command of Leitman tried to cross the barbed-wire fences close to the main gate. The guards on the watchtower aimed his fire on Leitman's group. I was one of the last to leave the camp.[32]

Pechersky's assumption that the field behind the camp commander's house was not mined was correct. He and the prisoners with him reached the forest without crossing any mines.

The first stage of the uprising—the quiet liquidation of the majority of the SS staff in the camp, among them the commanding officers—had been accomplished successfully. The only exception was Frenzel. However, the second stage of the uprising, the "ordinary" roll call and march toward the gate, was not carried out according to plan. A combination of events— among them the survival of Frenzel, the killing of the *Volksdeutsche* Kaiser near the gate of Camp I, which was seen by the Ukrainian guards, and the unexpected return to the camp of Erich Bauer—contributed to the fact that the second stage of the plan was carried out only in part. And although the leaders of the uprising had taken into account such a development and had formulated an alternative escape route through the fences and minefields, this alternative was not planned in detail. It remained more of a general idea than a true plan of action. Therefore, when the shooting began and the majority of prisoners began running in their confusion in all directions, the underground leadership lost control. Still, over half of the prisoners, about three hundred out of the six hundred who were in the main camp, succeeded in the evening twilight in crossing the fences and minefields and escaping into the forests.

PURSUIT AND ESCAPE FROM SOBIBOR

DISORDER AND CHAOS PREVAILED IN the camp until late into the night of October 14. The darkness that fell over the camp soon after the mass escape of the prisoners and the lack of electricity, which had been cut off by the rebels, made it very difficult for the few remaining SS men to take control and reinstate order in the camp. Only two of the five surviving SS men, Karl Frenzel and Erich Bauer, were active. Werner Dubois was wounded, and the two others, Franz Wulf and Willi Wendland, were somewhere in hiding during those hours. It took Frenzel and Bauer two to three hours to organize the Ukrainians and to gather part of the prisoners who had remained in the camp and lock them up in a barrack under strong guard. In the camp there were still prisoners who continued to resist; some of them were armed with axes or firearms. Searches were conducted to locate the killed SS men and hours passed until their bodies were discovered and gathered in one place.

While all this was going on, efforts were also made to contact the German security forces, who were stationed in the vicinity of Sobibor, request their help in restoring order in the camp, and organize a pursuit after the escape. However, only close to eight o'clock in the evening did Frenzel and Bauer succeed in reestablishing telephone communication with the outside world and issuing a call for help.

This call reached the SS, police, and army units stationed in the city of Chelm, forty kilometers south of Sobibor, since the area of Sobibor was under the administrative and security jurisdiction of the German authorities of Chelm. The first to arrive at Sobibor was a small unit of border police, which was in charge of the border between the General Government and the *Reichskommissariat* Ukraine and subordinate to the security police and SD. This unit numbered seven SS men under the command of SS *Untersturmführer* Adalbert Benda. They, with the help of the Ukrainian guards in the camp, succeeded in overcoming the last of the resisting prisoners and restoring control inside the camp. Benda wrote in his report: "The operation commando sent from the Border Police Commissariat in

Chelm combed the separate sub-camps inside the camp. Our men were fired at many times by the prisoners caught in the camp during the night of October 15, 1943, and in the early hours of October 16. [It should be October 14, 1943, and in the early hours of October 15. This report was submitted on March 17, 1944, and the dates given are mistakes.] During the combing of the camp itself, arms were used because the prisoners resisted arrest. A great number of prisoners were shot."[1]

Jakub Biskubicz, a prisoner who did not succeed in escaping with the bulk of the prisoners and who remained inside Camp II until late at night, testified:

> All the prisoners escaped. I remained alone.... I jumped over a 2 meter fence and reached the warehouse. It became dark, because in October night fell early; therefore the bullet fired in my direction didn't hit me. Until midnight I lay on the earth. I could hear shouts and screams from all directions. At midnight, I heard shooting close to me and the voices of Germans saying: "Nobody is here." They left. ... I reached Camp IV. I saw the open door of a watchtower. Nobody was around. I climbed the ladder of the tower and jumped outside over the fences and mines. I fell on the railway and escaped to the forest.[2]

Few of those who remained in the camp were as lucky as Biskubicz. About 150 were caught and locked into a barrack under a strong guard of Ukrainians. At midnight, the first squadron (company size) of the Mounted SS and Police Regiment III stationed in Chelm arrived by train to Sobibor as reinforcements. The commander of this squadron, Captain of the Security Police Erich Wullbrandt, testified:

> When I returned to Chelm from an operation against partisans in the Lublin district, I received an order to continue immediately to Sobibor. From the order it was clear that an uprising had taken place in the Jewish camp of Sobibor.... From the order we understood that the guards [in the camp] were still in danger; therefore, the commander of the Mounted Regiment III, Security Police Major Eggert, personally assumed command of our unit. It was feared that the Jews who had escaped would attack the camp to liberate the prisoners who remained there. To prevent such an eventuality, and for the safety of the Germans in the camp, our squadron, under my and Major Eggert's command, left for the operation.... Upon our arrival at the railway station of Sobibor, at the entrance to the camp, we were briefed by two members of the Waffen SS [Frenzel and Bauer] about the event.... When we arrived, we found that the corpses of the killed German members of the SS had been collected in one barrack. I personally saw the corpses. I think there were thirteen corpses in that room. ... According to the estimate at that time, about 50 percent of the prisoners had succeeded in escaping. The

remaining Jews were kept in their barracks. The watchtowers were manned by the foreign auxiliaries [Ukrainians]. . . . In the morning, the Jewish prisoners who [had been] shot [during the uprising] by the auxiliaries inside the camp were removed to one place. Their corpses were laid at the railway spur of the camp.[3]

The call for help from Sobibor also reached Security Battalion 689 of the German army, stationed in Chelm. This battalion was responsible for the security of military installations, including railways and bridges, and also for fighting the partisans who operated in the district. The battalion was subordinate to the military commander of the Lublin district, Lieutenant General Hilmar Moser. The commander of this battalion, Major Hans Wagner, testified:

The deputy camp commander [of Sobibor] telephoned battalion headquarters at 20:00 hours on October 14 and called for urgent armed help. The call was received by the battalion adjutant, First Lieutenant Wiertz. The deputy commander reported . . . that the Jewish prisoners had seized the camp armory and that out of the twenty-nine German SS officers and soldiers twelve were on vacation in Germany and out of the remaining seventeen SS men twelve had already been killed by rebellious Jews. . . . According to this report, some of the Ukrainian guards had collaborated with the rebels, but the majority of them had remained faithful. They, under the command of the surviving Germans, stood in desperate battle against the mutinous prisoners, most of whom had already escaped to the forests. I refused to extend armed help. Under no circumstances did I want to have anything to do with this camp and its organization. . . . About fifteen minutes later, the military commander of Chelm, a major in the German army, called and ordered me to send armed help immediately.

I again refused to extend help. . . . I have to note that for a long time there was a standing general order from the Area Military Commander from Cracow (General Haenicke, the commander of the military forces in the General Government) which stated that the German army, the Police and the SS had to extend help to each other in times of emergency without a specific order. Under such circumstances, the local military commander was empowered and obliged to issue orders and utilize those army units that were in his zone of operation.

After my refusal, the military commander of Chelm turned to our common military superior, the military commander of the Lublin district, General Moser. The general called me fifteen minutes later. Even to him I expressed my objection to extend help. He didn't order me, but said that he would turn to the Area Military Commander (in Cracow) to ascertain how the army should act in such a case. About a quarter of an hour later, General Moser informed me by telephone that the Area Military Commander, General Haenicke, said that we cannot forsake the fighting SS men and ordered that my battalion, with all its available forces, extend the requested help. . . . I could no longer refuse. I assigned a company of eighty men (not 100) under the command of Captain Wulf, the commander of company 4. . . . This unit arrived at the camp of Sobibor in the early morning (of October 15). By that time, the camp authorities had already quelled the uprising with its own forces, namely, with the Ukrainian guards. Most of the Jewish prisoners escaped; the remaining few hundred were surrounded.[4]

The killing of eleven SS men and two or three Ukrainians and *Volksdeutsche* guards, in addition to several wounded, produced turmoil among the German authorities in the General Government and was reported to the highest authorities in Berlin. It was a rare—and perhaps the only—case where prisoners, Jews or non-Jews, had revolted and had succeeded in a single action in liquidating such a large number of SS men.

A group of high-ranking SS officials headed by SS *Gruppenführer* Jacob Sporrenberg, the SS and police leader of the Lublin district who was put in charge of the camps after Odilo Globocnik left, and SS *Hauptsturmführer* Hermann Höfle arrived in Sobibor on the afternoon of October 15. After their arrival they received reports from Frenzel and from the commanders of the units who were carrying out the search and pursuit operation. Later they inspected the corpses of the killed SS men. Sporrenberg ordered the execution of all the remaining Jewish prisoners in the camp. There were at least 150 of them.

There were also prisoners in Camp III who had known nothing about the uprising until the shooting broke out. These prisoners were also killed, but whether they were included in the number of 150 or were in addition is unclear. All the prisoners who were in Sobibor that day were shot in Camp III by the Ukrainian guards at the command of the SS men. The shooting was carried out late in the afternoon of October 15.[5] This execution was the immediate response and revenge of the Nazi authorities to the slaying of the SS men and Ukrainians.

The pursuit of and searches for the escaping prisoners began in the morning hours of October 15. The German forces included a company of Army Security Battalion 689 and the First Squadron of the mounted SS and police, units of the border police, and Ukrainian guards from Sobibor. The Second Squadron of the mounted SS and police, which was operating in the sector of the Bug River, joined the forces engaged in the searches on October 16. Some units of the Third Squadron of the mounted SS and police joined the search forces later. The total strength of these forces reached between four hundred and five hundred soldiers and SS men. In addition, local police units in the nearby townships were alerted to carry out searches in their neighborhoods.[6]

According to the operation plan, the Second Squadron of the mounted SS and police and the border police units blocked the bridges and crossing points on the Bug River, which ran east of Sobibor. This part of the operation was to prevent the escaping prisoners from crossing the river and joining the Soviet partisans who were active there. The other forces encircled the entire area from the north, west, and south and combed the forests. The German air force, the Luftwaffe, allocated some airplanes to help the operating forces spot the escaping prisoners and guide the pursuers in the right direction. Whether there was a unified command over the whole operation or whether the army units and the SS forces operated separately, each with its own sector of activity, is difficult to establish.[7]

The fact that the searches and pursuit only started on the morning of October 15 gave the prisoners the entire night for an undisturbed head start. During the breakout from the camp, people ran in any direction they could in the hope of reaching the nearest forest and getting as far away as possible from Sobibor. After covering some distance from the camp, the individual escapees and small groups merged into larger groups, some of them numbering dozens of prisoners. But the prisoners were not familiar with the surrounding area of Sobibor, nor did they know in which direction to run. In some cases, after running the whole night, in the morning they discovered that they had run in a circle and were still very close to the camp.[8]

The large-scale search and pursuit action, in which all the German security forces stationed in the area of Sobibor took part, lasted four days, from the morning of October 15 until the evening of October 18. During October 19–21, the two mounted squadrons of the SS and police and a platoon of the security police from Lublin continued combing actions west of Sobibor in the forests of Dubeczno-Hansk and north of Chelm.[9] The main problem of the escaping prisoners during that period was to evade the German forces and get out of the area of the combing actions. Alexander Pechersky describes the escape of the prisoner group he was leading:

For some time we continued to hear shots from rifles and automatic weapons. This helped us orient ourselves. We knew that there, behind us, was the camp. Gradually the shooting became more distant, until it died down altogether.

It was already dark when shooting broke out again from the right. It sounded distant and faint.

I proposed that we continue going all through the night, and that we should go in a single file, one behind the other. I would be in front. Behind me, [Boris] Tsibulsky. Arkady [Vaispapir] would close the line. No smoking; no talking; no falling behind; no running ahead. If the man in front lies down, all would do the same. If a rocket flared up, all would lie down at once. There must be no panic no matter what happened.

We were out of the woods. For about 3 kilometers we walked through an open field. Then our path was blocked by a canal about 5 to 6 meters wide. The canal was deep, and it was impossible to wade through it, so we walked along the shore of the canal. Suddenly I noticed a group of people about 50 meters away. We all lay down at once. Arkady was given the task of investigating who they were.

At first he crawled on his belly; then he rose and ran up to the group. A few minutes later he returned. "Sasha, they're ours," he announced. "They found wooden stumps lying by the shore and are crossing over to the other side. Kalimali [Shubayev] is with them." We all crossed over the canal on these wooden stumps.

Shubayev had no news about Luka, but he had seen Shlomo [Leitman]. He said Shlomo was wounded before he managed to get into the woods. He had continued to run for a distance of about 3 kilometers and then his strength gave out. He begged to be shot.

What horrible, painful news that was! To break out of the camp and on the way to freedom to remain lying helpless.

By now our group numbered fifty-seven people. We covered another 5 kilometers and then heard the rumble of a passing train. Before us lay a broad open stretch of land, sparsely covered with short shrubs. We stopped. It was getting close to dawn, time to give some thought to the question of where we should spend the day. It was clear that the Germans would be pursuing us during the day. The woods in these parts were not very thick and could be easily combed in all directions.

I talked it over with Tsibulsky and Shubayev, and it was decided that the best thing to do would be to scatter around the bushes, precisely because it was an open space, not far from a railway line. Therefore it wouldn't occur to anyone to look for us there. But we would have to camouflage ourselves well, lie motionless, and not utter a sound. Before we took to the bushes, I sent out a few people to comb through them carefully for some distance on all sides. Throughout the day airplanes circled overhead, some quite low over the bushes where we lay. We heard the voices of the Poles who worked on the railway. Our people lay glued to the ground, covered with branches. No one moved until it grew dark. That's how the first day of our freedom passed. It was October 15, 1943.

Night fell. As we rose from our places, we noticed two figures approaching us. They moved cautiously. We guessed at once that they were our people. It turned out they had already been as far as the Bug and were now returning from there.

"Why didn't you cross?" we asked.

They reported that they had entered a hamlet not far from the river and were told that Germans had arrived at the shore during the night and that all crossings were heavily guarded.

We walked in single file, in the same order as yesterday: Tsibulsky and I were in front; Skubayev and Arkady were the last in line. After walking for about 5 kilometers we entered the woods and stopped.

It made no sense to continue together in so large a group. We would be too conspicuous. Also, it would be impossible to provide food for so many people. Therefore we divided ourselves into small groups, each going its own way.

My group consisted of nine people, including Shubayev, Boris Tsibulsky, Arkady Vaispapir, Michael ltzkowitch, Semion Mazurkiewitch. We headed east, with the polar stars as our compass. The nights were starry. Our first aim was to cross the Bug. To do that we had to find the proper place and the proper time. In quiet, deserted hamlets we obtained food and received vital information and directions. We were warned which places to avoid and where it would be advisable to stay over because there had been a breakout from the Sobibor camp, where people were being burned, and the Germans were combing the entire area in search of the escapees. We started out for the Stawki hamlets, about 1.5 kilometers from the Bug.[10]

Pechersky's departure raised fear and resentment among the remaining fifty prisoners. He and his men, all from the Minsk transport, took with them most of the group's weapons and the rest were left with one rifle; they felt themselves forsaken and leaderless. Tovia Blatt, who was with this group, claims that Pechersky did not even tell them he was leaving, but that he said he was going to reconnoiter the area and would soon return. Some other testimonies of survivors confirm Blatt's version.[11]

The fate of the remaining Jews after Pechersky and his group left is related by Shlomo Alster, a Polish Jew:

Sasha's people left us and went away. We remained without a leader. What could we do? Without arms and without a man to lead us. Together with us were French, Dutch, and Czechoslovakian Jews. They could not find their way without knowing the language and the surroundings. Like us, they also divided themselves into small groups. They went out to the road, which was full of SS men, and all of them were caught alive. Also the local people caught them one by one and brought them to Sobibor, where they were liquidated. None of them survived.

We, the Polish Jews, remained a small group. What should we do? To stay in the forest was dangerous, because either the Germans or the local people would catch us. We had to get away from this place, and from Sobibor—as far as possible. But this was not so simple—where could we go? I was hungry, my clothes were torn to pieces. I decided to go back to my native town, to Chelm, maybe there I could find some chance of survival. I couldn't see any other alternative.[12]

Pechersky's assumption that it would be almost impossible to find hiding places and food and escape the pursuing forces with a group of fifty-nine people was correct. Even well-armed partisan units who knew the area well split into small units when faced with the combing actions of larger German forces. Therefore, Pechersky's decision to split into small groups was justified from the military point of view. However, the few arms they possessed could have been divided among all the groups. Even one weapon in a group could be of help in obtaining food and sometimes even a deterrent to the local people who collaborated with the Germans.

Pechersky and his group succeeded in crossing the Bug River on the night of October 19–20, and three days later they met Soviet partisans in the area of Brest-Litovsk and joined up with them.[13]

Leon Feldhendler and a group of prisoners succeeded in hiding in the forest during the days when the German forces combed the whole area. Some other groups from among the Polish Jews also succeeded in avoiding the search units.[14]

It was a tremendous achievement on the part of the Jewish prisoners who did manage to get away, despite the relatively large ground forces involved in the operation, aided by air reconnaissance. Several factors contributed to the prisoners' success. The searches, which began only in the morning hours, allowed enough time for many prisoners to slip away from the camp area. The heavy woods in the region also hampered the searches from the planes. Furthermore, the Germans were mistaken in supposing that most of the escaped prisoners would head east to the Bug and therefore in stationing substantial forces at the Bug crossing points. In fact, most of them, especially the Polish Jews, headed into the General Government areas.

Of about three hundred Jews who escaped from Sobibor, one hundred were caught and shot during the four days that followed the uprising. All the others survived the pursuit action. In the monthly report of the First Mounted Squadron of the SS and police, which participated in this operation, it was stated: "In the period 14/10-18/10/43, the squadron took part in the operation against the Jews at the SS *Sonderkommando* Sobibor (40 km northeast of Chelm). From the number of 300 Jews who escaped, about 100 were liquidated in cooperation with the army and Border Police."[15] A few more of the escaping prisoners were caught during October 19–21.[16]

In view of the large German forces that were involved in the combing operations, which were even supported by airplanes, the search could not have been considered a success. Only one-third of the fleeing prisoners were caught. The rest escaped.

SURVIVAL AMONG THE LOCAL POPULATION

THE JEWISH PRISONERS WHO ESCAPED during the uprisings in Treblinka and Sobibor and were not caught in the first days of intensive searches faced the very serious problem of how to survive for a prolonged period in an area occupied by the Germans. Their success depended to a large extent on the attitude of the local population—first in the vicinity of the camps and later in the more distant areas of the General Government.

The local population in the areas around Treblinka and Sobibor was predominantly Polish, although there were some Ukrainian and Belorussian villages, mainly to the east of these camps. The escaping prisoners needed help to obtain food and to secure information about the surroundings, the whereabouts and activities of the local police and German security forces, and the safest direction to follow. They needed temporary shelter and places for more prolonged hiding. And the cooperation of the local population was important for Jews wishing to make contact with the partisans.

The escapees' fate was in the hands of peasants they happened upon while escaping through the fields, in the forests, or when they passed their houses. The peasants had the power to decide whether or not to turn the escapees over to the Germans, to use violence to capture and hand them over to the Germans, or to kill them by themselves. To encourage the aid of the local population, the Germans informed the peasants through the heads of the villages that anyone helping Jews would be harshly punished, and might even suffer the death penalty; and, on the other hand, they announced that anyone who captured and turned over a Jew or volunteered information as to the whereabouts of a Jew would get a special reward that included vodka and sugar.[1]

However, the attitude of the local population toward escaping prisoners was not only a function of the reward or punishment that they might receive from the Germans but also a result of the general prejudice against Jews. Anti-Semitism had deep roots in Poland, and the hatred toward the Jews was merely intensified by Nazi propaganda.

The general attitude and prevailing feelings toward the Jews among large segments of the Polish population at that time may be gleaned from the Polish underground newspaper *Narod* ("People"), a publication of *Unia* ("Unity"), a politically centrist, liberal, intellectual group, represented in the Polish Government-in-Exile, in London. On August 15, 1942, in the midst of the expulsion of the Jews from Warsaw to Treblinka, this underground publication printed a long article under the headline "The Slaughter of the Jews." The article was a critical survey of the relationship of the Polish Jews to Poland and the Poles. The Jews were blamed for their ingratitude of Poland's hospitality to them for many generations. They were described as a nation that regarded itself as a "Chosen People" similar to Nazi Germany. The Jews were accused of infiltrating Polish society in the period between the two world wars and defiling it by "Judaization." Furthermore, they were unfaithful to Poland when the Soviet Union attacked in September 1939. In general, the Jews were charged with hating Poland. In the last part of the article, it stated:

> If this will continue, within a short period, Warsaw will say good-bye to the last Jew. If it would be possible to conduct a funeral, the reaction would be interesting. Would sorrow or tears accompany the coffins, or perhaps joy? . . . The northern quarter [the part of Warsaw where the Jews lived] was inhabited for hundreds of years by hostile strangers. Hostile and strange both to our interests and mentality and hearts. Let us not show false feelings, unlike at funerals [where there are] professional mourners, let us be earnest and honest. . . . For the individual Jew human being, we feel sorry, and, if possible, let's extend help to the stray or hiding. . . . But let us not strive for an artificial sorrow for the dying nation that was not close to our hearts. In face of the execution of the verdict of history, let us be serious and honest.[2]

From this article it most definitely could be understood by the simple Pole that getting rid of a disloyal and hostile element is for the good of Poland. As this message was not published by an anti-Semitic party but by an intellectual liberal group, its view may definitely be seen as an expression of the true feelings toward the Jews by large segments of the Polish people. In this atmosphere, the escaping Jews could not expect widespread aid from the local population.

As mentioned previously, sections of the population in the areas around the death camps had grown rich as a result of the Jewish tragedy. The Ukrainian guards, who had taken large amounts of money and valuables from the victims, spent equally large amounts on vodka and girls in the nearby villages (see chapter 22). This newfound prosperity was an additional factor that encouraged the local people to cooperate with the German security forces. Even in areas distant from the camps, large sections of the local population had received—or taken over—houses, businesses, and property that had formerly belonged to Jews and which the Jews had had to leave behind when they were deported to the ghettos and death camps. Some of these local people were afraid that if the Jews survived, all this property would have to be returned to its rightful owners. In short, those who had escaped from the death camps were likely to be greeted with hostility when they sought sanctuary.

The rumors that the escapees carried large quantities of gold and money also did not work in their favor. There were peasants who were tempted to murder the escapees and rob them of their money. Unfortunately, there are no testimonies left from those Jews who were turned over to the Germans by the peasants, or who were murdered by them—they had no way of immortalizing their stories. However, in the testimonies of survivors, who for the most part remained alive thanks to the help they received from the local population, there are details and descriptions of the hostile attitude of part of the local people.

Tovia Blatt describes what happened to him and to two other escapees from Sobibor—Kostman and Wycen—in their attempt to find sanctuary among the local population. Blatt led his friends from Sobibor to his hometown of Izbica, where he had hoped to find a hiding place for the three of them with Polish friends of his family. However, when they finally reached the place, their request was denied with the excuse—justified to some extent—that the Poles were afraid. After wandering some more in the area of Izbica, they found a hiding place in the home of a farmer named Bojarski. In return for a substantial payment in gold and valuables that the escapees had taken with them from Sobibor, Bojarski set up a hiding place in the barn. At first Bojarski treated them well, but then he began cutting back on the food that he gave them until they were down to starvation rations; on the other hand, he kept demanding more and more money. The situation became so bad that they finally decided to leave the hiding place and try to find the partisans, but Bojarski was against their leaving, claiming that if they were caught they would reveal his name and the Germans would take revenge on him and his family. Using various excuses, he removed part of their clothing, and they were in fact kept as prisoners. After about five and a half months in hiding and various unpleasant incidents, Bojarski decided to get rid of them.

On the night of April 23, 1944, Bojarski and another two armed men appeared at the opening of the hiding place, shined a flashlight inside, and shot the three prisoners. After they saw that they were all bleeding, and thinking that they were dead, they took the money and valuables and left the place. Kostman had been killed by the shots, but Blatt and Wycen were only injured and had merely pretended to be dead. After they saw that Bojarski and the other men had gone into a neighboring house, Blatt and Wycen ran away. Blatt lived to see the liberation. Wycen, however, did not make it.[3]

There were other cases of escaping prisoners trying to find refuge in the areas of their former residences, using their knowledge of the places and people. Shlomo Alster, who had lived in Chelm before his deportation to Sobibor, described what happened to him after his escape:

> I reached Chelm, and there I met two other escapees from Sobibor, Pawroznik and Lerer. We found shelter in a cellar. . . . Lerer had a lot of money, dollars, and gold with him. . . . Pawroznik had an acquaintance in the market and he bought food for us. . . . Thus we survived for nine months. . . . Nobody would have imagined that three Jews were sitting in the center of Chelm at a time when no more Jews lived in the entire region. . . . Afterward I and Pawroznik wandered in the countryside and found a hiding place in the corn-fields until the summer of 1944, when we were liberated by the Soviet army.[4]

Some escapees succeeded in reaching Warsaw or other large towns, where they acquired Aryan identity cards and "melted" into the local population. Jacob Wiernik reached Warsaw after his escape from Treblinka and survived there with the help of the "Jewish National Committee," which was an underground organization operating there. Hanel Salomea, a girl with an Aryan appearance who had escaped from Sobibor, reached Cracow and found refuge as a Christian in the house of the "League of Catholic Women," where they did not even suspect that she was Jewish.[5]

Two Czechoslovakian Jews who escaped from Treblinka (Richard Glazer and Karl Unger) succeeded in reaching Czechoslovakia, acquiring Aryan papers there, and using them to be sent to work in Germany as foreign workers.

However, there were those among the escapees who did not dare return to the places where they had lived or who knew from the start that they could expect no help there. They wandered through the forests and villages in the hope that perhaps in this way they would survive until the liberation. Abraham Goldfarb, who was among the escapees from Treblinka, related:

> We walked in the direction of Sokolow-Podlaski. We approached a farmer and asked for food. The farmer informed on us to the police, and the gendarmes appeared immediately. We ran in all directions. I reached the forests called Puszcza Sterdynska. . . . Once I met a farmer in the forest and asked him for some food. He told me to gather mushrooms and that he would go and bring me bread. After a short time, he returned with another farmer.

They grabbed me, bound my hands, and demanded money and gold. They took out knives and threatened me that if I did not tell them where I had hidden the money they would stab me. I answered that I had been in the camp and that I had no money. They untied my hands, but wound a belt around my neck and informed me that they were taking me to the head of the village. On the way they beat me with a stick and I began to bleed. I thought they would kill me. In the meantime another three farmers arrived, and they led me to a wood. One pulled out a knife and said that for my own good I should give them my money, otherwise they would stab me to death. They warned me not to dare leave the wood because their people were everywhere and I would be caught; I had until the following morning to get the money that I had hidden. I ran from the forest and stopped at an isolated house near the wood. There they took pity on me. They gave me food and clothes and warned me not to stay in that area.... In the Puszcza Sterdynska were groups of Polish underground from the Armia Krajowa ("Home Army") and they cruelly killed Jews.[6]

Similar descriptions can be found in the testimonies of other survivors. Kalman Taigman from Treblinka mentioned in his testimony that Armia Krajowa men met him and his friends in the forest and shot at them.[7]

Indeed, more than a few of the escapees met their death in the forests from the bullets of German security forces, rightist and fascist groups of the Polish underground, or gangs of common criminals and outlaws who operated in those areas. Only a few dozen escapees succeeded in joining up with the Polish partisans of the *Armia Ludowa* (Al, "People's Army")—which was part of the leftist flank of the Polish underground in which there was a relatively large number of Jews—or with Jewish partisan units.

Mordechai Goldfarb, who escaped from Sobibor, told about what happened to him in the forests and how he joined a Jewish partisan unit:

Our group consisted of fourteen people, ten of whom were escapees from Sobibor and four Georgians who had escaped from the prison in Radom. After wandering in the forest, we reached the village of Hola. We thought in this area there should be partisans and, indeed, after a short time we met a group of sixteen armed men under the leadership of a Pole, Miszka Piatek.

They took us into their group and we remained together for about two weeks. However, we didn't feel comfortable as they were common thieves and we sought a way to be rid of them.... One night Miszka told us that we had to procure food and vodka. Five of us went out on the mission: three men from Sobibor—Yehuda Lerner, Boris, and I—one Georgian and one of the men from the local group. We reached the village of Kolacze and there we confiscated the food and liquor.... We returned to the forest, and at the first guard post of our camp we saw no one. We were surprised, especially when we saw that the second guard position was empty as well. We reached the camp. The fire was still burning and the people looked as if they were sleeping. We drew closer and saw that everyone had been killed. Six Jews and three Georgians were killed. Another Jew, Mendel the tailor, was wounded and asked that we kill him. We got away from the place quickly. We were afraid that Miszka was nearby and would shoot us. The local fellow who was with us disappeared immediately, and the Georgian also left us. We remained three wanderers. In the village of Kamien a farmer told us that nearby there was a group of Jewish partisans. Following the farmer's directions we walked 2 kilometers until we came to a house. We knocked on the door with trepidation. Suddenly someone shouted at us from a window: *"Amcha?"* (Jews) We happily replied: *"Amcha"* These were the people from the Jewish partisan unit of Yechiel Grynszpan. We fought there until the arrival of the Soviet army. On July 24, 1944, we joyously entered Lublin together with them all.[8]

Yechiel Grynszpan led a Jewish partisan unit that was active in the Parczew forest, northwest of Sobibor, from the end of 1942 or beginning of 1943. In the spring of 1943, Grynszpan's unit joined up with the Polish leftist partisans of the *Armia Ludowa*, but it remained a Jewish unit. Besides the never-ending danger presented by the German forces, Grynszpan's unit was also forced to fight against the *Armia Krajowa*, who ambushed the Jews in the forests. In addition to Mordechai Goldfarb and his friends, other people from Sobibor also reached Grynszpan's unit, among them Yitzchak Lichtman, Ada Lichtman, and a few women from Holland who had escaped with her from the camp (Ilana Safran, Selma Wijnberg, Katty Gokkes), a total of twelve people from Sobibor.[9]

Only a small number of the insurgents from the camps turned eastward and crossed the Bug River to the main areas of Soviet partisan activity.

The post-revolt escapees from Treblinka and Sobibor had absolutely no chance of finding relatively safe hiding places under German occupation. Those who escaped in periods before the revolt, especially in 1942, had usually returned to the ghettos, where they could find at least a temporary sanctuary. But those who escaped after the revolts did not even have this alternative open to them, as the last ghettos had already been liquidated. Therefore, most of the escapees tended to return to the places where they had lived prior to their internment, in the hope that their knowledge of the area and especially their acquaintance with a few local people might give them some chance of remaining alive.

On the whole, with some exceptions, the local population did not aid the escapees. Anti-Semitism, greediness, and the fear of German terror and punishment were all contributing factors. Yet it should also be noted that those who did succeed in remaining alive until the liberation were in part saved by the aid extended to them by the local population at critical junctures after their escape from the camps.

Survivors of the Sobibor uprising, just before the end of the war. YVA, 41EO7

Dov Freiberg, who was among those who escaped from Sobibor, summed up the difficult situation:

> We were murdered not only by Germans, but by Poles, Ukrainians, and partisans, especially the men of the *Armia Krajowa*, gangs and farmers. . . . More than once we considered suicide, after we saw that the whole world was against us. Every day of the ten months until the liberation is a story unto itself. Yet I would not have exchanged the whole terrible period in the forests for one day, even the best day, in Sobibor. There were also a few good Poles and Ukrainians. These people helped us and risked their lives because they had to fear every neighbor, every passerby, every child, who might inform on them.[10]

OPERATION REINHARD AND REPORTS ABOUT THE DEATH CAMPS IN POLISH WARTIME PUBLICATIONS

INFORMATION ABOUT THE OPERATION REINHARD death camps reached the Polish underground as soon as the mass-murder actions were begun there. The intelligence branch of the Polish underground had spread its network throughout the entire area of occupied Poland, even to the most remote places. The information collected by the underground was published from time to time in the *Biuletyn Informacyjny* ("Information Bulletin") of the command of the *Armia Krajowa* and was distributed clandestinely in occupied Poland.

These news items were also relayed to the Polish Government-in-Exile in London by the *Armia Krajowa* or the *Delegatura* (the delegate of the Polish Government-in-Exile from London in occupied Poland). The *Delegatura* was the political and civilian arm of the government in London, and a sort of underground government within Poland. The *Armia Krajowa* acted in conjunction with the *Delegatura* but was not subordinate to it. The *Delegatura* sent monthly reports, which sometimes covered dozens of pages, called *Pro memoria sytuacji w kraju* ("Notes on the Situation in the Country"). These reports were transferred to London via underground messengers who succeeded in reaching England by way of Sweden or Western Europe and Spain, although sometimes weeks passed before a report of this kind reached its destination. Certain reports were transmitted to London from underground radio stations that maintained continuous contact between Poland and the Government-in-Exile in London and with British intelligence services.[1] Jewish underground groups in Poland, like the Jewish National Committee and the Bund, also transferred broadcasts to London via the Polish underground, and, thus, also news of the deportations to the death camps and what was happening there.

"Reports on the Situation in Occupied Poland" were published in London periodically by the Polish Ministry-of-Interior-in-Exile. Some of these publications were retained in the underground archives in Poland and the archives of the Government-in-Exile in London. In the report of the *Delegatura* for April 1942, Belzec was mentioned:

The camp was fully completed a few days before March 17, 1942. From that day transports with Jews began to arrive from the direction of Lvov and Warsaw. . . . On the first day five transports arrived, afterward, one transport arrived daily from each direction. The transport enters the railway spur of Belzec camp after disembarkation, lasting half an hour, the train returns empty. . . . The observations of the local population (the camp is within sight and hearing distance of the inhabitants near the railway station) led all of them to one conclusion: that there is a mass murder of the Jews inside the camp. The following facts testify to this:

1. Between March 17 and April 13, about fifty-two transports (each of eighteen to thirty-five freight-cars with an average of 1,500 people) arrived in the camp.
2. No Jews left the camp, neither during the day nor the night.
3. No food was supplied to the camp (whereas bread and other food articles had been dispatched to the Jews who had worked earlier on the construction of the camp).
4. Lime was brought to the camp.
5. The transports arrived at a fixed time. Before the arrival of a transport, no Jews were seen in the camp.
6. After each transport, about two freight cars with clothing are removed from the camp to the railway stores. (The guards steal clothes.)
7. Jews in underwear were seen in the area of the camp.
8. In the area of the camp there are three barracks; they cannot accommodate even one-tenth of the Jews.
9. In the area of the camp, a strong odor can be smelled on warmer days.
10. The guards pay for vodka, which they drink in large quantities, with any requested sum, and frequently with watches and valuables.
11. Jews arrived in Belzec [the township] looking for a witness who would testify that Jews are being killed there. They were ready to pay 120,000 zloty. . . . They did not find a volunteer. . . . It is unknown by which means the Jews are liquidated in the camp. There are three assumptions: (1) electricity; (2) gas; (3) by pumping out the air.

With regard to (1): there is no visible source of electricity; with regard to (2): no supply of gas and no residue of the remaining gas after the ventilation of the gas chamber were observed; with regard to (3): there are no factors that deny this [possibility]. It was even verified that during the building of one of the barracks, the walls and floor were covered with metal sheets (for some purpose).

In the area of the camp huge pits were dug in the autumn. At that time it was assumed that there would be underground stores. Now the purpose of this work is clear. From the particular barrack where the Jews are taken for so-called disinfection, a narrow railway leads to these pits. It was observed that the "disinfected" Jews were transported to a common grave by this trolley.

In Belzec the term *Totenlager* ["death camp"] was heard in connection with the Jewish camp. The leadership of the camp is in the hands of twelve SS men (the commander is *Hauptmann* Wirth) who have forty guards for help.[2]

Another report from the *Delegatura* to the Government-in-Exile in London about Belzec was dated July 10, 1942:

According to information from a German employed in the extermination site, this place is located in Belzec, close to the railway station, and is fenced off by barbed wire. Inside and outside the fences Ukrainian sentries are posted. The extermination is carried out in the following manner: the train with the Jews, after its arrival at Belzec station, follows the spur until the fences that surround the place of extermination. There the railway workers are changed. From this place until the disembarkation point at the end of the spur, the train is driven by a German locomotive driver. After unloading, the men are taken to the barrack on the right, the women to the barrack on the left, where they have to remove their clothes, as if they were going to baths. After removing their clothes, both groups proceed to the third barrack, with an electrical floor, where the extermination is carried out. Afterward, the corpses are transferred by trolley to a trench behind the fence, which is 3 meters deep. This trench was dug by Jews, and all of them were subsequently liquidated. The Ukrainian guards on the spot have to be liquidated after the action is completed. The Ukrainian guards are lavishly provided with money and stolen valuables. For a liter of vodka, they pay 400 zloty; for a prostitute, 2,000 zloty plus jewelry.[3]

This report was published in London by the Polish Ministry of Interior at the beginning of 1943. Another report published by the ministry in the same year stated: "Near Belzec there are large gas chambers where Jews in groups of hundreds are gassed [simultaneously]. Their bodies are then cremated, and what remains is used as a fertilizer. In this way the Germans fulfill to the letter the *Führer*'s words that the Jews are the 'garbage of humanity.'"[4]

The reports about Belzec that reached London were handed over by the Polish Government-in-Exile to Dr. Ignacy Schwarzbart, a Jew and a member of the Polish National Council. On November 15, 1942, Schwartzbart published in London an open statement with all the known details about the extermination actions going on in Belzec.[5]

Sobibor was mentioned in the reports of the Polish underground only a few times, and no details were given. Hints that killings were going on in Sobibor reached Warsaw as early as the end of April or May 1942, at the start of the deportations to this camp. The report published in London by the Polish Ministry of Interior at the beginning of 1943 stated, "At this time (April-May) Warsaw heard the first terrible news of the camps in Sobibor (Wlodawa district) and in Belzec (southeastern Poland), where Jews were poisoned en masse in special gas chambers or electrocuted."[6]

There were no detailed reports about Sobibor and the extermination there published in 1942 or 1943. As this camp was built in a remote and desolate area, fewer transports were deported there and few deportees or prisoners succeeded in escaping; therefore, only very limited information about Sobibor reached the Polish underground and London.

News about Treblinka and the mass murder that was being perpetrated there reached the *Armia Krajowa* from the first weeks that the camp existed. The interest exhibited by the underground in what was going on in the desolate area of Treblinka dated from the early summer of 1941, when, in anticipation of the Soviet attack, German units were concentrated there and the labor and penal camp of Treblinka I was activated. This camp was first slated for Polish prisoners who were sent there for such crimes as not appearing for work, not handing over agricultural produce, food speculation, and other "minor" crimes. Jews from the area of Treblinka and from Germany were also brought there.

The order for the establishment of this camp was publicized in the official newspaper of the General Government, *Amtlicher Anzeigner,* on December 2, 1941, but the camp had been operational even earlier. However, in May 1942, when the Germans began erecting another camp in the vicinity of Treblinka it aroused the interest of the Polish underground.

The first transports from the Warsaw ghetto to the new camp—trains full of Jews that returned empty—set off a wave of rumors about what was happening inside the camp. The primary source for these rumors was the people who lived in the area and the Polish railway workers who transported the trains with the Jews until the railroad station in the village of Treblinka and returned them empty. Another and most important source was those Jews who, in the first days of the camp's operation, had succeeded in escaping. Franciszek Zabecki, a railway-traffic supervisor at Treblinka station and a member of the Polish underground, reconnoitered the area of the camp as early as the first days of its operation. He wrote:

> I rode my bicycle in order to find out what was going on there. The concrete road on which I rode was a straight distance of about 200 meters from the camp. I got off my bicycle as if I were fixing it. I fixed it for more than ten minutes. From the camp I heard screams of desperation and crying that pierced

the air, and songs and psalms and prayers of supplication in Yiddish and Polish reached my ears. Above all there was a constant rat-a-tat-tat of shots from machine guns.... The news of the tragedy in Treblinka was passed on to the world, but they could not prevent it. The fate of the Jews was sealed.[7]

General Tadeusz Bór-Komorowski, the second-in-command of the *Armia Krajowa,* wrote in his autobiography: "Not later than July 29 we learned from reports of the railway workers that transports were being taken to the concentration camp of Treblinka and that the Jews were disappearing there without trace. There can no longer be any doubt that the deportations are the beginning of extermination."[8]

In the Information Bulletin of the *Armia Krajowa* of August 17, 1942, there is a detailed reference to the extermination in Treblinka:

Report No. 30 (55)
... The progress in the liquidation of the Warsaw ghetto. The decrease in the number of inhabitants in the ghetto at the present stage totals 200,000 persons, that is, 50 percent of the situation that existed before July 22.... In the period between July 23 and August 7, the following transports left for Treblinka ... a total of 113,100 people. Besides these transports from Warsaw, every day additional trains from other cities reach Treblinka. For example, at the beginning of August a transport arrived from Radom, so that all together every day three transports arrive, each with sixty cars, of them fifty-eight with Jews. In each car there are 100 people. After the engine leaves the station, they force the Jews to undress in order to go, supposedly, to the showers. Actually they are taken to the gas chambers, exterminated there, and then buried in prepared pits, sometimes when they are still alive. The pits are dug with machines. The gas chambers are mobile, and they are situated above the pits. On August 5, there were 40,000 Jews in the camp, and every day 5,000 are killed. The Ukrainians, under German command, carry out the liquidation. By September 10, the Aktion in the Warsaw ghetto is supposed to end.[9]

In a comment attached to this report, it was noted that there was no corroboration from any other source for the item about "mobile gas chambers." In this report, Treblinka is mentioned without being called an extermination camp, and it is possible that it was not yet clear to the underground that two Treblinka camps now existed—the labor and penal camp, and the extermination camp.

In the *Information Bulletin* of September 8, 1942, the "Treblinka extermination camp" is first mentioned as separate from the labor camp.

Report No. 33 (58)
... The Treblinka extermination camp, the place where the Jews are being killed, is located near the labor camp. It is situated 5 kilometers from the

Treblinka station, and 2 kilometers from Poniatowo station. There is a direct telephone line to Malkinia. There is an old camp (for Poles) and a new camp whose construction is still underway (exclusively for Jews).... The extermination of the Jews is now carried out in a way that is completely independent of the old camp. A locomotive pushes the cars with the Jews to the platform. The Ukrainians remove the Jews from the cars and lead them to the "shower to bathe." This building is fenced off with barbed wire. They enter it in groups of 300–500 people. Each group is immediately closed hermetically inside, and gassed. The gas does not affect them immediately, because the Jews still have to continue on to the pits that are a few dozen meters away, and whose depth is 30 meters. There they fall unconscious, and a digger covers them with a thin layer of earth. Then another group arrives.... Soon we will relay an authentic testimony of a Jew who succeeded in escaping from Treblinka.[10]

In this edition of the *Bulletin*, there already appears an accurate description of the gas chambers as a permanent structure, and not as mobile units as was cited in the August 17 report; on the other hand, the description of the victims walking dozens of meters to the pits after the gassing is not true and is based on unreliable information.

The October 5 report stated:

The death camp continues its activity. Transports arrive from all areas of the General-Government (lately from Radom, Siedlce, and Miedzyrzec). At present, not twenty but only ten freight cars are taken to the platform, as it takes a long time to get rid of the corpses of those who died on the way (20–30 percent). The gas chambers are operated in the following system: outside the building, an engine works twenty-four hours a day. Its exhaust is connected to the wall of the barrack and through it the gas is introduced. The gas is a combination of poisonous liquid mixed with the gasoline from the engine and kills the people who are locked in. Within the camp, in addition to the Jewish workers, there is a Jewish orchestra and a group of Jewish women for entertaining the staff. By the end of August, 320,000 Jews were murdered in Treblinka.[11]

The *Information Bulletin* of October 23 reported the continued building in the extermination camp and the enlarged gas chambers with a new capacity of 750 people each, rather than the 350 previously.[12] This report related—albeit inaccurately—to the new building with ten new, larger gas chambers, which were built to replace the old structure, in which there had been three smaller gas chambers.

In the document dated November 15, 1942, a long, detailed description is given of the Treblinka camp. This document was prepared in the Warsaw ghetto as an appendix to another report, entitled "The Destruction of Jewish Warsaw," that was transmitted via the *Delegatura* to London on January 6, 1943. The appendix on Treblinka was entitled "Treblinka—The

Monument of Eternal Shame to the German People." In this document there is a description of the construction of the Treblinka extermination camp, its location, its size, and a detailed plan, including a sketch of the area. This report includes a description of the dozens of new gas chambers and other structures in the camp. With regard to the camp staff, it states that in addition to the Germans and Ukrainians there are also Jews, whom the document calls "Jewish auxiliaries," who are employed at auxiliary works, in sorting the clothes of the murdered and removing the corpses from the gas chambers and burying them. The document mentions the extremely difficult conditions under which the prisoners are kept, the daily killings among these Jews, and that their life expectancy in this camp was no more than two weeks. In the description of the way the transports were treated, there is reference to the deceptive plays of the Germans and a description of the extermination process from the moment the people disembarked on the platform—the way they were tortured—until they were led into the gas chambers, as well as the system of burying the corpses. In conclusion, it stated that by then two million Jews had been murdered in Treblinka—the majority of Polish Jewry. The report concludes by asking why the new gas chambers were built, as the majority of Polish Jewry had already been killed, and states that, according to one eyewitness, the Germans had already killed a group of Poles in the middle of August.[13]

This report is the first in which there is a comprehensive description of the Treblinka extermination camp. The facts are, for the most part, correct. Their source is escapees from the camp who reached the Warsaw ghetto and who gave testimony for the Ringelblum Archive and to Jewish underground groups in the Warsaw ghetto. This report is based therefore on the descriptions of witnesses who had seen for themselves the process of extermination, who had lived in the camp for days or weeks as prisoners, who had been employed at various jobs, and who had succeeded in escaping. The facts that they related on the basis of what they had seen were accurate, but the reference to two million Jews who had been murdered was incorrect. In the period to which the report refers, one-fourth to one-third of the number cited in the report had been murdered. Also the detail about the murder of a group of Poles in Treblinka was incorrect.

Another document that was transmitted by the *Delegatura* to London included material on the destruction of the Jews of Poland. There are two testimonies of escapees from Treblinka, a diagram of the camp, and reports on the extermination activities that were going on there. This document, sent to London at the end of March 1943, is long and detailed, like the report of November 15, 1942, and it contains a description of the camp, the extermination process, the life of the camp staff, and more. One testimony is of a Jewish officer from Warsaw who was in Treblinka for only five days and escaped in September 1942. The document also includes a section of the *Wiadomosci* (News) published by the underground Jewish National Committee in Warsaw, in which the process of extermination in Treblinka was described; a report on the high mortality rate in the trains on the way to the camp; and a report of the killings in the *Lazarett.*[14]

The fortnightly summaries of the Office of Information and Propaganda of the *Armia Krajowa* published in January 1943 contained news of deportations of Jews from the district of Bialystok to Treblinka. Appendix no. 45 to the fortnightly report of January 15, 1943, refers to the period of January 1–15: "... Treblinka. New transports of Jews to their death continue to arrive. For example: on November 20, 1942, forty freight cars arrived from Biala Podlaska; on November 21 and 22, every day forty freight cars from Bialystok; on November 24, forty freight cars from Grodno. During these five days, thirty-two freight cars with Jews' clothing were sent from Treblinka to the Reich. Lately there are transports with Jews from eastern Galicia and Rumania.[15]

Appendix no. 46, which was sent on January 31, 1943, refers to the period January 6–31, 1943:

> ... Treblinka. Now they are in the process of liquidating the remaining Jewish centers in the areas of Grodno and Bialystok. The victims are brought twice a week from collection camps in Kelbasin and Zabludow. The Jews stay in these camps three weeks on the average. The regime there is horrible, so only shadows of the people arrive in Treblinka.... Every night there are new victims from cold and hunger, typhus, dysentery, breakdowns; and the machine guns substantially lessen the transports to Treblinka. From the beginning of November, innovations were introduced in Treblinka: the women's hair is shorn before they undress. The hair is packed in bags. Organs are removed from the corpses and after certain treatment sent to army hospitals for transplants during surgical operations.[16]

These two reports include accurate information for the most part, but there are some inaccuracies: there were no transports to Treblinka with Jews from eastern Galicia or Rumania. And there is no basis to the item on the removal of organs from corpses for transplants in army hospitals.

In the report of July 9, 1943, there is a passage referring to the number of victims in several camps: "... the crimes in numbers. From the railroad documents they can estimate the number of people who were deported in dosed transports to Auschwitz, Belzec, and Treblinka. In this estimate, smaller groups and transports in automobiles were not included. From March 1942 until April [1943], 19,710 Poles were sent to Auschwitz, and 1,075,600 Jews to Treblinka and Belzec. The highest frequency of transports of Poles was in January (9,500 deportees). The largest number of Jews deported was in July 1942 (319,000), August (217,000), and September (280,000)."[17]

This report refers only to Treblinka and Belzec; there is no mention whatsoever of Sobibor. Fifteen months after Sobibor was in operation as a death camp, there were still few testimonies about it.

In 1943, a book was published in the United States entitled *The Black Book of Polish Jewry* in which there are descriptions of the persecution and extermination of the Jews of Poland; these descriptions were, in great part, based on the reports of the Polish underground that reached London. This book brought before the American and world public the mass extermination of the Jews that had been carried out in occupied Poland. The extermination activities in Belzec and Treblinka are described there at length and in detail, and dozens of pages are devoted to the subject. Sobibor is mentioned only twice in the entire book and, even then, only in a few words, as one of the places in which Jews were murdered.

The revolts in Treblinka and Sobibor were also mentioned in the Polish underground publications. In the weekly review of the main events that had occurred in Poland published on August 13, 1943, we find: "Treblinka set on fire. In Treblinka no. 2, besides a unit of SS and Ukrainians (160 men), there was a Jewish auxiliary group of 600 people who aided in the extermination activities. On the third of this month, this group attacked the guards, disarmed them, took over the arms storeroom, burned the buildings, and broke out to the forests. In the fighting, about 200 Jews fell. Germans and Ukrainians were injured, and evidently about fifty were killed."[18]

On August 10, 1943, the leftist underground newspaper in Warsaw, *Glos Warszawy* ("The Voice of Warsaw"), no. 49 (58), carried news of the uprising in Treblinka:

> News from Treblinka. Last week, news reached the capital on events in the notorious "death factory" Treblinka. Based on shreds of reports from various sources, the chain of events was as follows: in Treblinka there were still 3,000 Jews, who lived under the threatening guns of the Gestapo [and] were put to work burying the thousands of victims, [and who] serviced the gas chambers and did all kinds of other jobs. After a time, when they no longer had any strength, these miserable victims were murdered and replaced by others. Finally they rebelled. These desperate Jews killed a few dozen Gestapo, took over the arms storeroom and removed the weapons, set fire to some of the buildings, and escaped to the forests in the area. About 2,800 people, most of them armed, succeeded in escaping to the forests. As partisans they entered into battle with units sent against them in a punishment action, and caused them heavy losses.[19]

On August 18, the *Information Bulletin* published a report on the uprising in Treblinka, stating that the Jews killed thirty guards, took their arms, set fire to the camp, and about 1,800 escaped.[20]

On August 26, in a review of the situation in occupied Poland by the *Delegatura*, the uprising in Treblinka also appeared:

> ... bloody rebellion in Treblinka. In the Jewish Treblinka there were of late a few hundred Jewish craftsmen who were employed by the Germans, as well as workers at various jobs in the camp. Recently they were put to work at opening the mass graves of the Jews murdered in Treblinka and burning the bodies that were inside. Some of these Jews who still lived in Treblinka established an underground fighting organization. One day at the beginning of August, they found the right moment for action: some of the German/Ukrainian camp staff had left for a swim. The Jews attacked the rest of the staff, disarmed them, killed about fifty Germans and Ukrainians, and burned the barracks. All the Jews that were in the camp escaped to the forests in the vicinity of Treblinka. The Germans conducted extensive pursuits in these forests. Some of the Jews were caught and killed, some escaped.[21]

In the newspaper reviews of the underground in Poland from the end of 1943, published by the Ministry of Interior of the Government-in-Exile in London, which refer to the period September–October 1943, there are quotations from two underground newspapers in Poland—*The Struggle*, a paper with anti-Semitic leanings, and *W.N.R.*, the newspaper of the Polish Socialists and sympathetic to the Jews—and both of them carried a report on the uprising in Treblinka.[22]

In general, the reports on the uprising in Treblinka greatly exaggerate the number of rebels and the number of losses inflicted on the Germans and Ukrainians. The reason for the inaccuracies is primarily that the entire Polish underground had had no direct contact with the prisoners in Treblinka or with the Jewish underground that had been operating in the camp for many months. The source for earlier reports on Treblinka, which were usually reliable, was mostly Jews who had escaped from the camp or Polish railway workers who drove the trains. However, the reports on the uprising that are quoted here, although they were published a short time after the uprising, were based on inaccurate descriptions by the local population. The reports on the uprising that were published a few months later no longer repeat the numerical exaggerations. In the meantime, testimonies of survivors had been taken, and these contained more accurate details.

The uprising in Sobibor, like the other events there, was mentioned only briefly in the reports of the Polish underground. The report of the *Delegatura* in the second half of November 1943 stated: "During the liquidation of Sobibor in the middle of October, the Jews set fire to the barracks and crematorium, killed some gendarmes, and hundreds of them escaped into the forests."[23]

Some other reports about the uprising in Sobibor were dispatched by the Polish underground to London in the beginning of 1944. The Polish Ministry of Interior published a report in which it was stated: "In the second half of October, there was a bloody and successful rebellion of Jews in the death camp of Sobibor. The prisoners, who numbered a few hundred, killed several dozen oppressors, SS men and Ukrainians. After setting fire to the camp, all the prisoners escaped."[24]

The Polish underground—and especially the dominant element within it, which was organized in the *Armia Krajowa* and connected with the Government-in-Exile in London—knew what was going on in Treblinka and Belzec and, to a lesser extent, in Sobibor, from the start of the camps' operation and reported about it in their various publications. This underground took no practical steps to warn the Jews still in the various ghettos about the true purpose of the death camps and also did nothing to waylay the transports, such as sabotaging the trains and railroad tracks.

Stefan Korbonski, a leading figure in the Polish underground, who was in charge of broadcasts from Poland and clandestine radio contact with London, wrote in his memoirs that from the beginning of the deportation of the Jews from Warsaw to the death camps, radiograms reporting these events were sent to London regularly. Korbonski wrote that the Polish authorities in London, in contrast to the usual procedure did not respond to these broadcasts and nothing was mentioned on the BBC. He claims that he insistently demanded a reply:

> I sent a special radiogram in which I requested clarification of the reasons for their silence. My surprise grew when I did not receive any answer even to this radiogram.... This game went on for a few days, and evidently as a result of the daily alarms of the station in London, the government finally responded. The radiogram did not explain much. Its exact wording was: Not all your radiograms are appropriate for publication.... It was only about a month later that the BBC reported an item based on our information. Many months later, the entire matter was explained to me by an envoy of the government who was parachuted to the homeland: Your radiograms were not believed. The government did not believe them, and the British did not believe them. It was said that you exaggerated your anti-Nazi propaganda. Only when the British received confirmation of these facts from their sources was there consternation and the BBC transmitted your information.[25]

The Polish underground transmitted to London the reports on the death camps and the extermination of the Jews of Poland via its messengers and radio stations. It did not hide these facts nor delay their relay, and the reports reached the Polish Government-in-Exile in London and the British government. Both the Polish Government-in-Exile in London and the British government, which received these reports, responded to the information with indifference. Ignacy Schwarzbart and Szmul Zygielbojm, the Jewish representatives on the Polish National Council in London, to whom the Polish government conveyed these reports, requested and demanded that the Polish government publicize these reports and alert Britain and the United States to take the necessary action to stop the genocide of Poland's Jews; their requests were met with inaction and evasive responses. From its inception, the Polish Government-in-Exile attempted to make little of Polish Jewry's suffering and their incomparable and cruel destiny, presenting the general Polish population as victims of the German terror. Schwarzbart's and Zygielbojm's appeals and demands that the Polish Government-in-Exile instruct the *Armia Krajowa* to assist Poland's Jews went unanswered. Zygielbojm, in his great sorrow and despair and in an act of protest, after receiving the reports on the uprising and the liquidation of the Warsaw Ghetto, took his life in London on May 12, 1943.[26] Zygielbojm left a letter addressed to Wladyslaw Raczkiewicz, president of the Republic of Poland, and to its prime minister, Wladyslaw Sikorski, in which he wrote:

I am taking the liberty of addressing you, Sirs, these my last words, and through you to the Polish Government and the people of Poland, and to the governments and people of the Allies, and to the conscience of the whole world:

The latest news that has reached us from Poland makes it clear beyond any doubt that the Germans are now murdering the last remnants of the Jews in Poland with unbridled cruelty. Behind the walls of the ghetto the last act of this tragedy is now being played out.

The responsibility for the crime of the murder of the whole Jewish nationality in Poland rests first of all on those who are carrying it out, but indirectly it falls also upon the whole of humanity, on the peoples of the Allied nations and on their governments, who up to this day have not taken any real steps to halt this crime. By looking on passively upon this murder of defenseless millions—tortured children, women and men—they have become partners to the responsibility.

I am obliged to state that although the Polish Government contributed largely to the arousing of public opinion in the world, it still did not do enough. It did not do anything that was not routine, that might have been appropriate to the dimensions of the tragedy taking place in Poland.

By my death I wish to give expression to my most profound protest against the inaction in which the world watches and permits the destruction of the Jewish people.[27]

Despite the fact that numerous reports reached the British government from Polish sources and presumably also from British intelligence sources, these reports did not receive their due coverage on the BBC and on other British communications media. The British government was unwilling to take any military action whatsoever to disrupt the extermination by bombing the railway lines leading to the death camps or the camps themselves—and therefore did not call attention to the reports on extermination, opting instead to remain silent.

AN EVALUATION OF THE UPRISINGS AND THEIR RESULTS

THE UNDERGROUNDS IN BOTH TREBLINKA and Sobibor operated under extremely difficult and adverse conditions. The camps were small, easy to supervise, and offered no possible hiding places, and the prisoners were under the constant surveillance of the camp authorities. Yet the underground leaders still succeeded in organizing a clandestine group and preserving the secrecy of its existence from the Germans, Ukrainians, and the majority of their fellow prisoners. The fact that it was done attests to outstanding leadership, a sharp eye in selecting the members for the underground, and the manipulative ability to conceal the clandestine activities.

The underground in each camp operated independently; there was absolutely no contact between them. They were not even aware of the existence of the other camp and an underground organization there. Yet we find many similarities in the organization, plans, and activities in both camps. The conditions and structure of Treblinka and Sobibor were similar, and this was what probably dictated the way the organization and operation of the undergrounds developed. The leaders of the undergrounds came from the "elite" of the prisoners—the capos, heads of workshops, foremen. Even the size of the underground was similar in both camps—about fifty to sixty members.

Both undergrounds suffered setbacks and tragedies. In Treblinka it claimed the lives of Julian Chorazycki and Rakowski. And the failure to smuggle out grenades and detonators from the camp armory in April 1943 could very well have caused the discovery of the organization and the postponement of the planned uprising. In Sobibor, the planned escape cost the lives of Joseph Jacobs and seventy-two of his fellow Dutch Jews. The discovery of a tunnel in Camp III of Sobibor brought on a reprisal action and the shooting of 150 prisoners there. But in spite of all these failures and losses of human life, the idea of resistance was not snuffed out.

Both undergrounds tried to enlist the help of the Ukrainian guards. In Treblinka the effort was directed mainly at purchasing arms. In Sobibor they attempted to establish contact with partisans, to procure arms, and to receive help with the escape. Some Ukrainians with whom the underground leaders were in contact promised to extend help and received substantial sums of money and valuables for this purpose. But there were no positive results from these contacts. The one exception was when five Jewish prisoners escaped from the extermination area in Sobibor together with two Ukrainian guards. In all other cases, the Jews were cheated out of their money, or even betrayed, as in the case of Jacobs in Sobibor. The underground leadership in both camps finally reached the conclusion that no active help with arms or escape could be expected from the Ukrainian guards.

Even the hope that during the uprisings some of the Ukrainians who were former Soviet soldiers would join in the escape and the others would not fight against the Jews was not realized. The large majority remained faithful to the Germans, fought the Jewish rebels, and quelled the uprisings inside the camps. The hundreds of prisoners who were shot inside and close to the camps were in fact hit by the Ukrainian guards. Their loyalty to the Germans was particularly evident in Sobibor, where only two SS men remained active during the uprising, and the whole action against the escaped prisoners during these critical hours was carried out by the Ukrainians.

In Treblinka the underground included prisoners from the two separate sections of the camp—the Lower Camp and the extermination area. The transfer of Zialo Bloch, a leading figure of the underground in the Lower Camp, to the extermination area facilitated organizing the clandestine activity there. And the fact that the mason Jacob Wiernik had permission to go back and forth between the two parts of the camp also enabled the establishment of contacts and the coordination of activities. In fact, the uprising was carried out simultaneously and according to the same plan; prisoners from both sections of the camp met on the escape routes and mingled together. Jews from both parts were among the survivors.

In Sobibor the situation was different. There was no opportunity for contact between the prisoners in the two parts of the camp, and the undergrounds in each section operated independently. No information about the underground group in Camp III (extermination area) exists, except for the fact that a mass escape through a tunnel was planned and the digging required clandestine organization. As a result of the lack of contacts, the escape through the tunnel in Camp III, planned for the second half of September, was not coordinated with the uprising in the main camp a few weeks later, with the tragic outcome for the prisoners in Camp III. All those who were there when the tunnel was discovered were shot. The prisoners who were brought there as replacements were shot a day after the uprising. In both cases they were victims of reprisal actions. Had they only been aware of the conditions that prevailed in Sobibor in the late afternoon of October 14, when most of the SS men had already been liquidated, the prisoners in Camp III would have realized that they had a fair chance to escape during the uprising.

The plans for the uprisings in both camps called for them to begin in the afternoon while the prisoners and the SS men were dispersed at their workplaces. The darkness of the night was supposed to cover the escape and allow the prisoners more precious time to get as far from the camp as possible. In Treblinka the first stage of the uprising was aimed at removing the weapons from the armory; during the second stage they were to attack the SS men and take control of the camp. In Sobibor the first stage was the elimination of the SS men; the second stage was the escape. The plan in Sobibor did not call for taking control of the camp and destroying it as did the plan in Treblinka. The plan in Sobibor was less ambitious, with more modest aims, and, therefore, it had more chance to succeed. The implementation of the uprising plan was carried out more professionally from the military point of view in Sobibor than in Treblinka. This has to be attributed to Alexander Pechersky and the prisoners of war with him who had military training and combat experience.

Both plans were apt to succeed, but the tragic flaw in both was that alternative plans—in the event that action would not go according to plan—were never developed. And in both Treblinka—in the first stage—and Sobibor—in the second stage—without planned alternatives, the leaders lost control over people and events, and the organized action turned into an individual escape.

In Treblinka none of the leading figures of the underground, among them Galewski, Ze'ev Korland, and Zialo Bloch, survived the uprising. All of them fell during the outbreak from the camp or in the ensuing pursuit. In Sobibor, the two leaders of the uprising, Pechersky and Leon Feldhendler, succeeded in escaping and survived the war.

The local SS authorities feared being accused of negligence if it became known that clandestine activity had been organized in the camp. The responsible parties could have been tried and sentenced, which is what happened to the SS and police leader of the Warsaw district, Ferdinand Von Sammern, after the uprising in the ghetto there.

The commander of Treblinka, Franz Stangl, and his superiors in Lublin, Christian Wirth and Odilo Globocnik, downplayed the uprising and escape of the Jewish prisoners and tried to keep it a secret. Stangl claimed that all the prisoners who ran away from the camp during the uprising were caught within a few hours after their escape.[1] In fact, however, at that time three hundred to four hundred prisoners were still free outside the camp. In German reports, the uprising and mass escape from Treblinka were not mentioned. The fact that no German was killed during the uprising and only one was wounded made it possible to conceal the events in Treblinka, for when SS men were killed a report had to be submitted to the highest SS authorities in Berlin.

The uprising and escape in Sobibor could not be concealed. The call for help from this camp went out to various SS bodies and the highest army and civil authorities in the General Government. In addition, the killing of eleven SS men had to be reported immediately to SS headquarters in the Third Reich. On the day after the uprising, October 15, in a report of the Order Police in the Lublin district, it was stated that in Sobibor there had been a revolt of the Jewish prisoners; that they had overpowered the guards and seized the armory; that three hundred of them had fled in an unknown direction; and that nine SS men had been killed, one SS man had been wounded, one SS man had gone missing, and two foreign guards (Ukrainians) had been shot to death.[2] The uprising in Sobibor was also described in the reports of the Mounted Squadrons of the SS and police. The funeral of the killed SS men was attended by a high-ranking delegation from Hitler's chancellery in Berlin, because most of the killed SS men were former members of the euthanasia program and were in part subordinate to it.

The uprisings in Treblinka and Sobibor did not result in the closing of these death camps or stop the killing there. The decision to close these camps had been taken by the SS authorities before the uprisings. But the uprising in Treblinka did hasten the closing of the camp and the cessation of the killings there.

The uprising in Sobibor brought about a change in the plans for this camp. The original idea had been to turn Sobibor into a concentration camp for treating captured Soviet ammunition. Now it was decided that the Sobibor death camp would be entirely demolished and dismantled.

The uprisings in Treblinka and Sobibor can be considered a success from the point of view of the prisoners. Their main aim had been a mass escape and rescue of the camp inmates, all of whom were doomed to certain death. Even if most of the prisoners were killed during the uprisings and the ensuing pursuit, and less than one-third of the prisoners succeeded in escaping, we may still claim that this aim was achieved. This is most apparent if we take the alternative of Belzec, where no uprising took place. In this camp there were only two survivors, Rudolf Reder and Chaim Hirszman.

There were 850 prisoners in Treblinka on August 2. About 100 did not even attempt to escape, as most of them were too weak or sick. They were all shot on the spot. Half of those who participated in the uprising were killed during the uprising, in the camp or close to the fences. Approximately the same number—about 350 to 400 prisoners—succeeded in escaping. In the search and pursuit actions undertaken by the German security forces in the late afternoon and during the night of August 2, about 200 prisoners were caught and shot. Approximately 150 to 200 prisoners succeeded in evading the pursuit, but most of them did not survive by the time the area was liberated by the Soviet army and the *Armia Ludowa* (AL, Polish "People's Army"). No more than 70 prisoners from Treblinka remained alive at the end of the war.

In Sobibor there were about 600 prisoners on October 14, besides the 80 to 100 prisoners in Camp III. At least 150 prisoners, including those in Camp III, did not try to escape or were caught in the camp. They all were shot the following day. About 230 to 270 prisoners were killed during the uprising inside the camp or at the fences and minefield. During the searches and pursuit, 100 of the 300 prisoners who escaped from the camp were caught and shot. From the 200 prisoners who evaded the pursuit, about 130 to 150 found their death between that time and the liberation and 50 to 70 survived. All together about 120 to 130 prisoners from Sobibor and Treblinka survived the war.

The survival of these prisoners takes on an additional, important aspect. As part of Nazi Germany's attempt to hide the crimes they had committed, they strove not to leave any living witness to their evil acts. The survivors from Treblinka and Sobibor undermined this intention. They, the eyewitnesses, told the firsthand story of what had transpired in these camps.

The first booklets about what happened in these camps were published as early as 1944. While in the underground in Warsaw, Wiernik wrote his book *A Year in Treblinka*. In May 1944, Wiernik's manuscript was brought by a Polish underground courier to England, and at the end of that year it was published in the United States and Palestine. This was the first comprehensive publication by an eyewitness. Since that time many books, articles, and diaries have been written and published by the survivors of these camps. They also appeared as the main witnesses at the Treblinka and Sobibor war-crimes trials. Their testimonies are a primary source for historical research, including the research for this book.

PART IV

THE FINAL STAGE
OF OPERATION REINHARD

CHAPTER FORTY-SIX

OPERATION *ERNTEFEST* ("HARVEST FESTIVAL")

THE UPRISING OF THE JEWS in Treblinka and, to an even larger extent, the uprising in Sobibor and its aftermath shocked the German authorities in the General Government and throughout the higher echelons of the SS in Berlin. They became especially alarmed when they realized that what happened in Sobibor, with fewer than one thousand Jews, might happen in other camps in the Lublin district, where forty-two thousand to forty-five thousand Jews were still being kept as slave workers in German industrial enterprises. Labor camps under the command of the Operation Reinhard staff were located in Trawniki, Poniatowa, and other places in the Lublin district. There were also Jewish prisoners in the Majdanek concentration camp.[1]

In a conference held by Hans Frank in Cracow on October 19, 1943, five days after the Sobibor uprising, the issue of the Jews in the labor camps was raised. From the minutes of this conference:

> Police Major-General Hans Grunwald [the commander of the Order Police in the General Government] confirmed the data about the security situation given by SS *Oberführer* Bierkamp [the commander of the Security Police in the General Government]. . . . The camps with Jews in the General Government constituted a great danger, and the escape of the Jews from one of these camps [Sobibor] proved it. It was followed by a debate on that same problem. In connection with this, the Inspector of the Armament, General Schindler, SS *Oberführer* Bierkamp, and Major-General Grünwald were instructed by the Governor-General to inspect all the Jewish camps in the General Government in order to determine how many of the Jews there are used as a work force. The remainder were to be removed from the General Government.[2]

Himmler, however, did not wait for the results of the inspection of the camps as decided upon at the conference held by Hans Frank. He was determined to act quickly, before the example of Sobibor would influence prisoners in other camps. He decided to annihilate the Jews in these camps immediately. Friedrich Krüger, the higher SS and police leader of the General Government, was ordered by Himmler to carry out the liquidation action. The code name for this action was *Erntefest* ("Harvest Festival"). Krüger delegated this mission to Sporrenberg, the newly appointed SS and police leader of the Lublin district.[3]

The whole action was planned as a military operation. For reasons of secrecy and to prevent rumors about the killings from seeping out from one camp to another, Operation *Erntefest* had to be executed simultaneously in the three main camps: Poniatowa, Trawniki, and Majdanek. As such an action required large forces, several thousand police and SS men, including Waffen SS units, were concentrated for this operation from different places in the General Government and from East Prussia. The large forces, the element of surprise, and the swiftness of the operation were designed to safeguard against any resistance and provide the means to quell it quickly in the event that it should happen—what transpired in Sobibor would not be allowed to happen again.

On the eve of the *Erntefest* operation, there were between thirteen thousand to fifteen thousand Jews, including women and children, in the Poniatowa labor camp. Most of them had been transferred there from the Warsaw ghetto after the uprising, and they were working in the Walther C. Tobbens clothing enterprises. In the last days of October 1943, Jews from the camp were taken to dig two trenches close to the entrance gate of the camp. The Jews were told that these were defense trenches against air attacks and they were to be dug in zigzags. The length of both trenches was ninety-five meters, the width two meters, and the depth one and a half meters.[4]

Scharführer Heinrich Gley testified about what happened there on November 3:

> In November 1943—I don't remember the exact date—one night I was called to [Gottlieb] Hering [the commander of Poniatowa].... When I entered Hering's room, there were two police officers with him.... The officers informed Hering that the whole camp was surrounded by a police unit.... This police unit was under orders to liquidate all the Jews in the camp, without any exception. During the conversation, the officers expressed the opinion that the liquidation of the Jews was inevitable because otherwise security could not be guaranteed. Whether the assumption about the endangered security situation was based on the report of the successful uprising in Sobibor, I don't know....
>
> In the meantime all the Jews were ordered to concentrate in some specified places. They were separated in such a way that the Jews from the main camp were in the large hall and the Jews from the "settlement" were to line up at a square.
>
> From my room I could see how the Jews, entirely nude, were taken from the hall to the trench. This trench was zigzag. It was about 300–500 meters distant from the main hall. A tight chain of armed policemen guarded the

way. I could not see the shootings, but I heard the shootings. After the action was finished, I saw the corpses. . . .

In the evening, after completing the action, the police unit left. According to my estimation, the strength of the police unit was between 1,000–1,500 men.[5]

In the Poniatowa camp there was a Jewish Underground group, which had even succeeded in obtaining a few weapons. In the afternoon, when the killing action was approaching its end, a group of Jews closed in one of the barracks, members of the Underground group, resisted being taken to the trenches and opened fire on the SS men. They burned some of the nearby barracks that contained clothing. But the Germans set the barrack with the resisting Jews on fire, and all of them were burned alive. Polish firemen from the town of Opola Lubelski arrived to put out the fire in the clothing barracks, and some of these firemen testified that wounded Jews were also thrown into the burning barracks.[6]

About 150 Jews were left to clean the area and cremate the corpses of the killed. Fifty Jews who succeeded in hiding themselves during the shooting joined them. But two days after the massacre, these 200 Jews were shot because they refused to cremate the corpses. In their place, 120 Jews were brought from other camps to carry out this work.[7]

In the Trawniki labor camp there were between eight thousand and ten thousand Jews—men, women, and children—most of them from the Warsaw ghetto (according to a different source there were only six thousand Jews in Trawniki). The majority worked in the Schultz enterprises of furs, brushes, and so on. Like in Poniatowa, on November 3, 1943, the camp was surrounded by Waffen SS and police units. Early in the morning the Jews were driven from their barracks and taken in batches to the training camp of the SS auxiliaries in Trawniki. There they were forced to undress, put their clothes in a huge heap, and enter the trench, where they were shot. Those who arrived afterward were forced to lie on the corpses that had been shot before. When there was no more room in the trench in the training camp, some of the Jews were shot in the sand or in a gravel pit in the labor camp. To overcome the cries of the victims and the noise of the shooting, loudspeakers were installed in the camp and music was heard throughout the entire area. By late afternoon the murder action was completed. All the Jews had been shot, and the few Jews who had succeeded in escaping from the shooting site had been caught and shot.

A German manager of the Schultz enterprises in Trawniki, Kurt Ziemann, testified about the events on the morning of November 3:

The labor camp was surrounded. As we found out later, there was an entire SS battalion . . . young SS men from the Waffen SS. . . . We were asked to come to the headquarters of the training camp. . . . The commander of the Waffen SS unit announced to us that the enterprise would not be operational that day. . . . We could see that the Jews were taken in groups from the labor camp to the training camp. There they had to undress and put their clothes in a huge heap. Everything was done at a run. I could not see the execution place from where I was standing. The nude Jews disappeared behind a barrack. We merely heard the shooting. . . . The next morning I went to Warsaw for 3–5 days. When I returned, already at the station I could smell the odor of the corpses that had been cremated.[8]

A group of 100 to 120 Jews from the Milejow camp (east of Lublin) were brought to cremate the corpses of the murdered. After two or three weeks, when they finished the cremating work, they were also shot. They were shot in small groups, and each group had to cremate the corpses of the previous group. The last group was cremated by the Ukrainian guards.[9]

In the Majdanek concentration camp, the preparation for the action began in the last days of October. About three hundred prisoners dug for three days three trenches, each one hundred meters long and two meters deep, in the southern part of the camp, close to the new crematorium and the fences. About one hundred SS men came to Majdanek from other areas of the General Government and reinforced the camp staff. On November 2, 1943, two mobile loudspeakers were installed, one close to the trenches, the other close to the entrance gate of the camp. During the night of November 2–3, the guards around the camp were reinforced.[10]

At the morning roll call, all the Jewish prisoners, who were mixed in groups with other prisoners, were ordered to leave the rows and create a separate column. These Jews, together with those who were sick with typhus, were taken to the trenches and shot. The shooting began at six or seven in the morning and was covered by the dance music blaring from the loudspeakers. In the meantime columns of marching Jews from other camps in Lublin—those from the old airport, the DAW enterprises, and some other satellite camps of Majdanek—began arriving in Majdanek. All together there were about ten thousand Jews. They were brought to sub-camp V, which was close to the shooting site, and from there they were taken in groups of one hundred to a barrack and forced to undress. A passage was cut in the fences of sub-camp V, and, through it, the naked Jews were driven to the shooting site. The men and women were taken to the shooting site in separate groups. They were forced to lie down in the trenches and were shot by SS men standing on the edge of the pit. After the first groups were shot, the bottom of the trenches was full and all the others were forced to lie on top of those who had been shot before.

The shooting action lasted until five o'clock in the afternoon. The SS men who carried out the shooting were relieved by others a few times during the day, but the music coming from the loudspeakers played continuously. About eighteen thousand Jews were murdered that day in Majdanek.[11] Among the Jews concentrated in sub-camp V and waiting to be taken to the shooting site, there were some cases of suicide. There were also some acts of resistance. About twenty-five Jews who tried to find hiding places in the barracks of sub-camp V were found there the day after the shooting and were shot in the crematorium.

About three hundred men and three hundred women remained in Majdanek to take care of the clothes left by the murdered. After completing this work, the women were taken to Auschwitz. The men were taken to cremate the corpses of the murdered: after that they too were shot.[12]

With the completion of the *Erntefest* operation, only a few small labor camps under the authority of the German air force, with a population of about two thousand Jews, remained in the Lublin district.[13] The *Erntefest* operation was the last mass killing of the Jews who had still remained in the General Government and the closing *Aktion* of Operation Reinhard. Approximately thirty-nine thousand to forty-three thousand Jews were murdered during Operation *Erntefest*.

THE LIQUIDATION OF THE CAMPS AND THE TERMINATION OF OPERATION REINHARD

THE PRINCIPAL DECISION TO TERMINATE Operation Reinhard and close the death camps of Belzec, Sobibor, and Treblinka was taken by Heinrich Himmler during his visit to Lublin at the end of February and the beginning of March 1943 (see chapter 23). At that time almost all the Jews in the General Government had already been annihilated and the death camp of Auschwitz-Birkenau was in full operation and could meet the needs of the Nazi extermination machine. The final date for the closing of Belzec, Sobibor, and Treblinka now depended on when the cremation of the corpses would be completed. The SS authorities planned to leave absolutely no trace of the death camps. All construction in the camps was to be destroyed or evacuated. The whole area was to be cleaned of debris, plowed over, and trees were to be sown and planted.

BELZEC

The first camp to be dismantled and closed was Belzec.[1] The mass deportation to this camp stopped in December 1942. Some transports of Jews from the district of Lvov, which arrived in Belzec after this date, were sent from there to Sobibor. But the liquidation process took several months. *Scharführer* Werner Dubois, who was in Belzec at that time, testified:

> The transports to Belzec and, consequently, the gassing operations, stopped quite suddenly. . . . As staff members of the Belzec camp, we were informed that the place would be rebuilt completely. A working group of Jews, whose size I don't remember, was in charge of the demolition work. It is worth mention that at that time [March–April 1943] the cremation of the corpses was terminated and the graves were leveled. The camp was emptied entirely and leveled accordingly. I heard that some planting was done there. The Jewish work commando, after accomplishing this work, was taken to Sobibor. I remained in Belzec for two more days, together with some of my colleagues and guards, to carry out the last clearing and loading. . . . Some time later, when I was in Sobibor, I heard that during

the transport of the Jewish work commando from Belzec to Sobibor, some mutiny and shooting took place which led to some deaths.[2]

The transport of the Jewish prisoners from Belzec to Sobibor at the end of July 1943 was the closing act of this camp. When the prisoners left Belzec, they were told that they were going to Germany to work. Some escaped from the train (see chapter 33), and when the others arrived in Sobibor they grasped what truly awaited them. They resisted disembarking from the train and being taken to the gas chamber, but they were overcome and shot.

The last commander of Belzec, SS *Hauptsturmführer* Gottlieb Hering, was appointed commander of the Poniatowa labor camp. Most of the German staff from Belzec was sent to serve in Treblinka, Sobibor, and Poniatowa.

After the camp buildings were dismantled and the German and Ukrainian staff had left, people from the neighboring villages and townships started digging in the area of the camp, searching for gold and valuables. A Pole, Edward Luczynski, who lived in Belzec, testified: "After leveling and cleaning the area of the extermination camp, the Germans planted the area with small pines and left. At that moment, the whole area was plucked to pieces by the neighboring population, who were searching for gold and valuables. That's why the whole surface of the camp was covered with human bones, hair, ashes from cremated corpses, dentures, pots, and other objects."[3]

However, these diggings and searches endangered the German intent to erase the traces of their crimes and hide the very fact of the existence of a death camp in Belzec. Germans and Ukrainians from Sobibor and Treblinka were sent back to Belzec to prevent further diggings and to restore the "peaceful-looking" character of the place. To prevent future searches and digging, Operation Reinhard authorities decided to keep a permanent guard on the spot. A farm was built for a Ukrainian guard who would live there with his family. This precautionary measure was later adopted also in Treblinka and Sobibor. Odilo Globocnik wrote about this to Himmler: "For reasons of surveillance, in each camp a small farm was created which is occupied by a guard. An income must regularly be paid to him so that he can maintain the small farm."[4]

A group of twelve Ukrainians under the command of *Unterscharführer* Karl Schiffer came from Treblinka to build the farmhouse. Another group arrived from Sobibor to carry out afforestation work there. *Scharführer* Heinrich Unverhau testified about this group: "A few weeks before the uprising in Sobibor, I and three other SS men and a larger group of Ukrainian auxiliaries were again ordered to go to Belzec. We were doing afforestation work there. . . . We had to prevent the Poles from turning the whole area upside down in their searches for gold."[5]

The afforestation work was completed at the end of October 1943, before the winter set in and the last SS men and Ukrainians had left the place. A former Ukrainian guard from Belzec settled there with his family, and the Belzec death camp had turned into an "ordinary" farm.

TREBLINKA

The next camp to be liquidated was Treblinka. The last transports to this camp, before its closing, came from the Bialystok ghetto, where over twenty-five thousand Jews had lived until the second half of August 1943. All these Jews, according to the deportation plan, had to be sent to Treblinka in five train transports.[6] The transports, which included seventy-six freight cars, arrived in Treblinka on August 18 and 19. The other three transports passed through Treblinka, but continued on. One went to Majdanek, one to Auschwitz, and one with children to Theresienstadt.

The two transports from Bialystok were the last to arrive and be murdered in Treblinka. At that time the camp had already ceased to be fully operational. Part of it had been destroyed during the uprising a few weeks earlier, and only a few Jewish prisoners were still there to carry out the work connected with the extermination process. Therefore, the annihilation of the transports from Bialystok took more time than before the uprising. Only ten freight cars loaded with Jews could enter the camp simultaneously, as opposed to twenty previously. These difficulties were why the other transports from Bialystok, except for the one with the children, were sent to Majdanek and Auschwitz.[7]

The deportation and liquidation of the Jews from Bialystok was the last large-scale killing operation in which Globocnik and the Operation Reinhard staff were involved. Upon accomplishing this mission and in recognition of his work, Globocnik was promoted and appointed by Himmler as the higher SS and police leader in the Trieste area in northeast Italy. Another reason for Globocnik's transfer to Italy was his strained relationship with Governor General Hans Frank.[8] Moreover, the Germans were urgently needed at that time for reinforcements in Italy. This was after the downfall of Mussolini and the landing of the Allied forces in southern Italy and was a period of increased partisan activity in northern Italy.

Globocnik left Lublin in September 1943 and took with him to Italy a group of SS men and Ukrainians who had been under his command in Operation Reinhard, including Christian Wirth, Franz Stangl, and Franz Reichleitner. Gottlieb Hering, the commander of Belzec and later Poniatowa, joined them in Italy after Operation *Erntefest*.

For Stangl, the appointment to Italy was a pleasant surprise. Since the uprising of August 2 in Treblinka, he had been worried about being charged with responsibility for what had happened there. Stangl testified to his feelings after the uprising:

> They left me stewing for three weeks before Globocnik sent for me. It was my most difficult time. I was sure I would get all the blame. But as soon as I entered the office, Globocnik said: "You are transferred immediately to Trieste for antipartisan combat." I thought my bones would melt. I had been so sure they were going to say I had done something wrong, and now, on the contrary, I had what I always wanted. I was going to get out. And to Trieste, too, near home. I went back to Treblinka, but I only stayed three or four days, just enough time to prepare for the journey.[9]

Kurt Franz, Stangl's deputy, was appointed commander of Treblinka. He was responsible for dismantling the camp, destroying the gas chambers, and erasing all signs of the extermination camp. Franz had at his disposal some SS men and a group of Ukrainian guards. The physical work was carried out by about one hundred Jewish prisoners who remained there after the uprising. The work was accomplished during September–October 1943. A few days after the uprising in Sobibor, on October 20, thirty to fifty Jewish prisoners from Treblinka were sent to Sobibor to carry out the dismantling work there.[10]

In Treblinka about thirty Jewish prisoners remained, among them two women, to finish the work there. They were kept during the night in two closed freight cars on the railway spur. On November 17, the last transport, carrying equipment from the camp, departed. At the end of November, Kurt Franz received an order to demolish whatever yet remained in Treblinka and to take his men to Sobibor. Before Franz and his men left, the last Jewish prisoners were shot. Franz was in charge of the execution. The Jews were taken in groups of five and shot by three SS men. Before being shot, each group was forced to cremate the corpses of the five who had been shot before them; the last group was burned by the Ukrainians.[11] These thirty Jews were the last victims of Treblinka.

On the grounds of the former camp there were still sections of barbed wire, some pits, heaps of sand, and all kinds of articles—traces of the terrible tragedy that had occurred there. An agricultural farm was built on the site, and the bricks from the gas chambers were used for the farmhouse. A Ukrainian by the name of Strebel who had been a guard in Treblinka brought his family and began farming the area. The deserted fields of Treblinka were plowed, lupin was sown, and pine woods were planted.[12]

SOBIBOR

The last camp to be closed and demolished was Sobibor. After all the prisoners who had not escaped were shot there the day after the uprising, the

Jews who were brought to Sobibor from Treblinka carried out the dismantling work. They also loaded the ammunition from Camp IV onto trains.[13] As in Belzec and Treblinka, all the buildings in Sobibor were destroyed and a farm was built. Late in November, upon completing this work, all the remaining Jewish prisoners were murdered. They were taken to Camp III, forced to lie down side by side on the grills where the victims were cremated, and shot. The execution was carried out by *Oberscharführer* Gustav Wagner and the Ukrainian *Zugwachmünner* Alex Kaiser and Bodessa. The place was guarded by some other SS men and Ukrainians. The last SS men and Ukrainians left the camp in December 1943.[14]

THE TERMINATION OF GLOBOCNIK'S ECONOMIC ACTIVITY

While Operation Reinhard was in its closing phase and the death camps in various stages of liquidation, Globocnik was replaced as SS and police leader of the Lublin district by SS *Gruppenführer* Jacob Sporrenberg at the end of August or beginning of September 1943. However, the labor camps and the industrial enterprises of the SS in the Lublin district remained Globocnik's responsibility until October 22, 1943. Globocnik was then relieved of responsibility for the labor camps in the old airport of Lublin, in Trawniki, in Poniatowa, and from his post as director of the Eastern Industries.[15] All these camps were put under the command of the SS Economic and Administrative Main Office, headed by SS *Obergruppenführer* Oswald Pohl. But even then Globocnik was not officially exempted from his responsibility over all the assets, including valuables and money, taken from the victims of Operation Reinhard, valued at hundreds of millions of reichsmarks. On September 22, 1943, Himmler had already sent Globocnik a letter with a request to submit to him by December 31, 1943, a summary report concerning all the assets and economic achievements of Operation Reinhard. Globocnik wrote to Himmler from Trieste on November 3, 1943. The letter read:

> I concluded Operation Reinhard, which I directed in the General Government, on October 19, 1943, and have dissolved all the camps. I take the liberty of submitting the attached portfolio to you, *Reichsführer*, as my final statement. I have in the meantime handed over the labor camps to SS *Obergruppenführer* Pohl. . . .
>
> During a visit, you, *Reichsführer*, held out to me the prospect that a few Iron Crosses might be awarded for the special performance of this difficult task after the work had been concluded. . . . I beg to point out that such an award to the forces of the local SS and Police Leader was authorized for the work in Warsaw, which formed only a comparatively small part of the total work.[16]

On November 30, 1943, Himmler replied to Globocnik:

Dear Globocnik,

I confirm receipt of your letter dated November 4, 1943, and your noti-
fication regarding the termination of Operation Reinhard. Also I thank you
for the portfolio you sent me. I express to you my thanks and my acknowl-
edgement for the great and unique services which you performed for the entire German people by carrying out Operation Reinhard.
Heil Hitler!

Sincerely yours,
H. H. [Himmler][17]

In his letter Himmler did not refer to Globocnik's request that the Iron
Cross be awarded to leading figures of Operation Reinhard. His thanks
and acknowledgment were to suffice.

Globocnik submitted to Himmler a further report about the economic and administrative developments of Operation Reinhard on January 25,
1944. The report included a detailed appendix about the assets delivered
from Operation Reinhard—reichsmarks, foreign currency, precious metals, other valuables, and textiles. Globocnik knew that some circles in SS
headquarters, mainly those in the SS Economic and Administrative Main
Office, blamed him for not properly handling the economic matters of
Operation Reinhard, and even accused him of corruption. In his report he
wrote: "A certain odium still rests upon me to the effect that in all economic matters I did not maintain the necessary order. In this respect I must
advance indisputable proof that this is not so."

Globocnik asked Himmler to confirm that the delivery of the assets
was in proper order and that he was no longer responsible for any economic aspects of Operation Reinhard. A copy of this report was sent by Globocnik to *Obergruppenführer* Pohl. Globocnik was also worried about other
problems concerning his participation in Operation Reinhard. He wrote
in his report: "There is one additional factor to be added to the total ac-
counting of [Operation] Reinhard, which is, that the documents dealing
with it must be destroyed as soon as possible, after all the other basic works
concerning this matter have already been destroyed."[18]

In January 1944, the question of hiding his crimes began to bother
Globocnik, whereas a year and a half earlier, in August 1942, when asked
by visiting SS officers whether it would not be better, for reasons of secrecy, to cremate rather than to bury the corpses of the victims of Operation

Reinhard, Globocnik had answered, "We ought, on the contrary, to bury bronze tablets stating that it was we who had the courage to carry out this gigantic task." (See chapter 14.)

In the summer of 1942, Globocnik was still confident of Nazi Germany's ultimate victory and the annihilation of the Jewish people, and his part was to be a "glorious chapter" in the history of the Third Reich. But at the beginning of 1944, things seemed much gloomier. The German army was retreating on all fronts, and defeat was looming. The "gigantic task" Globocnik spoke of in August 1942—and, above all, his personal involvement in it—had to be hidden, erased from history. All the documents had to be destroyed, even those that did not relate directly to the murder of people but to money, textiles, and gold. Globocnik did not hesitate to mention this to Himmler in his last report on Operation Reinhard. And why should he? They had been partners in the "gigantic task" that had become the most gigantic crime of history.

LIQUIDATION OF THE MAJDANEK CONCENTRATION CAMP

At the close of Operation *Erntefest* (Operation Harvest Festival), the Germans left approximately six hundred Jews in Majdanek, half of whom were women, to burn the corpses of those murdered and sort their belongings. When the job was completed, the men were shot on the spot and the women were deported to Auschwitz. By early 1944, there were no more Jews in Majdanek. The camp continued to function as a concentration camp for thousands of Polish prisoners and other nationals. One of the camp's divisions served as a kind of hospital or more precisely, a holding pen for Soviet POWs who volunteered to serve the Germans and were wounded during the war.

With the progression of the Red Army toward the borders of the General Government, about 15,000 prisoners were transferred from Majdanek to Auschwitz and other camps throughout Germany during March and April 1944. During the massive Soviet counterattack, which began on June 22, 1944, the entire German front collapsed, with the group of the Central Armies entirely defeated. Within one month, the Soviet Army had advanced hundreds of kilometers westward, arriving at the outskirts of Lublin on July 22. The Soviet Army's appearance on the outskirts of Majdanek came as a complete surprise. On that day, about 1,000 of the camp prisoners were evacuated on foot. In their haste to leave, the SS did not manage to destroy the camp in time, but were able only to blow up part of the crematorium. The gas chambers and camp barracks remained intact. Polish prisoners, mainly peasants, fled. The Red Army found about 1,500 prisoners there, the vast majority war wounded from among the collaborators with the Germans. The latter were arrested and sent to POW camps in the Soviet Union. The liberators found huge piles of thousands of pairs of shoes taken from victims of the death camps and prepared for shipment to Germany.

Majdanek was the first concentration camp liberated by the Allied armies. Soviet, British, American, and other journalists were brought to see for themselves, and to photograph the evidence of the Nazis' crimes, which until then they had only heard about.

ASSESSING THE NUMBER OF VICTIMS
OF OPERATION REINHARD

IT IS DIFFICULT TO DETERMINE the precise number of Jews transported to the death camps of Belzec, Sobibor, and Treblinka as part of Operation Reinhard. This is since precise figures are lacking about the number of Jews in the areas from which they were transported to the death camps, due to conditions at the time and the Nazis' deportation policy. The data we have on the number of Jews living in areas of Poland before the war are taken from the last census conducted in 1931. From 1931 to the outbreak of war in 1939, there were changes in the demographics of the Jews in the cities and villages of Poland, due both to emigration and the continuing process of moving from towns to the larger cities as well as natural increase. Nevertheless, it is reasonable to assume that none of these processes generated significant change in the Jewish population figures in Poland on the eve of the German occupation.

More significant changes in the number of Jews in cities and towns of Poland began in the early years of the Second World War and the Nazi occupation, even prior to the beginning of the deportations to the death camps. From September to December 1939, Jews fled the German-occupied zones of Poland to the Soviet annexed areas—west Belarus and western Ukraine. Tens of thousands of Jews within the borders of the General Government fled or were deported from region to region, were concentrated in ghettos in the larger cites, or sent to forced labor camps. Thousands of Jews were shot during *Aktionen* that took place near their place of residence prior or during the liquidation of the ghettos. On the eve of the deportations to the death camps in 1942, there were, therefore, many localities without any Jews at all, while in other locations, the number of Jews was far greater than before the war.

The Wannsee Conference protocol noted that the General Government contained 2,284,000 Jews prior to Operation Reinhard, another 400,000 Jews in the Bezirk Bialystok, and 420,000 Jews in the incorporated areas of western Poland (which the protocol called Ostgebiete, "areas in the East"), for a total of 3,104,000 Jews.[1] In addition to the above, there were hundreds of thousands of Jews in eastern Poland, including west Belarus (the Generalkommissariat of Belorussia), areas of the Generalkommissariat of Wolhyn-Podolia (Polesia-Wolyn), as well as in the area of Vilna, annexed to the Generalkommissariat of Lithuania (including the cities of Pinsk, Brest-Litovsk, Rowno, Slonim, Baranowicze [or Baranovichi] and Nowogrodek, complete with their huge Jewish communities combined with hundreds of smaller Jewish communities in all of these areas). At least 250,000 Polish Jews fled or were deported deep into the Soviet Union. An estimated 3,300,000 to 3,350,000 Jews were in all of Poland on the eve of World War II. Based on these data, we can estimate that the number of Jews in the General Government was closer to 2,000,000—less than noted in the Wannsee Conference protocol.

Estimates of the number of Jews in the General Government murdered in the death camps of Belzec, Sobibor, and Treblinka and in the Majdanek concentration camp, which was also among the camps controlled by Odilo Globocnik and the Operation Reinhard general staff, are not based on reports by the camp commandants. There were never any written records of the killing activities in these camps: the entire operation was *Geheime Reichssache*—a secret matter of the Reich, and any written documentation on what was actually taking place in the death camps would have exposed the secret. The deportation orders and reports on their implementation were sometimes written down but usually given orally. Even the SS men who served in the camps were utterly prohibited from counting the number of Jews they murdered, or even to discuss the matter. SS *Unterscharführer* Robert Jührs, when asked at the Belzec war crimes trial on the number of Jews murdered in the camp, responded: "In the matter of this question, permit me to emphasize that we were explicitly prohibited from discussing numbers."[2] Furthermore, toward the end of the war, the Nazi authorities made sure to destroy the few extant documents; hence, after the war, only a very few German documents regarding the deportations were found.

The estimated number of Jews murdered in the camps during Operation Reinhard is consequently based on various sources, none of which provides a full or complete picture. One source comprises data on the number of Jews residing in cities from which they were deported to the camps involved in Operation Reinhard just before the war began. Other sources comprise, among others, documents and diaries left behind by the deported, survivor testimonies, testimonies at Nazi war crimes trials, and interrogation records by post-liberation Polish government agencies and public committees. However, Jews from hundreds of cities and villages were deported to the death camps and murdered, and we have no testimony at all about them. As for the number of Jews deported to Belzec, Sobibor, and Treblinka on known dates from known locations and murdered there, we must therefore add an estimated number of Jews who resided in the areas from which Jews were deported to these camps but about whom we have no information. Similarly, tens of thousands of Jews were transported to the General Government, mainly to the Lublin district, from areas of Western Poland annexed to Germany, as well as about 131,000 Jews from other European countries (see chapter 20).[3] In estimating the number of victims in each of the three death camps participating in Operation Reinhard detailed below in this chapter, what was taken into account was not only the majority who were murdered by asphyxiation in the gas chambers. It *aktionen* in the ghettos, in hiding places, or in attempted flight; those shot or killed in other ways as they attempted to escape from the trains; and those who died in the overcrowded cattle cars transporting the Jews to the camps.

In the General Government, the German authorities implemented a method of mass deportation to the death camps without preparing lists of names, and without even counting the number of those deported. The Jews were expelled from their homes, led on foot to the train stations, pushed into the overcrowded freight cars, transported to the camps, and murdered. Tens of thousands were shot in the ghettos and in escape attempts. The deportation was usually total. In cities where a few Jews were left (to work), the Germans counted those remaining, not those sent to be killed. Under these circumstances, it is difficult to obtain an accurate estimate of the number of victims from each city.

Some Reich railway system administration documents found after the war do provide certain facts on the number of trains at the disposal of the Operation to deport the Jews to the camps and the number of cars in each train. The Germans pushed 100 to 150 people into each freight car, and based on this figure we can form a general estimate of the number of Jews in each transport.

An additional source for estimating the number of those deported are the population registration records kept by the *Judenräte* of some of the ghettos. These censuses were usually conducted by order of the German authorities to exploit to the fullest the human resources in the ghetto for forced labor and in preparation for the transports. At times, the *Judenrat* initiated such a head count for food distribution purposes or to solve the housing problem more equally. Several documents with figures from these censuses were found after the Holocaust. At other times, the results were noted down in ghetto residents' diaries discovered after the war, in survivor memoirs, and community memorial books (*Yizkor* books) issued by the *Landsmannschaften* (organizations of survivors from specific cities and towns), which also comprise descriptions and number of Jews in the deportations. Survivor testimonies and testimonies from local non-Jewish witnesses to the deportations, as well as testimony from German officials at their postwar trials, are all important sources of information on the number of victims. These sources enable us to come closer to a more precise estimate of the number of Jews deported and murdered in Operation Reinhard's death camps.

An important research study from which we can learn about the timetables of the deportations from the cities and towns of the General Government, number of Jews deported from them, and the death camps which received them, is by Tatiana Bernstein, published in various publications by the Jewish Historical Institute in Warsaw. Another source is "The Table of the Holocaust of Polish Jewry," drawn up by Rabbi Yisral Schipansky and published in *Or Hamizrah* in New York, 1974. A more up-to-date source is the Encyclopedia of Jewish Communities, the project based on the *Pinkasei Hakehillot*, the Jewish community ledgers' volumes on eastern Galicia, western Galicia, Lublin, and Kielce published by Yad Vashem.

An important source for estimating the number of victims in Operation Reinhard are the documents that British intelligence succeeded in intercepting and decoding, including coded wireless messages from the SS, SiPo, and Orpo. These radio telegrams also referred to the destruction of the Jews and to Operation Reinhard and were first officially published in 1997. The decoded telegrams also mention Globocnik and his activities. Many of the thousands of decoded telegraphs were not recorded in their entirety, and the contents were not always understood. Many of the communications escaped the attention of British intelligence personnel who did not grasp their significance. Two of the telegrams not understood at the time, and whose meaning was clarified only since the turn of the millennium, were carefully studied to determine the number of Jews murdered in the death camps of Operation Reinhard. These telegrams were dispatched by SS *Sturmbanführer* Hermann Höfle from the Lublin headquarters of Operation Reinhard on January 11, 1943, and classified as top secret. The first, sent to Adolf Eichmann in Berlin at ten o'clock in the morning, comprised a report including the number of Jews murdered in

the operation's death camps, indicated only by their initials, during the last
two weeks of December 1942:

L [Lublin—Majdanek]	12,761
B [Belzec]	0
S [Sobibor]	515
T [Treblinka]	10,335
Total	23,611

Majdanek, defined as a concentration camp, is mentioned in this telegram
for the first time as a camp in which Jews were murdered. It was known
that the camp had three gas chambers to murder prisoners deemed unfit
for labor after a selection, and the Jews mentioned in this telegram were
murdered in these very gas chambers. There is no reliable information on
the location from which they were transported to Majdanek, but the assumption is they were Jews from approximately forty-two small forced labor camps from the area of Lublin and Radom. Following the Polish *Armi-
ja Ludowa*'s attack on the Janiszów forced labor camp, where about nine
hundred Jews were slaving, Heinrich Himmler ordered the liquidation of
the smaller labor camps with insufficient guards, and Majdanek was the
concentration camp closest to the smaller camps.[4] At Belzec, the roundups
to the death camps ended in mid-December, and transports of Jews were
no longer diverted there, which explains the zero figure in the list of deaths
for the second half of December 1942.

The second telegram was sent at 10:05, five minutes after the first.
Höfle sent it to Krakow, to SS *Obersturmbannführer* Franz Heim, deputy
head of the SiPo and the SD of the General Government (*Befehlshaber der
Sicherheitspolizei und des SD, BdS*), setting out detailed figures of the Jews
murdered in the death camps in Operation Reinhard through December
31, 1942:

L [Lublin—Majdanek]	24,733
B [Belzec]	434,508
S [Sobibor]	101,370
T [Treblinka]	71,355 [A second number 5 was not transcribed when the telegram was received; the figure for Treblinka should be 713,555].
Total	1,274,166[5]

The numbers of those killed mentioned in this telegram raised many
questions, since they are lower than the figures commonly accepted until

now, and lower than the data in this book. As for the Belzec camp, the numbers are final, since there were no more intakes of transports after mid-December 1942. Referring to Treblinka and Sobibor, the telegram mentioned partial numbers only: transports of Jews continued to arrive at Treblinka until August 1943 and to Sobibor up until early October 1943.

There is no doubt that Höfle sent these telegrams and that they were intercepted and decoded by British intelligence in real time. We can also state with assurance that Höfle had no reason to reduce the numbers of murdered. The question is: What was the source of these precise numbers, not only on the level of thousands, hundreds, and tens, but even on the level of units? This fact alone arouses doubts as to their reliability. As mentioned, the deportations from the ghettos and camps were accomplished without counting, as well as the process of killing in the camps. In the *aktionen* rounding up Jews to be deported from the ghettos and camps, deportees were crushed into the cattle cars until there was no more space—without a head count. When they arrived at the camps, they were rushed through the processes, herded into the gas chambers, the corpses then taken out to burial pits, all without counting as well. Apparently Höfle based his numbers on an overall estimate and partial reports, and to provide a semblance of reliability to his reports, he was "precise" to the units. It is reasonable to assume that the final total of victims in Belzec as well as Sobibor by the end of December 1942 were higher than the numbers stated in the second telegram.

Furthermore, in these two reports, Höfle refers to the number of those dead in the camps only, without taking into account the tens of thousands of Jews shot to death in their homes or hiding places in the ghetto, during the deportation roundups and during and after escape attempts. He does not take into account the thousands who jumped from the trains and fell to their death or were shot by guards accompanying the transports, and those who died under the inhuman conditions inside the trains on their way to the camps.

The detailed numbers in this book and the appendix, stated with as much precision as possible, are based on the estimate of the number of Jews living in those locations prior to the deportations. Even though most of the victims were murdered in the death camps, we have taken into account both those murdered and those who died during the roundups and on the trains. Peter Witte and Stephen Tyas mention the telegrams in their article, from which the numbers above are taken: "An unknown number of Jews, apparently tens of thousands, were shot during the 'cleansing' of the ghettos or in the forests. These numbers, without a doubt, are not included in these statistics."[6]

Polish historian Darius Libionka wrote in the introduction to his book on Operation Reinhard published in 2004: "By November 4, 1943 (Operation *Erntefest*), a total of close to 2,000,000 people were murdered in the ghettos, mass executions, and in Belzec, Sobibor, Treblinka, and Majdanek—more than the total of those murdered in the Auschwitz-Birkenau extermination camp. Not only the Jews of Poland were among the victims, but also Jews who were exiled to the General Government from Germany, Austria, Czechoslovakia, Slovakia, the Netherlands, and France."[7]

The number of Jews from these countries deported to the General Government, the great majority of whom were murdered in Operation Reinhard, was more than 131,000 (see chapter 20). Similarly, more than 13,000 Jews from the Reichskomissariat Östland were murdered in Sobibor (see chapter 19).

Our estimate of the total number of Jews murdered in Operation Reinhard and its affiliated operations, comprising the numbers stated by Höfle in his telegrams, is as follows: Belzec: 500,000–520,000; Sobibor, 250,000; Treblinka, 800,000–850,000; Majdanek, 60,000; Poniatowa and Trawniki, 20,000–25,000 (Operation *Erntefest*). The overall number is 1,600,000–1,735,000 murdered. Based on the estimated number of Jews living in the General Government as a little over 2,000,000, we can determine with certainty that hundreds of thousands of Jews, mainly from eastern Galicia (see chapters 2 and 8), were murdered before the deportation roundups to the camps, and during and after the deportations from the ghettos. Tens of thousands of Jews fled the ghettos, were captured, and were shot weeks and months after the deportations and on the death marches. Many tens of thousands died in the ghettos of starvation and disease. Several tens of thousands survived in the General Government in hiding, or thanks to Aryan papers, or were liberated by the Allies on German soil.

The tables of the deportations from the General Government and Bezirk Bialystok to the camps—Belzec, Sobibor, and Treblinka—listed in Appendix A are based on the aforementioned sources. To obtain more complete and more precise numbers, additional research and additional sources are needed. Perhaps in the future, they may be discovered in various archives, and perhaps we shall never know more precise figures. We must therefore remember that the tables are based on information we have up to the present time and are an estimate of the overall number of those murdered from each locality.

EPILOGUE

THE LARGEST SINGLE MASSACRE ACTION of the Holocaust, Operation Reinhard, which lasted twenty-one months, from March 1942 to November 1943, was carried out by, and accomplished according to the plans of, the Nazi extermination machine. It was an integral and substantial part of the overall plan for the "Final Solution of the Jewish problem."

The decision to implement Operation Reinhard, intended to annihilate the Jews of the General Government, was made during the first half of October 1941, approximately two months before Hitler's decision sometime in mid-December 1941 to entirely destroy all of the Jews of Europe. This was more than three months before the Wannsee Conference at which Reinhard Heydrich informed participants of the decision to annihilate the eleven million Jews of Europe. The five months that elapsed between the initial decision on Operation Reinhard until its launch in mid-March 1942 were necessary to plan and set up the organizational framework for the operation, construction of the Belzec death camp, and to bring together the German and Ukrainian personnel to manage and carry out the killings. Another four months and more elapsed until the operation reached its fullest extent, with the establishment of Sobibor and thereafter of Treblinka in July 1942

During the Final Solution of the problem of the Jews of Europe, at the point when total physical annihilation had commenced, three central decisions regarding the extermination and its timeframe were taken. The first decision related to the extermination of the Soviet Jews living within the June 22, 1941, borders. This decision was made over the course of a month, from the second half of July until the first half of August 1941, approximately six weeks after the German attack on the Soviet Union. This decision and its execution showed the Nazi leadership that the physical annihilation of millions of people was a possible solution to the Jewish problem and a means to destroy all of European Jewry.

The second decision on genocide was the decision on Operation Reinhard. This decision and its onset date was not part of the overall Nazi policy of extermination of all of the Jews of Europe and did not arise from it, since the overall policy of genocide was presented by Heydrich only at Wannsee. The decision on Operation Reinhard and its timing was dictated by the Nazi policy of *Drang nach Osten*—"spreading out to the East," meaning settling Germans in eastern Europe to bring about "Germanization" of the region. According to the plan thought up by Heinrich Himmler and Odilo Globocnik, Germanization was supposed to have begun in the Lublin district, disperse throughout the General Government, and serve as the connecting link to German settlement in the territories occupied in the Soviet Union. In order to clear an area for the German settlers, it was necessary first of all to get rid of the Jews and then to expel many of the Poles. Because there was no area to which they could deport the Jews of the Lublin district and of the entire General Government, it was decided to kill them without waiting for the overall plan for killing all of the Jews of Europe.

The third decision that concerned all of the Jews of Europe was Hitler's decision in the first half of December 1941, reflected in the program suggested by Heydrich at the Wannsee Conference (see chapter 2). The two decisions on extermination—the first to kill the Jews of the Soviet Union and the second on killing the Jews of the General Government—were indeed accepted prior to Hitler's overall plans for genocide, but definitely did receive his approval, and were compatible with the spirit of his speech in the Reichstag on January 30, 1939 (see the introduction).

The commanders of Operation Reinhard—Globocnik, Christian Wirth, and the SS men subordinate to them—succeeded in creating an efficient yet simple system of mass extermination by using relatively scanty resources. In each of the death camps—in Belzec, in Sobibor, and in Treblinka—a limited number of 20 to 35 Germans were stationed for purposes of command and supervision, and about 90 to 130 Ukrainians were responsible for guard duties and to prevent escape and resistance. All the physical work in the extermination process was imposed on 700 to 1,000 Jewish prisoners who were kept in each camp. The layout and structure of the camps were adapted to serve the extermination system and procedure. They were relatively small and compact, which enabled permanent and strict control over the entire area and all activities in the camp.

The material used to build the camps (lumber and bricks) and the means used for the extermination (a simple motor vehicle and ordinary petrol) were readily available in the immediate vicinity. Local workers and Jewish prisoners built the camps. All these elements made the entire operation independent of outside and distant factors. Anything needed for the smooth running of the extermination action could be procured in the surrounding areas within a short time. The killing system, as developed by Wirth, enabled the murder of tens of thousands of Jews every day in the three death camps under his jurisdiction.

The German authorities succeeded in keeping the erection of the camps and the activities there secret from the overwhelming majority of the victims throughout Operation Reinhard. Even when rumors or some information about Belzec and Treblinka and, to a much lesser extent, Sobibor reached the Jews still left in the ghettos of the General Government, the people were reluctant to believe them. It was much easier to accept the Nazi ruse that the deportees were destined for labor camps somewhere "in the East" where manpower was needed for wartime economic enterprises than to believe that innocent people were being sent to gas chambers. But even those who took the rumors about gas chambers and mass extermination seriously had no means of rescue for themselves and their families.

Nonetheless, as news reached the ghettoes of the true destination of the deportations, and of the fate of the deportees, it became more difficult to remove the Jews from the ghettoes and march them to the trains, requiring the Germans to allocate larger forces to execute the *Aktionen*. Tens of thousands of Jews prepared hiding places in the ghettoes, taking shelter there instead of reporting to the *Aktionen*, and many thousands fled to the forests. Thousands jumped off the trains as they were being transported to the camps. Only a scant few of these Jews survived. The majority of those in hiding were found and shot in their hiding places in the ghettoes or were burned to death when the Germans set the homes on fire. Those who fled to the forests were shot by their assailants, or murdered by peasants who coveted their possessions. And those who jumped from the trains met with a similar fate.

In the face of the hostility of the local population and the indifference or neutrality of the majority of them, together with the fear of the German terror, the chance to find refuge and to escape deportation was practically nil. The Germans further influenced the non-Jewish population by using embedded anti-Semitic feelings, bribery, and threats to encourage the capture and surrender of Jews in hiding or those who were attempting to escape. The Germans were the beneficiaries of the "noninterventionist" attitude of the local people, which kept them neutral and silent while their Jewish neighbors were dispatched to their death. This attitude, even if it was often motivated simply by fear of reprisals in case of extending help to Jews, contributed to the success of the Nazi extermination machine. The Jewish people, in order to survive, were in need of active help from the local people in providing hiding places, food, and Aryan documents. This was forthcoming neither from the local Polish population nor from the Polish

Underground. There were only a few exceptions to this general pattern of noninvolvement. The attitude of the majority of the Ukrainian population, which lived in the areas east of the camps, was even more hostile.

The Jews in the ghettos and in the camps were aware of the attitude of the local population and the slim chances of finding refuge among them. This, and the uncertainty of the destination and fate of the deportations, discouraged many from even considering escape. Nevertheless, many did try to escape during the deportations and from the trains. Very few survived.

The ruse continued even after the Jews arrived in the camps. Almost all of the victims went to the gas chambers believing that these were indeed baths. Secrecy, deception, and disguise on the one hand, and little chance for rescue or for hiding among the local population on the other hand, enabled the Nazis to keep their extermination machine running smoothly.

But those Jews who were selected for work in the camps and who were aware of what was going on there did not give up. Prisoners in Sobibor and Treblinka succeeded, despite the strict control and surveillance under which they were kept, in carrying out individual escapes and in staging an uprising accompanied by a mass escape. The uprisings ensured the survival of hundreds of prisoners and revealed the secrets of the death camps to the world. These survivors were the main witnesses at the Sobibor and Treblinka trials in the Federal Republic of Germany, as well as at other trials. The perpetrators did not succeed in their attempts to bury and burn the truth of the camps—and what transpired in them—together with the victims.

While Nazi Germany succeeded in keeping the aim of the deportations and the existence of the death camps secret from their victims, they did not succeed in preventing the truth about Belzec, Sobibor, and Treblinka from reaching the governments in London and Washington. In the initial stages of Operation Reinhard, information was transferred by the Polish Underground to the Polish Government-in-Exile in London and through their channels to the governments of Great Britain and the United States. As time passed, and especially toward the end of 1942, more and more detailed and accurate information reached the free world. It can be assumed that such information also reached the government of the Soviet Union.

No action followed this information. No steps were taken to warn the victims, to call on the local population and the Underground to help the victims, to bomb the railways or even the camps, to disrupt the smooth implementation of the deportations and extermination. The Jewish people were left to their fate.

The killing in the death camps of Operation Reinhard continued for twenty-one months. Tens of thousands of Jews who remained in several concentration camps in the General Government were murdered at Trawniki, Poniatowa, and Majdanek during the last stage of the Operation, camps that were all subject to the staff of Operation Reinhard. The conclusion of the operation to annihilate all of the Jews of the General Government were in the hands of the SS who felt a celebratory air as they completed their task, naming the killing action the *Erntefest*—Harvest Festival.

During Operation Reinhard, practically the entire Jewish population of the General Government were murdered together with the Jews of Bezirk Bialystok, as well as hundreds of thousands of Jews from the Third Reich and Jews from western and southern Europe (see the appendix and accompanying tables below for an estimate of the number of victims).

The silence that prevailed in the fields of Belzec, Sobibor, and Treblinka after the dismantling of the camps did not last long. While the Germans still controlled the area, and, to a greater extent, immediately after the liberation, in the summer of 1944, shameful scenes occurred on the sites of the former death camps. Rumors spread among the local population in the areas close to the camps, and even in more distant places, that not all the bodies had been burned and that some of the victims had been buried with their clothes without having undergone a search. The rumors claimed that in the seams and folds of the garments were hidden money, gold, and diamonds; there were also gold teeth that had not been removed. It was further said that the Jews who had been prisoners in the camps had buried great treasures. This was more than enough to bring people swarming all over the sites of the former death camps, digging and searching.

Rachel Auerbach, who visited Treblinka on November 7, 1945, as part of a delegation of the Polish State Committee for the Investigation of Nazi War Crimes on Polish Soil, described what she saw: "Masses of all kinds of pilferers and robbers with spades and shovels in their hands were there digging and searching and raking and straining the sand. They removed decaying limbs from the dust [and] bones and garbage that were thrown there. Would they not come upon even one hard coin or at least one gold tooth? They even dragged shells and unexploded bombs there, those hyenas and jackals in the disguise of man. They placed several together, set them off, and giant pits were dug in the desecrated ground saturated by the blood and the ashes of burned Jews."[1]

Scenes of this kind also took place in the fields of Belzec and Sobibor. The search for treasures continued. The area was dug up again and again, and each section of the land was checked thoroughly by local people and people from afar who tried their luck. These acts ceased only when the Polish government decided to turn the camp areas into national memorial sites. These memorials bear witness to the tragedies and massacres that were carried out on these sites and will remain for generations a mark of shame and disgrace, a reminder of the brutality and inhumanity that were the essence of Nazi Germany, and a warning to all peoples of the deadly dangers of racism and hatred.

APPENDIX A*

The Deportation of the Jews from the General Government, Bialystok General District, and Ostland

Table 1. Deportations to Belzec

A. District of Lublin

County	Town	Date of Deportation	Number of Deportees
Lublin	Lublin	March 17–April 14, 1942	30,000
	Piaski	March (end)	3,400
	Lubartow	April 9–10	800
Krasnystaw	Izbica	March 24	2,200
	Siennica Rozana	March (end)–April	272
Zamosc	Zamosc	April 11	3,000
	Cieszanow	April–May	1,300
	Tyszowce	May 22	580–800
	Komarow	May 23	1,000
	Laszczow	May 27	350
Janow	Krasnik	April 11–12	2,500
		November 1	3,000
	Zaklikow	November 3	2,000
	Janow Lubelski (via Zaklikow)	November	300
	Annapol (via Krasnik)	October–November	1,900

---

* After the Germans occupied Poland in September 1939 and established a civil administration, the General Government was divided into four districts (*Distrikte*); the annexation of the District of Galicia in 1941 made a total of five. The administrative subdivisions—counties (*Kreise*)—presented in this appendix reflect the situation during the General Government, not the divisions in prewar Poland.

Table 1. *Continued*

County	Town	Date of Deportation	Number of Deportees
	Modliborzyce (via Krasnik)	October–November	1,300
	Ulanow	October	1,100
	Zakrzowek (via Krasnik)	October–November	1,100
Bilgoraj	Bilgoraj	September 9–November 3	5,000
	Frampol	November 2	2,000
	Goraj	September 21	700
	Jozefow	November 2	1,800
	Krzeszow	November 2	500
	Szczebrzeszyn	May	280
		July 9	400
		November 20	2,000
	Tarnogrod	August 9–November 3	2,500

B. District of Galicia (Lvov)

County	Town	Date of Deportation	Number of Deportees
Lvov	Zolkiew	March 25–26, 1942	700
		November 22	2,000–2,500
	Lvov	March 15–April 1	15,000
		August 10–23	50,000–60,000
		November 18–21	8,000–10,000
	Bobrka	August 12	1,200–1,500
	Grodek Jagiellonski	August 13	2,500
	Mosciska	October 10	2,000
	Sadowa Wisznia	October	500
	Jaworow	November 7–8	1,300
	Kulikow	November 25	500
	Rudki	November	800
	Szczerzec	November 29–30	700
Rava Russkaya	Rava Russkaya	March 20	1,500
		July 29	1,200
		December 7–11	2,000–2,500
	Niemirow (via Rava Russkaya)	July 29	800

Table 1. *Continued*

County	Town	Date of Deportation	Number of Deportees
	Uhnow (via Rava Russkaya)	October (beginning)	2,000
	Lubaczow	October	2,000
	Lubycza Krolewska	October 4	500
	Oleszyce (via Lubaczow)	November	1,000
Czortkow	Czortkow	August 27	2,000
		October 5	500
	Borszczow	September 26	800
	Buczacz	October 17	1,600
		November 27	2,500
	Chorostkow	October 19	2,200
	Jezierzany	September 26	900
	Kopyczynce	September 30	1,000
	Korolowka	September 26	700
	Mielnica	September 26	2,000
	Monasterzyska	October 8	800
	Probuzna	September 30	1,500
	Skala-Podolska	September 26–27	700
	Tluste	July	300
		October 5	1,000
Brzezany	Brzezany	September 21	1,000–1,500
		December 4–5	1,000
	Bolszowce	September 21– October (end)	1,000
	Bukaczowce	September 21– October 26	700
	Bursztyn	September 21	200
		October 26	1,400
	Kozowa	September 21	1,000
	Narajow	September 21	900
		December 4–5	500
	Podhajce	September 21	1,000
		October 30	1,200
	Rohatyn	September 21	1,000
		December 8	1,500

Table 1. *Continued*

County	Town	Date of Deportation	Number of Deportees
Kamionka Strumilowa	Kamionka Strumilowa	September 15	1,500
	Lopatyn	October 28	hundreds
		October	400
	Radziechow	September 15	1,400
		October 7	1,000
	Sokal	September 17	2,000
		October 28	2,500
	Tartakow	October	900
	Witkow-Nowy	October	160
Drohobycz	Drohobycz	March 25, 1942	2,000
		August 8–17	2,500
		August 23–24	2,300
		November 9	1,000
	Boryslaw	August 4–6	5,000
		October	1,500
		November	2,000
	Sambor	August 4–6	4,000
		October 17–18	2,000
		October 22	2,000
	Stary Sambor	August 5–6	1,500
	Turka	August 4–8	5,000
Stanislawow	Stanislawow	March 31, 1942	5,000
		September 12	5,000
	Stryj	September 3–5	5,000
		October 17–18	2,000
		November	1,500
	Bolechow	August 3–6	2,000
		October 21	400
		November 20–23	300
	Chodorow	September 4–5	1,500
		October 18	350
	Brzozdowce	September 3–5	500
	Mikolajow	September 4	500
	Rozdol	September 4–5	1,600
	Skole	September 2–4	1,500

Table 1. *Continued*

County	Town	Date of Deportation	Number of Deportees
	Zydaczow	September 4–5	500–900
	Zurawno	September 4–5	500
Kolomyya	Kolomyya	April 3–4	5,000
		September 7	7,000
		October 11	4,000
	Peczenizyn	April	1,200
	Zablotow	April 11	400
	Sniatyn	April (beginning)	5,000
		September 7	1,500
	Horodenka	April 13	1,400
		September 9	1,500
Tarnopol	Tarnopol	August 29–31	4,000
		September 30	600–750
		November 8	2,500
	Jezierzany	September 26	700
	Jezierna	August 29	200
	Mikulince	August 31	1,200
	Skalat	August 31	600
		October 21	3,000
		November 9	1,100
	Trembowla	November 5	1,400
	Zbaraz	August 31– September 1	hundreds
		October 20–22	1,000
		November 8–9	1,000
	Zborob	August 29	1,000
Zloczow	Zloczow	August 30	2,700
		November 2–3	2,500
	Brody	September 19	2,500
		November 2	3,000
	Brzuchowice	August 26	250
	Olesko	August 29	470
	Pszemyslany	December 5	3,000
	Sasow	August 29	100
Przemysl	Przemysl	July 27– August 3	13,000

Table 1. *Continued*

County	Town	Date of Deportation	Number of Deportees
	Dobromil	July 29	1,700
	Lesko (via Zaslaw camp)	September 9	2,000
	Ustrzyki Dolne (via Zaslaw camp)	September 8	1,500
	Chyrow	July–August	900
	Bircza (via Przemysl)	July	1,000

C. District of Cracow

County	Town	Date of Deportation	Number of Deportees
Cracow	Cracow	June 1–6, 1942	5,000–6,000
		October 27–28	7,000
	Bochnia, Nowy-Wisnicz, Weiliczka, Dobczyce, Niepolomice, Gdow, Makow-Podhalanski, Jordanow, Skawina, Myslienica	August 25–30	14,000
Tarnow	Tarnow, Dobrowa	June 11–19	11,500
		July 24–25	1,800
	Tarnowska, Brzesko, Zabno, Tuchow, Zakliczyn	September 10–18	8,000
		November 15	2,500
Rzeszow	Rzeszow, Sokolow, Jawornik Polski, Glogow, Kolbuszowa, Czudec, Tyczyn, Blazowa, Strzyzow, Niebylec	July 7–18	22,000
Debica	Debica, Sedziszow, Baranow, Rozwadow, Tarnobrzeg, Pilzno, Radomysl, Ropczyce, Wielopole-Skrzynskie	July 21–25	12,000
Jaroslaw	Lancut, Lezajsk, Zolynia, Radymno (via Pelkin camp)	August (beginning)	10,000

Table 1. *Continued*

County	Town	Date of Deportation	Number of Deportees
Krosno	Krosno, Brzozow, Dukla, Jasienica, Korczyna, Rymanow	August 10–15	5,000
Jaslo	Jaslo, Biecz, Bobowa, Gorlice	August 16–20	16,000
Nowy Sącz	Nowy Sącz, Grybow, Stary Sącz, Krynica-Zdroj, Piwniczna, Lacko, Limanowa, Labowa	August 24–28	16,000
Nowy Targ	Nowy Targ, Rabka, Szczawnica, Czorsztyn Czarny Dunajec, Kroscienko	August 28–30	3,000
Miechow	Miechow, Dzialoszyce, Skalbmierz, Wolbrom, Slomniki, Proszowice	September 7	10,000
Sanok	Sanok, Lesko, Zagorz, Baligrod (via Zaslaw camp)	September 10–15	13,000

D. District of Radom

County	Town	Date of Deportation	Number of Deportees
Opatow	Sandomierz	October 29, 1942	3,230
	Zawichost	October 29	5,000

Table 2. Deportations to Sobibor

A. District of Lublin

County	Town	Date of Deportation	Number of Deportees
Pulawy	Pulawy	May 1942	2,500
	Opole	May 5	2,000
		May 12	2,000

Table 2. *Continued*

County	Town	Date of Deportation	Number of Deportees
	Deblin-Irena	May 6	2,500
	Ryki	May 7	3,000
	Jozefow nad Wisla	May 7	1,270
	Konskowola	May 8	1,580
	Baranow	May 8	1,500
	Markuszow	May 9	1,500
	Michow	May 10	2,500
	Lysobyki	May	500
Zamosc	Komarow	May 3	2,000
	Zamosc	May 15	5,000
Krasnystaw	Turobin	May 12	2,750
	Zolkiewka	May 12–15	1,000
	Gorzkow	May 13–14	2,000
	Krasnystaw	May 14–15	3,400
	Izbica	May 15	400
		October 22–30	5,000
		November 2	1,750
		January 1943	750
		April 1943	200
	Krasniczyn	June 6, 1942	800
Chelm	Chelm	May 21–23, 1942	4,300
		June (end)	300
		October 27–28, November 6	3,300
	Siedliszcze	May 18	630
		October 22	500
	Wlodawa	May 23	1,200
		October 24	5,000
		October 30	500
		April 30, 1943	2,000
	Reyowiec (via Chelm)	October 10, 1942	2,400
	Wojslowice	October	1,200
	Dubeczna	December	650
	Czycow, Kszywowierzba, Olchowiec, Pawlow, Sawin, Swierze, Uhrusk	October–November	3,000–4,000

Table 2. *Continued*

County	Town	Date of Deportation	Number of Deportees
Hrubieszow	Hrubieszow	June 1	3,049
		June 7–9	500
		October 28	2,000
	Belz	June 2	1,540
	Dubienka	June 2	2,670
	Grabowiec	June 8	1,200
	Uchanie	June 10	1,650
Biala-Podlaski	Biala-Podlaski	June 10–11	3,000
Lublin	Lubartow	October 11	3,000
	Leczna	October 23	3,000
		April 29, 1943	200
	Majdanek camp	July 1943	5,000

As this table shows, according to existing information, close to 100,000 Jews from the District of Lublin were deported to Sobibor. Based on the number of Jews who lived in small townships and villages in these areas before the war, and considering the thousands of Jews who were expelled or fled from territories in western Poland, which was annexed to Germany, and who found refuge in the Lublin area, the actual number of those who were deported to Sobibor is much higher. We may assume that the total number of Jews from the District of Lublin who were exterminated in Sobibor was about 130,000 to 140,000.

B. District of Galicia

About fifteen thousand to twenty-five thousand Jews were deported from Lvov and the other ghettos in the district of Galicia to Sobibor in the period between December 1942 and June 1943, after Belzec was closed.

Table 3. Deportations to Treblinka

A. The District of Warsaw

County	Town	Date of Deportation	Number of Deportees
Warsaw	Warsaw	July 22–August 28, 1942	199,500
	In the ghetto there were over 100,000 Jews expelled from the counties of Grojec, Lowicz, Skierniewice, Sochaczew and Blonie in February–March 1941.		

Table 3. *Continued*

County	Town	Date of Deportation	Number of Deportees
		September 3–12	52,000
		September 21	2,200
		January 18–22, 1943	6,000
		April 19–May 15	7,000
	Otwock, Falenica,	August 19–20, 1942	15,300
	Rembertow, Ludwisin,	October 3–4	9,000
	Radzymin, Wolomin,		
	Jadow		
Minsk	Minsk-Mazowiecki	August 21–22, 1942	6,100
Mazowiecki	Kaluszyn, Kolbiel,	September 15–27	9,900
	Mrozy Kuflew, Siennica,		
	Stanislawow,		
Siedlce	Siedlce	August 22–24	11,700
		September 26	
	November 30Mordy	August 22	3,800
	Losice	August 22	5,500
Sokolow-	Sokolow-Podlaski,	September 22–25	18,300
Węgrow	Węgrow, Stoczek		
	Kosow-Lacki		
	Sterdyn, Lochow		
Garwolin	Zelechow, Sobolew,	September 27–	20,000
	Sobienie-Jeziory, Parysow,	October 2, 1942	
	Laskarzew		

B. The District of Radom

County	Town	Date of Deportation	Number of Deportees
Radom	Radom	August 6, 1942	8,000
		August 16–17	20,000
		January 13, 1943	1,500
	Szydlowiec	September 23	10,000
		January 13, 1943	5,000
	Kozienice	September 27, 1942	13,000
	Glowaczow, Magnuszew,		
	Marianpol, Mniszew		
	Ryczywol,		
	Sieciechow, Stromiec,		

Table 3. *Continued*

County	Town	Date of Deportation	Number of Deportees
	Zwolen, Magnuszew, Trzebien, Kozienice, Gniewoszow, Garbatka, Janowice, Oblassy, Pionki, Policzna, Sarnow	September 29	10,000
	Gniewoszow (in addition to those sent through Zwolen)	November 15	1,000
Kielce	Kielce	August 20–24	20,000
	Checiny	September 12	4,300
	Bodzentyn	October 3	2,000
	Skarzysko-Kamienna, Suchedniow	September 22	3,000
Czestochowa	Czestochowa Ghetto	September 22–October 7	30,000
Radomsko	Radomsko	October 10–12	14,000
		January 6, 1943	4,000
	Zarki	October 6, 1942	800
	Koniecpol	October 7	1,600
Piotrkow	Piotrkow, Gorzkowice, Przyglow, Sulejow Kamiensk	October 15–25	27,500
Jedrzejow	Jedrzejow, Sedziszow, Szczekociny, Wloszczowa, Wodzislaw	September 16–25	16,500
Busko	Busko-Zdroj, Chmielnik Pacanow, Pinczow Nowy Korczyn	October 2–6	20,000
	Wislica, Stopnica	November 5–6	5,000
Konskie	Konskie, Gowarczow (via Konskie ghetto)	September 3–7	10,000

Table 3. *Continued*

County	Town	Date of Deportation	Number of Deportees
	Przedborz	October 9–12	4,000
	Radoszyce	November 3	4,000
Tomaszow-Mazowiecki,	Tomaszow-Mazowiecki Biala-Rawska, Drzewica Koluszki, Nowe Miasto Opoczno, Przysucha, Rawa Mazowiecka, Ujazd, Orzewicz Zarnow	October 22–November 2, 1942 January 6, 1943	42,800
Starachowice	Starachowice, Wierzbnik Chotcha Nowa Ilza, Lipsko Sienno, Tarlow Ciepielow	October 15–29, 1942	27,100
Opatow	Opatow	October 20, 1942	6,500
	Cmielow	October (end)	900
	Iwaniska	October 15	1,600
	Kunow	October (end)	500
	Klimontow	October 30	4,000
	Koprzywnica	October 31	1,600
	Lagow	October 7	2,000
	Ostrowiec	October 11–12	11,000
	Osiek	October 25	500
	Ozarow	October (end)	4,500
	Staszow	November 7	6,000
	Sandomierz	January 10, 1943	6,000

C. District of Lublin

County	Town	Date of Deportation	Number of Deportees
Biala-Podlaska	Biala-Podlaska	September 26–October 6, 1942	4,800

Table 3. *Continued*

County	Town	Date of Deportation	Number of Deportees
Radzyn	Parczew (including Jews from Kock)	August 19–25	5,500
	Miedzyrzec-Podlaski	August 25–26	11,000
	Radzyn	October 1	2,000
	Lukow		
	(including Jews	October 5–8	7,000
	from Adamow)	November 7	3,000

Table 4. Deportation of the Jews from Bialystok General District to Treblinka

Ghetto/Collection Camp (C.C.)	Details of Deportation from Ghettos or through Collection Camps	Date of Deportation	Number of Deportees
Bialystok ghetto	During this time, three transports of 20 freight cars left for Treblinka, each transport delivering about 2,000 deportees to the death camp. Another 4,000 people were deported on two transports to Auschwitz (General Administration, Eastern Railway [Geldof], Transport Order No. 552, February 1, 1943)	February 9–13, 1943	6,000
	The liquidation of the ghetto. Two transports of 76 freight cars left for Treblinka, and three transports left for Lublin (Majdanek). From Majdanek some 4,000 were deported to Auschwitz.	August 18–19, 1943	7,600
Jasionowka	In the ghetto there were 400 Jews from surrounding localities.	January 25, 1943	2,120

Table 4. *Continued*

Ghetto/Collection Camp (C.C.)	Details of Deportation from Ghettos or through Collection Camps	Date of Deportation	Number of Deportees
Bialystok C.C.	Knyszyn—1,300 Grodek-Bialystocki—1,380 Lapy—450 Choroszcz—400 Michalowo—750 Sokoly—850 Suprasl—170 Wasilkow—1,180 Zabludow—1,400 Kleszczele—400 Milejczyce—1,000	November 10– December 15, 1942	9,280
Bogusze C.C.	Goniądz—1,300 Trzcianne—1,200 Augustow—2,000 Grajewo—2,500 Rajgrod—600 Szczuczyn—1,500	November 10– December 15, 1942	9,100
Kelbasin C.C.	Druskieniki—500 Jeziory—2,000 Lunna—1,500 Ostryna—2,000 Porzecze—1,000 Skidel—3,000 Sopockinie—2,000 Dąbrowa—1,000 Indura—2,500 Janow—950 Krynki—5,000 Kuznica—1,000 Korycin—1,000 Odelsk—500 Sidra—350 Sokolka—8,000 Suchowola—5,100 Grodno—4,500—on December 19, 1942	November 10– December 15, 1942	38,900

Table 4. *Continued*

Ghetto/Collection Camp (C.C.)	Details of Deportation from Ghettos or through Collection Camps	Date of Deportation	Number of Deportees
	3,000 Jews were sent back to Grodno from Kelbasin C.C.		
Grodno	Over 10,000 Jews were deported in this action, most of them to Auschwitz, and one transport to Treblinka.	January 18–22, 1943	1,600
	The liquidation of the ghetto	February 14–19,1943	4,400
Volkovysk C.C.	Jalowka—850 Lyskow—600 Mosty—350 Porozow—1,000 Ros—1,000 Rozana—3,000 Swislocz—3,000 Wolkovysk—7,000 Wolfa—1,500 From this camp 2,000 were sent to Auschwitz and the rest to Treblinka.	November 10– December 15, 1942	16,300
County of Bielsk-Podlaski	In the ghetto of Bielsk-Podlaski there were 7,000 local Jews, and 4,000 more were brought there from Bocki, Bransk, Narew, and Orla during the first week of November. They were deported in eleven transports, 1,000 people in each transport.	November 2–11, 1942	11,000
	Ghetto of Ciechanowiec	October 15	3,300
	Siemiatycze	November 2–10	4,330

Table 5. The Deportations from Reichskommissariat Ostland to Sobibor

Area	Town	Date of Deportation	Number of Deportees
Generalkommissariat Belorussia	Lida	September 18–19, 1943	2,700
	Minsk	September 18–22	6,000
Generalkommissariat Lithuania	Vilna (Vilnius)	September 23–24	5,000

In most of the cities and townlets detailed in the above tables, Jews deported to death camps were counted along with tens of thousands of people shot to death in the round-ups, but we have no data on these numbers. However, referring to several locations, especially those with large Jewish communities, we do have data enabling an estimate of the number of people shot on site, not included in the number of those deported.

- In Lublin, during the roundups of March–April 1942, 5,500 to 6,000 people were shot.
- In Lvov, in late June 1942, 6,000 to 8,000 people were shot, with another approximately 10,000 shot in January 1943.
- In Radom, during the deportation roundups in August 1942, approximately 2,500 people were shot to death.
- In Kielce, during the deportation roundups in August 1942, approximately 2,500 people were shot to death.

These data show us that there was a widespread phenomenon of murdering Jews where they lived, repeated throughout all of the ghettos during the deportations, with numbers similar to the above or smaller. In addition, tens of thousands more Jews were shot to death, mainly in the district of Galicia, in organized murder actions separate from the roundups, and not associated with the roundups deporting Jews to the camps.

In addition to the figures on the transports of Jews set out in this appendix, tens of thousands of Jews were murdered in Belzec, Sobibor, and Treblinka, who were transported to these death camps from Germany, Austria, Slovakia, the Protectorate of Bohemia and Moravia (the Theresienstadt Gehtto), Greece, Yugoslavia, and France (see chapter 20).

APPENDIX B

The Fate of the Perpetrators of Operation Reinhard

Hans Frank, the head of the General Government, was arrested by the American army and sentenced to death by the Nuremberg International Military Court. He was hanged on October 16, 1946.

Josef Bühler, the secretary of state of the General Government, was sentenced to death by a Polish court and hanged in 1948.

Friedrich Wilhelm Krüger, the higher SS and police leader in the General Government, disappeared after the war. According to unconfirmed sources, he died on May 10, 1945.

Odilo Globocnik, the SS and police leader in the district of Lublin and in direct charge of Operation Reinhard, served from the autumn of 1943 in northern Italy as the higher SS and police leader. After the capitulation of Germany, he was taken by the British army to a prisoner-of-war camp, where he committed suicide on May 31, 1945.

Hermann Höfle, who was in charge of the "Main Department" of Operation Reinhard, was arrested in Austria as late as 1961. A year after his arrest, while incarcerated in a prison in Vienna, he committed suicide by hanging himself on August 21, 1962.

Christian Wirth, the inspector of the three death camps, Belzec, Sobibor, and Treblinka, commanded the "SS Task Force R," which was composed of former Operation Reinhard members from the autumn of 1943. This unit was engaged in anti-partisan and anti-Jewish actions in northern Italy in the area of Trieste-Fiume-Udine. All the Jews in these areas were to be concentrated in San Saba near Trieste and eventually executed. At Wirth's initiative a crematorium was even built there. Wirth was killed by partisans, near Trieste in May 1944.

Franz Stangl, the commander of Sobibor and Treblinka, was stationed in northern Italy, in the areas of Fiume and Udine, from the autumn of 1943 and engaged in actions against partisans and local Jews. After the war he escaped to Brazil; in 1967 he was discovered there, arrested, and extradited to the Federal Republic of Germany. He was tried in Dusseldorf in 1970 and was sentenced to life imprisonment. He died in prison a few months after the end of the trial.

Franz Reichleitner, the commander of Sobibor, was stationed in the area of Fiume in Italy from the autumn of 1943 and engaged in actions against partisans. He was killed by partisans.

Gottlieb Hering, the commander of Belzec and afterward of the Poniatowa camp, was in northern Italy, in the area of Trieste and San Saba, from the end of 1943. He did not survive the war.

Some of the SS men who had served in Belzec, Sobibor, and Treblinka were arrested in the Federal Republic of Germany and were brought to trial there.

A group of ten SS men who served in Treblinka, among them the deputy commander of the camp, Kurt Franz, were tried in Dusseldorf between October 12, 1964, and August 24, 1965. Kurt Franz and three other defendants were sentenced to life imprisonment; five defendants were sentenced to three to twelve years of imprisonment; one was acquitted.

The Sobibor trial, against twelve SS men who served in Sobibor, was held in the Court of Hagen and lasted from September 6, 1965, to December 20, 1966. During the trial, one of the defendants, Kurt Bolender, the former commander of Camp III—the extermination area—committed suicide. Of the other defendants, only six were sentenced to imprisonment: Karl Frenzel to life imprisonment and the others to three to eight years.

The Belzec trial in Munich lasted only three days, from January 18 to 21, 1965. The defendant was Josef Oberhauser. Some other SS men who had served in Belzec had also served in Sobibor and therefore had been defendants at the Sobibor trial. Oberhauser was sentenced to four and a half years' imprisonment.

In the Soviet Union, some trials of Ukrainians who had served in Operation Reinhard camps were held. At one of the trials, in Kiev, in 1962–1963, ten of the defendants were sentenced to death. The eleventh defendant received fifteen years' imprisonment. At a second trial, held in June 1965 in Kiev, three of the Ukrainian guardsmen who had served in Sobibor and Belzec were sentenced to death.

The majority of the SS men and Ukrainians who served in the death camps of Operation Reinhard were never brought to trial.

NOTES

INTRODUCTION

1. *Documents on the Holocaust: Selected Sources on the Destruction of the Jews of Germany and Austria, Poland, and the Soviet Union*, Yitzhak Arad, Israel Gutman, Abraham Margaliot, eds. (Lincoln: University of Nebraska Pressand Jerusalem: Yad Vashem , 1999, 2004), pp. 134–35 (hereafter, *Documents on the Holocaust*).

CHAPTER ONE: THE JEWS OF THE GENERAL GOVERNMENT, SEPTEMBER 1939–JUNE 1941: DEPORTATIONS AND GHETTOIZATION

1. Christopher R. Browning, *The Origins of the Final Solution: The Evolution of Nazi Jewish Policy, September 1939—March 1942* (Lincoln: University of Nebraska Press and Jerusalem: Yad Vashem, 2004), p. 36 (hereafter, Browning, *Origins*).

2. *Documents on the Holocaust*, 173–176. There were approximately six hundred thousand Jews living in Poland in areas annexed to the Third Reich whom Heydrich ordered deported to the General Government, of whom about four hundred thousand were from the Warthegau.

3. Ibid., p. 179.

4. Ibid., p. 178.

5. Klaus-Michael Mallmann, "'Człowieku, dziś świętuję tysięczny strzał 5 w potylicę': Policja Bezpieczeństwa a Shoa w Galicji Zachodniej," in Dariusz Libionka, ed., *Akcja Reinhardt: Zagłada Żydów w Generalnym Gubernatorstwie* (Warsaw: Instytut Pamięci Narodowej, 2004) (hereafter, *Akcja Reinhardt*), p. 94; Dieter Pohl, "Znaczenie dystryktu lubelskiego w 'ostatecznym rozwiązaniu kwestii żydowskiej,'" in *Akcja Reinhardt*, pp. 40–41; Browning, *Origins*, pp. 29–30. Browning specifies places, such as Różan, Błonie, and Pultusk, where dozens to hundreds of Jews were murdered during the first few weeks of the Nazi occupation.

6. Götz Aly, "'Jewish Resettlement': Reflections on the Political Prehistory of the Holocaust," in Ulrich Herbert, ed., *National Socialist Extermination Policies: Contemporary German Perspectives and Controversies* (New York: Berghahn Books, 2000), p. 59.

7. Heinz Höhne, *The Order of the Death's Head: The Story of Hitler's SS* (London: Secker and Warburg, 1970) (hereafter, Höhne), pp. 309–310.

8. Browning, *Origins*, p. 29.

9. Aly, "Jewish Resettlement," pp. 60–61.

10. Testimony of Zvi Pachter, in *Hayoetz Hamishpati Lamemshala Neged Adolf Eichmann: Eduyot* (Hebrew) (*The Eichmann Trial, Testimonies*, 2 vols., hereafter, *The Eichmann Trial, Testimonies*) (Jerusalem: Prime Minister's Office, Information Center, 1963), vol. 2, pp. 153–154.

11. Joseph Litvak, *Plitim Yehudim MiPolin BeVrit Hamo'atzut 1939–1946* (Hebrew; *Jewish Refugees from Poland in the Soviet Union 1939–1946*) (Jerusalem: The Institute of Contemporary Jewry, Hebrew University of Jerusalem, 1988), pp. 44–46.

12. Documents on German Foreign Policy, 1918–1945 (DGFP), ser. D (1937–1945), vol. 8, The War Years, Sept. 4, 1939–Mar. 18, 1940 (Washington, DC: US Govt. Print. Off., 1949–1983), p. 489.

13. Gerald Reitlinger, *The Final Solution: The Attempt to Exterminate the Jews of Europe, 1939–1945* (hereafter, Reitlinger), 2nd edition (London: Vallentine–Mitchell, 1968), pp. 51–52.

14. Vladimir Yampolski et al., *Organy gosudarstvennoi bezopasnosti v Velikoi 14, Otechestvennoi voine*, vol. 1, Nakanune (Moscow: Kniga i biznes, 1995), doc. no. 53, p. 118.

15. Browning, *Origins*, p. 121.

16. *Documents on the Holocaust*, p. 196.

17. Browning, *Origins*, p. 131.

18. Ibid., p. 81.

19. Ibid., pp. 87–89; Richard Breitman, *The Architect of Genocide: Himmler and the Final Solution* (Hannover and London: Bodley Head, 1991) (hereafter, Breitman), pp. 122–127.

20. Dieter Pohl, "The Murder of Jews of the General Government," in Herbert, *National Socialist Extermination Policies*, p. 86.

21. Yad Vashem Archives (hereafter, YVA), JM/19988 (previously labeled: M-33/895).

CHAPTER TWO: THE ROAD TO OPERATION REINHARD

1. Yitzhak Arad, *The Holocaust in the Soviet Union* (Lincoln and Jerusalem: University of Nebraska and Yad Vashem, 2009), pp. 52–54.

2. Ibid., 56–57.

3. Ulrich Herbert, "Extermination Policy: New Answers and Questions in the History of the 'Holocaust' in German Historiography," in Herbert, *National Socialist Extermination Policies*, p. 31; Browning, *Origins*, pp. 281–284; Arad, *The Holocaust in the Soviet Union*, pp. 129–133.

4. Yitzhak Arad, Shmuel Krakowski, and Shmuel Spector, eds., *The Einsatzgruppen Reports: Selections from the Dispatches of the Nazi Death Squads' Campaign against the Jews July 1941– January 1943* (New York, 1989), no. 26, p. 36; no. 56, p. 92; no. 66, p. 11; Raul Hilberg, *The Destruction of the European Jews* (New Haven and London, 2003), p. 301 (hereafter, Hilberg).

5. *Documents on the Holocaust*, pp. 398–400.

6. Hilberg, p. 343.

7. Nuremberg Documents, PS-510, cited from *Documents on the Holocaust*, pp. 350–352 (hereafter, Nuremberg Documents, PS-510).

8. Eugen Kogon, Hermann Langbein, and Adalbert Rückerl, eds., *Nationalsozialistische Massentötungen durch Giftgas*, Frankfurt am Main, 1983, p. 62 (hereafter, *Nationalsozialistische Massentötungen*); Breitman, p. 89.

9. *Nationalsozialistische Massentötungen*, p. 31; see also Breitman, p. 90.

10. Browning, *Origins*, p. 190.

11. *Nationalsozialistische Massentötungen*, p. 57; see also Breitman, pp. 197–198; Browning, *Origins*, p. 192.

12. *KL Auschwitz Seen by the SS Höss, Broad, Kremer*, 2nd ed. (Museum w Oswiecimu, 1978), pp. 92–95.

13. YVA, TR-10/959, pp. 45–47, the trial against Dr. Widmann (hereafter, Widmann); *Nationalsozialistische Massentötungen*, pp. 81–82; Breitman, pp. 201–202.

14. Edward Serwański, *Obóz Zaglady w Chełmnie nad Narem, 1941–1945* (Poznan, 1964), p. 45 (hereafter, Serwański); *Nationalsozialistische Massentötungen*, p. 84, gives the number of fifty to sixty people in the Saurer car and twenty-five to thirty people in the Diamond car.

15. *Nationalsozialistische Massentötungen*, pp. 84–86.

16. Nuremberg Documents, PS-510.

17. Nuremberg Documents, PS-710, cited from *Documents on the Holocaust*, p. 233.

18. Christian Gerlach, "The Wannsee Conference, the Fate of German Jews, and Hitler's Decision in Principle to Exterminate All European Jews," *B'shvil Hazikaron* (Hebrew) 42 (2001), pp. 30–31.

19. Nuremberg Documents, PS-2233.

20. Gerlach, "The Wannsee Conference," pp. 30–31.

21. Nuremberg Documents, NG-2586-G, cited from *Documents on the Holocaust*, pp. 253–256 (hereafter, Nuremberg Documents, NG-2586-G).

22. Nuremberg Documents, NG-2586-G.

23. Herbert, "Extermination Policy," p. 40.

24. Bogdan Musiał, "The Origins of 'Operation Reinhard': The Decision-Making Process for the Mass Murder of the Jews in the General Government," *Yad Vashem Studies* 28 (2000), pp. 113–153. See especially p. 129. Regarding the July 16, 1941, meeting, see Nuremberg Documents, L-221.

25. Richard Breitman described how Himmler built and expanded economically productive factories subject to the SS so as not to be financially dependent on the state treasury and the Nazi Party's financial organs. This would enable the SS to carry out its resettlement and other policies without the intervention of other government agencies. See Breitman, pp. 86–87, 184–185.

26. Pohl, "The Murder of Jews in the General Government," p. 87.

27. Musiał, "The Origins of 'Operation Reinhard,'" pp. 129–130.

28. Tadusz Zaderecki, *Bimshol Zlav Hakeres Bilvov* (Hebrew, *When the Swastika Ruled Lvov*) (Jerusalem: Yad Vashem, 1982), pp. 18–23; Arad, *The Holocaust in the Soviet Union*, pp. 89–91.

29. Zaderecki, *When the Swastika Ruled Lvov*, pp. 62–63; David Kahane, *Lvov Ghetto Diary* (Amherst: University of Massachusetts Press, 1990), p. 10 (hereafter, Kahane). According to other sources, there were two thousand victims. Petliura was assassinated in 1926 in Paris by Shalom Schwartzbard, a young Jew whose family were murdered by Petliura's soldiers in pogroms that took place in Ukraine during the civil war. Schwartzbard was tried in France and acquitted in a controversial trial.

30. Dieter Pohl, "Hans Krueger and the Murder of Jews in the Stanisławów Area," *Yad Vashem Studies* 26 (1998), pp. 239–264.

31. Eliyahu Yones, *Smoke in the Sand: The Jews of Lvov in the War Years, 1939–1944* (Jerusalem: Gefen, 2004), p. 187–188 (hereafter, Yones).

32. Thomas Sandkühler, "Anti-Jewish Policy and the Murder of the Jews in the District of Galicia, 1941/42," in Herbert, *National Socialist Extermination Policies*, pp. 108–109.

33. Pohl, "Hans Krueger and the Murder of the Jews," p. 245.

34. Ibid., p. 244. Dieter Pohl states the number of Jews in the city was then approximately forty thousand. This seems a bit excessive in light of the estimated number of murdered is the various *Aktionen*.

35. Ibid., pp. 251–253; Dieter Pohl, *Nationalsozialistische Judenverfolgung in Ostgalizien, 1941–1944* (Munich, 1997), pp. 144–147.

36. Danuta Dabrowska, Abraham Wein, and Aharon Weiss, eds. (Hebrew, *Encyclopedia of Jewish Communities,*), *Poland* vol. 2—*Eastern Galicia* (Jerusalem: Yad Vashem, 1976) pp. 473–474 (hereafter, *Pinkas HaKehillot: Eastern Galicia*).

37. Ibid., p. 77, 160, 180, 485, 518. Dieter Pohl attributes the scope of the genocide of the Jews of the Stanislawow area and its date, before the genocide in the rest of the General Government, to the personality of the SiPo commandant of the area, SS *Hauptsturmführer* Hans Krueger, who was extremely cruel. See Pohl, "Hans Krueger and the Murder of the Jews," pp. 251, 261–262. The first extermination *Aktion* after eastern Galicia was annexed to the General Government took place in Nadworna on October 6, 1941: more than 2,000 Jews were led into the forest adjacent to the city, where the Jews were shot by the German police and local Ukrainian policemen. Other communities in which thousands of Jews were murdered in roundups were Delyatin (approx. 1,950 murdered), Bolechów (approx. 1,000), Kosov (approx. 2,200), Sniatyn (500), Horodenka (approx. 2,500), Borysław (approx. 1,500), and Stryj (approx. 1,000).

38. Pohl, "The Murder of Jews in the General Government," p. 87.

39. Browning, *Origins*, pp. 324–326, 331, 365–366, 416–417; Herbert, *National Socialist Extermination Policies*, p. 28; see also Shmuel Krakowski, *Chełmno: A Small Village in Europe; The First Nazi Mass Extermination Camp* (Jerusalem: Yad Vashem, 2009).

40. On the murder of the Jews of Yugoslavia see Walter Manoschek, "The Extermination of Jews in Serbia," in Herbert, *National Socialist Extermination Policies*, pp. 163–185.

41. The data on the number of Jews in each country is imprecise yet may be considered to be a general estimate of the Jewish population of each country. It is important to note that included in the eleven million count were more than four hundred thousand Jews in the United Kingdom and neutral countries over which Germany had no control, as well as hundreds of thousands of Jews in North Africa (included in the figure of seven hundred thousand Jews in the unoccupied zone of France), which lowers the number of the Jews affected by Hitler's decision of early December 1941.

CHAPTER THREE: OPERATION REINHARD: ORGANIZATION AND MANPOWER

1. Nuremberg Documents, PS-1919, cited from *Documents on the Holocaust*, p.344.

2. Adalbert Rückerl, *Nationalsozialistische Vernichtungslager im Spiegel deutscher Strafprozesse: Belzec, Sobibor, Treblinka, Chelmno*(München: Deutscher Taschenbuch Verlag, 1977), pp. 117–118 (hereafter, Rückerl, *NS-Vernichtungslager*).

3. Nuremberg Documents, NO-426, affidavit of Viktor Brack, trial no. 1, at the so-called Doctors' Trials (hereafter, Brack-Nuremberg).

4. Nuremberg Documents, NO-205; see also Rückerl, *NS-Vernichtungslager*, pp. 117–119.

5. Gitta Sereny, *Into That Darkness: From Mercy Killing to Mass Murder* (London, 1974), p. 85 (hereafter, Sereny).

6. Patricia Heberer, "Ciągłość eksterminacji: Sprawcy 'T4' i 'Akcja Reinhardt,'" in *Akcja Reinhardt*, 83–84.

7. Rückerl, *NS-Vernichtungslager*, pp. 125–126. Cited in*Documents on the Holocaust*, pp. 274–275.

8. Josef Marszałek, *Majdanek* (Warszawa, 1981), pp. 54–55 (hereafter, Marszałek); Józef Marszałek, "Centralny Zarząd Budowlany SS i Policji w Lublinie," *Zeszyty Majdanka* 6 (1972): pp. 22–23.

9. YVA, TR-10/1102-1, the trial of Streibel, pp. 21–23 (hereafter, Streibel).

10. United States District Court, Southern District of Florida, Case 77-2668-Civ-NRC, 25/7/1978, *USA,Plaintiff v. Feodor Fedorenko, Defendant* (hereafter, Fedorenko Trial).

11. YVA, O-51/170.

12. Streibel, vol. 1, 32A.

13. Ibid., pp. 22–23; YVA, Streibel, vol. 2, TR-10/1102-2, pp. 2–3, 8–9.

14. Heberer, "Ciągłość eksterminacji," in *Akcja Reinhardt*, p. 111.

CHAPTER FOUR: BELZEC: CONSTRUCTION AND ESTABLISHING THE METHOD OF ANNIHILATION

1. *Obozy Hitlerowskie na ziemiach polskich 1939–1945* (Warszawa, 1979), p. 94 (hereafter, *Obozy Hitlerowskie*).

2. YVA, TR-10/1100, the trial of Josef Oberhauser (Landgericht München), pp. 7–8 (hereafter, Belzec-Oberhauser).

3. Ibid., Band 9, pp. 1782–1783.

4. Nuremberg Documents, PS-1553, statement by Gerstein, *Documents on the Holocaust*, pp. 347–350 (hereafter, Gerstein); Hilberg, pp. 936–937.

5. Belzec-Oberhauser, Band 6, pp. 1129–1130.

6. Ibid., p. 1131.

7. Ibid., p. 1116; Rückerl, *NS-Vernichtungslager*, p. 136.

8. *Ich, Adolf Eichmann, Ein historischer Zeugenbericht* (Leoni am Starnberger See, 1980), pp. 178–179.

9. Belzec-Oberhauser, Band 7, pp. 1288, 1384; Band 8, p. 1465.

10. Ibid., Band 8, p. 1508.

CHAPTER FIVE: CONSTRUCTION OF SOBIBOR

1. Streibel, TR-10/1102-2, pp. 28–29.
2. Sereny, pp. 109–111.
3. Rückerl, *NS-Vernichtungslager*, p. 163.
4. YVA, M-1-E/1255, Sonia Guter's testimony, Rejowiec (hereafter, Guter).
5. YVA, TR-10/1069, the Sobibor-Bolender trial, Düsseldorf, Band 9, p. 1784 (hereafter, Sobibor-Bolender); see also Rückerl, *NS-Vernichtungslager*, pp. 165–166.
6. Sobibor-Bolender, Band 8, p. 1166; Rückerl, *NS-Vernichtungslager*, pp. 158–165.
7. YVA, TR-10/730, Court ruling in Sobibor trial (hereafter, Court ruling—Sobibor trial), December 20, 1966, , pp. 124–126; YVA, TR-10/567, Bill of indictment against Kurt Bolender and others (hereafter, Indictment-Bolender and others), June 30, 1964, p. 146; SobiborBolender, Band 7, p. 1322.
8. Rückerl, *NS-Vernichtungslager*, p. 181.
9. YVA, O-3/7018, p. 4, testimony of Dov Freiberg (Hebrew), (hereafter, Freiberg [Hebrew]).

CHAPTER SIX: CONSTRUCTION OF TREBLINKA

1. Franciszek Ząbecki, *Wspomnienia dawne i nowe* (Warszawa, 1977), p. 35 (hereafter, Ząbecki).
2. YVA, TR-10/1074, the first Treblinka trial, the Kurt Franz trial, Dusseldorf, Band 11, pp. 2201, 2205, 2164 (hereafter, Treblinka-Franz). For the erection of Treblinka, see also YVA, O-3/560, p. 1, testimony of Wolf Shneidman, 1 (hereafter, Shneidman); and Abraham Katz, testimony to the Israel Police, TR-11, 1221, p. 2.
3. United Nations War Crimes Commission, Registered Number 7349/P/G/1367; Polish Charges against German War Criminals, case No. 1368, p. 9, January 5, 1948.
4. Rückerl, *NS-Vernichtungslager*, pp. 200–205.
5. *Faschismus-Getto-Massenmord, Dokumentation über Ausrottung und Widerstand der Juden in Polen wahrend des zweiten Weltkrieges* (Berlin, 1961), p. 304, photocopy of the document (hereafter, *Faschismus-Getto-Massenmord*).
6. Sobibor-Bolender, Band 9, p. 1785.

CHAPTER SEVEN: PREPARING FOR THE DEPORTATIONS

1. *Dokumenty i Materialy do Dziejow Okupacji niemieckiej w Polsce: Akcje i Wysiedlenia*, Wydawnictwa Centralnej Zydowskiej Komisji Historycznej (Warszawa-Lodz-Krakow, 1946), pp. 32–33 (hereafter, *Akcje i Wysiedlenia*); see also Reitlinger, p. 268.
2. *Faschismus-Getto-Massenmord*, p. 271.
3. Artur Eisenbach, *Hitlerowska Polityka zagłady Żydów* (Warszawa, 1961), p. 312 (hereafter, Eisenbach).
4. Ibid., p. 343.
5. Nuremberg Documents, NO-5574, cited from *Documents on the Holocaust*, pp. 275–276.
6. YVA, TR-10/835, the trial of Albert Ganzenmüller, the director general of the German railways, p. 204 (hereafter, Ganzenmüller).
7. YVA, 04/4-2, cited from *Documents on the Holocaust*, pp. 287–289.
8. Nuremberg Documents, NO-1611, cited from *Documents on the Holocaust*, pp. 289–290.
9. Hilberg, p. 200; Ganzenmüller, p. 100.
10. Ganzenmüller, pp. 103–104.
11. Höhne, *The Order of the Death's Head*, pp. 309–310.
12. Ganzenmüller, p. 110.
13. *Okupacja i ruch oporu w dzienniku Hansa Franka 1939–1945*, tom 1 (Warszawa, 1972), pp. 483–484, 487 (hereafter, *Frank's Diaries*).

14. Ganzenmüller, p. 208.

15. Rückerl, *NS-Vernichtungslager*, p. 114.

16. Ibid., p. 115.

17. Nuremberg Documents, PS-3688.

18. Ibid.

19. Jean Ancel, "Plans for Deportation of the Rumanian Jews," *Yad Vashem Studies* 16 (1984), pp. 386–390.

CHAPTER EIGHT: EXPULSION FROM THE GHETTOS

1. Streibel, TR-10/1102-7, pp. 4–11.

2. "Lublin," *Encyclopedia of the Holocaust*, ed. Israel Gutman, vol. 3 (New York: Macmillan, 1990), pp. 915–919.

3. *Teudut Migeto Lublin Yudenrat Lelo Derech* (Hebrew, *Documents from Lublin Ghetto: Judenrat without a Path*), Nachman Blumental, ed., vol. 6 ("From the Yad Vashem Archives"), (Jerusalem: Yad Vashem, 1967), pp. 310–312 (hereafter, *Documents from Lublin*). For the Polish original, also see pp. 242–243 on the English side of this edition.

4. YVA, TR-10/1061, Band III, pp. 446–447, the trial against J. Hoffman (hereafter, Hoffman).

5. Ida Rappaport-Glickstein, "The Ghettoes of Lublin and Majdan Tatarski, " in *Encyclopaedia of the Jewish Diaspora, Lublin*, Poland series, vol. 5 (Hebrew), (Jerusalem–Tel Aviv, 1957), pp. 694, 696–701.

6. David Silberklang, "Żydzi i pierwsze deportacje z dystryktu lubelskiego," in *Akcja Reinhardt*, pp. 58–59.

7. YVA, M-49-P/17, testimony of Dov Freiberg (Yiddish), pp. 2–3 (hereafter, Freiberg [Yiddish]). For more sources about deportations from small ghettos, see *Dokumenty i materiały z czasów okupacji niemieckiej w Polsce: Obozy*, Nachman Blumental, ed., (hereafter, *Dokumenty i Materiały, Obozy*), Lodz, 1946, p. 208.

8. Jacek Andrzej Młynarczyk, "Organizacja i realizacja 'Akcji Reinhardt' w dystrykcie radomskim," in *Akcja Reinhardt*, p. 189.

9. Streibel, TR-10/1102-7, pp. 51–54, see also Christopher Browning, *Ordinary Men: Reserve Police Battalion 101 and the Final Solution in Poland* (New York: HarperCollins, 1992), pp. 78–87.

10. *The Warsaw Diary of Adam Czerniakow: Prelude to Doom*, R. Hilberg, S. Staron, J. Kermisz, eds. (New York: Stein and Day, 1982), pp. 382–383 (hereafter, Czerniakow).

11. Ibid., p. 385.

12. *Encyclopedia of the Holocaust*, vol. 4, p. 1619.

13. Młynarczek, "Organizacja i realizacja," pp. 184–188.

14. Ibid., pp. 198–199. On July 17, 1942, Friedrich-Wilhelm Krüger, HSSPF of the General Government and Lieutenant General Max Schindler, armament inspector of the Wehrmacht in the General Government, discussed transporting Jews to work in the armament plants simultaneously with liquidation of the ghettos. In October 1942 an agreement of cooperation was signed between the Wehrmacht and the SS, on employing Jews in the armament plants. The agreement determined that Jews who had been working until then in enamel, clothing, arms, munitions, and the like up to that time would not be deported for the time being. From October 1942 onward, Jewish laborers needed for the arms industry, if only temporarily, were removed from the lists of those slated to be murdered.

15. Ibid., p. 193.

16. Sara Bender, *B'eretz Oyev: Yehudei Kielce vehasviva 1939–1946* (Hebrew, *In Enemy Land: The Jews of Kielce and the Region*) (Jerusalem: Yad Vashem, 2012), pp. 181–197 (hereafter, Bender, *B'eretz Oyev*); Młynarczek, "Organizacja i realizacja," p. 193.

17. Młynarczek, "Organizacja i realizacja," pp. 194, writes that more than thirty-three thousand Jews were deported from Czestochowa to Treblinka. Based on this data and on the

entry for Czestochowa in the *Encyclopedia of the Holocaust*, vol. 1, pp. 336–338, there were more than forty thousand Jews in the Czestochowa ghetto.

18. Bender, *B'eretz Oyev*, pp. 215–216; Młynarczek, "Organizacja i realizacja," pp. 195, 202.

19. *Encyclopedia of the Holocaust*, vol. 2, p. 832.

20. Pohl, "Hans Krueger and the Murder of the Jews," pp. 253–254.

21. *Pinkas HaKehillot: Eastern Galicia* , p. 474.

22. Arad, *The Holocaust in the Soviet Union*, pp. 223–228. As stated above, we estimate that out of the approximately 600,000 Jews remaining in eastern Galicia at the beginning of the German occupation, by mid-March 1942, after eight and a half months of occupation, 507,000–522,000 Jews remained in the district.

23. Nuremberg Documents, L-18.

24. Yones, p. 166; Kahane, pp. 48–49.

25. Yones, pp. 167–168, and Kahane, p. 72; note that sixty thousand Jews were deported in the *Aktion. Pinkas HaKehillot: Eastern Galicia*, p. 41, states that the deportees numbered fifty thousand. According to Dieter Pohl (in *Nationalsozialistische Judenverfolgung*, p. 221) this *Aktion* deported at least forty thousand people. This figure does not include those murdered in the ghetto.

26. *Pinkas HaKehillot: Eastern Galicia*, pp. 41–42; Kahane, pp. 78–83; Yones, pp. 170–171.

27. *Pinkas HaKehillot: Eastern Galicia*, pp. 374–376; Pohl, "Hans Krueger and the Murder of the Jews," pp. 257–258.

28. *Encyclopaedia of the Jewish Diaspora, Tarnopol*, Poland series, vol. 3 (Hebrew) (Jerusalem–Tel Aviv, 1955), pp. 408–410; *Pinkas HaKehillot: Eastern Galicia*, pp. 87–88.

29. *Pinkas HaKehillot: Eastern Galicia*, pp. 87–88.

30. *Encyclopedia of the Holocaust*, vol. 3, pp. 1201–1202; Mallmann, "Człowieku," p. 93. Yad Vashem recognized Battel as a Righteous Among the Nations on January 22, 1981, and Liedtke on June 24, 1993; see also *Encyclopedia of the Righteous among the Nations: Rescuers of Jews during the Holocaust—Europe (Part 1) and Other Countries* (Jerusalem: Yad Vashem, 2007), pp. 71–72, 119–120.

31. Pohl, *Nationalsozialistische Judenverfolgung*, p. 250, has stated that these figures are compatible with the official German data of 130,000 to 135,000 Jews in the district of Galicia. To this one needs to add an additional 10,000 to 15,000 Jews living in the ghettoes and camps as "illegals."

32. Nuremberg Documents, L-18, cited from *Documents on the Holocaust*, p. 339.

CHAPTER NINE: THE TRAINS OF DEATH

1. YVA, O-33/1291, testimony of Ada Lichtman, p. 10–11 (hereafter, A. Lichtman).

2. Abraham Krzepicki, "Treblinka" (hereafter, Krzepicki), *Biuletyn Żydowskiego Instytutu Historycznego* (hereafter, *BŻIH*), 1962, No. 43–44, pp. 86–89.

3. YVA, O-3/1846, pp. 12–13, testimony of Abraham Goldfarb (hereafter, A. Goldfarb).

4. Jerzy Królikowski, "Budowalem most Kolejowy w pobliżu Treblinki," *BŻIH*, No. 49, 1964, pp. 47–49 (hereafter, Królikowski).

5. Elimelech Feinzilber, *Churbn Siedlce* (Yiddish, "The Destruction of Siedlce") (Tel Aviv, 1952), pp. 34–35 (hereafter, Feinzilber).

6. Sereny, pp. 158–159.

7. Ganzenmüller, pp. 152–156.

8. Rückerl, *NS-Vernichtungslager*, p. 114.

9. Ząbecki, p. 47.

CHAPTER TEN: BELZEC: MARCH 17 TO JUNE 1942

1. *The Goebbels Diaries*, Louis P. Lochner, ed. (New York, 1948), pp. 175–176 (hereafter, *Goebbels Diaries*).

2. Belzec-Oberhauser, Band 6, pp. 1147–1148; Rückerl, *NS-Vernichtungslager*, p. 137.

3. YVA, TR-10/517, pp. 36–37.

4. Belzec-Oberhauser, Band 8, p. 1512–1513.

5. Rückerl, *NS-Vernichtungslager*, p. 139.

6. Belzec-Oberhauser, Band 8, pp. 1512–1513.

7. YVA, TR-10/517, pp. 33–34.

8. Sereny, p. 112.

9. Belzec-Oberhauser, Band 8, pp. 1483–1484.

10. Rückerl, *NS-Vernichtungslager*, pp. 136–137.

11. Tatiana Berenstein, "Martyrologia, opór i zagłada ludności żydowskiej w dystrykcie lubelskim," *BŻIH.*, No. 21, 1957 (hereafter, Berenstein, "Martyrologia"); Berenstein, "Eksterminacja ludności żydowskiej w dystrykcie Galicja, " *BŻIH.*, No. 61, 1967 (hereafter Berenstein, "Eksterminacja"); E. Podhorizer-Sandel, "O zagładzie Żydów w dystrykcie Krakowskim," *BŻIH.*, No. 30, 1959 (hereafter, Podhorizer-Sandel); Israel Schepansky, *Luach Hashoa shel Yahadut Polin* (Hebrew, "The Holocaust Calendar of Polish Jewry") (New York, 1974), No. 83–84, pp. 217–304.

12. YVA, TR-10/583, p. 1; YVA, TR-10/517, p. 34.

13. Rudolf Reder, *Belzec, Centralna Zydowski Komisja Historyczna* (CŻKH), Krakow, 1946, pp. 42–44 (hereafter, Reder).

14. Belzec-Oberhauser, Band 8, p. 1514.

CHAPTER ELEVEN: SOBIBOR: MAY TO JULY 1942

1. Sereny, pp. 110, 113.

2. Freiberg (Yiddish), pp. 4–5.

3. Belzec-Oberhauser, Band 7, pp. 1320–1321; see also Rückerl, *NS-Vernichtungslager*, pp. 166–168.

4. A. Lichtman, p. 18.

5. Sobibor-Bolender, Band 7, pp. 1308, 1433.

6. Court ruling—Sobibor trial, p. 243; Freiberg (Hebrew), p. 6.

7. Sobibor-Bolender, Band 4, p. 787.

8. A. Lichtman, p. 15; YVA, M-2/236, p. 2.

9. Court ruling—Sobibor trial, pp. 129–130.

10. YVA, M-49-E/1187, p. 4, the testimony of Herszl Cukerman (hereafter, Cukerman).

11. A. Lichtman, p. 17; YVA, M-2/236, pp. 2–3.

12. Freiberg (Hebrew), p. 5.

13. Cukerman, pp. 7–8.

14. Sobibor-Bolender, Band 7, p. 1429; YVA, Court ruling—Sobibor trial, pp. 248–249.

CHAPTER TWELVE: TREBLINKA: JULY 23 TO AUGUST 28, 1942

1. Ząbecki, pp. 39–40.

2. YVA, O-16/77, pp. 23–25, an anonymous testimony received by Yad Vashem from the Jewish Historical Institute in Warsaw.

3. Rückerl, *NS-Vernichtungslager*, p. 219.

4. Yisrael Gutman, *Mered Hanezurim: Mordechaj Anielewicz Vehahitkomemut Begeto Varsha* (Hebrew, *Revolt of the Besieged: Mordechaj Anielewicz and the Uprising of the Warsaw Ghetto*) (Tel Aviv and Jerusalem: Moreshet and Yad Vashem, 2013), p. 239.

5. A. Goldfarb, p. 13.

6. Eugen Kogon, *Der SS-Staat* (Bonn, 1974), p. 218 (hereafter, Kogon).

7. Krzepicki, pp. 43–44, 89–95.

8. A. Goldfarb, p. 15.

9. Jankiel Wiernik, *A Yor in Treblinke* (Yiddish, *A Year in Treblinka*) (New York: Undzer Tsayt Farlag, 1944), pp. 20–21 (hereafter, Wiernik).

10. Krzepicki, p. 108.

11. Berenstein, "Martyrologia"; Berenstein, "Eksterminacja"; Podhorizer-Sandel; Tatiana Brustin-Berenstein, "Deportacje i zagłada skupisk żydowskich w dystrykcie warszawskim," *BŻIH* No. 1 (3), 1952, pp. 83–125; Adam Rutkowski, "Martyrologia, walka i zagłada ludności żydowskiej w dystrykcie radomskim podczas okupacji hitlerowskiej." *BŻIH*, No. 15-16, 1955, pp. 75–182.

12. Treblinka-Franz, Band 10, p. 2030.

13. Ibid., Band 13, p. 3709.

CHAPTER THIRTEEN: REORGANIZATION IN TREBLINKA

1. Treblinka-Franz, Band 10, p. 1040.

2. YVA, TR-10/1074, the second Treblinka trial, the Franz Stangle trial, Band 13, p. 3696–3697 (hereafter, Treblinka-Stangl).

3. Treblinka-Franz, Band 8, p. 1493.

4. Sereny, pp. 161, 163.

5. Krzepicki, pp. 96–100.

6. Jerzy Rajgrodzki, "Jedenaście miesięcy w obozie zagłady w Treblince," *BŻIH*, No. 25, 1958, pp. 106–108 (hereafter, Rajgrodzki).

7. Szymon Datner, Janusz Gumkowski, Kazimierz Leszczinski, *War Crimes in Poland: Genocide 1939–1945* (Warsaw: Wydawnictwo Zachodnie, 1962), p. 278 (hereafter, *War Crimes in Poland*).

8. Ząbecki, p. 65.

9. Treblinka-Stangl, Band 13, pp. 3779–3780.

10. YVA, O-3/565, testimony of Boris (Kazik) Weinberg, pp. 1–4 (hereafter, Weinberg). He arrived in Treblinka from Warsaw and worked in the "Blue Command" for some time.

11. Krzepicki, p. 103.

12. Weinberg, pp. 4–5; see also Abraham Krzepicki, "Eighteen Days in Treblinka," in Alexander Donat, ed., *The Death Camp Treblinka* (New York, 1979), pp. 129–131 (hereafter, Donat); Sereny, p. 163.

13. Rückerl, *NS-Vernichtungslager*, p. 231.

14. Donat, p. 127.

15. Ibid., p. 132.

16. Yisrael Gutman, *Yehuday Varsha, 1939–1943* (Hebrew, *The Jews of Warsaw, 1939–1943*) (Jerusalem: Yad Vashem, 2012), pp. 345–350 (hereafter, Gutman).

CHAPTER FOURTEEN: THE MISSION OF GERSTEIN AND PFANNENSTIEL

1. Hilberg, p. 957–960; Reitlinger, p. 162.

2. Gerstein, April 26, 1945. The English translation was taken from Lucy Dawidowicz, ed., *A Holocaust Reader* (New York, 1976), pp. 104–109; see also *Documents on the Holocaust*, pp. 347–350.

3. Belzec-Oberhauser, Band 1, pp. 42–44, 135–149.

4. Hilberg, pp. 957–960.

CHAPTER FIFTEEN: JEWISH WORKING PRISONERS

1. Miriam Novitch, ed., *Sobibor, Martyrdom and Revolt* (New York, 1980), p. 146 (hereafter, Novitch).

2. Reder, pp. 39–40.

3. YVA, M-49-P/153, testimony of Tanhum Greenberg, pp. 17–18 (hereafter, Greenberg).

4. YVA, O-3/1586, testimony of Kalman Taigman, p. 2 (hereafter, Taigman).

5. Sereny, pp. 207–209.

6. Indictment-Bolender and others, p. 123.

7. Rückerl, *NS-Vernichtungslager*, pp. 158–161, 222; Reder, p. 40; Sereny, p. 198.

8. Rückerl, *NS-Vernichtungslager*, pp. 222–223.

9. Aron Gelbard, "19 Teg in Treblinke" (Yiddish, "Nineteen Days in Treblinka"), in *Encyclopaedia of the Jewish Diaspora, The Czestochowa Book*, vol. 2 (Jerusalem, 1967), p. 161 (hereafter, Gelbard-Czestochowa).

10. Reder, p. 51; Belzec-Oberhauser, Band 8, p. 1465.

11. Wiernik, p. 36.

CHAPTER SIXTEEN: WOMEN PRISONERS

1. A. Lichtman, p. 13.

2. Richard Rashke, *Escape from Sobibor* (Boston, 1982), pp. 96–97 (hereafter, Rashke); Novitch, pp. 50, 130–131.

3. Novitch, pp. 56, 72, 87.

4. Ibid., p. 131; A. Lichtman, p. 41.

5. Krzepicki, p. 105.

6. Bronka Sukno, testimony to the Israel Police, file PL/01121 (hereafter, Sukno).

7. Sereny, p. 247.

8. YVA, O-3/4039, 11, testimony of Eli Rozenberg (in German) (hereafter, Rozenberg). Rozenberg was from Warsaw and worked in the extermination area.

9. YVA O-3/4181, testimony of Sonia Lewkowicz (hereafter, Lewkowicz).

10. Sereny, pp. 208–209.

11. Ibid., p. 195.

12. Sobibor-Bolender, Band 4, pp. 789–790.

13. Court ruling—Sobibor trial; A. Lichtman, pp. 16–17.

14. Reder, pp. 55.

CHAPTER SEVENTEEN: IMPROVING EXTERMINATION TECHNIQUES AND INSTALLATIONS

1. Rückerl, *NS-Vernichtungslager*, p. 204; Treblinka-Franz, Band 10, pp. 2053–2055.

2. YVA, O-3/2267, pp. 7–8, testimony of Shlomo Helman (hereafter, Helman). He was one of the forty builders brought from Warsaw.

3. Wiernik, p. 25.

4. Sereny, p. 221; Rajgrodzki, p. 106.

5. Treblinka-Stangl, Band 13, p. 3702.

6. Treblinka-Franz, Band 10, pp. 2053–2055.

7. Rückerl, *NS-Vernichtungslager*, pp. 220–221.

8. Sereny, pp. 146–147; Jan Alexander Zaremba, *Treblinka* (Kielce, 1945), pp. 6–14 (hereafter Zaremba).

9. Sobibor-Bolender, Band 8, pp. 1542–1543.

10. Ibid., Band 7, p. 1308.

11. Ibid., pp. 1282–1283.

CHAPTER EIGHTEEN: THE ANNIHILATION OF THE JEWS IN THE GENERAL GOVERNMENT

1. *Biuletyn Glownej Komisji Badania Zbrodni Hitlerowskich w Polsce*, XIII, 1960, pp. 86–87. A testimony given by Franciszek Ząbecki, the inspector of railway traffic at Treblinka station, on December 21, 1945.

2. This refers to the documents published in the article by Peter Witte and Stephen Tyas, "A New Document on the Deportation and Murder of Jews during 'Einsatz Reinhardt' 1942,"

Holocaust and Genocide Studies, vol. 15, no. 3 (Winter 2001), pp. 468–486 (hereafter Witte and Tyas, "A New Document").

3. Reder, p. 45.

4. Rückerl, NS-Vernichtungslager, p. 143; Obozy Hitlerowskie, p. 94.

5. Gelbard-Czestochowa, p. 160.

6. Obozy Hitlerowskie, p. 528, states that at least seven hundred fifty thousand Jewish Polish citizens were murdered in Treblinka; Rückerl, NS-Vernichtungslager, p. 199, states that at least seven hundred thousand Jews were murdered in Treblinka.

7. Freiberg (Hebrew), pp. 9–10.

8. Court ruling—Sobibor trial, p. 144.

9. Freiberg (Hebrew), pp. 10–11.

10. Belzec-Oberhauser, Band 6, p. 1140; YVA, O-3/713, testimony of Tomasz (Tovia) Blatt, p. 67 (hereafter, Blatt).

11. A. Lichtman, pp. 26–27.

12. Dokumenty i Materialy, Obozy, p. 205.

13. Documents on the Holocaust, pp. 338–339. According to Katzmann's report, close to one hundred sixty thousand Jews from Galicia were "evacuated," that is, exterminated, in the period between November 1942 and the end of June 1943.

14. Tomasz Kranz, "Obóz koncentracyjny na Majdanku a 'Akcja Reinhardt,'" in Akcja Reinhardt, p. 236 (hereafter Kranz, "Obóz koncentracyjny").

15. Encyclopedia of the Holocaust, vol. 3, pp. 937–940.

16. Kranz, "Obóz koncentracyjny" pp. 238, 242–244

17. Nuremberg Documents, NO-1611, cited from Documents on the Holocaust, p. 290.

18. Eksterminacja Żydów na Ziemiach Polskich w okresie okupacji hitlerowskiej (Warszawa, 1957), pp. 311–316. (hereafter, Eksterminacja Żydów)

19. Nuremberg Documents, NO-5194; cited from Documents on the Holocaust, 334.

20. Documents on the Holocaust, p. 338.

21. Belzec-Oberhauser, Band 6, p. 1140.

22. Eksterminacja Żydów, pp. 338–339.

CHAPTER NINETEEN: DEPORTATIONS FROM BIALYSTOK GENERAL DISTRICT (BEZIRK BIALYSTOK) AND REICHSKOMMISSARIAT OSTLAND

1. Sara Bender, "'Akcja Reinhardt' w okręgu białostockim," in Akcja Reinhardt, pp. 206–207, 212 (heareafter, Bender, "Akcja Reinhardt").

2. Ibid., p. 207; Sara Bender, Mul Mavet Orev: Yehudey Bialystok Bemilhemet Haolam Hashniya 1939–1943 (Hebrew, As Death Lies in Wait: The Jews of Bialystok in World War II [1939–1943]) (Am Oved: Tel Aviv, 1997), p. 203 (hereafter, Bender, Mul Mavet Orev); Eisenbach, pp. 457–459.

3. Ganzenmüller, pp. 217–218.

4. Faschismus-Getto-Massenmord, p. 346; see also Rückerl, NS-Vernichtungslager, pp. 115–116.

5. Bender, Mul Mavet Orev, p. 211.

6. Ibid., p. 218.

7. YVA, M-11/19, testimony of Abraham Broide, pp. 5, 11 (hereafter, Broide).

8. Freiberg (Hebrew), p. 9–10.

9. Eisenbach, pp. 463–464; YVA, M-11/26.

10. YVA, TR-10/1112, the Zimmerman trial, testimony of Otto Hellwig, Band 1 (1–2), pp. 1–3 (hereafter, Hellwig); Bender, "'Akcja Reinhardt,'" pp. 214–215.

11. Bender, Mul Mavet Orev, pp. 280–281.

12. Nuremberg Documents, NO-2403; Documents on the Holocaust, pp. 456–457.

13. Sobibor-Bolender, Band 13, pp. 2575–2576; see also Sefer Lida (Hebrew) ("The Lida Book"), Alexander Manor, Yitzchak Ganozovitz (Ganoz), and Abba Landau, eds. (Tel Aviv: The

Association of Lida Descendants in Israel and the Lida Jews' Assistance Committee [Lida Relief] in the United States, 1970), pp. 314–315.

14. Alexander Pechersky, *Der Ufshtand in Sobibor* (Yiddish, "The Uprising in Sobibor") (Moscow, 1946), pp. 6–8 (hereafter, Pechersky).

15. Testimony of Yehuda Lerner, in Novitch, pp. 111–113 (hereafter, Lerner).

16. Pechersky, pp. 32, 40.

17. Yitzhak Arad, *Ghetto in Flames* (New York, 1982), pp. 431–432.

18. *Dokumenty i Materialy, Obozy,* p. 206.

19. Janina Kiełboń, "Deportacje Żydów do dystrktu lubelskiego (1939–1943)," in *Akcja Reinhardt*, pp. 175–177 (heareafter, Kiełbon, "Deportacje Żydów").

CHAPTER TWENTY: TRANSPORTS FROM OTHER EUROPEAN COUNTRIES

1. Robert Kuwałek, "Getta tranzytowe w dystrikcie lubelskim," in *Akcja Reinhardt*, pp. 139–142.

2. Ząbecki, p. 45.

3. Reitlinger, p. 165.

4. *Goebbels Diaries*, p. 176.

5. Kiełbon, "Deportacje Żydów," pp. 175–176.

6. Rückerl, *NS-Vernichtungslager*, p. 147.

7. YVA, O-51/88.

8. Martin Gilbert, *Atlas of the Holocaust* (Oxford, 1988), p. 92.

9. Wiernik, pp. 30–31.

10. Livia Rotkirchen, *Churban Yahadut Slovakia* (Hebrew, *The Destruction of Slovak Jewry*) (Jerusalem, 1961), p. 104; Kiełbon, "Deportacje Żydów," pp. 173–174.

11. YVA, M-2/236, pp. 67–69.

12. Rückerl, *NS-Vernichtungslager*, p. 148.

13. Ibid., pp. 147–148, 155; Reitlinger, p. 178.

14. Sereny, pp. 175–177; also see Ganzenmüller, p. 153.

15. Ganzenmüller, p. 158; Benjamin Arditi, *Yehudei Bulgaria Bi-Shnot Hamishtar Hanatzi 1940–1944* (Hebrew, *Bulgarian Jewry under the Nazi Regime 1940–1944*) (Holon, 1962), p. 155.

16. Alexander Matkowski, "The Destruction of Macedonian Jewry in 1943," *Yad Vashem Studies* 3 (1959), pp. 233–234 (hereafter, Matkowski).

17. Ibid., p. 244.

18. Ibid., pp. 246–250.

19. *The Crimes of the Fascist Occupants and Their Collaborators against Jews in Yugoslavia* (Belgrade, 1957), p. 195.

20. *Faschismus-Getto-Massenmord,* p. 353.

21. Treblinka-Stangl, Band 13, p. 3703; *War Crimes in Poland*, pp. 281–283, photocopies of these documents.

22. Shmuel Wilenberg, *Treblinka—Hamachane ve-Hamered* (Hebrew, "Treblinka—The Camp and the Uprising"), *Yalkut-Moreshet*, no. 5 (Tel Aviv, 1966), pp. 48–49 (hereafter, Wilenberg-Moreshet).

23. Wiernik, p. 40.

24. Serge Klarsfeld, *Memorial to the Jews Deported from France 1942–1944* (New York, 1983), pp. 396–397, 410–413.

25. YVA, O-3/4146, pp. 1–3.

26. Kiełbon, "Deportacje Żydów," pp. 176.

27. For a list of Jews deported from Holland to the extermination camps, see Hans Bloemendal, *In Memoriam* (Den Haag: Sdu Uitgeverij Koninginnegracht, 1995), and Guus Luijters, *In Memoriam, De gedeporteerde en vermoorde Joodse, Roma en sinti kinderen 1942–1945*

(Amsterdam: Nieuw Amsterdam, 2012). For a list of Jews deported to Sobibor, see Jules Schelvis, *Vernietigingskamp Sobibor* (Amsterdam: De Bataafsche Leeuw, 1993).

The Yad Vashem Archives contain twenty-five volumes with the names of all the Jews from Holland deported to the death camps. These monumental books were published by the Dutch government, based on the lists of the transports.

28. Novitch, pp. 71–72.
29. Ibid., p. 87.
30. Rückerl, *NS-Vernichtungslager*, p. 149.
31. Freiberg (Hebrew), p. 10.
32. *Dokumenty i Materialy, Obozy*, p. 205.
33. Kiełboń, "Deportacje Żydów," p. 177. According to Janina Kiełboń, during the course of Operation Reinhard, a total of 117,260 Jews were brought to the Lublin district and murdered there, as follows: 14,001 Czech Jews, 39,899 Jews from Slovakia, 19,050 Jews from Germany, 6,000 Jews from Austria, 34,310 Jews from Holland, and 4,000 Jews from France.

In addition to these numbers, 11,359 Jews from Greek Thrace and Yugoslav Macedonia and approximately 2,800 Jews from Thessaloniki need to be added, bringing the number of Jews brought from European countries into the Lublin district and murdered in Operation Reinhard camps to 131,419.

CHAPTER TWENTY-ONE: THE EXTERMINATION OF GYPSIES

1. Hans Günther, *Rassenkunde des dt. Volkes* (München, 1926), pp. 420–427. The Gypsies were also referred to by the Nazis as "professional thieves," "do-nothings, work-shy, loiterers, and criminals." See Michael Zimmerman, "The National Socialist 'Solution of the Gypsy Question,'" in Herbert, *National Socialist Extermination Policies*, p. 195.
2. Browning, *Origins*, pp. 180–181.
3. Hilberg, pp. 214–216, 1072–1074; Reitlinger, p. 90.
4. Hans-Joachim Doring, *Die Zigeuner in Nationalsozialistischen Staat* (Hamburg, 1964), pp. 215–218.
5. Reitlinger, pp. 125, 200, 488–489.
6. Czerniakow, pp. 346–347, 351, 364–368, 375.
7. Cited from Joseph Kermish, "Emmanuel Ringelblum's Notes Hitherto Unpublished," *Yad Vashem Studies* 7 (1968), pp. 177–178; see also Chaim Aharon Kaplan, *Scroll of Agony: The Warsaw Diary of Chaim A. Kaplan*, Abraham I. Katsh, ed., Bloomington and Washington, DC: Indiana University Press in association with the United States Holocaust Memorial Museum, 1999.
8. Wiernik, p. 35; Sereny, p. 212.
9. Ząbecki, p. 91.
10. Heniek Shperling, *Fun Letzten Churbn* (Yiddish, "From Last Destruction"), No. 6, (München, 1947), p. 11 (hereafter, Shperling).
11. Wiernik, p. 51.
12. Testimony of Shimon Goldberg, in *Dokumenty i Materialy, Obozy*, p. 181 (hereafter, Goldberg).
13. Freiberg (Hebrew), p. 8.
14. Belzec-Oberhauser, Band 6, p. 1154.
15. *Główna Komisja Badania Zbrodni Hitlerowskich w Polsce*, Warsaw, April 1983, International Scientific Session: Stanislaw Zabierowski, pp. 5–6; Cezary Jabłoński, pp. 9–10; Loch Mroz, p. 13.

CHAPTER TWENTY-TWO: THE ECONOMIC PLUNDER

1. Rückerl, *NS-Vernichtungslager*, pp. 109–111.
2. Sobibor-Bolender, Band 3, p. 439; Belzec-Oberhauser, Band 7, p. 1342.
3. Sobibor-Bolender, Band 13, pp. 2683–2684.
4. YVA, O-3/3131, testimony of Oscar Strawczinski, pp. 9–11 (hereafter, Strawczinski).

5. Testimony of Abraham Lindwaser, in *The Eichmann Trial, Testimonies*, vol. 2, p. 1109.

6. Treblinka-Franz, Band 10, p. 2088.

7. YVA, O-3/547, testimony of Shmuel Rajzman, p. 187 (hereafter, Rajzman).

8. Ząbecki, pp. 72–73.

9. Sobibor-Bolender, Band 8, pp. 1556–1557.

10. Nuremberg Documents, PS-4024.

11. Ibid., NO-1257.

12. Ibid., L-18; *Documents on the Holocaust*, pp. 335–341.

13. Nuremberg Documents, PS-4024.

14. Sereny, pp. 162–163.

15. Ibid., p. 160; Treblinka-Stangl, Band 13, pp. 3709–3710.

16. Donat, p. 101, the testimony of Krzepicki.

17. Rashke, pp. 13–14, 93–94.

18. Ząbecki, pp. 74–75.

19. Nuremberg Documents, PS-4024.

20. Sobibor-Bolender, Band 7, 1425.

21. Królikowski, p. 55.

22. Wiernik, p. 34; see also Sereny, pp. 193–194.

CHAPTER TWENTY-THREE: HIMMLER'S VISIT TO SOBIBOR AND TREBLINKA

1. Nuremberg Documents, NO-2494.

2. Sobibor-Bolender, Band 6, p. 1190, and Band 4, p. 769.

3. A. Lichtman, pp. 47–48.

4. Freiberg (Hebrew), p. 8; Blatt, pp. 66–67; *Documenty i Materialy, Obozy*, p. 211.

5. Sobibor-Bolender, Band 4, pp. 768–769.

6. Greenberg, pp. 28–29.

7. YVA, O-68, Christian Wirth's personal file. The original is in the Berlin Documentation Center (BDC).

8. Ibid.

9. Rückerl, *NS-Vernichtungslager*, p. 176. The complete document is quoted there.

10. Ibid., p. 177. The complete document is quoted there.

11. Ibid., p. 178. The complete document is quoted there.

CHAPTER TWENTY-FOUR: THE ERASURE OF THE CRIMES

1. Nuremberg Documents, NO-3947.

2. Serwański, pp. 53–57; Hilberg, pp. 1042–1044.

3. *Documents on the Holocaust*, p. 348.

4. Sobibor-Bolender, Band 13, pp. 2561–2562; see also Rückerl, *NS-Vernichtungslager*, p. 173.

5. Sobibor-Bolender, Band 9, p. 1743.

6. *Dokumenty i Materialy, Obozy*, p. 203.

7. Rückerl, *NS-Vernichtungslager*, p. 173; Freiberg (Hebrew), p. 11.

8. Belzec-Oberhauser, Band 9, pp. 1697–1698.

9. Ibid., Band 6, p. 1187.

10. Ibid., p. 1154.

11. Rückerl, *NS-Vernichtungslager*, pp. 205–206.

12. Treblinka-Franz, Band 10, p. 2057.

13. YVA, O-33/4821, testimony of Yechiel Reichman, pp. 41–42 (hereafter, Reichman).

14. Wiernik, p. 39.

15. A. Goldfarb, pp. 17–18.

16. Mieczysław Chodźko, "Wspomnienia Treblinkarza," *BŻIH*, No. 27, 1958, p. 93.

1. *Nationalsozialistische Massentötungen*, p. 53.
2. Sereny, pp. 53–54.
3. Belzec-Oberhauser, Band 9, p. 1731.
4. Sereny, pp. 113–114.
5. Treblinka-Stangl, Band 13, pp. 37–40.
6. Sereny, p. 200.
7. Ibid., pp. 200–201.
8. Ibid., p. 164.
9. Jacek Andrzej Młynarczyk, "Treblinka—obóz śmierci Akcji Reinhardt," in *Akcja Reinhardt*, p. 218.
10. Belzec-Oberhauser, Band 5, p. 964.
11. Reder, pp. 59–60.
12. Belzec-Oberhauser, Band 6, p. 1145.
13. Moshe Bahir, "The Big Sobiber Uprising (3)," *Pirsumei Muzeon Halochamim VeahPartizanim* (Hebrew, *Publications of the Museum of the Combatants and Partisans*) 19 (Tel Aviv: Museum of the Combatants, 1973), p. 39 (hereafter, Bahir, "The Big Sobiber Uprising (3)").
14. Novitch, pp. 157–158.
15. Strawczinski, pp. 11–12.
16. YVA, TR-10/833, pp. 132–135, Kurt Franz trial. According to the testimony given to the Israel police on June 14, 1961, by Bronka Sukno, a survivor of Treblinka, Kurt Franz was a homosexual and had sexual relations with a prisoner in the camp. His name is in the testimony.
17. Zaremba, p. 21 (this publication includes testimonies by survivors, taken in 1944–1945, immediately after the liberation of eastern Poland); Wiernik, pp. 45–46; Sereny, p. 259.
18. Bahir, "The Big Sobiber Uprising (3)," p. 34.
19. A. Lichtman, pp. 36–37.
20. Sobibor-Bolender, Band 8, p. 1582.
21. Ibid., Band 6, p. 1111.
22. Indictment-Bolender and others, p. 210.
23. Sobibor-Bolender, Band 8, p. 1591.
24. Bahir, "The Big Sobiber Uprising (3)," p. 37.
25. Rajgrodzki, pp. 111–112.
26. Shperling, p. 12.
27. Bahir, "The Big Sobiber Uprising (3)," p. 35; A. Lichtman, p. 16.
28. A. Lichtman, pp. 16–17.
29. Wiernik, p. 25.
30. Sereny, p. 188.
31. A. Lichtman, p. 28.
32. Sobibor-Bolender, Band 4, p. 712.
33. Novitch, p. 64.
34. Rozenberg, p. 6. Ivan Demianiuk lived in Germany after the war ended and in 1951 immigrated to the United States. He concealed the fact of his service for Nazi Germany on his American citizenship application. Years later, Jewish survivors of Treblinka identified him, leading to his arrest and trial. In 1981, he was stripped of his American citizenship and was extradited to Israel in 1986. During his trial in 1987–1988 he was sentenced to death for his role in abusing and murdering Jews at Treblinka. He won his appeal before the Israeli High Court based on uncertainties about his identity and was expelled to the United States. Demianiuk was extradited to Germany and was tried there in 2011, following the discovery of documents regarding his service at Sobibor. Convicted of aiding and abetting in the murder of twenty-nine thousand Jews at Sobibor, he was sentenced to five years in prison. Ivan Demianiuk died in March 2012, before his appeal came before the court.

35. Wiernik, pp. 29–30.

36. Sobibor-Bolender, Band 8, pp. 1593–1594.

37. See bibliography.

CHAPTER TWENTY-SIX: THE PRISONERS' DAILY LIFE

1. Reder, p. 52.

2. Freiberg (Hebrew), pp. 6–7.

3. Reder, p. 52.

4. Sobibor-Bolender, Band 6, p. 1185.

5. Reder, p. 52.

6. Wilenberg-Moreshet, p. 28; see also Rückerl, *NS-Vernichtungslager*, p. 213.

7. Wilenberg-Moreshet, p. 34.

8. Shmuel Wilenberg, "Uprising in Treblinka" (Hebrew), *Yad Vashem News* 25/26 (1961), p. 34 (hereafter, Wilenberg–Yad Vashem).

9. Reder, p. 59.

10. Reichman, p. 12.

11. Wilenberg-Moreshet, p. 32.

12. Reichman, pp. 11–12.

13. Freiberg (Hebrew), p. 13.

14. Reder, p. 53.

CHAPTER TWENTY-SEVEN: THE PRISONERS AND THE DEPORTEES

1. Reichman, p. 6.

2. Testimony of David Milgroim in *Miparashat Hashoa: Machanot Haavoda BePolin* (Hebrew, *The Holocaust Account: Extermination Camps in Poland*), Israel Kloisner, ed. (Jerusalem: Rubin Mass Publishers, 1947), pp. 155–156.

3. Gelbard-Czestochowa, pp. 163–164.

4. Donat, pp. 110–111, the testimony of Krzepicki.

5. Pechersky, p. 29.

6. Reichman, pp. 15–16.

7. Wilenberg-Moreshet, p. 44.

8. Rashke, pp. 122–123.

9. Strawczinski, p. 6; see also YVA, O-3/550, testimony of Alexander Kudlik, YVA, O-3/550, p. 4 (hereafter, Kudlik).

CHAPTER TWENTY-EIGHT: FAITH AND RELIGION

1. Donat, p. 111.

2. Rahske, p. 62; see also Novitch, pp. 157–158.

3. Krzepicki, p. 100.

4. Reichman, p. 12.

5. Reder, p. 53.

6. A. Lichtman, p. 36.

7. Rozenberg, pp. 7–8; see also Wiernik, p. 42, and Helman, p. 13.

8. YVA, O-3/2212, testimony of Mordechai Goldfarb, p. 25 (hereafter, M. Goldfarb). See also Rückerl, *NS-Vernichtungslager*, p. 195; A. Lichtman, p. 45; and Pechersky, p. 48.

CHAPTER TWENTY-NINE: DISEASES, EPIDEMICS, AND SUICIDE

1. Strawczinski, pp. 34–35.

2. Wiernik, p. 34.

3. Wilenberg-Moreshet, p. 50.

4. Ibid., p. 46.

5. YVA, O-3/2309, testimony of Yitzhak Lichtman, p. 11 (hereafter, Y. Lichtman).

6. Rajgrodzki, pp. 109–110.

7. Reichman, pp. 54–55.

8. Rückerl, *NS-Vernichtungslager*, pp. 231–232.

9. A. Lichtman, pp. 32–33.

10. Novitch, p. 60.

11. A. Lichtman, p. 11.

12. Reichman, pp. 26–27, 53.

13. Rozenberg, p. 7; Wiernik, p. 29.

14. *The Eichmann Trial, Testimonies*, p. 1111.

15. Rozenberg, p. 7.

16. Freiberg (Hebrew), p. 6.

17. Rashke, p. 103.

CHAPTER THIRTY: SOCIAL LIFE

1. *Dokumenty i Materialy, Obozy*, p. 204.

2. Reder, pp. 56–57.

3. Ibid., pp. 41, 54, 61.

4. Freiberg (Hebrew), p. 4.

5. A. Lichtman, p. 49.

6. Rashke, pp. 110–111.

7. Blatt, pp. 56–57, 66, 68–69.

8. A. Lichtman, pp. 19–20; Freiberg (Hebrew), p. 13; Rashke, pp. 98–99.

9. Pechersky, pp. 28–29, 32.

10. YVA, M-1-E/651, testimony of Chaskel Menche (Yiddish), p. 4 (hereafter, Menche).

11. A. Lichtman, p. 49.

12. Rashke, p. 102.

13. Pechersky, pp. 30–35.

14. Bialowicz, YVA, O-18, The Stone Collection, see YVA, O-3/4144, p. 3, the testimony of Philip Bialowicz. The document states "Gestapo."

15. Krzepicki, p. 108.

16. Strawczinski, pp. 30–33.

17. Ibid., p. 34.

18. Rückerl, *NS-Vernichtungslager*, p. 213; Zaremba, p. 26.

19. Rückerl, *NS-Vernichtungslager*, pp. 215, 234.

20. Rajgrodzki, pp. 104–108.

21. Ibid., p. 113.

22. Ibid., p. 111; see also Sereny, pp. 194–195; Helman, p. 13; Rozenberg, p. 11.

23. Strawczinski, p. 14; Rajgrodzki, p. 109.

CHAPTER THIRTY-ONE: THE COGNIZANCE AND REACTION OF THE VICTIMS IN OCCUPIED POLAND

1. *Documents from Lublin*, pp. 317, 319–320.

2. Kahane, pp. 46–47.

3. Tadeusz Pankiewicz, *Apteka w getcie Krakowskim* (Krakow, 1982), p. 128 (hereafter, Pankiewicz).

4. Gerszon Taffet, *Zagłada żydów żółkiewskich* (Lodz, 1946), p. 27 (hereafter, Taffet).

5. Y. Lichtman, p. 1; see also Abraham Margolis, YVA, O-3/7019, p. 2 (hereafter, Margolis-YVA).

6. YVA, M-10-AR-1/704, the underground newspaper *Nowe Tory* (Polish, "New Tracks"), March–April 1942 (hereafter, *Nowe Tory*).

7. Ibid.; YVA, M-10-AR-1/690, the underground newspaper *Yediot* (Yiddish, "News") 6 (June 9, 1942) (hereafter, *Yediot*).

8. Wiernik, p. 10.

9. *Plock—Toldot Kehilla Atikat Yomin Be-Polin* (Hebrew, *Plock—The History of an Ancient Community in Poland*), testimony of Marian Platkiewicz (Tel Aviv, 1967), p. 546 (hereafter, Platkiewicz).

10. Krzepicki, p. 86; Taigman, p. 2.

11. Pankiewicz, pp. 129–130.

12. YVA, M-10-AR-2/329, the underground newspaper *Oif der Vach* (Yiddish, "On Guard") 1 (September 20, 1942) (hereafter, *Oif der Vach*).

13. YVA, O-3/4139, the testimony of Abraham Wang (hereafter, Wang).

14. Reder, pp. 35–37.

15. *Encyclopaedia of the Jewish Diaspora, Grodno,* Poland series, vol. 9 (Hebrew) (Jerusalem, 1973), pp. 564–565.

CHAPTER THIRTY-TWO: ESCAPES FROM THE TRAINS AND SPONTANEOUS ACTS OF RESISTANCE

1. Królikowski, pp. 49–50.

2. Feinzilber, p. 141.

3. Rückerl, *NS-Vernichtungslager*, pp. 56–60.

4. *Bleter fun Geshichte* (Yiddish, "Pages from History") (Warsaw, 1969), Volume XVII, pp. 174–176.

5. Ibid., pp. 176–177.

6. YVA, O-3/4192, testimony of Shlomo Alster, p. 6 (hereafter, Alster).

7. YVA, O-3/4138, testimony of Israel Trager, pp. 1–2 (hereafter, Trager).

8. Novitch, p. 49.

9. Strawczinski, p. 17.

10. Taigman, pp. 7–8; see also Wilenberg-Moreshet, p. 30.

11. Wiernik, pp. 40–41.

12. YVA, O-3/2352, the Sobibor collective testimony (hereafter, Collective Evidence), Jacob Biskubicz, p. 50.

13. Ibid., p. 62.

14. Ibid., pp. 62–63.

15. Pechersky, pp. 40–41; see also Collective Evidence, p. 24.

16. The Archives of the Central Committee of PZPR (Polish United Workers Party), "Delegation of the Polish Government in Exile," 202/III file 7, p. 126. Documents from the year 1942.

CHAPTER THIRTY-THREE: ESCAPES FROM THE CAMPS

1. *Fun Letzten Churbn* (Yiddish, "From Last Destruction"), No. 3 (Munich, October–November, 1946), pp. 46–48. A testimony from Treblinka.

2. Krzepicki, pp. 133–134; Kogon, p. 218.

3. *The Czestochowa Book* (Yiddish, Yizkor book), New York, 1958, pp. 57–59.

4. Gelbard-Czestochowa, p. 163.

5. *Akcje i Wysiedlenia*, p. 290.

6. Kogon, p. 229; Abraham Lewin, *Pinkaso shel Hamore MiYehudia* (Hebrew, *Notes from the Teacher of Yehudia*) (Tel Aviv, 1969), p. 115; Gutman, pp. 367–369.

7. Strawczinski, pp. 23–24.

8. Ibid., pp. 24–25.

9. Shperling, p. 14; Taigman, p. 10.

10. Sereny, p. 196.

11. Wilenberg-Moreshet, pp. 36–37.

12. Wiernik, pp. 42–45; Rozenberg, pp. 9–10.

13. Arie Neiberg, *Haacharonim* (Hebrew, "The Last") (Merchavia, 1958), pp. 98, 190–191.

14. Taffet, pp. 27–29.

15. Pankiewicz, p. 130.

16. Reder, pp. 63–64.

17. YVA, M-49-E/1476, testimony of Pola Hirszman, p. 4.

18. Ibid., p. 7. For further information regarding Chaim Hirszman and the circumstances of his death see Dariusz Libionka, "The Life Story of Chaim Hirszman: Remembrance of the Holocaust and Reflections on Postwar Polish-Jewish Relations," *Yad Vashem Studies* 34 (2006), pp. 219–247.

19. Novitch, p. 109.

20. See Tatiana Berenstein, "Obozy pracy przymusowej dla Żydów w dystrykcie lubelskim," *BŻIH*, No. 24, 1957, p. 16. Based on a report of the Gendarmerie in Chelm on January 7, 1943; Rückerl, *NS-Vernichtungslager*, p. 186.

21. Blatt, pp. 69–70; Freiberg (Hebrew), p. 8; YVA, O-62/27, testimony of Hanel Salomea, p. 3 (hereafter, Salomea).

22. A. Lichtman, p. 51; testimony of Feldhendler, in *Dokumenty i Materialy, Obozy*, p. 205 (herafter, Feldhendler).

23. A. Lichtman, p. 38; Blatt, p. 73.

24. Sobibor-Bolender, Band 4, p. 708.

25. Rashke, p. 147; Adam Rutkowski, *Ruch oporu w Hitlerowskim Obozie Stracen Sobibor, BŻIH.*, No. 65–66, 1968, p. 20 (hereafter, Rutkowski).

26. A. Lichtman, p. 24.

CHAPTER THIRTY-FOUR: THE UNDERGROUND IN TREBLINKA

1. Strawczinski, p. 26; Rajgrodzki, p. 109; Platkiewicz, p. 549.

2. Strawczinski, p. 47.

3. Wilenberg-Yad Vashem, p. 34.

4. *Ruch Podziemny w ghettach i obozach, Materialy i Dokumenty*, 1946, C.Z.K.H., B. Ajzensztain, Powstanie w Treblince, p. 189 (hereafter, Ajzensztain). According to the testimony of Richard Glazer, as recorded by Gitta Sereny, p. 210, the reason for Bloch's transfer was that Kurt Küttner, the Lower Camp commander, began to suspect certain unusual activities among the prisoners, and, instinctively, his suspicion fell on Bloch. Therefore, he sent him to the extermination area. See Sereny, p. 210.

5. Tanhum Greenberg, "The Uprising in Treblinka," (Hebrew) in *Moreshet*, vol. V, 1966 (hereafter, Greenberg-Moreshet), pp. 59–60, states that some pistols were purchased from outside the camp by people from the Camouflage Team. But there is no confirmation and no additional corroboration of this statement.

6. Ibid., p. 60; Wilenberg-Moreshet, p. 53.

7. Sereny, p. 206.

8. Greenberg-Moreshet, p. 60.

9. Wilenberg-Moreshet, p. 47.

10. YVA, O-3/556, testimony of Eugeny Turowski, p. 4 (hereafter, Turowski).

11. Strawczinski, pp. 49–50.

12. Greenberg-Moreshet, p. 61. Greenberg testified that he, as a former soldier, was called to Rakowski, the camp elder, who showed him a grenade and asked him whether the grenade was good for action. It was he who found that there was no detonator inside.

13. Strawczinski, pp. 51–52; Greenberg-Moreshet, p. 61.

14. YVA, M-49-P/118, testimony of Moshe Kleiman, p. 43 (hereafter, Kleiman); Wilenberg-Moreshet, p. 51.

15. Wilenberg-Moreshet, p. 52; Strawczinski, p. 50; Stanislav Kon, "The Uprising in Treblinka," in *Sefer Milchamot Ha-Getaot* (Hebrew, *The Ghetto War Book*), Yitshak Zukerman and Moshe Basok, eds. (Tel Aviv), p. 536 (hereafter, Kon).

16. Wilenberg-Moreshet, p. 54.

17. Strawczinski, pp. 54–55; Sereny, p. 182.

18. Platkiewicz, p. 548; Ajzensztain, p. 189.

19. A. Goldfarb, p. 26.

20. Wiernik, pp. 45–46; Rozenberg, p. 12.

21. Wiernik, p. 38.

22. A. Goldfarb, pp. 28–29.

23. Wiernik, p. 54.

24. Ibid., p. 52.

25. Reichman, p. 61; Taigman, p. 19; Rajgrodzki, p. 115.

CHAPTER THIRTY-FIVE: THE PLAN FOR THE UPRISING IN TREBLINKA

1. Wiernik, p. 56.

2. Testimony of Shmuel Rajzman, in *Dokumenty i Materialy, Obozy*, p. 188 (hereafter, Rajzman-*Dokumenty*); Strawczinski, p. 56.

3. Lewkowicz, p. 7; Ząbecki, p. 84.

4. Strawczinski, p. 56.

5. Shmuel Rajzman, "The Uprising in Treblinka," in *Kehillat Wengrow, Sefer Zikaron* (Hebrew and Yiddish, *Memorial Book of the Community of Wengrow*) (Tel Aviv: 1961), p. 221 (hereafter, Rajzman-*Wengrow*); Sereny, p. 246.

6. Kon, p. 537.

7. Wiernik, p. 54.

8. A. Goldfarb, p. 25.

9. Wiernik, p. 57.

CHAPTER THIRTY-SIX: AUGUST 2, 1943: THE UPRISING IN TREBLINKA

1. Lewkowicz, p. 1.

2. Wiernik, pp. 57–58.

3. Sereny, p. 238; Ząbecki, p. 94.

4. Platkiewicz, p. 550.

5. Kudlik, p. 7; Kon p. 537.

6. Platkiewicz, p. 549; Wilenberg-Moreshet, p. 56.

7. Shneidman, p. 4; Taigman, p. 14.

8. Rozenberg, p. 13.

9. Wiernik, pp. 57–58; A. Goldfarb, p. 25; Helman, p. 14.

10. Rozenberg, p. 3; Wiernik, p. 58.

11. Strawczinski, p. 57; Shneidman, p. 4.

12. Platkiewicz, pp. 549–550; Wilenberg-Moreshet, p. 57.

13. Sereny, pp. 241–242.

14. Strawczinski, pp. 58–59; Kudlik, p. 7.

15. Wilenberg-Moreshet, pp. 56–58.

16. Lewkowicz, p. 5; Wiernik, pp. 59–60; Rozenberg, p. 13; A. Goldfarb, p. 26; Reichman, pp. 62–63; Rajgrodzki, p. 116.

17. Rajgrodzki, p. 116.

18. Sereny, pp. 239–240.

CHAPTER THIRTY-SEVEN: PURSUIT AND ESCAPE FROM TREBLINKA

1. Królikowski, p. 53; see also Ząbecki, p. 95.
2. Sereny, p. 247.
3. Rajgrodzki, pp. 116–117.
4. Reichman, p. 63.
5. Platkiewicz, p. 551.
6. YVA, M-49-E/106, testimony of Leon Perelsztain, p. 8 (hereafter, Perelsztain).
7. Lewkowicz, p. 5.

CHAPTER THIRTY-EIGHT: IDEAS AND ORGANIZATION FOR RESISTANCE IN SOBIBOR

1. Rutkowski, p. 13.
2. There are several different versions of the exact wording of the note. *Dokumenty i Materialy, Obozy,* pp. 207, 213.
3. A. Lichtman, p. 37.
4. Cukerman, pp. 9–12.
5. Testimony of Bialowicz; Rutkowski, in Novitch, p. 68, pp. 14–15 (hereafter, Bialowicz).
6. Cukerman, pp. 13–14.
7. YVA O-16/464, testimony of Feldhendler's wife (hereafter, Feldhendler's wife); Blatt, p. 77; Rutkowski, p. 16.
8. Testimony of Dov Freiberg, in *The Eichmann Trial, Testimonies,* vol. 2 (hereafter, Freiberg–Eichmann Trial), p. 1040.
9. Feldhendler's wife, pp. 13–14; Rutkowski, p. 15.
10. Rutkowski, p. 16.
11. Freiberg–Eichmann Trial, p. 1040; Feldhendler's wife, pp. 11–12, Rutkowski, p. 22; Cukerman, pp. 18–19.
12. A. Lichtman, p. 25.
13. Ibid.; Cukerman, pp. 18–19; Rashke, p. 149.
14. A. Lichtman, p. 30; Rutkowski, p. 21; Moshe Bahir, "The Big Sobiber Uprising (4)," *Pirsumei Muzeon Halochamim VeahPartizanim* (Hebrew, *Publications of the Museum of the Combatants and Partisans*) p. 21 (Tel Aviv: Museum of the Combatants, 1974), , p. 12 (hereafter, Bahir, "The Big Sobiber Uprising (4),"); YVA, O-3/4141, testimony of Izak Rotenberg, p. 3 (hereafter, Rotenberg).
15. Blatt, p. 65; Cukerman, p. 20.

CHAPTER THIRTY-NINE: THE UNDERGROUND IN SOBIBOR

1. Pechersky, pp. 13–15.
2. Ibid., p. 17.
3. Ibid., p. 25.
4. Ibid., pp. 32–34.
5. Ibid., pp. 22–24.
6. Ibid., pp. 26–27.
7. Ibid., p. 41; Rutkowski, pp. 27–28, states that Wajspapir, a prisoner of war, was also a member of the Underground Committee.
8. YVA, O-33/1047, testimony of Semion Rosenfeld, p. 45 (hereafter, Rosenfeld).
9. Valentin Tomin and A. Sinelnikov, *Vozvrashchenie nezhelatelno,* Moscow, 1964, pp. 135–136 (hereafter, Tomin-Sinelnikov).
10. Pechersky, pp. 30–31.
11. Tomin-Sinelnikov, pp. 144–147, 151–152.

12. Pechersky, p. 31.

13. Ibid., pp. 31–32.

14. Rückerl, *NS-Vernichtungslager*, p. 195; Tomin-Sinelnikov, pp. 153–155.

15. Pechersky, p. 44.

16. Ibid., pp. 31–32.

17. Ibid., pp. 38–39.

18. Ibid., pp. 39–40.

CHAPTER FORTY: THE PLAN FOR THE UPRISING IN SOBIBOR

1. Pechersky, pp. 40–41; Blatt, p. 78.

2. Rückerl, *NS-Vernichtungslager*, p. 195; Pechersky, p. 48; Rashke, p. 201.

3. Pechersky, p. 42. Pechersky does not mention the meeting held on October 11.

4. Ibid., p. 42.

5. Ibid., p. 44; Rashke, pp. 205–206.

6. Rosenfeld, p. 5.

7. Pechersky, pp. 43–44.

8. Rashke, p. 207.

9. Bahir, "The Big Sobiber Uprising (4)," p. 14; Rutkowski, p. 31.

10. Rashke, pp. 209–210; Rutkowski, pp. 330–331; Blatt, p. 78; Pechersky does not mention October 13 as the day fixed for the uprising or the subsequent postponement.

11. YVA, O-33/1052, Pechersky's memoirs in Russian, p. 81 (hereafter, Pechersky-Russian). These memoirs are based on the booklet published in Moscow in 1946, with some small additions. It was written by Pechersky in 1972 in his hometown of Rostov.

12. A. Lichtman, pp. 54–59.

13. Pechersky-Russian, p. 81.

CHAPTER FORTY-ONE: OCTOBER 14, 1943: THE UPRISING IN SOBIBOR

1. A. Lichtman, pp. 55–56; Rashke, p. 211; Rutkowski, p. 32.

2. Pechersky-Russian, p. 82.

3. Ibid., pp. 82–83.

4. Pechersky, pp. 47–49.

5. Blatt, p. 79; Pechersky-Russian, p. 86.

6. Rashke, p. 216.

7. Ibid., pp. 216–217.

8. Pechersky-Russian, p. 84; Rosenfeld, p. 6.

9. Pechersky, pp. 49–50.

10. Ibid., pp. 51–53.

11. Pechersky-Russian, p. 85.

12. YVA, O-3/4137, testimony of Yehuda Lerner, p. 2 (hereafter, Lerner-YVA); Pechersky-Russian, p. 85.

13. Rashke, p. 222, writes that Klat was killed by Rosenfeld and Vaispapir. However, Rosenfeld testified that his duty was to kill Frenzel, and, in his description of his activity during the uprising, he does not mention killing Klat.

14. Blatt, p. 80.

15. Rashke, p. 225; testimony of Abraham Margolis, in Collective Evidence, pp. 74–75 (hereafter, Margolis).

16. A. Lichtman, p. 55.

17. Pechersky, pp. 50–51.

18. Ibid., pp. 53–54.

19. Ibid., p. 54; Rashke, pp. 227–228.

20. YVA, 2688/127-0, pp. 4–5, Pechersky's story as told on a Soviet radio station (hereafter, Perchersky-radio).

21. Rosenfeld, pp. 5–6.

22. Pechersky-Russian, p. 87.

23. Collective Evidence, pp. 76–77.

24. Pechersky, p. 55.

25. Ibid., p. 56.

26. Sobibor-Bolender, Band 4, pp. 808–809.

27. M. Goldfarb, p. 26.

28. Collective Evidence, p. 72; *The Eichmann Trial, Testimonies*, p. 1061.

29. Court ruling-Sobibor trial, pp. 140–143.

30. A. Lichtman, pp. 56–57.

31. Sobibor-Bolender, Band 7, pp. 1338–1339.

32. Pechersky-Russian, pp. 89–90.

CHAPTER FORTY-TWO: PURSUIT AND ESCAPE FROM SOBIBOR

1. Novitch, pp. 166–167.

2. Collective Evidence, p. 72.

3. Sobibor-Bolender, Band 9, pp. 1795–1798.

4. Ibid., Band 3, pp. 562–564.

5. Ibid., p. 564; Band 6, p. 113; Indictment-Bolender and others, p. 141.

6. Wojciech Zyśko, "Eksterminacyjna działalność Truppenpolizei w dystrykcie lubelskim w, latach 1943–1944," *Zeszyty Majdanka* 6 (1972), pp. 186–188 (hereafter Zyśko, *Zeszyty Majdanka* 6), monthly reports of the First, Second, and Third Squadrons of the mounted SS and police, covering the period September 26 to October 25, 1943.

7. This description of the operation plan by the pursuit forces is based on the reports mentioned in note 6, testimonies of survivors, and the tasks of the units taking part in the action. (The border police was permanently assigned to guarding the bridges and crossing points on the Bug River.)

8. A. Lichtman, p. 58; M. Goldfarb, p. 27.

9. Zyśko, *Zeszyty Majdanka* 6, p. 186.

10. Pechersky, pp. 58–62.

11. Blatt, p. 83; the Yiddish publication in the Soviet Union *Sovietish Heimland* ("Soviet Homeland"), 1970, No. 5, pp. 134–136 (hereafter, Pechersky-Homeland), carried an article by Pechersky, who quotes a former prisoner of Sobibor, Boris Tabarinsky: "Our group included fifty people. You decided that we should split into small groups [as it was] easier to hide. It was clear that everyone wanted to remain in your group. You selected the Soviet boys and said that you were going with them to look for food." Tabarinsky was included in Pechersky's group.

12. Alster, pp. 15–16.

13. Pechersky, p. 64.

14. Feldhendler's wife, p. 21.

15. Zyśko, *Zeszyty Majdanka* 6, p. 186–187.

16. Ibid., p. 187.

CHAPTER FORTY-THREE: SURVIVAL AMONG
THE LOCAL POPULATION

1. Ząbecki, p. 95, wrote about the warning issued to the local population; see also Taigman, p. 8.

2. YVA, microfilm JM-3686.

3. Blatt, pp. 87–100.

4. Alster, pp. 16–19.

5. Salomea, p. 4.

6. A. Goldfarb, pp. 27–29.

7. Taigman, p. 15; Rajzman, p. 11; Reichman, p. 67.

8. M. Goldfarb, pp. 29–32.

9. A. Lichtman, p. 63.

10. Freiberg (Hebrew), p. 16.

CHAPTER FORTY-FOUR: OPERATION REINHARD AND REPORTS ABOUT THE DEATH CAMPS IN POLISH WARTIME PUBLICATIONS

1. Krystyna Marczewska and Wladyslaw Wazniewski, "Treblinka w swietle akt Delegatury Rzadu na Kraj, *Biuletyn glownej Komisji Badania Zbrodni Hitlerowskich w Polsce*, XIX (Warsaw, 1968), pp. 129–130 (hereafter, Papers of the Delegatura).

2. YVA, O-25/140-8; Ireneusz Caban, Zygmunt Mańkowski, *Zwiazek Walki Zbrojnej, i, Armia Krajowa w Okregu Lubelskim* (Lublin: Wydawnictwo Lubelskie, 1971), part two/vol. 2, pp. 34–35.

3. YVA, M-2/196, the Schwarzbart Collection (hereafter, Schwarzbart Collection); *Armia Krajowa w Dokumentach 1939–1945*, Book Two, June 1941–April 1943 (London, 1973), p. 288.

4. Schwarzbart Collection.

5. Jacob Apenszlak, ed., *The Black Book of Polish Jewry: An Account of the Martyrdom of Polish Jewry under the Nazi Occupation* (New York, 1943), p. 131. Schwarzbart represented the Zionists in London on the Polish National Council (similar to a parliament). Szmul Zygielbojm was an additional Bund Party representative.

6. Schwarzbart Collection.

7. Ząbecki, pp. 36, 38, 45.

8. Tadeusz Bór-Komorowski, *The Secret Army* (London: Victor Gollancz, 1950), p. 99.

9. Papers of the Delegatura, pp. 136–137.

10. Ibid., pp. 137–138.

11. Ibid., pp. 138–139.

12. Ibid., p. 139.

13. Ibid., pp. 139–145.

14. Ibid., pp. 145–146.

15. Ibid., p. 154.

16. Ibid., pp. 154–155.

17. Ibid., p. 155.

18. Ibid., pp. 155–156.

19. *Faschismus-Getto-Massenmord*, p. 557.

20. Papers of the Delegatura, p. 156.

21. Ibid., p. 156.

22. YVA, M-2/1215, London, 1943.

23. YVA, O-25, see Delegatura documents.

24. YVA, M-2/216.

25. Stefan Korboński, *W Imieniu Rzeczypospolitej*, Paris, 1954, pp. 253–254.

26. Daniel Blatman, "Reakcje żydowskich działaczy i organizacji żydowskich na wiadomożci z Polski (1942–1943)" in *Akcja Reinhardt*, pp. 274, 277–282.

27. *Documents on the Holocaust*, pp. 324–326.

CHAPTER FORTY-FIVE: AN EVALUATION OF THE UPRISINGS AND THEIR RESULTS

1. Sereny, p. 247.

2. *Faschismus-Getto-Massenmord*, p. 565.

1. For the number of Jews in these camps, see *Obozy Hitlerowskie*, pp. 308, 397, 523.
2. *Frank's Diaries*, Book 2, p. 242.
3. Stanisław Piotrowski, *Misja Odyla Globocnika* (Warszawa, 1949), quotations from Sporrenberg's trial (hereafter, Piotrowski).
4. Ryszard Gicewicz, "Obóz pracy w Poniatowej (1941–1943)," *Zeszyty Majdanka* 10 (1980), p. 102 (hereafter Gicewicz, *Zeszyty Majdanka* 10).
5. Belzec-Oberhauser, Band 8, pp. 1538–1539. The "settlement" was a part of the Poniatowa labor camp, where some Jewish prisoners were living.
6. Gicewicz, *Zeszyty Majdanka* 10, pp. 100, 103.
7. Ibid., p. 103.
8. YVA, TR-10/1145-Z, the trial of Birmes-Gollak, Band 22, pp. 3732–3735 (hereafter, Birmes-Gollak).
9. Streibel, pp. 16–21.
10. Marszałek, p. 128.
11. Ibid., pp. 129–130; *Przezyli Majdanek*, testimonies of survivors of Majdanek published by the Museum of Majdanek (Lublin, 1980), pp. 15–16 (hereafter, *Survived Majdanek*).
12. Marszałek, p. 130; testimony of Ida Mazower, in *Survived Majdanek*, pp. 276–277.
13. Piotrowski, p. 58; Marszałek, p. 131. These Jews remained in the camps of Zamosc, Pulawy, and Biala-Podlaska.

CHAPTER FORTY-SEVEN: THE LIQUIDATION OF THE CAMPS AND THE TERMINATION OF OPERATION REINHARD

1. Belzec-Oberhauser, Band 6, p. 1140.
2. Ibid., Band 7, pp. 1402–1403; Sobibor-Bolender, Band 3, p. 483.
3. Belzec-Oberhauser, Band 6, pp. 1141, 1152.
4. Nuremberg Documents, PS-4024, p. 2.
5. Sobibor-Bolender, Band 3, p. 713; Court ruling—Sobibor trial, p. 302; Treblinka-Franz, Band 10, p. 2009.
6. Ganzenmüller, Band 3, Ganzenmüller's trial, the transport order No. 290 of August 17, 1943, issued by the Directorate of the German Railways in Konigsberg; Ząbecki, p. 96.
7. The transport with 1,200 children was sent to Theresienstadt. This transport was connected with the possible exchange for Germans in Allied custody, but nothing came of the plan. Some weeks later, the children were sent to the gas chambers in Auschwitz.
8. Piotrowski, p. 15.
9. Sereny, p. 249.
10. Rückerl, *NS-Vernichtungslager*, p. 129.
11. Ibid., pp. 240–242.
12. Ząbecki, p. 99.
13. Court ruling—Sobibor trial, p. 352.
14. Ibid., p. 353; Sobibor-Bolender, Band 3, p. 441; Indictment-Bolender and others, pp. 141.
15. Nuremberg Documents, PS-4024, pp. 4–5.
16. Ibid., p. 29.
17. Ibid., p. 30.
18. Ibid., pp. 1, 9.

CHAPTER FORTY-EIGHT: ASSESSING THE NUMBER OF VICTIMS OF OPERATION REINHARD

1. Neither the source for these data nor their precision is clear.
2. Rückerl, *NS-Vernichtungslager*, p. 143.

3. Kiełboń, "Deportacje Żydów," p. 170. Kiełboń notes there that between 1939 and 1941, 30,800 Jews were deported from areas of western Poland annexed to Germany into the Lublin district, and added to them were an additional 7,100 Jewish POWs from the Polish army.

4. Witte and Tyas, "A New Document," pp. 469–472.

5. Ibid., p. 470.

6. Ibid., pp. 473–474.

7. *Akcja Reinhardt*, p. 7.

Epilogue

1. Rochel Auerbach, *Af di Felder fun Treblinke* (Yiddish, *On the Fields of Treblinka*), Der Zentraler Yiddisher Historishe Komisye baim Z. K. fun Poilishe Yidn (The Central Historical Commission of the Central Committee of Polish Jews) (Warsaw, Lodz, and Cracow, 1947), p. 101.

BIBLIOGRAPHY

Ajzenstain. *Ruch Podziemny w ghettach i obozach, Materialy i Dokumenty*, CŻKH, B. Ajzensztain, Powstanie w Treblince, 1946.

Akcje i Wysiedlenia. Dokumenty i Materialy do Dziejow Okupacji niemieckiej w Polsce: Akcje i Wysiedlenia, Wydawnictwa Centralnej Zydowskiej Komisji Historycznej, Warszawa-Lodz-Krakow, 1946.

Alster, Shlomo. YVA, O-3/4192, testimony of Shlomo Alster.

Aly, Götz. "'Jewish Resettlement': Reflections on the Political Prehistory of the Holocaust," in Ulrich Herbert, ed., *National Socialist Extermination Policies: Contemporary German Perspectives and Controversies*, New York, 2000, 53–82.

Ancel, Jean. "Plans for Deportation of the Rumanian Jews," *Yad Vashem Studies* 16 (1984), 381–420.

Apenszlak, Jacob, ed. *The Black Book of Polish Jewry: An Account of the Martyrdom of Polish Jewry under the Nazi Occupation*, New York, 1943.

Arad, Yitzhak. *Ghetto in Flames*, New York, 1982.

———. *The Holocaust in the Soviet Union: Selected Sources on the Destruction of the Jews of Germany and Austria, Poland, and the Soviet Union*, Lincoln and Jerusalem: University of Nebraska and Yad Vashem, 2009.

Arad, Yitzhak, Shmuel Krakowski, and Shmuel Spector, eds., *The Einsatzgruppen Reports: Selections from the Dispatches of the Nazi Death Squads' Campaign against the Jews July 1941–January 1943*, New York, 1989.

Arditi, Benjamin. *Yehudei Bulgaria Bi-Shnot Hamishtar Hanatzi 1940–1944* (Hebrew, *Bulgarian Jewry under the Nazi Regime 1940–1944*), Holon, 1962.

Armia Krajowa w Dokumentach 1939–1945, Book Two, June 1941–April 1943, London, 1973.

Auerbach, Rochel. *Af di Felder fun Treblinke* (Yiddish, *On the Fields of Treblinka*), Der Zentraler Yiddisher Historishe Komisye baim Z. K. fun Poilishe Yidn (The Central Historical Commission of the Central Committee of Polish Jews), Warsaw, Lodz, and Cracow, 1947.

Bahir, Moshe. "The Big Sobiber Uprising (3)," *Pirsumei Muzeon Halochamim VeahPartizanim* (Hebrew, *Publications of the Museum of the Combatants and Partisans*) 19, Tel Aviv, 1973.

——— "The Big Sobiber Uprising (4)," *Pirsumei Muzeon Halochamim VeahPartizanim* (Hebrew, *Publications of the Museum of the Combatants and Partisans*) 21, Tel Aviv, 1974.

Belzec-Oberhauser. YVA, TR-10/1100, the trial of Josef Oberhauser, Landgericht München.

Bender, Sara. "'Akcja Reinhardt' w okręgu białostockim," in Dariusz Libionka, ed., *Akcja Reinhardt: Zagłada Żydów w Generalnym Gubernatorstwie*, 203–216, Warsaw, 2004.

———. *Mul Mavet Orev: Yehudey Bialystok Bemilhemet Haolam Hashniya, 1939–1943* (Hebrew, *As Death Lies in Wait: The Jews of Bialystok in World War II [1939–1943]*), Tel-Aviv, 1997.

———. *B'eretz Oyev: Yehudei Kielce vehasviva, 1939–1946* (Hebrew, *In Enemy Land: The Jews of Kielce and the Region*), Jerusalem, 2012.

Berenstein, Tatiana. "Martyrologia, opór i zagłada ludności żydowskiej w dystrykcie lubelskim," *BŻIH*, No. 21, 1957, 21–92.

———"Eksterminacja ludności żydowskiej w dystrykcie Galicja (1941–1943)," *BŻIH*, No. 61, 1967, 3–58.

———"Deportacje i zagłada skupisk żydowskich w dystrykcie warszawskim," *BŻIH* No. 1(3), 1952, 83–125.

——— "Obozy pracy przymusowej dla Żydów w dystrykcie lubelskim," *BŻIH*, No. 24, 1957, 3–20.

Bialowicz, Philip. YVA, O-18, the Stone Collection (see YVA, O-3/4144). testimony of Philip Bialowicz.

Bialowicz, Simha. Testimony of Bialowicz, in *Sobibor, Martyrdom and Revolt*, Miriam Novitch, ed., New York, 1980.

Birmes-Gollak. YVA, TR-10/1145-Z, the trial of Birmes-Gollak.

Biskubicz, Jacob. In YVA, O-3/2352, Collective Evidence.

Blatt, Tomasz. YVA, O-3/713, testimony of Tomasz (Tovia) Blatt.

Blatman, Daniel. "Reakcje żydowskich działaczy i organizacji żydowskich na wiadomożci z Polski (1942–1943)," in Dariusz Libionka, ed., *Akcja Reinhardt: Zagłada Żydów w Generalnym Gubernatorstwie*, 267–282, Warsaw, 2004.

Bleter fun Geshicte (Yiddish, "Pages from History"), Warsaw, 1969. See Volume XVII.

Bloemendal, Hans. *In Memoriam*. Den Haag, 1995.

Bór-Komorowski, Tadeusz. *The Secret Army*, London, 1950.

Brack-Nuremberg. Nuremberg Documents, NO-426, affidavit of Viktor Brack, trial no. 1, at the so-called Doctors' Trials.

Breitman. Richard. *The Architect of Genocide: Himmler and the Final Solution*, Hannover and London, 1991.

Broide, Abraham. YVA, M-11/19, testimony of Abraham Broide.

Browning, Christopher R. *Ordinary Men: Reserve Police Battalion 101 and the Final Solution in Poland*, New York: Harper Collins, 1992

———. *The Origins of the Final Solution: The Evolution of Nazi Jewish Policy, September 1939– March 1942*, Lincoln, NE, and Jerusalem, 2004.

BŻIH. Biuletyn Żydowskiego Instytutu Historycznego.

Caban, Ireneusz, and Zygmunt Mańkowski. *Zwiazek Walki Zbrojnej, i, Armia Krajowa w, Okregu Lubelskim*, Part Two, Documents, Lublin, 1971.

Chodźko, Mieczysław. "Wspomnienia Treblinkarza," *BŻIH*, No. 27, 1958, 93–104.

Collective Evidence. YVA, O-3/2352, the Sobibor collective testimony.

Court ruling-Sobibor trial. YVA, TR-10/730, Court ruling in Sobibor trial.

The Crimes of the Fascist Occupants and Their Collaborators against Jews in Yugoslavia, Belgrade, 1957.

Cukerman, Herszl. YVA, M-49-E/1187, testimony of Herszl Cukerman.

Czerniakow, Adam. *The Warsaw Diary of Adam Czerniakow: Prelude to Doom*, Raul Hilberg, Stansilaw Staron, Josef. Kermisz, eds., New York, 1982.

Czestochowa. The Czestochowa Book (Yiddish, Yizkor book,), New York, 1958.

CŻKH Centralna Żydouski Komisja Historyczna.

Datner, Szymon, Janusz Gumkowski and Kazimierz Leszczinski. *War Crimes in Poland: Genocide 1939–1945*, Warsaw, 1962.

Dawidowicz, Lucy, ed. *A Holocaust Reader*, New York, 1976.

Teudut Migeto Lublin Yudenrat Lelo Derech (Hebrew, *Documents from Lublin Ghetto*), Nachman Blumental, ed., vol. 6 ("From the Yad Vashem Archives"), Jerusalem, 1967.

Documents on the Holocaust: Selected Sources on the Destruction of the Jews of Germany and Austria, Poland, and the Soviet Union. Yitzhak Arad, Israel Gutman, Abraham Margaliot, eds. Lincoln: University of Nebraska Press and Jerusalem: Yad Vashem, 1999, 2004.

Documents on German Foreign Policy, 1918–1945 (DGFP), ser. D (1937–1945), vol. 8, The War Years, September 4, 1939–March 18, 1940 (Washington, DC: US Govt. Print. Off., 1949–1983).

Dokumenty i Materialy, z czasów okupacji niemieckiej w Polsce: Obozy, Nachman Blumental, ed., Lodz, 1946.

Donat, Alexander. *The Death Camp Treblinka*, New York, 1979. (See Abraham Krzepicki, "Eighteen Days in Treblinka," therein.)

Doring, Hans-Joachim. *Die Zigeuner in Nationalsozialistischen Staat*, Hamburg, 1964.

Eisenbach, Artur. *Hitlerowska polityka zagłady Żydów*, Warszawa, 1961.

Eksterminacja Żydów, na Ziemiach Polskich w oknesje okupacji hitlerowskiej, Warszawa, 1957.

Encyclopedia of the Holocaust, ed. Israel Gutman, vol. 3, New York, 1990.

Encyclopaedia of the Jewish Diaspora, The Czestochowa Book, vol. 2 (Hebrew and Yiddish), Jerusalem, 1967.

Encyclopaedia of the Jewish Diaspora, Grodno, Poland series, vol. 9 (Hebrew), Jerusalem, 1973.

Encyclopaedia of the Jewish Diaspora, Lublin, Poland series vol. 5 (Hebrew), Jerusalem–Tel Aviv, 1957.

Encyclopaedia of the Jewish Diaspora, Tarnopol, Poland series, vol. 3 (Hebrew), Jerusalem–Tel Aviv, 1955.

Encyclopedia of the Righteous among the Nations: Rescuers of Jews during the Holocaust— Europe (Part 1) and Other Countries, Jerusalem: Yad Vashem, 2007.

Faschismus-Getto-Massenmord. Faschismus-Getto-Massenmord, Dokumentation über Ausrottung und Widerstand der Juden in Polen wahrend des zweiten Weltkrieges, Berlin, 1961.

Fedorenko Trial. United States District Court, Southern District of Florida, Case 77-2668-Civ-NRC, July 25, 1978. *USA, Plaintiff, v. Feodor Fedorenko, Defendant.*

Feinzilber, Elimelech. *Churbn Siedlce* (Yiddish, "The Destruction of Siedlce"), Tel Aviv, 1952.

Feldhendler, Leon. Testimony of Leon Feldhendler, in *Dokumenty i Materialy, Obozy*, p. 205.

Feldhendler's wife. YVA, O-16/464, testimony of Leon Feldhendler's wife.

Frank's Diaries. Okupacja i ruch oporu w dzienniku Hansa Franka 1939–1945, tom 1, Warszawa, 1972.

Freiberg, Dov (Hebrew). YVA, O-3/7018, testimony of Dov Freiberg (Hebrew).

Freiberg, Dov (Yiddish). YVA, M-49-P/17, testimony of Dov Freiberg (Yiddish).

Freiberg, Dov. *Hayoetz Hamishpati Lamemshala Neged Adolf Eichmann: Eduyot* (Hebrew, *The Eichmann Trial, Testimonies*), 2 vols., Prime Minister's Office, Information Center, Jerusalem, 1963; see testimony of Dov Freiberg therein (Freiberg–Eichmann Trial).

Fun Letzten Churbn (Yiddish, "From Last Destruction"), Münich.

Ganzenmüller. YVA, TR-10/835, the trial of Albert Ganzenmüller, the director general of the German railways. (See also YVA, TR-10/1107.)

Gelbard-Czestochowa. Aron Gelbard. "19 Teg in Treblinke" (Yiddish, "Nineteen Days in Treblinka"), in *Encyclopaedia of the Jewish Diaspora, The Czestochowa Book*, vol. 2, Jerusalem, 1967.

Gerlach, Christian. "The Wannsee Conference, the Fate of German Jews, and Hitler's Decision in Principle to Exterminate All European Jews," *B'shvil Hazikaron* (Hebrew) 42 (2001), 22–40.

Gerstein. Nuremberg Documents, PS-1553, statement by Kurt Gerstein, April 26, 1945.

Gicewicz, *Zeszyty Majdanka* 10. Gicewicz, Ryszard. "Obóz pracy w Poniatowej (1941–1943)," *Zeszyty Majdanka* 10 (1980), 88–104.

Gilbert, Martin. *Atlas of the Holocaust*, Oxford, 1988.

Glazer, Richard. Testimony recorded in Gitta Sereny, *Into that Darkness: From Mercy Killing to Mass Murder*, London, 1974.

Goebbels Diaries. The Goebbels Diaries, Louis P. Lochner, ed., New York, 1948.

Goldberg, Shimon. Testimony of Shimon Goldberg, in *Dokumenty i Materialy, Obozy*.

Goldfarb, A. YVA, O-3/1846, testimony of Abraham Goldfarb.

Goldfarb, M. YVA, O-3/2212, testimony of Mordechai Goldfarb.

Greenberg, Tanhum. YVA, M-49-P/153, testimony of Tanhum Greenberg.

Greenberg-Moreshet, Tanhum Greenberg, "The Uprising in Treblinka," in *Moreshet*, vol. V, 1966.

Gunther, Hans. *Rassenkunde des dt. Volkes*, München, 1926.

Guter, Sonia. YVA, M-1-E /1255, testimony of Sonia Guter, Rejowiec.

Gutman, Iisrael. *Mered Hanezurim: Mordechaj Anielewicz Vehahitkomemut Begeto Varsha* (Hebrew, *Revolt of the Besieged: Mordechaj Anielewicz and the Uprising of the Warsaw Ghetto*), Tel Aviv and Jerusalem: Moreshet and Yad Vashem, 2013.

———. *Yehuday Varsha 1939–1943* (Hebrew, *The Jews of Warsaw 1939–1943*) Jerusalem, 2012.

Heberer, Patricia. "Ciągłość eksterminacji: Sprawcy 'T4' i "Akcja Reinhardt,'" in Dariusz Libionka, ed., *Akcja Reinhardt: Zagłada Żydów w Generalnym Gubernatorstwie*, 69–84 Warsaw, 2004.

Hellwig, Otto. YVA, TR-10/1112, the Zimmerman trial, testimony of Otto Hellwig.

Helman, Shlomo. YVA, O-3/2267, testimony of Shlomo Helman.

Herbert, Ulrich. "Extermination Policy: New Answers and Questions in the History of the 'Holocaust' in German Historiography," in Ulrich Herbert, ed., *National Socialist Extermination Policies: Contemporary German Perspectives and Controversies*, 1–52, New York, 2000.

Herbert, Ulrich, ed. *National Socialist Extermination Policies: Contemporary German Perspectives and Controversies*, New York, 2000.

Hilberg, Raul. *The Destruction of the European Jews*, New Haven and London, 2003.

Hirszman, Pola. YVA, M-49-E/1476, testimony of Pola Hirszman.

Hoffman, J. YVA, TR-10/1061, the trial against J. Hoffman.

Höhne, Heinz. *The Order of the Death's Head: The Story of Hitler's S.S.*, London, 1970.

Ich, Adolf Eichmann, Ein historischer Zeugenbericht, Leoni am Starnberger See, 1980.

Indictment-Bolender and others. YVA, TR-10/567, Bill of indictment against Kurt Bolender and others.

Główna Komisja Badania Zbrodni Hitlerowskich w, Polsce. International Scientific Session, Warsaw, April 1983.

Kahane, David. *Lvov Ghetto Diary*, Amherst: University of Massachusetts Press, 1990.

Kaplan, Chaim Aharon. *Scroll of Agony: The Warsaw Diary of Chaim A. Kaplan*, Abraham I. Katsh ed., Bloomington and Washington, DC, 1999.

Katz, Abraham. Testimony to the Israel Police, 1221.

Kermish, Joseph. "Emmanuel Ringelblum's Notes Hitherto Unpublished," *Yad Vashem Studies* 7 (1968), 173–183.

Kiełboń, Janina. "Deportacje Żydów do dystrktu lubelskiego (1939–1943)," in Dariusz Libionka, Dariusz, ed., *Akcja Reinhardt: Zagłada Żydów w Generalnym Gubernatorstwie*, 161–181, Warsaw, 2004.

Klarsfeld, Serge. *Memorial to the Jews Deported from France 1942–1944*, New York, 1983.

KL Auschwitz Seen by the SS Höss, Broad, Kremer, 2nd ed., Museum w Oswiecimu, 1978.

Kleiman, Moshe. YVA, M-49-P/118, testimony of Moshe Kleiman.

Kogon, Eugen. *Der SS-Staat*, Bonn, 1974.

———. *The Theory and Practice of Hell*, London, 1950.

Kon, Stanislav. "The Uprising in Treblinka," in *Sefer Milchamot Ha-Getaot* (Hebrew, *The Ghetto War Book*), Yitshak Zukerman and Moshe Basok, eds., Tel Aviv, 1955.

Korboński, Stefan. *W Imieniu Rzeczypospolitej*, Paris, 1954.

Krakowski, Shmuel. *Chełmno: A Small Village in Europe; The First Nazi Mass Extermination Camp*, Jerusalem: Yad Vashem, 2009.

Kranz, Tomasz. "Obóz koncentracyjny na Majdanku a Akcja Reinhardt," in Dariusz Libionka, ed., *Akcja Reinhardt: Zagłada Żydów w Generalnym Gubernatorstwie*, 233–247, Warsaw, 2004.

Królikowski, Jerzy. "Budowalem most Kolejowy w poblizu Treblinki," *BŻIH*, No. 49, 1964, 46–57.

Krzepicki, Abraham. "Treblinka," *BŻIH*, No. 43–44, 1962, 84–106.

Kudlik, Alexander. YVA, O-3/550, testimony of Alexander Kudlik.

Kuwałek, Robert. "Getta tranzytowe w dystrikcie lubelskim," in Dariusz Libionka, ed., *Akcja Reinhardt: Zagłada Żydów w Generalnym Gubernatorstwie*, 138–160, Warsaw, 2004.

Lerner, Yehuda. Testimony of Yehuda Lerner, in *Sobibor, Martyrdom and Revolt*, Miriam Novitch, ed., New York, 1980.

Lerner-YVA. YVA, O-3/4137, testimony of Yehuda Lerner.

Lewin, Abraham. *Pinkaso shel Hamore MiYehudia* (Hebrew, *Notes from the Teacher of Yehudia*), Tel Aviv, 1969.

Lewkowicz. YVA, O-3/4181, testimony of Sonia Lewkowicz.

Libionka, Dariusz, ed. *Akcja Reinhardt: Zagłada Żydów w Generalnym Gubernatorstwie*, Warsaw, 2004.

Libionka, Dariusz. "The Life Story of Chaim Hirszman: Remembrance of the Holocaust and Reflections on Postwar Polish-Jewish Relations," *Yad Vashem Studies* 34 (2006), 219–247.

Lichtman, A. YVA, O-33/1291, testimony of Ada Lichtman.

Lichtman, Y. YVA, O-3/2309, testimony of Yitzhak Lichtman.

Lindwaser, Abraham. *Hayoetz Hamishpati Lamemshala Neged Adolf Eichmann: Eduyot* (Hebrew, *The Eichmann Trial, Testimonies*), 2 vols., Prime Minister's Office, Information Center, Jerusalem, 1963; see testimony of Abraham Lindwaser, therein (Lindwaser-Eichmann Trial).

Litvak, Joseph. *Plitim Yehudim MiPolin BeVrit Hamo'atzut 1939–1946* (Hebrew, *Jewish Refugees from Poland in the Soviet Union 1939–1946*), Jerusalem, 1988.

Luijters, Guus. *In Memoriam, De gedeporteerde en vermoorde Joodse, Roma en sinti kinderen 1942–1945*, Amsterdam, 2012.

Mallmann, Klaus-Michael. "'Człowieku, dziś świętuję tysięczny strzał 5 w potylicę': Policja Bezpieczeństwa a Shoa w Galicji Zachodniej," in Dariusz Libionka, ed., *Akcja Reinhardt: Zagłada Żydów w Generalnym Gubernatorstwie*, 85–102, Warsaw, 2004.

Margolis. Testimony of Abraham Margolis, in YVA, O-3/2352, Collective Evidence Sobibor.

Margolis-YVA. YVA, O-3/7019, testimony of Abraham Margolis.

Manoschek, Walter. "The Extermination of Jews in Serbia," in Ulrich Herbert, ed., *National Socialist Extermination Policies: Contemporary German Perspectives and Controversies*, 163–185, New York, 2000.

Marczewska, Krystyna, and Wladyslaw Wazniewski. Papers of the Delegatura. "Treblinka w swietle akt Delegatury Rzadu na Kraj," *Biuletyn glownej Komisji Badania Zbrodni Hitlerowskich w Polsce*, XIX, Warsaw, 1968.

Marszałek, Józef. "Centralny Zarząd Budowlany SS i Policji w Lublinie," *Zeszyty Majdanka* 6 (1972), 5–45.

———. *Majdanek*, Warszawa, 1981.

Matkowski, Alexander. "The Destruction of Macedonian Jewry in 1943," *Yad Vashem Studies* 3 (1959), 203–258.

Mazower, Ida. Testimony of Ida Mazower, in *Survived Majdanek*.

Menche, Chaskel. YVA, M-1-E/651, testimony of Chaskel Menche.

Milgroim, David. Testimony in *Miparashat Hashoa*.

Miparashat Hashoa: Machanot Haavoda BePolin (Hebrew, *The Holocaust Account: Extermination Camps in Poland*), Israel Kloisner, ed., Jerusalem, 1947.

Młynarczyk, Jacek Andrzej. "Organizacja i realizacja 'akcji Reinhardt' w dystrykcie radomskim," in Dariusz Libionka, ed., *Akcja Reinhardt: Zaginha Żagin w Generalnym Gubernatorstwie*. 182–202, Warsaw, 2004.

———. "Treblinka—obóz śmierci 'akcji Reinhardt,'" in Dariusz Libionka, ed., *Akcja Reinhardt: Zagłada Żydów w Generalnym Gubernatorstwie*, 217–232, Warsaw, 2004.

Musiał, Bogdan. "'The Origins of 'Operation Reinhard': The Decision-Making Process for the Mass Murder of the Jews in the General Government," in *Yad Vashem Studies* 28 (2000), 113–153.

Nationalsozialistische Massentötungen. Eugen Kogon, Hermann Langbein, and Adalbert Rückerl, eds., *Nationalsozialistische Massentötungen durch Giftgas*, Frankfurt am Main, 1983.

Neiberg, Arie. *Haacharonim* (Hebrew, *The Last*), Merchavia, 1958.

Novitch, Miriam, ed. *Sobibor, Martyrdom and Revolt*, New York, 1980.

Nowe Tory. YVA, M-10-AR-1/704, the underground newspaper *Nowe Tory* (Polish, "New Tracks"). Nuremberg Documents.

Obozy Hitlerowskie. Obozy Hitlerowskie na ziemiach polskich 1939–1945, Warszawa, 1979.

Oif der Vach. YVA, M-10-AR-2/329, the underground newspaper *Oif der Vach* (Yiddish, "On Guard").

Pachter, Zvi. *Hayoetz Hamishpati Lamemshala Neged Adolf Eichmann: Eduyot* (Hebrew, *The Eichmann Trial, Testimonies*), 2 vols., Prime Minister's Office, Information Center, Jerusalem, 1963, vol. 2; see testimony of Zvi Pachter, therein.

Pankiewicz, Tadeusz. *Apteka w getcie Krakowskim*, Krakow, 1982.

Pechersky, Alexander. *Der Ufshtand in Sobibor* (Yiddish, "The Uprising in Sobibor"), Moscow, 1946.

Pechersky-Homeland. *Sovietish Heimland* (Yiddish, "Soviet Homeland"), 1970, No. 5, article by Pechersky. A Yiddish publication in the Soviet Union.

Pechersky-radio. YVA, 2688/127-0, Alexander Pechersky's story as told on a Soviet radio station.

Pechersky-Russian. YVA, O-33/1052, Alexander Pechersky's memoirs in Russian.

Perelsztain. YVA, O-M-49-E /106, testimony of Leon Perelsztain.

Pinkas HaKehillot (Hebrew, *Encyclopedia of Jewish Communities*) Poland vol. 2—*Eastern Galicia*, Dabrowska, Danuta, Abraham Wein, and Aharon Weiss, eds., Jerusalem, 1976.

Piotrowski, Stanisław. *Misja Odyla Globocnika*, Warszawa, 1949.

Pirsumei Muzeon Halochamim VeahPartizanim (Hebrew, *Publication of the Museum of the Combatants and Partisans*), Tel Aviv, April 1973.

Platkiewicz, Marian. *Plock—Toldot Kehilla Atikat Yomin Be-Polin* (Hebrew, *Plock—The History of an Ancient Community in Poland*), testimony of Marian Platkiewicz, Tel Aviv, 1967.

Pohl, Dieter. "Hans Krueger and the Murder of Jews in the Stanisławów Area," *Yad Vashem Studies* 26 (1998) 239–264.

———. "The Murder of Jews of the General Government," in Ulrich Herbert, ed., *National Socialist Extermination Policies: Contemporary German Perspectives and Controversies*, 83–103, New York, 2000.

———. *Nationalsozialistische Judenverfolgung in Ostgalizien, 1941–1944*, Munich, 1997. 497

———. "Znaczenie dystryktu lubelskiego w 'ostatecznym rozwiązaniu kwestii żydowskiej,'" in Dariusz Libionka, ed., *Akcja Reinhardt: Zagłada Żydów w Generalnym Gubernatorstwie*, 39–53, Warsaw, 2004.

Rajgrodzki, Jerzy. "Jedenaście miesięcy w obozie zagłady w Treblince," *BŻIH*, No. 25, 1958, 101–118.

Rajzman, Shmuel. YVA, O-3/547, testimony of Shmuel Rajzman.

Rajzman-*Dokumenty*. Testimony of Shmuel Rajzman, in *Dokumenty i Materialy, Obozy*.

Rajzman-*Wengrow*. Shmuel Rajzman, "The Uprising in Treblinka," in *Kehillat Wengrow, Sefer Zikaron* (Hebrew and Yiddish, *Memorial Book of the Community of Wengrow*), Tel Aviv, 1961.

Rashke, Richard. *Escape from Sobibor*, Boston, 1982.

Reder, Rudolf. *Belzec*, CŻKH, Krakow, 1946.

Reichman, Yechiel. YVA, O-33/4821, testimony of Yechiel Reichman.

Reitlinger, Gerald. *The Final Solution: The Attempt to Exterminate the Jews of Europe, 1939–1945*, 2nd ed., London, 1968.

Rosenfeld, Semion. YVA, O-33/1047, testimony of Semion Rosenfeld.

Rotenberg, Izak. YVA, O-3/4141, testimony of Izak Rotenberg.

Rotkirchen, Livia. *Churban Yahadut Slovakia* (Hebrew, "The Destruction of Slovak Jewry"), Jerusalem, 1961.

Rozenberg, Eli. YVA, O-3/4039, testimony of Eli Rozenberg (in German).

Rückerl, Adalbert. *Nationalsozialistische Vernichtungslager im Spiegel deutscher Strafprozesse: Belzec, Sobibor, Treblinka, Chelmno*, München: Deutscher Taschenbuch Verlag, 1977.

Rutkowski, Adam. "Ruch oporu w hitlerowskim Obozie stracen Sobibor," *BŻIH*, No. 65–66, 1968, 3–49.

———. "Martyrologia, walka i zagłada ludności żydowskiej w dystrykcie radomskim podczas okupacji hitlerowskiej." *BŻIH*, No. 15-16, 1955, 75–182.

Salomea, Hanel. YVA, O-62/27, testimony of Hanel Salomea.

Sandkühler, Thomas. "Anti-Jewish Policy and the Murder of the Jews in the District of Galicia, 1941/42," in Ulrich Herbert, ed., *National Socialist Extermination Policies: Contemporary German Perspectives and Controversies*, 104–127, New York, 2000.

Schelvis, Jules. *Vernietigingskamp Sobibor*, Amsterdam: De Bataafsche Leeuw, 1993.

Schepansky, Israel. *Luach Hashoa shel Yahadut Polin* (Hebrew, "The Holocaust Calendar of Polish Jewry"), New York, 1974.

Schwarzbart Collection. YVA, M-2/196, the Schwarzbart Collection.

Sefer Lida (Hebrew, "The Lida Book"), A. Manor, Y. Ganozovitz (Ganoz), A. Landau, eds., Tel Aviv: The Association of Lida Descendants in Israel and the Lida Jews' Assistance Committee (Lida Relief) in the United States, 1970.

Sefer Milchamot Ha-Getaot (Hebrew, *The Ghetto War Book*), Yitshak Zukerman and Moshe Basok, eds., Tel Aviv, 1955.

Sereny, Gitta. *Into That Darkness: From Mercy Killing to Mass Murder*, London, 1974.

Serwański, Edward. *Obóz Zaglady w Chełmnie nad Narem, 1941–1945*, Poznan, 1964.

Shneidman, Wolf. YVA, O-3/560, testimony of Wolf Shneidman.

Shperling, Heniek. *Fun Letzten Churbn* (Yiddish, "From Last Destruction"), No. 6, München, 1947.

Silberklang, David. "Żydzi i pierwsze deportacje z dystryktu lubelskiego," in Dariusz Libionka, ed., *Akcja Reinhardt: Zagłada Żydów w Generalnym Gubernatorstwie*, 54–68, Warsaw, 2004.

Sobibor-Bolender. YVA, TR-10/1069, the Sobibor-Bolender trial, Düsseldorf.

Strawczinski, Oscar. YVA, O-3/3131, testimony of Oscar Strawczinski.

Streibel. YVA, TR-10/1102, the trial of Streibel.

Sukno, Bronka. Testimony to the Israel Police, file PL/01121.

Survived Majdanek. Przezyli Majdanek, testimonies of survivors of Majdanek, published by the Museum of Majdanek, Lublin, 1980.

Taffet, Gerszon. *Zagłada żydów żółkiewskich*, Lodz, 1946.

Tiagman, Kalman. YVA, O-3/1586, testimony of Kalman Taigman.

Tomin-Sinelnikov, Valentin Tomin, and A. Sinelnikov, *Vozvrashchenie nezhelatelno*, Moscow, 1964.

Trager, Israel. YVA, O-3/4138, testimony of Israel Trager.

Treblinka-Franz. YVA, TR-10/1074, the first Treblinka trial, the Kurt Franz trial Düsseldorf. (See also YVA, TR-10/833.)

Treblinka-Stangl. YVA, TR-10/1074, the second Treblinka trial, the Franz Stangl trial.

Turowski, Eugeny. YVA, O-3/556, testimony of Eugeny Turowski.

Wang, Abraham. YVA, O-3/4139, testimony of Abraham Wang.

Weinberg. YVA, O-3/565, testimony of Boris (Kazik) Weinberg.

Wengrow. Kehillat Wengrow, Sefer Zikaron (*Memorial Book of the Community of Wengrow*), Tel Aviv, 1961.

Widmann. YVA, TR-10/959, the trial against Dr. Widmann.

Wiernik, Jankiel. *A Yor in Treblinka* (Yiddish, *A Year in Treblinka*), New York, 1944.

Wilenberg-Moreshet, and Shmuel Wilenberg. *Treblinka—Hamachane ve-Hamered* (Hebrew, "Treblinka—The Camp and the Uprising"), *Yalkut-Moreshet*, no. 5, Tel Aviv, 1966, 25–58.

Wilenberg–Yad Vashem, and Shmuel Wilenberg. "Uprising in Treblinka" (Hebrew) *Yad Vashem News* 25/26 (1961).

Wirth, Christian. YVA, O-68, Christian Wirth's personal file. The original is in the Berlin Documentation Center.

Witte, Peter, and Stephen Tyas. "A New Document on the Deportation and Murder of Jews during 'Einsatz Reinhardt' 1942," *Holocaust and Genocide Studies* 15, no. 3 (Winter 2001), 468–486.

Yad Vashem Studies.

Yampolski, Vladimir, et al., *Organy gosudarstvennoi bezopasnosti v Velikoi 14, Otechestvennoi voine*, vol. 1, Nakanune, Moscow, 1995.

Yediot. YVA, M-10-AR-1/690, the underground newspaper *Yediot* (Yiddish, "News").

Yones, Eliyahu. *Smoke in the Sand: The Jews of Lvov in the War Years, 1939–1944*, Jerusalem, Gefen, 2004.

YVA. Yad Vashem Archives.

Ząbecki, Franciszek. *Wspomnienia dawne i nowe*, Warszawa, 1977.

———. *Biuletyn Glowne: Komisji Badania Zbrodni Hitlerowskich w Polsce*, XIII, 1960, 86–87, a testimony given by Franciszek Ząbecki on December 21, 1945.

Zaderecki, Tadusz. *Bimshol Zlav Hakeres Bilvov* (Hebrew, *When the Swastika Ruled Lvov*), Jerusalem, 1982.

Zaremba, Jan Alexander. *Treblinka*, Kielce, 1945.

Zeszyty Majdanka 6 (1972); 9 (1977); 10 (1980).

Zimmerman, Michael. "The National Socialist 'Solution of the Gypsy Question,'" in
Ulrich Herbert, ed., *National Socialist Extermination Policies: Contemporary German Perspectives and Controversies*, 186–209, New York, 2000.
Zyśko, Wojciech. "Eksterminacyjna działalność Truppenpolizei w dystrykcie lubelskim w, latach 1943–1944," *Zeszyty Majdanka* 6 (1972), 155–210.

499

INDEX

DR. YITZHAK ARAD (né Itzhak Rudnicki) was born in 1926 in Święciany (now Švenčionys, Lithuania). He is an Israeli historian, a former Soviet partisan, and a retired IDF Brigadier General. He served as the Chairman of the Directorate of Yad Vashem – The World Holocaust Remembrance Center in Jerusalem from 1972 to 1993. Following his retirement, he continues to research and write about the holocaust.

Dr. Arad has a PhD in philosophy from Tel Aviv University and is the author and editor of numerous publications, including *The Partisan: From the Valley of Death to Mount Zion* (1979); *Ghetto in Flames: The Struggle and Destruction of the Jews in Vilna in the Holocaust* (1980); *Belzec, Sobibor, Treblinka: The Operation Reinhard Death Camps* (1987); *The Holocaust in the Soviet Union* (2009); and *In the Shadow of the Red Banner* (2010).